Zone 1
Zone 2
Zone 3
Zone 4
Zone 5
Zone 6
Zone 7
Zone 8
Zone 9
Zone 10

THE ILLUSTRATED ENCYCLOPEDIA OF PERENNIALS

THE ILLUSTRATED ENCYCLOPEDIA OF PERENNIALS

A unique reference guide to more than 1500 plants with comprehensive descriptions and planting information

PROFESSOR MARSHALL CRAIGMYLE

PUBLISHED BY
SALAMANDER BOOKS LIMITED
LONDON

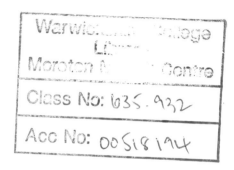

DEDICATED TO SADIE

A Salamander Book

Published by Salamander Books Ltd.
8 Blenheim Court
Brewery Road
London N7 9NT
United Kingdom

1 3 5 7 9 8 6 4 2

ISBN 1 84065 071 0

Credits
Managing Editor: Charlotte Davies
Editor: Candida Frith-MacDonald
Designers: John Heritage, Mark Holt
Indexer: Amanda O'Neill
Film set: SX Composing Ltd, England
Reproduction: Studio Tec, England
Printed in Spain

Acknowledgements
I am indebted to many persons and establishments for help or encouragement, or both, in the preparation of this book. To Mrs Jane Sterndale-Bennett, Chairman of the Hardy Plant Society, Dr. Dilys Davies, past Chairman of the Hardy Plant Society, and Mr Michael Upward, past secretary of the Alpine Garden Society I owe a substantial debt of gratitude for their ongoing help and interest. I am indebted to Geyata Ajilvski for help in identifying the Flora of Texas, to C. Ritchie Bell for help with the Flora of North Carolina, and to Rod Saunders for help with the South African Flora. I owe a substantial debt of gratitude to those members of the Hardy Plant Society in whose gardens many of the photographs were taken, and to the members in particular of the South Wales Group, and those groups which hosted Hardy Plant Society Autumn Weekends which I attended, viz. The Worcester Group, the Hampshire Group and the Hertfordshire Group; but for these the project would not have been possible.

In addition I owe much gratitude for photographic opportunities in many nurseries, and in particular Messrs. Blooms of Bressingham, Cotswold Garden Flowers (Bob Brown), Apple Court Nursery (Diana Grenfell and Roger Grounds), Bernie Stevens, the Nursery, St. David's, Pembrokeshire, the Perennial Nursery, St. David's, Pembrokeshire (Mrs. P. Symons), Wye Valley Plants, Tintern (Adrian and Elsa Wood). I am indebted to the Director of The Royal Botanic Garden, Edinburgh for permission to use the following illustrations taken in Logan Botanic Garden: *Aciphylla aurea*; *Aciphylla glaucescens*; *Celmisia coriacea*; *Erysimum* 'Bowles Mauve'; *Fuchsia splendens*; *Kniphofia thompsonii* var. *snowdenii*; *Meconopsis betonicifolia*; *Meconopsis* x *sheldonii* 'Slieve Donard'; *Ranunculus lyalii*; *Rodgersia aesculifolia*; *Salvia leucantha*; and *Salvia microphylla*.

I am indebted also to the Director, Sissinghurst Castle Garden, Kent for permission to use several photographs taken in the garden; to Dr Smart for permission to use the picture of the bog garden in Marwood Hill Garden , Barnstaple (p.17) and to Mrs Jane Sterndale-Bennett for permission to use the picture of the hot colours bed at White Windows, Longparish (p.18). I am also indebted to several nurseries for supplying me with catalogues on request, and in particular Jacques Amand, Harrow, Middlesex, Blooms of Bressingham, Diss, Norfolk, and Messrs Parkers, Dutch Bulbs Ltd. I owe many thanks to successive librarians of Pershore College of Horticulture for extending the use of the College Library to me over the years.

My final thanks go to Ms Anne McDowall, formerly of Salamander Books Ltd, for her enthusiasm for the project, and with whom the basic plan of the book was devised, to the staff of Salamander Books for all their help and encouragement, and to Ms Candida Frith-Macdonald. Last, but by no means least, my thanks go to my wife for tolerating for several years, many long winter evenings alone while I sat at the computer.

M.B.L. CRAIGMYLE M.B. Ch. B. M.D.

Additional Pictures
Page 1 *Dicentra spectabilis* forma *alba* A.G.M, Page 2 *Allium cristophii* 'Star of Persia', Page 4 Iris 'Tinkerbell', Page 5 *Paeonia officinalis* Common peony

CONTENTS

PERENNIALS IN THE GARDEN

PERENNIALS GIVE A GARDEN ITS CHARACTER. While trees and shrubs form the permanent backbone of a garden, providing form and structure that endure for years and cannot easily be changed, many of them are primarily background plants, contributing little in the way of showy flowers or extravagant foliage. At the other extreme, annuals provide seasonal colour and variety but must be renewed each year, allowing the gardener to ring the changes but increasing the labour involved in the garden. Perennials provide colour and a variety of form that last for years, and it is worth choosing them carefully. Fortunately, this is a wide and varied group of plants. While many of the world's most interesting annuals come from warm, Mediterranean-type climates, and require some help and care to grow in other conditions, perennials are well-represented in the flora of diverse habitats in all regions of the world. There is a range of perennial plants to suit every situation in the garden, from a dry stone wall to a bog garden or pond. Perennials have been important in garden design for centuries. Their influence stretches from the notorious tulip mania, in which fortunes were made and lost, to the humble cottage garden. Classic garden design featured the herbaceous border, its selection of perennials carefully graded with taller plants at the back and shorter specimens at the front, shown against the backdrop of an immaculately clipped evergreen hedge or a mellow brick wall, and appreciated from an expanse of smooth lawn. Since the end of the nineteenth century, this approach has been giving way to island beds and less regimented plantings. Increased travel means that modern gardens often show the influences of exotic locations and foreign styles. Gardens today are also often designed with concern for water conservation and other environmental issues, and so look to the natural landscape and wild plant groupings for inspiration. These considerations affect small gardens as well as great ones: even the modestly sized suburban plot may now revolve around a gravel garden, miniature wildflower meadow, or wildlife pond. Such gardens have the great advantage to the modern gardener of being less labour intensive, and here the perennial comes into its own, returning to bloom again year after year.

A fine example of the traditional deep herbaceous border, here at Packwood House, in Warwickshire, owned by the National Trust.

A PERENNIAL PLANT is one that lives for three or more years, with some perennials living for many more than that. They are distinct from annual plants, which live for one year, and biennials, which live for two, but some very beautiful perennials are short-lived (see p.295), and our gardens would be all the poorer were they restricted to plants of the long-lived variety.

Perennials have developed different strategies for surviving over winter. A perennial plant may disappear below ground completely in winter, in which case it is described as herbaceous, or it may retain some of its leaves throughout the year, in which case it is described as semi-evergreen, or all of them, in which case it is described as evergreen. The great majority of perennial plants are herbaceous. Most of them are also fibrous-rooted, but some have a swollen underground stem in the form of a bulb, a corm, a rhizome, or a tuber. These are all devices for storing energy, enabling a plant to overwinter underground, where it is protected from cold. For the average gardener, the subtle botanical differences between bulbs, corms, rhizomes or tubers are unlikely to be important, although the particular techniques used in dividing them vary (see p.22). Subshrubs are also included in this book because they associate well with perennials in mixed borders; they produce woody mature growth that survives the cold, as well as some soft growth, which dies back in the winter.

Perennial plants come from many different regions of the world, and as a result they vary enormously in their tolerance of cold. The term "hardy" is used to describe a plant that can survive through the winter outside, and "tender" to describe a plant that requires protection under glass, but these constrictions vary from place to place. In temperate climates, many less hardy or tender perennials are treated as annuals and discarded in the autumn; conversely, in many countries of the world, plants that we think of as tender can be left to overwinter in the open ground. As a result, it is necessary to define the terms whenever they are used. The Royal Horticultural Society uses a scale from H1 (needs heated protection under glass) to H4 (generally hardy in the British Isles), but its publications also give specific minimum temperatures for plants. In mainland Europe, systems with more bands, with narrower ranges, are used, but all of these remain fairly general and so provide necessarily limited help. In this book, a system of climatic zones based on minimum winter temperates has been used (see p.10), as this gives the most reliable and universal guide to a plant's needs.

HOW PLANTS ARE NAMED

The world of plant nomenclature can be complex and may seem confusing at first. Plant names are liable to change as botanical study advances, and many out-of-date names remain in common use for some years. All plants described in the plant directory include the plant's name in binominal nomenclature – that is, a generic name followed by a specific name. The plants are listed alphabetically by species name. The authority for the terminology is *The Plant Finder*, 1999–2000 Edition, published by the Royal Horticultural Society, London, England. The terms used can be defined as follows:

Division The broadest categories, for example Pteridophyta (ferns) or Angiospermae (flowering plants).

Order For example Ranunculales, which includes three families. The name of an order always ends with the suffix '-ales'.

Family This term is used to classify plants into groups exhibiting similar characteristics such as flower and foliage form. These names usually end in -aceae, for example Liliaceae. The family name is given for every plant in the plant directory. In some cases, names have changed, and both are given, as with Asteraceae/Compositae.

Genus A genus is a group of similar species. Each genus has a Latin name, which has its first letter in capitals and which also forms the first half of the binominal nomenclature system, by which all plants are identified, and which is always written in italics, for example *Lilium formosanum*, in which *Lilium* is the genus or generic name.

Species The basic unit of plant nomenclature is a species: a group of plants with the same characteristics, interbreeding freely, usually in a distinct geographical range. The specific name forms the second word of the binominal nomenclature, and is written in italics, but without an initial capital letter. It usually indicates a characteristic of the plant, for example *lancifolia*, meaning that the leaves are lance-shaped, or the origin of the plant, as in *formosanum*, meaning "as found in Formosa". A species grows in the wild somewhere in the world, and usually all plants are of fairly uniform appearance and habit, and can be propagated by seed. Further adaptation of the system of nomenclature divides species into lesser categories as described below.

Subspecies This denotes naturally ocurring plants that have subtle differences from the species. The name is written in italics, with the word subspecies usually abbreviated as 'subsp.' and not given in italics, for example *Aconitum napellus* subsp. *vulgare*.

Variety This describes a variation, between a subspecies and a form, that is sufficiently distinct to have its own name. The word variety is not written in italics, and is abbreviated to 'var.', for example *Agapanthus campanulatus* var. *albidus*.

Forma This lowest of the subclassifications, is not italicised and is abbreviated to 'f.', for example *Allium carinatum* subsp. *pulchellum* f. *album*. It denotes characteristics that may be important to a gardener but which are genetically minor, such as flower colour.

Hybrids These are the result of a sexual union between two species or two genera, and are distinguished by having an "x" in their name. An interspecific hybrid is expressed with the "x" before the specific name, for example *Potentilla* x *tonguei*, while an intergeneric hybrid is expressed with the "x" before the generic name, for example, x *Solidaster luteus*. Hybrids must be propagated vegetatively from cuttings if they are to come true to type. It is possible to take seed, but only a percentage of the progeny will be true to type.

Above: *The much-hybridised genus Crocosmia has given rise to cultivars such as* Crocosmia x crocosmiiflora *'Emily McKenzie', which has large, bright orange flowers with deeper-coloured markings in the throats. Plants bred for the garden are often more lush in habit than the species, or have larger, bolder flowers.*

Cultivars An abbreviation of the description "cultivated variety", this is a plant raised deliberately in cultivation. Cultivar names are not given in italics, but are put in inverted commas, for example *Agapanthus* 'Bressingham Blue'. A cultivar may be a hybrid, but the name is also used generally to cover sports; these are spontaneous genetic mutations of a portion of a plant, producing atypical foliage or flowers, or both. Some sports are unstable, and revert rapidly to the parent type. Many variegated plants originated as sports. Due to their origins, most cultivars need to be propagated vegetatively, rather than from seed. The rules that govern cultivar names have been considerably tightened over the years, excluding proper names and Latin words for new cultivars. Some breeders now register trade names for their plants that are more marketable than the true cultivar names; such plants are marked "Regd." in this and other books, and the name is legally controlled.

HARDINESS ZONES

The first consideration when choosing a perennial to be grown in the garden all year round is whether it is hardy in your area. The United States Department of Agriculture (USDA) has developed a system of temperature zones as a basis for assessing which plants can be grown in different areas. The zones are based on the annual average minimum temperature in an area, and are illustrated on the maps below and opposite of Europe, North America, Australia, New Zealand and South Africa. The maps have been divided into the USDA climatic zones, numbered from Zone 1, the coldest, with a winter minimum of -50°F (-44°C), up to Zone 11, the warmest, with a minimum of +40°F (+5°C). Every entry in the directory section of this book cites the plant's hardiness zone. To establish whether a perennial will be hardy in your garden, refer to the map of hardiness zones and find the rating for your area. Any plant with a zonal rating equal to or lower than the rating for your area will be hardy in your garden. Thus if your area is rated Zone 7, all plants graded from Zone 1 to Zone 7 will survive and flower at the average minimum winter temperature there and plants graded Zone 8 to Zone 11 will not. However, Zone 8 plants may be grown outside provided they are given protection in the form of a deep mulch of bracken or leaves, a pane of glass or a cloche, all of which keep the plants dry and help them substantially in surviving the winter. Zone 9 to Zone 11 plants can be grown out of doors in summer in a Zone 7 area, but will have to be lifted and kept under glass in winter or, alternatively, grown in containers and brought into a conservatory or greenhouse over winter.

Another consideration is that every garden has a number of microclimates – that is, some parts of the garden are warmer than others. It may be that the zonal rating for your area does not apply to all of your garden. So if your garden is rated Zone 7, the warmest corner, such as at the foot of a south-facing wall, may well be Zone 8. The only way to find out is to experiment by growing Zone 8-rated plants in that site.

Temperature ranges

ZONE 1: Below-50°F (Below -45°C)
ZONE 2: -50 to -35°F (-45 to -37°C)
ZONE 3: -35 to -20°F (-37 to 29°C)
ZONE 4: -20 to -10°F (-29 to 23°C)
ZONE 5: -10 to-5°F (-23 to -21°C)
ZONE 6: -5 to 5°F (-21 to -15°C)
ZONE 7: 5 to 10°F (-15 to -12°C)
ZONE 8: 10 to 20°F (-12 to -7°C)
ZONE 9: 20 to 30°F (-7 to -1°C)
ZONE 10: 30 to 40°F (-I to 4°C)
ZONE 11: Above +40°F (Above +5°C)

Zone 1
Zone 2
Zone 3
Zone 4
Zone 5
Zone 6
Zone 7
Zone 8
Zone 9
Zone 10
Zone 11

Western Europe

North America

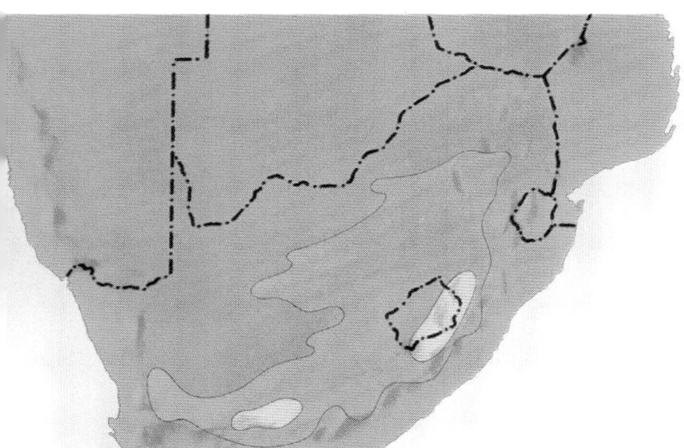

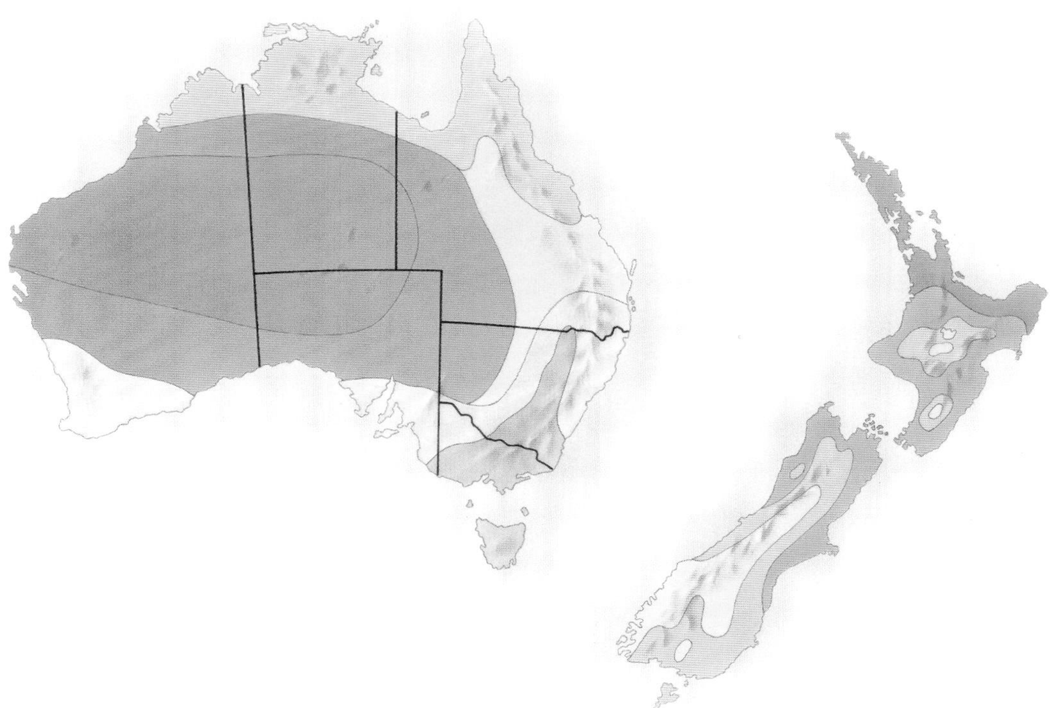

The Southern Hemisphere

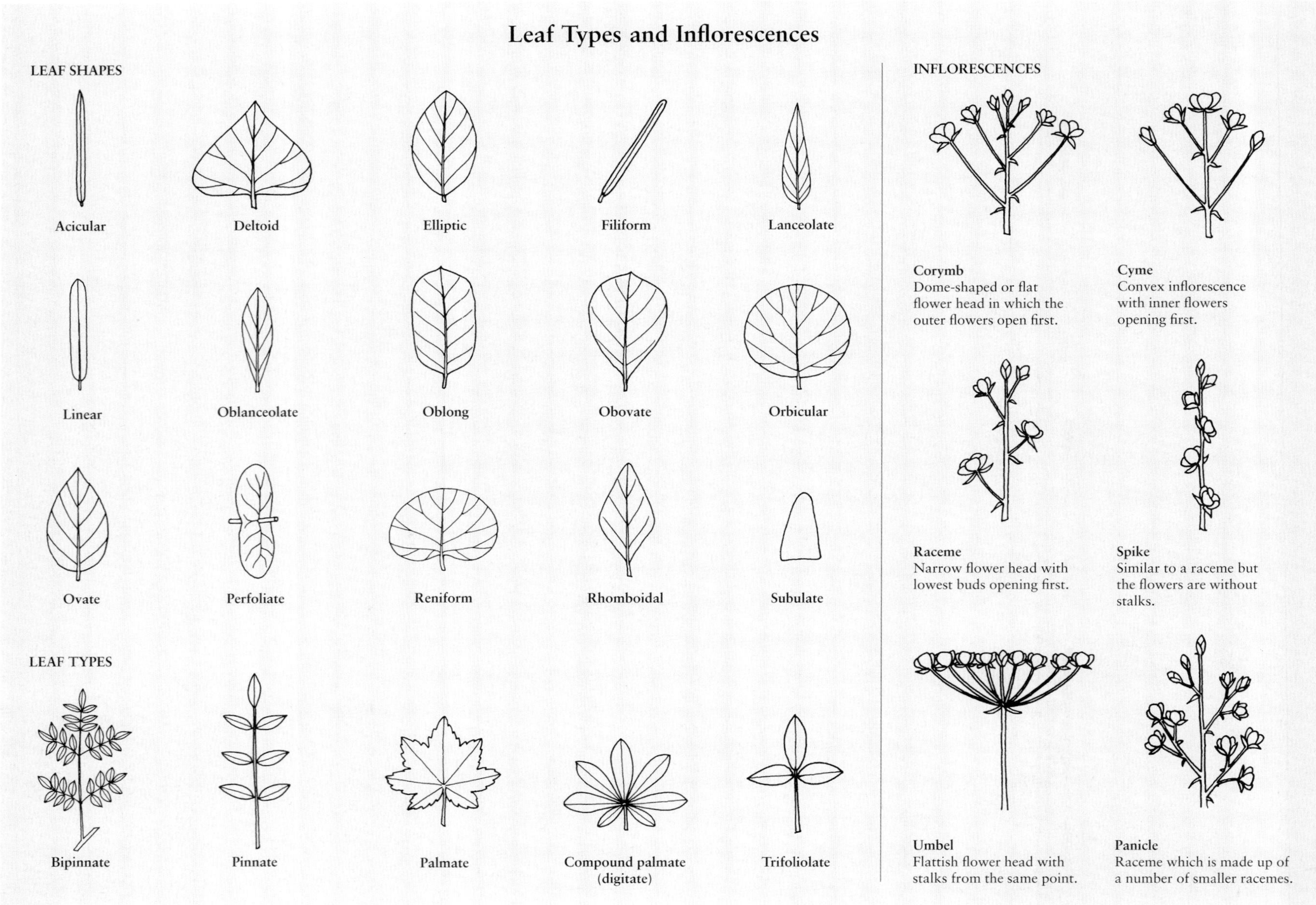

PLANNING A PERENNIAL GARDEN

In the past, the main way in which perennials were grown was in conventional herbaceous borders. These were frequently mixed, in the sense that shrubs were included. These borders were long and needed to be deep to be effective. They usually had a high wall or hedge behind, with the result that the plants grew at an angle towards the light. Wind then tended to cascade over the wall and flatten the plants, and much time-consuming staking was required.

Island beds, pioneered by the famous nurseryman Alan Bloom in his garden in Bressingham, in Norfolk, have several advantages over herbaceous borders. Provided the bed is not underneath overhanging trees or in the shade of buildings, the plants grow vertically, and much less staking is required. A further great advantage of the narrow island bed is that the plants are much more accessible for general maintenance such as deadheading, cutting or staking, and unless the bed is very large, it is not necessary to trample through it for such purposes. Shrubs are less likely to be incorporated into island beds of perennials, but it is not unusual to see subshrubs, such as *Fuchsia, Helianthemum, Phygelius* and others included in these beds, as they are so akin to perennials in many respects, and thus many are included in this book. Island beds of shade-loving perennials can of course be created in densely shaded areas, or in dappled shade for those which prefer half-shade. Island beds are also better suited to the small garden.

A development that has been spearheaded on mainland Europe is the inclusion of grasses in beds and borders, and along with this a "loosening up" of the planting, with plants of different heights being more intermingled, so that tall plants with an open, airy habit may be grown at the edge of a bed, with plants behind seen as if through a veil. Such plantings may be strongly architectural, or may tend towards a wilder, more natural look: they are perhaps not for all gardens, but they do provide a lower-maintenance option.

Above: *A visual guide to the different leaf shapes and types of inflorescence described in the plant directory section.*

Right: *Exuberant planting spills onto the path from these double borders at Crathes Castle in Grampian, owned by the National Trust for Scotland.*

Above: *Tender plants, such as some fuchsias, are best grown in containers that can be moved in winter. Here,* Fuchsia *'Gartenmeister Bonstedt' grows in a sandstone basket urn on the main terrace at Powis Castle, in Wales.*
Right: Aubrieta, Alyssum *and* Iberis *cascading down a stone wall show the opportunity for varied planting afforded by a change in levels or a raised bed.*

Conditions in the garden can affect planting as much as stylistic preferences. Containers can be used for perennial plants, and this is a useful method for gardens in temperate climes, because tender plants grown in this way can easily be brought under cover or indoors for the winter. However, it is not necessary to restrict their use to tender plants. All perennials may be grown in this way, but the containers of those that are to be left in the open garden all year round must not be small, or the plant may either dry out in summer or succumb to frost in winter because the roots are too near the cold sides of the container. For the older or wheelchair-bound gardener, containers allow plants to be raised up to levels where they can more easily be tended, smelled, and viewed close at hand. Planting in raised beds has many of the same advantages as using containers. The flowers are brought nearer and can therefore be more readily appreciated, and maintenance is easier. Raised beds have the further advantage that trailing plants can be grown on and in their walls, increasing both the selection of plant types that can be grown and the area that is available for planting, both of which are important considerations in small gardens.

You might design either part or the whole of the garden specifically to attract and support local wildlife. Labour-intensive lawns may quickly be turned into something resembling a wildflower meadow (although a true meadow takes time and care to establish), and plants chosen to feed beneficial insects incorporated (see p.294 for suitable plants). A wildlife-friendly garden will usually succeed better in its aims if it includes a pond or a bog garden. These can both be created with pond liners. In a garden that is naturally waterlogged, it is better not to fight the prevailing conditions, but to make a virtue of necessity. There are plenty of attractive, even dramatic plants that will thrive in bog conditions (see page 292).

At the opposite end of the spectrum, the need to conserve water has resulted in a rise in recent years in the popularity of gardens designed to cope with dry summers without the need for constant watering. Thirsty lawns are replaced by paving with planting pockets or mulches of gravel, at best laid over weed-suppressing membranes, options that reduce both maintenance and evaporation. Such gravel gardens often feature tough perennials from Mediterranean climates. Perhaps the most famous gravel planting is in Beth Chatto's garden at Elmstead Market in Essex, a planting developed specifically to explore and show the diverse and beautiful range of plants that will survive naturally with little or no watering in a low-rainfall area (for drought-tolerant plants see p.291).

Perennials that actively dislike wet, particularly winter wet, can be grown in scree beds. These have a covering of several inches of coarse grit, and have several advantages. They keep the neck of a plant, where it is most likely to rot in a wet winter, dry, and they provide excellent drainage, minimizing plant losses in wet winters. Scree beds are also relatively maintenance-free, and the scree garden planted up with perennials is almost totally maintenance-free.

Below: *These alpine plants growing in a scree bed were photographed in Hartpury, Gloucestershire, where they survive the winters in spite of the high level of winter wet in the area. It is necessary to plan such a bed carefully to create a natural look. Larger pieces of stone in the design here help in this. Always ensure that stone does not come from environmentally sensitive areas.*

COMBINING PERENNIALS

There are many possible arrangements for planting perennials in any garden. The usual way of combining perennials is simply to grow all kinds – flowering, foliage, bulbs, ferns, grasses and sub-shrubs – together, intermingling plants with differing contours to give a pleasant architectural outline. This has many advantages, mainly that it offers points of interest throughout the seasons. Also, since many bulbs are spring-flowering, the gaps they leave as their foliage dies down are soon filled by herbaceous perennials coming into leaf. This sort of mixed planting also helps to guard against pests or diseases associated with one plant type gaining a hold.

Below: *This planting of moisture-loving perennials, in Marwood Hill Garden, Barnstaple, in Devon, shows what can be achieved by gardening with the prevailing circumstances. The area, at the bottom of a slope, is a damp location that provides many bog plants with the reliably moist conditions that they require throughout the year to flourish.*

There are however, many other interesting possibilities for those who would like to take a more structured or thematic approach. Some gardeners prefer to create very specific mixed plantings using "companion planting", holding that certain plant combinations benefit the health of the plants; this is a subject for a specialist book.

Those with the luxury of space may plant a one-season garden or bed. There are enough perennials of interest in each season for this to be a possibility for any one of them. The drawback, especially of a summer border is that the planting lacks interest for the rest of the year. Other seasonal beds can be planted with annuals in summer.

Many gardeners combine plants on the basis of colour. The all-white garden, as in the famous example at Sissinghurst, is popular, but any colour can be accommodated in a planting of perennials. A scheme of two colours broadens the range of plants. Blue and gold make a very pleasing combination, as do red and yellow, but not all colours mix, so they must be chosen carefully. In a looser approach, hot-coloured flowers complement each other and will have great impact, while cool-coloured flowers create a restful atmosphere.

Another approach is to combine plants according to their type. Gardeners usually have their favourite genera, and often choose to grow only these. Beds composed entirely of tulips, narcissi, irises, lilies, hostas, pinks, geraniums, columbines, cannas, campanulas or Michaelmas daisies are all common sights. A less restrictive theme would be to use one class of plant, such as grasses, flowering plants or ferns – ferneries were very popular in the 19th century.

Other groupings may be suggested by the area of the garden and its use. In an area directly outside a door or window, highly visible all year, a bed of evergreens (see p.290) may be appropriate. In part of the garden used mainly in fine summer weather, an abundance of flowers over a long season (see p.290) may be a priority. For a low-maintenance garden, ground-cover planting (see pp.292–93) will be essential. And in difficult, shady areas, only a grouping of shade-lovers (see pp.290–91) will succeed.

Left: *Bold red* Crocosmia *combines with yellow* Ligularia *and* Kniphofia *in a high-impact hot border.*

Below: *This well-planned combination of spires, rounded shapes and trailing plants is at the National Trust's Packwood House, in Warwickshire.*

CHOOSING PERENNIALS

When choosing perennials, one of the most important considerations is whether they suit your conditions . Do not assume that if a plant is bought locally it will be hardy in that area: a sales centre may have brought the plants from a long way off, even from another country. Many smaller nurseries do their own propagating, and so their plants may well be hardy locally; but always check first. Also, it is easiest to garden with the soil type and moisture level; there is little to be gained from trying to grow acid-loving plants in chalky soil or moisture-loving plants in a dry, free-draining soil. If some favourites must be included, be prepared to grow them in either containers or specially prepared beds, and to take extra care of them.

Another factor is the space available. The width of a plant has to be known to decide how many are needed to make a good-sized clump; for some, as many as five may be required. Also consider how far they spread. This is especially important in small gardens, and must be established beforehand. Some perennials, such as *Geranium* 'Ann Folkard', may spread several feet. Some perennials spread rapidly and invasively by underground stolons (see p.296).

Even in a large garden, invasive perennials can be a nuisance: they spread through neighbouring plants, grow up through them, and can cause them to die off, so are best avoided. Some perennials also seed themselves so freely that they become a nuisance (see p.295). At the other end of the scale, some perennials are very short-lived, (see p.295) and whilst there are many beautiful garden plants in this category, the gaps they leave behind need to be filled.

It is also important to look ahead to flowering time to ensure that colour clashes do not occur. It is useful to draw a plan of the area in each season before planting to ensure that these points are taken into account, and when planting out, start by placing the plants on the bed in their pots to ensure they are well-spaced before planting.

There are also practical human needs to consider. Allergies and asthma are on the increase, and our understanding of which plants trigger reactions is improving. Plants in the Asteraceae/Compositae family are the worst, but by no means the only, offenders in this.

Above: *Careful planning has produced this spectacular flowering display in a border at Jenkyn Place, near Bentley in Hampshire. It is best to see the plants in flower and compare colours before planning such a planting: even within a single colour the range of shades and tones can be surprisingly wide.*

Gardeners who suffer should avoid plants that cause skin irritation (see p.295), or which may trigger an allergic reaction (see p.293), and choose those plants which are least likely to cause a reaction (see p.293). In gardens that will be used by young children, it is best to avoid plants that are harmful if eaten, and in particular those plants with berries or poisonous swollen roots (see p.295). Some perennials need to be lifted and divided every few years to keep them in healthy trim, (see p.296) and should be avoided by infirm gardeners, or those with little time to spare. By avoiding perennials which are likely to be troublesome to them, any gardener can plant a garden that will be a pleasure for many years.

Planting and Maintaining Perennials

Since the advent of "containerisation", it has become possible to buy perennials all year round. This does not mean, however, that they can be planted all year round. Spring and autumn are good times to plant; spring is preferable in cold countries, giving the plant time to establish a root system before the onset of winter. Grasses and grey-leaved perennials transplant best in spring. Summer planting is possible, but there is the risk of the plant drying out, with disastrous results. Winter planting should be avoided if the ground is, or may become, frozen or waterlogged.

When planting perennials, keep in mind that the plants are likely to remain *in situ* for a number of years, and so thorough preparation of the ground is vital. This entails making sure that the drainage is good, removing all perennial weeds, digging over the site and incorporating as much humus as possible, and in particular, matter that is slow to disintegrate, such as bark.

Some perennials are tap-rooted, and resent transplantation (see p.296) so these should be placed with particular care: plant according to their needs, rather than taking a chance, and note the height when fully grown, so that it is not awkwardly placed. All plants should be allowed sufficient room for growth, and not surrounded too closely with others.

Once they are established, perennials are remarkably low-maintenance plants; nevertheless any garden requires a certain amount of work. The following tasks will all need to be carried out on a regular basis.

Weeding It is impossible to prevent annual grasses and perennial weeds such as dandelions from seeding into beds. Weeding can be performed either by hand or by hoe. The former is preferable, because hoeing can damage root systems, but is more tiring. Some plants, such as *Eremurus*, are surface-rooting, and should never be hoed around.

Mulching The most desirable, albeit expensive, way of keeping weeds to a minimum is to mulch on a regular basis, say once or twice a season. An organic mulch will also nourish plants as it disintegrates. A mulch should be applied only when the ground is wet; if it is not possible to wait for rain, water beforehand.

Staking The most important consideration here is to provide the support early, before the plants have flopped over. After that the task is twice as difficult. Many of the commercially available staking devices are designed on the principle that the plant grows up through a circular grid, so the device should be in place early in the growth cycle. However, there are many others that are designed to be put in place only after the plant has made considerable growth; all are vastly superior to the old-fashioned bamboo cane and string method. One favoured method is to use Christmas trees; the side branches of these can be cut off and put in place early, allowing the plant to grow up through them, or later, to provide support around the edges of the plants.

Dead-heading This is a very important task for three reasons. Firstly, it prevents energy going into the setting of seed and instead allows the plant to put its effort into building up reserves for the winter. Secondly, for some plants, it will result in a second flush of flowers later in the season. Thirdly, it will prevent many plants from self-seeding too freely.

Feeding Beds of perennials that lie undisturbed for many years will require feeding on a regular basis. The more mulching they receive, the less feeding they will require, since organic mulches decompose and feed the soil in the long run. However, nitrogen-rich fertilisers early in the growing season will help to build up a strong plant, and phosphate-rich feeds at flowering time will help to improve the quality of bloom.

Watering To water is tedious, time-consuming, and sometimes expensive, but necessary at times. The first golden rule of watering is to water thoroughly, or not at all, since repeated surface watering encourages plants to form surface roots at the expense of deep ones, which is courting disaster. The second golden rule is to do so late in the day, and not in the morning, as during the day much of the water will be lost by transpiration. It is always worth conserving water by diverting down-pipes into water butts.

Combatting pests and diseases The number of pests and diseases affecting plants is extensive, but perennials suffer less than most other plants, one reason for their increasing popularity. No category of plant, however, is entirely problem-free.

The major pest of perennials is the snail or slug. Common slug and snail killers contain metaldehyde, a potent poison. The dead slugs will be eaten by hedgehogs and birds (especially in suburban areas where every garden may be laced), and the poison may get into the hands of children. Slug and snail killers that are aluminium-sulphate based do not harm wildlife, but are more readily rendered ineffective by rain, needing to be renewed after each shower. Bell cloches are very useful in protecting new growth in spring, because the cloche prevents the slug killer from becoming ineffective after rain. The cloches should be removed when a healthy plant has been established. Slug traps, which are filled with beer, milk or other suitably tempting liquids, and in which the slugs drown, are also effective: be sure to place them with the edge a little above ground level so that beneficial beetles do not fall in. Biological controls, in the form of nematodes that parasitise slugs, are a more expensive, but effective and environmentally friendly alternative. Hedgehogs are the most natural solution of all, hence the importance of not endangering them with metaldehyde.

As regards disease, the problem common to many perennials is powdery mildew, which is particularly prevalent in very wet areas. It is disfiguring, debilitating, and often fatal. Chemical fungicides barely control it, and some plants, such as *Phlox paniculata* and *Aster novi-belgii*, are untreatable. Affected growth should be cut down and disposed of, but not composted or burned. It is often best simply to grow something else if the problem persists.

PROPAGATING PERENNIALS

Perennials can be propagated by seed, by division, and by cuttings.

Seed Species will come true from seed, but even these will show some variation in the progeny. Varieties, forms and sports and most cultivars cannot be propagated by seed if they are required to come true. The seedlings will vary widely, with only a few similar to the parent plant. Seed of *Gentiana, Helleborus,* and *Primula* must be sown fresh; be patient, as the seed will germinate the following spring, or even the spring after that. *Pulsatilla* must also be sown fresh, but germinates at once, as will seeds of the Ranunculaceae family. Most other seeds should be sown in spring. Use sterile seed compost and leave fine seeds on the surface, but lightly cover larger seeds. The largest seeds, such as *Lupinus* and *Baptisia*, have tough coats that must be chipped or abraded before sowing.

Cuttings These can be of stems or basal growth, generally taken in spring, or of roots, taken in late winter. A sandy soil should be used for rooting, preferably with bottom heat.

Division Most perennials can be increased easily by lifting and dividing established, congested plants. For herbaceous perennials, this should be carried out during the dormant period, and as a rule, division should take place in spring or autumn. The roots of the plants determine the best method of dividing the plant. Plants with fibrous roots, such as *Aster novae-angliae* (New England daisy), *Aster novi-belgii* (Michaelmas daisy), *Leucanthemum* × *superbum* (shasta daisy), *Rudbeckia* (coneflower) and *Helenium* (sneezeweed) can be increased by lifting and carefully dividing the complete roots. Plants with fleshy roots and woody crowns, such as *Delphinium* and *Lupinus* (lupins) can be propagated by lifting the crowns and using a sharp knife to cut through them, or by taking cuttings from young shoots in spring. Rhizomatous plants, such as *Iris germanica*, have thick, tough roots; these can be lifted and, using a sharp knife, the young roots around the outside of the clump divided into pieces 5–7.5cm (2–3in) long, each containing a few strong leaves. Dust the cut surfaces with fungicide then replant them to the same depth,

Below: *Division is an easy and inexpensive way to increase many herbaceous perennials. Once a border is established with these plants it is easy to lift and divide them every three or four years.* Helenium autumnale *'Pumilum magnificum', a yellow autumn daisy, offers a sunny splash of bright yellow blooms from late summer through to the end of autumn. Congested clumps should be divided by division after flowering in autumn or in spring.*

using the dark mark on the stem indicating the previous level as a guide. Discard the old, woody, central parts. Tuberous genera such as *Paeonia* should also be divided using a sharp knife, ensuring that each section of the tuber has good growing points. Both cormous and bulbous perennials increase freely at the root, and all that is necessary is separation of the offsets, best done when the plant is dormant. Only tap-rooted perennials cannot be propagated by division and must be increased by seed or cuttings.

Most perennials are fibrous-rooted, so the method of division for these is worth describing in more detail; all fibrous-rooted plants can be increased in this way, either by pulling the outer shoots apart with roots attached, or by dividing the root ball with a spade or with garden forks held back-to-back (as below). They can be divided at any time between early autumn and mid-spring, as long as the soil is not frozen or waterlogged. Usually this means in autumn when the weather is mild, but it is advisable to wait until spring in extremely cold and frost-prone areas.

When dividing fibrous-rooted plants, first cut down all stems to within a few inches of the ground. Clear these away and make sure that the soil is free from debris, including weeds. Use a garden fork to dig up the clump, taking care not to sever too many roots. To divide the plant, push two garden forks back-to-back down through the centre of the clump, then lever the handles together to force the roots apart. Ensure that the forks are both pushed in fully; otherwise the upper part of the clump will tear away from the base. Select and pull away young parts from the outside of the clump for replanting. Discard the woody, central area, which is the oldest part, and remove the roots of perennial weeds at the same time.

If the roots are extremely matted, wash them in water and part them gently with a plant label or a pointed stick. Replant the pieces before their roots become dry; if they cannot be replanted at once, wrap them in wet sacking. Ensure that the soil into which they are to be planted is also moist; water thoroughly several days before planting, so that excess moisture has time to drain away. Water again after planting and regularly through the growing season.

If the divided parts are particularly small, increase their size by planting them into a nursery bed for one or two years before putting them in their permanent positions in a border. If the parent plant is especially fine and a large number of new plants are wanted, pot very small pieces into 7.5cm (3in) pots and place in a cold frame until they are large enough to be planted into a garden. This is most important if the clump is divided in autumn.

1 Cut down all stems so that the crown of the plant can be seen. Use a garden fork to dig up the clump, taking care not to damage the roots.

2 Insert two garden forks into the clump back-to-back, and lever their handles together. Small plants are best divided with handforks.

1

2

3 Gently pull the clump into small pieces, but not very small unless a large number of plants are required. Discard the old, woody central part.

4 Replant the young pieces soon after the clump has been divided. Do not allow the roots to become dry; cover them with damp sacking if planting is delayed.

3

4

THE PLANT DIRECTORY

MORE THAN 1500 plant entries are featured in the directory. Each entry is illustrated with a colour picture of the plant *in situ*, and gives the botanical and common name or names; the height and spread of the plant in metric and imperial measures; the required aspect and type of soil; hardiness rating, and suitable propagation methods. There is a brief description of the plant, giving any appropriate information about the root system or the area in which the plant originated, and detailing the the form and colour of the flower and the foliage. The Royal Horticultural Society in the UK carries out extensive trials of all categories of plants, and the accolade of the Award of Garden Merit is given to the most outstanding plants. A plant which has the Award of Garden Merit will have the letters A.G.M. after its name. Positive and negative attributes of each plant are given in the form of symbols, explained below and on the bookmark.

KEY TO SYMBOLS

Positive Attribute Symbols

- Long flowering
- Repeat flowering
- Aromatic/Perfumed
- Evergreen
- Architectural plant
- Good cut flower
- Good for winter drying
- Drought-tolerant
- Attracts butterflies/bees
- Attractive seedheads/berries
- Low allergen
- Attractive foliage

Negative Attribute Symbols

- Insignificant flowers
- Short-lived plant
- Requires staking
- Invasive plant
- Seeds everywhere
- Prone to slug/snail damage
- Regular lifting and dividing
- Resents disturbance
- Prone to powdery mildew
- Highly allergenic
- Poisonous/skin irritant

Herbaceous border at Bramdean House, in midsummer

Acaena caesiiglauca
(Rosaceae)

Common names: Bidi-bidi;
New Zealand burr
Height: 12cm (5in)
Spread: To 1m (3ft)
Aspect: Sun or half-shade
Soil: Well-drained
Hardiness: Zone 6
Propagation: Seed, in autumn; softwood cuttings, in spring; division, in spring or autumn

Semi-prostrate, evergreen subshrub. Leaves glaucous, pinnate, with 7–13 obovate leaflets. Flowerheads spherical, followed by reddish-brown burrs in late summer.

Acaena microphylla
'Kupferteppich'
(Rosaceae)

Common name: Copper carpet
Height: 5cm (2in)
Spread 60cm (24in)
Aspect: Sun or half shade
Soil: Must not be waterlogged
Hardiness: Zone 6
Propagation: Seed, in autumn; softwood cuttings, in spring; division, in spring or autumn

Prostrate, evergreen subshrub. Leaves bronze, pinnate, with 9–15 rounded leaflets. Flowerheads spherical, small, followed by red burrs. Good for rock garden or wall.

Acanthus dioscoridis
var. *perringii*
(Acanthaceae)

Common name: Bear's breeches
Height: 40cm (16in)
Spread: 60cm (24in)
Aspect: Sun or half shade
Soil: Well-drained
Hardiness: Zone 8
Propagation: Seed, in spring; division, in spring or autumn; root cuttings, in winter

Evergreen with running, fleshy rootstalk. Leaves spiny, pinnatifid, grey-green, rosetted. Racemes of pink flowers with green bracts, late spring to late summer. Shy-flowering.

Acanthus hungaricus
(Acanthaceae)

Common name: Bear's breeches
Height: 1.2m (4ft)
Spread: 90cm (3ft)
Aspect: Sun or half shade
Soil: Well-drained
Hardiness: Zone 8
Propagation: Seed, in spring; division, in spring or autumn; root cuttings, in winter

Clump-forming evergreen. Leaves oblong-obovate, dark green, deeply lobed. Racemes of pale pink or white flowers, bracts tinged purple, early to midsummer.

Acanthus mollis
(Acanthaceae)

Common name: Bear's breeches
Height: To 1.5m (5ft)
Spread: 90cm (3ft)
Aspect: Sun or half shade
Soil: Well-drained
Hardiness: Zone 6
Propagation: Seed, in spring; division, in spring or autumn; root cuttings, in winter

Clump-forming, architectural evergreen with obovate, dark green, deeply lobed, shiny leaves. Flowers in racemes, white, with purple-shaded bracts, in late summer.

Acanthus spinosus
A.G.M.
(Acanthaceae)

Common name: Bear's breeches
Height: To 1.2m (4ft)
Spread: 60cm (2ft)
Aspect: Sun or half shade
Soil: Well-drained
Hardiness: Zone 6
Propagation: Seed, in spring; division, in spring or autumn; root cuttings, in winter

Clump-forming, architectural evergreen. Leaves spiny, oblong, deeply cut, arching, dark green. Tall raceme of soft mauve flowers and purple bracts, from late spring.

ACHILLEA (Compositae)
Yarrow • Milfoil • Sneezewort

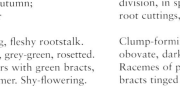

A genus of some 80 species, from various habitats in the temperate northern hemisphere. The daisy-like flowerheads usually lack ray petals, so have only disc florets, and are closely packed in tight corymbs, borne on stout stems. They exhibit a wide range of colour. All are attractive to both bees and butterflies. The foliage is feathery, save for that of *A. ptarmica*, and some are evergreen. The flowerheads last a long time, and are good for cutting and drying for the winter, and suitable for flower arrangements in both fresh and dry states. *Achillea* do best in full sun with good drainage, but they are only reasonably tolerant of drought, so a moisture-retentive soil is best. They grow well in coastal areas. Drawbacks are that they are prone to powdery mildew, and some forms require staking. *A. millefolium* (Zone 2) and *A. ptarmica* (Zone 5), both rhizomatous, can be as invasive as weeds. All the rest are well-behaved, except that they may die out in the centre and usually have to be lifted and divided every few years, and the healthy outer edges replanted. Many species and cultivars hold an Award of Garden Merit; some not illustrated here are *A. ageratifolia* (Zone 3), *A.* × *lewisii* 'King Edward' (Zone 5), and *A. tomentosa* (Zone 3).

Achillea
'Coronation Gold' A.G.M.
(Asteraceae/Compositae)

Common name: Yarrow
Height: 90cm (36in)
Spread: 45cm (18in)
Aspect: Sun
Soil: Humus-rich
Hardiness: Zone 6
Propagation: Division, in spring

Clump-forming evergreen with pinnatifid, oblong, grey-green leaves. Corymbs 10cm (4in) across of golden-yellow flowerheads, from midsummer. Good for small gardens.

Achillea
'Credo'
(Asteraceae/Compositae)

Common names: Milfoil; yarrow
Height: 1.2m (4ft)
Spread: 60cm (2ft)
Aspect: Sun
Soil: Humus-rich
Hardiness: Zone 6
Propagation: Division, in spring

Clump-forming perennial with feathery, pale green leaves and corymbs of pale yellow flowerheads, ageing to cream, in summer.

Achillea
'Fanal'
(Asteraceae/Compositae)

Common name: Yarrow
Height: 75cm (30in)
Spread: 60cm (24in)
Aspect: Sun
Soil: Humus-rich
Hardiness: Zone 2
Propagation: Division, in spring

Mat-forming hybrid with linear, 2-pinnate, grey-green leaves. Corymbs 15cm (6in) across of bright red flowerheads with yellow discs. Flowers fade as they age.

Achillea filipendula
'Gold Plate' A.G.M.
(Asteraceae/Compositae)

Common name: Yarrow
Height: 1.2m (4ft)
Spread: 45cm (18in)
Aspect: Sun
Soil: Humus-rich
Hardiness: Zone 3
Propagation: Division, in spring

Clump-forming evergreen. Rosettes of mid- to grey-green, oblong, 1- or 2-pinnate leaves. Bright yellow flowerheads in corymbs 15cm (6in) across, early summer to early autumn.

Achillea
'Forncett Candy'
(Asteraceae/Compositae)

Common name: Yarrow
Height: 90cm (36in)
Spread: 45cm (18in)
Aspect: Sun
Soil: Humus-rich
Hardiness: Zone 6
Propagation: Division, in spring

Clump-forming evergreen, with fern-like, grey-green leaves. Abundant pale pink flowerheads, fading to almost white in corymbs 15cm (6in) across, in summer.

Achillea
'Huteri'
(Asteraceae/Compositae)

Common name: Yarrow
Height: 60cm (24in)
Spread: 30cm (12in)
Aspect: Sun
Soil: Humus-rich
Hardiness: Zone 6
Propagation: Division, in spring

A bushy cultivar, with linear, pinnate leaves of silver-grey. Flowerheads with white ray florets are borne in corymbs in summer.

Achillea millefolium
'Cerise Queen'
(Asteraceae/Compositae)

Common name: Yarrow
Height: 60cm (2ft)
Spread: 60cm (2ft)
Aspect: Sun
Soil: Humus-rich
Hardiness: Zone 2
Propagation: Division, in spring

Rhizomatous, mat-forming cultivar. Leaves linear to lance-shaped, pinnatisect, dark green. Corymbs of magenta flowerheads with white discs in summer. Highly invasive.

Achillea
'Moonshine' A.G.M.
(Asteraceae/Compositae)

Common name: Yarrow
Height: 60cm (2ft)
Spread: 60cm (2ft)
Aspect: Sun
Soil: Humus-rich
Hardiness: Zone 7
Propagation: Division, in spring

Clump-forming evergreen with linear to lance-shaped, grey-green, pinnatifid leaves. Corymbs 15cm (6in) across of light yellow flowerheads, early summer to early autumn.

Achillea ptarmica
'Nana Compacta'
(Asteraceae/Compositae)

Common name: Sneezewort
Height: 30cm (12in)
Spread: 60cm (24in)
Aspect: Sun
Soil: Humus-rich
Hardiness: Zone 5
Propagation: Division, in spring

Rhizomatous perennial. Leaves linear to lance-shaped, toothed, dark green. Corymbs of off-white flowers with grey-green centres in summer. Too invasive for borders.

Achillea ptarmica
'Stephanie Cohen'
(Asteraceae/Compositae)

Common name: Sneezewort
Height: 75cm (30in)
Spread: 80cm (32in)
Aspect: Sun
Soil: Any
Hardiness: Zone 5
Propagation: Division, in spring

A handsome but invasive cultivar. Foliage linear to lance-shaped, toothed, green. Pale pink flowers with darker centres, borne in corymbs from early to late summer.

Aciphylla aurea
(Apiaceae/Umbelliferae)

Common names: Bayonet plant; spear grass
Height: 1m (3ft)
Spread: 1m (3ft)
Aspect: Full sun
Soil: Moist but well-drained, humus-rich
Hardiness: Zone 5
Propagation: Seed, when ripe

Rosettes of strap-like, 2-pinnate grey-green leaves with spiny tips and gold edges. Many golden-brown, star-shaped flowers. Needs both sexes and warm summers to fruit.

Aciphylla glaucescens
(Apiaceae/Umbelliferae)

Common names: Bayonet plant; spear grass
Height: 1m (3ft)
Spread: 1m (3ft)
Aspect: Full sun
Soil: Moist but well-drained, humus-rich
Hardiness: Zone 8
Propagation: Seed, when ripe

Rosettes of narrow, 3-pinnate, strap-like leaves, silver-grey, spiny-tipped and edged. Yellow-green, star-shaped flowers. Needs both sexes and a warm climate to fruit.

ACONITUM (Ranunculaceae)
Monkshood • Aconite • Wolf's bane

A genus of about 100 species from woodlands, grasslands and scrub in the northern hemisphere. They are tuberous-rooted, except for *A. lycotonum* subsp. *vulparia*. The distinctive flowers have hoods composed of sepals, giving one of the common names, which provide the shape and colour and hide the petals. They are carried in tall panicles or racemes, well above the foliage. The leaves are generally of a rich green, and ovate, round, palmately lobed or kidney-shaped. All *Aconitum* need to be lifted and divided every few years; the taller forms, although good architectural plants for woodland or border, will also require staking. It is important to note that all parts of these plants are highly poisonous if eaten. There are no particularly tempting-looking fruits, but it is still safest to say that the genus should not be grown in a garden where there are children. Contact with the foliage may also cause skin irritation, but handled with care they make good cut flowers, and are popular with flower-arrangers. The flowers are not allergenic. Other Award of Garden Merit varieties that have not been illustrated here are *A.* 'Bressingham Spire' (Zone 4), *A. carmichaelii* 'Kelmscott' (Zone 3), and *A.* 'Spark's Variety' (Zone 4).

Aconitum x *cammarum*
'Bicolor' A.G.M.
(Ranunculaceae)

Common name: Monkshood
Height: 1.2m (4ft)
Spread: 1.2m (4ft)
Aspect: Sun or half shade
Soil: Moist, fertile, humus-rich
Hardiness: Zone 3
Propagation: Division, in autumn

A very hardy perennial. Foliage ovate to round, deeply lobed, glossy, dark green. Blue and white flowers in loose arching panicles from midsummer.

Aconitum septentrionale
'Ivorine'
(Ranunculaceae)

Common name: Monkshood
Height: 90cm (36in)
Spread: 45cm (18in)
Aspect: Sun or half shade
Soil: Moist, fertile, cool
Hardiness: Zone 5
Propagation: Division, in autumn

Very attractive perennial with deeply lobed, rounded, rich green leaves. Ivory flowers in spike-like racemes in late spring and early summer; largest in a cool, moist climate.

Aconitum lycoctonum subsp. *vulparia* (Ranunculaceae)

Common name: Wolf's bane
Height: To 1.5m (5ft)
Spread: 30cm (1ft)
Aspect: Sun or half shade
Soil: Moist, fertile, humus-rich
Hardiness: Zone 3
Propagation: Seed, in spring; division, in autumn

An erect, very hardy perennial with round, lobed, rich green leaves. Panicles of hooded, pale yellow flowers are borne from mid- to late summer.

Aconitum lycoctonum, subsp. *vulparia* 'Albidum' (Ranunculaceae)

Common name: Wolf's bane
Height: To 1.5m (5ft)
Spread: 30cm (1ft)
Aspect: Sun or half shade
Soil: Moist, fertile, humus-rich
Hardiness: Zone 3
Propagation: Division, in autumn

A very hardy, handsome perennial. Erect stems. Leaves dark green, rounded, with 5 to 9 lobes. Flowers in panicles, hooded, pure white.

Aconitum napellus (Ranunculaceae)

Common name: Monkshood
Height: To 1.5m (5ft)
Spread: 30cm (1ft)
Aspect: Sun or half shade
Soil: Moist, fertile, humus-rich
Hardiness: Zone 6
Propagation: Seed, in spring; division, in autumn

Erect, with rounded, deeply-lobed, often toothed, dark green leaves. Panicles of flowers are intense indigo-blue in the best forms. Very variable; buy in bloom.

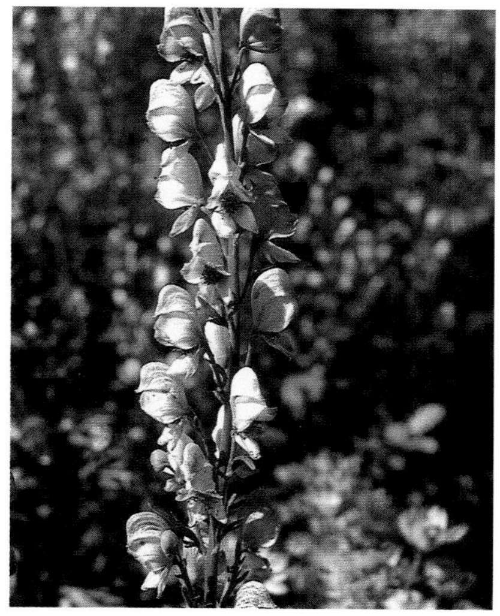

Aconitum napellus subsp. *vulgare* 'Albidum' (Ranunculaceae)

Common name: Monkshood
Height: To 1.5m (5ft)
Spread: 30cm (1ft)
Aspect: Sun or half shade
Soil: Moist, fertile, humus-rich
Hardiness: Zone 6
Propagation: Division, in autumn.

Erect, with handsome foliage of rounded, deeply lobed, toothed, dark green leaves. Panicles of grey-white flowers in mid- to late summer.

Actaea alba A.G.M. (Ranunculacae)

Common names: Doll's eyes; white baneberry
Height: 90cm (3ft)
Spread: 60cm (2ft)
Aspect: Half shade
Soil: Cool, moist, fertile, humus-rich
Hardiness: Zone 3
Propagation: Seed, in autumn; division, in spring

Rhizomatous woodland plant with 2-, 3-, or 5-ternate, toothed, green leaves. Tiny white flowers in spherical racemes are followed by clusters of extremely toxic white berries.

Actaea rubra A.G.M. (Ranunculaceae)

Common name: Red baneberry
Height: 45cm (18in)
Spread: 30cm (12in)
Aspect: Half shade
Soil: Cool, moist, fertile, humus-rich
Hardiness: Zone 3
Propagation: Seed, in autumn; division, in spring

Woodlander with 2- or 3-pinnate leaves of up to 15 ovate leaflets. Small racemes of white, ovoid flowers in spring to summer, followed by shiny, red, highly toxic berries.

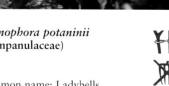

Adenophora asiatica (Campanulaceae)

Common name: Ladybells
Height: 30cm (12in)
Spread: 15cm (6in)
Aspect: Sun or half shade
Soil: Moist, well-drained, humus-rich
Hardiness: Zone 5
Propagation: Seed, in autumn; cuttings in spring; no division

A charming fleshy-rooted perennial. Leaves ovate, toothed, mid-green. Flowers bell-shaped, pendent, pale lavender-blue, in terminal racemes, in mid- to late summer.

Adenophora potaninii (Campanulaceae)

Common name: Ladybells
Height: To 90cm (3ft)
Spread: 30cm (1ft)
Aspect: Sun or half shade
Soil: Moist, well-drained, humus-rich
Hardiness: Zone 3
Propagation: Seed, in autumn; cuttings, in spring

Reliable perennial with lax stems and ovate to lance-shaped, toothed leaves. Racemes of pendent, open, bell-shaped, violet-blue flowers in mid- to late summer.

Adiantum aleuticum
A.G.M.
(Adiantaceae/Pteridaceae)

Common name: Aleutian maidenhair fern
Height: 75cm (30in)
Spread: 75cm (30in)
Aspect: Sun or half shade
Soil: Moist, well-drained, humus-rich
Hardiness: Zone 4
Propagation: Spores, in warmth when ripe; division, in spring

Rhizomatous, deciduous fern. Fronds pale to mid-green, kidney-shaped to broadly ovate, pedate, with oblong segments and black stalks and midribs.

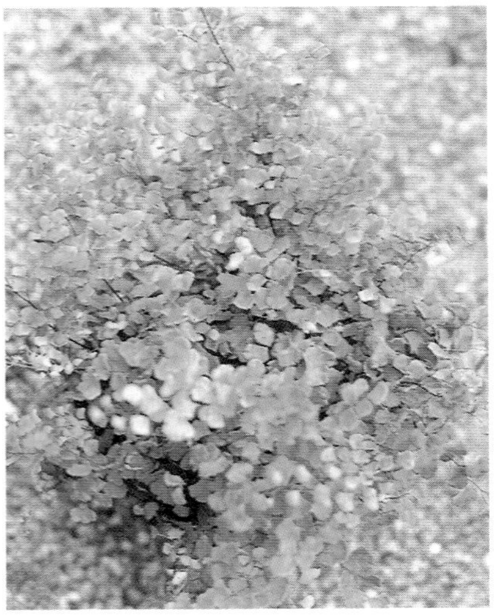

Adiantum capillus-veneris
(Adiantaceae/Pteridaceae)

Common name: True maidenhair fern
Height: 30cm (12in)
Spread: 45cm (18in)
Aspect: Half shade
Soil: Moist, well-drained, alkaline, fertile
Hardiness: Zone 8
Propagation: Spores, in warmth when ripe; division, in spring

Creeping, rhizomatous fern, evergreen down to -2°C (28°F). Fronds arching, bronze-pink, turning green, 2- or 3-pinnate, triangular. Pinnae fan-shaped, stems black.

Adiantum pedatum
A.G.M.
(Adiantaceae/Pteridaceae)

Common name: Five-fingered maidenhair fern
Height: 40cm (16in)
Spread: 40cm (16in)
Aspect: Half-shade
Soil: Moist, well drained, fertile
Hardiness: Zone 5
Propagation: Spores, in warmth in autumn; division, in spring

Deciduous, creeping, rhizomatous fern. Fronds ovate to kidney-shaped, pinnate, mid-green. Segments oblong or triangular, upper edges lobed or toothed. Stems black.

Aegopodium podagraria
'Variegatum'
(Apiaceae/Umbelliferae)

Common name: Variegated ground elder
Height: 60cm (2ft)
Spread: Indefinite
Aspect: Full or half shade
Soil: Any
Hardiness: Zone 2
Propagation: Division, in spring

Invasive rhizomatous plant. Leaves ovate, green, cream-edged. Insignificant white flowers. Grow in difficult dry shade or in a container; dead-head before it sets seed.

Aeonium cuneatum
(Crassulaceae)

Common names: None
Height: 2m (6ft)
Spread: 50cm (20in)
Aspect: Half shade
Soil: Well-drained, fertile
Hardiness: Zone 9
Propagation: Seed, in warmth in spring; cuttings, in spring

Showy, evergreen succulent. Tidy rosettes of fleshy leaves on clustered, basal shoots. Spike-like panicle of star-shaped, yellow flowers in spring and summer.

Aethionema schistosum
(Brassicaceae/Cruciferae)

Common name: Stone cress
Height: 10cm (4in)
Spread: 30cm (12in)
Aspect: Sun
Soil: Well-drained
Hardiness: Zone 6
Propagation: Seed, in spring

Upright, free-flowering; for border front or rock garden. Narrow, linear, acuminate, crowded leaves. Tight raceme of 4-petalled, tiny pink flowers in spring. From Turkey.

Aethionema
'Warley Rose' A.G.M.
(Brassicaceae/Cruciferae)

Common name: Stone cress
Height: 20cm (8in)
Spread: 20cm (8in)
Aspect: Sun
Soil: Well-drained
Hardiness: Zone 7
Propagation: Softwood cuttings, in spring or autumn

Free-flowering but short-lived dwarf subshrub. Leaves linear, blue-grey. Small pink flowers in tight racemes in spring and early summer. Good wall plant.

Agapanthus
'Blue Imp'
(Alliaceae/Liliaceae)

Common names: African blue lily
Height: 30cm (12in)
Spread: 20cm (8in)
Aspect: Full sun
Soil: Moist, well-drained, fertile
Hardiness: Zone 7
Propagation: Division, in late spring

Choice dwarf form, ideal for small gardens. Deciduous, strap-shaped, dark green leaves. Large umbels of deep blue flowers in late summer.

AGAPANTHUS (Alliaceae/Liliaceae)
African blue lily

A genus of about 10 perennials from southern Africa. They are vigorous, and form large clumps. The foliage is strap-shaped, often arching, and of a deep green; some species are evergreen, but the hybrid forms are all deciduous. The inflorescence is an umbel, which may be rounded, pendent or intermediate between the two. The individual flowers may be tubular, trumpet-shaped or bell-shaped, and are usually blue in colour, although white forms exist. They are followed by attractive seed heads. The roots are very brittle, so the genus does not transplant well: they should be moved whilst in growth, if at all. *Agapanthus* are generally fairly hardy, but in cold areas they should be mulched over winter if left in the open ground; they make excellent container plants that can be moved under some protection in winter. The evergreen species, originating in coastal areas, are tender and should have winter protection. All make good flowers for cutting; the seed heads also dry well, and are liked by flower-arrangers. Other Award of Garden Merit forms not included in this selection are *A. africanus* and *A. africanus* 'Albus' (both Zone 9), *A. caulescens* (Zone 7), *A.* 'Loch Hope' (Zone 7) and *A. praecox* 'Variegatus' (Zone 9).

***Agapanthus* 'Bressingham Blue'**
(Alliaceae/Liliaceae)

Common name: African blue lily
Height: 90cm (36in)
Spread: 45cm (18in)
Aspect: Full sun
Soil: Moist, well-drained, fertile
Hardiness: Zone 7
Propagation: Division, in late spring

Very robust cultivar. Trumpet-shaped, intensely amethyst-blue flowers in huge, rounded umbels in mid- to late summer. Strap-like, deep green leaves.

Agapanthus campanulatus
(Alliaceae/Liliaceae)

Common name: African blue lily
Height: 1.2m (4ft)
Spread: 45cm (18in)
Aspect: Full sun
Soil: Moist, well-drained, fertile
Hardiness: Zone 7
Propagation: Division, in late spring

Vigorous, clump-forming species. Narrow, strap-like, grey-green leaves. Bell-shaped flowers of pale or dark blue in rounded umbels on strong stems.

Agapanthus campanulatus* var. *albidus
(Alliaceae:Liliaceae)

Common name: African blue lily
Height: To 1.2m (4ft)
Spread: 45cm (18in)
Aspect: Full sun
Soil: Moist, well-drained, fertile
Hardiness: Zone 7
Propagation: Division, in late spring

A white-flowered form of the species. Vigorous and clump-forming, with narrow, strap-like, grey-green leaves. Rounded umbels of bell-shaped flowers.

***Agapanthus* 'Lilliput'**
(Alliaceae/Liliaceae)

Common name: African blue lily
Height: 40cm (16in)
Spread: 40cm (16in)
Aspect: Full sun
Soil: Moist, well-drained, fertile
Hardiness: Zone 7
Propagation: Division, in late spring

Clump-forming dwarf form, ideal for small gardens. Umbels rounded or intermediate, flowers trumpet-shaped and deep blue, in mid- to late summer.

***Agastache* 'Firebird'**
(Labiatae/Lamiaceae)

Common name: Mexican hyssop
Height: 60cm (2ft)
Spread: 30cm (1ft)
Aspect: Full sun
Soil: Well-drained, fertile
Hardiness: Zone 8
Propagation: Semi-ripe cuttings, in late summer

A short-lived cultivar with lance-shaped to ovate, grey-green, aromatic leaves. Spikes of tubular, two-lipped, long-lasting, copper-red flowers from midsummer to early autumn.

Agastache foeniculum
(Labiatae/Lamiaceae)

Common names: Anise hyssop
Height: 1.5m (5ft)
Spread: 30cm (1ft)
Aspect: Full sun
Soil: Well-drained, fertile
Hardiness: Zone 8
Propagation: Semi-ripe cuttings, in late summer

Upright, aniseed-scented plant. Veined, ovate to lance-shaped leaves, downy beneath. Blue flowers with lilac bracts and calyces, in spikes from midsummer to early autumn.

*Bugle (*Ajuga reptans*) flowering in an oak wood in Monkswood, UK*

Agastache mexicana
(Labiatae/Lamiaceae)

Common name: Mexican hyssop
Height: 90cm (3ft)
Spread: 30cm (1ft)
Aspect: Full sun
Soil: Well-drained, fertile
Hardiness: Zone 9
Propagation: Semi-ripe cuttings, in early summer

Short-lived, bushy perennial with aromatic foliage. Ovate to lance-shaped, green leaves. Flowers rosy-red, in tall spikes, from mid- to late summer.

Agave americana
'Marginata'
(Agavaceae)

Common names: Century plant; maguey
Height: 2m (6ft)
Spread: 3m (10ft)
Aspect: Full sun
Soil: Sharply-drained, acidic
Hardiness: Zone 9
Propagation: Seed, in warmth in spring; offsets, in spring or autumn

Succulent from Central America. Rosette of lance-shaped, grey-green leaves with spiny yellow edges. May produce panicles of yellow flowers in summer; monocarpic.

ADDITIONAL AGAVES with an A.G.M. (all Zone 9)

A. americana 'Mediopicta'

A. americana 'Variegata'

A. filifera

A. parviflora

A. potatorium

A. stricta

A. victoria-reginae

Ajania pacifica
(Asteraceae/Compositae)

Common names: None
Height: 30cm (1ft)
Spread: 90cm (3ft)
Aspect: Full sun
Soil: Well-drained, poor
Hardiness: Zone 6
Propagation: Seed, cuttings, or division, all in spring

Mound-forming Asian subshrub, spreading by runners. Leaves ovate, lobed, silky, grey-green, edged white. Flowers yellow buttons, in corymbs in autumn.

Ajuga reptans
'Atropurpurea' A.G.M.
(Labiatae: Lamiaceae)

Common name: Bugle
Height: 15cm (6in)
Spread: 90cm (36in)
Aspect: Half shade; protect from midday sun
Soil: Moist
Hardiness: Zone 6
Propagation: Softwood cuttings, in spring

Rhizomatous, creeping ground cover. Ovate to oblong-spoon-shaped, dark purple leaves. Whorled spikes of dark blue flowers in spring and early summer.

Ajuga reptans
'Burgundy Glow' A.G.M.
(Labiatae/Lamiaceae)

Common name: Bugle
Height: 15cm (6in)
Spread: To 90cm (36in)
Aspect: Half shade; protect from midday sun
Soil: Moist
Hardiness: Zone 6
Propagation: Softwood cuttings, in spring

Rhizomatous, creeping ground cover. Ovate to spoon-shaped leaves are silvery green, flushed dark red. Blue flowers in hairy-stemmed spikes in spring to early summer.

Ajuga reptans
'Multicolor' syn. 'Rainbow'
(Labiatae/Lamiaceae)

Common name: Bugle
Height: 15cm (6in)
Spread: 1m (36in)
Aspect: Half shade; protect from midday sun
Soil: Moist
Hardiness: Zone 6
Propagation: Softwood cuttings, in spring

Rhizomatous, creeping ground cover. Ovate to spoon-shaped leaves, reddish-bronze and green, splashed pink and cream. Spikes of dark blue flowers in spring to early summer.

Albuca altissima
(Hyacinthaceae/Liliaceae)

Common names: None
Height: 45cm (18in)
Spread: 30cm (12in)
Aspect: Full sun
Soil: Well-drained, fertile
Hardiness: Zone 9
Propagation: Seed, in spring; bulbils, in autumn

Bulbous plant from South Africa. Glabrous, green, lanceolate leaves. Trumpet-shaped, white flowers, with a broad green median stripe, in a loose raceme in late summer.

Albuca humilis
(Hyacintheae/Liliaceae)

Common names: None
Height: 10cm (4in)
Spread: 5cm (2in)
Aspect: Sun
Soil: Well-drained, fertile
Hardiness: Zone 7
Propagation: Seed, in warmth in spring; offsets, in autumn

Bulbous perennial. Leaves narrow, linear, green, basal. Flowers narrow, white bells, outer tepals striped green, inner ones tipped yellow, in late spring and early summer.

Alcea rosea
(Malvaceae)

Common name: Hollyhock
Height: 2m (6ft)
Spread: 1m (3ft)
Aspect: Sun
Soil: Well-drained, fertile
Hardiness: Zone 3
Propagation: Seed, *in situ* in summer

Well-loved perennial. Leaves rounded, hairy, lobed, green. Long terminal racemes of yellow, white, pink or purple, single flowers in early and midsummer. Dries well.

Alcea rosea
'Chater's Double'
(Malvaceae)

Common name: Hollyhock
Height: 2.5m (8ft)
Spread: 60cm (2ft)
Aspect: Sun
Soil: Well-drained, fertile
Hardiness: Zone 3
Propagation: Seed, *in situ* in summer

Race with fully double, paeony-like flowers in many shades in early and midsummer. Leaves round, hairy, green. Grow as annuals if hollyhock rust is a problem.

Alchemilla alpina
(Rosaceae)

Common name: Alpine lady's mantle
Height: 12cm (5in)
Spread: 50cm (20in)
Aspect: Sun or half shade
Soil: Moist, humus-rich
Hardiness: Zone 3
Propagation: Seed, in spring; division, in spring or autumn

Creeping, mat-forming, woody perennial. Kidney-shaped or rounded, lobed, white-edged green leaves, silver beneath. Straggly cymes of tiny, yellow flowers in summer.

Alchemilla mollis
A.G.M.
(Rosaceae)

Common name: Lady's mantle
Height: 60cm (2ft)
Spread: 90cm (3ft)
Aspect: Sun or half shade
Soil: Moist, humus-rich
Hardiness: Zone 3
Propagation: Seed, in spring; division, in spring or autumn

Handsome, clump-forming ground cover. Leaves rounded, lobed, toothed, pale green, softly hairy. Tiny greenish-yellow flowers in lax cymes from spring to autumn.

Alisma plantago-aquatica
(Alismataceae)

Common name: Water plantain
Height: 75cm (30in)
Spread: 75cm (30in)
Aspect: Sun
Soil: Marginal or in water 15–30cm (6–12in) deep
Hardiness: Zone 6
Propagation: Seed, when ripe; division, in spring

Rhizomatous, deciduous aquatic marginal. Basal rosettes of elliptic to lance-shaped, grey-green leaves. Huge, branched panicle of tiny white flowers in mid- and late summer.

ALLIUM (Liliaceae)
Onion

Huge genus of some 700 species from a wide range of habitats in the northern hemisphere. They may be bulbous or rhizomatous, and are grown for culinary or ornamental value or both. All enjoy full sun, and most prefer well-drained soil. Hardiness varies: many are reliably hardy, but there are some tender species. Most are deciduous. The flowerheads are umbels, which may be ovoid, round or pendent in shape; individual flowers are cup-, bell- or star-shaped. All alliums make good cut flowers, although the aggressive onion odour may not be to everyone's liking, and they are much used fresh and dried by flower-arrangers. Contact with the bulbs may cause skin irritation, or exacerbate existing allergic skin disease. Many alliums are well-behaved garden plants, and twenty-one carry an Award of Garden Merit as ornamental plants. Others spread like pernicious weeds: those that carry bulbils in the flowerhead, such as *A. carinatum* (Zone 7), *A. vineale* (Zone 5) and *A. scorodoprasum* (Zone 7), should be avoided in most situations, as they come up everywhere. Other promiscuous alliums to be treated with caution are *A. canadense* (Zone 4), *A. ampeloprasum* var. *bulbiferum* (Zone 6), *A. paradoxum* (Zone 8) and *A. roseum* (Zone 8).

Allium angulosum
(Alliaceae/Liliaceae)

Common name: Mouse garlic
Height: 45cm (18in)
Spread: 30cm (12in)
Aspect: Sun
Soil: Moist, fertile
Hardiness: Zone 5
Propagation: Seed, in spring; offsets, in autumn

Bulbous onion with linear to strap-like, rich, shiny, green basal leaves, sharply keeled underneath. Flowers are pale lilac, in hemispherical umbels on stout stems.

Allium carinatum subsp. *pulchellum* A.G.M.
(Alliaceae/Liliaceae)

Common name: Keeled garlic
Height: 60cm (24in)
Spread: 10cm (4in)
Aspect: Sun
Soil: Well-drained, fertile
Hardiness: Zone 7
Propagation: Seed, in spring; offsets, in autumn

Bulbous evergreen perennial with mid-green, linear, basal leaves. Rich purple, bell-shaped flowers in elongated, dense umbel. Slowly forms clumps. From S. Europe.

Allium cernuum
(Alliaceae/Liliaceae)

Common names: Nodding onion; wild onion
Height: 60cm (24in)
Spread: 10cm (4in)
Aspect: Sun
Soil: Well-drained, fertile
Hardiness: Zone 6
Propagation: Seed, in spring; offsets, in autumn

An easy-going, vigorous, bulbous plant with deep pink, bell-shaped flowers in a drooping umbel. The leaves are narrow, dark green basal straps.

Allium cristophii A.G.M.
(Alliaceae/Liliaceae)

Common names: Star of Persia
Height: 60cm (24in)
Spread: 20cm (8in)
Aspect: Sun
Soil: Well-drained, fertile
Hardiness: Zone 5
Propagation: Seed, in spring; offsets, in autumn

Popular bulbous perennial. Leaves basal, strap-like, grey-green. Bears purplish-pink, star-shaped flowers with a metallic sheen in large, spherical umbels in early summer.

Allium flavum A.G.M.
(Alliaceae/Liliaceae)

Common name: Small yellow onion
Height: 40cm (16in)
Spread: 10cm (4in)
Aspect: Sun
Soil: Well-drained, fertile
Hardiness: Zone 7
Propagation: Seed, in spring; offsets, in autumn

Very variable, bulbous onion. Leaves strap-shaped, glaucous, green. Up to 60 bright yellow, bell-shaped, pendent flowers in a loose umbel in summer.

Allium giganteum A.G.M.
(Alliaceae/Liliaceae)

Common names: None
Height: 2m (6ft)
Spread: 20cm (8in)
Aspect: Sun
Soil: Well-drained, fertile
Hardiness: Zone 5
Propagation: Seed, in spring; offsets, in autumn

Bulbous allium with pale green, strap-like basal leaves that wither before flowering. Large, dense umbel of up to 60 lilac-pink, star-shaped flowers in summer.

Allium 'Globemaster' A.G.M.
(Alliaceae/Liliaceae)

Common names: None
Height: 80cm (32in)
Spread: 20cm (8in)
Aspect: Sun
Soil: Well-drained, fertile
Hardiness: Zone 7
Propagation: Offsets, in autumn

Very desirable hybrid with strap-shaped, grey-green basal leaves. Numerous dark violet, star-shaped flowers in an umbel 15–20cm (6–8in) across, in summer.

Allium karataviense A.G.M.
(Alliaceae/Liliaceae)

Common names: None
Height: 25cm (10in)
Spread: 10cm (4in)
Aspect: Sun
Soil: Well-drained, fertile
Hardiness: Zone 4
Propagation: Seed, in spring; offsets, in autumn

Bulbous species from Central Asia. Paired, elliptic, grey-green or grey-purple, horizontal basal leaves. Large umbel of many pale pink, star-shaped flowers in summer.

Allium moly
A.G.M.
(Alliaceae/Liliaceae)

Common names: Golden garlic, lily leek, yellow onion
Height: 25cm (10in)
Spread: 10cm (4in)
Aspect: Sun or half shade
Soil: Well-drained, fertile
Hardiness: Zone 3
Propagation: Seed, in spring; offsets, in autumn

Bulbous woodland plant with grey-green, lance-shaped basal leaves. The umbel is dense, with up to 30 star-shaped golden-yellow flowers in summer. From Europe.

Allium nigrum
(Alliaceae/Liliaceae)

Common names: None
Height: 35cm (14in)
Spread: 8cm (3in)
Aspect: Sun
Soil: Well-drained, fertile
Hardiness: Zone 4
Propagation: Seed, in spring; offsets, in autumn

Bulbous Mediterranean perennial with grey-green, lance-shaped, basal leaves. Off-white, cup-shaped flowers with prominent, dark green ovaries, in a flattened umbel, summer.

Allium oreophilum
A.G.M.
(Alliaceae/Liliaceae)

Common names: None
Height: 20cm (8in)
Spread: 5cm (2in)
Aspect: Sun
Soil: Well-drained, fertile
Hardiness: Zone 4
Propagation: Seed, in spring; offsets, in autumn

Bulbous perennial. Leaves basal, linear, mid-green. Umbel very loose, with some 15 long-lasting, bell-shaped, strong pink flowers, each tepal with a dark midrib.

Allium
'Purple Sensation' A.G.M.
(Alliaceae/Liliaceae)

Common names: None
Height: 1m (36in)
Spread: 8cm (3in)
Aspect: Sun
Soil: Well-drained, fertile
Hardiness: Zone 2
Propagation: Offsets, in autumn

Free-flowering, bulbous hybrid of unknown parentage. Basal, grey-green, strap-shaped leaves. Tight, spherical umbel of over 50 star-shaped, dark violet flowers in summer.

Allium schoenoprasum
'Forescate'
(Alliaceae/Liliaceae)

Common name: Chives
Height: 60cm (24in)
Spread: 8cm (3in)
Aspect: Sun
Soil: Well-drained, fertile
Hardiness: Zone 1
Propagation: Offsets, in autumn

Rhizomatous allium grown for its edible leaves, which are hollow, dark green cylinders, and for its dense umbels of bright pinkish-purple flowers in summer.

Allium schubertii
(Alliaceae/Liliaceae)

Common names: None
Height: 60cm (24in)
Spread: 20cm (8in)
Aspect: Sun
Soil: Well, drained, fertile
Hardiness: Zone 5
Propagation: Seed, in spring; offsets, in autumn

Bulbous allium. The strap-like, bright green basal leaves die back before early-summer flowering. Pale lilac flowers have pedicels of unequal length, so umbel appears shaggy.

Allium senescens
(Alliaceae/Liliaceae)

Common names: None
Height: 60cm (24in)
Spread: 5cm (2in)
Aspect: Sun
Soil: Well-drained, fertile
Hardiness: Zone 1
Propagation: Seed, in spring; offsets, in autumn

Vigorous, bulbous perennial. Strap-shaped, short, mid-green basal leaves. Pink, cup-shaped, long-lasting flowers in a dense umbel of 30 in early and midsummer.

Allium sphaerocephalon
(Alliaceae/Liliaceae)

Common names: Round-headed leek
Height: 90cm (36in)
Spread: 8cm (3in)
Aspect: Sun
Soil: well-drained, fertile
Hardiness: Zone 1
Propagation: Seed, in spring; offsets, in autumn

Bulbous allium. Leaves are basal, linear, mid-green. Flowers are bell-shaped, dark pink or red-brown, in dense, ovoid umbel in summer; bulbils may form in the umbel.

*The rounded umbels of Star of Persia (*Allium christophii*) against Lady's Mantle (*Alchemilla mollis*) and Lavandula.*

Allium unifolium
(Alliaceae/Liliaceae)

Common name: One-leaved onion
Height: 25cm (10in)
Spread: 5cm (2in)
Aspect: Sun
Soil: Well-drained, fertile
Hardiness: Zone 4
Propagation: Seed, in spring; offsets, in autumn

Bulbous North American perennial. Short, linear, grey-green basal leaves die back before flowering in spring. Flowers clear pink, large, open, bell-shaped, in umbels.

ADDITIONAL ALLIUMS with an A.G.M.

A. 'Beau Regard' (Zone 8)

A. beesianum (Zone 8)

A. caeruleum (Zone 7)

A. carinatum subsp. *pulchellum* (Zone 7)

A. 'Gladiator' (Zone 7)

A. hollandicum (Zone 8)

A. hollandicum 'Purple Sensation' (Zone 8)

A. insubricum (Zone 8)

Aloe ferox
(Aloeaceae/Liliaceae)

Common name: Cape aloe
Height: 3m (10ft)
Spread: 1.5m (5ft)
Aspect: Full sun
Soil: Well-drained, fertile
Hardiness: Zone 9
Propagation: Seed, when ripe: offsets, in late spring, early summer

Evergreen succulent with a rosette of dull-green, fleshy, lance-shaped leaves with red teeth. Large, erect panicle of scarlet flowers in summer. Conservatory plant in cold areas.

Aloe tenuior
(Aloeaceae/Liliaceae)

Common names: None
Height: 3m (10ft)
Spread: 60cm (2ft)
Aspect: Full sun
Soil: Well-drained, fertile
Hardiness: Zone 9
Propagation: Seed, when ripe; offsets in late spring to early summer

Evergreen, succulent perennial from South Africa. Forms a rosette of linear, glaucous, toothed leaves. Bears orange-yellow flowers in a panicle in summer.

ALOES with an A.G.M.

A. aristata (Zone 9)

A. bakeri (Zone 10)

A. melanocantha (Zone 9)

A. rauhii (Zone 10)

A. somaliensis (Zone 10)

A. 'Variegata' (Zone 9)

A. vera (Zone 8)

Alonsoa warscewiczii
A.G.M.
(Scrophulariaceae)

Common names: Musk flower
Height: 60cm (2ft)
Spread: 30cm (1ft)
Aspect: Full sun
Soil: Well-drained, fertile
Hardiness: Zone 9
Propagation: Seed, in warmth in spring or late summer

Evergreen, bushy subshrub. Leaves ovate to lance-shaped, toothed, dark green. Spurred, deep pink flowers in loose racemes, summer to autumn. Treat as annual in cold areas.

Alopecurus pratensis
'Aureovariegatus'
(Graminae/Poaceae)

Common names: Foxtail grass
Height: 1.2m (4ft)
Spread: 60cm (2ft)
Aspect: Sun or half shade
Soil: Well-drained, fertile
Hardiness: Zone 5
Propagation: Seed, when ripe; division, in spring or autumn

Perennial grass that clumps up rapidly. Leaves basal, linear, striped yellow and green. Long, dense panicles of green or purple spikelets in spring to midsummer.

Alstroemeria aurea
(Alstroemeriaceae)

Common names: None
Height: 1m (36in)
Spread: 45cm (18in)
Aspect: Sun or partial shade
Soil: Moist, well-drained, fertile
Hardiness: Zone 7
Propagation: Seed, when ripe; division, in spring or autumn

Tuberous perennial. Leaves linear to lance-shaped, mid-green. Terminal 3- to 7-rayed umbels, each with up to 3 yellow or orange flowers, in summer. Can be invasive.

ALSTROEMERIA (Alstroemeriaceae)
Peruvian Lily • Lily of the Incas

A genus of some 50 species of perennials from South America, found in mountains and grasslands. *Alstroemeria* are tuberous, and will spread rapidly to form large clumps; they can even become invasive if the conditions suit them. The tubers should be handled carefully, and are best left undisturbed once planted. They have extremely handsome flowers, and a long flowering season, making them valuable border plants. They also make excellent cut flowers, and are popular with flower-arrangers and grown commercially for florists. A few species are tender, but many are marginally hardy in most areas, and can be grown outside if they are given a sunny spot and covered with a dry mulch through winter. Contact with the foliage may cause exacerbation of a skin allergy. The tubers should be planted 20cm (8in) deep. Thirty forms have an Award of Garden Merit, including the popular Ligtu Hybrids, a name covering many crosses, principally of *A. ligtu* and *A. haemantha*. Also holding an A.G.M. are the 'Princess' strain: this is a registered name, and the botanically preferred name is given as a synonym in the panel at right; the plants are most likely to be sold under the former, but may be found in books under the latter.

Alstroemeria
Ligtu Hybrids A.G.M.
(Alstroemeriaceae)

Common names: None
Height: 1m (36in)
Spread: 45cm (18in)
Aspect: Sun or half shade
Soil: Moist, well-drained, fertile
Hardiness: Zone 7
Propagation: Seed, when ripe; division, in spring or autumn

Vigorous hybrids with a wide range of colours, such as this deep red. Leaves linear to lance-shaped, mid-green. Flowers in terminal, 3- to 7-rayed racemes, summer.

Alstroemeria
Ligtu Hybrids A.G.M.
(Alstroemeriaceae)

Common names: None
Height: 1m (36in)
Spread: 45cm (18in)
Aspect: Sun or half shade
Soil: Moist, well-drained, fertile
Hardiness: Zone 7
Propagation: Seed, when ripe; division, in spring or autumn

Two-tone yellow and cream colour break in the Ligtu Hybrid range. Leaves linear to lance-shaped, mid-green. Terminal, 3- to 7-rayed racemes of flowers in summer.

Alstroemeria psittacina
(Alstroemeriaceae)

Common names: None
Height: 1m (36in)
Spread: 45cm (18in)
Aspect: Sun or half shade
Soil: Moist, well-drained, fertile
Hardiness: Zone 7
Propagation: Seed, when ripe; division, in spring or autumn

Tuberous species with grey-green, linear to lance-shaped leaves. Flowers in 4- to 6-rayed panicles, each ray having up to 3 green and red flowers, in summer.

Alstroemeria
'Solent Wings'
(Alstroemeriaceae)

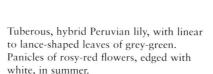

Common names: None
Height: 1m (36in)
Spread: 45cm (18in)
Aspect: Sun or half shade
Soil: Moist, well-drained, fertile
Hardiness: Zone 7
Propagation: Division, in spring or autumn

Tuberous, hybrid Peruvian lily, with linear to lance-shaped leaves of grey-green. Panicles of rosy-red flowers, edged with white, in summer.

ADDITIONAL ALSTROEMERIAS with an A.G.M.

A. 'Alhambra' (Zone 7)

A. 'Amanda' (Zone 9)

A. 'Amor' (Zone 9)

A. 'Apollo' (Zone 7)

A. 'Bianca' (Zone 9)

A. 'Coronet' (Zone 7)

A. 'Diamond' (Zone 9)

A. 'Fiona' (Zone 9)

A. 'Flaming Star' (Zone 7)

A. 'Friendship' (Zone 7)

A. 'Golden Delight' (Zone 7)

A. 'Helios' (Zone 9)

A. 'Orange Delight' (Zone 7)

A. 'Orange Gem' (Zone 7)

A. 'Orange Glory' (Zone 7)

A. 'Rebecca' (Zone 9)

A. 'Rhapsody' (Zone 9)

A. 'Princess Carmina'®, syn. 'Stasilva' (Zone 7)

A. 'Princess Caroline'®, syn. 'Staroko' (Zone 7)

A. 'Princess Grace'®, syn. 'Starodo' (Zone 7)

A. 'Princess Juliana'®, syn. 'Staterpa' (Zone 7)

A. 'Princess Mira'®, syn. 'Stapripur' (Zone 7)

A. 'Queen Elizabeth the Queen Mother'®, syn. 'Stamoli' (Zone 7)

A. 'Solent Crest' (Zone 7)

A. 'Solent Rose' (Zone 7)

A. 'Tiara' (Zone 9)

A. 'White Libelle' (Zone 9)

A. ' Yellow Friendship' (Zone 7)

A. 'Yellow Crown' (Zone 7)

Alstroemeria 'White Apollo' (Alstroemeriaceae)

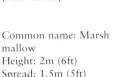

Common names: None
Height: 1m (36in)
Spread: 45cm (18in)
Aspect: Sun or half shade
Soil: Moist, well-drained, fertile
Hardiness: Zone 7
Propagation: Division, in spring or autumn

Very handsome hybrid with terminal clusters of pure white, orange-throated flowers, streaked brown, in summer. Leaves linear to lance-shaped.

Althaea cannabina (Malvaceae)

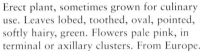

Common name: Mallow
Height: 2m (6ft)
Spread: 75cm (30in)
Aspect: Any, but best in sun
Soil: Moist, well-drained, fertile
Hardiness: Zone 4
Propagation: Seed, in summer

Erect, woody-stemmed plant for the larger garden. Leaves dark green, paler beneath, hairy, round, lobed. Small, pink flowers in axillary clusters, summer to early autumn.

Althaea officinalis (Malvaceae)

Common name: Marsh mallow
Height: 2m (6ft)
Spread: 1.5m (5ft)
Aspect: Any, but best in sun
Soil: Moist, well-drained, fertile
Hardiness: Zone 3
Propagation: Seed, in summer

Erect plant, sometimes grown for culinary use. Leaves lobed, toothed, oval, pointed, softly hairy, green. Flowers pale pink, in terminal or axillary clusters. From Europe.

Alyssum montanum 'Berggold' (Brassicaceae/Cruciferae)

Common name: Madwort
Height: 15cm (6in)
Spread: 60cm (24in) or more
Aspect: Sun
Soil: Well-drained, humus-rich
Hardiness: Zone 6
Propagation: Seed, in spring or autumn; cuttings, in summer

Prostrate, mat-forming evergreen with grey, oblong-obovate leaves in rosettes. Bears racemes of yellow, fragrant flowerheads in early summer. An excellent wall plant.

Alyssum spinosum 'Roseum' A.G.M. (Brassicaceae/Cruciferae)

Common names: None
Height: 40cm (16in)
Spread: 50cm (20in)
Aspect: Sun
Soil: Well-drained, humus-rich
Hardiness: Zone 6
Propagation: Seed, in autumn or spring; cuttings, in summer

Rounded, compact, evergreen subshrub; spiny and densely branched. Leaves small, obovate, grey-green. Flowers cross-shaped, 4-petalled, pale or dark pink, in racemes.

Amaryllis belladonna (Amaryllidaceae)

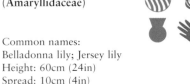

Common names: Belladonna lily; Jersey lily
Height: 60cm (24in)
Spread: 10cm (4in)
Aspect: Full sun
Soil: Well-drained
Hardiness: Zone 9
Propagation: Seed, in warmth when ripe; offsets, in spring

Bulbous perennial. Umbels of funnel-shaped, scented, purplish-pink flowers in autumn; strap-shaped, fleshy leaves in early winter. Protect from frost. Needs a dry dormancy.

Amicia zygomeris (Leguminosae/Papilionaceae)

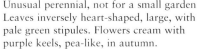

Common names: None
Height: 2m (6ft)
Spread: 1.2m (4ft)
Aspect: Full sun
Soil: Well-drained, fertile
Hardiness: Zone 9
Propagation: Seed, in warmth in spring; cuttings, in spring and summer

Unusual perennial, not for a small garden. Leaves inversely heart-shaped, large, with pale green stipules. Flowers cream with purple keels, pea-like, in autumn.

Amsonia tabernaemontana (Apocynaceae)

Common names: None
Height: 60cm (24in)
Spread: 45cm (18in)
Aspect: Sun
Soil: Moist, well-drained
Hardiness: Zone 8
Propagation: Seed or division, in spring

Clump-forming perennial. Small, ovate or elliptic, matt, dark green leaves. Pale blue flowers in dense panicles from spring to midsummer. Milky sap may irritate skin.

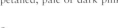

Anagallis monellii
A.G.M.
(Primulaceae)

Common name: Blue pimpernel
Height: 20cm (8in)
Spread: 40cm (16in)
Aspect: Full sun
Soil: Moist, well-drained, fertile
Hardiness: Zone 7
Propagation: Seed or division, both in spring

Sprawling, short-lived perennial with mid-green, lance-shaped to elliptic, stalkless leaves. Open, 5-petalled, deep blue flowers in summer. From S.E. Europe.

Anaphalis triplinervis
A.G.M.
(Asteraceae/Compositae)

Common name: Pearl everlasting
Height: 90cm (3ft)
Spread: 60cm (3ft)
Aspect: Sun or half shade
Soil: Well-drained, fertile, humus-rich
Hardiness: Zone 5
Propagation: Seed or division, both in spring

Perennial with spoon-shaped, pale grey-green leaves, white-woolly underneath. Corymbs of yellow flowers with white bracts in summer. From S.W. China.

Anchusa azurea
(Boraginaceae)

Common name: Alkanet
Height: 1.5m (5ft)
Spread: 60cm (2ft)
Aspect: Full sun
Soil: Moist, well-drained, fertile
Hardiness: Zone 3
Propagation: Seed or basal cuttings, both in spring

Clump-forming, Mediterranean perennial. Leaves linear to lance-shaped, hairy, dark green. Panicles of open, gentian-blue flowers in early summer.

Anchusa azurea
'Feltham Pride'
(Boraginaceae)

Common name: Alkanet
Height: 90cm (3ft)
Spread: 60cm (2ft)
Aspect: Full sun
Soil: Moist, well-drained, fertile
Hardiness: Zone 3
Propagation: Basal cuttings, in spring; root cuttings, in winter

A compact cultivar, sometimes grown as a biennial, with linear to lance-shaped leaves of mid- to dark green. Clear, bright blue flowers in early summer.

Anchusa
'Loddon Royalist' A.G.M.
(Boraginaceae)

Common name: Alkanet
Height: 90cm (3ft)
Spread: 60cm (2ft)
Aspect: Full sun
Soil: Moist, well-drained, fertile
Hardiness: Zone 3
Propagation: Basal cuttings, in spring; root cuttings, in winter

Sturdy hybrid, but it may still need to be staked in exposed areas. Leaves linear to lance-shaped, mid-green. Panicle of deep blue flowers in early summer.

ANEMONE (Ranunculaceae)
Windflower

This large genus contains some 120 species of perennials, with open, saucer- to cup-shaped flowers, with a prominent boss of stamens, and lobed, dissected foliage. They originate in a wide range of habitats across both the northern and southern hemispheres, and they vary widely in their character and in cultural requirements as a result. Some are good specimens for the border, others are more suitable for rock gardens or naturalizing in woodlands. For the purposes of cultivation requirements, anemones can be divided into three broad groups:

Spring-flowering, tuberous or rhizomatous species that come from Alpine or woodland areas.

Spring- or early summer-flowering, tuberous species from the Mediterranean and regions of Central Asia that have hot, dry summers.

Summer- or autumn-flowering, fibrous-rooted, tall, herbaceous species from open sites.

All these types are covered here, but the third category will form the main group. Some anemones are poisonous, and the sap of all may cause skin irritation. All are unfortunately prone to powdery mildew, and slug damage.

Anemone blanda
A.G.M.
(Ranunculaceae)

Common names: None
Height: 15cm (6in)
Spread: 15cm (6in)
Aspect: Sun or half shade
Soil: Well-drained, humus-rich
Hardiness: Zone 5
Propagation: Seed, when ripe; offsets, in summer

Tuberous, woodland perennial from Turkey. Leaves 3-palmate, triangular or oval, deep green. Flowers solitary, single, with deep blue tepals, in spring.

This lovely white form was a 'sport' from a red-flowered variety in the garden of M. Jobert in 1858.

Anemone blanda
'White Splendour' A.G.M.
(Ranunculaceae)

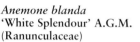

Common names: None
Height: 15cm (6in)
Spread: 15cm (6in)
Aspect: Full sun or half shade
Soil: Well-drained, humus-rich
Hardiness: Zone 5
Propagation: Seed, when ripe; offsets, in summer

Spring flowers have pure white tepals with pinkish reverse. Leaves oval or triangular, 3-palmate, dark green. One of a few A.G.M. cultivars of this species.

Anemone coronaria
De Caen Group
(Ranunculaceae)

Common names: Florists' anemone; wind poppy
Height: 45cm (18in)
Spread: 15cm (6in)
Aspect: Full sun
Soil: Porous, gritty
Hardiness: Zone 8
Propagation: Seed, when ripe; offsets, in summer

Clones with single, long-stemmed flowers with 5–8 tepals in a wide range of colours. Oval, 3-palmate, mid-green basal and stem leaves. Tuberous; keep dry after flowering.

Anemone coronoria
St. Brigid Group
(Ranunculaceae)

Common names: Florists' anemone; wind poppy
Height: 45cm (18in)
Spread: 15cm (6in)
Aspect: Full sun
Soil: Porous
Hardiness: Zone 8
Propagation: Seed, when ripe; offsets, in summer

Leaves mid-green, 3-palmate, round or oval. Solitary, fully double flowers in a wide range of colours, on long stems in spring. Tuberous; keep dry after flowering.

Anemone cylindrica
(Ranunculaceae)

Common names: None
Height: 60cm (24in)
Spread: 10cm (4in)
Aspect: Half shade
Soil: Well-drained, humus-rich
Hardiness: Zone 6
Propagation: Seed, when ripe

Fibrous-rooted, cushion-forming, rosetted perennial. Leaves linear to elliptic, glossy green. Flowers in early spring, white with a yellow-green eye, on long stems.

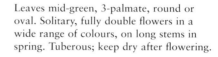

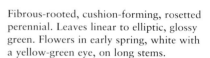

Anemone hupehensis
'Hadspen Abundance'
A.G.M. (Ranunculaceae)

Common names: None
Height: 90cm (36in)
Spread: 40cm (16in)
Aspect: Sun or half shade
Soil: Moist, fertile, humus-rich
Hardiness: Zone 6
Propagation: Division, in spring or autumn

Fibrous-rooted, suckering perennial. Oval, 3-palmate, long-stalked, basal, dark green leaves. Umbels of up to 15 flowers, each with 5 or 6 deep pink tepals, in autumn.

Anemone hupehensis var. *japonica* 'Prinz Heinrich'
A.G.M. (Ranunculaceae)

Common names: None
Height: 90cm (36in)
Spread: 40cm (16in)
Aspect: Sun or half shade
Soil: Moist, fertile, humus-rich
Hardiness: Zone 6
Propagation: Division, in spring or autumn

Fibrous-rooted, suckering hybrid. Leaves oval, 3-palmate, basal, dark green. Umbels of up to 15 flowers, each with 5 or 6 dark pink tepals, in mid- to late summer.

Anemone x *hybrida*
'Honorine Jobert' A.G.M.
(Ranunculaceae)

Common name: Japanese anemone
Height: 1.2m (4ft)
Spread: Indefinite
Aspect: Sun or half shade
Soil: Moist, fertile, humus-rich
Hardiness: Zone 6
Propagation: Division, in spring or autumn

Vigorous, suckering, woody hybrid. Oval, 3-palmate, toothed, mid-green leaves. Umbel of up to 20 pure white flowers, the reverse pinkish, in autumn.

Anemone x *hybrida*
'Elegans'
(Ranunculaceae)

Common name: Japanese anemone
Height: 1.2m (4ft)
Spread: Indefinite
Aspect: Sun or half shade
Soil: Moist, well-drained, humus-rich
Hardiness: Zone 6
Propagation: Division, in spring or autumn

A cloned selection of this popular, vigorous plant. Leaves 3-palmate, oval, mid-green. Single pink flowers in umbels of up to 20 over a long period in autumn.

Anemone x *hybrida* 'Margarete' (Ranunculaceae)

Common name: Japanese anemone
Height: 90cm (3ft)
Spread: Indefinite
Aspect: Sun or half shade
Soil: Moist, fertile, humus-rich
Hardiness: Zone 6
Propagation: Division, in spring or autumn

A vigorous, cloned selection of this popular perennial. Umbels of semi-double, deep pink flowers in autumn. Leaves oval, 3-palmate, mid-green.

Anemone x *hybrida* 'Pamina' (Ranunculaceae)

Common name: Japanese anemone
Height: 80cm (32in)
Spread: Indefinite
Aspect: Sun or half shade
Soil: Moist, fertile, humus-rich
Hardiness: Zone 6
Propagation: Division, in spring or autumn

Cloned selection, slightly smaller than most, with oval, 3-palmate, mid-green leaves and umbels of single, lilac-pink flowers with rounded tepals.

Anemone x *hybrida* 'Whirlwind' (Ranunculaceae)

Common name: Japanese anemone
Height: 1.2m (4ft)
Spread: Indefinite
Aspect: Sun or half shade
Soil: Moist, fertile, humus-rich
Hardiness: Zone 6
Propagation: Division, in spring or autumn

Cloned selection of the popular Japanese anemone with umbels of semi-double, white flowers, sometimes with a centre of greenish, whorled tepals.

Anemone x *lesseri* (Ranunculaceae)

Common names: None
Height: 40cm (16in)
Spread: 30cm (12in)
Aspect: Sun or half shade
Soil: Well-drained, humus-rich
Hardiness: Zone 3
Propagation: Seed, when ripe

Fibrous-rooted hybrid. Large, round, 3- to 5-palmate leaves; leaflets lobed, toothed. Reddish-pink, purple, yellow or white flowers, singly or in umbels, in summer.

Anemone leveillei (Ranunculaceae)

Common names: None
Height: 60cm (2ft)
Spread: 30cm (1ft)
Aspect: Half shade
Soil: Moist, humus-rich
Hardiness: Zone 6
Propagation: Seed, when ripe

Fibrous-rooted perennial. Leaves kidney-shaped, 3-lobed, deeply divided, toothed, mid-green. Flowers white, with 8 tepals, the reverse hairy and pink, in summer.

Anemone multifida (Ranunculaceae)

Common names: None
Height: 30cm (12in)
Spread: 15cm (6in)
Aspect: Sun or half shade
Soil: Well-drained, humus-rich
Hardiness: Zone 2
Propagation: Seed, when ripe

Sturdy, vigorous, rhizomatous perennial. Handsome, rounded, palmate, mid-green stem and basal leaves. Umbels of 2 or 3 creamy yellow flowers with 5–9 tepals.

Anemone nemorosa A.G.M. (Ranunculaceae)

Common names: Windflower; wood anemone
Height: 15cm (6in)
Spread: 30cm (12in) or more
Aspect: Half shade
Soil: Moist, well-drained, humus-rich
Hardiness: Zone 5
Propagation: Seed, when ripe; offsets, in autumn

Creeping, rhizomatous woodlander. Leaves round, 3-palmate; leaflets lobed and toothed, mid-green. Flowers are solitary, white, with 6–8 tepals, in spring and early summer.

Anemone nemorosa 'Robinsoniana' A.G.M. (Ranunculaceae)

Common names: Windflower; wood anemone
Height: 15cm (6in)
Spread: 30cm (12in)
Aspect: Half shade
Soil: Well-drained, humus-rich
Hardiness: Zone 5
Propagation: Division, in spring or autumn

Cloned selection of the species, with large, pale lavender-pink flowers with creamy grey undersides. One of a few cultivars of *A. nemorosa* to carry an A.G.M.

Anemone rivularis
(Ranunculaceae)

Common names: None
Height: 90cm (3ft)
Spread: 30cm (1ft)
Aspect: Sun or half shade
Soil: Well-drained, humus-rich
Hardiness: Zone 7
Propagation: Seed, when ripe

Fibrous-rooted, clump-forming anemone. Long-stalked, round, 3-palmate or 3-lobed, hairy, toothed basal and stem leaves. Umbels of white flowers in spring and autumn.

Anemonella thalictroides
(Ranunculaceae)

Common name: Rue anemone
Height: 10cm (4in)
Spread: 30cm (12in)
Aspect: Half shade
Soil: Moist, well-drained, humus-rich
Hardiness: Zone 4
Propagation: Seed, when ripe

Clump-forming, tuberous woodlander. Blue-green, fern-like, 3-ternate leaves. Pale pink, cup-shaped flowers in loose umbels, spring to early summer. Hates waterlogged soil.

Anemonopsis macrophylla
(Ranunculaceae)

Common names: None
Height: 80cm (32in)
Spread: 45cm (18in)
Aspect: Half shade
Soil: Moist, acidic, humus-rich
Hardiness: Zone 4
Propagation: Seed, when ripe; division, in summer

Woodlander with glossy leaves, 3-ternate; toothed lobes ovate-oblong. Loose racemes of nodding, cup-shaped flowers, sepals lilac and petals violet, mid- to late summer.

Angelica archangelica
(Apiaceae/Umbelliferae)

Common names: Archangel; garden angelica; wild parsnip
Height: 2m (6ft)
Spread: 1m (3ft)
Aspect: Full or half shade
Soil: Moist, deep, fertile, humus-rich
Hardiness: Zone 4
Propagation: Seed, when ripe; plant out when small

Herbaceous, monocarpic herb. Leaves mid-green, 2- or 3-pinnate, with lance-shaped, toothed leaflets. Umbels of greenish-yellow flowers on stiff stems, early to midsummer.

Angelica gigas
(Apiaceae/Umbelliferae)

Common names: None
Height: to 2m (6ft)
Spread: 1.2m (4ft)
Aspect: Full or half shade
Soil: Moist, deep, fertile, humus-rich
Hardiness: Zone 4
Propagation: Seed, when ripe

Large perennial for damp sites. Leaves very large, 3-ternate; leaflets lobed, diamond-ovate. Dense umbel of purple flowers and bracts with red stems, summer to autumn.

Anigozanthos manglesii
A.G.M.
(Haemodoraceae)

Common names: Cat's paw; Mangles' kangaroo paw
Height: 1.2m (4ft)
Spread: 60cm (2ft)
Aspect: Full sun
Soil: Moist, well-drained, sandy, humus-rich
Hardiness: Zone 9
Propagation: Seed, in warmth when ripe

Clump-forming evergreen. Leaves lance- to strap-shaped, grey-green. Flowers 2-lipped, tubular, yellow-green, with dense, pale green hairs outside, red inside, spring to summer.

Anisodontea capensis
(Malvaceae)

Common names: None
Height: 1m (36in)
Spread: 80cm (32in)
Aspect: Full sun
Soil: Well-drained, fertile
Hardiness: Zone 9
Propagation: Seed, in warmth in spring; semi-ripe cuttings, in summer

Woody evergreen. Leaves ovate-triangular, hairy, mid-green, shallowly lobed. Flowers solitary or in racemes of 2 or 3, pale pink, cup-shaped, in summer to autumn.

Anomatheca laxa var. *alba*
(Iridaceae)

Common names: None
Height: 30cm (12in)
Spread: 5cm (2in)
Aspect: Full sun
Soil: Gritty, fertile
Hardiness: Zone 8
Propagation: Seed, in warmth in spring; division, in spring

Cormous perennial. Leaves lance-shaped, flat, mid-green. Flowers in racemes, open, pure white, followed by brown capsules of red seeds. Self-seeds, but not invasively.

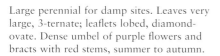

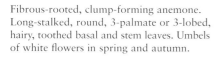

Antennaria dioica
(Asteraceae/Compositae)

Common names: Cats'ears; pussy toes
Height: 10cm (4in)
Spread: 40cm (16in)
Aspect: Full sun
Soil: Well-drained, fertile
Hardiness: Zone 5
Propagation: Seed, in spring or autumn

Mat-forming, stoloniferous ground cover. Spoon-shaped, grey-green leaves, very hairy beneath. Corymbs of fluffy, pink or white, everlasting flowers in late spring to summer.

ANTHEMIS (Asteraceae/Compositae)
Dog Fennel

Genus of some 100 mat- or clump-forming species originating in Europe, northern Africa, Turkey, the Caucasus and Iran. *Anthemis* make very useful border plants, with a long flowering season extending from late spring to the end of summer, and beautiful, filigree, aromatic, evergreen foliage when they are not in flower. Smaller types also suit rock gardens. The flowerheads are daisy-like, with white or yellow ray florets and yellow disc florets, and some of the species will make good cut flowers. Although the genus as a whole is not long-lived (*A. tinctoria* in particular is notable for this), all are easily propagated from seed or cuttings. A plant's life can also be extended by shearing it over in autumn just after flowering is over. This will ensure that new basal growth is encouraged, which will take the plant through the winter. Shearing also helps to keep the plants from becoming mildewed, a particular problem of *Anthemis*; they come from sunny, well-drained sites in the wild, and wet winters are greatly disliked by all species. They do not transplant well, but should nevertheless be divided regularly in spring. Despite these drawbacks, these plants provide the gardener with rewards that make them well worth all the effort.

Anthemis punctata subsp. *cupaniana* A.G.M.
(Asteraceae/Compositae)

Common name: Dog fennel
Height: 30cm (1ft)
Spread: 90cm (3ft)
Aspect: Full sun
Soil: Well-drained, gritty
Hardiness: Zone 6
Propagation: Seed, division or basal cuttings, all in spring

Evergreen with aromatic, ovate-obovate, pinnatisect, silver-grey leaves, grey-green in winter. Flowers daisy-like, white, long-lasting, in early summer. From Sicily.

Anthemis tinctoria
'E.C. Buxton'
(Asteraceae/Compositae)

Common names: Golden marguerite; ox-eye chamomile
Height: 70cm (28in)
Spread: 60cm (24in)
Aspect: Full sun
Soil: Well-drained, gritty
Hardiness: Zone 6
Propagation: Division or basal cuttings, both in spring

A selected form with lemon-yellow, daisy-like flowerheads above aromatic, evergreen, handsome foliage. Leaves are ovate-obovate, pinnatisect, grey-green.

Anthemis 'Grallagh Gold'
(Asteraceae/Compositae)

Common names: Golden marguerite; ox-eye chamomile
Height: 80cm (32in)
Spread: 60cm (24in)
Aspect: Full sun
Soil: Well-drained, gritty
Hardiness: Zone 6
Propagation: Division or basal cuttings, both in spring

A selected form with intense gold, daisy-like flowerheads. Leaves are evergreen, aromatic, ovate-obovate, pinnatisect, and grey-green.

Anthemis tinctoria
'Sauce Hollandaise'
(Asteraceae/Compositae)

Common names: Golden marguerite; ox-eye chamomile
Height: 60cm (2ft)
Spread: 60cm (2ft)
Aspect: Full sun
Soil: Well-drained, gritty
Hardiness: Zone 6
Propagation: Division or basal cuttings, both in spring

Cloned selection. Flowers have near-white ray petals, contrasting with yellow boss. Foliage is evergreen, ovate-obovate, aromatic, pinnatisect and grey-green.

Anthemis tinctoria
'Wargrave'
(Asteraceae/Compositae)

Common names: Golden marguerite; ox-eye chamomile
Height: 60cm (2ft)
Spread: 60cm (2ft)
Aspect: Full sun
Soil: Well-drained, gritty
Hardiness: Zone 6
Propagation: Division or basal cuttings, both in spring

Cultivar with daisy-like flowerheads of pale, soft yellow. Leaves are aromatic, evergreen, ovate-obovate, pinnatisect, and grey-green.

Anthemis tinctoria *'Wargrave', a fine variety with lemon yellow flowers on long stems.*

Anthericum liliago
(Anthericaceae/Liliaceae)

Common name: St Bernard's lily
Height: 90cm (3ft)
Spread: 30cm (1ft)
Aspect: Full sun
Soil: Well-drained, fertile
Hardiness: Zone 7
Propagation: Seed, in spring or autumn; division, in spring

Clump-forming, rhizomatous perennial. Leaves grassy, mid-green. Panicles of open, lily-like, white flowers in late spring, early summer, followed by attractive seed heads.

Anthriscus sylvestris
(Apiaceae/Umbelliferae)

Common names: Cow parsley; Queen Anne's lace
Height 1m (3ft)
Spread: 30cm (1ft)
Aspect: Sun or half shade
Soil: Well-drained
Hardiness: Zone 7
Propagation: Seed, in spring or autumn

Short-lived clump-forming perennial. Leaves 3-pinnate, with ovate pinnatifid leaflets. Umbels of tiny white flowers from mid-spring to summer.

Anthriscus sylvestris
'Ravenswing'
(Apiaceae/Umbelliferae)

Common names: Cow parsley; Queen Anne's lace
Height: 1m (3ft)
Spread: 30cm (1ft)
Aspect: Sun or half shade
Soil: Well-drained
Hardiness: Zone 7
Propagation: Seed, in spring or autumn

A dark-leaved form of the species. Leaves lacy, dark purple-brown, 3-pinnate; leaflets ovate, pinnatifid. Loose umbels of small, white flowers in spring to early summer.

Antirrhinum hispanicum
(Scrophulariaceae)

Common name: Snapdragon
Height: 20cm (8in)
Spread: 30cm (12in)
Aspect: Full sun
Soil: Sharply drained, fertile
Hardiness: Zone 7
Propagation: Softwood cuttings, in summer

Short-lived subshrub. Leaves lance-shaped to orbicular, green. Flowers white or pale pink, lip streaked red, perfumed, 2-lipped, in loose racemes, late summer. From Spain.

Antirrhinum majus
'Taff's White'
(Scrophulariaceae)

Common name: Snapdragon
Height: 60cm (2ft)
Spread: 60cm (2ft)
Aspect: Full sun
Soil: Sharply drained
Hardiness: Zone 7
Propagation: Softwood cuttings, in summer

Cloned selection of the garden snapdragon, grown as an annual. Leaves lance-shaped, glossy green, edged cream. Flowers fragrant, 2-lipped, white, in summer to autumn.

AQUILEGIA (Ranunculaceae)
Columbine

A genus of some 70 species from a wide range of habitats, from mountain to woodland, widely distributed across the northern hemisphere. The larger species and their cultivars, covered here, are popular garden plants and an almost indispensable element of the classic cottage garden. Their flowering season forms a useful bridge over the gap between the spring- and summer-flowering genera, and a wide range of colours is available. The flowers are distinctive, often bicoloured, with hooked spurs, and carried either singly or in panicles. The basal leaves are also distinctive and attractive. Some enthusiasts have beds devoted entirely to columbines, and later in the season dig them out to replace them with summer bedding. They do have the drawback of being short-lived, but this is mitigated by their tendency to grow very readily from seed; they will also self-seed abundantly in the garden, and any seedling with poor flowers can be taken out, as there will be plenty of better examples. Columbines do not transplant well, so seed should be sown *in situ*, or the seedlings should be planted out when they are still small. Contact with the sap may cause skin irritation, and all members of the genus are poisonous.

Aquilegia canadensis
A.G.M.
(Ranunculaceae)

Common name: Canadian columbine
Height: 90cm (3ft)
Spread: 30cm (1ft)
Aspect: Sun or half shade
Soil: Moist, well-drained
Hardiness: Zone 3
Propagation: Seed, when ripe or in spring

Clump-forming, with 2-ternate, fern-like, green leaves. Racemes of up to 20 nodding flowers, sepals scarlet, petals lemon, spurs red, from mid-spring to early summer.

Aquilegia chrysantha 'Yellow Queen' (Ranunculaceae)

Common name: Columbine
Height: 90cm (3ft)
Spread: 60cm (2ft)
Aspect: Sun or half shade
Soil: Moist, well-drained
Hardiness: Zone 3
Propagation: Division, in spring

Cloned selection with fern-like, 3-ternate leaves, of ovate, green leaflets. Racemes of 4–12 flowers with pale yellow petals and golden-yellow sepals in spring to summer.

Aquilegia Mrs Scott-Elliot Hybrids (Ranunculaceae)

Common name: Columbine
Height: 90cm (3ft)
Spread: 60cm (2ft)
Aspect: Sun or half shade
Soil: Moist, well-drained
Hardiness: Zone 3
Propagation: Seed, in autumn or spring

Robust hybrid strain. Leaves 2-ternately lobed, mid-green. Flowers in racemes, in a range of colours and bicolours, from spring to midsummer.

Aquilegia Music Series A.G.M. (Ranunculaceae)

Common name: Columbine
Height: 45cm (18in)
Spread: 45cm (18in)
Aspect: Sun or half shade
Soil: Moist, well-drained
Hardiness: Zone 3
Propagation: Seed, in autumn or spring

Hybrid strain of compact and robust plants with 2-ternate, mid-green leaves. Long-spurred flowers in a range of colours and bicolours in spring to summer.

Aquilegia vulgaris (Ranunculaceae)

Common name: Granny's bonnet
Height: 90cm (3ft)
Spread: 60cm (2ft)
Aspect: Sun or half shade
Soil: Moist, well-drained
Hardiness: Zone 3
Propagation: Seed, in spring or autumn

Stiff, upright plant with 2-ternately lobed, mid-green leaves. Terminal racemes of 5–15 pendent or horizontal, blue, pink, white or violet flowers in spring to early summer.

Aquilegia vulgaris var. *stellata* 'Nora Barlow' A.G.M. (Ranunculaceae)

Common name: Granny's bonnet
Height: 90cm (3ft)
Spread: 60cm (2ft)
Aspect: Sun or half shade
Soil: Moist, well-drained
Hardiness: Zone 3
Propagation: Division, in spring

Selected form with fully double, pompon flowers. Tepals are red and green, spurless, and quilted. Good proportion of seedlings come true if plant is grown in isolation.

Aquilegia vulgaris var. *stellata* (Ranunculaceae)

Common name: granny's bonnet
Height: 90cm (3ft)
Spread: 60cm (2ft)
Aspect: Sun or half shade
Soil: Moist, well-drained
Hardiness: Zone 3
Propagation: Seed, in autumn or spring

Variety with spurless flowers with tepals that spread, resembling flowers of clematis (*see pp.79–80*), in shades of blue or pink. Leaves 2-ternately lobed, mid-green.

Aquilegia vulgaris 'William Guiness' (Ranunculaceae)

Common name: Granny's bonnet
Height: 70cm (28in)
Spread: 60cm (24in)
Aspect: Sun or half shade
Soil: Moist, well-drained
Hardiness: Zone 3
Propagation: Division, in spring

Selected form with dark purple to black flowers, with sepals tipped white, in terminal racemes. Leaves are mid-green and 2-ternately lobed.

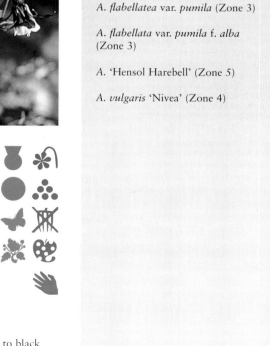

ADDITIONAL AQUILEGIAS with an A.G.M.

A. bertolonii (Zone 5)

A. caerulea (Zone 3)

A. flabellata (Zone 3)

A. flabellatea var. *pumila* (Zone 3)

A. flabellata var. *pumila* f. *alba* (Zone 3)

A. 'Hensol Harebell' (Zone 5)

A. vulgaris 'Nivea' (Zone 4)

Arabis blepharophylla
'Frühlingszauber' A.G.M.
(Brassicaceae/Cruciferae)

Common name: Rock cress
Height: 10cm (4in)
Spread: 20cm (8in)
Aspect: Full sun
Soil: Well-drained
Hardiness: Zone 7
Propagation: Seed, in autumn

Compact, short-lived, evergreen perennial. Forms a rosette of toothed, obovate, dark green leaves. Racemes of dark pink-purple, fragrant flowers in spring to early summer.

Arabis procurrens
'Variegata' A.G.M.
(Brassicaceae/Cruciferae)

Common name: Rock cress
Height: 8cm (3in)
Spread: 40cm (16in)
Aspect: Full sun
Soil: Well-drained, gritty
Hardiness: Zone 5
Propagation: Seed, in autumn

Creeping evergreen with rosettes of oblong-lance-shaped leaves, glossy mid-green, edged cream, sometimes tinged pink. Racemes of white flowers, in spring. Superb wall plant.

Arctotheca calendula
(Asteraceae/Compositae)

Common names: None
Height: 50cm (20in)
Spread: Indefinite
Aspect: Full sun
Soil: Well-drained
Hardiness: Zone 9
Propagation: Seed, in warmth in spring; division, in spring

Creeping, rhizomatous, spreading plant. Rosettes of pinnatifid, oblong, green leaves, white-woolly beneath. Flowers in spring or early summer, yellow, purple-tinted beneath.

Arctotis fastuosa
'Zulu Prince'
(Asteraceae/Compositae)

Common names: African daisy; monarch of the veldt
Height: 60cm (24in)
Spread: 40cm (16in)
Aspect: Full sun
Soil: Moist, well-drained, gritty
Hardiness: Zone 9
Propagation: Seed, in warmth in spring or summer

Creeping perennial often treated as annual. Silvery white, elliptic, lobed leaves. Solitary flowers; cream ray florets, black triangles at the bases, midsummer to early autumn.

Arctotis × *hybrida*
(Asteraceae/Compositae)

Common names: African daisy; monarch of the veldt
Height: 60cm (2ft)
Spread: 30cm (1ft)
Aspect: Full sun
Soil: Moist, well-drained, gritty
Hardiness: Zone 9
Propagation: Seed, in warmth in spring or autumn

Range of hybrids. Flowers solitary, single, in red, yellow, pink, white, or orange; some with darker marks on ray florets. Leaves silvery, felted, elliptic, lobed, wavy-edged.

Arenaria montana
A.G.M.
(Caryophyllaceae)

Common name: Sandwort
Height: 5cm (2in)
Spread: 30cm (12in)
Aspect: Full sun
Soil: Moist, well-drained, gritty
Hardiness: Zone 4
Propagation: Seed, in autumn; division, in spring

An evergreen, prostrate plant with grey-green, lance-shaped leaves. Flowers solitary or in cymes of a few flowers, white, in late spring. Good wall plant.

Argyranthemum frutescens
subsp. *canariae* A.G.M.
(Asteraceae/Compositae)

Common name: Marguerite
Height: 60cm (2ft)
Spread: 60cm (2ft)
Aspect: Full sun
Soil: Well-drained
Hardiness: Zone 9
Propagation: Seed, in warmth in spring

Free-flowering subshrub with pinnatisect, dissected, green leaves. Flowers in loose corymbs, white or very pale pink, spring to autumn. From the Canary Islands.

Argyranthemum
'Jamaica Primrose' A.G.M.
(Asteraceae/Compositae)

Common name: Marguerite
Height: 1m (3ft)
Spread: 1m (3ft)
Aspect: Full sun
Soil: Well-drained
Hardiness: Zone 9
Propagation: Greenwood cuttings, in spring

Hybrid, evergreen subshrub, often grown as an annual. Leaves pinnatisect, toothed, grey-green. Flowers solitary, single, pale yellow, with darker disc. Long-flowering.

Argyranthemum 'Vancouver' A.G.M. (Asteraceae/Compositae)

Common name: Marguerite
Height: 1m (3ft)
Spread: 80cm (32in)
Aspect: Full sun
Soil: Well-drained
Hardiness: Zone 9
Propagation: Greenwood cuttings, in spring

Handsome, evergreen, hybrid subshrub. Leaves pinnatisect, greyish-green. Solitary, double, anemone-centred flowers, spring to autumn. Ray florets pink, disc florets rose.

ADDITIONAL ARGYRANTHEMUMS with an A.G.M. (all Zone 9)

A. 'Cornish Gold'

A. 'Donington Hero'

A. foeniculaceum 'Royal Haze'

A. gracile 'Chelsea Girl'

A. 'Levada Cream'

A. 'Mary Cheek'

A. 'Petite Pink'

A. 'Qinta White'

A. 'Snow Storm'

Arisaema amurense (Araceae)

Common name: Himalayan cobra lily
Height: 45cm (18in)
Spread: 15cm (6in)
Aspect: Half shade, cool
Soil: Moist, acidic, humus-rich
Hardiness: Zone 6
Propagation: Seed, in autumn or spring; offsets, in autumn

Tuberous. Large, solitary leaf, with 5 linear to lance-shaped leaflets. Flowering spathe green striped white and purple, may be followed by berries if both sexes grown.

Arisaema candidissimum A.G.M. (Araceae)

Common name: Himalayan cobra lily
Height: 30cm (12in)
Spread: 45cm (18in)
Aspect: Half shade, cool
Soil: Moist, humus-rich
Hardiness: Zone 6
Propagation: Seed, in autumn or spring; offsets, in autumn

Tuberous plant. Spathe white striped pink, scented; appears late, so mark position. Large, 3-palmate leaves with ovate leaflets follow. Will fruit if male and female grown.

Arisaema triphyllum (Araceae)

Common name: Jack-in-the-pulpit
Height: 30cm (1ft)
Spread: 30cm (1ft)
Aspect: Half shade, cool
Soil: Moist, humus-rich
Hardiness: Zone 4
Propagation: Seed, in autumn or spring; offsets, in autumn

A tuberous species. Leaves three-lobed, green. Spathe hooded, green, striped purple and white, may be followed by berries if plants of both sexes are grown.

Arisarum proboscideum (Araceae)

Common name: Mouse plant
Height: 20cm (8in)
Spread: Indefinite
Aspect: Half shade, woodland
Soil: Moist, humus-rich
Hardiness: Zone 7
Propagation: Seed, in spring; division, in autumn

Rhizomatous, mat-forming perennial. Dark green, glossy, arrow-shaped leaves. Hooded, dark brown-purple spathe, with a long tip like a mouse's tail. Can be invasive.

Aristea ecklonii (Iridaceae)

Common names: None
Height: 60cm (24in)
Spread: 45cm (18in)
Aspect: Full sun
Soil: Moist, well-drained, humus-rich
Hardiness: Zone 9
Propagation: Seed, in warmth in spring

Rhizomatous evergreen, forming tangled clumps. Lance-shaped, stem-clasping, and linear basal leaves. Panicles of lilac or blue, saucer-shaped flowers, lasting a day, summer.

Aristea major (Iridaceae)

Common names: None
Height: 1.5m (5ft)
Spread: 45cm (18in)
Aspect: Full sun
Soil: Well-drained, humus-rich
Hardiness: Zone 8
Propagation: Seed, in warmth in spring

Handsome, rhizomatous evergreen. Leaves both lance-shaped basal and long, linear stem. Flowers in panicles in summer; purple or blue, saucer-shaped, closing at night.

Armeria maritima
(Plumbaginaceae)

Common name: Sea thrift
Height: 30cm (1ft)
Spread: 30cm (1ft)
Aspect: Full sun
Soil: Well-drained
Hardiness: Zone 4
Propagation: Seed or division, both in spring

Clump-forming evergreen, with a cushion of linear, dark green leaves. Red, pink or white, cup-shaped flowers, in spherical heads in spring and early summer.

Armeria maritima
'Alba'
(Plumbaginaceae)

Common name: White sea thrift
Height: 30cm (1ft)
Spread: 30cm (1ft)
Aspect: Full sun
Soil: Well-drained
Hardiness: Zone 4
Propagation: Seed or division, both in spring

White variant of the species. Leaves in a tight cushion, evergreen, linear, dark green. Small, spherical heads of cup-shaped, white flowers in early summer.

Armeria maritima
'Vindictive' A.G.M.
(Plumbaginaceae)

Common names: None
Height: 15cm (6in)
Spread: 10cm (4in)
Aspect: Full sun
Soil: Well-drained
Hardiness: Zone 4
Propagation: Division, in spring

Compact, dwarf selected form; shorter stems than the species, bearing spherical heads of rose-pink, cup-shaped flowers. Leaves evergreen, linear, in a cushion.

Armoracia rusticana
(Brassicaceae/Cruciferae)

Common names: Horseradish; red cole
Height: 1m (3ft)
Spread: 60cm (2ft)
Aspect: Full sun
Soil: Moist, well-drained, fertile
Hardiness: Zone 5
Propagation: Division, in winter

Clump-forming perennial cultivated for the culinary use of its roots. Leaves dark green, oblong-ovate, toothed. Flowers in terminal panicles, small, white. Sap may irritate.

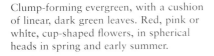

Artemisia lactiflora **A.G.M.**
(Asteraceae/Compositae)

Common name: White mugwort
Height: 1.5m (5ft)
Spread: 60cm (2ft)
Aspect: Full sun
Soil: Moist, well-drained, fertile
Hardiness: Zone 4
Propagation: Seed or division, both in autumn or spring

Clump-forming culinary herb with deeply cut, pinnatisect, dark green leaves. Bears long-lasting white flowers, in panicles, from late summer to mid-autumn.

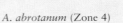

Artemisia schmidtiana
'Nana' A.G.M.
(Asteraceae/Compositae)

Common names: None
Height: 10cm (4in)
Spread: 30cm (12in)
Aspect: Full sun
Soil: Well-drained, fertile
Hardiness: Zone 4
Propagation: Seed or division, both in spring or autumn

Dwarf, rhizomatous, evergreen culinary herb. Leaves pinnatisect, with linear lobes, silky-hairy, silver. Panicles of many small, yellow flowers, ageing to cream, in summer.

ADDITIONAL ARTEMISIAS with an A.G.M.

A. abrotanum (Zone 4)

A. absinthum 'Lambrook Mist' (Zone 4)

A. absinthum 'Lambrook Silver' (Zone 4)

A. alba 'Canescens' (Zone 6)

A. caucasica (Zone 5)

A. frigida (Zone 4)

A. ludoviciana 'Silver Queen' (Zone 5)

A. ludoviciana 'Valerie Finnis' (Zone 5)

A. pontica (Zone 4)

A. 'Powis Castle' (Zone 8)

Arthropodium candidum **'Maculatum'**
(Anthericaceae/Liliaceae)

Common names: None
Height: 20cm (8in)
Spread: 10cm (4in)
Aspect: Full sun
Soil: Well-drained, gritty, fertile
Hardiness: Zone 8
Propagation: Seed, in autumn or spring; division, in spring

Tuberous perennial. Leaves linear, dull flesh-pink, mottled bronze. Flowers tiny, white, in racemes or panicles, in early to midsummer. Just big enough for a border.

An autumn show of Artemisia *backed by* Sedum in the gardens of Powis Castle.

Arum italicum
(Araceae)

Common name: Lords and ladies
Height: 30cm (12in)
Spread: 15cm (6in)
Aspect: Sun or half shade
Soil: Well-drained, humus-rich
Hardiness: Zone 6
Propagation: Seed, in autumn; division, after flowering

Woodlander with large, cream spathes in early summer, then spikes of red berries. Leaves spear- to arrow-shaped, green, in late autumn. All parts toxic and irritant.

Arum italicum subsp. *italicum* 'Marmoratum' A.G.M. (Araceae)

Common name: Lords and ladies
Height: 30cm (12in)
Spread: 15cm (6in)
Aspect: Sun or half shade
Soil: Well-drained, humus-rich
Hardiness: Zone 6
Propagation: Seed, in autumn; division, after flowering

Variegated form of the species, with green, cream-veined, spear- to arrow-shaped leaves. Cream spathes followed by spikes of red berries. All parts toxic and irritant.

Aruncus dioicus
A.G.M.
(Rosaceae)

Common name: Goatsbeard
Height: 2m (6ft)
Spread: 1.2m (4ft)
Aspect: Full or half shade
Soil: Moist, fertile
Hardiness: Zone 7
Propagation: Seed or division, both in spring or autumn

Rhizomatous woodlander. Leaves fern-like, toothed, 2-pinnate; leaflets ovate. Dioecious: female flowers greenish, males more upright, creamy-white, in loose panicles in summer.

Aruncus dioicus
'Glasnevin'
(Rosaceae)

Common name: Goatsbeard
Height: 2m (6ft)
Spread: 1.2m (4ft)
Aspect: Full or half shade
Soil: Moist, fertile
Hardiness: Zone 7
Propagation: Seed or division, both in spring or autumn

Selected form with pendulous panicles, better in male plants than female. Dead-head females to prevent seeding. Leaves fern-like, toothed, 2-pinnate; leaflets ovate.

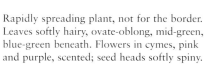

Asarina procumbens
(Scrophulariaceae)

Common name: Twining snapdragon
Height: 5cm (2in)
Spread: 60cm (24in)
Aspect: Half shade
Soil: Well-drained, gritty, fertile
Hardiness: Zone 7
Propagation: Seed, in warmth in spring

Evergreen, trailing, brittle-stemmed plant. Leaves kidney-shaped, lobed, hairy, dark green. Flowers snapdragon-like, cream with yellow throats, in summer. Good on walls.

Asclepias incarnata
(Asclepiadaceae)

Common name: Swamp milkweed
Height: 1.2m (4ft)
Spread: 60cm (2ft)
Aspect: Full sun
Soil: Moist, humus-rich
Hardiness: Zone 3
Propagation: Seed or division, both in spring

Good marginal plant. Leaves elliptic-ovate, mid-green. Clustered cymes of flowers with pink-purple, reflexed petals and paler horns, in summer to autumn. Silky seed heads.

Asclepias syriaca
(Asclepiadaceae)

Common names: Milkweed; silkweed
Height: 2m (6ft)
Spread: Indefinite
Aspect: Full sun
Soil: Well-drained, fertile
Hardiness: Zone 3
Propagation: Seed or division, both in spring

Rapidly spreading plant, not for the border. Leaves softly hairy, ovate-oblong, mid-green, blue-green beneath. Flowers in cymes, pink and purple, scented; seed heads softly spiny.

Asclepias tuberosa
(Asclepiadaceae)

Common name: Butterfly weed
Height: 90cm (3ft)
Spread: 30cm (1ft)
Aspect: Full sun
Soil: Well-drained, fertile, humus-rich
Hardiness: Zone 3
Propagation: Seed or division, both in spring

Handsome but difficult, tuberous perennial. Leaves lance-shaped to ovate-oblong, hairy, mid-green. Flowers in cymes, orange, in summer to autumn; seed heads nodding.

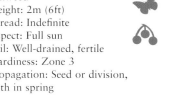

Asphodeline lutea
(Asphodelaceae/Liliaceae)

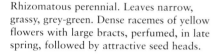

Common names: King's spear; yellow asphodel
Height: 1.5m (5ft)
Spread: 30cm (1ft)
Aspect: Full sun
Soil: Well-drained, gritty, fertile
Hardiness: Zone 7
Propagation: Seed, in spring; division, in autumn

Rhizomatous perennial. Leaves narrow, grassy, grey-green. Dense racemes of yellow flowers with large bracts, perfumed, in late spring, followed by attractive seed heads.

Asphodelus albus
(Asphodelaceae/Liliaceae)

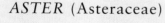

Common name: Asphodel
Height: 90cm (36in)
Spread: 30cm (12in)
Aspect: Full sun
Soil: Well-drained, gritty, humus-rich
Hardiness: Zone 6
Propagation: Seed or division, both in spring

Clump-forming perennial. Leaves linear, grassy, keeled, mid-green. Flowers white, brown-veined, star-shaped, with brownish bracts, in few-branched racemes in spring.

Asphodelus ramosus
(Asphodelaceae/Liliaceae)

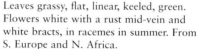

Common name: Asphodel
Height: 1.5m (5ft)
Spread: 30cm (1ft)
Aspect: Sun
Soil: Well-drained, gritty, humus-rich
Hardiness: Zone 7
Propagation: Seed or division, both in spring

Leaves grassy, flat, linear, keeled, green. Flowers white with a rust mid-vein and white bracts, in racemes in summer. From S. Europe and N. Africa.

Asplenium scolopendrium
A.G.M.
(Aspleniaceae)

Common name: Hart's tongue fern
Height: 70cm (28in)
Spread: 60cm (24in)
Aspect: Half shade
Soil: Moist, well-drained, gritty
Hardiness: Zone 5
Propagation: Seed, in warmth in spring; division, in spring

Evergreen terrestrial fern. Fronds strap-shaped, fleshy, glossy, green. Remove old fronds in spring to allow new to develop. Good wall plant.

ASTER (Asteraceae)

Large genus of some 150 species, including annuals, biennials and a few subshrubs as well as perennials. They are found chiefly in the northern hemisphere, and in North America in particular, although some subshrubs originate in South Africa. Asters grow in a wide range of habitats, from woodland to mountain, and so come in all shapes and sizes; they also vary in their degrees of hardiness. Their varying cultural requirements mean that there are asters to suit a range of garden situations, from scree beds to woodlands and stream edges. They all have similar inflorescences: daisy-like flowerheads with ray florets usually of white, pink, purple or blue, and disc florets in shades of yellow. There are a few exceptions to this, with yellow ray florets or pink disc florets. All asters are prone to slug damage, and the many cultivars of *A. novi-belgii*, the Michaelmas daisy, are very prone to powdery mildew; it may not be possible to grow them at all in a wet garden, even with constant care. Taller species and cultivars may need staking, and some will need to be lifted and divided every few years to maintain their vigour. Nonetheless, these are valuable late-season plants. Many of them hold an Award of Garden Merit; some that have not been profiled in detail are listed on p.58.

Aster alpinus
var. *albus*
(Asteraceae/Compositae)

Common name: White alpine aster
Height: 25cm (10in)
Spread: 45cm (18in)
Aspect: Full sun
Soil: Well-drained, gritty
Hardiness: Zone 3
Propagation: Seed, in spring or autumn

White form of a mostly violet species. Mid-green, narrow, lance-shaped leaves. Flowers solitary, single, with white petals and yellow disc florets, spring and early summer.

Aster amellus
'King George' A.G.M.
(Asteraceae/Compositae)

Common name: None
Height: 45cm (18in)
Spread: 45cm (18in)
Aspect: Sun
Soil: Well-drained, alkaline, gritty
Hardiness: Zone 5
Propagation: Division, in spring

Clump-forming, with lance-shaped leaves of mid-green. Flowers in late summer to autumn, large, violet-blue with a yellow boss. One of a few cultivars with an A.G.M.

Aster divaricatus
(Asteraceae/Compositae)

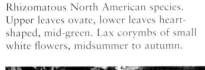

Common names: None
Height: 60cm (2ft)
Spread: 60cm (2ft)
Aspect: Half shade
Soil: Moist
Hardiness: Zone 4
Propagation: Seed or division, both in spring

Rhizomatous North American species. Upper leaves ovate, lower leaves heart-shaped, mid-green. Lax corymbs of small white flowers, midsummer to autumn.

Aster ericoides
(Asteraceae/Compositae)

Common names: None
Height: 1m (3ft)
Spread: 40cm (16in)
Aspect: Half shade
Soil: Moist
Hardiness: Zone 3
Propagation: Seed or division, both in spring

Lax, freely branching, slender-stemmed perennial. Leaves linear-lance-shaped, green. Loose panicles of small white flowers from summer to autumn. From North America.

Aster × *frikartii*
(Asteraceae/Compositae)

Common names: None
Height: 80cm (32in)
Spread: 45cm (18in)
Aspect: Full sun
Soil: Well-drained, gritty
Hardiness: Zone 4
Propagation: Division, in spring

Hybrid of garden origin. Leaves ovate, rough, green. Flowers in loose corymbs, light purple-blue, with orange discs, in late summer to autumn.

Aster × *frikartii*
'Mönch' A.G.M.
(Asteraceae/Compositae)

Common names: None
Height: 70cm (28in)
Spread: 40cm (16in)
Aspect: Full sun
Soil: Well-drained, gritty
Hardiness: Zone 4
Propagation: Division, in spring

Cloned selection, widely grown on account of its very long flowering season, from summer to early autumn. The flowers are of a more intense colour than the type.

Aster lateriflorus
(Asteraceae/Compositae)

Common name: Calico aster
Height: 1m (3ft)
Spread: 30cm (1ft)
Aspect: Half shade
Soil: Moist, good drainage
Hardiness: Zone 3
Propagation: Seed, in spring

Clump-forming species. Leaves mid-green, linear-oblong. Flowers white, with pink disc florets, on spreading, branched stems from midsummer to autumn.

Aster macrophyllus
(Asteraceae/Compositae)

Common names: None
Height: 1m (3ft)
Spread: 80cm (28in)
Aspect: Half or full shade
Soil: Moist
Hardiness: Zone 3
Propagation: Seed, in spring

Invasive aster; good ground cover. Large leaves, heart-shaped, toothed, green. Flowers in corymbs, small, starry, pale violet fading to white, yellow disc florets, in autumn.

Aster novae-angliae 'Andenken an Alma Pötschke' A.G.M.
(Asteraceae/Compositae)

Common name: New England aster
Height: 1.2m (4ft)
Spread: 60cm (2ft)
Aspect: Sun or half shade
Soil: Moist, fertile
Hardiness: Zone 2
Propagation: Division, in spring

Cloned selection of a rhizomatous aster. Leaves lance-shaped, mid-green. Flowers in sprays, bright salmon-pink with yellow disc florets, in autumn. Very desirable.

Aster novae-angliae
'Lye End Beauty'
(Asteraceae/Compositae)

Common name: New England aster
Height: 1.7m (5½ft)
Spread: 80cm (32in)
Aspect: Sun or half shade
Soil: Moist, fertile
Hardiness: Zone 2
Propagation: Division, in spring

Lovely clone of a rhizomatous species. Leaves lance-shaped, mid-green. Flowers in sprays, ray florets lilac, disc florets yellow, in autumn. One of many named varieties.

This large-flowered aster, Aster amellus *'King George', has soft blue-violet blooms borne on 60cm (2ft) stems.*

Aster novi-belgii
'Jenny'
(Asteraceae/Compositae)

Common names: Michaelmas daisy; New York aster
Height: 1.2m (4ft)
Spread: 90cm (3ft)
Aspect: Full sun or half shade
Soil: Moist, fertile
Hardiness: Zone 2
Propagation: Division, in spring

One of many cultivars of this rhizomatous aster, very prone to powdery mildew. Leaves lance-shaped, green. Double, purple-red flowers with yellow disc florets in autumn.

Aster sedifolius
(Asteraceae/Compositae)

Common names: None
Height: 1.2m (4ft)
Spread: 60cm (2ft)
Aspect: Full sun
Soil: Well-drained, fertile
Hardiness: Zone 6
Propagation: Seed, in spring or autumn

Leaves lance-shaped, green. Starry, lilac flowers with yellow disc florets, on weak stems. The form 'Nanus' is much more compact, with flowers of a deeper blue.

Aster thomsonii
'Nanus'
(Asteraceae/Compositae)

Common names: None
Height: 45cm (18in)
Spread: 25cm (10in)
Aspect: Half shade
Soil: Moist, fertile
Hardiness: Zone 7
Propagation: Seed, in spring or autumn

Dwarf cultivar. Leaves elliptic to ovate, toothed, green. Flowers in terminal sprays, blue-lilac, star-shaped, long-lasting, in summer to early autumn.

Aster tongolensis
'Wartburgstern'
(Asteraceae/Compositae)

Common names: None
Height: 50cm (20in)
Spread: 50cm (20in)
Aspect: Full sun
Soil: Well-drained, fertile
Hardiness: Zone 8
Propagation: Division, in spring

Selected form of a rhizomatous, mat-forming species. Leaves hairy, elliptic, dark green. Flowers solitary, single, in summer; violet-blue ray florets, orange disc florets.

ADDITIONAL ASTERS with an A.G.M.

A. 'Coombe Fishacre' (Zone 3)

A. *cordifolius* 'Chieftain' (Zone 3)

A. *cordifolius* 'Sweet Lavender' (Zone 3)

A. *ericoides* 'Blue Star' (Zone 3)

A. *ericoides* 'Brimstone'(Zone 3)

A. *ericoides* 'Golden Spray' (Zone 3)

A. *ericoides* 'Pink Cloud' (Zone 3)

A. 'Kylie' (Zone 3)

A. 'Little Carlow' (Zone 3)

A. 'Ochtendgloren' (Zone 3)

A. 'Photograph' (Zone 3)

A. *pilosus* var. *demotus* (Zone 5)

A. *pringlei* 'Monte Cassino' (Zone 4)

A. 'Ringdove' (Zone 3)

A. *turbinellus* (Zone 5)

Asteriscus maritimus
(Asteraceae)

Common names: None
Height: 25cm (10in)
Spread: 20cm (8in)
Aspect: Sun
Soil: Well-drained, gritty
Hardiness: Zone 8
Propagation: Seed, in warmth in spring

Good wall plant from the Canary and Cape Verde Islands. Leaves oblong to spoon-shaped, hairy. Bears solitary, single, orange-yellow flowers in autumn.

ASTILBE (Saxifragaceae)
Spiraea

There are only about a dozen species in this small genus; they are rhizomatous and clump-forming, and found in the wild in moist areas, on stream banks and in the woodlands of North America and south-east Asia. The vast majority of the astilbes in cultivation are interspecific hybrids of complex parentage, arising from crosses between *A.* x *arendsii* (Zone 6), *A. astilboides* (Zone 6), *A. chinensis* (Zone 5), *A. japonica* (Zone 5), *A. simplicifolia* (Zone 7) and *A. thunbergii* (Zone 7). Many deservedly hold an Award of Garden Merit. They are easy-to-please, being fairly hardy and tolerant of sun or half shade and of boggy or dry soil. Their divided, toothed foliage is handsome, and they make excellent ground cover or bog or marginal plants. Astilbes are also long-flowering, with tapering, usually open panicles of flowers, in shades of white or cream through pinks to rich red, in summer. These do not require staking, and are followed by attractive seed heads, which will persist on the plants throughout the winter. The flowers unfortunately fade quickly when cut, but the seed heads dry well. In all, they are almost exemplary perennials. Their only drawback is that they do require regular division and replanting if they are to stay at their best.

Astilbe chinensis var. *pumila* A.G.M.
(Saxifragaceae)

Common names: None
Height: 25cm (10in)
Spread: 20cm (8in)
Aspect: Sun or half shade
Soil: Moist or boggy
Hardiness: Zone 5
Propagation: Division, in autumn or winter

Highly desirable astilbe from China, with 3-ternate, toothed, hairy leaves of red-green. Flowers in dense, conical panicles of reddish-pink in late summer.

Astilbe x *arendsii* 'Feuer'
(Saxifragaceae)

Common names: None
Height: 60cm (24in)
Spread: 45cm (18in)
Aspect: Sun or half shade
Soil: Moist or boggy
Hardiness: Zone 6
Propagation: Division, in autumn or winter

A striking hybrid cultivar with flowers of a distinctive coral-red, in open panicles in summer. Handsome lobed, toothed, dark green leaves.

Astilbe x *arendsii* 'Glut'
(Saxifragaceae)

Common names: None
Height: 60cm (24in)
Spread: 45cm (18in)
Aspect: Sun or half shade
Soil: Moist or boggy
Hardiness: Zone 6
Propagation: Division, in autumn or winter

A very desirable, compact hybrid astilbe. Foliage deep green, lobed, toothed. Crowded panicles of deep crimson-red flowers in summer.

Astilbe 'Jo Ophorst'
(Saxifragaceae)

Common names: None
Height: 1.2m (4ft)
Spread: 60cm (2ft)
Aspect: Sun or half shade
Soil: Moist or boggy
Hardiness: Zone 6
Propagation: Division, in autumn or winter

An *Astilbe* x *chinensis* var. *davidii* hybrid, taller than most; it has panicles of pink flowers with a hint of lilac, in late summer. Leaves 3-ternate, toothed.

Astilbe chinensis var. *taquetii* 'Purpurlanze'
(Saxifragaceae)

Common names: None
Height: 1.2m (4ft)
Spread: 90cm (3ft)
Aspect: Half shade or sun
Soil: Prefers moist or boggy
Hardiness: Zone 5
Propagation: Division, in autumn or winter

An astilbe for the dry garden, as it will tolerate this better than most. Tall, elegant panicles of purple-red in late summer to early autumn.

Astilbe 'Red Sentinel'
(Saxifragaceae)

Common names: None
Height: 1m (3ft)
Spread: 50cm (20in)
Aspect: Sun or half shade
Soil: Moist or boggy
Hardiness: Zone 5
Propagation: Division, in autumn or winter

Clump-forming *A. japonica* hybrid, with dark green, toothed leaves. Erect panicles of dark crimson flowers are carried above the foliage in summer.

Astilbe 'Rheinland' A.G.M.
(Saxifragaceae)

Common names: None
Height: 50cm (20in)
Spread: 45cm (18in)
Aspect: Sun or half shade
Soil: Moist or boggy
Hardiness: Zone 5
Propagation: Division, in autumn or winter

A. japonica hybrid, clump-forming, with mid-green foliage, and dense, upright panicles of deep pink flowers throughout the summer.

ADDITIONAL ASTILBES with an A.G.M.

A. x *arendsii* 'Brautschleier' (Zone 6)

A. x *arendsii* 'Fanal' (Zone 6)

A. 'Bronce Elegans' (Zone 7)

A. chinensis var. *taquetii* 'Superba' (Zone 5)

A. x *crispa* 'Perkeo' (Zone 6)

A. glaberrima var. *saxatilis* (Zone 6)

A. simplicifolia (Zone 7)

A. 'Straussenfeder' (Zone 7)

Astilbe
'Sprite' A.G.M.
(Saxifragaceae)

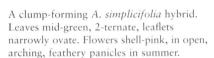

Common names: None
Height: 50cm (20in)
Spread: 1m (3ft)
Aspect: Sun or half shade
Soil: Moist or boggy
Hardiness: Zone 7
Propagation: Division, in autumn or winter

A clump-forming *A. simplicifolia* hybrid. Leaves mid-green, 2-ternate, leaflets narrowly ovate. Flowers shell-pink, in open, arching, feathery panicles in summer.

ASTRANTIA (Apiaceae/Umbelliferae)
Hattie's pincushion • Masterwort

This is a small genus of some ten clump-forming perennials, found across Europe and into western Asia, of which just two are in general cultivation. Their natural habitats are mountain woodlands and stream margins; they are reliably hardy, and they will grow in either sun or half shade. In the garden they will also suit a mixed border as long as it remains moist at all times. *Astrantia* form basal rosettes of handsome, palmate green leaves, but with the exception of *A. major* 'Sunningdale Variegated' they are primarily grown for their airy sprays of small flowers. These have five petals, and each is surrounded by a showy ruff of papery bracts in shades of pink and red; they are carried above the foliage on tall, wiry stems. They will self-seed freely about the garden, so if this is not desired plants should be scrupulously dead-headed after flowering in summer: the flowers and their bracts will dry well for winter, and they are extremely popular for flower arrangements in either the fresh or the dried state. *Astrantia* will attract both bees and butterflies into the garden, but they are unfortunately also liked by slugs. Another drawback of the genus is that they are prone to powdery mildew.

Astrantia major
(Apiaceae/Umbelliferae)

Common name: Masterwort
Height: 90cm (36in)
Spread: 45cm (18in)
Aspect: Sun or half shade
Soil: Moist, fertile, humus-rich
Hardiness: Zone 6
Propagation: Seed, when ripe

Clump-forming plant. Basal rosette of green leaves with up to 7 lobes. Umbels of small, white flowers backed by green-veined white bracts, in summer, often again in autumn.

Astrantia major
'Hadspen Blood'
(Apiaceae/Umbelliferae)

Common name: Masterwort
Height: 90cm (36in)
Spread: 45cm (18in)
Aspect: Sun or half shade
Soil: Moist, fertile, humus-rich
Hardiness: Zone 6
Propagation: Seed, when ripe

A handsome cultivar with dark red flowers, surrounded by matching dark red bracts, in summer. The species is from C. and E. Europe.

Astrantia major rubra
(Apiaceae/Umbelliferae)

Common name: Masterwort
Height: 90cm (36in)
Spread: 45cm (18in)
Aspect: Sun or half shade
Soil: Moist, fertile, humus-rich
Hardiness: Zone 6
Propagation: Division, in spring

Handsome cultivar with plum flowers surrounded by pinkish bracts, in summer. A favourite for flower-arranging. Basal rosette of green leaves with up to 7 lobes.

Astrantia major
'Shaggy' A.G.M.
(Apiaceae/Umbelliferae)

Common name: Masterwort
Height: 90cm (36in)
Spread: 45cm (18in)
Aspect: Sun or half shade
Soil: Moist, fertile, humus-rich
Hardiness: Zone 6
Propagation: Division, in spring

Extremely attractive cultivar, sometimes sold as 'Margery Fish'. Leaves very deeply cut. Flowers in summer with very long and sharp-pointed bracts, with green tips.

Astrantia major
'Ruby Wedding'
(Apiaceae/Umbelliferae)

Common name: Masterwort
Height: 90cm (3ft)
Spread: 45cm (18in)
Aspect: Sun or half shade
Soil: Moist, fertile, humus-rich
Hardiness: Zone 6
Propagation: Division, in spring

Handsome cultivar with particularly attractive toothed foliage. Flowers in summer, with plum-coloured petals and bracts. A favourite for flower arranging.

Astrantia major
'Roma'
(Apiaceae/Umbelliferae)

Common name: Masterwort
Height: 90cm (36in)
Spread: 45cm (18in)
Aspect: Sun or half shade
Soil: Moist, fertile, humus-rich
Hardiness: Zone 6
Propagation: Division, in spring

Cultivar with deep pink flowers and bracts in summer. Very popular for fresh or dried flower arrangements. Leaves green, with up to 7 lobes, in basal rosettes.

Astrantia major 'Sunningdale Variegated' A.G.M.
(Apiaceae/Umbelliferae)

Common name: Masterwort
Height: 90cm (36in)
Spread: 45cm (18in)
Aspect: Full sun
Soil: Moist, fertile, humus-rich
Hardiness: Zone 6
Propagation: Division, in spring

Cultivar grown for both flower and foliage. Leaves have either cream lobes or cream edges. Flowers have bracts of pale pink. Grow in full sun for maximum leaf colour.

Astrantia maxima
A.G.M.
(Apiaceae/Umbelliferae)

Common name: Masterwort
Height: 60cm (2ft)
Spread: 30cm (1ft)
Aspect: Sun or half shade
Soil: Moist, fertile, humus-rich
Hardiness: Zone 6
Propagation: Seed or division, both in spring

Clump-forming perennial. Leaves green, with handsome, deeply-divided lobes. Flowers small, pink, surrounded by sharp, pink bracts, in umbels, early to midsummer.

Athyrium filix-femina
A.G.M.
(Athyriaceae)

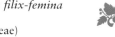

Common name: Lady fern
Height: 1.2m (4ft)
Spread: 90cm (3ft)
Aspect: Shade
Soil: Moist, acidic, fertile, humus-rich
Hardiness: Zone 5
Propagation: Spores in heat when ripe; division, in spring

Rhizomatous, deciduous, variable fern. Fronds light green, 2- or 3-pinnate, lance-shaped. Pinnae elliptic, segments oblong to lance-shaped. Stalks sometimes reddish.

Aubrieta
'Red Carpet'
(Brassicaceae/Cruciferae)

Common name: Aubrietia
Height: 5cm (2in)
Spread: 60cm (24in) or more
Aspect: Full sun
Soil: Well-drained, neutral or alkaline, gritty
Hardiness: Zone 7
Propagation: Softwood cuttings, in early summer

One of several hybrid cultivars; good wall plant or ground cover. Leaves evergreen, oblong, hairy, mid-green. Flowers bright scarlet, 4-petalled. Trim after flowering.

Aurinia saxatilis
A.G.M.
(Brassicaceae/Cruciferae)

Common name: Gold dust
Height: 25cm (10in)
Spread: 40cm (16in)
Aspect: Full sun
Soil: Well-drained, gritty, fertile
Hardiness: Zone 3
Propagation: Seed, in autumn

Mound-forming evergreen. Leaves in rosettes, obovate, hairy, toothed, grey-green. Flowers in panicles, yellow, in spring and early summer. Good in a wall.

Bacopa monnieri
(Scrophulariaceae)

Common name: Water hyssop
Height: 10cm (4in)
Spread: 40cm (16in)
Aspect: Sun
Soil: Aquatic or marginal
Hardiness: Zone 8
Propagation: Division, in spring

Aquatic or semi-aquatic, mat-forming, creeping plant. Leaves spoon-shaped, apex dentate. Flowers small, 5-petalled, white or pale pink, summer. Worldwide distribution.

Ballota
'All Hallows Green'
(Labiatae/Lamiaceae)

Common names: None
Height: 60cm (2 ft)
Spread: 75cm (30in)
Aspect: Full sun
Soil: Well-drained, poor, gritty
Hardiness: Zone 8
Propagation: Softwood cuttings, in spring

Evergreen subshrub with lime-green, heart-shaped, aromatic, woolly leaves. Flowers small, two-lipped, pale green, with green calyces, in mid- to late summer.

Ballota pseudodictamnus
A.G.M.
(Labiatae/Lamiaceae)

Common names: None
Height: 50cm (20in)
Spread: 60cm (24in)
Aspect: Full sun
Soil: Well-drained, poor, gritty
Hardiness: Zone 8
Propagation: Softwood cuttings, in spring

Evergreen subshrub. Leaves ovate, greyish-to yellowish-green. Flowers on white-woolly stems, white or pinkish-white with pale green calyces. Dislikes winter wet.

Baptisia australis
A.G.M.
(Leguminosae/Papilionaceae)

Common name: False or wild indigo
Height: 1.5m (5ft)
Spread: 60cm (2ft)
Aspect: Full sun
Soil: Sharply drained, gritty
Hardiness: Zone 5
Propagation: Seed, when ripe; division, in spring

Erect or spreading plant. Leaves palmate, with inversely lance-shaped leaflets, deep green. Flowers in racemes, pea-like, indigo-blue, followed by inflated seed heads.

Begonia grandis
subsp. *evansiana*
(Begoniaceae)

Common name: Begonia
Height: 80cm (32in)
Spread: 30cm (12in)
Aspect: Full sun or half shade
Soil: Moist, fertile, humus-rich
Hardiness: Zone 8
Propagation: Bulbils, in autumn

Tuberous begonia with ovate, olive-green leaves. Pendent cymes of perfumed, bright pink flowers on tallish, branched stems in summer. Produces plenty of bulbils.

Belamcanda chinensis
(Iridaceae)

Common names: Blackberry; leopard lily
Height: 90cm (36in)
Spread: 20cm (8in)
Aspect: Sun or half shade
Soil: Moisture-retentive but well-drained
Hardiness: Zone 8
Propagation: Seed or division, in spring

Rhizomatous, short-lived perennial. Leaves sword-shaped, green. Flowers orange, with maroon spots, in summer, followed by handsome, open seed heads; seeds black.

Bellis perennis
(Asteraceae/Compositae)

Common name: Common daisy
Height: 20cm (8in)
Spread: 20cm (8in)
Aspect: Sun or half shade
Soil: Well-drained, fertile
Hardiness: Zone 4
Propagation: Seed or division, both in spring

Well-known evergreen. Leaves obovate to spoon-shaped, green. Flowers solitary, single or double; disc florets yellow, ray florets white, red, or pink. Good ground cover.

Bellis perennis
'Pomponette' A.G.M.
(Asteraceae/Compositae)

Common name: Common daisy
Height: 20cm (8in)
Spread: 20cm (8in)
Aspect: Sun or half shade
Soil: Well-drained, fertile
Hardiness: Zone 4
Propagation: Seed or division, both in spring

Cloned selection. Leaves spoon-shaped to obovate, green. Flowerheads fully double, with quilled petals. Evergreen ground cover. Treat as a biennial in cold areas.

Bellium crassifolium canescens
(Asteraceae/Compositae)

Common names: None
Height: 15cm (6in)
Spread: 20cm (8in)
Aspect: Half shade
Soil: Well-drained, fertile
Hardiness: Zone 8
Propagation: Seed, in spring

Mediterranean species, at home in coastal gardens. Leaves elliptic to spoon-shaped, fleshy, green. Flowers solitary, white, with yellow discs, in summer.

Bergenia cordifolia
(Saxifragaceae)

Common name: Elephants' ears
Height: 60cm (24in)
Spread: 80cm (32in)
Aspect: Sun or half shade
Soil: Moist, well-drained, humus-rich
Hardiness: Zone 3
Propagation: Division, in spring or autumn

Evergreen from Siberia. Leaves round or heart-shaped, mid-green, flushed purple in winter. Panicles of pink flowers on long, strong, red stems, late winter to early spring.

BERGENIA (Saxifragaceae)
Elephant's ears

This genus from the moorlands, woodlands and meadows of Central and East Asia, contains only some half dozen or so species; however, these hybridise very readily and so have given rise to a large number of named-variety hybrids. They are all evergreen and rhizomatous, and generally hardy. Elephant's ears are extremely useful perennials, as they will grow in sun or shade and in dry or wet soil. The leaves are distinctive: large, round, glossy and leathery, in rosettes, and colouring up well in winter, particularly in poor soil. They make excellent ground cover, and are good in a woodland situation. The flowering cymes are also handsome, and provide particularly welcome colour when they appear in winter and early spring. The flowers last well in water, and the leaves will last for weeks, which gives them great appeal for flower-arrangers. They are suitable plants for those with allergies. They do benefit from regular lifting and dividing, but this is also the best way to propagate, as plants in gardens where more than one type is growing will produce hybrid seeds. Slugs can be a problem. Other cultivars with an Award of Garden Merit are 'Bressingham White' (Zone 4) and *B. cordifolia* 'Purpurea' (Zone 3).

***Bergenia* 'Silberlicht' A.G.M.**
(Saxifragaceae)

Common name: Elephant's ears
Height: 45cm (18in)
Spread: 60cm (24in)
Aspect: Sun or half shade
Soil: Moist, well-drained, humus-rich
Hardiness: Zone 6
Propagation: Division, in autumn or spring

Hybrid with large, broad, obovate green leaves with scalloped edges. White flowers in early and mid-spring age to pink, and have pink sepals.

***Bergenia* 'Sunningdale'**
(Saxifragaceae)

Common name: Elephant's ears
Height: 45cm (18in)
Spread: 60cm (24in)
Aspect: Sun or half shade
Soil: Moist, well-drained, humus-rich
Hardiness: Zone 3
Propagation: Division, in autumn or spring

Clump-forming hybrid with large, round or obovate leaves, deep green turning red in winter. Flowers rich lilac-magenta, on long red stems in early and midwinter.

***Blechnum spicant* A.G.M.**
(Blechnaceae)

Common name: Hard fern
Height: 50cm (20in)
Spread: 60cm (24in)
Aspect: Half or deep shade
Soil: Moist, acidic, humus-rich
Hardiness: Zone 5
Propagation: Spores, in late summer

Evergreen, rhizomatous fern. Lance-shaped, sterile, dark green fronds, pinnate and pinnatifid with oblong pinnae, surround taller, fertile fronds with linear pinnae.

Bletilla striata
(Orchidaceae)

Common names: None
Height: 60cm (2ft)
Spread: 60cm (2ft)
Aspect: Half shade
Soil: Moist, well-drained, humus-rich
Hardiness: Zone 7
Propagation: Division, in spring

Terrestrial, deciduous orchid. Pseudobulbs flattened, each producing 3 or 4 oblong to lance-shaped green leaves. Terminal racemes of magenta flowers, spring to early summer.

***Bletilla striata* 'Albostriata'**
(Orchidaceae)

Common names: None
Height: 60cm (2ft)
Spread: 60cm (2ft)
Aspect: Half shade; protect from midday summer sun
Soil: Moist, well-drained, humus-rich
Hardiness: Zone 7
Propagation: Division, in spring

A selected form with white flowers, flushed pink, in spring to summer. Leaves oblong to lance-shaped, green. Grow in a peat bed or a woodland garden.

***Brunnera macrophylla* A.G.M.**
(Boraginaceae)

Common names: None
Height: 60cm (2ft)
Spread: 60cm (2ft)
Aspect: Half or full shade
Soil: Moist, well-drained, humus-rich
Hardiness: Zone 3
Propagation: Seed or division, both in spring

Rhizomatous woodland or ground-cover plant. Leaves large and green; basal leaves heart-shaped, stem leaves elliptic. Flowers in panicles, bright blue, in spring.

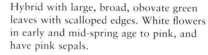

The delicate bright blue flowers of Brunnera macrophylla *appear above a bed of large heart-shaped leaves.*

Brunnera macrophylla
'Dawson's White'
(Boraginaceae)

Common names: None
Height: 60cm (2ft)
Spread: 60cm (2ft)
Aspect: Half or full shade
Soil: Moist, well-drained, humus-rich
Hardiness: Zone 3
Propagation: Division, in spring

Handsome variegated cultivar, good in woodland. Leaves large, elliptic and heart-shaped with wide cream margins. Flowers blue. Will not come true from seed.

Brunnera macrophylla
'Hadspen Cream' A.G.M.
(Boraginaceae)

Common names: None
Height: 60cm (2ft)
Spread: 60cm (2ft)
Aspect: Half or full shade
Soil: Moist, well-drained, humus-rich
Hardiness: Zone 3
Propagation: Division, in spring

Variegated clone, with large, cream-edged, elliptic and heart-shaped leaves, contrasting well with the bright blue flowers. Suits a woodland setting, and good for cutting.

Brunsvigia subacaulis
(Amaryllidaceae/Liliaceae)

Common names: None
Height: 45cm (18in)
Spread: 20cm (8in)
Aspect: Full sun
Soil: Sharply-drained, gritty
Hardiness: Zone 9
Propagation: Seed, in warmth in spring; offsets, in autumn

Bulbous perennial. Bright crimson flowers should appear before leaves, but may not do so for years. Leaves long, strap-shaped, dark green. From South Africa.

Buglossoides purpurocaerulea
(Boraginaceae)

Common names: None
Height: 60cm (2ft)
Spread: Indefinite
Aspect: Full sun; protect from midday sun
Soil: Well-drained, fertile
Hardiness: Zone 6
Propagation: Division, in spring

Rhizomatous ground cover; non-flowering shoots root as they run, spreading rapidly. Leaves dark green, lance-shaped. Flowers are small, purple, in erect cymes.

Bulbine alooides
(Asphodelaceae/Liliaceae)

Common names: None
Height: 30cm (12in)
Spread: 15cm (6in)
Aspect: Full sun
Soil: Well-drained, gritty
Hardiness: Zone 9
Propagation: Seed, in warmth in spring; division, in spring

Clump-forming perennial from South Africa, with compact rosettes of green, fleshy, lance-shaped leaves. Racemes of yellow, star-shaped flowers in spring.

Bulbinella hookeri
(Asphodelaceae/Liliaceae)

Common names: None
Height: 60cm (24in)
Spread: 30cm (18in)
Aspect: Sun or half shade
Soil: Well-drained, neutral or acidic
Hardiness: Zone 8
Propagation: Seed, when ripe; division, in autumn

Fleshy-rooted perennial from South Africa with rosettes of grass-like, succulent leaves. Flowers star-shaped, yellow, in dense racemes, in spring to summer.

Buphthalmum salicifolium
(Asteraceae/Compositae)

Common name: Ox eye
Height: 60cm (24in)
Spread: 45cm (18in)
Aspect: Full sun
Soil: Dry, gritty, poor
Hardiness: Zone 4
Propagation: Seed or division, both in spring

Leaves narrow, lance-shaped or obovate, dark green. Flowers yellow, inula-like daisies on erect stems all summer long, especially if dead-headed regularly.

Bupleurum falcatum
(Apiaceae/Umbelliferae)

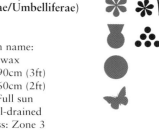

Common name: Thorow-wax
Height: 90cm (3ft)
Spread: 60cm (2ft)
Aspect: Full sun
Soil: Well-drained
Hardiness: Zone 3
Propagation: Seed or division, both in spring

Leaves narrow, linear, green. Yellow flowers in umbels, similar to the familiar *Gypsophila paniculata* (*see p.140*), not spectacular but lasting for many weeks.

Bupleurum fruticosum
(Apiaceae/Umbelliferae)

Common name: Shrubby hare's ear
Height: 2m (6ft)
Spread: 3m (9ft)
Aspect: Full sun
Soil: Any, well-drained
Hardiness: Zone 7
Propagation: Seed or division, both in spring

Dense, evergreen subshrub, too large for the small garden. Leaves obovate, blue-green. Flowers starry, yellow, in umbels, summer to autumn. Good seaside plant.

Butomus umbellatus A.G.M.
(Butomaceae)

Common names: Flowering rush; water gladiolus
Height: 1.2m (4ft)
Spread: 45cm (18in)
Aspect: Full sun
Soil: Marginal, or aquatic to 35cm (10in) deep
Hardiness: Zone 5
Propagation: Seed, in mud in spring; division, in spring

Rhizomatous aquatic perennial. Leaves long, radical, green, turning bronze. Flowers numerous, perfumed, pink, in umbels in late summer.

Cacalia glabra
(Asteraceae)

Common names: None
Height: 80cm (32in)
Spread: 45cm (18in)
Aspect: Sun
Soil: Well-drained
Hardiness: Zone 6
Propagation: Seed, in spring

Leaves kidney-shaped, coarse, pale green, with glabrous undersides. Flattish corymbs of small, pink flowers in spring. European member of a widely distributed genus.

Calamintha grandiflora 'Variegata'
(Labiatae/Lamiaceae)

Common name: Calamint
Height: 45cm (18in)
Spread: 45cm (18in)
Aspect: Sun or half shade
Soil: Moist, well-drained
Hardiness: Zone 5
Propagation: Seed or division, both in spring

Rhizomatous culinary herb; good ground cover. Leaves aromatic, ovate, toothed, variegated green and cream. Pink flowers in lax cymes, in summer.

Calamintha nepeta
(Labiatae/Lamiaceae)

Common name: Lesser calamint
Height: 45cm (18in)
Spread: 80cm (32in)
Aspect: Sun or half shade
Soil: Moist, well-drained
Hardiness: Zone 6
Propagation: Seed or division, both in spring

Aromatic culinary herb; good ground cover. Leaves ovate, hairy, green. Pink flowers in branching cymes of up to 15, in summer. From Eurasia and N. Africa.

Calamintha nepeta subsp. *glandulosa* 'White Cloud'
(Labiatae/Lamiaceae)

Common name: Lesser calamint
Height: 45cm (18in)
Spread: 80cm (32in)
Aspect: Sun or half shade
Soil: Moist, well-drained
Hardiness: Zone 6
Propagation: Seed or division, both in spring

Long-flowering, cloned selection; good for culinary use or ground cover. Flowers white, in branching cymes, spring and summer. Leaves aromatic, ovate, hairy, green.

Calandrinia grandiflora
(Portulacaceae)

Common names: None
Height: 1m (36in)
Spread: 45cm (18in)
Aspect: Full sun
Soil: Sharply drained, acidic, humus-rich
Hardiness: Zone 7
Propagation: Seed, in spring; stem cuttings, in spring

An evergreen species from Chile, often grown as an annual in cold areas. Leaves fleshy, elliptic, green. Flowers in racemes, cup-shaped, magenta, in summer.

Calanthe discolor
(Orchidaceae)

Common names: None
Height: 20cm (8in)
Spread: 20cm (8in)
Aspect: Half shade
Soil: Well-drained, gritty, humus-rich
Hardiness: Zone 8
Propagation: Division, after flowering

Evergreen terrestrial orchid from Korea, Japan and Taiwan. Leaves oblong, green. Flowers in erect racemes of up to 10, purplish with pink lips.

Calceolaria biflora
(Scrophulariaceae)

Common names: Pouch flower; slipper flower; slipperwort
Height: 20cm (8in)
Spread: 20cm (8in)
Aspect: Sun or half shade
Soil: Porous, acidic, fertile
Hardiness: Zone 6
Propagation: Seed, in autumn or spring; division, in spring

Rhizomatous evergreen from South America. Leaves in rosettes, oblong, toothed, dark green. Flowers yellow, 2-lipped, in loose racemes of up to 8, all summer long.

Calceolaria integrifolia A.G.M.
(Scrophulariaceae)

Common names: Pouch flower; slipper flower; slipperwort
Height: 1m (3ft)
Spread: 30cm (1ft)
Aspect: Sun or half shade
Soil: Porous, acidic, fertile
Hardiness: Zone 9
Propagation: Seed, in autumn or spring; division, in spring

Lax subshrub. Leaves grey-green, ovate to lance-shaped, toothed. Flowers in cymes of as many as 35, yellow, all summer long. Usually treated as an annual in cold areas.

Calceolaria polyrhiza
(Scrophulariaceae)

Common names: Pouch flower; slipper flower; slipperwort
Height: 8cm (3in)
Spread: 20cm (8in)
Aspect: Sun or half shade
Soil: Gritty, acidic, fertile
Hardiness: Zone 9
Propagation: Seed, in autumn or spring; division, in spring

Rhizomatous, dwarf evergeen from Chile and Argentina. Leaves ovate, toothed, green. Cymes of up to 6 yellow flowers, spotted red, in summer. Good for an alpine house.

Calceolaria tenella
(Scrophulariaceae)

Common names: Pouch flower; slipper flower; slipperwort
Height: 8cm (3in)
Spread: 45cm (18in)
Aspect: Sun or half shade
Soil: Gritty, acidic, fertile
Hardiness: Zone 9
Propagation: Seed, in autumn or spring; division, in spring

An evergreen, creeping perennial from Chile. Leaves ovate, toothed, light green. Three-flowered cymes of pouched, yellow, red-spotted blooms, in summer.

Caltha palustris
'Flore Pleno' A.G.M.
(Ranunculaceae)

Common names: Kingcup; marsh marigold
Height: 25cm (10in)
Spread: 25cm (10in)
Aspect: Full sun
Soil: Marginal aquatic
Hardiness: Zone 3
Propagation: Division, in autumn or spring

Rhizomatous marginal plant for temperate climates. Leaves kidney-shaped, toothed, deep green. Flowers in corymbs, yellow, waxy, fully double.

Camassia leichtlinii
subsp. _leichtlinii_ A.G.M.
(Hyacinthaceae/Liliaceae)

Common name: Quamash
Height: 1.2m (4ft)
Spread: 10cm (4in)
Aspect: Sun or half shade
Soil: Moist, well-drained, humus-rich
Hardiness: Zone 3
Propagation: Seed, when ripe; offsets, in summer

Bulbous perennial from the western U.S.A. Leaves linear, green. Flowers in racemes, star-shaped, off-white, in late spring. The flowering season is very short.

Camassia leichtlinii
'Semiplena'
(Hyacinthaceae/Liliaceae)

Common name: Quamash
Height: 1.2m (4ft)
Spread: 10cm (4in)
Aspect: Sun or half shade
Soil: Moist, well-drained, humus-rich
Hardiness: Zone 3
Propagation: Offsets, in summer

Semi-double, sterile form (so cannot be raised from seed). Flowers in dense racemes, star-shaped, cream; short season in spring. Bulbs become crowded very quickly.

Camassia quamash
(Hyacinthaceae/Liliaceae)

Common name: Quamash
Height: 90cm (36in)
Spread: 5cm (2in)
Aspect: Sun or half shade
Soil: Moist, well-drained, humus-rich
Hardiness: Zone 5
Propagation: Seed, when ripe; offsets, in summer

Edible, bulbous plant from North America. Leaves linear, green. Flowers starry, cup-shaped, blue, in racemes; short season in late spring. Can be naturalised in grass.

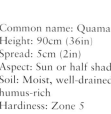

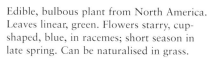

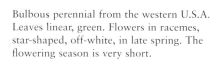

CAMPANULA (Campanulaceae)
Bellflower

This is a very large genus, containing some 300 species, including annuals and biennials as well as perennials. They are found in very diverse habitats in temperate southern Europe, Turkey and Asia. The species therefore have differing cultivation requirements, but as a whole they are fairly undemanding, and will grow in sun or dappled shade if given a soil that is well-drained and fertile. There is a campanula to suit most situations in a garden, from wall plants to borders, as the habits vary from trailing or spreading to clump-forming or upright; the taller varieties of the latter may require staking. Campanula flowers also show a wide variety of shapes, from tubular and bell-shaped to star-shaped, and intermediates between these. The flowering season is long, from late spring through the summer. Some species are rampant and invasive, and to be avoided unless you have plenty of room for them to spread or are willing to confine them to a container. Species that fall into this category are *C. persicifolia*, *C. pulla*, and *C. takesimana*; *C. persicifolia* will also self-seed liberally around the garden unless it is dead-headed. The only other disadvantage is that they are prone to attack by slugs and snails.

Campanula barbata
(Campanulaceae)

Common name: Bearded bellflower
Height: 30cm (12in)
Spread: 20cm (8in)
Aspect: Sun or half shade
Soil: Moist, well-drained
Hardiness: Zone 6
Propagation: Seed, in autumn

Short-lived perennial from the Alps and Norway. Leaves oblong, hairy, toothed, green. Flowers in one-sided racemes, pendent, blue, bell-shaped, in late spring.

Campanula
'Burghaltii' AG.M.
(Campanulaceae)

Common name: Bellflower
Height: 60cm (2ft)
Spread: 30cm (1ft)
Aspect: Sun or half shade
Soil: Moist, well-drained, alkaline, fertile
Hardiness: Zone 7
Propagation: Division, in spring or autumn

Hybrid between *C. punctata* and *C. latifolia*. Basal leaves heart-shaped, stem leaves ovate, green. Pendent, tubular, lavender flowers, in racemes in summer.

Campanula carpatica
A.G.M.
(Campanulaceae)

Common name: Alpine bellflower
Height: 20cm (8in)
Spread: 60cm (24in)
Aspect: Sun or half shade
Soil: Moist, well-drained
Hardiness: Zone 3
Propagation: Seed, in autumn

Clump-forming plant from the Carpathians. Leaves basal, ovate, toothed, green. Flowers solitary, upturned, open bells, blue, white, or violet, over a long period in summer.

Campanula carpatica
'Blaue Clips'
(Campanulaceae)

Common name: Bellflower
Height: 30cm (1ft)
Spread: 30cm (1ft)
Aspect: Sun or half shade
Soil: Moist, well-drained
Hardiness: Zone 3
Propagation: Division, in spring or autumn

Compact hybrid; comes almost true from seed. Very free-flowering; remontant if sheared after flowering. Flowers light sky blue, in summer. May need staking.

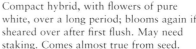

Campanula carpatica
'Weisse Clips'
(Campanulaceae)

Common name: Bellflower
Height: 30cm (1ft)
Spread: 30cm (1ft)
Aspect: Sun or half shade
Soil: Moist, well-drained
Hardiness: Zone 3
Propagation: Division, in spring or autumn

Compact hybrid, with flowers of pure white, over a long period; blooms again if sheared over after first flush. May need staking. Comes almost true from seed.

Campanula cochleariifolia
A.G.M.
(Campanulaceae)

Common name: Fairies' thimbles
Height: 10cm (4in)
Spread: 30cm (12in)
Aspect: Sun or half shade
Soil: Moist, well-drained
Hardiness: Zone 6
Propagation: Seed, in autumn

Rhizomatous, rosette-forming, miniature. Leaves round, toothed, green. Flowers solitary, blue, pendent, bells, in summer. Charming plant from the Alps.

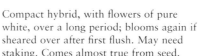

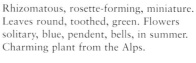

Campanula
'Elizabeth'
(Campanulaceae)

Common name: Bellflower
Height: 40cm (16in)
Spread: 40cm (16in)
Aspect: Sun or half shade
Soil: Moist, well-drained
Hardiness: Zone 7
Propagation: Division, in spring or autumn

A rhizomatous hybrid from *C. takesimana*. Leaves in rosettes, heart-shaped. Flowers in racemes, pendent bells, reddish, cream inside; late summer. Good ground cover.

Campanula garganica
'Dickson's Gold'
(Campanulaceae)

Common name: Bellflower
Height: 5cm (2in)
Spread: 30cm (12in)
Aspect: Sun or half shade
Soil: Moist, well-drained
Hardiness: Zone 5
Propagation: Division, in spring or autumn

Attractive *C. garganica* hybrid. Leaves ovate to heart-shaped, toothed; the yellow colour is a striking contrast to the blue of the upward-facing, starry flowers.

Campanula glomerata
'Superba' A.G.M.
(Campanulaceae)

Common name: Clustered bellflower
Height: 60cm. (2ft.)
Spread: Indefinite
Aspect: Sun or half shade
Soil: Moist, well-drained, alkaline
Hardiness: Zone 2
Propagation: Seed, in spring

Leaves ovate to lance-shaped, toothed, deep green. Flowers in dense racemes, tubular, violet-purple. Flowers again if sheared after first flush. From Europe and Asia.

Campanula glomerata
var. *alba*
(Campanulaceae)

Common names: Clustered bellflower
Height: 60cm (2ft)
Spread: Indefinite
Aspect: Sun or half shade
Soil: Moist, well-drained, alkaline
Hardiness: Zone 2
Propagation: Division, in spring or autumn

Pure white sport of a purplish-flowered species. Leaves ovate to lance-shaped, round-toothed. May need staking. Will flower twice if sheared after first flush.

Campanula
'Kent Belle'
(Campanulaceae)

Common name: Bellflower
Height: 75cm (30in)
Spread: 30cm (12in)
Aspect: Sun or half shade
Soil: Moist, well-drained
Hardiness: Zone 3
Propagation: Division, in spring or autumn

This very handsome hybrid is a recent introduction. Tall stems bear large, silky, shining bells, deep violet in colour. Leaves ovate, toothed, green.

Campanula lactiflora
'Loddon Anna' A.G.M.
(Campanulaceae)

Common name: Milky bellflower
Height: 90cm (3ft)
Spread: 60cm (2ft)
Aspect: Sun or half shade
Soil: Moist, well-drained, alkaline, fertile
Hardiness: Zone 5
Propagation: Division, in spring or autumn

Cloned cultivar of an undemanding species. Leaves ovate, toothed, green. Flowers lilac-pink bells in conical panicles, early summer to autumn. Flowers twice if dead-headed.

Campanula lactiflora
'Pritchard's Variety.' A.G.M.
(Campanulaceae)

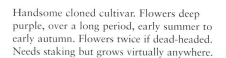

Common name: Milky bellflower
Height: 75cm (30in)
Spread: 60cm (24in)
Aspect: Sun or half shade
Soil: Moist, well-drained, alkaline, fertile
Hardiness: Zone 5
Propagation: Division, in spring or autumn

Handsome cloned cultivar. Flowers deep purple, over a long period, early summer to early autumn. Flowers twice if dead-headed. Needs staking but grows virtually anywhere.

Campanula latifolia
'Alba'
(Campanulaceae)

Common name: Bellflower
Height: 1.2m (4ft)
Spread: 60cm (2ft)
Aspect: Sun or half shade
Soil: Moist, well-drained, alkaline, fertile
Hardiness: Zone 3
Propagation: Seed, in spring; division, in spring or autumn

Vigorous perennial. Basal leaves toothed, ovate-oblong, rough-surfaced, green; stem leaves similar, pointed. Flowers in spiky racemes, open, tubular, white, in summer.

Campanula latiloba **'Hidcote Amethyst' A.G.M.** (Campanulaceae)

Common name: Bellflower
Height: 90cm (36in)
Spread: 45cm (18in)
Aspect: Sun or half shade
Soil: Moist, well-drained, alkaline, fertile
Hardiness: Zone 3
Propagation: Division, in spring or autumn

Handsome clone of a species from Turkey. Leaves basal, lance-shaped, toothed, green. Flowers cup-shaped, pale amethyst, shaded purple, in racemes, in mid- and late summer.

Campanula persicifolia 'Alba' (Campanulaceae)

Common name: Peach-leaved bellflower
Height: 90cm (36in)
Spread: 45cm (18in)
Aspect: Sun or half shade
Soil: Moist, well-drained, alkaline, fertile
Hardiness: Zone 3
Propagation: Seed, in spring; division, in spring or autumn

Evergreen (rare in campanulas), rhizomatous plant. Rosettes of basal, narrow, toothed, green leaves. Racemes of cup-shaped, pure white flowers in early and midsummer.

Campanula persicifolia 'Chettle Charm' (Campanulaceae)

Common name: Peach-leaved bellflower
Height: 90cm (3ft)
Spread: 30cm (1ft)
Aspect: Sun or half shade
Soil: Moist, well-drained, alkaline, fertile
Hardiness: Zone 3
Propagation: Division, in spring or autumn

Cloned cultivar of rhizomatous, unusual evergreen species. Leaves lance-shaped to oblong-ovate, toothed. Racemes of creamy-white flowers, tinted blue, in summer.

Campanula persicifolia 'Telham Beauty' (Campanulaceae)

Common name: Peach-leaved bellflower
Height: 90cm (3ft)
Spread: 30cm (1ft)
Aspect: Sun or half shade
Soil: Moist, well-drained, alkaline, fertile
Hardiness: Zone 3
Propagation: Division, spring or autumn

Cloned cultivar; rhizomatous, evergreen. Leaves basal, toothed, lance-shaped to oblong-obovate. Flowers very large, blue, in summer and again in autumn.

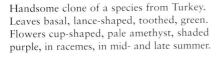

Campanula pulla (Campanulaceae)

Common name: Bellflower
Height: 20cm (8in)
Spread: 30cm (12in)
Aspect: Sun or half shade
Soil: Moist, well-drained
Hardiness: Zone 6
Propagation: Seed in autumn

An invasive perennial from the Alps. Leaves in basal rosettes, spoon-shaped, toothed, green, shiny. Flowers solitary, bell-shaped, pendent, deep purple, in spring to summer.

Campanula pyramidalis (Campanulaceae)

Common name: Chimney bellflower
Height: To 3m (6ft)
Spread: 60cm (2ft)
Aspect: Sun or half shade
Soil: Moist, well-drained, alkaline, fertile
Hardiness: Zone 8
Propagation: Seed, in spring; division, spring or autumn

A short-lived perennial often treated as a biennial. Leaves in rosettes, ovate, toothed, green. Flowers in racemes, cup-shaped, fragrant, blue, from late spring to summer.

Campanula rotundifolia (Campanulaceae)

Common names: Harebell; Scottish bluebell
Height: 30cm (1ft)
Spread: 30cm (1ft)
Aspect: Sun or half shade
Soil: Moist, well-drained
Hardiness: Zone 3
Propagation: Seed in spring

Spreads by underground runners. Leaves basal, round, toothed, green. Flowers fragrant, cup-shaped, pale blue or white, in racemes in late spring to summer.

Campanula takesimana (Campanulaceae)

Common names: None
Height: 80cm (32in)
Spread: Indefinite
Aspect: Sun or half shade
Soil: Well-drained
Hardiness: Zone 7
Propagation: Seed, in spring; division, in spring or autumn

Highly invasive rhizomatous species. Leaves glossy, heart-shaped, green. Flowers in arching sprays, off-white, flushed pink or brown, pendent, bell-shaped, in summer.

Campanula lactiflora *'Pouffe', a charming miniature campanula with small green hummocks covered in lavender-blue flowers.*

ADDITIONAL CAMPANULAS with an A.G.M.

C. arvatica (Zone 7)

C. betulifolia (Zone 5)

C. betulifolia 'Birch Hybrid' (Zone 4)

C. chamissonis 'Superba' (Zone 2)

C. formanekiana (Zone 7)

C. 'G.F. Wilson' (Zone 5)

C. garganica (Zone 5)

C. garganica 'W.H. Paine' (Zone 5)

C. garganica 'Superba' (Zone 5)

C. isophylla (Zone 7)

C. isophylla 'Alba' (Zone 7)

C. isophylla 'Mayi' (Zone 7)

C. 'Joe Elliott' (Zone 6)

C. lactiflora 'Alba' (Zone 5)

C. latiloba 'Alba' (Zone 3)

C. latiloba 'Highcliffe Variety' (Zone 3)

C. latiloba 'Percy Piper' (Zone 3)

C. persicifolia 'Fleur de Neige' (Zone 3)

C. portenschlagiana (Zone 4)

C. poscharskiana 'Stella' (Zone 3)

C. raineri (Zone 6)

C. tommassiniana (Zone 6)

Campanula trachelium
(Campanulaceae)

Common names: Bats-in-the-belfry; nettle-leaved bellflower; throatwort
Height: 90cm (3ft)
Spread: 30cm (1ft)
Aspect: Sun or half shade
Soil: Well-drained, alkaline, fertile
Hardiness: Zone 3
Propagation: Seed, in spring; division, in spring or autumn

Woody-based Mediterranean species. Leaves nettle-like, ovate, toothed, mid-green. Flowers tubular, blue or white, in short racemes in mid- to late summer.

Canna indica
(Cannaceae)

Common names: Arrowroot; Indian shot
Height: To 2m (6ft)
Spread: 60cm (2ft)
Aspect: Sun
Soil: Well-drained, fertile, humus-rich
Hardiness: Zone 8
Propagation: Seed, in warmth in spring; division, in spring

Rhizomatous South American plant. Leaves broad, elliptic, large, bronze-green. Flowers in racemes to panicles, iris-like, orange or red, summer to autumn; best dead-headed.

Canna
'King Midas'
(Cannaceae)

Common names: None
Height: 1.5m (5ft)
Spread: 60cm (2ft)
Aspect: Sun
Soil: Well-drained, fertile, humus-rich
Hardiness: Zone 8
Propagation: Division, in spring

Rhizomatous hybrid of complex origin. Leaves, large, broad, dark green. Flowers in raceme, gladiolus-like, yellow with orange markings, midsummer to early autumn.

Canna
'Striata'
(Cannaceae)

Common names: None
Height: 1.5m (5ft)
Spread: 50cm (20in)
Aspect: Sun
Soil: Well-drained, fertile, humus-rich
Hardiness: Zone 8
Propagation: Division, in spring

Handsome perennial of uncertain origins. Leaves large, broad, pale green with bright yellow veins. Flowers gladiolus-like, orange, in racemes, midsummer to early autumn.

Cardamine pentaphyllos
(Brassicaceae/Cruciferae)

Common name: Bittercress
Height: 60cm (2ft)
Spread: 30cm (1ft)
Aspect: Half or full shade
Soil: Moist, humus-rich
Hardiness: Zone 6
Propagation: Seed or division, both in spring

Clump-forming, rhizomatous perennial. Leaves 5-palmate, leaflets green, toothed, lance-shaped. Flowers in lax racemes, pink, white or lilac, late spring and early summer.

Cardamine pratensis
'Flore Pleno' A.G.M.
(Brassicaceae/Cruciferae)

Common names: Cuckoo flower; lady's smock
Height: 20cm (8in)
Spread: 30cm (12in)
Aspect: Half or full shade
Soil: Moist, humus-rich
Hardiness: Zone 4
Propagation: Seed, in autumn or spring; division, in spring

Rhizomatous perennial. Leaves in rosettes, pinnate; leaflets ovate-round, deep green, glossy. Flowers in panicles, lilac-pink, double. Produces plantlets in leaf clusters.

Cardiocrinum giganteum **A.G.M.**
(Liliaceae)

Common name: Giant lily
Height: To 4m (12ft)
Spread: 45cm (18in)
Aspect: Half shade
Soil: Moist, well-drained, humus-rich
Hardiness: Zone 7
Propagation: Seed, when ripe; offsets, after flowering

Bulbous perennial, forming rosettes of large, broad, ovate, glossy leaves. Flowers large, trumpet-shaped, nodding, perfumed, white, in racemes of up to 20 in summer.

CAREX (Cyperaceae)
Sedge

This is an extremely large genus, containing some 1,500 or more rhizomatous or tufted species, most of which are evergreen, but some of which are herbaceous. Sedges are found naturally in a very wide range of habitats, and spread all over the world, so it is impossible to generalise about their cultural requirements as a genus; this also means that it is possible to find a sedge to suit every situation in every garden. They are generally hardy, but there are a few that are not. Large numbers of species and selections are in cultivation; however, many of these have little or no garden value. Out of all of them, two cultivars alone, *C. elata* 'Aurea' and *C. oshimensis* 'Evergold' (Zone 7) have achieved an Award of Garden Merit. For the most part, sedges are grown for their foliage, which is linear and grass-like, and may be flushed yellow or variegated. Flowers are grass-like, mostly in shades of brown and often inconspicuous, but a few sedges do also have attractive inflorescences. They are carried in panicles, generally short and spiked, sometimes longer or drooping, as in *C. pendula*. Without exception, sedges should be avoided by anyone who is seeking to create a low-allergen garden.

Carex comans
(Cyperaceae)

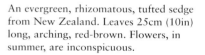

Common name: Sedge
Height: 40cm (16in)
Spread: 75cm (30in)
Aspect: Sun or half shade
Soil: Moist; dislikes extreme wet or dry conditions
Hardiness: Zone 7
Propagation: Seed, in warmth in spring; division, in early summer

An evergreen, rhizomatous, tufted sedge from New Zealand. Leaves 25cm (10in) long, arching, red-brown. Flowers, in summer, are inconspicuous.

Carex elata
'Aurea' A.G.M.
(Cyperaceae)

Common names: Bowles' golden sedge; tufted sedge
Height: 70cm (28in)
Spread: 45cm (18in)
Aspect: Sun or half shade
Soil: Moist to wet
Hardiness: Zone 7
Propagation: Division, in late spring

Deciduous, rhizomatous species. Leaves to 60cm (24in), golden-yellow, green-edged. Insignificant flowers in spring to summer; males are tall, above leaves, females shorter.

Carex pendula
(Cyperaceae)

Common names: Drooping, pendulous or weeping sedge
Height: 1.5m (5ft)
Spread: 1.5m (5ft)
Aspect: Sun or half shade
Soil: Moist to wet, fertile
Hardiness: Zone 8
Propagation: Division, in late spring

Evergreen, tufted sedge. Leaves 90cm (3ft), keeled, shiny, green, blue-green beneath. Flowers in catkin-like cylinders, dark brown, spring to summer. Stems upright or arching.

Carex testacea
(Cyperaceae)

Common name: Wood sedge
Height: 1.5m (5ft)
Spread: 1.5m (5ft)
Aspect: Sun or half shade
Soil: Moist; dislikes extreme wet or dry conditions
Hardiness: Zone 7
Propagation: Seed, in warmth in spring

Tufted evergreen species. Leaves arching, 60cm (2ft), pale green, orange-brown in full sun. Flower spikes brown, cylindrical, 60cm (2ft), in summer; seed heads longer.

Carlina acaulis
(Asteraceae/Compositae)

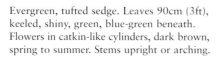

Common name: Stemless carline thistle
Height: 10cm (4in)
Spread: 25cm (10in)
Aspect: Sun
Soil: Very well-drained, poor
Hardiness: Zone 4
Propagation: Seed in autumn

Short-lived perennial from the Alps. Leaves in rosettes, pinnatisect, oblong, spiny. Flowers stemless, spiky, silvery, off-white bracts around a brown disc in summer.

Catananche caerulea
'Major' A.G.M.
(Asteraceae/Compositae)

Common names: Blue cupidone; Cupid's dart
Height: 90cm (3ft)
Spread: 30cm (1ft)
Aspect: Full sun
Soil: Well-drained
Hardiness: Zone 7
Propagation: Seed or division, both in spring

Handsome cultivar of a plant from S.W. Europe. Leaves linear, grassy, hairy, grey-green. Flowers solitary, dark-centred, lilac-blue, surrounded by bracts to match.

Catananche caerulea
'Alba'
(Asteraceae/Compositae)

Common name: White Cupid's dart
Height: 90cm (3ft)
Spread: 30cm (1ft)
Aspect: Full sun
Soil: Well-drained
Hardiness: Zone 7
Propagation: Seed or division, both in spring

White cultivar, often treated as a biennial. Solitary flowers have lilac-blue centres, pure white ray florets and bracts. Linear, grassy, hairy leaves are grey-green.

Cautleya gracilis
(Zingiberaceae)

Common names: None
Height: 45cm (18in)
Spread: 25cm (10in)
Aspect: Half shade
Soil: Moist, humus-rich
Hardiness: Zone 8
Propagation: Seed, in warmth in spring; division, in spring

Woodlander; plant rhizomes 15cm (6in) deep. Leaves broad, lance-shaped, glossy, green, reddish-grey beneath. Flowers yellow, bracts red-brown, in spikes in late summer.

Cautleya spicata
(Zingiberaceae)

Common names: None
Height: 60cm (24in)
Spread: 45cm (18in)
Aspect: Half shade
Soil: Moist, humus-rich
Hardiness: Zone 8
Propagation: Seed, in warmth in spring; division, in spring

Rhizomatous Himalayan species. Leaves broad, lance-shaped, shiny, mid-green. Flowers yellow, two-lipped, with orange bracts, in stiff spikes in late summer.

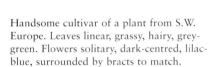

Cedronella canariensis
(Labiatae/Lamiaceae)

Common name: Balm of Gilead
Height: 1m (3ft)
Spread: 60cm (2ft)
Aspect: Full sun
Soil: Well-drained, fertile
Hardiness: Zone 9
Propagation: Seed, in warmth in spring; softwood cuttings, in spring

Short-lived plant from the Canary Islands. Leaves aromatic, 3-palmate, green, used in herb teas and pot-pourri. Two-lipped, pink, white or lilac flowers, in whorls in summer.

Celmisia coriacea
(Asteraceae/Compositae)

Common name: New Zealand daisy
Height: 60cm (24in)
Spread: 30cm (18in)
Aspect: Sun or half shade
Soil: Moist, well-drained, humus-rich
Hardiness: Zone 7
Propagation: Seed, when ripe; division, in spring

Rhizomatous evergreen; tricky in dry, warm areas. Leaves lance-shaped, grey-green, silky, hairy. Flowers late spring to summer, solitary; ray florets white, disc yellow.

Celmisia hookeri
(Asteraceae/Compositae)

Common name: New Zealand daisy
Height: 30cm (1ft)
Spread: 60cm (2ft)
Aspect: Sun or half shade
Soil: Moist, well-drained, acidic, humus-rich
Hardiness: Zone 7
Propagation: Seed, when ripe; division, in spring

Tufted evergreen from New Zealand. Good seaside plant; not for hot, dry areas. Leaves broad, oblong, glossy, deep green, felty white beneath. Solitary flowers; white, yellow disc.

Celmisia spectabilis
(Asteraceae/Compositae)

Common name: New Zealand daisy
Height: 30cm (1ft)
Spread: 30cm (1ft)
Aspect: Sun or half shade
Soil: Moist, well-drained, acidic, humus-rich
Hardiness: Zone 7
Propagation: Seed, when ripe; division, in spring

Clump-forming, rhizomatous evergreen, not for hot, dry sites. Leaves glossy, silvery green above, felty white beneath, oblong. Flowers solitary, ray florets white, disc florets yellow.

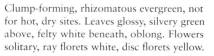

Centaurea bella
(Asteraceae/Compositae)

Common names: Hardheads; knapweed
Height: 30cm (12in)
Spread: 45cm (18in)
Aspect: Sun
Soil: Well-drained
Hardiness: Zone 6
Propagation: Seed, in spring; division, in spring or autumn

Clump-forming plant from the Caucasus. Leaves obovate, pinnatifid, feathery, green, hairy beneath. Flowers solitary, florets lobed, purple-pink, in summer.

Centaurea dealbata 'Steenbergii'
(Asteraceae/Compositae)

Common names: Hardheads; knapweed; Persian cornflower
Height: 60cm (2ft)
Spread: 60cm (2ft)
Aspect: Sun
Soil: Well-drained
Hardiness: Zone 3
Propagation: Seed, in spring; division, in spring or autumn

Undemanding, clump-forming perennial from the Caucasus. Leaves obovate, pinnatisect, green, with grey-green undersides. Flowers pink, in midsummer.

Centaurea hypoleuca 'John Coutts'
(Asteraceae/Compositae)

Common names: Hardheads; knapweed
Height: 60cm (24in)
Spread: 45cm (18in)
Aspect: Sun
Soil: Well-drained
Hardiness: Zone 5
Propagation: Seed, in spring; division, in spring or autumn

Cultivar of a species from the Caucasus. Leaves lance-shaped, pinnatifid, wavy-edged, green, white beneath. Flowers rose-pink, solitary, fragrant, long-lasting, in summer.

Centaurea macrocephala
(Asteraceae/Compositae)

Common names: Globe cornflower; hardheads; knapweed
Height: 1.5m (6ft)
Spread: 60cm (2ft)
Aspect: Sun
Soil: Well-drained
Hardiness: Zone 3
Propagation: Seed, in spring; division, in spring or autumn

Vigorous perennial from the Caucasus and Turkey. Leaves green, broad, lance-shaped, pinnatifid. Flowers large, yellow, with a basal support of brown, papery bracts.

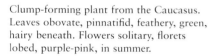

Centaurea montana
(Asteraceae/Compositae)

Common names: Hardheads; knapweed; mountain bluet
Height: 45cm (18in)
Spread: 60cm (24in)
Aspect: Sun
Soil: Well-drained
Hardiness: Zone 3
Propagation: Seed, in spring; division, in spring or autumn

Rhizomatous perennial. Leaves ovate, green, woolly beneath. Widely spaced florets give red-violet flowers a lacy look. Dead-head for more flowers and to prevent self-seeding.

Centaurea montana alba
(Asteraceae/Compositae)

Common names: Hardheads; knapweed; white mountain bluet
Height: 45cm (18in)
Spread: 60cm (24in)
Aspect: Sun
Soil: Well-drained
Hardiness: Zone 3
Propagation: Seed, in spring; division, in spring or autumn

Rhizomatous perennial. Leaves lance-shaped to ovate, pinnatified, green, woolly beneath. Flowers solitary, white, lacy. Dead-head for more flowers and to prevent self-seeding.

Centaurium erythraea
(Gentianaceae)

Common name: Common centaury
Height: 10cm (4in)
Spread: 5cm (2in)
Aspect: Sun or half shade
Soil: Moist, well-drained
Hardiness: Zone 8
Propagation: Seed, when ripe; division, in spring

Short-lived perennial from Europe and Weste Asia. Leaves basal, obovate, grey-green, prominently veined. Flowers in flat-topped cymes, pink, in summer.

Centranthus ruber
(Valerianaceae)

Common name: Valerian
Height: 1m (3ft)
Spread: 1m (3ft)
Aspect: Sun
Soil: Well-drained, poor, alkaline
Hardiness: Zone 7
Propagation: Seed, in spring

Woody, much-branched perennial. Leaves fleshy, glaucous, ovate to lance-shaped. Dense cymes, of small, pink or red, fragrant flowers all summer; cut back after flowering.

Popular for its large brownish leaves, Canna × hybrida *'King Humbert' also boasts brilliant orange blooms.*

***Centranthus ruber* 'Albus'**
(Valerianaceae)

Common name: White valerian
Height: 1m (3ft)
Spread: 1m (3ft)
Aspect: Sun
Soil: Well-drained, poor, alkaline
Hardiness: Zone 7
Propagation: Seed, in spring

Woody, branching plant. Leaves ovate to lance-shaped, fleshy, green, glaucous. White, fragrant, in dense cymes. Cut after flowering for more flowers and to prevent self-seeding.

Cephalaria gigantea
(Dipsacaceae)

Common name: Giant scabious
Height: 2m (6ft)
Spread: 80cm (32in)
Aspect: Sun or half shade
Soil: Moist, well-drained, fertile
Hardiness: Zone 6
Propagation: Seed or division, both in spring

Clump-forming perennial. Leaves toothed, pinnatifid-pinnatisect, lobes oblong, toothed, green. Flowers on branching stems, solitary, scabious-like, primrose, in summer.

Cerastium tomentosum
(Caryophyllaceae)

Common name: Snow-in-summer
Height: 8cm (3in)
Spread: Indefinite
Aspect: Sun
Soil: Well-drained
Hardiness: Zone 4
Propagation: Seed, in autumn; division, in spring

Rampant, invasive perennial from Italy and Sicily. Leaves lance-shaped to linear, white-woolly. Flowers star-shaped, white, in cymes, all summer. Superb wall plant.

***Chaerophyllum hirsutum* 'Roseum'**
(Apiaceae/Umbelliferae)

Common names: None
Height: 60cm (24in)
Spread: 30cm (18in)
Aspect: Sun or half shade
Soil: Moist, fertile
Hardiness: Zone 6
Propagation: Seed, when ripe

Tap-rooted perennial. Leaves aromatic, 2- or 3-pinnate; lobes ovate, toothed. Pink flowers in compound umbels, late spring to early summer. Flowers again if dead-headed.

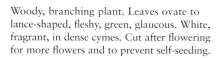

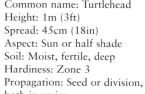

***Chamaemelum nobile* 'Flore Pleno'**
(Asteraceae/Compositae)

Common name: Double Roman chamomile
Height: 30cm (12in)
Spread: 45cm (18in)
Aspect: Sun
Soil: Gritty, well-drained
Hardiness: Zone 4
Propagation: Seed, *in situ* in spring

Mat-forming, aromatic herb. Leaves fresh green, pinnate, feathery. Flowers double, ray florets cream, disc florets yellow, in summer. Highly allergenic, skin irritant.

Chelidonium majus
(Papaveraceae)

Common name: Greater celandine
Height: 60cm (24in)
Spread: 20cm (8in)
Aspect: Any, but best in half shade
Soil: Any
Hardiness: Zone 6
Propagation: Seed in spring

Clump-forming, woodland plant. Leaves lobed-pinnatisect, scalloped, green. Small, yellow, 4-petalled flowers in umbels, in summer. Highly allergenic and skin irritant.

***Chelidonium majus* 'Flore Pleno'**
(Papaveraceae)

Common name: Double greater celandine
Height: 60cm (2ft)
Spread: 20cm (8in)
Aspect: Any
Soil: Any
Hardiness: Zone 6
Propagation: Seed, in spring

Cultivar with double flowers, larger than in the species. Leaves green, lobed-pinnatisect, scalloped. Will grow anywhere, self-seeds freely. Skin-irritant and very allergenic.

Chelone glabra
(Scrophulariaceae)

Common name: Turtlehead
Height: 1m (3ft)
Spread: 45cm (18in)
Aspect: Sun or half shade
Soil: Moist, fertile, deep
Hardiness: Zone 3
Propagation: Seed or division, both in spring

Sturdy perennial from the U.S.A. Leaves ovate to lance-shaped, green. White flowers, tinged pink, 2-lipped, very weather-resistant, in dense terminal racemes in autumn.

Chelone obliqua
(Scrophulariaceae)

Common name: Turtle head
Height: 60cm (2ft)
Spread: 30cm (1ft)
Aspect: Sun or half shade
Soil: Moist, fertile, deep
Hardiness: Zone 3
Propagation: Seed or division, both in spring

Erect, sturdy plant from the U.S.A. Leaves lance-shaped to elliptic, toothed, green, boldly veined. Flowers in terminal racemes, deep pink, resembling turtle heads, autumn.

Chiastophyllum oppositifolium A.G.M.
(Crassulaceae)

Common names: None
Height: 20cm (8in)
Spread: 15cm (6in)
Aspect: Half shade
Soil: Moist, well-drained
Hardiness: Zone 7
Propagation: Seed, in autumn; cuttings, in summer

Rhizomatous, mat-forming evergreen. Leaves ovate-round, wavy-edged, fleshy, green. Arching, branched racemes of bell-shaped yellow flowers, spring to summer.

Chrysanthemum weyrichii
(Asteraceae/Compositae)

Common names: None
Height: 30cm (12in)
Spread: 45cm (18in)
Aspect: Sun
Soil: Moist, well-drained, fertile
Hardiness: Zone 4
Propagation: Seed, in autumn; division, in spring or autumn

Rhizomatous, mat-forming perennial from Russia. Leaves aromatic, 5-lobed, round, green. Flowers daisy-like, ray florets pink and disc florets yellow, in autumn.

Chrysanthemum yezoense A.G.M.
(Asteraceae/Compositae)

Common names: None
Height: 30cm (12in)
Spread: 45cm (18in)
Aspect: Sun
Soil: Moist, well-drained
Hardiness: Zone 3
Propagation: Seed, in autumn; division in spring or autumn

Perennial from Japan. Leaves fleshy, ovate, pinnate, lobes oblong. Flowers single, ray florets white, disc florets yellow, weather-resistant, in branching sprays, in autumn.

Chrysogonum virginianum
(Asteraceae/Compositae)

Common names: Golden knee; golden star
Height: 25cm (10in)
Spread: 25cm (10in)
Aspect:sun or half shade
Soil: Moist, well-drained, humus-rich
Hardiness: Zone 5
Propagation: Seed, when ripe; division, in spring or autumn

Rhizomatous, evergreen woodland ground cover. Leaves ovate, hairy, green. Flowers solitary, star-shaped, 5-petalled, yellow, from early spring to late summer.

Cicerbita plumieri
(Asteraceae/Compositae)

Common names: None
Height: 1.2m (4ft)
Spread: 45cm (18in)
Aspect: Sun or half shade
Soil: Moist, acidic, fertile, humus-rich
Hardiness: Zone 5
Propagation: Seed or division, both in spring

Perennial from N. Europe. Leaves basal, green, pinnatifid-pinnatisect. Flowers in erect panicles, florets strap-shaped, lilac, from summer to early autumn.

Cichorium intybus A.G.M.
(Asteraceae/Compositae)

Common name: Chicory
Height: 1.2m (4ft)
Spread: 60cm (2ft)
Aspect: Sun
Soil: Well-drained, fertile
Hardiness: Zone 3
Propagation: Seed, in autumn or spring

Clump-forming, tap-rooted, culinary herb. Leaves basal, inverse lance-shaped, toothed, green. Flowers on branched stems, florets strap-shaped, blue, closed by midday.

Cimicifuga racemosa A.G.M.
(Ranunculaceae)

Common name: Black snake root
Height: 2m (6ft)
Spread: 60cm (2ft)
Aspect: Half shade
Soil: Moist, fertile, humus-rich
Hardiness: Zone 4
Propagation: Seed, when ripe; division, in spring

Clump-forming perennial. Leaves basal, green, 2- or 3-ternate; lobes oblong, toothed. Racemes, sometimes arched, of offensive-smelling white flowers, in summer.

Cimicifuga simplex
(Ranunculaceae)

Common name: Bugbane
Height: 1.2m (4ft)
Spread: 60cm (2ft)
Aspect: Half shade
Soil: Moist, well-drained, fertile
Hardiness: Zone 5
Propagation: Seed, when ripe; division, in spring

Clump-forming woodlander. Leaves basal, 3-ternate; leaflets ovate, purplish-green. Malodorous white flowers in bottle-brush racemes white, in autumn. No staking.

Cimicifuga simplex var. *simplex* 'Atropurpurea'
(Ranunculaceae)

Common name: Bugbane
Height: 1.2m (4ft)
Spread: 60cm (2ft)
Aspect: Half shade
Soil: Moist, well-drained, fertile
Hardiness: Zone 5
Propagation: Seed, when ripe; division, in spring

Cloned form with purple foliage, stems and buds. Leaves basal, 3-ternate; leaflets ovate. White, malodorous flowers in bottle-brush racemes in autumn. No staking needed.

Cirsium rivulare 'Atropurpureum'
(Asteraceae/Compositae)

Common name: Plume thistle
Height: 1.2m (4ft)
Spread: 60cm (2ft)
Aspect: Sun
Soil: Moist, well-drained
Hardiness: Zone 5
Propagation: Seed or division, both in spring

Leaves prickly, green, elliptic to lance-shaped, entire-pinnatifid. Flowers on erect stems, spherical, crimson-purple, early and midsummer. Dead-head to stop self-seeding.

Cirsium spinosissimum
(Asteraceae/Compositae)

Common names: None
Height: 1.2m (4ft)
Spread: 70cm (28in)
Aspect: Sun
Soil: Moist, gritty, humus-rich
Hardiness: Zone 5
Propagation: Seed or division, both in spring

Alpine species. Leaves whitish-green, oblong to lance-shaped, pinnatifid; lobes ovate, spiny. Flowerheads cream-white, backed by narrow, prickly bracts, mid- to late summer.

Claytonia megarhiza
(Portulacaceae)

Common name: Spring beauty
Height: 5cm (2in)
Spread: 15cm (6in)
Aspect: Sun
Soil: Well-drained, gritty, humus-rich
Hardiness: Zone 4
Propagation: Seed, in autumn

Short-lived, tap-rooted evergreen from the Rocky Mountains. Leaves fleshy, spoon-shaped, deep green. Flowers cup-shaped, white, in racemes on short stems in spring.

Claytonia virginica
(Portulacaceae)

Common name: Spring beauty
Height: 30cm (12in)
Spread: 20cm (8in)
Aspect: Half shade
Soil: Well-drained, gritty, humus-rich
Hardiness: Zone 6
Propagation: Seed, in autumn

Cormous perennial from eastern North America. Leaves basal, linear, fleshy, green. Small flowers in racemes, pink with red veins, in spring.

Clematis × *eriostemon* 'Hendersonii'
(Ranunculaceae)

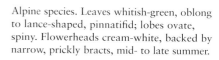

Common names: None
Height: To 5m (15ft)
Spread: 1m (3ft)
Aspect: Sun or half shade
Soil: Well-drained, fertile, humus-rich
Hardiness: Zone 4
Propagation: Division, in spring

Hybrid herbaceous clematis; suits a mixed border. Flowers solitary, bell-shaped, blue, tinted indigo, with recurved tips and cream anthers. Only for the large garden.

Clematis heracleifolia
(Ranunculaceae)

Common names: None
Height: 90cm (3ft)
Spread: 1.2m (4ft)
Aspect: Sun
Soil: Well-drained, fertile, humus-rich
Hardiness: Zone 3
Propagation: Division, in spring

Herbaceous clematis from China. Leaves 3-lobed, toothed, green. Flowers scented, in racemes, blue, in summer, followed by good seed heads. Not for the small garden.

Clematis heracleifolia var. *davidiana*
(Ranunculaceae)

Common names: None
Height: 90cm (3ft)
Spread: 1.2m (4ft)
Aspect: Sun
Soil: Well-drained, fertile, humus-rich
Hardiness: Zone 3
Propagation: Division, in spring

A form of this late, large-flowered species with rich blue flowers. The sepals are more spreading and less reflexed than in the species, giving a more substantial flower.

Clematis integrifolia
(Ranunculaceae)

Common names: None
Height: 60cm (2ft)
Spread: 1.5m (5ft)
Aspect: Sun
Soil: Well-drained, fertile, humus-rich
Hardiness: Zone 3
Propagation: Division in spring

Herbaceous clematis from C. Europe. Leaves inverse lance-shaped to elliptic, downy. Flowers solitary, mid-blue bells, in summer, followed by silvery seed heads.

Clematis integrifolia 'Rosea' A.G.M.
(Ranunculaceae)

Common names: None
Height: 60cm (2ft)
Spread: 1m (3ft)
Aspect: Sun
Soil: Well-drained, fertile, humus-rich
Hardiness: Zone 3
Propagation: Division, in spring

Cloned cultivar with perfumed, sugar-pink flowers with darker undersides, in summer. Leaves inverse lance-shaped to elliptic, downy. Suitable for the small garden.

Clintonia umbellulata
(Convallariaceae/Liliaceae)

Common name: Speckled wood lily
Height: 30cm (12in)
Spread: 15cm (6in)
Aspect: Half or full shade
Soil: Acid, moist, fertile, humus-rich
Hardiness: Zone 4
Propagation: Seed or division, both in autumn

Rhizomatous, hardy perennial. Bright green, glossy, oblong-oblanceolate leaves. White flowers, spotted green and purple, in dense umbels, late spring to summer. Seeds black.

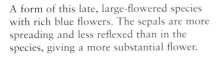

Clivia nobilis
(Amaryllidaceae)

Common name: Kaffir lily
Height 40cm (16in)
Spread: 30cm (12in)
Aspect: Half shade
Soil: Well-drained, fertile, humus-rich
Hardiness: Zone 10
Propagation: Seed, in warmth when ripe; division, in winter or spring

Bulbous evergreen from South Africa. Strap-shaped, basal, bright green leaves. Flowers narrow trumpets, scarlet with green mouths, in pendent umbels, spring and summer.

Codonopsis clematidea
(Campanulaceae)

Common name: Bonnet bellflower
Height: 60cm (2ft)
Spread: 60cm (2ft)
Aspect: Sun or half shade
Soil: Moist, well-drained, humus-rich
Hardiness: Zone 4
Propagation: Seed, in autumn or spring

Branched, scrambling plant from C. Asia. Leaves ovate-acuminate. Flowers solitary, nodding, bell-shaped, pale blue; beautiful black, yellow and blue marks inside.

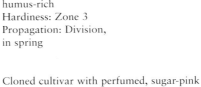

Colchicum autumnale
(Colchicaceae/Liliaceae)

Common name: Autumn crocus
Height: 15cm (6in)
Spread: 8cm (3in)
Aspect: Sun
Soil: Well-drained, fertile, humus-rich
Hardiness: Zone 5
Propagation: Offsets, in summer

European species of cormous perennial. Flowers lavender-pink goblets, in autumn, before erect, lance-shaped, green leaves. All parts are poisonous and irritate skin.

Colchicum bivonae
(Colchicaceae/Liliaceae)

Common name: Autumn crocus
Height: 15cm (6in)
Spread: 10cm (4in)
Aspect: Sun
Soil: Well-drained, fertile, humus-rich
Hardiness: Zone 6
Propagation: Seed, when ripe; offsets, in summer

Cormous perennial from Italy and Turkey. Flowers perfumed, tessellated, purplish-pink goblets with cream centres, before strap-shaped leaves, autumn. All parts poisonous.

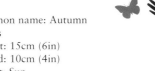

Colchicum byzantinum
A.G.M.
(Colchicaceae/Liliaceae)

Common name: Autumn crocus
Height: 12cm (5in)
Spread: 10cm (4in)
Aspect: Sun
Soil: Well-drained, fertile, humus-rich
Hardiness: Zone 6
Propagation: Seed, when ripe; offsets, in summer

Vigorous, probably hybrid, cormous plant. Flowers open funnels, lilac, in autumn, before elliptic to lance-shaped, ribbed leaves. All parts poisonous and irritant.

Commelina coelestis
(Commelinaceae)

Common names: Day flower; widow's tears
Height: 90cm (36in)
Spread: 45cm (18in)
Aspect: Sun or half shade
Soil: Well-drained, fertile
Hardiness: Zone 8
Propagation: Seed, in warmth in spring; division, in spring

Clump-forming, erect tuberous plant from Central and South America. Leaves lance-shaped to oblong, mid-green. Flowers in cymes, vivid blue, late summer to autumn.

Convallaria majalis
A.G.M.
(Convallariaceae/Liliaceae)

Common name: Lily of the valley
Height: 25cm (10in)
Spread: 45cm (18in)
Aspect: Half or full shade
Soil: Moist, fertile, humus-rich
Hardiness: Zone 3
Propagation: Flesh-free seeds, when ripe; division, in autumn

Rhizomatous, woodland ground cover. Leaves basal, elliptic, smooth, mid-green. Arching racemes of perfumed, spherical, white bells, late spring. Seeds mildly toxic.

Convolvulus althaeoides subsp. *tenuissimus*
(Convolvulaceae)

Common name: Bindweed
Height: 15cm (6in)
Spread: Indefinite
Aspect: Sun
Soil: Well-drained, gritty
Hardiness: Zone 8
Propagation: Seed, in warmth in spring

Invasive, trailing or climbing perennial from S. Europe. Leaves ovate, lobed, silver-green. Flowers open funnels, clear pink, in mid- to late summer. Best confined in a tub.

Convolvulus sabatius
A.G.M.
(Convolvulaceae)

Common name: Bindweed
Height: 15cm (6in)
Spread: 50cm (20in)
Aspect: Sun
Soil: Well-drained, gritty
Hardiness: Zone 8
Propagation: Seed, in warmth in spring

Trailing perennial from Italy, Spain, and N. Africa. Leaves oblong to broadly ovate, mid-green. Flowers open cups, lavender-blue, from summer to early autumn.

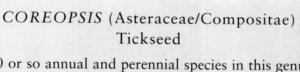

COREOPSIS (Asteraceae/Compositae)
Tickseed

The 100 or so annual and perennial species in this genus all originate in Mexico and Central and North America. All the perennials are fairly hardy, in spite of the generally southerly bias in the distribution of the genus in the wild. *Coreopsis* are found naturally in woodlands and open grasslands; in the garden, their daisy-like, usually bright yellow flowerheads make an eye-catching addition to an annual or perennial border. Many species, such as *C. grandiflora* (Zone 7) and *C. verticillata* (Zone 6), can be short-lived; because of this tendency, and the ability of most species to flower well in their first year when grown from seed, some are more commonly cultivated as annuals. Perennial *Coreopsis* are easy-going spreaders, so if they are not grown as annuals they must be lifted and divided every few years to keep them vigorous. Although they are upright in habit, *Coreopsis* do not, as a rule, require staking; some of the taller cultivars may, however, benefit from support. All will repeat-flower if dead-headed. The flowerheads are attractive to both bees and butterflies; they also make good cut flowers for arrangements, as they last well in water. Unfotunately, they are without exception highly allergenic.

Coreopsis grandiflora
(Asteraceae/Compositae)

Common name: Tickseed
Height: 90cm (36in)
Spread: 45cm (18in)
Aspect: Sun or half shade
Soil: Well-drained, fertile
Hardiness: Zone 7
Propagation: Seed, in spring; division, in autumn

Clump-forming perennial from the U.S.A. Leaves lance-shaped to palmately lobed. Flowers solitary, single, yellow; ray florets have jagged edges. Spring to late summer.

Coreopsis grandiflora
'Early Sunrise'
(Asteraceae/Compositae)

Common name: Tickseed
Height: 45cm (18in)
Spread: 45cm (18in)
Aspect: Sun or half shade
Soil: Well-drained, fertile
Hardiness: Zone 7
Propagation: Division, in spring

Selected, double-flowered form, with jagged ray florets of golden yellow, flushed orange near the centre, in late spring to summer. Leaves lance-shaped or palmately lobed.

Coreopsis grandiflora
'Sunray'
(Asteraceae/Compositae)

Common name: Tickseed
Height: 75cm (30in)
Spread: 45cm (18in)
Aspect: Sun or half shade
Soil: Well-drained, fertile
Hardiness: Zone 7
Propagation: Division, in spring

A selected form, often treated as an annual, with semi-double, deep yellow flowers in late spring to summer. Leaves lance-shaped or palmately lobed.

Coreopsis rosea
'American Dream'
(Asteraceae/Compositae)

Common name: Tickseed
Height: 60cm (24in)
Spread: 30cm (18in)
Aspect: Sun or half shade
Soil: Well-drained, fertile
Hardiness: Zone 4
Propagation: Division, in spring

A selected form of a species from North America. Leaves linear, bright green. Flowers solitary, single, in midsummer; ray florets deep pink, disc florets yellow.

Coreopsis verticillata
'Grandiflora' A.G.M.
(Asteraceae/Compositae)

Common name: Tickseed
Height: 80cm (32in)
Spread: 45cm (18in)
Aspect: Sun or half shade
Soil: Well-drained, fertile
Hardiness: Zone 6
Propagation: Seed or division, both in spring

Bushy, rhizomatous perennial. Leaves are mid-green, deeply incised, 3-pinnate; lobes filamentous, linear. Yellow flowers in loose corymbs, early summer to early autumn.

Coreopsis verticillata
'Moonbeam'
(Asteraceae/Compositae)

Common name: Tickseed
Height: 50cm (20in)
Spread: 45cm (18in)
Aspect: Sun or half shade
Soil: Well-drained, fertile
Hardiness: Zone 6
Propagation: Division, in spring

A selected form of the species with flowers of lemon-yellow, all summer long. Leaves are mid-green, deeply incised, 3-pinnate; lobes linear, filamentous.

Coreopsis verticillata
'Zagreb'
(Asteraceae/Compositae)

Common name: Tickseed
Height: 30cm (1ft)
Spread: 30cm (1ft)
Aspect: Sun or half shade
Soil: Well-drained, fertile
Hardiness: Zone 6
Propagation: Division, in spring

Drought-resistant, cloned cultivar, with flowers of golden-yellow all summer. Mid-green leaves are deeply incised, 3-pinnate, with linear, filamentous lobes.

Coriaria terminalis
(Coriariaceae)

Common names: None
Height: 1m (3ft)
Spread: 2m (6ft)
Aspect: Sun
Soil: Well-drained, fertile
Hardiness: Zone 8
Propagation: Seed, in warmth in spring; division, in spring

Rhizomatous, deciduous subshrub. Leaves alternate, lance-shaped, glossy-green. Insignificant flowers are followed by black berries with poisonous seeds.

Coriaria terminalis
var. *xanthocarpa*
(Coriariaceae)

Common names: None
Height: 90cm (3ft)
Spread: 1.5m (5ft)
Aspect: Sun
Soil: Well-drained, fertile
Hardiness: Zone 8
Propagation: Seed, in warmth in spring; division, in spring

Rhizomatous, deciduous subshrub. Shoots arching, leaves lance-shaped, bright green. Insignificant flowers, followed by berries of translucent yellow with poisonous seeds.

The starry yellow flowers of Coreopsis verticillata *are borne from midsummer through to autumn.*

Cornus canadensis
A.G.M.
(Cornaceae)

Common names: Cornel; dogwood
Height: 15cm (6in)
Spread: Indefinite
Aspect: Sun or half shade
Soil: Moist, acidic
Hardiness: Zone 2
Propagation: Division, in spring or autumn

Highly invasive plant. Leaves lance-shaped to oval, mid-green. Flowers tiny, green, with large, white, pink-tinted bracts, spring and early summer, followed by red berries.

Cortaderia selloana
'Pumila' A.G.M.
(Poaceae/Bambusoideae)

Common name: Pampas grass
Height: To 1.5m (5ft)
Spread: 90cm (3ft)
Aspect: Sun
Soil: Well-drained, fertile
Hardiness: Zone 8
Propagation: Seed, in warmth in spring; division, in spring

Dwarf clone of a tall species; the only form for small gardens. Leaves long, razor-edged (wear gloves), arching, glaucous. Flowering panicles erect, silvery-yellow, in autumn.

Cortaderia selloana
'Rendatleri'
(Poaceae/Bambusoideae)

Common name: Pampas grass
Height: 2.5m (8ft)
Spread: 2m (6ft)
Aspect: Sun
Soil: Well-drained, fertile
Hardiness: Zone 8
Propagation: Seed, in warmth in spring; division, in spring

Pampas grass with most attractive pinkish-purple panicles. Place at the back of the border: razor-sharp leaf-blades will cut nearby plants in a wind. Wear gloves.

Cortusa matthiolii
(Primulaceae)

Common names: None
Height: 30cm (12in)
Spread: 15cm (6in)
Aspect: Half shade
Soil: Moist, well-drained, fertile, humus-rich
Hardiness: Zone 7
Propagation: Seed, when ripe; division, in spring

European woodlander, for cool, moist sites. Leaves basal, round- or heart-shaped, mid-green. Flowers in one-sided umbels, bell-shaped, pink, late spring and early summer.

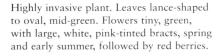

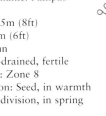

Corydalis cheilanthifolia
(Papaveraceae)

Common names: None
Height: 30cm (12in)
Spread: 25cm (10in)
Aspect: Sun or half shade
Soil: Well-drained, fertile
Hardiness: Zone 6
Propagation: Seed, when ripe; division, in autumn

Fibrous-rooted evergreen. Leaves fern-like, 2- or 3-pinnate, leaflets lance-shaped to linear, tinted bronze. Deep yellow flowers in racemes, spring to summer. Good wall plant.

Corydalis flexuosa
(Papaveraceae)

Common names: None
Height: 30cm (12in)
Spread: 20cm (8in)
Aspect: Half shade
Soil: Moist, well-drained, humus-rich
Hardiness: Zone 7
Propagation: Seed, when ripe; division, in autumn

Woodlander from China. Leaves 2-ternate, leaflets ovate, glaucous green. Brilliant blue flowers in terminal and axillary racemes, late spring to summer. Summer dormant.

Corydalis lutea
(Papaveraceae)

Common names: None
Height: 40cm (16in)
Spread: 30cm (12in)
Aspect: Sun or half shade
Soil: Moist, well-drained, fertile, humus-rich
Hardiness: Zone 6
Propagation: Seed, when ripe; division, in autumn

Rhizomatous, mound-forming, evergreen woodlander. Leaves mid-green, fern-like, 2- or 3-pinnate; leaflets obovate, 3-lobed. Flowers yellow, in racemes, all summer.

Corydalis ochroleuca
(Papaveraceae)

Common names: None
Height: 30cm (12in)
Spread: 30cm (12in)
Aspect: Sun or half shade
Soil: Moist, well-drained, fertile
Hardiness: Zone 5
Propagation: Seed, when ripe; division, in autumn

Evergreen, fibrous-rooted woodlander. Leaves 2- or 3-pinnate, leaflets obovate. Flowers in small racemes, white, with yellow throats, late spring to early summer.

Corydalis ophiocarpa
(Papaveraceae)

Common names: None
Height: 75cm (30in)
Spread: 30cm (12in)
Aspect: Sun or half shade
Soil: Moist, well-drained, fertile, humus-rich
Hardiness: Zone 6
Propagation: Seed, when ripe; division, in autumn

Perennial from the E. Himalayas. Leaves in a dense rosette, 2-pinnate, grey-green. Flowers in a crowded terminal raceme, ivory, the inner petals tipped red, in spring.

Corydalis solida
A.G.M.
(Papaveraceae)

Common name: Fumewort
Height: 30cm (12in)
Spread: 15cm (6in)
Aspect: Sun or half shade
Soil: Sharply drained, gritty
Hardiness: Zone 6
Propagation: Seed, when ripe; division, in autumn

Tuberous perennial from N. Europe. Leaves grey-green, 2- or 3-ternate; leaflets ovate, deeply dissected. Flowers pale lilac-pink, red or white, in dense spiky racemes, in spring.

Cosmos atrosanguineus
(Asteraceae/Compositae)

Common name: Chocolate cosmos
Height: 75cm (30in)
Spread: 45cm (18in)
Aspect: Sun
Soil: Moist, well-drained, fertile
Hardiness: Zone 8
Propagation: Seed, in warmth in late spring

Spreading, with pinnate or 2-pinnate leaves; lobes ovate to diamond-shaped. Solitary, single, velvety, chocolate-scented, maroon flowers, summer to autumn.

Crambe cordifolia
A.G.M.
(Brassicaceae/Cruciferae)

Common name: Greater sea kale
Height: 2m (6ft)
Spread: 1.5m (5ft)
Aspect: Sun
Soil: Well-drained, fertile
Hardiness: Zone 6
Propagation: Seed or division, both in spring

Coastal plant. Leaves large, ovate to kidney-shaped, toothed, deep green. Flowers tiny, perfumed, cross-shaped, white, in branched panicles, in late spring and early summer.

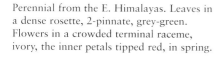

Crambe maritima
(Brassicaceae/Cruciferae)

Common name: Sea kale
Height: 80cm (32in)
Spread: 60cm (24in)
Aspect: Sun
Soil: Well-drained, fertile
Hardiness: Zone 5
Propagation: Seed or division, both in spring

Culinary herb from coastal Europe and the Black Sea. Leaves glaucous green, large, ovate, twisted. Flowers in dense racemes, small, perfumed, white, from late spring.

Crepis incana
A.G.M.
(Asteraceae/Compositae)

Common name: Pink dandelion
Height: 30cm (1ft)
Spread: 30cm (1ft)
Aspect: Full sun
Soil: Any well-drained
Hardiness: Zone 8
Propagation: Seed, when ripe

Perennial from Greece. Leaves dandelion-like, inverse lance-shaped, pinnatifid, grey-green. Corymbs of dandelion-like, bright pink flowers. Flowers well if dead-headed.

Crinum macowanii
(Amaryllidaceae)

Common names: Pyjama lily
Height: 60cm (24in)
Spread: 15cm (6in)
Aspect: Sun
Soil: Moist, well-drained, fertile, humus-rich
Hardiness: Zone 9
Propagation: Seed, in warmth when ripe; offsets, in spring

Bulbous plant from South Africa. Leaves basal straps, wavy-edged, green. Flowers in umbels, perfumed, white or pink, with a red stripe on each tepal. All parts toxic.

Crinum × powellii
A.G.M.
(Amaryllidaceae)

Common names: Cape lily
Height: 1.2m (4ft)
Spread: 30cm (1ft)
Aspect: Sun
Soil: Moist, well-drained, fertile, humus-rich
Hardiness: Zone 6
Propagation: Seed or offsets, both in spring

Deciduous, bulbous hybrid of garden origin. Leaves long, arching, green straps. Flowers perfumed, flared, pink trumpets, in umbels late summer to autumn. All parts toxic.

Crinum x *powellii* 'Album' A.G.M. (Amaryllidaceae)

Common names: White cape lily
Height: 1.2m (4ft)
Spread: 30cm (1ft)
Aspect: Sun
Soil: Moist, well-drained, fertile, humus-rich
Hardiness: Zone 6
Propagation: Seed or offsets, both in spring

White form of deciduous, bulbous hybrid. Flared, scented trumpet flowers marginally bigger than the pink form. Leaves long, arching, green straps. All parts toxic.

CROCOSMIA (Iridaceae)
Montbretia

This genus of cormous perennials consists of some half a dozen species from South Africa, which have been hybridised extensively since the end of the 19th century. The original cross was made in 1882, in France, between *C. pottsii* and *C. aurea*, and given the unwieldy label *C.* x *crocosmiiflora*. The terminology has become very complex, and is often given only in part; here, they are dealt with in alphabetical order of the cultivar name, as is common practice. The hybrids are extremely handsome and useful plants, generally a great improvement on the wild forms. Their degree of hardiness varies, but most are fairly hardy. The corms form "chains" in time, with new corms growing on old corms, and must be lifted and divided when the clumps become too dense; the old corms should not be detached in the process, as they are stores of nourishment for the new ones. The leaves are erect, linear to lance-shaped, pleated or ribbed, and green or brownish-green. The flowers are in spikes, which may be branched or unbranched, carried on wiry stems, and are followed by attractive seed capsules. Both the leaves and the flowering spikes last well in water, and montbretias are popular for flower-arranging; they are low-allergen plants.

Crocosmia x *crocosmiiflora* 'Citronella' (Iridaceae)

Common name: Montbretia
Height: 60cm (24in)
Spread: 10cm (4in)
Aspect: Sun or half shade
Soil: Moist, well-drained, fertile, humus-rich
Hardiness: Zone 7
Propagation: Division, in spring

A hybrid cultivar with flowers of pale yellow in upright to slightly arched, branching spikes, in late summer. Leaves are pale green.

Crocosmia 'Emberglow' (Iridaceae)

Common name: Montbretia
Height: 75cm (30in)
Spread: 10cm (4in)
Aspect: Sun or half shade
Soil: Moist, well-drained, humus-rich, fertile
Hardiness: Zone 7
Propagation: Division in spring

A hybrid with mid-green foliage and flowers of dark red, arranged in 2 neat rows along arching, branching spikes, in late summer.

Crocosmia x *crocosmiiflora* 'Emily McKenzie' (Iridaceae)

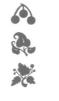

Common name: Montbretia
Height: 60cm (24in)
Spread: 10cm (4in)
Aspect: Sun or half shade
Soil: Moist, well-drained, fertile, humus-rich
Hardiness: Zone 7
Propagation: Division, in spring

A hybrid with mid-green foliage and large, downward-facing flowers of bright orange, with mahogany markings in the throat, in late summer.

Crocosmia 'Firebird' (Iridaceae)

Common name: Montbretia
Height: 80cm (32in)
Spread: 10cm (4in)
Aspect: Sun or half shade
Soil: Moist, well-drained, fertile, humus-rich
Hardiness: Zone 7
Propagation: Division, in spring

Robust hybrid bearing vibrant orange-red, upward-facing flowers in late summer, in generally unbranched spikes. Leaves are mid-green.

Crocosmia x *crocosmiiflora* 'Jackanapes' (Iridaceae)

Common name: Montbretia
Height: 60cm (24in)
Spread: 10cm (4in)
Aspect: Sun or half shade
Soil: Moist, well-drained, fertile, humus-rich
Hardiness: Zone 7
Propagation: Division, in spring

Striking hybrid with large, bicoloured flowers of red and orange in late summer, on freely branching, arching stems above mid-green foliage.

Crocosmia x *crocosmiiflora*
'Lady Hamilton'
(Iridaceae)

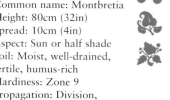

Common name: Montbretia
Height: 80cm (32in)
Spread: 10cm (4in)
Aspect: Sun or half shade
Soil: Moist, well-drained, fertile, humus-rich
Hardiness: Zone 9
Propagation: Division, in spring

A hybrid with leaves of mid-green and flowers of rich yellow with apricot centres. Flowers are borne on upright, branching stems, in late summer.

Crocosmia
'Lucifer' A.G.M.
(Iridaceae)

Common name: Montbretia
Height: 1m (36in)
Spread: 10cm (4in)
Aspect: Sun or half shade
Soil: Moist, well-drained, fertile, humus-rich
Hardiness: Zone 7
Propagation: Division, in spring

Very popular, dependable hybrid with flowers of intense, deep tomato-red in late summer, on branching, slightly arched spikes. Leaves are pleated, mid-green.

Crocosmia masoniorum
AG.M.
(Iridaceae)

Common name: Montbretia
Height: 1.2m (4ft)
Spread: 10cm (4in)
Aspect: Sun or half shade
Soil: Moist, well-drained, fertile, humus-rich
Hardiness: Zone 7
Propagation: Seed, when ripe; division, in spring

Large, robust species from South Africa. Leaves long, pleated, mid-green. Flowers upward-facing, orange-red, in arching spikes, in summer.

Crocosmia paniculata
(Iridaceae)

Common name: Montbretia
Height: 1.2m (4ft)
Spread: 10cm (4in)
Aspect: Sun or half shade
Soil: Moist, well-drained, fertile, humus-rich
Hardiness: Zone 8
Propagation: Seed, when ripe; division, in spring

Large species from South Africa, with pleated leaves of olive-green. Flowering spike branched, flowers orange-red, downturned, in late summer.

Crocosmia
'Severn Sunrise'
(Iridaceae)

Common name: Montbretia
Height: 80cm (32in)
Spread: 10cm (4in)
Aspect: Sun or half shade
Soil: Moist, well-drained, fertile, humus-rich
Hardiness: Zone 7
Propagation: Division, in spring

A hybrid with flowers of glowing orange with lighter throats, in generally upright, branching spikes, above leaves of mid-green, in late summer.

Crocosmia x *crocosmiiflora*
'Solfaterre' A.G.M.
(Iridaceae)

Common name: Montbretia
Height: 80cm (32in)
Spread: 10cm (4in)
Aspect: Sun or half shade
Soil: Moist, well-drained, fertile, humus-rich
Hardiness: Zone 8
Propagation: Division, in spring

Very old hybrid with unusual, bronze-coloured leaves. Bears flowers of apricot-yellow in late summer. Excellent for flower arrangements.

Crocosmia
'Vulcan'
(Iridaceae)

Common name: Montbretia
Height: 80cm (32in)
Spread: 10cm (4in)
Aspect: Sun or half shade
Soil: Moist, well-drained, fertile, humus-rich
Hardiness: Zone 7
Propagation: Division, in spring

A hybrid with mid-green leaves, and spikes of plentiful, outward-facing flowers of vibrant orange-red colour, borne in late summer.

Crocosmia
'Walburton Yellow'
(Iridaceae)

Common name: Montbretia
Height: 80cm (32in)
Spread: 10cm (4in)
Aspect: Sun or half shade
Soil: Moist, well-drained, fertile, humus-rich
Hardiness: Zone
Propagation: Division, in spring

Modern hybrid with typical large, upward-facing flowers of clear yellow colour, carried in spikes above mid-green foliage, in late summer.

CROCUS (Iridacae)
Crocus

These cormous perennials of varying hardiness are found naturally in Europe, North Africa, and through the Middle East to China. They are suitable for planting at the edges of beds or borders, and flower in spring or autumn. Their flowers are goblets, formed by six tepals, the outer three opening to reveal the inner three, which may be of a different colour. Some are perfumed. The foliage is linear, semi-erect, mid-green, with a silver or pale green central stripe. In the spring-flowering types, the foliage appears with, or just after the flowers; in some of the autumn-flowering types it may appear before the flowers. Crocuses are universally deciduous. An Award of Garden Merit has been bestowed on no fewer than 39 crocuses, and it is for the specialist book to cover them in detail. The representatives of the genus here are all but one spring-flowering, and all but one hold an A.G.M. Those which require a dry summer dormancy are not covered here, since they need an alpine house or bulb frame; other types are easy to grow. All they ask is sun and good drainage, and they will increase and will require regular lifting and division. Wildlife can be a problem: sparrows pull the flowers apart, and garden rodents may eat the corms.

Crocus chrysanthus
'Blue Pearl' A.G.M.
(Iridaceae)

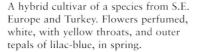

Common name: Crocus
Height: 7cm (3in)
Spread: 5cm (2in)
Aspect: Sun
Soil: Well-drained, gritty, fertile
Hardiness: Zone 4
Propagation: Offsets, in summer

A hybrid cultivar of a species from S.E. Europe and Turkey. Flowers perfumed, white, with yellow throats, and outer tepals of lilac-blue, in spring.

Crocus chrysanthus
'Cream Beauty' A.G.M.
(Iridaceae)

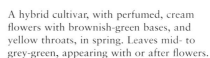

Common name: Crocus
Height: 7cm (3in)
Spread: 5cm (2in)
Aspect: Sun
Soil: Moist, well-drained, gritty
Hardiness: Zone 4
Propagation: Offsets, in summer

A hybrid cultivar, with perfumed, cream flowers with brownish-green bases, and yellow throats, in spring. Leaves mid- to grey-green, appearing with or after flowers.

Crocus kotschyanus
A.G.M.
(Iridaceae)

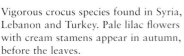

Common name: Crocus
Height: 10cm (4in)
Spread: 6cm (3in)
Aspect: Sun
Soil: Dry in summer, gritty
Hardiness: Zone 5
Propagation: Seed, when ripe; offsets, in summer

Vigorous crocus species found in Syria, Lebanon and Turkey. Pale lilac flowers with cream stamens appear in autumn, before the leaves.

Crocus x *luteus*
'Golden Yellow' A.G.M.
(Iridaceae)

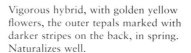

Common name: Crocus
Height: 10cm (4in)
Spread: 5cm (2in)
Aspect: Sun
Soil: Well-drained, gritty
Hardiness: Zone 4
Propagation: Offsets, in summer

Vigorous hybrid, with golden yellow flowers, the outer tepals marked with darker stripes on the back, in spring. Naturalizes well.

Crocus tomassinianus
'Ruby Giant'
(Iridaceae)

Common name: Crocus
Height: 10cm (4in)
Spread: 3cm (1in)
Aspect: Sun
Soil: Well-drained, gritty
Hardiness: Zone 5
Propagation: Offsets, in summer

Clump-forming, vigorous crocus that naturalizes well. Bears rich reddish-pink flowers in spring. A sterile hybrid cultivar, so does not set seed.

Crocus chrysanthus
'Snow Bunting' A.G.M.
(Iridaceae)

Common name: Crocus
Height: 8cm (3in)
Spread: 5cm (2in)
Aspect: Sun
Soil: Well-drained, gritty
Hardiness: Zone 4
Propagation: Offsets, in summer

A vigorous hybrid cultivar, flowering in spring. White flowers may have faint, feathery bluish markings. Mid- to grey-green leaves with or after the flowers.

Spring would not be spring without the ubiquitous crocus. Here a beautiful display is complemented by a wood of Silver Birch.

Cyrtanthus brachyscyphus
(Amaryllidaceae)

Common name: Fire lily
Height 30cm (12in)
Spread: 10cm (4in)
Aspect: Sun
Soil: Well-drained, fertile, humus-rich
Hardiness: Zone 9
Propagation: Seed, in warmth when ripe; offsets, in spring

Deciduous, bulbous perennial from South Africa. Leaves lance-shaped, semi-erect, green. Flowers in umbels, tubular, red, in spring to summer.

Dactylis glomerata
'Variegata'
(Graminae/Poaceae)

Common names: Cocksfoot; orchard grass
Height: 45cm (18in)
Spread: 25cm (10in)
Aspect: Sun or half shade
Soil: Well-drained, fertile
Hardiness: Zone 5
Propagation: Division, in spring

Clump-forming, evergreen, perennial grass from Eurasia and N. Africa. Leaves linear, variegated cream. Flowering spike one-sided, pale green.

Dactylorhiza elata
A.G.M.
(Orchidaceae)

Common name: Robust marsh orchid
Height: 60cm (24in)
Spread: 15cm (6in)
Aspect: Half shade
Soil: Well-drained, moist, humus-rich
Hardiness: Zone 6
Propagation: Division, in spring

Tuberous, terrestrial orchid. Leaves linear to lance-shaped, green, may be spotted brown. Flowers in dense terminal racemes, purple, with bracts, late spring. Easy in right place.

Dactylorhiza foliosa
A.G.M.
(Orchidaceae)

Common name: Madeiran orchid
Height: 60cm (24in)
Spread: 15cm (6in)
Aspect: Half shade
Soil: Well-drained, moist, humus-rich
Hardiness: Zone 7
Propagation: Division, in spring

Terrestrial, tuberous orchid. Lance-shaped, green leaves, can be spotted brown. Flowers in racemes, pink or purple, with bracts, late spring to early summer. Easy in right place.

Dactylorhiza fuchsii
(Orchidaceae)

Common name: Common spotted orchid
Height: 60cm (24in)
Spread: 15cm (6in)
Aspect: Half shade
Soil: Moist, well-drained, humus-rich
Hardiness: Zone 6
Propagation: Division, in spring

Terrestrial, tuberous, deciduous orchid. Leaves lance-shaped, spotted purple. Dense terminal umbels of flowers, late spring and early summer, mauve. Easy in right place.

Dactylorhiza praetermissa
(Orchidaceae)

Common name: Southern marsh orchid
Height: 60cm (24in)
Spread: 15cm (6in)
Aspect: Half shade
Soil: Moist, well-drained, humus-rich
Hardiness: Zone 6
Propagation: Division, in spring

Tuberous, terrestrial, deciduous orchid from N. Europe. Leaves lance-shaped, can be spotted. Flowers in dense umbel, pale garnet, with bracts. Easy in right conditions.

Dahlia
'Bishop of Llandaff' A.G.M.
(Asteraceae/Compositae)

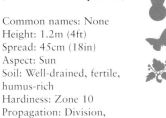

Common names: None
Height: 1.2m (4ft)
Spread: 45cm (18in)
Aspect: Sun
Soil: Well-drained, fertile, humus-rich
Hardiness: Zone 10
Propagation: Division, in spring

Hybrid dahlia in the 'miscellaneous' classification. Leaves pinnate, lobes oval, toothed, black-red. Paeony-flowered, blooms semi-double, bright red.

Dahlia merckii
(Asteraceae/Compositae)

Common names: None
Height: 2m (6ft)
Spread: 1m (3ft)
Aspect: Sun
Soil: Well-drained, fertile, humus-rich
Hardiness: Zone 9
Propagation: Division, in spring

Tuberous perennial from Mexico. Leaves pinnate, green. Flowers on many-branched stems, single pink, purple or white, with yellow disc florets.

Cynara cardunculus A.G.M. (Asteraceae/Compositae)

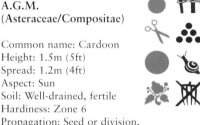

Common name: Cardoon
Height: 1.5m (5ft)
Spread: 1.2m (4ft)
Aspect: Sun
Soil: Well-drained, fertile
Hardiness: Zone 6
Propagation: Seed or division, both in spring

Clump-forming perennial from Morocco and the S.W. Mediterranean. Leaves silver, spiny, pinnatifid; blanched midribs edible. Flowers huge thistles, on woolly stems.

Cynara baetica subsp. *maroccana* (Asteraceae/Compositae)

Common names: None
Height: 1m (3ft)
Spread: 60cm (2ft)
Aspect: Sun
Soil: Well-drained, gritty, fertile
Hardiness: Zone 8
Propagation: Seed or division, both in spring

Clump-forming perennial from Morocco. Leaves pinnatisect; lobes linear, toothed, spiny, with white woolly undersides. Flower purple, thistle-like, good for drying.

Cynara scolymus (Asteraceae/Compositae)

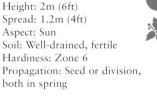

Common name: Globe artichoke
Height: 2m (6ft)
Spread: 1.2m (4ft)
Aspect: Sun
Soil: Well-drained, fertile
Hardiness: Zone 6
Propagation: Seed or division, both in spring

Culinary plant from the N. Mediterranean. Leaves pinnatifid, grey-green, pointed, white-woolly underneath. Flower purple, with big bracts, in autumn, edible as a bud.

Cynoglossum nervosum (Boraginaceae)

Common name: Hound's tongue
Height: 80cm (32in)
Spread: 60cm (2ft)
Aspect: Sun or half shade
Soil: Well-drained, moist
Hardiness: Zone 5
Propagation: Seed or division, both in spring

Perennial from N. India and W. Pakistan. Leaves lance-shaped to oblong, hairy, bright green. Cymes of intense blue, forget-me-not flowers, spring to summer. Feed sparingly.

Cypella herbertii (Iridaceae)

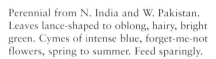

Common names: None
Height: 60cm (2ft)
Spread: 10cm (4in)
Aspect: Sun
Soil: Well-drained, sandy, humus-rich
Hardiness: Zone 9
Propagation: Seed, in warmth when ripe

Bulbous perennial from South America. Lance-shaped to linear, pleated leaves. Outer tepals of flowers mustard, inner tepals brown, spotted or streaked purple, summer.

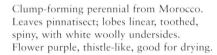

Cypripedium acaule (Orchidaceae)

Common name: Lady's slipper orchid
Height: 25cm (10in)
Spread: 25cm (10in)
Aspect: Half shade
Soil: Moist, acidic, fertile, humus-rich
Hardiness: Zone 5
Propagation: Division, in spring

Terrestrial, rhizomatous orchid from North America. Leaves paired, elliptic. Flower solitary, nodding, brown-green, with pink lips, in summer. Extremely difficult to grow.

Cypripedium calceolus (Orchidaceae)

Common name: Lady's slipper orchid
Height: 40cm (16in)
Spread: 40cm (16in)
Aspect: Half shade
Soil: Moist, acidic, fertile, humus-rich
Hardiness: Zone 5
Propagation: Division, in spring

Terrestrial rhizomatous orchid. Leaves ovate-elliptic, dark green. Flower single or paired, brown-purple, petals twisted, lips large, yellow. Very difficult in cultivation.

Cypripedium reginae (Orchidaceae)

Common name: Showy lady's slipper
Height: 75cm (30in)
Spread: 30cm (12in)
Aspect: Half shade
Soil: Moist, acidic, fertile, humus-rich
Hardiness: Zone 4
Propagation: Division, in spring

Terrestrial rhizomatous orchid from North America. Leaves ovate to lance-shaped. Flowers single or paired, white, with rose-pink lips, in summer. Very difficult to grow.

Cyrtanthus brachyscyphus
(Amaryllidaceae)

Common name: Fire lily
Height 30cm (12in)
Spread: 10cm (4in)
Aspect: Sun
Soil: Well-drained, fertile, humus-rich
Hardiness: Zone 9
Propagation: Seed, in warmth when ripe; offsets, in spring

Deciduous, bulbous perennial from South Africa. Leaves lance-shaped, semi-erect, green. Flowers in umbels, tubular, red, in spring to summer.

Dactylis glomerata
'Variegata'
(Graminae/Poaceae)

Common names: Cocksfoot; orchard grass
Height: 45cm (18in)
Spread: 25cm (10in)
Aspect: Sun or half shade
Soil: Well-drained, fertile
Hardiness: Zone 5
Propagation: Division, in spring

Clump-forming, evergreen, perennial grass from Eurasia and N. Africa. Leaves linear, variegated cream. Flowering spike one-sided, pale green.

Dactylorhiza elata
A.G.M.
(Orchidaceae)

Common name: Robust marsh orchid
Height: 60cm (24in)
Spread: 15cm (6in)
Aspect: Half shade
Soil: Well-drained, moist, humus-rich
Hardiness: Zone 6
Propagation: Division, in spring

Tuberous, terrestrial orchid. Leaves linear to lance-shaped, green, may be spotted brown. Flowers in dense terminal racemes, purple, with bracts, late spring. Easy in right place.

Dactylorhiza foliosa
A.G.M.
(Orchidaceae)

Common name: Madeiran orchid
Height: 60cm (24in)
Spread: 15cm (6in)
Aspect: Half shade
Soil: Well-drained, moist, humus-rich
Hardiness: Zone 7
Propagation: Division, in spring

Terrestrial, tuberous orchid. Lance-shaped, green leaves, can be spotted brown. Flowers in racemes, pink or purple, with bracts, late spring to early summer. Easy in right place.

Dactylorhiza fuchsii
(Orchidaceae)

Common name: Common spotted orchid
Height: 60cm (24in)
Spread: 15cm (6in)
Aspect: Half shade
Soil: Moist, well-drained, humus-rich
Hardiness: Zone 6
Propagation: Division, in spring

Terrestrial, tuberous, deciduous orchid. Leaves lance-shaped, spotted purple. Dense terminal umbels of flowers, late spring and early summer, mauve. Easy in right place.

Dactylorhiza praetermissa
(Orchidaceae)

Common name: Southern marsh orchid
Height: 60cm (24in)
Spread: 15cm (6in)
Aspect: Half shade
Soil: Moist, well-drained, humus-rich
Hardiness: Zone 6
Propagation: Division, in spring

Tuberous, terrestrial, deciduous orchid from N. Europe. Leaves lance-shaped, can be spotted. Flowers in dense umbel, pale garnet, with bracts. Easy in right conditions.

Dahlia
'Bishop of Llandaff' A.G.M.
(Asteraceae/Compositae)

Common names: None
Height: 1.2m (4ft)
Spread: 45cm (18in)
Aspect: Sun
Soil: Well-drained, fertile, humus-rich
Hardiness: Zone 10
Propagation: Division, in spring

Hybrid dahlia in the 'miscellaneous' classification. Leaves pinnate, lobes oval, toothed, black-red. Paeony-flowered, blooms semi-double, bright red.

Dahlia merckii
(Asteraceae/Compositae)

Common names: None
Height: 2m (6ft)
Spread: 1m (3ft)
Aspect: Sun
Soil: Well-drained, fertile, humus-rich
Hardiness: Zone 9
Propagation: Division, in spring

Tuberous perennial from Mexico. Leaves pinnate, green. Flowers on many-branched stems, single pink, purple or white, with yellow disc florets.

Darmera peltata
A.G.M.
(Saxifragaceae)

Common name: Umbrella plant
Height: 2m (6ft)
Spread: 1.5m (5ft)
Aspect: Sun or half shade
Soil: Marginal aquatic
Hardiness: Zone 6
Propagation: Seed or division, both in spring

Rhizomatous marginal plant from the U.S.A. Leaves large, peltate, round, deeply lobed, toothed, veined, deep green. Flowers on tall stems in large cymes, pink, in spring.

Davallia mariesii
A.G.M.
(Davalliaceae)

Common name: Squirrel's foot fern
Height: 15cm (6in)
Spread: Indefinite
Aspect: Half shade
Soil: Moist, gritty, humus-rich
Hardiness: Zone 9
Propagation: Spores, in warmth when ripe; division, in spring

Rhizomatous, deciduous, creeping fern from E. Asia. Fronds 3- to 4-pinnate, finely cut, broad, mid-green. Segments linear or triangular.

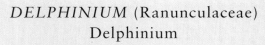

DELPHINIUM (Ranunculaceae)
Delphinium

Genus of some 250 species, from all parts of the world except the Arctic, Australia and Antarctica. Most are fibrous-rooted; a few are tuberous. The best-known delphiniums are the tall hybrids with dense spires of flowers, but some species are small enough for the rock garden. The leaves are toothed and 3-, 5- or 7-lobed. Tall hybrids almost always need staking. They make excellent cut flowers, and are prized by flower-arrangers. Delphiniums are low in allergens, but all parts are poisonous and skin-irritant. They are prone to powdery mildew, slugs and snails. They are classified in three groups.

Belladonna Group Upright, to 1.2m (4ft), branching, with palmately lobed leaves and loose spikes of elfin-cap-like single flowers with spurs up to 3cm (1¼in), in early and late summer.

Elatum Group Clump-forming, to over 1.7m (5½ft), with tapering flower spikes and similar smaller, later-flowering lateral shoots in late spring to early summer, again in autumn if cut back; flowers single to double, with 5 large outer sepals and an 'eye' of 8 inner sepals. The most popular type.

Pacific Hybrids Short-lived, grown as annuals or biennials. Over 1.7m (5½ft) tall, and bloom in spring and early summer. Flowers are semi-double and short-lived.

Delphinium beesianum
'Cliveden Beauty'
(Ranunculaceae)

Common names: None
Height: 1.2m (4ft)
Spread: 45cm (18in)
Aspect: Sun
Soil: Well-drained, fertile
Hardiness: Zone 3
Propagation: Heeled basal cuttings, in spring

Belladonna Group delphinium: upright, suits a border. Branching stems bear flowers of sky blue in very loose, open spikes, early and late summer.

Delphinium beesianum
'Peace'
(Ranunculaceae)

Common names: None
Height: 1.2m (4ft)
Spread: 45cm (18in)
Aspect: Sun
Soil: Well-drained, fertile
Hardiness: Zone 3
Propagation: Heeled basal cuttings, in spring

Belladonna Group delphinium with flowers of intense blue, borne in open spikes in early and late summer. Suits a border or island bed.

Delphinium beesianum
'Volkerfrieden'
(Ranunculaceae)

Common names: None
Height: 1.2m (4ft)
Spread: 45cm (18in)
Aspect: Sun
Soil: Well-drained, fertile
Hardiness: Zone 3
Propagation: Heeled basal cuttings, in spring

Vigorous Belladonna Group delphinium: upright, suitable for a border or island bed. Bears flowers of deep blue in early and late summer.

Delphinium
Blue Jade Group
(Ranunculaceae)

Common names: None
Height: 1.5m (5ft)
Spread: 60cm (2ft)
Aspect: Sun
Soil: Well-drained, fertile
Hardiness: Zone 3
Propagation: Heeled basal cuttings, in spring

Clump-forming Elatum group, with large flowers of mid-blue with darker eyes, borne in dense spikes. Among the shorter examples of this group.

Delphinium *'Dora Larkan' displays branched spikes of pretty blue flowers.*

Delphinium cashmerianum
(Ranunculaceae)

Common names: None
Height: 40cm (16in)
Spread: 15cm (6in)
Aspect: Sun
Soil: Well-drained, fertile
Hardiness: Zone 5
Propagation: Seed, in spring

Perennial from the W. Himalayas. Leaves round, toothed, 5- to 7-lobed, green. Dark blue-purple, single flowers in open panicles, in early and again in late summer.

Delphinium
'Galahad'
(Ranunculaceae)

Common names: None
Height: 1.7m (5½ft)
Spread: 75cm (30in)
Aspect: Sun
Soil: Well-drained, fertile
Hardiness: Zone 3
Propagation: Seed, in spring

Pacific Hybrid delphinium, grown as an annual or biennial. Large, short-lived flowers of pure white. Suits a border or island bed.

Delphinium grandiflorum
'Blue Butterfly'
(Ranunculaceae)

Common names: None
Height: 40cm (16in)
Spread: 20cm (8in)
Aspect: Sun
Soil: Well-drained, fertile
Hardiness: Zone 3
Propagation: Seed, in spring

Selected form of a short-lived perennial from Japan and China to Siberia. Leaves 5-lobed, lobes narrowly divided. Flowers in open panicles, single, bright blue, early summer.

Delphinium
Magic Fountain Series
(Ranunculaceae)

Common names: None
Height: 1.5m (5ft)
Spread: 60cm (2ft)
Aspect: Sun
Soil: Well-drained, fertile
Hardiness: Zone 3
Propagation: Seed, in spring

Series with flowers in a range of colours, from the Elatum Group. One of the shorter examples of the group; suits a border or an island bed.

Delphinium nudicaule
(Ranunculaceae)

Common names: None
Height: 60cm (24in)
Spread: 20cm (8in)
Aspect: Sun
Soil: Well-drained, fertile
Hardiness: Zone 8
Propagation: Seed, in spring

Short-lived perennial from California. Leaves 3- to 5-lobed, fleshy, green. Flowers in open panicles, single, funnel-shaped, vermilion with yellow throats, in summer.

Delphinium speciosum
(Ranunculaceae)

Common names: None
Height: 75cm (30in)
Spread: 30cm (12in)
Aspect: Sun
Soil: Well-drained, fertile
Hardiness: Zone 6
Propagation: Seed, in spring

Perennial from the Caucasus and C. Asia. Leaves 3- to 5-lobed, segments broad, toothed, subdivided further. Flowers in racemes, intense blue, in summer.

ADDITIONAL HYBRID DELPHINIUMS with an A.G.M. (all Zone 5)

D. 'Blue Dawn'

D. 'Blue Nile'

D. 'Bruce'

D. 'Conspicuous'

D. 'Emily Hawkins'

D. 'Fanfare'

D. 'Faust'

D. 'Fenella'

D. 'Gillian Dallas'

D. 'Langdon's Royal Flush'

D. 'Loch Leven'

D. 'Lord Butler'

D. 'Mighty Atom'

D. 'Rosemary Brock'

D. 'Spindrift'

D. 'Summerfield Miranda'

D. 'Sungleam'

Desmodium elegans
(Leguminosae/Papilionaceae)

Common names: Beggarweed; tick trefoil
Height: 1.5m (5ft)
Spread: 1.5m (5ft)
Aspect: Sun
Soil: Well-drained
Hardiness: Zone 6
Propagation: Seed, in autumn; softwood cuttings, in spring

Deciduous subshrub. Leaves long, 3-pinnate, leaflets obovate, green above, grey below. Flowers in terminal panicles, pea-like, pink, from late summer to autumn.

Dianella nigra
(Liliaceae/Phormiaceae)

Common name: New Zealand blueberry
Height: 60cm (24in)
Spread: 45cm (18in)
Aspect: Sun or half shade
Soil: Well-drained, acidic, fertile, humus-rich
Hardiness: Zone 9
Propagation: Seed, in warmth in spring; division, in spring

Evergreen woodlander from New Zealand. Leaves grassy, linear to lance-shaped, dark green. Loose panicles of small, off-white flowers in summer, then black berries.

Dianella tasmanica
(Liliaceae/Phormiaceae)

Common name: Tasmanian blueberry
Height: 1.2m (4ft)
Spread: 45cm (18in)
Aspect: Sun or half shade
Soil: Well-drained, acidic, fertile, humus-rich
Hardiness: Zone 9
Propagation: Seed, in warmth in spring; division, in spring

Rhizomatous evergreen from Tasmania and S.E. Australia. Leaves stiff, rough-edged. strap-like. Lavender flowers in branching panicles in summer, then blue berries.

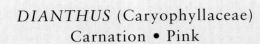

DIANTHUS (Caryophyllaceae)
Carnation • Pink

Widely grown genus of some 300 species from Eurasia and Africa, with one from arctic America.They are evergreen and long-flowering, with perfumed flowers, excellent for cutting. All *Dianthus* ask is a gritty, well-drained soil, in sun. They may flower themselves to death, but are generally short-lived and must be replaced on a regular basis, from cuttings in late summer. They are also loved by pigeons and rabbits. All are highly allergenic. There are four major categories, of which only the last is included here.

Perpetual-flowering Carnations: Grown under glass for exhibition or the cut-flower trade.

Malmaison Carnations: Grown under glass for exhibition or the cut-flower trade.

Border Carnations: Summer-flowering, sometimes clove-scented, fully double garden plants in a range of colours and fancy or picotee-edged. They were derived initially from *D. plumarius*, but lineage is now obscure.

Pinks: Summer-flowering garden plants, grouped into alpine, old-fashioned or modern. They may be single or double, clove-scented or not. Sterile 'mule' pinks are crosses between border carnations and sweet William (*D. barbatus*).

Dianthus callizonus
(Caryophyllaceae)

Common name: Pink
Height: 20cm (8in)
Spread: 30cm (12in)
Aspect: Sun
Soil: Well-drained
Hardiness: Zone 5
Propagation: Cuttings of non-flowering shoots, in summer

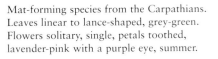

Mat-forming species from the Carpathians. Leaves linear to lance-shaped, grey-green. Flowers solitary, single, petals toothed, lavender-pink with a purple eye, summer.

***Dianthus* 'Cranmere Pool' A.G.M.**
(Caryophyllaceae)

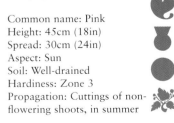

Common name: Pink
Height: 45cm (18in)
Spread: 30cm (24in)
Aspect: Sun
Soil: Well-drained
Hardiness: Zone 3
Propagation: Cuttings of non-flowering shoots, in summer

Hybrid garden pink cultivar, with double flowers which are off-white with a rich magenta centre, slightly toothed, and scented, in summer.

***Dianthus* 'Dainty Dame'**
(Caryophyllaceae)

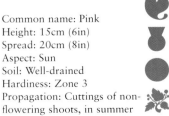

Common name: Pink
Height: 15cm (6in)
Spread: 20cm (8in)
Aspect: Sun
Soil: Well-drained
Hardiness: Zone 3
Propagation: Cuttings of non-flowering shoots, in summer

A compact, hybrid pink cultivar with perfumed, single, white flowers with a deep maroon eye, the petals slightly toothed, in summer.

***Dianthus deltoides* A.G.M.**
(Caryophyllaceae)

Common name: Maiden pink
Height: 20cm (8in)
Spread: 30cm (12in)
Aspect: Sun
Soil: Well-drained
Hardiness: Zone 3
Propagation: Cuttings of non-flowering shoots, in summer

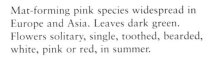

Mat-forming pink species widespread in Europe and Asia. Leaves dark green. Flowers solitary, single, toothed, bearded, white, pink or red, in summer.

Dianthus deltoides
'Leuchtfunk'
(Caryophyllaceae)

Common name: Maiden pink
Height: 20cm (8in)
Spread: 30cm (12in)
Aspect: Sun
Soil: Well-drained
Hardiness: Zone 3
Propagation: Cuttings of non-flowering shoots, in summer

A cloned selection of the mat-forming maiden pink species, bearing abundant flowers of intense cerise, in summer. Leaves dark green.

Dianthus
'Devon Dove'® A.G.M.
(Caryophyllaceae)

Common name: Pink
Height: 45cm (18in)
Spread: 30cm (12in)
Aspect: Sun
Soil: Well-drained
Hardiness: Zone 3
Propagation: Cuttings of non-flowering shoots, in summer

A hybrid pink cultivar bearing double flowers of pure white, petals toothed, bearded, in summer. Leaves and stems a bloomy blue-green.

Dianthus
'Dewdrop'
(Caryophyllaceae)

Common name: Pink
Height: 45cm (18in)
Spread: 30cm (12in)
Aspect: Sun
Soil: Well-drained
Hardiness: Zone 3
Propagation: Cuttings of non-flowering shoots, in summer

Hybrid pink cultivar with semi-double white flowers, with dark markings at the centre, petals toothed, in summer. Leaves are linear.

Dianthus
'Doris' A.G.M.
(Caryophyllaceae)

Common names: Pink
Height: 45cm (18in)
Spread: 30cm (12in)
Aspect: Sun
Soil: Any, well-drained
Hardiness: Zone 3
Propagation: Cuttings of non-flowering shoots, in summer

Modern hybrid pink with perfumed, double, bicoloured flowers of pale pink with a dark pink centre, petals toothed, in summer.

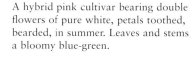

Dianthus
'Gran's Favourite' A.G.M.
(Caryophyllaceae)

Common name: Laced pink
Height: 30cm (12in)
Spread: 20cm (8in)
Aspect: Sun
Soil: Well-drained
Hardiness: Zone 3
Propagation: Cuttings of non-flowering shoots, in summer

Popular, mound-forming, laced, modern pink with clove-scented, double white flowers, with pink centres and edges, in summer.

Dianthus gratianopolitanus
A.G.M.
(Caryophyllaceae)

Common name: Cheddar pink
Height: 15cm (6in)
Spread: 35cm (15in)
Aspect: Sun
Soil: Well-drained
Hardiness: Zone 3
Propagation: Cuttings of non-flowering shoots, in summer

A mat-forming species from N.W. and C. Europe. Leaves grey-green. Flowers single, solitary, intensely perfumed, deep pink, in summer. Petals toothed, bearded.

Dianthus
'Haytor Rock' A.G.M.
(Caryophyllaceae)

Common name: Modern clove pink
Height: 45cm (18in)
Spread: 30cm (12in)
Aspect: Sun
Soil: Any, well-drained
Hardiness: Zone 3
Propagation: Cuttings of non-flowering shoots, in summer

Excellent modern hybrid pink bearing flushes of clove-scented, double, pink flowers, streaked red, in summer. Leaves grey-green.

Dianthus
'Houndspool Ruby' A.G.M.
(Caryophyllaceae)

Common name: Modern pink
Height: 45cm (18in)
Spread: 20cm (8in)
Aspect: Sun
Soil: Any well-drained
Hardiness: Zone 3
Propagation: Cuttings of non-flowering shoots, in summer

Clump-forming modern pink with double, bicoloured flowers of ruby-red with currant-red centres, in flushes through summer. Leaves grey-green.

Dianthus
'Inshriach Dazzler' A.G.M.
(Caryophyllaceae)

Common names: Alpine pink
Height: 10cm (4in)
Spread: 15cm (6in)
Aspect: Sun
Soil: Well-drained
Hardiness: Zone 3
Propagation: Cuttings of non-flowering shoots, in summer

An alpine pink with solitary, single flowers of deep carmine-red with fringed petals, carried on short stems, in summer. Good for border edge or rock garden.

Dianthus knappii
(Caryophyllaceae)

Common name: Pink
Height: 40cm (16in)
Spread: 30cm (12in)
Aspect: Sun
Soil: Well-drained
Hardiness: Zone 3
Propagation: Seed, in spring or autumn

The only yellow-flowered species. Flowers on long stems, in few-flowered clusters, yellow, with a purple spot near the base, in summer. From the W. Balkans.

Dianthus
'Mrs. Sinkins'
(Caryophyllaceae)

Common name: Old-fashioned pink
Height: 45cm (18in)
Spread: 30cm (12in)
Aspect: Sun
Soil: Well-drained
Hardiness: Zone 3
Propagation: Cuttings of non-flowering shoots, in summer

A popular, old-fashioned self with one flush of flowers, in summer. Flowers are shaggy, double, fringed, white, and strongly perfumed; calyces tend to split.

Dianthus myrtinervius
(Caryophyllaceae)

Common name: Pink
Height: 5cm (2in)
Spread: 20cm (8in)
Aspect: Sun
Soil: Well-drained
Hardiness: Zone 7
Propagation: Seed, in autumn or spring

Mat-forming species from the Balkans and Greece. Leaves lance, bright green. Flowers solitary, single, deep pink, with a pale eye, in summer.

Dianthus pavonius
A.G.M.
(Caryophyllaceae)

Common name: Pink
Height: 8cm (3in)
Spread: 20cm (8in)
Aspect: Sun
Soil: Well-drained
Hardiness: Zone 4
Propagation: Seed, in autumn or spring

Mat-forming perennial from the Alps. Leaves linear, grey-green. Flowers solitary, single, toothed, bearded, deep pink in summer. Good for border or rock garden.

Dianthus
'Prince Charming'
(Caryophyllaceae)

Common name: Pink
Height: 10cm (4in)
Spread: 20cm (8in)
Aspect: Sun
Soil: Well-drained
Hardiness: Zone 3
Propagation: Seed, in autumn or spring.

A small pink with single flowers, of a washed-out pink in colour. Leaves are linear and green. Suitable for the edge of a border or for a rock garden.

Dianthus
'Queen of Henri'
(Caryophyllaceae)

Common name: Pink
Height: 45cm (18in)
Spread: 20cm (8in)
Aspect: Sun
Soil: Well-drained
Hardiness: Zone 3
Propagation: Cuttings of non-flowering shoots, in summer

Modern pink with patterned, perfumed flowers. The centres of the petals are white, their edges laced with pink. Leaves are grey-green.

Dianthus
'Rose Joy' A.G.M.
(Caryophyllaceae)

Common name: Pink
Height: 45cm (18in)
Spread: 20cm (8in)
Aspect: Sun
Soil: Well-drained
Hardiness: Zone 3
Propagation: Cuttings of non-flowering shoots, in summer

Dependable modern pink with double, toothed, pink-purple flowers, in clusters of 2–3, in flushes through summer. Foliage is grey-green.

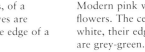

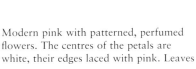

The sweetly scented garden pink Dianthus pavonius *has solitary flowers and grey-green leaves.*

Dianthus
'Royal Velvet'
(Caryophyllaceae)

Common name: Pink
Height: 45cm (18in)
Spread: 20cm (8in)
Aspect: Sun
Soil: Well-drained
Hardiness: Zone 3
Propagation: Cuttings of non-flowering shoots, in summer

A modern hybrid pink, with single, laced, pink flowers, blotched white, in flushes through summer. Foliage is linear and grey-green.

Dianthus superbus
(Caryophyllaceae)

Common name: Superb pink
Height: 20cm (8in)
Spread: 20cm (8in)
Aspect: Sun
Soil: Well-drained
Hardiness: Zone 4
Propagation: Seed, in autumn or spring

Species from the mountains of Eurasia. Leaves linear, green. Flowers single, solitary or in pairs, perfumed, purple-pink, with deeply-fringed petals, in summer.

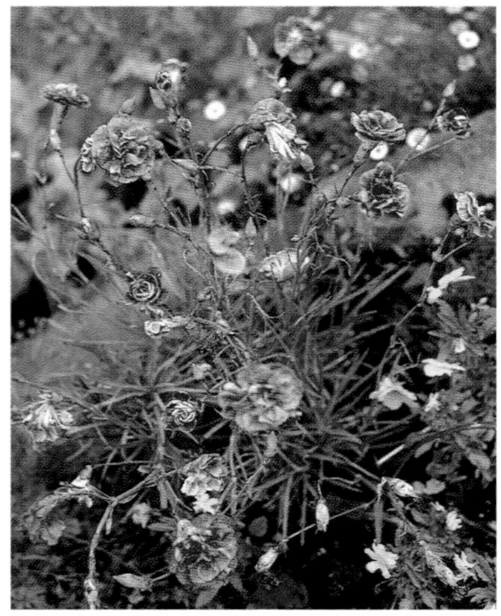

Dianthus
'Valda Wyatt' A.G.M.
(Caryophyllaceae)

Common name: Modern pink
Height: 30cm (1ft)
Spread: 30cm (1ft)
Aspect: Sun
Soil: Well-drained
Hardiness: Zone 3
Propagation: Cuttings of non-flowering shoots, in summer

Modern bicoloured pink with double, clove-scented flowers of lavender-pink, with deeper pink centres, in flushes through summer.

Dianthus
'Waithman Beauty'
(Caryophyllaceae)

Common name: Modern pink
Height: 30cm (12in)
Spread: 20cm (8in)
Aspect: Sun
Soil: Well-drained
Hardiness: Zone 3
Propagation: Cuttings of non-flowering shoots, in summer

A modern hybrid pink with flowers of deep pink, blotched white and with white centres, in flushes in summer. Leaves are linear, grey-green.

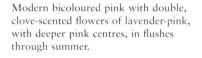

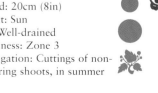

Dianthus
'Whatfield Joy'
(Caryophyllaceae)

Common name: Modern pink
Height: 20cm (8in)
Spread: 10cm (4in)
Aspect: Sun
Soil: Well-drained
Hardiness: Zone 3
Propagation: Cuttings of non-flowering shoots, in summer

A modern hybrid pink with single, small flowers of rose pink, with a paler centre, borne in flushes in summer. Leaves are linear and green.

Dianthus
'Widecombe Fair'
(Caryophyllaceae)

Common name: Modern pink
Height: 30cm (12in)
Spread: 20cm (8in)
Aspect: Sun
Soil: Well-drained
Hardiness: Zone 3
Propagation: Cuttings of non-flowering shoots, in summer

Modern hybrid pink with double, clove-scented, peach flowers, which open to blush pink, in flushes through summer. Leaves are linear, grey-green.

DIASCIA (Scrophulariaceae)
Twinspur

There are some 50 or so erect to creeping or trailing, annual and short-lived perennial species in this genus. They originate in the southern regions of the African continent, and consequentially they are for the most part not very hardy. They are, however, relatively recent arrivals, and some are proving hardier than thought at first, surviving in Zone 9 or even into Zone 8, provided they are given protection from excessive winter wet. They prefer moist soil, but do not tolerate waterlogged conditions. Diascias are chiefly valued for their long flowering season. The flowers are invariably pink or salmon-coloured, and borne in racemes on stems that range from erect to prostrate. They are tubular and five-lobed; the two upper lobes are spurred and have curious sacs marked with yellow and purple patches, known as "windows", at the base. They should be dead-headed regularly to prolong flowering. The foliage is mid-green, linear to ovate, and toothed, and sometimes evergreen. Diascias also benefit from a shearing-over in late summer, and this provides a useful source of cuttings for propagation, either to safeguard in case of winter losses or to replace plants that have passed their best every few years.

Diascia
'Coral Belle'®, syn. 'Hecbel'
(Scrophulariaceae)

Common name: Twinspur
Height: 30cm (12in)
Spread: 20cm (8in)
Aspect: Sun
Soil: Moist, well-drained, fertile
Hardiness: Zone 8
Propagation: Cuttings, spring or summer

A hybrid *Diascia*. Leaves ovate to lance-shaped, mid-green. Racemes of flowers, coral-pink in colour, all summer long. Good for the fornt of a border.

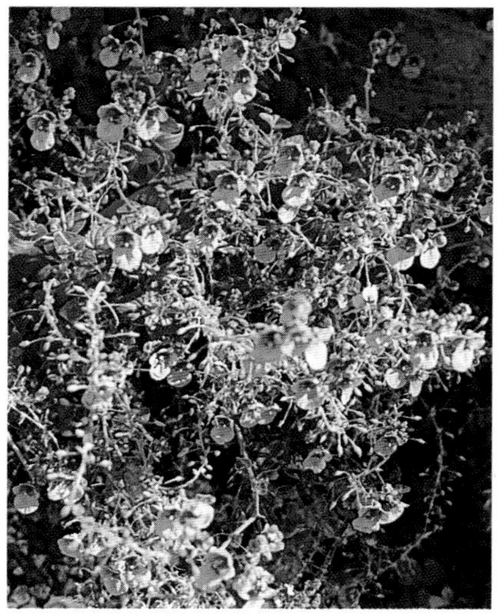

Diascia fetcaniensis
(Scrophulariaceae)

Common name: Twinspur
Height: 25cm (10in)
Spread: 30cm (12in)
Aspect: Sun
Soil: Moist, well-drained, fertile
Hardiness: Zone 8
Propagation: Seed, in warmth in spring; cuttings, in spring

Species from the Drakensberg mountains of southern Africa. Leaves ovate, hairy, green. Flowers in loose racemes, rose-pink, spurs downturned, summer and early autumn.

Diascia
'Joyce's Choice' A.G.M.
(Scrophulariaceae)

Common name: Twinspur
Height: 30cm (12in)
Spread: 20cm (8in)
Aspect: Sun
Soil: Moist, well-drained, fertile
Hardiness: Zone 8
Propagation: Cuttings, in spring or summer

Reliable hybrid *Diascia*. Leaves ovate-linear, mid-green. Flowers in loose racemes, bicoloured light and dark yellowish-pink, all summer.

Diascia
'Lady Valerie' A.G.M.
(Scrophulariaceae)

Common name: Twinspur
Height: 30cm (12in)
Spread: 20cm (8in)
Aspect: Sun
Soil: Moist, well-drained, fertile
Hardiness: Zone 8
Propagation: Cuttings, in spring or summer

A hybrid *Diascia*. Leaves ovate to heart-shaped, mid-green. Flowers of a strong yellowish-pink are carried in loose racemes all summer.

Diascia rigescens
A.G.M.
(Scrophulariaceae)

Common name: Twinspur
Height: 30cm (12in)
Spread: 40cm (16in)
Aspect: Sun
Soil: Moist, well-drained, fertile
Hardiness: Zone 8
Propagation: Seed or cuttings, both in spring

Trailing species from South Africa. Leaves heart-shaped, toothed, mid-green. Flowers in dense racemes, deep pink, in summer. Flops over if not staked.

Diascia
'Rose Queen'
(Scrophulariaceae)

Common name: Twinspur
Height: 45cm (18in)
Spread: 30cm (12in)
Aspect: Sun
Soil: Moist, well-drained, fertile
Hardiness: Zone 8
Propagation: Cuttings, in spring or summer

A very floriferous and handsome hybrid *Diascia* cultivar with flowers of a most intense pink, borne in loose racemes all summer long.

Diascia
'Ruby Field' A.G.M.
(Scrophulariaceae)

Common name: Twinspur
Height: 25cm (10in)
Spread: 45cm (18in)
Aspect: Sun
Soil: Moist, well-drained, fertile
Hardiness: Zone 8
Propagation: Cuttings, in spring or summer

An early hybrid *Diascia* cultivar. Leaves heart-shaped, mid-green. Very prolific in flowering, bearing masses of salmon-pink flowers all summer.

Diascia vigilis
A.G.M.
(Scrophulariaceae)

Common name: Twinspur
Height: 30cm (12in)
Spread: 45cm (18in)
Aspect: Sun
Soil: Moist, well-drained, fertile
Hardiness: Zone 8
Propagation: Seed or cuttings, both in spring

Species from the Drakensberg mountains of southern Africa. Leaves ovate to lance-shaped, toothed, fleshy. Flowers in loose racemes, clear pink, all summer.

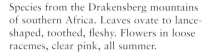

DICENTRA (Fumariaceae/Papaveraceae)
Bleeding heart

A genus of some 20 or so annuals and perennials found in both Asia and North America, originating for the most part in moist woodland habitats. They may be rhizomatous, tuberous, or have fleshy tap roots. All are reliably hardy. The foliage is much-divided, fern-like, and silver-grey; some species are evergreen, but most are deciduous. The flowers are pendent, carried in arching panicles or racemes. They are highly distinctive: the two outer petals are pouched, giving a generally heart-shaped outline, while the two inner petals form a hood over the anthers. This curious appearance has earned the plants in the genus a variety of common names, from bleeding heart (most often used for *D. spectabilis*) to Dutchman's breeches. They last well in water, and make excellent and unusual cut flowers; they and the foliage are valuable for flower arrangements. Most of the perennials in the genus make good border plants, but one or two are simply too invasive and better placed in a woodland garden. *D. spectabilis* is not long-lived. *Dicentra* are low in allergens, but all parts of the plants are poisonous and skin irritant. Their preferred conditions are half shade and moist, fertile soil, but they are drought-tolerant.

Dicentra
'Adrian Bloom'
(Fumariaceae/Papaveraceae)

Common name: Bleeding heart
Height: 40cm (16in)
Spread: 45cm (18in)
Aspect: Half shade
Soil: Moist, well-drained, fertile
Hardiness: Zone 5
Propagation: Division, in spring or just after the leaves die down

Clump-forming, rhizomatous hybrid. Leaves pinnate, lobes long, grey-green. Flowers in narrow racemes, carmine, in late spring and sporadically to autumn.

Dicentra
'Pearl Drops'
(Fumariaceae/Papaveraceae)

Common name: Bleeding heart
Height: 30cm (12in)
Spread: 45cm (18in)
Aspect: Half shade
Soil: Moist, well-drained, fertile
Hardiness: Zone 5
Propagation: Division, in spring or just after the leaves die down

Rhizomatous, invasive, hybrid cultivar. Leaves lobed, glaucous blue-green. Flowers white, tinted pink, in racemes from mid-spring to summer.

Dicentra scandens
(Fumariaceae/Papaveraceae)

Common name: Bleeding heart
Height: 1.5m (5ft)
Spread: 45cm (18in)
Aspect: Half shade
Soil: Moist, well-drained, fertile
Hardiness: Zone 6
Propagation: Seed, when ripe or in spring

Scrambling or climbing species. Leaves deeply lobed, segments ovate to lance-shaped, mid-green. Long racemes of yellow flowers, on leafy, wiry stems, in summer.

Dicentra spectabilis
A.G.M.
(Fumariaceae/Papaveraceae)

Common name: Bleeding heart
Height: 1m (36in)
Spread: 45cm (18in)
Aspect: Half shade
Soil: Moist, well-drained, fertile
Hardiness: Zone 6
Propagation: Seed, when ripe or in spring

Clump-forming species. Leaves 2-ternate, lobes ovate to cut, mid-green. Flowers in arching racemes, outer petals rose-pink, inner ones white, spring to early summer.

Dicentra spectabilis
'Alba' A.G.M.
(Papaveraceae)

Common name: Bleeding heart
Height: 1.2m (4ft)
Spread: 45cm (18in)
Aspect: Half shade
Soil: Moist, well-drained, fertile
Hardiness: Zone 6
Propagation: Seed, when ripe or in spring

Pure white form of the species, and more robust and longer-lived. Late spring to midsummer. Woodlander from Siberia, China and Korea.

Dicentra
'Spring Morning'
(Fumariaceae/Papaveraceae)

Common name: Bleeding heart
Height: 45cm (18in)
Spread: 45cm (18in)
Aspect: Half shade
Soil: Moist, well-drained, fertile
Hardiness: Zone 5
Propagation: Division, in spring or just after the leaves die down

Clump-forming, rhizomatous hybrid, with finely divided, dark green leaves, which contrast well with the racemes of pale pink, nodding flowers.

This form of Bleeding heart Dicentra spectabilis *'alba' has arching racemes of pure white flowers.*

Dicksonia antarctica
A.G.M.
(Cyathaceae/Dicksoniaceae)

Common names: Soft tree fern; woolly tree-fern
Height: To 5m (15ft)
Spread: To 4m (12ft)
Aspect: Half or full shade
Soil: Acidic, humus-rich
Hardiness: Zone 8
Propagation: Spores, when ripe

Rhizomatous, tree-like fern from Australia and Tasmania. Fronds 2- to 3-pinnate, pale green, darkening with age, evergreen in mild climates. Trunk up to 60cm (2ft) across.

Dictamnus albus
A.G.M.
(Rutaceae)

Common names: Burning bush; dittany
Height: 90cm (3ft)
Spread: 60cm (2ft)
Aspect: Sun or half shade
Soil: Dry, well-drained
Hardiness: Zone 3
Propagation: Seed, when ripe; division, in spring or autumn

Leaves pinnate, spiny, lemon-scented, green. Flowers in long, open racemes, white. Oil in flowers and fruit aromatic; can be ignited on hot days. Toxic, skin-irritant, allergenic.

Dictamnus albus
var. *purpureus* A.G.M.
(Rutaceae)

Common name: Burning bush
Height: 90cm (3ft)
Spread: 60cm (2ft)
Aspect: Sun or half shade
Soil: Dry, well-drained
Hardiness: Zone 3
Propagation: Seed, when ripe; division, in spring or autumn

Purple-flowered form. Leaves pinnate, spiny, lemon-scented, green. Flowers in long, open racemes. On hot days oil in flowers and fruit can be ignited. Toxic, irritant, allergenic.

Dierama pendulum
(Iridaceae)

Common name: Angel's fishing-rod
Height: 2m (6ft)
Spread: 60cm (2ft)
Aspect: Sun
Soil: Well-drained, humus-rich
Hardiness: Zone 7
Propagation: Seed, when ripe; division, in spring

Cormous evergreen from South Africa. Leaves basal, arching, grass-like, grey-green. Flowers bell-shaped, pendent, pink, on arching stems in summer. Seed heads good.

Dierama pulcherrimum
(Iridaceae)

Common name: Angel's fishing rod
Height: 1.5m (5ft)
Spread: 60cm (2ft)
Aspect: Sun
Soil: Well-drained, humus-rich
Hardiness: Zone 7
Propagation: Seed, when ripe; division, in spring

Cormous evergreen from South Africa and Zimbabwe. Leaves basal, grassy, green. Flowers tubular to bell-shaped, white or pink, pendent, on arching stems, summer.

Dietes bicolor
(Iridaceae)

Common name: Fortnight lily
Height: 90cm (3ft)
Spread: 30cm (1ft)
Aspect: Sun or half shade
Soil: Moist, well-drained
Hardiness: Zone 9
Propagation: Seed, in autumn or spring

Rhizomatous evergreen from Africa. Leaves basal, erect, leathery, sword-shaped, pale green. Flowers flat; 3 cream tepals have a brown spot at the base, spring to summer.

Dietes grandiflora
(Iridaceae)

Common name: Wild iris
Height: 1m (3ft)
Spread: 30cm (1ft)
Aspect: Sun or half shade
Soil: Moist, well-drained
Hardiness: Zone 9
Propagation: Seed, in autumn or spring

Rhizomatous plant from South Africa. Erect linear, leathery, pale green, basal leaves. Flat, evanescent flowers; 3 white tepals marked mauve and yellow, spring and early summer.

Digitalis ferruginea
(Scrophulariaceae)

Common name: Rusty foxglove
Height: 1.2m (4ft)
Spread: 45cm (18in)
Aspect: Half shade
Soil: Moist, avoiding extremes of wet or dry, humus-rich
Hardiness: Zone 7
Propagation: Seed, in spring

Tall woodlander. Dark green, oblong, entire leaves in rosettes. Flowers in long narrow spikes, golden-brown, veined red-brown inside, in summer. Toxic and skin-irritant.

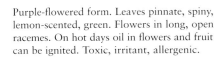

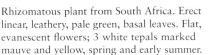

DIGITALIS (Scrophulariaceae)
Foxglove

There are 20 or so biennial and short-lived perennial species from Eurasia and North Africa in this genuas. They are tall, architectural plants which do not require staking except in very exposed situations. They are fine woodland plants. Most are perennial, but in Britain they all tend to be thought of as biennial because the native *D. purpurea* is that; this species, too, can be perennial, but the flowers deteriorate markedly in later years. Foxgloves self-seed, so the fact that they are short-lived is not really a problem. Their self-seeding is not invasive, with the seedlings appearing around the base of the parent plant, but if it is a problem dead-heading will cure it. They are very drought-tolerant, but they are prone to powdery mildew. The foliage is handsome, oblong to obovate, toothed or entire, mid-green, growing in basal rosettes. The flowers are in upright racemes, which are usually one-sided, and are open bells or tubules in a range of golden or purple shades, often marked with spots or veins inside. They are very attractive to bees, and an imposing addition to flower arrangements. They are low in allergens, so suitable for the gardener with allergies, but all parts of the plant are poisonous and contact can irritate skin.

Digitalis
'Glory of Roundway'
(Scrophulariaceae)

Common name: Foxglove
Height: 90cm (36in)
Spread: 30cm (12in)
Aspect: Half shade
Soil: Moist, avoiding wet or dry extremes, humus-rich
Hardiness: Zone 5
Propagation: Division, in spring

Hybrid foxglove cultivar with tall racemes of funnel-shaped, flowers of pale yellow, tinted pink, in summer. Good woodland plant. All parts toxic and skin-irritant.

Digitalis grandiflora
A.G.M.
(Scrophulariaceae)

Common name: Yellow foxglove
Height: 1m (3ft)
Spread: 45cm (18in)
Aspect: Half shade
Soil: Humus-rich
Hardiness: Zone 4
Propagation: Seed, in spring

Woodlander from Europe to Siberia. Leaves ovate-oblong, toothed, veined, mid-green. Raceme of pale yellow tubular flowers in early to mid-summer. Toxic and irritant.

Digitalis
'John Innes Tetra'
(Scrophulariaceae)

Common name: Foxglove
Height: 90cm (36in)
Spread: 30cm (12in)
Aspect: Half shade
Soil: Humus-rich
Hardiness: Zone 6
Propagation: Division, in spring

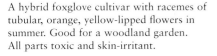

A hybrid foxglove cultivar with racemes of tubular, orange, yellow-lipped flowers in summer. Good for a woodland garden. All parts toxic and skin-irritant.

Digitalis lanata
A.G.M.
(Scrophulariaceae)

Common name: Grecian foxglove
Height: 60cm (2ft)
Spread: 30cm (1ft)
Aspect: Half shade
Soil: Humus-rich
Hardiness: Zone 7
Propagation: Seed, in spring

Woodland species. Leaves oblong to lance-shaped, mid-green. Dense raceme of cream to fawn flowers, veined brown, pale lower lip, in midsummer. Toxic and skin irritant.

Digitalis lutea
(Scrophulariaceae)

Common name: Straw foxglove
Height: 60cm (2ft)
Spread: 30cm (1ft)
Aspect: Half shade
Soil: Humus-rich
Hardiness: Zone 4
Propagation: Seed, in spring

Woodland species. Leaves glossy, green, inverse-lance-shaped to oblong, toothed. Slim raceme of pale yellow flowers, early- to midsummer. Toxic and skin irritant.

Digitalis* × *mertonensis
A.G.M.
(Scrophulariaceae)

Common names: None
Height: 90cm (36in)
Spread: 30cm (1ft)
Aspect: Half shade
Soil: Humus-rich
Hardiness: Zone 5
Propagation: Division, in spring

Tetraploid hybrid; comes true from seed. Leaves toothed, veined, glossy, lance-shaped to ovate. Racemes of pinkish-buff flowers, spring to early summer. Toxic and irritant.

Digitalis purpurea
(Scrophulariaceae)

Common name: Common foxglove
Height: To 2m (6ft)
Spread: 60cm (2ft)
Aspect: Half shade
Soil: Humus-rich
Hardiness: Zone 6
Propagation: Seed, in spring

Biennial or short-lived perennial European species. Leaves lance-shaped, toothed, deep green. Flowers in one-sided racemes, pink, purple or white. Toxic and skin irritant.

Dionaea muscipula
(Droseraceae)

Common name: Venus' fly-trap
Height: 30cm (12in)
Spread: 15cm (6in)
Aspect: Sun
Soil: Moist, acidic
Hardiness: Zone 8
Propagation: Seed, in warmth in spring

Rosette-forming, insectivorous species from North America. Leaves yellow-green, stalks winged, spiny-edged. Flowers in umbels on bare stalks, white, early to midsummer.

Diphylleia cymosa
(Berberidaceae)

Common name: Umbrella leaf
Height: 1m (3ft)
Spread: 30cm (1ft)
Aspect: Full or half shade
Soil: Moist, humus-rich
Hardiness: Zone 7
Propagation: Seed or division, both in spring

Rhizomatous woodlander. Leaves large, peltate, toothed, dark green. Flowers in terminal cymes, white, bowl-shaped, in late spring to early summer; blue berries follow.

Diplarrhena moraea
(Iridaceae)

Common names: None
Height: 60cm (24in)
Spread: 25cm (10in)
Aspect: Sun or half shade
Soil: Moist, well-drained, gritty, acidic
Hardiness: Zone 7
Propagation: Seed or division, both in spring

Rhizomatous plant from Australia. Leaves basal, long, linear, dark green. Flowers scented, white; purple and yellow marks on inner tepals, in late spring to early summer.

Disa uniflora
(Orchidaceae)

Common name: Pride of table mountain
Height: 60cm (24in)
Spread: 20cm (8in)
Aspect: Half shade
Soil: Peaty, mossy, gritty
Hardiness: Zone 10
Propagation: Division, after growth starts

Terrestrial orchid from South Africa. Leaves lance-shaped, green. Short raceme of up to 10 flowers in summer, red with gold veins. Not easy; keep cool and shaded in summer.

Disporum smithii
(Convallariaceae/Liliaceae)

Common name: Fairy bells
Height: 60cm (2ft)
Spread: 30cm (1ft)
Aspect: Half shade
Soil: Moist, well-drained, humus-rich
Hardiness: Zone 6
Propagation: Seed, in autumn; division, in spring

Rhizomatous woodlander. Leaves ovate to lance-shaped, scalloped, green. Flowers in umbels, pendent, tubular, greenish-white, in spring; orange berries in late summer.

Dodecatheon meadia
A.G.M.
(Primulaceae)

Common name: Shooting stars
Height: 40cm (16in)
Spread: 25cm (10in)
Aspect: Sun or half shade
Soil: Moist, well-drained, acidic, humus-rich
Hardiness: Zone 3
Propagation: Seed, when ripe, after cold exposure; division, in spring

Clump-forming woodlander from the U.S.A. Leaves ovate to spoon-shaped, mid-green. Flowers in umbels, magenta, in spring. *D. meadia* f. *album* also has an A.G.M.

Dodecatheon pulchellum
A.G.M.
(Primulaceae)

Common name: Shooting stars
Height: 35cm (14in)
Spread: 15cm (6in)
Aspect: Sun or half shade
Soil: Moist, well-drained, acidic, humus-rich
Hardiness: Zone 5
Propagation: Seed, when ripe, after cold exposure; division, in spring

Clump-forming woodlander from western North America. Leaves spoon-shaped to ovate, mid green. Flowers in umbels of up to 20, cerise, in spring.

Doronicum orientale 'Magnificum' (Asteraceae/Compositae)

Common name: Leopard's bane
Height: 50cm (20in)
Spread: 90cm (36in)
Aspect: Half shade
Soil: Moist, humus-rich
Hardiness: Zone 5
Propagation: Seed, in spring; division, in autumn

Spreading, rhizomatous woodlander from Europe and the near East. Leaves basal, ovate, scalloped, mid-green. Flowers large, solitary, yellow daisies, mid- to late spring.

Doronicum pardalianches (Asteraceae Compositae)

Common name: Leopard's bane
Height: 90cm (3ft)
Spread: 90cm (3ft)
Aspect: Half shade
Soil: Moist, humus-rich
Hardiness: Zone 6
Propagation: Seed, in spring; division, in autumn

Spreading, rhizomatous woodlander from Europe. Leaves basal, ovate, toothed, hairy, mid-green. Flowers yellow, daisy-like, in corymbs, spring to midsummer.

Doronicum plantagineum (Asteraceae/Compositae)

Common name: Leopards bane
Height: 80cm (32in)
Spread: 45cm (18in)
Aspect: Half shade
Soil: Moist, humus-rich
Hardiness: Zone 6
Propagation: Seed, in spring; division, in autumn

Rhizomatous woodlander from W. Europe. Leaves basal, ovate, hairy, mid-green; die down soon after flowering. Flowers on branching stems, yellow, in late spring.

Draba longisiliqua A.G.M. (Brassicaceae/Cruciferae)

Common name: Whitlow grass
Height: 10cm (4in)
Spread: 20cm (8in)
Aspect: Sun; protect against winter wet
Soil: Sharply-drained, gritty
Hardiness: Zone 6
Propagation: Seed, after cold exposure, in autumn

Cushion-forming evergreen. Rosettes of leaves, obovate, grey-hairy. Flowers yellow, in dense, short racemes, in spring. Grow in alpine house or cover with glass in winter.

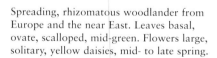

Dracunculus vulgaris (Araceae)

Common name: Dragon arum
Height: 1.5m (5ft)
Spread: 60cm (2ft)
Aspect: Sun, but tolerates half shade
Soil: Well-drained, dry in summer, humus-rich
Hardiness: Zone 9
Propagation: Offsets, in autumn or spring

Tuberous Mediterranean woodlander. Basal, pedate, deep green leaves; brownish marks. Flowers spring to summer; maroon spathe, black spadix, malodorous. May bear berries.

Dryas octopetala A.G.M. (Rosaceae)

Common name: Mountain avens
Height: 10cm (4in)
Spread: 1m (36in)
Aspect: Sun or half shade
Soil: Well-drained, gritty, humus-rich
Hardiness: Zone 2
Propagation: Seed, when ripe; softwood cuttings, in summer

Subshrub from Europe. Leaves ovate, scalloped, green. Flowers almost stemless, upward-facing, white with yellow stamens, in late spring to early summer.

Dryopteris affinis A.G.M. (Aspidiaceae/ Dryopteridaceae)

Common name: Golden male fern
Height: 90cm (3ft)
Spread: 90cm (3ft)
Aspect: Half shade
Soil: Moist, humus-rich
Hardiness: Zone 6
Propagation: Spores, in warmth when ripe

Evergreen, rhizomatous, terrestrial fern. Fronds lance-shaped, 2-pinnate, pale green, turning dark green, with a dark spot where each pinna joins the brown midrib.

Echinacea pallida (Asteraceae/Compositae)

Common name: Pink coneflower
Height: 1.2m (4ft)
Spread: 45cm (18in)
Aspect: Sun
Soil: Well-drained, humus-rich
Hardiness: Zone 5
Propagation: Seed, in spring; division, in autumn or spring

Rhizomatous perennial from the U.S.A. Leaves linear to lance-shaped, bristly, dark green. Flowers daisy-like, disc florets brown, ray florets drooping, pale pink, late summer.

Echinacea purpurea
(Asteraceae/Compositae)

Common name: Purple coneflower
Height: 1.5m (5ft)
Spread: 45cm (18in)
Aspect: Sun
Soil: Well-drained, humus-rich
Hardiness: Zone 3
Propagation: Seed, in spring; division, in spring or autumn

Rhizomatous perennial from the U.S.A. Leaves ovate, toothed, smooth, green. Flowers solitary, single, ray florets reflexed, purple, disc florets golden-brown.

Echinacea purpurea
'Robert Bloom'
(Asteraceae/Compositae)

Common name: Purple coneflower
Height: 1.5m (5ft)
Spread: 45cm (18in)
Aspect: Sun
Soil: Well-drained, humus-rich
Hardiness: Zone 3
Propagation: Seed, in spring; division, in spring or autumn

A selected form of *E. purpurea*. Flowers mauve-crimson, reflexed ray florets, with prominent discs of orange-brown. Leaves toothed, ovate, smooth.

Echinacea purpurea
'Magnus'
(Asteraceae/Compositae)

Common name: Great purple coneflower
Height: 1.5m (5ft)
Spread: 45cm (18in)
Aspect: Sun
Soil: Well-drained, humus-rich
Hardiness: Zone 3
Propagation: Seed, in spring; division, in spring or autumn

Large-flowered form of *E. purpurea,* in which the flowerheads are 18cm (7in) across. Ray florets held almost horizontal. Leaves ovate, toothed, smooth, green.

Echinacea purpurea
'White Lustre'
(Asteraceae/Compositae)

Common name: White coneflower
Height: 1.5m (5ft)
Spread: 45cm (18in)
Aspect: Sun
Soil: Well-drained, humus-rich
Hardiness: Zone 3
Propagation: Seed, in spring; division, in spring or autumn

White form of *E. purpurea*. Flowers have creamy-white, reflexed ray florets, and orange-brown disc florets. Leaves ovate, toothed, smooth, green.

Echinacea purpurea
'White Swan'
(Asteraceae/Compositae)

Common name: White coneflower
Height: 1.5m (5ft)
Spread: 45cm (18in)
Aspect: Sun
Soil: Well-drained, humus-rich
Hardiness: Zone 3
Propagation: Seed, in spring; division, in spring or autumn

Selected white form of *E. purpurea*. Flowers are large, with white ray florets and orange-brown disc florets. Leaves are ovate, toothed, smooth, green.

Echinops bannaticus
(Asteraceae/Compositae)

Common name: Globe thistle
Height: 1.2m (4ft)
Spread: 60cm (2ft)
Aspect: Sun
Soil: Well-drained, poor
Hardiness: Zone 3
Propagation: Seed, in mid-spring; division, in spring or autumn

Clump-forming perennial from S.E. Europe. Leaves ovate, spiny, hairy, pinnatisect, grey-green. Flowers terminal, spherical, blue-grey, with bristly bracts, late summer.

Echinops ritro
A.G.M.
(Asteraceae/Compositae)

Common name: Globe thistle
Height: 60cm (24in)
Spread: 45cm (18in)
Aspect: Sun
Soil: Well-drained, poor
Hardiness: Zone 3
Propagation: Seed, in mid-spring; division, in spring or autumn

Clump-forming plant. Leaves oblong, pinnatisect, spiny, dark green, cobwebby above, white-downy beneath. Flowerhead spherical, bright blue, in late summer.

Echium pininana
(Boraginaceae)

Common name: Bugloss
Height: 4m (12ft)
Spread: 90cm (3ft)
Aspect: Sun
Soil: Well-drained, fertile
Hardiness: Zone 9
Propagation: Seed, in warmth in summer

Leaves in rosettes, lance-shaped, silver-hairy. Flowers in huge panicle-like cyme, blue, funnel-shaped, with big bracts. Toxic and skin-irritant. From the Canary Islands.

Echium wildpretii
(Boraginaceae)

Common names: None
Height: 2m (6ft)
Spread: 60cm (2ft)
Aspect: Sun
Soil: Well-drained, fertile
Hardiness: Zone 9
Propagation: Seed, in warmth in summer

Perennial from the Canary islands. Leaves in a basal rosette, narrow, lance-shaped, hairy, pale green. Flowers in dense cymes, funnel-shaped, red, late spring to summer.

Edraianthus pumilio
A.G.M.
(Campanulaceae)

Common name: Grassy bells
Height: 2.5cm (1in)
Spread: 15cm (6in)
Aspect: Sun
Soil: Sharply drained, gritty, chalky
Hardiness: Zone 6
Propagation: Seed, in autumn; softwood cuttings, in summer

Dwarf, cushion-forming perennial from Dalmatia. Leaves linear, hairy, silver-green. Flowers solitary, stemless, upturned bells, deep purple-blue, in early summer.

Elsholtzia stauntonii
(Labiatae/Lamiaceae)

Common name: Mint bush
Height: 1.2m (4ft)
Spread: 1m (3ft)
Aspect: Sun
Soil: Well-drained, fertile
Hardiness: Zone 4
Propagation: Seed, in warmth when ripe; softwood cuttings, in summer

Deciduous subshrub with toothed, lance-shaped, mid-green leaves, ageing red, mint-scented. Flowers small, purple-pink; dense panicles or racemes, late summer to autumn.

Elymus hispidus
(Graminae/Poaceae)

Common name: Blue wheatgrass
Height: 75cm (30in)
Spread: 40cm (16in)
Aspect: Sun
Soil: Moist, well-drained, fertile
Hardiness: Zone 5
Propagation: Seed, *in situ* in autumn or spring

Non-invasive evergreen grass from Eurasia. Leaves silvery blue, ridged below, upright then arching. Dense, wheat-like flower panicle in summer, silver-blue turning beige.

Elymus magellanicus
(Graminae/Poaceae)

Common name: Wild rye
Height: 15cm (6in)
Spread: 30cm (12in)
Aspect: Sun
Soil: Moist, well-drained, fertile
Hardiness: Zone 5
Propagation: Seed, *in situ* in autumn or spring

Mound-forming, tufted grass from South America. Leaves linear, folded, blue. Flower spike lax or prostrate, bearing up to 7 flowers, all summer long.

Eomecon chionantha
(Papaveraceae)

Common name: Snow poppy
Height: 40 cm (16in)
Spread: Indefinite
Aspect: Half shade
Soil: Moist, well-drained, humus-rich
Hardiness: Zone 7
Propagation: Seed or division, both in spring

Invasive woodlander from E. China. Leaves handsome, leathery, kidney-shaped, green. Flowers like white poppies, in loose panicles, from late spring to midsummer.

Epilobium angustifolium
(Onagraceae)

Common name: Rosebay willow herb
Height: 1.5m (5ft)
Spread: 1m (3ft)
Aspect: Sun or half shade
Soil: Moist, well-drained, humus-rich
Hardiness: Zone 3
Propagation: Seed, when ripe; division, in spring or autumn

Highly invasive, rhizomatous plant. Leaves lance-shaped, mid-green. Flowers in racemes, pink saucers, from summer to early autumn. Self-seeds very prolifically.

Epilobium angustifolium
var. *album*
(Onagraceae)

Common name: White rosebay willowherb
Height: 1.5m (5ft)
Spread: 1m (3ft)
Aspect: Sun or half shade
Soil: Moist, well-drained, humus-rich
Hardiness: Zone 3
Propagation: Seed, when ripe; division, in spring or autumn

White-flowered form; flowers in racemes from summer to early autumn. Claimed to be less invasive than the usual form of the species, but still a liberal self-seeder.

Epimedium × versicolor *'Sulphureum' has attractive red-brown lobed leaves that turn green.*

Epilobium dodonaei
(Onagraceae)

Common name: Willow herb
Height: 90cm (36in)
Spread: 20cm (8in)
Aspect: Sun or half shade
Soil: Moist, well-drained, humus-rich
Hardiness: Zone 6
Propagation: Seed, when ripe; division, in spring or autumn

An invasive perennial from C. Europe to W. Asia. Leaves linear, toothed, hairy, mid-green. Flowers in loose terminal racemes, dark pink-purple, all summer.

Epilobium glabellum
(Onagraceae)

Common name: Willow herb
Height: 20cm (8in)
Spread: 20cm (8in)
Aspect: Half shade
Soil: Moist, well-drained, humus-rich
Hardiness: Zone 8
Propagation: Seed, when ripe; division, in spring or autumn

Clump-forming woodland ground cover. Leaves elliptic-ovate, toothed, dark green. Flowers solitary, on branching stems, white or pink, summer. Evergreen in mild areas.

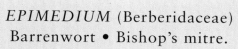

EPIMEDIUM (Berberidaceae)
Barrenwort • Bishop's mitre.

A genus of some 40 rhizomatous, clump-forming, perennial species, of varying hardiness, found from the Mediterranean across to temperate regions of East Asia. Their natural habitat is woodland or shady scrub, and they all prefer a sheltered and partly shaded site. Some species are evergreen, others semi-evergreen, yet others deciduous. All have handsome, mainly basal foliage, and will make excellent ground cover, especially in a woodland or other partly shaded situation; smaller types are suitable for a rock garden. New growth in spring may be tinted bronze, and the leaves of many deciduous species colour attractively in autumn. The foliage of the semi-evergreen and deciduous types should be sheared over in late winter before new growth begins, to show the flowers to their best. Although *Epimedium* are not spectacular when in bloom, they have a quiet charm. The individual flowers are delicate in appearance. They are mainly cup- or saucer-shaped and composed of two sets of four tepals surrounding four petals; these often have elongated spurs. They are nodding, in shades of pink, purple, buff, white or yellow, and carried in erect to arching racemes or panicles on slender stems. *Epimedium* are low in allergens.

Epimedium davidii
(Berberidaceae)

Common names: None
Height: 30cm (12in)
Spread: 45cm (18in)
Aspect: Half shade
Soil: Moist, well-drained, fertile, humus-rich
Hardiness: Zone 7
Propagation: Seed, when ripe; division, in autumn

Clump-forming evergreen from W China. Leaves bronze ageing to green, 3-palmate, lobes ovate to lance-shaped. Flowers yellow, with curved spurs, spring to early summer.

Epimedium grandiflorum
A.G.M.
(Berberidaceae)

Common names: None
Height: 30cm (1ft)
Spread: 30cm (1ft)
Aspect: Half shade,
Soil: Moist, well-drained, fertile, humus-rich
Hardiness: Zone 5
Propagation: Seed, when ripe; division, in autumn

Rhizomatous, deciduous plant. Leaves lobed, leaflets ovate to heart-shaped, spiny-edged, bronze turning green. Flowers pink, white, purple or yellow, spurred, in spring.

Epimedium* × *rubrum
A.G.M.
(Berberidaceae)

Common names: None
Height: 30cm (1ft)
Spread: 30cm (1ft)
Aspect: Half shade
Soil: Moist, well-drained, fertile, humus-rich
Hardiness: Zone 5
Propagation: Seed, when ripe; division, in autumn

Rhizomatous, semi-evergreen perennial of garden origin. Leaves 2-ternate, lobes spiny, ovate, pointed, red turning brown, lasting over winter. Flowers red and cream, spring.

Epimedium* × *versicolor
'Sulphureum' A.G.M.
(Berberidaceae)

Common names: None
Height: 30cm (1ft)
Spread: 1m (3ft)
Aspect: Half shade
Soil: Moist, well-drained, fertile, humus-rich
Hardiness: Zone 5
Propagation: Seed, when ripe; division, in autumn

Rhizomatous, evergreen perennial of garden origin. Leaves lobed, 5-11 ovate, spiny leaflets, red-brown turning green. Flowers deep yellow, spurs long, in spring.

Epimedium × *youngianum* **'Roseum'**
(Berberidaceae)

Common names: None
Height: 30cm (1ft)
Spread: 30cm (1ft)
Aspect: Half shade
Soil: Moist, well-drained, humus-rich, fertile
Hardiness: Zone 5
Propagation: Seed, when ripe; division, in autumn

Deciduous rhizomatous perennial with ovate leaves, sometimes spotted or with pale green centres and dark green edges. Flowers dusky pink, in spring.

Epipactis gigantea
(Orchidaceae)

Common name: Giant helleborine
Height: 40cm (16in)
Spread: To 1m (3ft)
Aspect: Half or full shade
Soil: Moist, well-drained, humus-rich
Hardiness: Zone 6
Propagation: Division, such that each piece has an eye, in spring

Rhizomatous terrestrial orchid. Ovate to lance-shaped, green leaves. Flowers nodding, in spikes, greenish-yellow, veined maroon and brown. Spreads rapidly in ideal sites.

Eranthis hyemalis
A.G.M
(Ranunculaceae)

Common name: Winter aconite
Height: 8cm (3in)
Spread: 5cm (2in)
Aspect: Sun or half shade
Soil: Reliably moist through summer, fertile, humus-rich
Hardiness: Zone 5
Propagation: Seed or division, both in spring

Tuberous perennial from S. Europe. Basal leaves lobed-pinnate, green. Stem leaves in a ruff below flower, dissected, bright green. Flowers yellow cups. All parts poisonous.

Eremurus himalaicus
(Asphodelaceae/Liliaceae)

Common names: Desert candle; foxtail lily
Height: 2m (6ft)
Spread: 60cm (2ft)
Aspect: Sun
Soil: Gritty, well-drained, fertile
Hardiness: Zone 3
Propagation: Seed, in autumn; division, after flowering

Fleshy-rooted perennial. Leaves in rosettes, linear, green. Flowers in tall racemes, white, spring to early summer. Must have winter cold to flower. Do not dig near base.

Eremurus robustus
(Asphodelaceae/Liliaceae)

Common names: Desert candle; foxtail lily
Height: 3m (10ft)
Spread: 1m (3ft)
Aspect: Sun
Soil: Well-drained, gritty, fertile
Hardiness: Zone 6
Propagation: Seed, in autumn; division, after flowering

Perennial from C. Asia. Leaves blue-green strap-shaped, rough-edged. Flowers pink, in racemes, in early to midsummer. Needs winter cold to flower. Do not dig near base.

Eremurus stenophyllus
(Asphodelaceae/Liliaceae)

Common names: Desert candle; foxtail lily
Height: 1m (3ft)
Spread: 60cm (2ft)
Aspect: Sun
Soil: Well-drained, gritty, fertile
Hardiness: Zone 5
Propagation: Seed, in autumn; division, after flowering

Perennial from W. Asia, Iran and Pakistan. Leaves linear, hairy, grey-green. Flowers in racemes, yellow, fading to orange, early to midsummer. Do not dig or hoe near base.

ERIGERON (Asteraceae/Compositae)
Fleabane

There are over 200 species in this genus, most of them perennials; their main distribution in the wild is in North America. They range from mat- or mound-forming alpines to taller, clump forming border types. They are invaluable border perennials, with several excellent characteristics. They have a long flowering season: *Erigeron karvinskianus* is the longest-flowering of all hardy perennials, blooming non-stop for up to six months; few gardeners could ask for more. They are easy-going, requiring only sun and reasonably fertile, well-drained soil; some of the alpines benefit from protection against excessive winter wet. Almost all are reliably hardy, and they are excellent for coastal gardens, *E. glaucus* especially so. They are much appreciated by bees and butterflies in the garden, and also by flower arrangers, as they last very well in water if picked when open. There have to be disadvantages, and as a genus they need to be lifted and divided every few years. Some of the taller hybrids do require staking, and slugs are fond of the new growth in spring. All *Erigeron* are unfortunately highly allergenic, and so should be avoided by allergic gardeners (note that this is not the only genus commonly called fleabane).

Erigeron aurantiacus
(Asteraceae/Compositae)

Common name: Orange daisy
Height: 30cm (1ft)
Spread: 30cm (1ft)
Aspect: Sun
Soil: Well-drained, fertile, humus-rich
Hardiness: Zone 6
Propagation: Seed or division, both in spring

Clump-forming perennial from Turkestan. Leaves spoon-shaped to elliptic, velvety, green. Flowerheads solitary, single, bright orange with yellow discs, in summer.

Erigeron
'Charity'
(Asteraceae/Compositae)

Common names: Fleabane
Height: 60cm (24in)
Spread: 45cm (18in)
Aspect: Sun
Soil: Well-drained, fertile, humus-rich
Hardiness: Zone 5
Propagation: Division, in spring

Clump-forming hybrid cultivar. Leaves mid-green, lance-shaped. Flowerheads lilac-pink with yellow discs, semi-double, in early and midsummer.

Erigeron compositus
(Asteraceae/Compositae)

Common name: Cutleaf daisy
Height: 15cm (6in)
Spread: 10cm (4in)
Aspect: Sun
Soil: Well-drained, fertile, humus-rich
Hardiness: Zone 5
Propagation: Seed or division, both in spring

Cushion-forming perennial. Leaves 3- or 4-ternate, lobed, hairy, grey-green. Yellow-centred, pale blue, white or pink, solitary, single flowerheads, in summer. Self-seeds.

Erigeron
'Dignity'
(Asteraceae/Compositae)

Common name: Fleabane
Height: 50cm. (20in.)
Spread: 45cm. (18in.)
Aspect: Sun
Soil: Well-drained, fertile, humus-rich
Hardiness: Zone 5
Propagation: Division, in spring

Hybrid fleabane cultivar with lance- to spoon-shaped leaves, and violet-mauve flowerheads with yellow centres in early and midsummer.

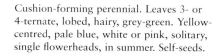

Erigeron
'Four Winds'
(Asteraceae/Compositae)

Common name: Fleabane
Height: 50cm (20in)
Spread: 45cm (18in)
Aspect: Sun
Soil: Well-drained, fertile, humus-rich
Hardiness: Zone 5
Propagation: Division, in spring

Hybrid cultivar with lance-shaped, mid-green leaves, and solitary, single flowerheads of strong pink with yellow centres, in early and midsummer.

Erigeron glaucus
(Asteraceae/Compositae)

Common name: Beach aster
Height: 30cm (12in)
Spread: 45cm (18in)
Aspect: Sun
Soil: Well-drained, fertile, humus-rich
Hardiness: Zone 3
Propagation: Seed or division, both in spring

Coastal species. Leaves lance-shaped to obovate, glaucous green. Flowerheads solitary, semi-double, pale mauve with yellow discs, late spring to midsummer.

Erigeron karvinskianus
A.G.M.
(Asteraceae/Compositae)

Common names: None
Height: 30cm (1ft)
Spread: 1m (3ft)
Aspect: Sun
Soil: Well-drained, fertile, humus-rich
Hardiness: Zone 7
Propagation: Seed or division, both in spring

Vigorous, spreading; excellent wall plant. Leaves hairy, grey-green, lance-shaped. Flowerheads single, small, white turning pink, summer to early winter in mild areas.

Erigeron philadelphicus
(Asteraceae/Compositae)

Common names: None
Height: 60cm (2ft)
Spread: 30cm (1ft)
Aspect: Sun
Soil: Well-drained, moist
Hardiness: Zone 2
Propagation: Seed or division, both in spring

Species from northern U.S.A. and Canada. Leaves obovate, hairy, scalloped, green. Flowerheads solitary, single, rose-lilac, with a yellow disc.

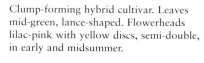

Erigeron
'Rotes Meer'
(Asteraceae/Compositae)

Common names: None
Height: 60cm (2ft)
Spread: 60cm (2ft)
Aspect: Sun
Soil: Well-drained, fertile, humus-rich
Hardiness: Zone 5
Propagation: Division, in autumn

Hybrid fleabane cultivar with semi-double flowerheads of a deep red with yellow centres, borne in summer. Leaves are spoon-shaped.

Erigeron
'Schneewitschen'
(Asteraceae/Compositae)

Common names: None
Height: 70cm (28in)
Spread: 60cm (24in)
Aspect: Sun
Soil: Well-drained, fertile, humus-rich
Hardiness: Zone 3
Propagation: Division, in spring

A hybrid garden cultivar bearing single flowerheads of purest white, with yellow centres, in summer. Good in a herbaceous or a mixed border.

Erigeron
'Serenity'
(Asteraceae/Compositae)

Common names: None
Height: 75cm (30in)
Spread: 45cm (18in)
Aspect: Sun
Soil: Well-drained, fertile, humus-rich
Hardiness: Zone 5
Propagation: Division, in spring

Hybrid cultivar of lax habit, bearing semi-double flowerheads of violet-mauve, in corymbs, in early and midsummer. Leaves are lance-shaped.

Erinus alpinus
A.G.M.
(Scrophulariaceae)

Common name: Fairy foxglove
Height: 10cm (4in)
Spread: 10cm (4in)
Aspect: Sun or half shade
Soil: Well-drained
Hardiness: Zone 6
Propagation: Seed, in autumn

Semi-evergreen. Inverse-lance-shaped, sticky leaves. Flowers 2-lipped, pink, purple or white in short racemes, late spring to early summer. May repeat-flower if dead-headed.

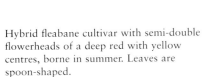

Eriogonum umbellatum
(Polygonaceae)

Common name: Sulphur flower
Height: 30cm (1ft)
Spread: 1m (3ft)
Aspect: Sun
Soil: Well-drained, gritty
Hardiness: Zone 7
Propagation: Seed, in autumn; cuttings, in spring

Leaves in rosettes, ovate, mid-green, white undersides. Yellow flowers turning red, in umbels, in summer. Hates winter wet. Not always free-flowering. Trim after flowering.

Eriogonum umbellatum
var. *torreyanum*
(Polygonaceae)

Common name: Sulphur flower
Height: 30cm (1ft)
Spread: 1m (3ft)
Aspect: Sun
Soil: Well-drained, gritty
Hardiness: Zone 7
Propagation: Seed, in autumn; cuttings, in spring

Subshrub from U.S.A. Leaves ovate, shiny, dark green. Flowers in umbels, yellow, with pronounced bracts, in summer. Free-flowering, in contrast to the species.

Eriophyllum lanatum
(Asteraceae/Compositae)

Common names: Golden yarrow; woolly sunflower
Height: 60 cm (2ft)
Spread: 60cm (2ft)
Aspect: Sun
Soil: Well-drained, gritty
Hardiness: Zone 5
Propagation: Seed, in autumn; division, in spring

Perennial from W. North America. Leaves divided, white-woolly, silver-grey. Flowers solitary or in corymbs, yellow, spring to summer. Can be invasive.

Erodium carvifolium
(Geraniaceae)

Common names: Heron's bill; stork's bill
Height: 35cm (14in)
Spread: 20cm (8in)
Aspect: Sun
Soil: Well-drained, gritty, humus-rich
Hardiness: Zone 7
Propagation: Seed, when ripe; division, in spring

Long-flowering plant from Spain. Leaves basal, 2-pinnate, green with white midrib. Flowers in umbels of up to 10, deep pink, over a long period in spring and summer.

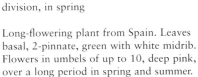

ERODIUM (Geraniaceae)
Heron's bill • Stork's bill

A genus of some 60 species distributed across Europe, Asia, North Africa, North and South America and Australia. Most are perennials, but the genus also includes annuals and both deciduous and evergreen subshrubs. Most are reliably hardy, but one or two are less so; all are drought-tolerant. *Erodium* are invaluable garden plants, on account of their long flowering season, which stretches from spring to late summer, and their handsome foliage. The leaves may be lobed, pinnatisect, or pinnate. The flowers are usually borne in umbels, but sometimes singly, and range in colour from pink to purple, often with darker veins or markings, as well as some yellow or white examples. They are five-petalled and geranium-like, but can be distinguished by their stamens: *Erodium* have five stamens, whereas geraniums have ten. Some types are too small for a border and are best grown in a rock garden, but others are excellent plants for the front of the border. All make good plants for coastal gardens. They are easy to cultivate, provided they have a sunny position and good drainage, and they do not require staking. They do have a tendency to self-seed, so should be cut back after flowering if this is not desired.

Erodium
'Fran's Choice'
(Geraniaceae)

Common names: Heron's bill; stork's bill
Height: 20cm (8in)
Spread: 20cm (8in)
Aspect: Sun
Soil: Well-drained, gritty, humus-rich
Hardiness: Zone 7
Propagation: Seed, when ripe; division, in spring

Hybrid, clump-forming cultivar. Leaves pinnatisect, toothed, mid-green. Flowers borne in short terminal umbels, pink, in summer.

Erodium manescaui
(Geraniaceae)

Common names: Heron's bill; stork's bill
Height: 45cm (18in)
Spread: 20cm (8in)
Aspect: Sun
Soil: Well-drained, gritty, humus-rich
Hardiness: Zone 6
Propagation: Seed, when ripe; division, in spring

Clump-forming. Leaves toothed, hairy, mid-green, pinnate; lobes ovate. Flowers in long-stemmed umbels, magenta, upper two petals spotted, spring to summer.

Erodium
'Merstham Pink'
(Geraniaceae)

Common names: Heron's bill; stork's bill
Height: 22cm (9in)
Spread: 25cm (10in)
Aspect: Sun
Soil: Well-drained, gritty, humus-rich
Hardiness: Zone 6
Propagation: Division, in spring

Hybrid cultivar; superb wall plant. Leaves fern-like or carrot-like, dark green. Flowers in umbels, pink, over a long period, in summer to autumn.

Erodium pelargoniiflorum
(Geraniaceae)

Common names: Heron's bill; stork's bill
Height: 30cm (1ft)
Spread: 30cm (1ft)
Aspect: Sun
Soil: Well-drained, gritty, humus-rich
Hardiness: Zone 6
Propagation: Seed, when ripe; division, in spring

Species from Anatolia. Leaves mid-green, pelargonium-like, ovate-cordate, lobed. Flowers in umbels, white, upper two petals spotted purple, over a long period, summer.

ERYNGIUM (Apiaceae/Umbelliferae)
Sea holly

A genus of over 200 species, which can be split into "old-world" and "new-world". The species from dry regions of North Africa, Turkey, Asia, China and Korea are usually tap-rooted, and have rounded leaves and congested, white or blue flowerheads with conspicuous bracts. Those from wet regions of South America and warm regions of Central and North America are usually fibrous-rooted and evergreen, with long, narrow leaves and flowers of greenish-white or purple. They are excellent border plants, especially for coastal gardens, and can be long-flowering. Eryngiums usually have spiny, silver-veined leaves in basal rosettes; wear gloves when handling. The flowerhead is a rounded, crowded head of small, stalkless flowers, like that of a thistle. Flowers dry well, and are useful for flower-arranging either fresh or dry. Eryngiums like a position in sun and well-drained soil, which should not be too rich, or they will make soft growth and suffer from powdery mildew. They attract bees and butterflies, and are low in allergens. They dislike transplantation, so should be sited carefully in the first instance. Some will self-seed, especially *E. giganteum*, and some require staking.

Eryngium agavifolium
(Apiaceae/Umbelliferae)

Common name: Sea holly
Height: 1.5m (5ft)
Spread: 60cm (2ft)
Aspect: Sun
Soil: Moist, well-drained, fertile
Hardiness: Zone 7
Propagation: Seed, when ripe; division, in spring

Rosette-forming evergreen from Argentina. Leaves sword-shaped, toothed, glossy. Flowers in cylindrical umbels, greenish-white, bracts spiny or entire, late summer.

Eryngium alpinum
A.G.M.
(Apiaceae/Umbelliferae)

Common name: Sea holly
Height: 70cm (28in)
Spread: 45cm (18in)
Aspect: Sun
Soil: Well-drained to dry, poor, humus-rich
Hardiness: Zone 5
Propagation: Seed, when ripe; division, in spring

Tap-rooted European species. Basal leaves spiny and heart-shaped; stem, 3-lobed. Flowers in cylindrical umbels, steely-blue or white, with bracts, summer to autumn.

Eryngium alpinum
'Amethyst'
(Apiaceae/Umbelliferae)

Common name: Sea holly
Height: 70cm (28in)
Spread: 45cm (18in)
Aspect: Sun
Soil: Well-drained to dry, poor, humus-rich
Hardiness: Zone 5
Propagation: Seed, when ripe; division, in spring

Cloned selection of *E. alpinum*, in which the flowers are smaller and violet-blue. Is tap-rooted, so resents disturbance. Basal leaves spiny, heart-shaped; stem, 3-lobed.

Eryngium alpinum
'Slieve Donard'
(Apiaceae/Umbelliferae)

Common name: Sea holly
Height: 70cm (28in)
Spread: 45cm (18in)
Aspect: Sun
Soil: Well-drained to dry, poor, humus-rich
Hardiness: Zone 5
Propagation: Seed, when ripe; division, in spring

Cloned selection of *E. alpinum*, with flowers and bracts of creamy-green, in summer to autumn. Basal leaves spiny, heart-shaped; stem leaves, 3-lobed.

Eryngium bourgatii
(Apiaceae/Umbelliferae)

Common name: Sea holly
Height: 45cm (18in)
Spread: 30cm (12in)
Aspect: Sun
Soil: Well-drained to dry, poor, humus-rich
Hardiness: Zone 5
Propagation: Seed, when ripe; division, in spring

Tap-rooted species from the Pyrenees. Dark green, silver-veined, rounded, pinnatifid, spiny leaves. Flowers in cylindrical umbels, blue with silver bracts, mid- to late summer.

Eryngium bourgatii
'Picos'
(Apiaceae/Umbelliferae)

Common name: Sea holly
Height: 45cm (18in)
Spread: 30cm (12in)
Aspect: Sun
Soil: Well-drained to dry, poor, humus-rich
Hardiness: Zone 5
Propagation: Division, in spring

Cloned selection of *E. bourgatii*, with bright blue flowers and silver bracts in summer. Rounded, pinnatifid, spiny, dark green, silver-veined leaves. Very desirable.

Eryngium eburneum
(Apiaceae/Umbelliferae)

Common name: Sea holly
Height: 1.2m (4ft)
Spread: 30cm (1ft)
Aspect: Sun
Soil: Moist but well-drained, humus-rich, fertile
Hardiness: Zone 5
Propagation: Seed, when ripe; division, in spring

Evergreen from South America. Leaves in a rosette, narrow, linear, spiny, mid-green. Spherical umbels of grey-green flowers and bracts on branched stems, late summer.

Eryngium giganteum
A.G.M.
(Apiaceae/Umbelliferae)

Common name: Miss Willmott's ghost
Height: 90cm (3ft)
Spread: 30cm (1ft)
Aspect: Sun
Soil: Well-drained to dry, poor, humus-rich
Hardiness: Zone 5
Propagation: Seed when ripe

Short-lived or monocarpic species. Leaves heart-shaped, basal, and stem, ovate, spiny, silver-veined, mid-green. Branched umbels of steel-blue flowers with silver-grey bracts.

Eryngium horridum
(Apiaceae/Umbelliferae)

Common name: Sea holly
Height: 3m (10ft)
Spread: 1m (3ft)
Aspect: Sun
Soil: Moist but well-drained, fertile
Hardiness: Zone 5
Propagation: Seed, when ripe; division, in spring

Species from Brazil and Argentina. Leaves linear, arched, mid-green. Flowerheads spherical, on branching stems, in summer. Unspectacular, but unusual.

Eryngium × *oliverianum* A.G.M.
(Apiaceae/Umbelliferae)

Common name: Sea holly
Height: 90cm (36in)
Spread: 45cm (18in)
Aspect: Sun
Soil: Well-drained to dry, poor
Hardiness: Zone 5
Propagation: Division, in autumn

Tap-rooted, deciduous garden hybrid. Basal leaves ovate, 3-lobed, spiny, dark green; stem leaves 4- to 5-palmately lobed. Flowers and bracts silver-blue, summer to autumn.

Eryngium pandanifolium
(Apiaceae/Umbelliferae)

Common name: Sea holly
Height: 4m. (12ft.)
Spread: 2m. (6ft.)
Aspect: Sun
Soil: Moist, well-drained, fertile
Hardiness: Zone 8
Propagation: Seed when ripe; division in spring

Clump-forming species from Argentina and Brazil. Leaves linear, spiny, silver-green. Flowers brown-purple with dark bracts, in cylindrical umbels, late summer to autumn.

Eryngium proteiflorum
(Apiaceae/Umbelliferae)

Common name: Sea holly
Height: 90cm (3ft)
Spread: 60cm (2ft)
Aspect: Sun
Soil: Well-drained to dry, poor
Hardiness: Zone 8
Propagation: Seed, when ripe; division, in autumn

Tap-rooted evergreen from Mexico. Leaves in rosettes, linear, spiny-edged, silvery green. Flowers in cylindrical umbels, grey-blue, with spiny bracts, in spring.

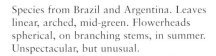

Eryngium × *tripartitum* A.G.M.
(Apiaceae/Umbelliferae)

Common name: Sea holly
Height: 90cm (36in)
Spread: 50cm (20in)
Aspect: Sun
Soil: Well-drained, poor
Hardiness: Zone 5
Propagation: Seed, when ripe; division, in spring

Tap-rooted Mediterranean species. Leaves ovate, 3-lobed, toothed, dark green. Violet-blue flowers with blue-grey bracts, in spherical umbels, in summer to autumn.

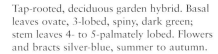

Erysimum alpinum syn. *E. heiraciifolium*
(Brassicaceae/Cruciferae)

Common name: Alpine wallflower
Height: 15cm (6in)
Spread: 15cm (6in)
Aspect: Sun
Soil: Well-drained, fertile
Hardiness: Zone 6
Propagation: Seed, in spring

Dwarf wallflower from Scandinavia, with lance-shaped, mid-green leaves and perfumed, sulphur-yellow flowers, borne in racemes in summer.

Erysimum 'Bowles Mauve' A.G.M.
(Brassicaceae/Cruciferae)

Common name: Wallflower
Height: 75cm (30in)
Spread: 60cm (24in)
Aspect: Sun
Soil: Well-drained, fertile
Hardiness: Zone 7
Propagation: Heeled softwood cuttings, in spring or summer.

Strong, evergreen, hybrid, woody subshrub. Leaves lance-shaped, grey-green. Mauve flowers in racemes on long stems, over a long period from early spring to summer.

Erysimum linifolium 'Variegatum'
(Brassicaceae/Cruciferae)

Common name: Wallflower
Height: 70cm (28in)
Spread: 25cm (10in)
Aspect: Sun
Soil: Well-drained, fertile
Hardiness: Zone 6
Propagation: Heeled softwood cuttings, in spring or summer

Mat-forming, woody evergreen with grey-green, white-variegated, narrow, linear to lance-shaped leaves. Lilac flowers in long racemes on long stems, spring to autumn.

Erysimum
'Orange Flame'
(Brassicaceae/Cruciferae)

Common name: Wallflower
Height: 10cm (4in)
Spread: 30cm (12in)
Aspect: Sun
Soil: Well-drained, fertile
Hardiness: Zone 7
Propagation: Heeled softwood cuttings, in spring or summer

Mat-forming, creeping, evergreen, hybrid perennial. Leaves inverse lance-shaped, dark green. Flowers in lax racemes, orange, from spring to autumn.

ERYTHRONIUM (Liliaceae)
Trout lily • Dog's tooth violet

There are some 22 clump-forming, bulbous species in this genus. They are found in open meadow and deciduous woodland habitats, distributed across Eurasia and North America, and as a consequence they are suited to a range of garden situations, from a rock garden or mixed border to a woodland planting. They are hardy, and grow well in acidic, moisture-retentive but well-drained conditions, in dappled half shade. The bulbs are tooth-like, with long points, and should be planted vertically in the autumn, quite deeply; there should be 12cm (5in) of soil above the top of the bulb. Bulbs should never be bought in the dry state, nor allowed to dry out when dividing established clumps, as they will give you only limited success at best, and they may not recover at all. The leaves are basal and invariably handsome, being glossy, green and often mottled, marbled or otherwise marked with bronze, maroon, or white. The nodding, bell- to hat-shaped flowers are borne singly or in clusters of up to ten, at the tops of erect, leafless stems. They have a delicate, charming appearance, with recurved tepals in shades of white, yellow, pink or purple, and prominent stamens. The only significant problem is attack by slugs and snails.

Erythronium californicum
'White Beauty' A.G.M.
(Liliaceae)

Common name: Trout lily
Height: 35cm (14in)
Spread: 10cm (4in)
Aspect: Half shade
Soil: Well-drained, acidic, humus-rich
Hardiness: Zone 5
Propagation: Division, after flowering

Cloned selection of a bulbous woodlander. Leaves elliptic, deep green, mottled cream. Flowers 1–3 per stem, pendent, cream, with white anthers and prominent stamens.

Erythronium dens-canis
A.G.M.
(Liliaceae)

Common name: Dog's tooth violet
Height: 15cm (6in)
Spread: 10cm (4in)
Aspect: Sun or half shade
Soil: Well-drained, acidic, humus-rich
Hardiness: Zone 3
Propagation: Division, after flowering

Eurasian species. Leaves elliptic-oblong, mid-green, marbled brown. Flowers downturned, solitary, pink, white or lilac with purple anthers, in spring.

Erythronium grandiflorum
(Liliaceae)

Common name: Avalanche lily
Height: 30cm (12in)
Spread: 10cm (4in)
Aspect: Half shade
Soil: Well-drained, acidic, humus-rich
Hardiness: Zone 3
Propagation: Division, after flowering

Species from the western U.S.A. Leaves elliptic, bright green. Flowers 1–3 per stem, golden-yellow, with distinctive stigmas and anthers, in spring.

Erythronium helenae
(Liliaceae)

Common name: Trout lily
Height: 35cm (14in)
Spread: 15cm (6in)
Aspect: Half shade
Soil: Well-drained, acidic, humus-rich
Hardiness: Zone 5
Propagation: Division, after flowering

A species from California, closely related to *E. oregonum* and *E. californicum*. Leaves elliptic, bright green. Flowers cream, with yellow centres, in spring.

Erythronium
'Pagoda' A.G.M.
(Liliaceae)

Common name: Trout lily
Height: 35cm (14in)
Spread: 10cm (4in)
Aspect: Half shade
Soil: Well-drained, acidic, humus-rich
Hardiness: Zone 5
Propagation: Division, after flowering

A vigorous hybrid cultivar. Leaves elliptic, deep green, mottled. Flowers, up to 10 per stem, are yellow, with dark yellow anthers, in spring.

Dog's tooth violet, Erythronium dens-canis, *is a low-growing plant with beautifully marked leaves and delicate blooms.*

Erythronium tuolumnense A.G.M.
(Liliaceae)

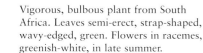

Common name: Trout lily
Height: 35cm (14in)
Spread: 8cm (3in)
Aspect: Half shade
Soil: Well-drained, acidic, humus-rich
Hardiness: Zone 5
Propagation: Division, after flowering

Vigorous species from C. California. Leaves elliptic, pale green. Flowers bright yellow, strongly recurved, with yellow anthers, up to 7 on a stem, in spring.

Eucomis autumnalis
(Hyacinthaceae/Liliaceae)

Common names: Pineapple flower; pineapple lily
Height: 30cm (12in)
Spread: 20cm (8in)
Aspect: Sun
Soil: Well-drained, dry in winter, fertile
Hardiness: Zone 8
Propagation: Offsets in spring

Bulbous, with a basal rosette of strap-like, broad, wavy-edged leaves. Small, starry, greenish-white flowers in racemes topped by spiky bracts, late summer to autumn.

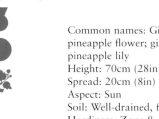

Eucomis bicolor
(Hyacinthaceae/Liliaceae)

Common names: Pineapple flower; pineapple lily
Height: 60cm (24in)
Spread: 20cm (8in)
Aspect: Sun
Soil: Well-drained, fertile
Hardiness: Zone 8
Propagation: Offsets in spring

Bulbous plant. Leaves broad straps, wavy-edged, bright green. Flowers in racemes, topped by pineapple-like, pink-edged green bracts, in late summer and autumn.

Eucomis pallidiflora
(Hyacithaceae/Liliaceae)

Common names: Giant pineapple flower; giant pineapple lily
Height: 70cm (28in)
Spread: 20cm (8in)
Aspect: Sun
Soil: Well-drained, fertile
Hardiness: Zone 8
Propagation: Offsets in spring

Vigorous, bulbous plant from South Africa. Leaves semi-erect, strap-shaped, wavy-edged, green. Flowers in racemes, greenish-white, in late summer.

Eupatorium album
(Asteraceae/Compositae)

Common name: Hemp agrimony
Height: 1m (3ft)
Spread: 30cm (1ft)
Aspect: Sun or half shade
Soil: Moist
Hardiness: Zone 4
Propagation: Seed or division, both in spring

Coarse woodland or waterside plant from the eastern U.S.A. Leaves oblong to lance-shaped, toothed, mid-green. Tubular, white flowers in corymbs.

Eupatorium purpureum
(Asteraceae/Compositae)

Common names: Joe Pye weed
Height: 2m (6ft)
Spread: 1m (3ft)
Aspect: Sun or half shade
Soil: Moist
Hardiness: Zone 4
Propagation: Seed or division, both in spring

Clump-forming plant. Leaves lance-shaped, toothed, mid-green tinged purple. Tubular flowers in terminal panicles, pink, from midsummer to early autumn.

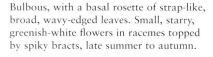

EUPHORBIA (Euphorbiaceae)
Spurge

A vast genus containing over 2000 species, from annuals and perennials to succulents and shrubs, from many habitats in many parts of the world. As a consequence, their cultural requirements differ widely. They range from extremely ? hardy to tender, and may be evergreen, semi-evergreen or deciduous. Nearly all bear highly characteristic "cyathia", small cups of long-lasting bracts that may be green, yellow, red, brown or purple, cupping nectaries and insignificant flowers with much-reduced parts. In the perennial and shrubby species, these are carried in dense clusters. The leaves are very varied, and often ephemeral. Gardeners tend to be polarised into enthusiasm or antipathy towards this genus. Some species are too invasive to be included in the garden, especially *E. cyparissias* (Zone 4) and *E. pseudovirgata* (Zone 6). Others, such as *E. lathyris* (Zone 6), *E. hybernia* (Zone 7), *E. coralloides* (Zone 8) and *E. wallichii* (Zone 7) will self-seed prolifically. All euphorbias resent disturbance, so site them carefully at the outset. All are useful for flower-arranging, in the fresh and the dry state, but it must be noted that all parts of euphorbias are poisonous and bleed a skin-irritant milky sap, and the flowers are also highly allergenic.

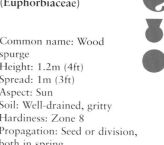

Euphorbia amygdaloides
(Euphorbiaceae)

Common name: Wood spurge
Height: 80cm (32in)
Spread: 30cm (12in)
Aspect: Half shade
Soil: Moist, humus-rich
Hardiness: Zone 7
Propagation: Seed or division, both in spring

Evergreen from Europe, Turkey and the Caucasus. Leaves obovate, matt, green. Cymes of green-yellow involucres and cyathia from mid-spring to early summer.

***Euphorbia amygdaloides* 'Purpurea'**
(Euphorbiaceae)

Common name: Wood spurge
Height: 80cm (32in)
Spread: 30cm (12in)
Aspect: Half shade
Soil: Moist, humus-rich
Hardiness: Zone 7
Propagation: Seed or division, both in spring

A variant of the species with obovate, purple leaves. Involucres and cyathia are acid yellow, in cymes from mid-spring to early summer.

***Euphorbia amygdaloides* var. *robbiae* A.G.M.**
(Euphorbiaceae)

Common name: Mrs. Robb's bonnet
Height: 80cm (32in)
Spread: 30cm (12in)
Aspect: Sun or half shade
Soil: Moist
Hardiness: Zone 7
Propagation: Division, in spring

A select form of *E. amygdaloides*. Spreads by rhizomes, and may be invasive. Leaves broad, leathery, shiny green. Cymes to 18cm (7in) tall, less dense than in species.

Euphorbia characias
(Euphorbiaceae)

Common name: Wood spurge
Height: 1.2m (4ft)
Spread: 1m (3ft)
Aspect: Sun
Soil: Well-drained, gritty
Hardiness: Zone 8
Propagation: Seed or division, both in spring

Evergreen Mediterranean subshrub. Leaves linear, grey-green. Cyathia yellow-green, cupped by green involucres, in dense terminal cymes in spring and summer.

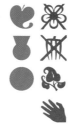

***Euphorbia characias* subsp. *characias* A.G.M.**
(Euphorbiaceae)

Common name: Wood spurge
Height: 1.2m (4ft)
Spread: 1m (3ft)
Aspect: Sun
Soil: Well-drained, gritty
Hardiness: Zone 8
Propagation: Division, in spring

A variant of *E. characias* in which the nectaries in the cyathia are dark reddish-brown, with notched or short horns. Leaves are linear, grey-green.

***Euphorbia characias* subsp. *wulfenii* A.G.M.**
(Euphorbiaceae)

Common names: None
Height: 1.2m (4ft)
Spread: 1m (3ft)
Aspect: Sun
Soil: Well-drained, gritty
Hardiness: Zone 7
Propagation: Division, in spring

Popular variant of *E. characias* in which the cyathia and nectaries are yellow-green. The leaves are linear and grey-green, as in the species.

***Euphorbia characias* subsp. *wulfenii* 'Variegata'**
(Euphorbiaceae)

Common names: None
Height: 1.2m (4ft)
Spread: 1m (3ft)
Aspect: Sun
Soil: Well-drained, gritty
Hardiness: Zone 7
Propagation: Division, in spring

Cultivar of *E. characias* subsp. *wulfenii* in which the leaves are edged with cream. The cyathia and nectaries are yellow-green, the involucres green.

***Euphorbia cyparissias* 'Fens Ruby'**
(Euphorbiaceae)

Common name: Cypress spurge
Height: 40cm (16in)
Spread: 40cm (16in)
Aspect: Sun
Soil: Well-drained
Hardiness: Zone 4
Propagation: Division, in spring

Selected form of a rhizomatous, invasive species from Europe. Leaves feathery, linear, blue-green. Cyathia and involucres yellow-green, in terminal cymes.

Euphorbia dulcis
'Chameleon'
(Euphorbiaceae)

Common names: Milkweed; spurge
Height: 30cm (1ft)
Spread: 30cm (1ft)
Aspect: Shade
Soil: Moist, humus-rich
Hardiness: Zone 5
Propagation: Division, in spring

Form of a rhizomatous species from Europe. Leaves inverse lance-shaped, purple. Cyathia and involucres yellow-green, tinted purple.

Euphorbia griffithii
'Fireglow'
(Euphorbiaceae)

Common names: Milkweed; spurge
Height: 90cm (3ft)
Spread: 60cm (2ft)
Aspect: Half shade
Soil: Moist, humus-rich
Hardiness: Zone 5
Propagation: Division, in spring

Selected form of a rhizomatous species. Leaves lance-shaped, dark green, midribs red; good in autumn. Flowers, early summer in cymes; involucres red, cyathia yellow.

Euphorbia polychroma
A.G.M.
(Euphorbiaceae)

Common name: Spurge
Height: 40cm (16in)
Spread: 60cm (24in)
Aspect: Sun or half shade
Soil: Well-drained, humus-rich
Hardiness: Zone 6
Propagation: Seed or division, both in spring

Herbaceous species from Europe to Turkey. Leaves obovate, dark green. Flowers in terminal cymes, cyathia yellow, involucres yellow-green, mid-spring to midsummer.

Euphorbia polychroma
'Candy'
(Euphorbiaceae)

Common names: Milkweed; spurge
Height: 40cm (16in)
Spread: 60cm (24in)
Aspect: Sun or half shade
Soil: Well-drained, humus-rich
Hardiness: Zone 6
Propagation: Seed or division, both in spring

A variant of the species with stems and obovate leaves of dark purple. Cyathia and involucres a paler yellow. Flowers in terminal cymes, mid-spring to midsummer.

Fascicularia bicolor
(Bromeliaceae)

Common names: None
Height: 45cm (18in)
Spread: 60cm (24in)
Aspect: Sun
Soil: Sharply drained, poor
Hardiness: Zone 8
Propagation: Seed or division, both in spring

Rosetted, evergreen, terrestrial bromeliad. Leaves arching, long, tough, spiny, green; inner leaves turn red as corymb of blue flowers and white bracts appears in summer.

Felicia petiolata
(Asteraceae/Compositae)

Common name: Blue daisy
Height: 1m (3ft)
Spread: 1m (3ft)
Aspect: Sun
Soil: Sharply drained, fertile
Hardiness: Zone 9
Propagation: Stem-tip cuttings, in autumn

Prostrate plant from South Africa. Leaves lanceolate, green. Flowers daisy-like, pink or white, with yellow centres, over long periods in summer. Not for damp climates.

Ferula communis
(Apiaceae/Umbelliferae)

Common names: Giant fennel
Height: To 3m (10ft)
Spread: 60cm (2ft)
Aspect: Sun
Soil: Well-drained, fertile
Hardiness: Zone 8
Propagation: Seed, when ripe

Tap-rooted, inedible plant. Leaves green, malodorous, finely divided. Slow to flower; umbels of yellow, white or purple in summer. *(See also* Foeniculum *p.123).*

Festuca glauca
'Elijah Blue'
(Graminae/Poaceae)

Common name: Blue fescue
Height: 30cm (12in)
Spread: 25cm (10in)
Aspect: Sun
Soil: Well-drained to dry
Hardiness: Zone 5
Propagation: Division, in spring

Evergreen grass. Leaves blue-green, narrow, linear. Flowers brownish-green, in dense panicles, in early and midsummer. Regular division keeps foliage colour good.

Festuca ovina
'Tetra Gold'
(Graminae/Poaceae)

Common name: Fescue
Height: 30cm (12in)
Spread: 25cm (10in)
Aspect: Sun
Soil: Dry, well-drained
Hardiness: Zone 5
Propagation: Division, in spring

Hybrid evergreen grass. Leaves narrow, linear, yellow-green. Dense panicle of brown flowers, in early and midsummer. Regular division keeps leaf colour brilliant.

Filipendula purpurea
A.G.M.
(Rosaceae)

Common name: Dropwort; meadowsweet
Height: 1.2m (4ft)
Spread: 60cm (2ft)
Aspect: Sun or half shade
Soil: Moist, well-drained, fertile, humus-rich
Hardiness: Zone 6
Propagation: Seed or division, both in autumn or spring

Perennial from Japan. Leaves toothed, pinnate, leaflets 5- to 7-lobed, green. Flowers perfumed, red fading to pink, in crowded corymbs, in mid- to late summer.

Filipendula ulmaria
'Variegata'
(Rosaceae)

Common names: Dropwort; meadowsweet
Height: 90cm (3ft)
Spread: 60cm (2ft)
Aspect: Sun or half shade
Soil: Moist, well-drained, fertile, humus-rich
Hardiness: Zone 2
Propagation: Seed or division, both in autumn or spring

Species from Europe and W. Asia. Leaves pinnate, veined, inverse lance-shaped, green, striped or marked yellow. Flowers in dense, branching corymbs, creamy-white, summer.

Filipendula vulgaris
(Rosaceae)

Common name: Dropwort
Height: 60cm (24in)
Spread: 45cm (18in)
Aspect: Sun
Soil: Dry, well-drained
Hardiness: Zone 3
Propagation: Seed or division, both in autumn or spring

Rhizomatous species from Eurasia. Leaves pinnate, fern-like, toothed, dark green. Flowers perfumed, in loose corymbs, white, in early and midsummer.

Foeniculum vulgare
'Purpureum'
(Apiaceae/Umbelliferae)

Common name: Fennel (edible)
Height: 1.8m (6ft)
Spread: 60cm (2ft)
Aspect: Sun
Soil: Moist, well-drained, fertile
Hardiness: Zone 5
Propagation: Seed, in warmth or *in situ*, in spring

Deep-rooting herb from S. Europe. Leaves aromatic, bronze-purple, hair-like, finely cut. Flowers tiny, yellow, on branching stems, in compound umbels, mid- to late summer.

Fragaria
'Lipstick'
(Rosaceae)

Common name: Strawberry
Height: 15cm (6in)
Spread: Indefinite
Aspect: Sun or half shade
Soil: Moist, well-drained, fertile
Hardiness: Zone 5
Propagation: Plantlets from runners, at any time

Sterile, stoloniferous ground cover. Leaves 3-palmate, lobes toothed, broad, ovate. Flowers single, in cymes, cerise, spring to autumn. Evergreen in mild areas.

Fragaria
'Pink Panda'®
(Rosaceae)

Common name: Strawberry
Height: 15cm (6in)
Spread: Indefinite
Aspect: Sun or half shade
Soil: Moist, well-drained, fertile
Hardiness: Zone 5
Propagation: Plantlets from runners, at any time

Stoloniferous, sterile ground cover. Leaves 3-palmate, lobes broad, ovate, toothed, bright green, evergreen in mild areas. Pink, single flowers in cymes, spring to autumn.

Fragaria vesca
(Rosaceae)

Common name: Alpine strawberry
Height: 20cm (8in)
Spread: Indefinite
Aspect: Sun or half shade
Soil: Moist, well-drained, fertile
Hardiness: Zone 5
Propagation: Plantlets from runners, at any time

Stoloniferous ground cover species. Leaves 3-palmate, lobes ovate, toothed, bright green. Flowers in cymes, white, followed by small, red, edible fruits.

An unusual and impressive plant, Fritillaria imperialis *bears drooping flowers and a crown of leaves on a tall stem.*

Francoa sonchifolia
(Saxifragaceae)

Common name: Bridal wreath
Height: 1m (3ft)
Spread: 45cm (18in)
Aspect: Sun or half shade
Soil: Moist, well-drained, humus-rich
Hardiness: Zone 7
Propagation: Seed or division, both in spring

Evergreen perennial from Chile. Leaves in a basal rosette, hairy, broad, deeply lobed, green. Flowers in tall, compact racemes, pink, with deep pink marks, in summer.

Francoa sonchifolia
Rodgerson's form
(Saxifragaceae)

Common names: Bridal wreath
Height: 1m (3ft)
Spread: 45cm (18in)
Aspect: Sun or half shade
Soil: Moist, well-drained, humus-rich
Hardiness: Zone 7
Propagation: Seed or division, both in spring

Selected form of this evergreen woodlander from Chile. Basal rosette of hairy, broad, deeply lobed leaves. Tall flowering raceme of dark pink flowers.

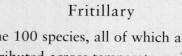

FRITILLARIA (Liliaceae)
Fritillary

A genus of some 100 species, all of which are bulbous perennials, distributed across temperate regions of the northern hemisphere. They are found especially in south-western Asia, the Mediterranean area and western North America, and come from a wide range of habitats, and consequently vary in their cultural requirements, but all are hardy. Fritillaries range in size from diminutive species, suitable only for the rock garden, to tall plants, eminently suitable for beds or borders, and woodland species. However, some species require more particular conditions, which in wet regions can be met only by growing them in a bulb frame or alpine house; the smaller species are for the dedicated exhibitor. The fragile bulbs require careful handling. The leaves are for the greater part lance-shaped or linear. The flowers are usually pendulous, and tubular to bell- or saucer-shaped, with 6 tepals. They are often marked with a distinctive checked, or "tessellated", pattern. Flowers are borne singly or in terminal racemes or umbels; in some types, most notably *F. imperialis*, there is a cluster of leaf-like bracts above the flowers. Unfortunately, nearly all fritillaries have a distinctly unpleasant smell.

Fritillaria acmopetala
A.G.M.
(Liliaceae)

Common name: Fritillary
Height: 40cm (16in)
Spread: 8cm (3in)
Aspect: Sun
Soil: Well-drained, fertile
Hardiness: Zone 7
Propagation: Offsets, in summer; seed, gathered in autumn, kept cold until spring, then sown in warmth

Bulbous perennial from E. Mediterranean. Leaves linear, blue-green. Flowers bell-shaped, pendent, pale green to brown, in late spring.

Fritillaria hermonis
subsp. *amana*
(Liliaceae)

Common name: Fritillary
Height: 30cm (12in)
Spread: 7cm (3in)
Aspect: Sun
Soil: Sharply drained, fertile
Hardiness: Zone 8
Propagation: Offsets, in summer; seed, gathered in autumn, kept cold until spring, then sown in warmth

Bulbous plant from the Lebanon to Turkey. Leaves lance-shaped, glaucous grey-green. Flowers single or paired, pendent bells, green, tessellated brown or purple, spring.

Fritillaria imperialis
(Liliaceae)

Common name: Crown imperial
Height: 1.2m (4ft)
Spread: 30cm (1ft)
Aspect: Sun
Soil: Well-drained, dry in summer, limy, fertile
Hardiness: Zone 4
Propagation: Offsets, after foliage dies down

Handsome, bulbous species. Leaves lance-shaped, in whorls. Flowers in umbels, pendent, orange, crowned by leaf-like bracts, late spring. Plant 20cm (8in) deep.

Fritillaria imperialis
'Maxima Lutea' A.G.M.
(Liliaceae)

Common name: Yellow crown imperial
Height: 1.2m (4ft)
Spread: 30cm (12in)
Aspect: Sun
Soil: Well-drained, dry in summer, limy, fertile
Hardiness: Zone 4
Propagation: Offsets, after foliage dies down

Variant of the species with yellow flowers, pendent, in umbels, crowned by leaf-like bracts, late spring. Leaves lance-shaped, in whorls. Plant 20cm (8in) deep.

Fritillaria imperialis
'Rubra'
(Liliaceae)

Common name: Crown imperial
Height: 1.2m (4ft)
Spread: 30cm (1ft)
Aspect: Sun
Soil: Well-drained, limy, fertile
Hardiness: Zone 4
Propagation: Offsets, after foliage dies down

Very handsome, a crown of leaf-like bracts on top of the red flower, but demanding; given sun, lime, potash, and deep planting, it may flower. Leaves lance-shaped.

Fritillaria meleagris
A.G.M.
(Liliaceae)

Common name: Snake's head fritillary
Height: 30cm (12in)
Spread: 10cm. (4in)
Aspect: Sun or half shade
Soil: Humus-rich
Hardiness: Zone 4
Propagation: Offsets, after foliage dies down

Bulbous Eurasian species. Leaves grey-green, linear. Flowers pendent, solitary or paired bells, white or purple, with bold tesselation, spring. Also shown is F. *alba*, A.G.M.

Fritillaria michailovskyi
A.G.M.
(Liliaceae)

Common name: Fritillary
Height: 15cm (6in)
Spread: 5cm (2in)
Aspect: Sun
Soil: Sharply drained, dry during dormancy, fertile
Hardiness: Zone 7
Propagation: Offsets, after foliage dies down

Handsome species from Turkey. Leaves lance-shaped, mid-green. Flowers pendent bells, purple-brown, yellow-edged tepals, in umbels in late spring.

Fritillaria persica
(Liliaceae)

Common name: Persian fritillary
Height: 1m (36in)
Spread: 10cm (4in)
Aspect: Sun
Soil: Well-drained, gritty, fertile
Hardiness: Zone 5
Propagation: Offsets, after foliage dies down

Robust bulbous species from Turkey, best in hot, dry areas. Leaves lance-shaped, glaucous green. Flowers purple or brown-green, pendent bells, in racemes, in spring.

Fritillaria pudica
(Liliaceae)

Common name: Yellow fritillary
Height: 15cm (6in)
Spread: 5cm (2in)
Aspect: Sun
Soil: Well-drained, dry during dormancy, fertile
Hardiness: Zone 6
Propagation: Offsets, after foliage has died down

Bulbous species from North America. Mid-green, lance-shaped leaves. Flowers solitary or paired, pendent bells, yellow or orange-yellow, in early spring. Dislikes wet.

FUCHSIA (Onagraceae)
Fuchsia

A genus of subshrubs from Central and South America and New Zealand, of only 100 or so species, but with over 8000 hybrids in cultivation. They are mostly deciduous and mostly tender, but some are hardy, and some are evergreen, especially in warm regions. They are happy in any soil that is reliably moist, and have a flowering season from midsummer to autumn. The flowers are handsome, and unique. They are pendent, in terminal clusters, and tubular or bell-shaped, with long tubes, widely spread sepals, and below these a skirt of petals; these may be of a similar colour, or of different colours. The number of petals varies; 4 in single-flowered types, between 5 and 7 in semi-double varieties, and more than 8 in fully double varieties. The group derived from *Fuchsia triphylla* is single-flowered, with very long tubes. Fuchsias in cold areas need the warmest corner of the garden; even then, frost will kill off much of the top growth in winter. In very cold areas, give them a winter mulch to protect from frost. They are excellent plants for mixed beds or borders, or hanging baskets, but will not grow under trees. Trailing types are good for baskets. A few are grown for their foliage value, rather than their flowers; all have berries after flowering.

Fuchsia
'Bicentennial'
(Onagraceae)

Common names: None
Height: 45cm (18in)
Spread: 60cm (24in)
Aspect: Sun or half shade
Soil: Moist, well-drained
Hardiness: Zone 9
Propagation: Softwood cuttings, in spring

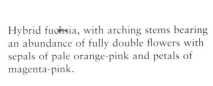

Hybrid fuchsia, with arching stems bearing an abundance of fully double flowers with sepals of pale orange-pink and petals of magenta-pink.

Fuchsia
'Genii' A.G.M.
(Onagraceae)

Common names: None
Height: 90cm (3ft)
Spread: 90cm (3ft)
Aspect: Sun or half shade
Soil: Moist, well-drained
Hardiness: Zone 9
Propagation: Softwood cuttings, in spring

Hybrid fuchsia grown principally for its foliage value. Leaves broadly ovate, lime-green. Flowers small, single, tubes and sepals red, corolla purple.

Fuchsia
'Coralle' A.G.M.
(Onagraceae)

Common names: None
Height: 90cm (3ft)
Spread: 60cm (2ft)
Aspect: Sun or half shade
Soil: Well-drained, moist
Hardiness: Zone 9
Propagation: Softwood cuttings, in spring

Upright Triphylla group hybrid. Olive-green leaves. Flowers in terminal clusters on strong stems; long, tapering orange tubes, salmon-pink sepals and corolla.

Fuchsia
'Madame Cornélissen' A.G.M. (Onagraceae)

Common names: None
Height: 90cm (3ft)
Spread: 30cm (1ft)
Aspect: Sun or half shade
Soil: Moist, well-drained
Hardiness: Zone6
Propagation: Softwood cuttings, in spring

Strong, upright hybrid fuchsia. Medium-sized, semi-double or double flowers have red tubes, recurved red sepals, and a white corolla, from midsummer to late autumn.

Fuchsia magellanica
'Versicolor' A.G.M.
(Onagraceae)

Common names: Ladies' ear-drops
Height: 1m (3ft)
Spread: 1.5m (5ft)
Aspect: Sun or half shade
Soil: Moist, well-drained
Hardiness: Zone 6
Propagation: Softwood cuttings, in spring

Species fuchsia. Leaves copper in the early season, grey-green with pink tips later. Flowers small, with red tubes, red, wide-spreading sepals, and purple corollas.

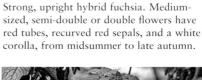

Fuchsia
'Phénoménal'
(Onagraceae)

Common names: None
Height: 30cm (1ft)
Spread: 30cm (1ft)
Aspect: Sun or half shade
Soil: Moist, well-drained
Hardiness: Zone 8
Propagation: Softwood cuttings, in spring

Hybrid fuchsia with very large, double flowers. Tube and sepals red, corolla mauve-purple. Long flowering, from summer to late autumn.

Fuchsia
'Reading Show'
(Onagraceae)

Common names: None
Height: 30cm (1ft)
Spread: 30cm (1ft)
Aspect: Sun or half shade
Soil: Moist, well-drained
Hardiness: Zone 8
Propagation: Softwood cuttings, in spring

Long-flowering hybrid fuchsia. Very large, double flowers, with red tube and sepals and a deep blue corolla with a red base, from summer to late autumn.

Fuchsia splendens
A.G.M.
(Onagraceae)

Common names: None
Height: 2m (6ft)
Spread: 1m (3ft)
Aspect: Sun or half shade
Soil: Moist, well-drained
Hardiness: Zone 9
Propagation: Seed, in warmth in spring; softwood cuttings, in spring

Species from Mexico and Costa Rica. Ovate, toothed, hairy, green leaves. Small, solitary flowers; tubes broad and orange, sepals green with a red base, petals green.

Fuchsia
'Thalia' A.G.M.
(Onagraceae)

Common names: None
Height: 90cm (3ft)
Spread: 90cm (3ft)
Aspect: Sun
Soil: Moist, well-drained
Hardiness: Zone 9
Propagation: Softwood cuttings, in spring

Triphylla group fuchsia. Leaves deep olive-green, velvety. Flowers in terminal clusters, long, slim, red; tubes and sepals red, petals orange-red, in summer.

Fuchsia
'Thornley's Hardy'
(Onagraceae)

Common names: None
Height: 30cm (12in)
Spread: 20cm (8in)
Aspect: Sun or half shade
Soil: Moist, well-drained
Hardiness: Zone 5
Propagation: Softwood cuttings, in spring

Hybrid fuchsia, with a sprawling habit. Flowers pendent, small. Tube creamy-white, sepals spreading and creamy-white, corolla deep rose-pink.

Fuchsia
'Tom West'
(Onagraceae)

Common names: None
Height: 60cm (2ft)
Spread: 60cm (2ft)
Aspect: Sun or half shade
Soil: Moist, well-drained
Hardiness: Zone 9
Propagation: Softwood cuttings, in spring

Hybrid fuchsia, grown principally for its foliage. Leaves variegated green and cream, and veined pink. Flowers small, single; tubes and sepals red, corolla purple.

Gaillardia
'Burgunder'
(Asteraceae/Compositae)

Common name: Blanket flower
Height: 60cm (2ft)
Spread: 45cm (18in)
Aspect: Sun
Soil: Well-drained, gritty, poor
Hardiness: Zone 4
Propagation: Softwood cuttings, in spring

Hybrid of garden origin. Leaves basal, in rosettes, inverse lance-shaped, grey or green. Flowers daisy-like, single, dark wine-red, from summer to early autumn.

Gaillardia
'Kobold'
(Asteraceae/Compositae)

Common name: Blanket flower
Height: 30cm (12in)
Spread: 45cm (18in)
Aspect: Sun
Soil: Well-drained, gritty, poor
Hardiness: Zone 4
Propagation: Softwood cuttings, in spring

Hybrid, known also as 'Goblin'. Leaves basal, in rosettes, green. Flowers single, ray florets red with yellow tips, disc florets deep red, summer to early autumn.

Galanthus nivalis
A.G.M.
(Amaryllidaceae)

Common name: Snowdrop
Height: 10cm (4in)
Spread: 10cm (4in)
Aspect: Half shade
Soil: Moist, well-drained, humus-rich
Hardiness: Zone 4
Propagation: Division, after flowering

Bulbous woodlander from N. Europe. Leaves narrow, glaucous. Flowers solitary, scented, white; inner tepals marked green at tip, late winter. All parts toxic and irritant.

Galega x *hartlandii*
'Alba' A.G.M.
(Leguminosae/Papilionaceae)

Common name: Goat's rue
Height: 1.5m (5ft)
Spread: 90cm (3ft)
Aspect: Sun or half shade
Soil: Moist
Hardiness: Zone 4
Propagation: Seed, in spring; division, in autumn or spring

Clump-forming perennial. Leaves pinnate, leaflets oval, green. Flowers in erect axillary racemes, pea-like, white, from early summer to early autumn.

Galega officinalis
(Leguminosae/Papilionaceae)

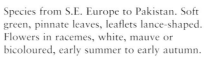

Common name: Goat's rue
Height: 1.5m (5ft)
Spread: 90cm (3ft)
Aspect: Sun or half shade
Soil: Moist
Hardiness: Zone 4
Propagation: Seed, in spring; division in early or late winter

Species from S.E. Europe to Pakistan. Soft green, pinnate leaves, leaflets lance-shaped. Flowers in racemes, white, mauve or bicoloured, early summer to early autumn.

Galium odoratum
(Rubiaceae)

Common name: Lady's bedstraw
Height: 45cm (18in)
Spread: Indefinite
Aspect: Sun or half shade
Soil: Moist, humus-rich
Hardiness: Zone 5
Propagation: Seed, when ripe; division, in spring or autumn

Rhizomatous plant from N. Africa, Europe and Siberia. Leaves lance-shaped, emerald green, whorled. Small, starry, scented, white flowers in cymes, late spring to midsummer.

Galtonia candicans
(Hyacinthaceae/Liliaceae)

Common name: Summer hyacinth
Height: 1.2m (4ft)
Spread: 10cm (4in)
Aspect: Sun
Soil: Moist, well-drained, fertile
Hardiness: Zone 6
Propagation: Seed or offsets, both in spring

Bulbous, moist-grassland plant from South Africa. Leaves lance-shaped, grey-green. Flowers in tall slim racemes, pendent, scented, tubular, white, in late summer.

Galtonia princeps
(Hyacinthaceae/Liliaceae)

Common name: Summer hyacinth
Height: 90cm (36in)
Spread: 10cm (4in)
Aspect: Sun
Soil: Moist, well-drained, fertile
Hardiness: Zone 8
Propagation: Seed or offsets, both in spring

Bulbous species from southern Africa. Flowers rather smaller than those of *G. candicans*, and tinted green, in late summer. Leaves lance-shaped, green.

Galtonia viridiflora
A.G.M.
(Hyacinthaceae/Liliaceae)

Common name: Summer hyacinth
Height: 1m (36in)
Spread: 10cm (4in)
Aspect: Sun
Soil: Moist, well-drained, fertile
Hardiness: Zone 8
Propagation: Seed or offsets, both in spring

Bulbous perennial from Southern Africa. Leaves lance-shaped, grey-green. Flowers in tallish, compact racemes of up to 30, trumpet-shaped, pendent, pale green.

Gaura lindheimeri
A.G.M.
(Onagraceae)

Common name:White gaura
Height: 1.5m (5ft)
Spread: 90cm (3ft)
Aspect: Sun
Soil: Well-drained, gritty
Hardiness: Zone 4
Propagation: Seed or division, both in spring

Clump-forming plant from Louisiana and Texas. Flowers in loose panicles, white, summer to autumn. Graceful in a wind. Leaves lance- to spoon-shaped, toothed.

Gaura lindheimeri
'Siskiyou Pink'
(Onagraceae)

Common name: Pink gaura
Height: 1.5m (5ft)
Spread: 90cm (3ft)
Aspect: Sun
Soil: Well-drained, gritty
Hardiness: Zone 4
Propagation: Seed or division, both in spring

Delightful form of the species. Flowers in loose panicles, pale and deep pink, over a long period from summer to autumn. Leaves lance- to spoon-shaped, toothed.

Gazania
Chansonette Series A.G.M.
(Asteraceae/Compositae)

Common name: Treasure flower
Height: 20cm (8in)
Spread: 20cm (8in)
Aspect: Sun
Soil: Well-drained, gritty
Hardiness: Zone 9
Propagation: Seed, in warmth in spring; cuttings, in autumn

Selected hybrids of evergreens from tropical Africa. Leaves basal, lance-shaped, glossy green above, grey-felted below. Single pink, yellow, orange or bronze flowers, summer.

Gazania
Daybreak Series A.G.M.
(Asteraceae /Compositae)

Common name: Treasure flower
Height: 20cm (8in)
Spread: 20cm (8in)
Aspect: Sun
Soil: Well-drained, gritty
Hardiness: Zone 9
Propagation: Seed, in warmth in spring; cuttings, in autumn

Hybrids of evergreens from tropical Africa. Leaves lance-shaped, green above, white-felted below. Flowers single, solitary, white, orange, yellow or pink, spring and summer.

Gazania
Talent Series A.G.M.
(Asteraceae/Compositae)

Common name: Treasure flower
Height: 20cm (8in)
Spread: 20cm (8in)
Aspect: Sun
Soil: Well-drained, gritty
Hardiness: Zone 9
Propagation: Seed, in warmth in spring; cuttings, in autumn

Selected hybrids of evergreens from tropical Africa. Leaves lance-shaped, grey-felted above and below. Flowers single, solitary, yellow, brown, orange or pink, in summer.

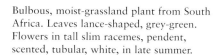

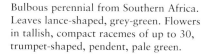

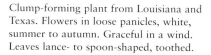

Gentiana angustifolia
(Gentianaceae)

Common names: None
Height: 10cm (4in)
Spread: 30cm (12in)
Aspect: Sun
Soil: Well-drained, light, humus-rich
Hardiness: Zone 7
Propagation: Seed or division, both in spring

Evergreen perennial from the Pyrenees, Alps, and Jura mountains. Leaves lance-shaped, in rosettes. Flowers on short stems, deep blue, single, trumpet-shaped, early summer.

Gentiana asclepiadea
A.G.M.
(Gentianaceae)

Common name: Willow gentian
Height: 90cm (36in)
Spread: 45cm (18in)
Aspect: Half shade
Soil: Moist, well-drained, acidic, humus-rich
Hardiness: Zone 6
Propagation: Seed, when ripe; division, in spring

Clump-forming herbaceous species from C. and S. Europe. Leaves willow-like, lance-shaped to ovate, pointed. Axillary clusters of flowers on arching stems, blue trumpets.

Gentiana asclepiadea
var. *alba*
(Gentianaceae)

Common name: White willow gentian
Height: 90cm (36in)
Spread: 45cm (18in)
Aspect: Sun
Soil: Well-drained, light, humus-rich
Hardiness: Zone 6
Propagation: Seed or division, both in spring

Naturally occuring form of the species, bearing white flowers on more upright stems. Leaves lance-shaped to ovate, pointed, willow-like.

Gentiana lutea
(Gentianaceae)

Common names: Bitterwort; yellow gentian
Height: 2m (6ft)
Spread: 60cm (2ft)
Aspect: Sun
Soil: Well-drained, humus-rich
Hardiness: Zone 4
Propagation: Seed or division, both in spring

Robust, fleshy-rooted mountain species. Basal leaves blue-green, ovate, ribbed; stem leaves paired, ovate, green. Flowers yellow, star-shaped, in clusters of up to 10, summer.

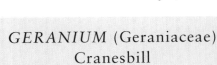

Gentiana septemfida
A.G.M.
(Gentianaceae)

Common name: Crested gentian
Height: 20cm (8in)
Spread: 30cm (12in)
Aspect: Sun
Soil: Moist, well-drained, humus-rich
Hardiness: Zone 3
Propagation: Seed or division, both in spring

Spreading, herbaceous species from Turkey to C. Asia. Leaves ovate, pointed, paired. Flowers in terminal clusters, narrow bells, bright blue, white throats, in summer.

Gentiana tibetica
(Gentianaceae)

Common name: Tibetan gentian
Height: 60cm (24in)
Spread: 20cm (8in)
Aspect: Sun
Soil: Well-drained, humus-rich
Hardiness: Zone 6
Propagation: Seed or division, both in spring

Species from Tibet. Basal leaves broad, lance, green; stem leaves linear. Flowers in dense terminal racemes, white, surrounded by apical leaves, in summer.

GERANIUM (Geraniaceae)
Cranesbill

A genus of over 300 species from temperate regions of both hemispheres. The perennial species are indispensable for beds and borders: they have beautiful flowers, make excellent ground cover, and are easy to grow and long-lived. They do dislike waterlogged soil: this is reflected in their distribution in the wild, where they are found in all habitats except boggy ones. They are a diverse group, and vary in both their degree of hardiness and their cultural requirements. *G. malviflorum* (Zone 8) is unusual in that it makes top-growth over winter, flowers in spring, and disappears till winter. Geranium flowers are mostly saucer-shaped, but may be flat or stellate; they may be borne in umbels, panicles or cymes. The leaves are basal and stem, palmately lobed, and often deeply divided and toothed; some species are evergreen. Many geranium species are floppy or scramble, and most need support of some kind to make them look reasonable. All should be sheared over in the autumn to encourage new basal growth. All are low-allergen plants, and most are drought-tolerant. *G. nodosum* (Zone 6) and *G. procurrens* (Zone 7) root as they touch the soil, and *G. thunbergii* (Zone 7) self-seeds to an unacceptable degree, so must be dead-headed.

Geranium
'Ann Folkard' A.G.M.
(Geraniaceae)

Common names: None
Height: 60cm (2ft)
Spread: 1.5m (5ft)
Aspect: Sun or half shade
Soil: Well-drained
Hardiness: Zone 7
Propagation: Division, in spring

Hybrid scrambling ground cover. Leaves 5-lobed, toothed, yellow at first, turning green. Flowers saucer-shaped, magenta with dark centres and veining, all summer.

Geranium cinereum
'Ballerina' A.G.M.
(Geraniaceae)

Common names: None
Height: 15cm (6in)
Spread: 30cm (12in)
Aspect: Sun or half shade
Soil: Well-drained
Hardiness: Zone 5
Propagation: Division, in spring

Long-flowering hybrid evergreen. Leaves 5- to 7-lobed, divisions 3-lobed, grey-green. Flowers cup-shaped, upward-facing, pale pink veined dark pink, spring to summer.

Geranium cinereum
var. *subcaulescens* A.G.M.
(Geraniaceae)

Common names: None
Height: 15cm (6in)
Spread: 30cm (12in)
Aspect: Sun or half shade
Soil: Well-drained
Hardiness: Zone 5
Propagation: Seed or division, both in spring

Species from Italy, the Balkans and Turkey. Leaves deeply lobed, deep green. Flowers on longish stems, brilliant magenta with black centres, in summer.

Geranium himalayense
(Geraniaceae)

Common names: None
Height: 45cm (18in)
Spread: 60cm (24in)
Aspect: Any
Soil: Well-drained
Hardiness: Zone 4
Propagation: Seed or division, both in spring

Rhizomatous species. Leaves basal, 7-lobed, veined, green, colourful in autumn. Loose cymes of flowers, saucer-shaped, deep blue, in flushes from early summer to autumn.

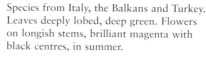

Geranium himalayense
'Plenum'
(Geraniaceae)

Common names: None
Height: 25cm (10in)
Spread: 60cm (24in)
Aspect: Any
Soil: Well-drained
Hardiness: Zone 4
Propagation: Seed or division, both in spring

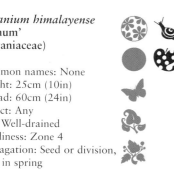

Fully double form of *G. himalayense*. More compact than the single form, and with smaller leaves. Flowers purplish-pink, shaded blue, darkly veined.

Geranium ibericum
subsp. *jubatum*
(Geraniaceae)

Common names: None
Height: 50cm (20in)
Spread: 60cm (24in)
Aspect: Sun or half shade
Soil: Well-drained
Hardiness: Zone 6
Propagation: Seed or division, both in spring

Clump-forming; 9- to 11-lobed, basal, hairy, leaves. Cymes of violet-blue, cup-shaped, upward-facing flowers in flushes from early summer. From Turkey, Iran, the Caucasus.

Geranium incanum
(Geraniaceae)

Common names: None
Height: 40cm (16in)
Spread: 60cm (24in)
Aspect: Sun
Soil: Well-drained
Hardiness: Zone 9
Propagation: Seed or division, both in spring

Evergreen from South Africa. Leaves basal, filigree, aromatic, deeply cut into 5 toothed, lobed, grey-green segments. Loose cymes of dark pink flowers, summer to autumn.

Geranium
'Johnson's Blue' A.G.M.
(Geraniaceae)

Common names: None
Height: 45cm (18in)
Spread: 75cm (30in)
Aspect: Sun or half shade
Soil: Well-drained
Hardiness: Zone 4
Propagation: Division, in spring

Rhizomatous hybrid. Leaves 7-lobed, basal; leaflets further lobed, toothed, mid-green. Flowers in loose cymes, blue saucers with pink centres, in summer.

The clump-forming Geranium psilostemon *bears cymes of deep-purple flowers in late summer.*

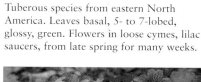

Geranium macrorrhizum
'Ingwersen's Variety' A.G.M. (Geraniaceae)

Common names: None
Height: 30cm (1ft)
Spread: 60cm (2ft)
Aspect: Sun or half shade
Soil: Well-drained
Hardiness: Zone 4
Propagation: Division, in spring

Cloned selection of a rhizomatous species. Leaves 7-lobed, toothed, aromatic, sticky, light green. Flowers flat, pale pink, calyx inflated, stamens prominent, early summer.

Geranium maculatum
(Geraniaceae)

Common names: None
Height: 60cm (24in)
Spread: 45cm (18in)
Aspect: Sun
Soil: Moist, well-drained
Hardiness: Zone 4
Propagation: Seed or division, both in spring

Tuberous species from eastern North America. Leaves basal, 5- to 7-lobed, glossy, green. Flowers in loose cymes, lilac saucers, from late spring for many weeks.

Geranium maderense
A.G.M.
(Geraniaceae)

Common names: None
Height: 1.5m (5ft)
Spread: 1.5m (5ft)
Aspect: Sun
Soil: Well-drained
Hardiness: Zone 9
Propagation: Seed or division, both in spring

Species from Madeira. Bright green, basal, 5- to 7-lobed, toothed leaves. Panicles of flat, pale-veined magenta flowers on purple-hairy stems, spring to late summer.

Geranium × *oxonianum*
'Rose Clair'
(Geraniaceae)

Common names: None
Height: 90cm (3ft)
Spread: 60cm (2ft)
Aspect: Sun or half shade
Soil: Well-drained
Hardiness: Zone 5
Propagation: Division, in spring

Clump-forming, robust hybrid. Leaves basal, 5-lobed, each with 5 leaflets, green, toothed, veined. Flowers in loose cymes, pink, fading to white, spring to autumn.

Geranium phaeum
(Geraniaceae)

Common name: Mourning widow
Height: 60cm (2ft)
Spread: 45cm (18in)
Aspect: Half or full shade
Soil: Moist, well-drained
Hardiness: Zone 5
Propagation: Seed or division, both in spring

Herbaceous species from the mountains of Eurasia. Leaves basal, 7- to 9-lobed, green. Flowers in cymes, violet-blue, black, white, or maroon in late spring and early summer.

Geranium
'Phillippe Vapelle'
(Geraniaceae)

Common names: None
Height: 40cm (16in)
Spread: 30cm (12in)
Aspect: Sun or half shade
Soil: Well-drained
Hardiness: Zone 7
Propagation: Division, in spring

A hybrid of *G. renardii* × *G. platypetalum*. Leaves basal, lobed, softly hairy, blue-grey. Flowers large, blue-purple, with bold, dark veins, long period from spring to summer.

Geranium pratense
(Geraniaceae)

Common name: Meadow cranesbill
Height: 90cm (3ft)
Spread: 60cm (2ft)
Aspect: Sun or half shade
Soil: Well-drained
Hardiness: Zone 5
Propagation: Seed or division, both in spring

Herbaceous species from Europe to China. Leaves basal, 7 to 9 deeply divided lobes, toothed, green. Flowers in dense cymes, blue, violet or white saucers, in summer.

Geranium pratense
'Mrs. Kendall Clark'
A.G.M. (Geraniaceae)

Common names: None
Height: 90cm (3ft)
Spread: 60cm (2ft)
Aspect: Sun or half shade
Soil: Well-drained
Hardiness: Zone 5
Propagation: Division, in spring

Cloned selection of the species. Leaves basal, 7- to 9-lobed, toothed, mid-green. Flowers in umbels, saucer-shaped, pearl-grey, over a long period in summer.

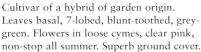

Geranium pratense 'Plenum Violaceum' A.G.M. (Geraniaceae)

Common names: None
Height: 90cm (3ft)
Spread: 60cm (2ft)
Aspect: Sun or half shade
Soil: Well-drained
Hardiness: Zone 5
Propagation: Division, in spring

Double-flowered form. Leaves basal, lobed, toothed, mid-green. Flowers in dense cymes, rich, deep violet-blue saucers, tinged purple in the centre, over a long period in summer.

Geranium psilostemon A.G.M. (Geraniaceae)

Common name: Armenian cranesbill
Height: 1.2m (4ft)
Spread: 1.2m (4ft)
Aspect: Sun or half shade
Soil: Well-drained
Hardiness: Zone 6
Propagation: Seed or division, both in spring

Clump-forming; leaves basal, lobed, toothed, green, red in spring and autumn. Flowers large, deep purple, black centres and veins, in loose cymes; very long period in summer.

Geranium pyrenaicum 'Bill Wallis' (Geraniaceae)

Common names: None
Height: 60cm (2ft)
Spread: 30cm (1ft)
Aspect: Sun or half shade
Soil: Well-drained
Hardiness: Zone 7
Propagation: Seed, in spring

Cultivar of an evergreen species. Leaves small, lobed, mid-green. Flowers small, in loose cymes, rich purple; long period in summer. Self-seeds; comes true from seed.

Geranium x riversleaianum 'Mavis Simpson' (Geraniaceae)

Common names: None
Height: 30cm (1ft)
Spread: 1.2m (4ft)
Aspect: Sun or half shade
Soil: Well-drained
Hardiness: Zone 7
Propagation: Division, in spring

Cultivar of a hybrid of garden origin. Leaves basal, 7-lobed, blunt-toothed, grey-green. Flowers in loose cymes, clear pink, non-stop all summer. Superb ground cover.

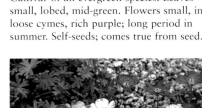

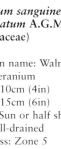

Geranium x riversleaianum 'Russell Pritchard' A.G.M. (Geraniaceae)

Common names: None
Height: 30cm (1ft)
Spread: 1m (3ft)
Aspect: Sun or half shade
Soil: Well-drained
Hardiness: Zone 7
Propagation: Division, in spring

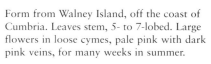

Cultivar of a garden hybrid. Leaves basal, 7-lobed, toothed, grey-green. Flowers in loose cymes, dark magenta, over long periods in summer. Excellent ground cover.

Geranium sanguineum 'Elsbeth' (Geraniaceae)

Common name: Bloody cranesbill
Height: 20cm (8in)
Spread: 30cm (12in)
Aspect: Sun or half shade
Soil: Well-drained
Hardiness: Zone 5
Propagation: Division, in spring

Cloned selection of a rhizomatous European species. Leaves stem, 5- to 7-lobed, toothed, mid-green. Flowers in loose cymes, large, bright purple saucers, spring to summer.

Geranium sanguineum 'Shepherd's Warning' A.G.M. (Geraniaceae)

Common names: None
Height: 15cm (6in)
Spread: 15cm (6in)
Aspect: Sun or half shade
Soil: Well-drained
Hardiness: Zone 5
Propagation: Division, in spring

Cultivar of a rhizomatous species, low-growing, mat-forming, and with flowers of deep pink which fade to white, in summer. Excellent ground cover.

Geranium sanguineum var. striatum A.G.M. (Geraniaceae)

Common name: Walney island geranium
Height: 10cm (4in)
Spread: 15cm (6in)
Aspect: Sun or half shade
Soil: Well-drained
Hardiness: Zone 5
Propagation: Seed or division, both in spring

Form from Walney Island, off the coast of Cumbria. Leaves stem, 5- to 7-lobed. Large flowers in loose cymes, pale pink with dark pink veins, for many weeks in summer.

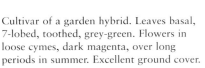

Hardy geraniums will spread to make attractive ground cover; some, such as Geranium himalayense *will even flourish in deep shade.*

***Geranium sanguineum* var. *striatum* 'Splendens'**
(Geraniaceae)

Common names: None
Height: 45cm (18in)
Spread: 30cm (12in)
Aspect: Sun or half shade
Soil: Well-drained
Hardiness: Zone 5
Propagation: Seed or division, both in spring

One of the taller cultivars of the species. Leaves stem, 5- to 7-lobed, mid-green. Flowers large, deep pink with darker veins, in summer.

***Geranium* 'Stanhoe'**
(Geraniaceae)

Common names: None
Height: 20cm (8in)
Spread: 20cm (8in)
Aspect: Sun or half shade
Soil: Well-drained
Hardiness: Zone 7
Propagation: Division, in spring

A hybrid of garden origin, between *G. sessiliflorum* and *G. traversii*. Leaves small, round, hairy, grey-green. Flowers delicate pink, from midsummer to autumn.

***Geranium sylvaticum* 'Album' A.G.M.**
(Geraniaceae)

Common name: Wood cranesbill
Height: 75cm (30in)
Spread: 60cm (24in)
Aspect: Sun or half shade
Soil: Moist, well-drained
Hardiness: Zone 4
Propagation: Seed or division, both in spring

Clump-forming geranium. Leaves basal, 7-lobed, lobes deeply cut, toothed. Flowers in dense cymes, white, blue or pink saucers, in spring and early summer.

***Geranium sylvaticum* 'Amy Doncaster'**
(Geraniaceae)

Common names: None
Height: 75cm (30in)
Spread: 60cm (24in)
Aspect: Sun or half shade
Soil: Moist, well-drained
Hardiness: Zone 4
Propagation: Division, in spring

Cloned cultivar of the woodland geranium, with flowers of deep blue with white eyes, in spring and summer. Leaves basal, 7-lobed, lobes deeply cut, toothed.

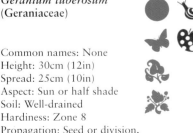

Geranium tuberosum
(Geraniaceae)

Common names: None
Height: 30cm (12in)
Spread: 25cm (10in)
Aspect: Sun or half shade
Soil: Well-drained
Hardiness: Zone 8
Propagation: Seed or division, both in spring

Mediterranean species. Summer-dormant; makes deeply cut, toothed, mid-green leaves over winter and bears loose cymes of bright pink flowers with dark veins in spring.

***Geranium wallichianum* 'Buxton's Variety' A.G.M.**
(Geraniaceae)

Common names: None
Height: 30cm (1ft)
Spread: 1m (3ft)
Aspect: Sun or half shade
Soil: Well-drained
Hardiness: Zone 7
Propagation: Division, in spring

Cultivar of a trailing species from Kashmir and Afghanistan. Leaves 3- to 5-lobed, toothed. Flowers in loose cymes, large, sky-blue saucers, from midsummer to autumn.

Gerbera jamesonii
(Asteraceae/Compositae)

Common names: Barberton daisy; Transvaal daisy
Height: 45cm (18in)
Spread: 60cm (24in)
Aspect: Sun
Soil: Well-drained, fertile
Hardiness: Zone 8
Propagation: Seed in warmth or division, both in spring

From Indonesia, Madagascar and South Africa. Leaves inverse lance-shaped, lobed, woolly below. Flowers solitary, single, red with yellow centres, spring to late summer.

***Geum* 'Dolly North'**
(Rosaceae)

Common name: Avens
Height: 60cm (2ft)
Spread: 60cm (2ft)
Aspect: Sun or half shade
Soil: Well-drained, fertile
Hardiness: Zone 5
Propagation: Seed or division, both in autumn or spring

A *Geum chiloense* hybrid. Leaves basal, in rosettes, pinnate, leaflets heart- to kidney-shaped, wrinkled. Flowers glowing orange, in cymes on branched stems, early summer.

GEUM (Rosaceae)
Avens

A genus of some 50 species, all perennial and hardy, from temperate and polar regions of both hemispheres, with the exception of Australia. Their natural habitats range from mountainsides to woodlands and damp meadows, and they will grow in just about any soil as long as it is not waterlogged. They prefer full sun, but will tolerate light or dappled shade. Avens have handsome, evergreen foliage, mainly borne in basal rosettes. They are very useful border plants, since they bloom in early summer before the main summer flowering season, and can be persuaded to repeat-flower by dead-heading. The flowers, in pink, red, orange, yellow or cream, are open and bowl- to saucer-shaped. In the garden they are much appreciated by bees, and they are also excellent for cutting and low in allergens. One drawback of this genus is that they do begin to flower less well after a few years, and will become free-flowering again only if they are lifted and divided, with the old, woody growth being discarded, and only the soft, new growth replanted. By far the best time to do this is in late spring; division at other times will mean losing a year's flowering. They can be grown from seed, but tend to hybridise readily.

Geum coccineum
(Rosaceae)

Common name: Avens
Height: 50cm (20in)
Spread: 30cm (12in)
Aspect: Sun or half shade
Soil: Well-drained, fertile
Hardiness: Zone 4
Propagation: Seed or division, both in spring or autumn

An evergreen perennial from the Balkans. Leaves basal, pinnate, hairy, and stem, entire, toothed. Flowers in cymes, brick-red with yellow stamens, in early summer.

Geum
'Lady Stratheden' A.G.M.
(Rosaceae)

Common name: Avens
Height: 60cm (2ft)
Spread: 60cm (2ft)
Aspect: Sun or half shade
Soil: Well-drained, fertile
Hardiness: Zone 6
Propagation: Seed or division, both in spring or autumn

A *Geum chiloense* hybrid. Leaves pinnate, hairy, lobes kidney-shaped to ovate. Flowers semi-double, in cymes of up to 5, yellow, all summer.

Geum
'Mrs J. Bradshaw' A.G.M.
(Rosaceae)

Common name: Avens
Height: 60cm (2ft)
Spread: 60cm (2ft)
Aspect: Sun or half shade
Soil: Well-drained, fertile
Hardiness: Zone 6
Propagation: Seed or division, both in spring or autumn

A *Geum chiloense* hybrid. Leaves pinnate, hairy, lobes ovate to heart-shaped, mid-green. Flowers in cymes of up to 5, semi-double, red, from early to late summer.

Geum
'Prinses Juliana'
(Rosaceae)

Common name: Avens
Height: 60cm (2ft)
Spread: 60cm (2ft)
Aspect: Sun or half shade
Soil: Well-drained, fertile
Hardiness: Zone 5
Propagation: Seed or division, both in spring or autumn

A *Geum chiloense* hybrid. Leaves pinnate, hairy, lobes ovate to heart-shaped, mid-green. Flowers in cymes of up to 5, semi-double, strong yellow, early and midsummer.

Geum rivale
(Rosaceae)

Common name: Water avens
Height: 60cm (24in)
Spread: 45cm (18in)
Aspect: Sun or half shade
Soil: Wet or marginal aquatic, humus-rich
Hardiness: Zone 3
Propagation: Seed or division, both in spring or autumn

European species. Leaves in basal rosettes, pinnate, obovate, veined, scalloped. Cymes of flowers, pendent, orange-yellow or pink bells, from late spring to midsummer.

Geum
'Tangerine'
(Rosaceae)

Common name: Avens
Height: 30cm (1ft)
Spread: 30cm (1ft)
Aspect: Sun or half shade
Soil: Moist, fertile
Hardiness: Zone 3
Propagation: Division, in spring or autumn

Geum rivale hybrid. Leaves in basal rosettes, pinnate, obovate to wedge-shaped, dark green, scalloped. Flowers in cymes, orange, pendent saucers, late spring to midsummer.

Gillenia trifoliata
A.G.M.
(Rosaceae)

Common names: Bowman's root; Indian physic
Height: 1m (3ft)
Spread: 60cm (2ft)
Aspect: Half shade
Soil: Moist, well-drained, acidic
Hardiness: Zone 4
Propagation: Seed or division, both in spring or autumn

Rhizomatous woodlander. Leaves 3-palmate, toothed, veined, leaflets ovoid, bronze-green. Flowers asymmetric, starry, white; long period from spring to late summer.

GLADIOLUS (Iridaceae)
Gladiolus

A genus of almost 200 species of cormous perennials from many countries, especially Africa, and South Africa in particular, Madagascar, the Arabian peninsula and western Asia. Some are hardy, but others are half-hardy or tender. All like sun and well-drained, fertile soil. The genus has been hybridised extensively for the flower trade and exhibition: over 10,000 cultivars and hybrids exist, and new ones are produced continually. There are different ways of classifying them; of most use to the gardener is the grouping of most into Grandiflorus, Nanus and Primulinus. Grandiflorus are tall, with a single, long, dense spike of many large flowers. Nanus are shorter, with 2 or 3 dense spikes of small flowers. Both of these groups are tender and need lifting each year. Primulinus, with a single loose spike of many flowers, contain some that can be left in the ground all year round in warmer areas. For the greater part, they do not need staking. Some species, *G. papilio* and *G. communis* subsp. *byzantinus* for example, are invasive; in transplanting them, make sure that all the tiny cormlets are moved as well, or they will make plants of flowering size by the next season. They make excellent cut flowers, and are low in allergens.

Gladiolus callianthus
A.G.M.
(Iridaceae)

Classification: Species
Height: 1m (3ft)
Spread: 10cm (4in)
Aspect: Sun
Soil: Well-drained, fertile
Hardiness: Zone 9
Propagation: Seed, in warmth in spring; offsets when dormant

Tender species, formerly *Acidanthera*. Leaves basal, erect, linear, green. Flowers in arching spikes, scented, white with a purple throat, in late summer and early autumn.

Gladiolus cardinalis
(Iridaceae)

Classification: Species
Height: 90cm (36in)
Spread: 10cm (4in)
Aspect: Sun
Soil: Well-drained, fertile
Hardiness: Zone 9
Propagation: Seed, in warmth in spring; offsets, when dormant

A tender, cormous perennial from South Africa. Leaves basal, erect, linear, green. Flowers in spikes of up to 12, funnel-shaped, bright red with white flash on each tepal.

Gladiolus communis subsp. *byzantinus* A.G.M.
(Iridaceae)

Classification: Species
Height: 1m (3ft)
Spread: 10cm (4in)
Aspect: Sun
Soil: Well-drained, fertile
Hardiness: Zone 6
Propagation: Seed, in spring; offsets, when dormant

Invasive type. Leaves basal, erect, linear, green. Flowers in spikes of up to 20, funnel-shaped, magenta with pale streaks on the lower tepal. Divide regularly.

Gladiolus
'Green Woodpecker'
A.G.M. (Iridaceae)

Classification: Grandiflorus
Height: 1.5m (5ft)
Spread: 12cm (5in)
Aspect: Sun
Soil: Well-drained, fertile
Hardiness: Zone 9
Propagation: Offsets, when dormant

Leaves basal, erect, linear, green. Flowers in spikes of up to 25, ruffled, green-yellow with red marks on the throat, in mid- and late summer.

Gladiolus papilio
(Iridaceae)

Classification: Species
Height: 90cm (36in)
Spread: 8cm (3in)
Aspect: Sum
Soil: Well-drained, fertile
Hardiness: Zone 8
Propagation: Offsets, when dormant

Highly invasive species from South Africa. Leaves basal, erect to arching, linear, mid-green. Flowers in spikes of up to 5, hooded, grey-green with red internal marks.

Gladiolus
'The Bride' A.G.M.
(Iridaceae)

Classification: Cardinalis hybrid
Height: 60cm (24in)
Spread: 5cm (2in)
Aspect: Sun
Soil: Well-drained, fertile
Hardiness: Zone 8
Propagation: Offsets, when dormant

Hybrid cultivar. Leaves basal, erect, linear, mid-green. Flowering spike of up to 6 white flowers, marked pink on the lower tepal, from early spring to early summer.

Gladiolus tristis
(Iridaceae)

Classification: Species
Height: 1.5m (5ft)
Spread: 5cm (2in)
Aspect: Sun
Soil: Well-drained, fertile
Hardiness: Zone 7
Propagation: Seed, in spring; offsets, when dormant

South African species. Leaves basal, erect, linear. Tall spike of up to 20 open funnel-shaped, scented flowers, creamy-white, with dark flushing or dots, in spring.

Glaucium flavum
(Papaveraceae)

Common name: Yellow horned poppy
Height: 90cm (36in)
Spread: 45cm (18in)
Aspect: Sun
Soil: Well-drained, fertile
Hardiness: Zone 7
Propagation: Seed, sown *in situ* in spring or autumn

Rosette-forming, short-lived, coastal plant. Leaves pinnatifid, lobes toothed, rough, glaucous blue-green. Flowers single, yellow, in summer, followed by good seed heads.

Glaucium flavum
f. fulvum
(Papaveraceae)

Common name: Horned poppy
Height: 90cm (36in)
Spread: 45cm (18in)
Aspect: Sun
Soil: Well-drained, fertile
Hardiness: Zone 7
Propagation: Seed, sown *in situ* in spring or autumn

Form of the species with flowers of bright orange, in summer, followed by long, curved seed pods. Short-lived, but self-seeds; resents disturbance.

Glyceria maxima
var. variegata
(Graminae/Poaceae)

Common names: Manna grass; sweet grass
Height: 70cm (28in)
Spread: Indefinite
Aspect: Sun
Soil: Water to 15cm (6in) deep
Hardiness: Zone 5
Propagation: Division, in spring

Rhizomatous, aquatic grass from Europe and Asia. Leaves narrow straps, striped cream, white and green. Flowers in panicles, purplish-green, in mid- to late summer.

Glycyrrhiza glabra
(Leguminosae/Papilionaceae)

Common names: Liquorice; sweetwood
Height: 1m (3ft)
Spread: 45cm (18in)
Aspect: Sun
Soil: Moist, deep, fertile
Hardiness: Zone 8
Propagation: Seed or division, both in spring

Tap-rooted plant from the Mediterranean to SW Asia. Leaves pinnate, leaflets ovate, sticky, glandular, pale green. Flowers in racemes, pale blue and white, late summer.

Goniolimon tataricum
(Plumbaginaceae)

Common name: Tatarian statice
Height: 30cm (1ft)
Spread: 30cm (1ft)
Aspect: Sun
Soil: Well-drained, gritty
Hardiness: Zone 4
Propagation: Seed, in spring

Rosette-forming plant. Leaves inverse lance-shaped, smooth, leathery, pale green. Wide panicles of tubular flowers, white sepals and red petals. Excellent for cutting and drying.

Grindelia chiloensis
(Asteraceae/Compositae)

Common names: Gum plant; rosinweed; tarweed
Height: 1m (3ft)
Spread: 1m (3ft)
Aspect: Sun
Soil: Well-drained
Hardiness: Zone 6
Propagation: Seed, in spring; semi-ripe cuttings, in summer

Evergreen subshrub from Argentina and Chile. Leaves basal, inverse lance-shaped, grey-green. Flowers solitary, semi-double, yellow, on long stalks, over summer.

Gypsophila paniculata
(Caryophyllaceae)

Common name: Baby's breath
Height: 1.2m (4ft)
Spread: 1.2m (4ft)
Aspect: Sun
Soil: Well-drained, gritty
Hardiness: Zone 4
Propagation: Seed, in warmth in winter to spring

Tap-rooted plant. Leaves lance-shaped to linear, glaucous-green. Loose panicles of many small, white, trumpet flowers, over a long period in mid- and late summer.

Gypsophila repens
A.G.M.
(Caryophyllaceae)

Common name: Baby's breath
Height: 20cm (8in)
Spread: 30cm (12in)
Aspect: Sun
Soil: Well-drained, gritty
Hardiness: Zone 4
Propagation: Seed, in warmth in winter to spring

Mat-forming perennial from the mountains of S Europe. Leaves linear, mid-green. Flowers in loose panicles, white or pink, over a long period in summer.

Gypsophila
'Rosenschleier' A.G.M.
(Caryophyllaceae)

Common name: Baby's breath
Height: 45cm (18in)
Spread: 45cm (18in)
Aspect: Sun
Soil: Well-drained, gritty
Hardiness: Zone 4
Propagation: Seed, in warmth in winter to spring

A robust, semi-evergreen hybrid. Leaves lance-shaped to linear, blue-green. Flowers in loose, many-flowered panicles, double, white, turning pink, mid- to late summer.

Hacquetia epipactis
A.G.M.
(Apiaceae/Umbelliferae)

Common names: None
Height: 5cm (2in)
Spread: 20cm (8in)
Aspect: Half shade
Soil: Moist, well-drained, acidic, humus-rich
Hardiness: Zone 7
Propagation: Seed, when ripe; division, in spring

Rhizomatous; sole species in genus. Tiny, yellow flowers with large, green bracts in late winter, followed by round, lime green, 3-lobed leaves, each lobe wedge-shaped.

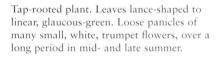

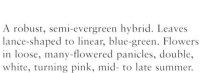

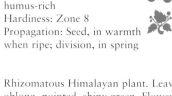

Hakonechloa macra
'Mediovariegata'
(Graminae/Poaceae)

Common names: None
Height: 45cm (18in)
Spread: 45cm (18in)
Aspect: Sun or half shade
Soil: Moist, well-drained, humus-rich
Hardiness: Zone 5
Propagation: Division, in spring

Leaves arching, linear, green, with median stripes and asymmetric narrow margins of pale yellow. Panicles of pale green spikelets, late summer to mid-autumn.

Haplopappus glutinosus
(Asteraceae/Compositae)

Common names: None
Height: 15cm (6in)
Spread: 30cm (12in)
Aspect: Sun
Soil: Sharply drained, fertile, protected from winter wet
Hardiness: Zone 9
Propagation: Seed, when ripe or in spring

An evergreen, tender perennial from Chile and Argentina. Leaves in dense cushions, oblong, lobed or pinnatisect, sticky, green. Flowers solitary, single, yellow, in summer.

Hedychium densiflorum
(Zingiberaceae)

Common name: Ginger lily
Height: 5m (15ft)
Spread: 2m (6ft)
Aspect: Sun or half shade
Soil: Moist, well-drained, humus-rich
Hardiness: Zone 8
Propagation: Seed, in warmth when ripe; division, in spring

Rhizomatous Himalayan plant. Leaves oblong, pointed, shiny green. Flowers in dense, cylindrical racemes, tubular, scented, orange or yellow, in late summer.

Hedychium forrestii
(Zingiberaceae)

Common name: Ginger lily
Height: 1.5m (5ft)
Spread: 60cm (2ft)
Aspect: Sun or half shade
Soil: Moist, well-drained, humus-rich
Hardiness: Zone 9
Propagation: Seed, in warmth when ripe; division, in spring

Tender, rhizomatous perennial from China. Leaves narrow, lance-shaped, veined, green. Flowers in racemes, white, in late summer and early autumn. Excellent for cutting.

Hedychium yunnanense
(Zingiberaceae)

Common name: Ginger lily
Height: 1m (3ft)
Spread: 60cm (2ft)
Aspect: Sun or half shade
Soil: Moist, well-drained, humus-rich
Hardiness: Zone 9
Propagation: Seed, in warmth when ripe; division, in spring

Tender, rhizomatous species from Yunnan. Leaves broad obovate, shiny green. Raceme of white, deeply divided flowers with orange bracts; attractive seed heads.

Hedysarum coronarium
(Leguminosae/Papilionaceae)

Common name: French honeysuckle
Height: 1m (3ft)
Spread: 60cm (2ft)
Aspect: Sun
Soil: Well-drained, gritty
Hardiness: Zone 3
Propagation: Seed, when ripe or in spring

Perennial from the Mediterranean. Leaves pinnate, with up to 15 obovate leaflets, mid-green. Flowers in racemes, perfumed, deep red, pea-like, on erect stems in spring.

HELENIUM (Asteraceae/Compositae)
Helen's flower • Sneezeweed

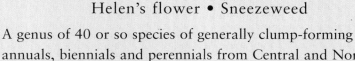

A genus of 40 or so species of generally clump-forming annuals, biennials and perennials from Central and North America. Their natural habitats are woodland edges or grasslands and are usually damp, and they will do well in a sunny position. The genus has been much hybridised, such that there is a large number of hybrids of uncertain parentage, but of great value in the garden. Sneezeweeds flower over long periods in late summer and autumn, and the earlier-flowering types can be persuaded to flower again if dead-headed. The flowers are daisy-like, with prominent discs of yellow or brown, and ray florets of yellow, orange and red, bringing rich autumn tints in the border. They are much-visited by bees and butterflies, providing valuable late food. The foliage is mid-green, lance-shaped, and unspectacular. The taller species and cultivars usually need to be staked, and all become congested fairly rapidly, so it is necessary to lift and divide them every few years or so. Thew flowers are excellent for cutting, and are popular for flower-arranging, but they are named sneezeweed for a reason, being highly allergenic. The plants are also poisonous, and contact with the foliage can cause skin irritation.

Helenium autumnale
(Asteraceae/Compositae)

Common names: Helen's flower; sneezeweed
Height: 1.5m (5ft)
Spread: 45cm (18in)
Aspect: Sun
Soil: Moist, well-drained, fertile
Hardiness: Zone 3
Propagation: Seed, in spring; division, in spring or autumn

A perennial from North America. Leaves lance-shaped, toothed, mid-green. Flowers solitary, ray florets yellow, disc florets brown, from late summer to mid-autumn.

Helenium
'Crimson Beauty'
(Asteraceae/Compositae)

Common names: Helen's flower; sneezeweed
Height: 1.2m (4ft)
Spread: 60cm (2ft)
Aspect: Sun
Soil: Moist, well-drained, humus-rich
Hardiness: Zone 3
Propagation: Seed, in spring; division, in spring or autumn

A very hardy hybrid cultivar. Leaves ovate, mid-green. Flowers solitary, ray florets bright red, disc florets brown, from late summer to mid-autumn.

Helenium
'Goldene Jugend'
(Asteraceae/Compositae)

Common names: Helen's flower; sneezeweed
Height: 80cm (32in)
Spread: 60cm (24in)
Aspect: Sun
Soil: Moist, well-drained, humus-rich
Hardiness: Zone 5
Propagation: Seed, in spring; division, in spring or autumn

A hybrid cultivar. Leaves ovate, mid-green. Flowers solitary, ray florets yellow, disc florets pale brown, over a long period in early and midsummer.

Helenium
'Moerheim Beauty'
(Asteraceae/Compositae)

Common names: Helen's flower; sneezeweed
Height: 90cm (3ft)
Spread: 60cm (2ft)
Aspect: Sun
Soil: Moist, well-drained, humus-rich
Hardiness: Zone 3
Propagation: Seed, in spring; division, in spring or autumn

Very hardy hybrid *Helenium*. Leaves ovate, mid-green. Flowers solitary, ray florets dark, coppery-red, disc florets brown, over a long period from early to late summer.

Helenium
'Sahin's Early Flowerer'
(Asteraceae/Compositae)

Common names: Helen's flower; sneezeweed
Height: 90cm (3ft)
Spread: 60cm (2ft)
Aspect: Sun
Soil: Moist, well-drained, humus-rich
Hardiness: Zone 5
Propagation: Seed, in spring; division, in spring or autumn

A hybrid *Helenium*. Leaves ovate, mid-green. Flowers single, ray florets bright red, disc florets dark brown, in late spring to midsummer.

Helenium
'Waldtraut'
(Asteraceae/Compositae)

Common names: Helen's flower; sneezeweed
Height: 90cm (3ft)
Spread: 60cm (2ft)
Aspect: Sun
Soil: Moist, well-drained, humus-rich
Hardiness: Zone 3
Propagation: Seed, in spring; division, in spring or autumn

Very hardy hybrid *Helenium*. Leaves ovate, mid-green. Flowers single, ray florets orange, disc florets brown, over a long period in late summer and early autumn.

Helianthemum
'Ben Fhada'
(Cistaceae)

Common name: Rock rose
Height: 20cm (8in)
Spread: 20cm (8in)
Aspect: Sun
Soil: Well-drained, fertile
Hardiness: Zone 6
Propagation: Softwood cuttings, in spring to early summer

Subshrub, evergreen in mild areas. Leaves oblong to linear, grey-green. Flowers yellow with an orange centre, 5-petalled saucers, in cymes; long period in late spring to summer.

Helianthemum
'Fireball'
(Cistaceae)

Common name: Rock rose
Height: 20cm (8in)
Spread: 30cm (12in)
Aspect: Sun
Soil: Well-drained, fertile
Hardiness: Zone 6
Propagation: Softwood cuttings, in spring to early summer

Hybrid, evergreen or semi-evergreen subshrub. Leaves oblong, grey-green. Flowers in cymes, double, bright scarlet, over a long period in late spring to summer.

Helianthemum
'Laurenson's Pink'
(Cistaceae)

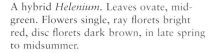

Common name: Rock rose
Height: 20cm (8in)
Spread: 30cm (12in)
Aspect: Sun
Soil: Well-drained, fertile
Hardiness: Zone 6
Propagation: Softwood cuttings, in spring to summer

A hybrid subshrub. Leaves linear, mid-green. Flowers in cymes, single, pale pink with an orange centre, over a long period in spring to midsummer.

Helianthemum nummularium
(Cistaceae)

Common name: Rock rose
Height: 20cm (8in)
Spread: 30cm (12in)
Aspect: Sun
Soil: Well-drained, fertile
Hardiness: Zone 6
Propagation: Seed, when ripe or in spring

Subshrub from mainland Europe. Leaves ovate to lance-shaped, grey-green. Flowers in cymes, single, petals deep pink, paler at base; long period from spring to summer.

HELIANTHUS (Asteraceae/Compositae)
Sunflower

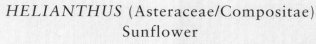

A genus of some 80 species, annual and perennial, from North, Central and South America. They are generally tall, coarse plants demanding quite a bit of space; the taller, spreading types are best in a wild garden. They require full sun and good drainage, and should not be overfed, as this will result in more foliage than flowers. There are many cultivars and hybrids, and the nomenclature of these is highly confused and liable to change frequently. Sunflowers are grown for their large, daisy-like flowers with usually yellow ray florets and brown, purple or yellow disc florets; these are borne over long periods in summer, and long, hot summers are needed for good flowering. The flowers of perennial species are generally smaller than those of the annuals. They attract bees and are excellent for cutting; unfortunately they are also highly allergenic. Sunflowers are prone to powdery mildew, and so should not be allowed to dry out in summer. Slugs are fond of their new growth in spring. Some will spread aggressively, and it is necessary to dig around them annually to sever the spreading roots. They need to be staked, and they must be lifted and divided every few years. Contact with the foliage may cause skin irritation.

Helianthus decapetalus
(Asteraceae/Compositae)

Common name: Thin-leaf sunflower
Height: 1.2m (4ft)
Spread: Indefinite
Aspect: Sun
Soil: Moist, well-drained, humus-rich
Hardiness: Zone 5
Propagation: Division, in spring or autumn

Rampant, rhizomatous species. Leaves ovate to lance-shaped, smooth above, hairy-rough below. Flowers single, daisy-like, yellow with brown centres, late summer to autumn.

Helianthus doronicoides
(Asteraceae/Compositae)

Common name: Sunflower
Height: 1.5m (5ft)
Spread: 60cm (2ft)
Aspect: Sun
Soil: Moist, well-drained, humus-rich
Hardiness: Zone 4
Propagation: Division, in spring or autumn

Invasive herbaceous species from the U.S.A. Leaves ovate to lance-shaped, large, bristly. Flowers single, daisy-like, lemon, over a long period from summer to autumn.

Helianthus
'Lemon Queen'
(Asteraceae/Compositae)

Common name: Sunflower
Height: 1.8m (6ft)
Spread: 1.2m (4ft)
Aspect: Sun
Soil: Moist, well-drained, humus-rich
Hardiness: Zone 5
Propagation: Division, in spring or autumn

Hybrid sunflower. Leaves ovate, veined, dark green. Flowers pale yellow, daisy-like, with darker yellow centres, over a long period in late summer to autumn.

Helianthus × *multiflorus*
(Asteraceae/Compositae)

Common name: Sunflower
Height: 2m (6ft)
Spread: 1m (3ft)
Aspect: Sun
Soil: Moist, well-drained, humus-rich
Hardiness: Zone 5
Propagation: Division, in spring or autumn

Clump-forming garden hybrid. Leaves ovate to lance-shaped, hairy, deep green. Flowers with yellow ray florets and brown disc florets, over a long period from late summer.

Helianthus × *multiflorus*
'Loddon Gold' A.G.M.
(Asteraceae/Compositae)

Common name: Sunflower
Height: 1.5m (5ft)
Spread: 90cm (3ft)
Aspect: Sun
Soil: Moist, well-drained humus-rich
Hardiness: Zone 5
Propagation: Division, in spring or autumn

Hybrid, also called *Helianthus* 'Loddon Gold'. Leaves lance-shaped to ovate, hairy, dark green. Flowers double, rich yellow; long period from late summer onwards.

Helianthus × *multiflorus*
'Triomphe de Gand'
(Asteraceae/Compositae)

Common name: Sunflower
Height: 1.2m (4ft)
Spread: 90cm (3ft)
Aspect: Sun
Soil: Moist, well-drained, humus-rich
Hardiness: Zone 5
Propagation: Division, in spring or autumn

Hybrid, also called *Helianthus* 'Triomphe de Gand'. Leaves ovate to lance-shaped, hairy, dark green. Flowers large, single, yellow, disc florets quilled, in late summer.

Helianthus salicifolius
(Asteraceae/Compositae)

Common name: Willow-leaved sunflower
Height: 2.5m (8ft)
Spread: 90cm (3ft)
Aspect: Sun
Soil: Moist, well-drained, humus-rich
Hardiness: Zone 4
Propagation: Division, in spring or autumn

Rhizomatous species from the U.S.A. Very handsome foliage, arching, linear to lance-shaped, bright green. Flowers single, yellow, over a long period from early autumn.

Helichrysum italicum
A.G.M.
(Asteraceae/Compositae)

Common name: Sunflower
Height: 60cm (2ft)
Spread: 90cm (3ft)
Aspect: Sun
Soil: Well-drained, protected from winter wet
Hardiness: Zone 8
Propagation: Seed or division, both in spring

Evergreen subshrub from S Europe. Leaves linear, aromatic, silver-grey. Flowers dark yellow, "everlasting" in corymbs on long stems; long period from summer to autumn.

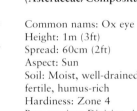

Helichrysum 'Schwefellicht'
(Asteraceae/Compositae)

Common names: None
Height: 40cm (16in)
Spread: 30cm (12in)
Aspect: Sun
Soil: Well-drained, protected from winter wet
Hardiness: Zone 6
Propagation: Seed or division, both in spring

A hybrid herbaceous perennial. Leaves lance-shaped, woolly, silver-white. Flowers "everlasting", fluffy, yellow, in tight corymbs, in late summer.

Helictotrichon sempervirens A.G.M.
(Graminae/Poaceae)

Common name: Blue oat grass
Height: 1.2m (4ft)
Spread: 60cm (2ft)
Aspect: Sun
Soil: Well-drained
Hardiness: Zone 5
Propagation: Seed or division, both in spring

Evergreen perennial grass from Europe. Leaves linear, flat or rolled, blue-grey. Flowers in stiff spikelets, straw-coloured, shiny, in panicles in early to midsummer.

Heliopsis helianthoides 'Ballerina'
(Asteraceae/Compositae)

Common name: Ox eye
Height: 1m (3ft)
Spread: 60cm (2ft)
Aspect: Sun
Soil: Moist, well-drained, fertile, humus-rich
Hardiness: Zone 4
Propagation: Division, in spring or autumn

Hybrid cultivar. Leaves ovate to lance-shaped, toothed, mid-green. Flowers semi-double, yellow with orange discs, on branching stems, summer to early autumn.

Heliopsis helianthoides 'Canary Bird'
(Asteraceae/Compositae)

Common nams: Ox eye
Height: 1m (3ft)
Spread: 60cm (2ft)
Aspect: Sun
Soil: Moist, well-drained, fertile, humus-rich
Hardiness: Zone 4
Propagation: Division, in spring or autumn

Hybrid cultivar. Leaves ovate to lance-shaped, toothed, mid-green. Flowers semi-double, yellow with dark centres, from midsummer to early autumn.

Heliopsis helianthoides 'Gigantea'
(Asteraceae/Compositae)

Common name: Ox eye
Height: 1.2m (4ft)
Spread: 60cm (2ft)
Aspect: Sun
Soil: Well-drained, fertile, humus-rich
Hardiness: Zone 4
Propagation: Division, in spring or autumn

A hardy cultivar. Leaves ovate to lance-shaped, toothed, mid-green. Flowers semi-double, yellow with dark centres, from midsummer to early autumn.

Heliopsis helianthoides var. *scabra* 'Light of Loddon'
(Asteraceae/Compositae)

Common name: Ox eye
Height: 1.2m (4ft)
Spread: 60cm (2ft)
Aspect: Sun
Soil: Well-drained, fertile, humus-rich
Hardiness: Zone 4
Propagation: Division, in spring or autumn

Hardy cultivar. Leaves lance-shaped to ovate, toothed, dark green. Flowers semi-double, with yellow ray florets and brown disc florets, midsummer to early autumn.

HELLEBORUS (Ranunculaceae)
Hellebore

A small genus of only 15 or so rhizomatous species, but one that gives the gardener some handsome weather-resistant winter flowers of excellent quality and form. They are native to central and eastern Europe and western Asia. Their natural habitats vary quite considerably, from rocky scrub and grassland to woodland, and so their cultural requirements also vary; some do well in full sun, and are good in a sunny border, whilst others enjoy dappled shade, and are excellent for naturalizing in a woodland garden. Some species perform best if their soil is acidic, but others prefer alkaline conditions; what they all have in common is a dislike of soils with extremes of wetness or dryness. All hellebores are reliably hardy. The flowers appear in late winter and spring and vary from open saucer-shaped to bell-shaped and tubular; each has 5 tepals, numerous stamens, and leafy bracts. They range in colour from pure white through to deep purple, with some spotted and green types. The foliage may be evergreen or deciduous, and is leathery, toothed and dark green. Hellebores are high-allergen plants, and all parts are poisonous and may also cause skin irritation on contact, so they are best avoided by the allergic gardener.

Helleborus argutifolius
A.G.M.
(Ranunculaceae)

Common name: Corsican hellebore
Height: 1.2m (4ft)
Spread: 90cm (3ft)
Aspect: Sun or half shade
Soil: Alkaline, humus-rich
Hardiness: Zone 7
Propagation: Seed, when ripe; division, in spring or autumn

Species from Corsica and Sardinia. Leaves 3-lobed, leaflets elliptic, spiny-toothed, dark green, leathery. Pendent, pale green flowers in dense cymes, late winter to early spring.

Helleborus argutifolius
'Pacific Frost'
(Ranunculaceae)

Common name: Corsican hellebore
Height: 1.2m (4ft)
Spread: 90cm (3ft)
Aspect: Half shade
Soil: Alkaline, humus-rich
Hardiness: Zone 7
Propagation: Division, in spring or autumn

Grown for its outstanding leaves, blotched pale green and silver, ovate. Flowers in many-flowered cymes, pendent, pale green, in late winter to early spring.

Helleborus niger
A.G.M.
(Ranunculaceae)

Common name: Christmas rose
Height: 30cm (12in)
Spread: 45cm (18 in)
Aspect: Half shade
Soil: Alkaline, humus-rich
Hardiness: Zone 3
Propagation: Seed, when ripe; division, in spring or autumn

Species from central Europe. Leaves dark green, oblong to lance-shaped, apex toothed. Flowers solitary or paired, white saucers, pink-flushed, in late winter to early spring.

Helleborus odorus
(Ranunculaceae)

Common name: Hellebore
Height: 50cm (20in)
Spread: 50cm (20in)
Aspect: Sun or half shade
Soil: Alkaline, humus-rich
Hardiness: Zone 6
Propagation: Seed, when ripe; division, in spring or autumn

Leaves dark green, basal, pedate, 3 lateral leaflets; each divided into 3–5 toothed lobes. Cymes of up to 5 green, fragrant, saucer-shaped flowers, late winter to early spring.

Helleborus orientalis
hybrid
(Ranunculaceae)

Common name: Lenten rose
Height: 50cm (20in)
Spread: 45cm (18in)
Aspect: Sun or half shade
Soil: Alkaline, humus-rich
Hardiness: Zone 6
Propagation: Division, in spring or autumn

Leaves leathery, basal, pedate, deep green, with 7 to 9 elliptic leaflets. Flowers outward-facing, deep-pink saucers, midwinter to mid-spring. One of many cultivars.

Helleborus orientalis
hybrid
(Ranunculaceae)

Common name: Lenten rose
Height: 50cm (20in)
Spread: 45cm (18in)
Aspect: Sun or half shade
Soil: Alkaline, humus-rich
Hardiness: Zone 6
Propagation: Division, in spring or autumn

Leaves basal, leathery, pedate, deep green, with 7 to 9 elliptic leaflets. Flowers pale pink, downward-facing saucers, midwinter to mid-spring. One of many cultivars.

Helleborus* × *sternyii
Blackthorn Group A.G.M.
(Ranunculaceae)

Common name: Hellebore
Height: 35cm (14in)
Spread: 30cm (12in)
Aspect: Sun or half shade
Soil: Alkaline, humus-rich
Hardiness: Zone 7
Propagation: Seed, when ripe; division, in spring or autumn

Hybrid evergreen hellebore. Leaves with 3 elliptic leaflets, boldly veined, greyish-green. Flowers in many-flowered cymes, green, suffused pink, from midwinter to spring.

Helleborus viridis
(Ranunculaceae)

Common name: Green hellebore
Height: 40cm (16in)
Spread: 45cm (18in)
Aspect: Sun or half shade
Soil: Alkaline, humus-rich
Hardiness: Zone 6
Propagation: Seed, when ripe; division, in spring or autumn

Evergreen species. Leaves basal, with up to 13 oblong leaflets, mid-green. Flowers in cymes of up to 4, pendent, green, in winter or early spring.

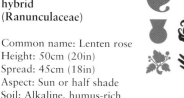

The flowers of daylilies, such as the star-shaped Hemerocallis *'Burford', can light up a border all summer.*

Heloniopsis orientalis
(Liliaceae/Melanthiaceae)

Common names: None
Height: 20cm (8in)
Spread: 20cm (8in)
Aspect: Half shade
Soil: Moist, well-drained, acidic, humus-rich
Hardiness: Zone 7
Propagation: Seed, in spring or autumn; division, in spring

Rhizomatous, evergreen woodlander. Leaves broad, lance-shaped, leathery, pale green. Flowers pink, nodding funnels, in racemes of up to 10.

HEMEROCALLIS (Hemerocallidaceae/Liliaceae)
Day Lily

A genus of about 15 perennials from Japan, China and Korea. They have been extensively hybridised, however, to the extent that 30,000 hybrids are in cultivation. They are clump-forming, and need to be lifted and divided every few years. *Hemerocallis fulva* and *H. lilio-asphodelus* are as invasive as weeds, however, and should not be admitted to the small garden. They will thrive in sun or light shade, and are not demanding as to soil type, so long as it is not too dry. The foliage is grassy, arching, and bright green; it may be evergreen or semi-evergreen, and disguises the fading leaves of spring-flowering bulbs well. The flowering stems are stout, and staking is not usually required. The flowers may be circular, triangular, stellate, or spider-shaped in outline, and may be single or double. They are summer-flowering. Each flower lasts for just one day (or one night in the case of the nocturnal varieties, which open in the late afternoon); but is usually followed by a succession of others. Some are perfumed. Daylilies are indispensable plants for the mixed border, and are good for ground cover. They make excellent cut flowers, and are cherished by flower-arrangers. They are low in allergens, and suitable for allergic gardeners.

Hemerocallis
'Amersham'
(Hemerocallidaceae/Liliaceae)

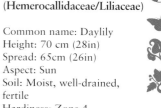

Common name: Daylily
Height: 70 cm (28in)
Spread: 65cm (26in)
Aspect: Sun
Soil: Moist, well-drained, fertile
Hardiness: Zone 4
Propagation: Division, in spring or autumn

A deciduous, hybrid daylily bearing a succession of single, star-shaped flowers of striking dark red with a contrasting yellow throat.

Hemerocallis
'Bette Davis Eyes'
(Hemerocallidaceae/Liliaceae)

Common name: Daylily
Height: 65cm (26in)
Spread: 65cm (26in)
Aspect: Sun
Soil: Moist, well-drained, fertile
Hardiness: Zone 4
Propagation: Division, in spring or autumn

A hardy, hybrid *Hemerocallis* cultivar with a succession of circular flowers of a delicate, peach-pink colour, with a dark magenta throat.

Hemerocallis
'Black Magic'
(Hemerocallidaceae/Liliacea)

Common name: Daylily
Height: 60cm (2ft)
Spread: 60cm (2ft)
Aspect: Sun
Soil: Moist, well-drained, fertile
Hardiness: Zone 4
Propagation: Division, in spring or autumn

A hardy, hybrid *Hemerocallis* with star-shaped flowers of rich maroon, with a central pale stripe on each petal, and a yellow throat.

Hemerocallis
'Cartwheels' A.G.M.
(Hemerocallidaceae/Liliaceae)

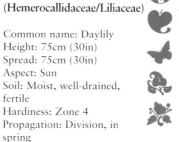

Common name: Daylily
Height: 75cm (30in)
Spread: 75cm (30in)
Aspect: Sun
Soil: Moist, well-drained, fertile
Hardiness: Zone 4
Propagation: Division, in spring

A hardy, evergreen, nocturnal-flowering hybrid daylily. A free-flowering cultivar, with star-shaped flowers of clear, unmarked yellow.

Hemerocallis
'Chemistry'
(Hemerocallidaceae/Liliaceae)

Common name: Daylily
Height: 70cm (28in)
Spread: 70cm (28in)
Aspect: Sun
Soil: Moist, well-drained, fertile
Hardiness: Zone 4
Propagation: Division, in spring or autumn

A hardy, hybrid daylily with a succession of star-shaped flowers of amber, marked with a brown ring near the centre and an orange throat.

Hemerocallis
'Chicago Royal Robe'
(Hemerocallidaceae/Liliaceae)

Common name: Daylily
Height: 60cm (24in)
Spread: 15cm (6in)
Aspect: Sun
Soil: Moist, well-drained, humus-rich
Hardiness: Zone 4
Propagation: Division, in spring or autumn

A hardy, semi-evergreen, hybrid daylily with a succession of large, perfumed, circular flowers of dark purple with a yellow-green throat.

Hemerocallis
'Chicago Sunrise'
(Hemerocallidaceae/Liliaceae)

Common name: Daylily
Height: 70cm (28in)
Spread: 15cm (6in)
Aspect: Sun
Soil: Moist, well-drained, humus-rich
Hardiness: Zone 4
Propagation: Division, in spring or autumn

Free-flowering, hardy, semi-evergreen hybrid daylily, with a succession of circular, clear yellow flowers with a darker throat, from midsummer.

Hemerocallis
'Corky' A.G.M.
(Hemerocallidaceae/Liliaceae)

Common name: Daylily
Height: 80cm (32in)
Spread: 9cm (3in)
Aspect: Sun
Soil: Moist, well-drained, humus-rich
Hardiness: Zone 4
Propagation: Division, in spring

Very free-flowering, evergreen, hardy hybrid daylily, with black stems, mahogany buds, and small, star-shaped flowers of lemon-yellow, in midsummer.

Hemerocallis.
'Golden Scroll'
(Hemerocallidaceae/Liliaceae)

Common name: Daylily
Height: 48cm (19in)
Spread: 15cm (6in)
Aspect: Sun
Soil: Moist, well-drained, humus-rich
Hardiness: Zone 4
Propagation: Division, in spring or autumn

A hybrid daylily with lush foliage and ruffled, circular, muted tangerine-orange to deep peach flowers, with a green throat, in late summer.

Hemerocallis
'King Haiglar'
(Hemerocallidaceae/Liliaceae)

Common name: Daylily
Height: 70cm (28in)
Spread: 13cm (5in)
Aspect: Sun
Soil: Moist, well-drained, humus-rich
Hardiness: Zone 4
Propagation: Division, in spring or autumn

A very free-flowering, hybrid daylily cultivar bearing large flowers of rich scarlet, with a small yellow throat, in midsummer.

Hemerocallis
'Lady Neva'
(Hemerocallidaceae/Liliaceae)

Common name: Daylily
Height: 90cm (36in)
Spread: 22cm (9in)
Aspect: Sun
Soil: Moist, well-drained, humus-rich
Hardiness: Zone 4
Propagation: Division, in spring or autumn

A hybrid daylily with ruffled flowers of buff to bright yellow, marked maroon; throat flared, yellow, filaments yellow, anthers grey.

Hemerocallis
'Little Grapette'
(Hemerocallidaceae/Liliaceae)

Common name: Daylily
Height: 30cm (12in)
Spread: 45cm (18in)
Aspect: Sun
Soil: Moist, well-drained, fertile
Hardiness: Zone 4
Propagation: Division, in spring or autumn

A hybrid daylily with star-shaped flowers of deep purple with a green throat, in midsummer. Shorter daylilies such as this are excellent for containers.

Hemerocallis
'Mighty Mogul'
(Hemerocallidaceae/Liliaceae)

Common name: Daylily
Height: 90cm (36in)
Spread: 45cm (18in)
Aspect: Sun
Soil: Moist, well-drained, humus-rich
Hardiness: Zone 4
Propagation: Division, in spring

A hybrid daylily with a succession of bright scarlet flowers with a yellow throat. The petals are reflexed and have slightly ruffled edges.

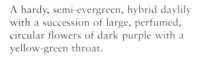

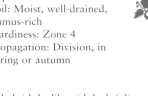

Hemerocallis
'Stella de Oro' A.G.M.
(Hemerocallidaceae/Liliaceae)

Common name: Daylily
Height: 30cm (12in)
Spread: 45cm (18in)
Aspect: Sun
Soil: Moist, well-drained, humus-rich
Hardiness: Zone 4
Propagation: Division, in spring

A vigorous, free-flowering, hybrid evergreen daylily, with a succession of circular, bright yellow flowers on slender stems in early summer.

Hesperis matronalis
(Brassicaceae/Cruciferae)

Common names: Dame's violet; sweet rocket
Height: 90cm (36in)
Spread: 45cm (18in)
Aspect: Sun or half shade
Soil: Moist, well-drained, fertile
Hardiness: Zone 3
Propagation: Seed, sown *in situ* in spring

Short-lived, rosette-forming plant from Asia and Europe. Leaves dark green, ovate, toothed, hairy. Flowers perfumed, lilac-purple, in panicles, spring to midsummer.

Heuchera cylindrica
'Greenfinch'
(Saxifragaceae)

Common names: Coral bells; coral flower
Height: 90cm (3ft)
Spread: 60cm (2ft)
Aspect: Any
Soil: Moist, well-drained, fertile
Hardiness: Zone 4
Propagation: Division, in autumn.

Cloned cultivar. Leaves round, scalloped, dark green, mottled pale green. Flowers in panicles on tall spikes, green, from mid-spring to midsummer. Good ground cover.

Heuchera micrantha
var. *diversifolia*
'Palace Purple' A.G.M.

Common names: Coral bells; coral flower
Height: 60cm (2ft)
Spread: 60cm (2ft)
Aspect: Any
Soil: Moist, well-drained, fertile
Hardiness: Zone 5
Propagation: Division, in autumn

Leaves large, shiny, jagged, metallic bronze. Flowers in very tall, loose panicles, cream, anthers red, followed by good seed heads in early summer. Good ground cover.

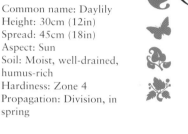

Heuchera
'Persian Carpet'
(Saxifragaceae)

Common names: Coral bells; coral flower
Height: 35cm (14in)
Spread: 60cm (24in)
Aspect: Any
Soil: Moist, well-drained, fertile
Hardiness: Zone 7
Propagation: Division, in autumn

Hybrid with large, round, metallic, silvery red-purple leaves. Flowers on tall spikes in panicles, greenish, in early summer. Handsome ground cover. Liked by bees.

Heuchera
'Pewter Moon'
(Saxifragaceae)

Common names: Coral bells; coral flower
Height: 40cm (16in)
Spread: 30cm (12in)
Aspect: Any
Soil: Moist, well-drained, fertile
Hardiness: Zone 7
Propagation: Division, in autumn

Hybrid with ovate to heart-shaped leaves, bronze-purple, marbled grey. Flowers in panicles, ice-pink, in early summer. A good evergreen ground cover for shade.

Heuchera
'Rachel'
(Saxifragaceae)

Common names: Coral bells; coral flower
Height: 30cm (1ft)
Spread: 30cm (1ft)
Aspect: Any
Soil: Moist, well-drained, fertile
Hardiness: Zone 7
Propagation: Division, in autumn

Hybrid with rounded, lobed, toothed leaves of dark green with bronzed edges. Flowers in erect panicles, pale pink, in early summer. Evergreen ground cover for shade.

Heuchera
'Red Spangles' A.G.M.
(Saxifragaceae)

Common names: Coral bells; coral flower
Height: 50cm (20in)
Spread: 25cm (10in)
Aspect: Any
Soil: Moist, well-drained, fertile
Hardiness: Zone 4
Propagation: Division, in autumn

Hybrid with round, lobed, toothed leaves of dark green, marbled pale green. Flowers in short, open panicles, scarlet, all summer. Evergreen ground cover for shade.

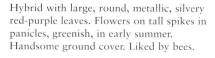

x *Heucherella alba* 'Bridget Bloom' (Saxifragaceae)

Common names: None
Height: 40cm (16in)
Spread: 30cm (12in)
Aspect: Any
Soil: Moist, well-drained, fertile, acidic
Hardiness: Zone 5
Propagation: Division, in autumn or spring

Evergreen hybrid of *Heuchera* and *Tiarella*. Leaves ovate, 7- to 9-lobed, toothed, green. Panicles of tiny, pink flowers in late spring and again in autumn. Ground cover.

x *Heucherella alba* 'Rosalie' (Saxifragaceae)

Common names: None
Height: 40cm (16in)
Spread: 20cm (8in)
Aspect: Any
Soil: Moist, well-drained, fertile, acidic
Hardiness: Zone 5
Propagation: Division, in spring or autumn

Hybrid of *Heuchera* and *Tiarella*. Leaves ovate, 7- to 9-lobed, toothed, green, veined brown. Flowers in panicles, tiny, pale pink, in spring and again in autumn.

Hieracium lanatum (Asteraceae/Compositae)

Common name: Hawkweed
Height: 45cm (18in)
Spread: 20cm (8in)
Aspect: Sun
Soil: Well-drained, poor
Hardiness: Zone 7
Propagation: Seed, in autumn or spring; division, in spring

Clump-forming. Leaves linear to lance-shaped, densely white-hairy, grey-green, margined white. Loose panicles of semi-double, chrome-yellow flowers, in summer.

Hieracium maculatum (Asteraceae/Compositae)

Common name: Hawkweed
Height: 80cm (32in)
Spread: 20cm (8in)
Aspect: Sun
Soil: Well-drained, poor
Hardiness: Zone 6
Propagation: Seed, in autumn or spring; division, in spring

Leaves ovate to lance-shaped, toothed, dark green, spotted brown-purple. Flowers in corymbs, yellow daisies. Seeds everywhere, so dead-head after flowering.

Hordeum jubatum (Graminae/Poaceae)

Common names: Squirreltail barley; squirreltail grass
Height: 50cm (20in)
Spread: 30cm (12in)
Aspect: Sun
Soil: Well-drained, fertile
Hardiness: Zone 5
Propagation: Seed, sown *in situ* in spring or autumn

Grass from Asia and North America. Leaves erect to arching, linear, pale green. Dense, broad panicles of arched, silky, bristled spikelets in early and midsummer.

HOSTA (Hostaceae/Liliaceae)
Plantain lily

A genus of some 70 species from E. Russia, China, Japan and Korea. They are soundly perennial, and are grown principally for their foliage value. Some of them have very nice flowers, and therefore qualify on both accounts. Some give a second, albeit brief, display in autumn. The leaves may be round, ovate or lance- or heart-shaped, 12–50cm (5–20in) in length, and come in all shades of green, solid or with margins or centres marked with variegation in shades from white to rich yellow. The flowers are in one-sided racemes, and may be bell- or trumpet-shaped. Hostas will grow in sun or full shade, but flower better in sun; the yellow-foliaged types do best in sun. They demand moisture at the roots, and more so when in full sun, so must be watered in dry spells; the foliage will wilt as a warning. They respond readily to division at almost any time of year. The great scourge of the genus is the attention of the slug and snail families; should they nibble the emergent shoots, the leaves will be scarred for the rest of the season, so take preventative measures early in spring. Hostas are good plants for the allergic gardener, since they are low in allergens.The foliage and flowers are very useful in flower-arranging.

Hosta crispula A.G.M. (Hostaceae/Liliaceae)

Common name: Plantain lily
Height: 90cm (3ft)
Spread: 90cm (3ft)
Aspect: Full shade
Soil: Moist, well-drained, fertile
Hardiness: Zone 5
Propagation: Division, in autumn or spring

Leaves lance- to heart-shaped, edges scalloped, deep green margined irregularly in white. Flowers lavender-white, funnel-shaped, on leafy scapes in summer.

Hosta
'Eric Smith'
(Hostaceae/Liliaceae)

Common name: Plantain lily
Height: 1.2m (4ft)
Spread: 60cm (2ft)
Aspect: Any
Soil: Moist, well-drained, fertile
Hardiness: Zone 5
Propagation: Division, in autumn or spring

A hardy hybrid in the Tardiana Group. Leaves large, rounded, bluish-green. Flowers lilac-pink funnels on tall, leafy scapes, in midsummer.

Hosta
'Frances Williams' A.G.M.
(Hostaceae/Liliaceae)

Common name: Plantain lily
Height: 65cm (26in)
Spread: 1m (36in)
Aspect: Full or half shade
Soil: Moist, well-drained, fertile
Hardiness: Zone 5
Propagation: Division, in spring or autumn

Clump-forming hybrid. Leaves glaucous blue-green, margined yellow-green, heart-shaped. Flowers grey-white bells on scapes, in early summer. Relatively slug-resistant.

Hosta
'Ground Master'
(Hostaceae/Liliaceae)

Common name: Plantain lily
Height: 50cm (20in)
Spread: 55cm (22in)
Aspect: Full or half shade
Soil: Moist, well-drained, fertile
Hardiness: Zone 5
Propagation: Division, in autumn or spring

Hybrid cultivar. Leaves ovate to lance-shaped, matt green, with irregular wavy margins of cream, fading to white. Flowers on scapes, purple funnels, in summer.

Hosta
'Honeybells' A.G.M.
(Hostaceae/Liliaceae)

Common name: Plantain lily
Height: 90cm (3ft)
Spread: 1.2m (4ft)
Aspect: Half shade or sun
Soil: Moist, well-drained, fertile
Hardiness: Zone 5
Propagation: Division, in autumn or spring

A robust hybrid. Leaves ovate or heart-shaped, wavy-edged, strongly veined, luminous pale green. Flowers perfumed, white bells, on leafy scapes in late summer.

Hosta plantaginea
(Hostaceae/Liliaceae)

Common name: Plantain lily
Height: 75cm (30in)
Spread: 1m (3ft)
Aspect: Half shade or sun
Soil: Moist, well-drained, fertile
Hardiness: Zone 5
Propagation: Division, in autumn or spring

Leaves glossy pale green, ovate to heart-shaped, veins prominent. Flowers scented, white trumpets, on leafy scapes, late summer to autumn. Shy-flowering in cold areas.

Hosta rohdeifolia
(Hostaceae/Liliaceae)

Common name: Plantain lily
Height: 1m (36in)
Spread: 45cm (18in)
Aspect: Full or half shade
Soil: Moist, well-drained, fertile
Hardiness: Zone 5
Propagation: Division, in autumn or spring

A species from Japan. Leaves lance- to inverse-lance-shaped, olive-green. Flowers on leafy scapes, purple funnels, with dark purple stripes, in summer.

Hosta
'Royal Standard' A.G.M.
(Hostaceae/Liliaceae)

Common name: Plantain lily
Height: 1m (3ft)
Spread: 1.2m (4ft)
Aspect: Any
Soil: Moist, well-drained, fertile
Hardiness: Zone 5
Propagation: Division, in autumn or spring

Robust, hybrid perennial. Leaves ovate to heart-shaped, ribbed, shiny pale green. Flowers white, perfumed funnels on leafy scapes in late summer.

Hosta sieboldiana
(Hostaceae/Liliaceae)

Common name: Plantain lily
Height: 1m (3ft)
Spread: 1.2m (4ft)
Aspect: Half shade or sun
Soil: Moist, well-drained, fertile
Hardiness: Zone 5
Propagation: Division, in autumn or spring

Species from Japan. Leaves large, ovate to heart-shaped, thick, grey-green, green or blue. Flowers in leafy scapes, pale lilac-grey bells, in early summer.

Hosta
'So Sweet'
(Hostaceae/Liliaceae)

Common name: Plantain lily
Height: 60cm (24in)
Spread: 55cm (22in)
Aspect: Half shade or sun
Soil: Moist, well-drained, fertile
Hardiness: Zone 5
Propagation: Division, in autumn or spring

Hybrid with ovate to lance-shaped, glossy, mid-green leaves, margined creamy-white. Flowers white, purple-striped, fragrant, funnel-shaped, in mid- and late summer.

Hosta
'Sun Power'
(Hostaceae/Liliaceae)

Common name: Plantain lily
Height: 1.2m (4ft)
Spread: 1m (3ft)
Aspect: Full or half shade
Soil: Moist, well-drained, fertile
Hardiness: Zone 5
Propagation: Division, in autumn or spring

A hybrid perennial. Leaves ovate to heart-shaped, bright yellow or yellow-green. Flowers pale lavender or white, on leafy scapes in summer.

Hosta
'Sweet Susan'
(Hostaceae/Liliaceae)

Common name: Plantain lily
Height: 45cm (18in)
Spread: 70cm (28in)
Aspect: Half shade or sun
Soil: Moist, well-drained
Hardiness: Zone 5
Propagation: Division, in autumn or spring

Hybrid with large, heart-shaped, mid-green leaves. Flowers funnel-shaped, perfumed, white, edged purple, on leafy scapes in early and again in late summer.

Hosta
'Tall Boy'
(Hostaceae/Liliaceae)

Common name: Plantain lily
Height: 1m (3ft)
Spread: 1m (3ft)
Aspect: Any
Soil: Moist, well-drained, fertile
Hardiness: Zone 5
Propagation: Division, in autumn or spring

A hybrid perennial. Leaves ovate, green. Flowers funnel-shaped, purple, in dense racemes on leafy scapes well above the leaves, in late summer.

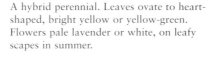

Hosta undulata
var. *undulata* A.G.M.
(Hostaceae/Liliaceae)

Common name: Plantain lily
Height: 80cm (32in)
Spread: 45cm (18in)
Aspect: Any
Soil: Moist, well-drained, fertile
Hardiness: Zone 5
Propagation: Division, in autumn or spring

Leaves lance-shaped to elliptic, twisted, green with pronounced central white band. Flowers on arching, leafy scapes, mauve, funnel-shaped, in early and mid-summer.

Hosta
'Wide Brim' A.G.M.
(Hostaceae/Liliaceae)

Common name: Plantain lily
Height: 55cm (22in)
Spread: 1m (36in)
Aspect: Any
Soil: Moist, well-drained, fertile
Hardiness: Zone 5
Propagation: Division, in autumn or spring

Clump-forming hybrid. Leaves relatively small, heart-shaped, puckered, dark green, margined cream. Flowers pale lavender funnels, in summer.

Houttuynia cordata
'Chameleon'
(Saururaceae)

Common names: None
Height: 30cm (1ft)
Spread: Indefinite
Aspect: Sun
Soil: Moist, humus-rich, fertile
Hardiness: Zone 5
Propagation: Division in spring

Rampant ground cover. Leaves aromatic, ovate or heart-shaped, heavily variegated in red, yellow and green. Flowers tiny, green-yellow, with white bracts, in spring.

Houttuynia cordata
'Flore Pleno'
(Saururaceae)

Common names: None
Height: 30cm (1ft)
Spread: Indefinite
Aspect: Sun or half shade
Soil: Moist, humus-rich, fertile
Hardiness: Zone 5
Propagation: Division, in spring

Highly invasive, rhizomatous woodlander. Leaves aromatic, ovate or heart-shaped, grey-green. Flowers tiny, green-yellow, with pure white bracts. Ground cover in shade.

One of the taller hostas, 'Tall Boy' makes an impact when massed in a border.

Hyacinthoides non-scripta var. *alba*
(Hyacinthaceae/Liliaceae)

Common name: English bluebell
Height: 40cm (16in)
Spread: 10cm (4in)
Aspect: Half shade
Soil: Moist, well-drained, fertile, humus-rich
Hardiness: Zone 5
Propagation: Offsets, in summer

Vigorous, bulbous, woodlander. Leaves linear, glossy, dark green. Flowers in one-sided, arched racemes, pendent, perfumed, bell-shaped, white. Spreads rapidly.

Hyacinthoides non-scripta var. *rosea*
(Hyacinthaceae/Liliaceae)

Common name: English bluebell
Height: 40cm (16in)
Spread: 10cm (4in)
Aspect: Half shade
Soil: Moist, well-drained, fertile, humus-rich
Hardiness: Zone 5
Propagation: Offsets, in summer

Vigorous, bulbous woodlander. Leaves linear, glossy-green. Flowers in one-sided, arching racemes, lilac-pink, perfumed, bell-shaped. Excellent in half shade.

Hyacinthus orientalis 'Blue Jacket' A.G.M.
(Hyacinthaceae/Liliaceae)

Common name: Hyacinth
Height: 30cm (12in)
Spread: 8cm (3in)
Aspect: Sun or half shade
Soil: Well-drained, fertile
Hardiness: Zone 5
Propagation: Offsets, in summer

Hybrid of a bulbous plant from the Middle East. Leaves linear, channelled, green. Flowers in dense, erect racemes, perfumed, single, tubular, navy blue, in early spring.

Hyacinthus orientalis 'City of Haarlem' A.G.M.
(Hyacinthaceae/Liliaceae)

Common name: Hyacinth
Height: 30cm (12in)
Spread: 8cm (3in)
Aspect: Sun or half shade
Soil: Well-drained, fertile
Hardiness: Zone 5
Propagation: Offsets, in summer

Hybrid cultivar. Leaves linear, channelled, green. Flowers in erect, dense racemes of up to 40, perfumed, tubular, primrose, in early spring.

Hyacinthus orientalis 'Gipsy Queen' A.G.M.
(Hyacinthaceae/Liliaceae)

Common name: Hyacinth
Height: 30cm (12in)
Spread: 8cm (3in)
Aspect: Sun or half shade
Soil: Well-drained, fertile
Hardiness: Zone 5
Propagation: Offsets, in summer

Hybrid cultivar. Leaves linear, channelled, green. Flowers in erect racemes of up to 40, perfumed, tubular, single, salmon-pink, in early spring.

Hyacinthus orientalis 'L'Innocence' A.G.M.
(Hyacinthaceae/Liliaceae)

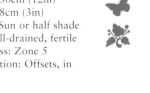

Common name: Hyacinth
Height: 30cm (12in)
Spread: 8cm (3in)
Aspect: Sun or half shade
Soil: Well-drained, fertile
Hardiness: Zone 5
Propagation: Offsets, in summer

Hybrid cultivar. Leaves linear, channelled, green. Flowers in erect racemes of up to 40, single, perfumed, tubular, pure white, in early spring.

Hylomecon japonica
(Papaveraceae)

Common names: None
Height: 20cm (8in)
Spread: 45cm (18in)
Aspect: Half or full shade
Soil: Moist, well-drained, acidic, humus-rich
Hardiness: Zone 7
Propagation: Seed, when ripe; division, in spring

Rhizomatous woodlander. Leaves pinnate, lobes ovate, toothed, pale green. Flowers solitary, single, 4-petalled cups, chrome yellow, from spring to summer.

Hymenocallis × festalis
(Amaryllidaceae)

Common name: Spider lily
Height: 80cm (32in)
Spread: 30cm (12in)
Aspect: Sun or half shade
Soil: Moist, well-drained, fertile
Hardiness: Zone 9
Propagation: Seed, in warmth when ripe; offsets, in summer

Evergreen, tender, bulbous garden hybrid. Leaves basal, oblong, shiny, green. Flowers in umbels on erect stems, white, perfumed, central cup, petals long and twisted.

Hypericum cerastioides
(Clusiaceae/Guttiferae)

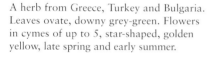

Common name: St. John's wort
Height: 20cm (8in)
Spread: 45cm (18in)
Aspect: Sun
Soil: Well-drained, gritty
Hardiness: Zone 7
Propagation: Division, in spring or autumn

A herb from Greece, Turkey and Bulgaria. Leaves ovate, downy grey-green. Flowers in cymes of up to 5, star-shaped, golden yellow, late spring and early summer.

Hypericum olympicum
A.G.M.
(Clusiaceae/Guttiferae)

Common name: St. John's wort
Height: 30cm (1ft)
Spread: 30cm (1ft)
Aspect: Sun
Soil: Well-drained, gritty
Hardiness: Zone 6
Propagation: Greenwood cuttings, in summer

A subshrub from Greece and Turkey. Leaves oblong, pointed, grey-green. Flowers in cymes of up to 5, star-shaped, deep yellow, in summer.

Hypericum perforatum
(Clusiaceae/Guttiferae)

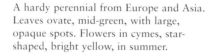

Common name: Perforate St. John's wort
Height: 1.2m (4ft)
Spread: 60cm (2ft)
Aspect: Sun
Soil: Well-drained, gritty
Hardiness: Zone 3
Propagation: Division, in spring or autumn

A hardy perennial from Europe and Asia. Leaves ovate, mid-green, with large, opaque spots. Flowers in cymes, star-shaped, bright yellow, in summer.

Hyssopus officinalis
f. *albus*
(Labiatae/Lamiaceae)

Common name: Hyssop
Height: 60cm (2ft)
Spread: 90cm (3ft)
Aspect: Sun
Soil: Well-drained, fertile
Hardiness: Zone 3
Propagation: Seed, in autumn

Hardy, aromatic subshrub. Leaves linear, mid-green. Flowers funnel-shaped, scented, whorled, white (deep blue in the species), in spikes, from midsummer to autumn.

Iberis sempervirens
'Pinky Perpetual'
(Brassicaceae/Cruciferae)

Common name: Candytuft
Height: 30cm (12in)
Spread: 40cm (16in)
Aspect: Sun
Soil: Moist, well-drained, fertile
Hardiness: Zone 4
Propagation: Softwood cuttings, in late spring

Hardy, evergreen subshrub from Europe. Leaves linear, short, dark green. Flowers pink, in racemes, in late spring and early summer. The species has white flowers.

Iberis sempervirens
'Weisser Zwerg'
(Brassicaceae/Cruciferae)

Common name: Candytuft
Height: 10cm (4in)
Spread: 20cm (8in)
Aspect: Sun
Soil: Moist, well-drained, fertile
Hardiness: Zone 4
Propagation: Softwood cuttings, in late spring

A very compact cloned selection. Leaves are short, linear, dark green. Bears a profusion of white, stemless flowers in spring.

Impatiens tinctoria
(Balsaminaceae)

Common name: Balsam
Height: 2.2m (7ft)
Spread: 1m (3ft)
Aspect: Half shade
Soil: Moist, well-drained, humus-rich
Hardiness: Zone 10
Propagation: Seed, in warmth in early spring

Robust, tuberous plant. Leaves oblong to lance-shaped, toothed, spirally arranged, green. Flowers in racemes, white, scented, with a violet throat, summer to autumn.

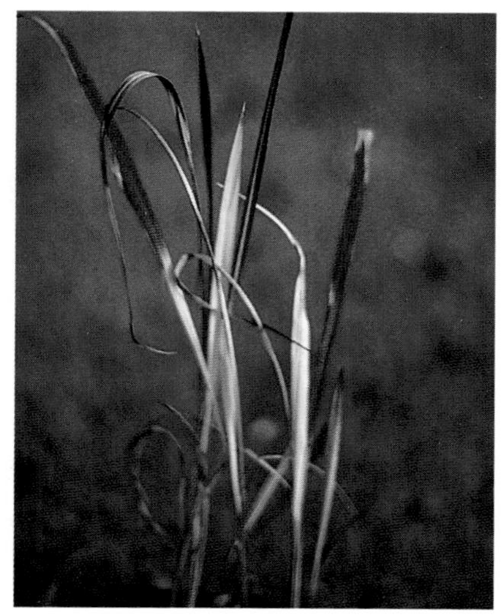

Imperata cylindrica
'Rubra'
(Graminae/Poaceae)

Common name: Japanese blood grass
Height: 60cm (2ft)
Spread: 30cm (1ft)
Aspect: Sun or half shade
Soil: Moist, well-drained, humus-rich
Hardiness: Zone 8
Propagation: Division, in spring

Half-hardy grass from Japan. Leaves linear, flat, pale green, turning bright red from the tips downwards. Panicles of fluffy, silvery spikelets in late summer in warm areas.

INCARVILLEA (Bignoniaceae)
Poor man's orchid

A genus of some 15 or so annuals and taprooted perennials from rocky mountains and high-altitude grasslands of Central and Eastern Asia. The flowers are held high, singly or in panicles or racemes, on stiff stems, and are tubular to trumpet-shaped, with 5 petals. They are mostly purple or pink in colour, but white forms exist; flowering time is early or midsummer. The foliage is dark green, and the alternate leaves pinnate or pinnatisect. *Incarvillea* would be worth taking some time over, but in fact they are easy and accommodating plants; the delicate, exotic look of the flowers belies the fact that these plants are hardy or half-hardy. They are suitable for either a rock garden or a mixed border. They have carrot-like roots, and so resent disturbance once they have become established. They should be planted with their crowns 8–10cm (3–4in) below the soil surface, and damage to the fleshy roots should be avoided at all costs. Some protection should be given from very high levels of wet in winter, and a mulch protection used in prolonged frosts. *Incarvillea* are easy to grow from seed, but they will take three years to flower, except for *I. arguta*, which may well flower in its first season.

Incarvillea arguta
(Bignoniaceae)

Common names: None
Height: 90cm (3ft)
Spread: 30cm (1ft)
Aspect: Sun, shade in summer
Soil: Moist, well-drained, fertile
Hardiness: Zone 8
Propagation: Seed, in spring or autumn

Leaves pinnate, deep green, leaflets lance-shaped, toothed. Flowers in racemes of up to 20, pendent, tubular, pink or white, in early and midsummer.

Incarvillea delavayi
(Bignoniaceae)

Common name: Pink bignonia
Height: 60cm (2ft)
Spread: 30cm (1ft)
Aspect: Sun, shade in summer
Soil: Moist, well-drained, fertile
Hardiness: Zone 6
Propagation: Seed, in spring or autumn

Tap-rooted plant from China. Leaves dark green, pinnate, leaflets lance-shaped, toothed. Flowers in racemes of up to 10, purple-pink, in early and midsummer.

Incarvillea delavayi f. *alba*
(Bignoniaceae)

Common name: White bignonia
Height: 60cm (2ft)
Spread: 30cm (1ft)
Aspect: Sun, shade in summer
Soil: Moist, well-drained, fertile
Hardiness: Zone 6
Propagation: Seed, in spring or autumn

Leaves dark green, pinnate, leaflets lance-shaped, toothed, terminal segment large. Flowers in racemes of up to 10, white with a yellow throat, in early and midsummer.

Incarvillea delavayi
'Bees Pink'
(Bignoniaceae)

Common name: Pink bignonia
Height: 60cm (2ft)
Spread: 30cm (1ft)
Aspect: Sun, shade in summer
Soil: Moist, well-drained, fertile
Hardiness: Zone 6
Propagation: Division, in spring

Selected form of the species. Leaves dark green, pinnate, leaflets lance-shaped, toothed. Flowers in racemes of up to 10, pink trumpets, in early and midsummer.

Incarvillea mairei
(Bignoniaceae)

Common names: None
Height: 50cm (20in)
Spread: 30cm (12in)
Aspect: Sun, shade in summer
Soil: Moist, well-drained, fertile
Hardiness: Zone 4
Propagation: Seed, in spring or autumn

Leaves dark green, pinnate, leaflets ovate, toothed. Few-flowered racemes of purple-crimson trumpets with a yellow throat, in early summer.

Incarvillea sinensis
'Alba'
(Bignoniaceae)

Common names: None
Height: 85cm (34in)
Spread: 30cm (12in)
Aspect: Sun
Soil: Moist, well-drained, fertile
Hardiness: Zone 4
Propagation: Seed, in spring or autumn

Tap-rooted plant from China and Nepal. Leaves dark green, pinnatisect, pinnae linear to lance-shaped. Tall, few-flowered racemes of white trumpets, in late summer.

Incarvillea 'Snowtop' (Bignoniaceae)

Common names: None
Height: 60cm (2ft)
Spread: 30cm (1ft)
Aspect: Sun
Soil: Moist, well-drained, fertile
Hardiness: Zone 6
Propagation: Division, in spring, with care

Hardy hybrid. Pure white flowers in summer. Dies down very early, so mark the position well, to prevent damaging the roots of the dormant plant.

Incarvillea zhongdianensis (Bignoniaceae)

Common names: None
Height: 40cm (16in)
Spread: 20cm (8in)
Aspect: Sun
Soil: Moist, well-drained, fertile
Hardiness: Zone 7
Propagation: Seed, in autumn or spring

Recent introduction (as *I. compacta*) from China. Foliage dark glossy-green. Flowers of a glorious purplish-pink, with a yellow throat. Should become very popular.

INULA (Asteraceae/Compositae)

A genus of some 100 species, mostly perennial, but including some annuals and biennials; all the perennial species are hardy, easy to grow, and some (for example, *Inula hookeri* and *I. racemosa*) are frankly invasive. Their native habitats, ranging across temperate and tropical regions of Asia, Africa and Europe, range from moist, shady lowlands to sunny and mountainous areas. They will grow in any soil, but prefer a moisture-retentive one; if they become too dry they are prone to powdery mildew. *I magnifica* will even grow in boggy soil. All species suit a sunny position, but *I. ensifolia* will tolerate light shade, and *I. hookeri* prefers half shade. In general, the robust, taller species naturalize well in wildflower gardens, although some need to be staked if they are not supported by other plants, and the smaller types are a good choice for growing in rock gardens. *I. helenium* has been cultivated as a medicinal herb; its roots were once used to produce an expectorant. The flowers, borne singly or in corymbs in summer, are yellow or orange and daisy-like, and are much visited by bees and butterflies. Some are good for cutting. The foliage is unremarkable; the basal leaves are large, sometimes toothed or hairy, and the stem leaves are progressively smaller as they ascend.

Inula acaulis (Asteraceae/Compositae)

Common names: None
Height: 10cm (4in)
Spread: 30cm (1ft)
Aspect: Sun
Soil: Moist, well-drained,
Hardiness: Zone 6
Propagation: Seed or division, both in spring or autumn

Choice, compact, rhizomatous species from Asia. Leaves inversely lance-shaped, mid-green. Flowers solitary, single, ray florets yellow, disc florets brown, in summer.

Inula ensifolia (Asteraceae/Compositae)

Common names: None
Height: 60cm (2ft)
Spread: 30cm (1ft)
Aspect: Sun or half shade
Soil: Moist, well-drained, fertile
Hardiness: Zone 5
Propagation: Seed or division, both in spring or autumn

Rhizomatous, free-flowering species. Leaves stemless, linear, mid-green. Flowers in corymbs or solitary, single, daisy-like, golden-yellow, in mid- to late summer.

Inula helenium (Asteraceae/Compositae)

Common name: Elecampane
Height: 1.5m (5ft)
Spread: 90cm (3ft)
Aspect: Sun
Soil: Moist, well-drained, fertile
Hardiness: Zone 5
Propagation: Seed or division, both in spring or autumn

A medicinal rhizomatous plant. Leaves in basal rosette, ovate, toothed, mid-green. Flowers in corymbs or solitary, single, daisy-like, yellow, in mid- and late summer.

Inula hookeri (Asteraceae/Compositae)

Common names: None
Height: 80cm (32in)
Spread: Indefinite
Aspect: Half shade
Soil: Moist, well-drained, fertile
Hardiness: Zone 6
Propagation: Seed or division, both in spring or autumn

Invasive species. Leaves ovate, toothed, hairy, green. Flowers solitary or in heads of 2 or 3, single, ray florets thin, pale yellow, in late summer to mid-autumn.

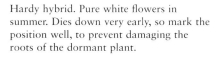

Inula magnifica
(Asteraceae/Compositae)

Common names: None
Height: 1.8m (6ft)
Spread: 90cm (3ft)
Aspect: Sun
Soil: Moist, well-drained, fertile
Hardiness: Zone 6
Propagation: Seed or division, both in spring or autumn

Species from the Caucasus. Leaves very large, elliptic-ovate, dark green. Single, daisy-like flowers in corymbs of up to 20, golden-yellow, in late summer.

Inula orientalis
(Asteraceae/Compositae)

Common names: None
Height: 1m (3ft)
Spread: 60cm (2ft)
Aspect: Sun
Soil: Moist, well-drained, fertile
Hardiness: Zone 6
Propagation: Seed or division, both in spring or autumn

Rhizomatous species. Leaves ovate-elliptic, toothed, hairy, mid-green. Solitary, yellow daisy-like flowers, with reflexed and incurved ray florets, in summer.

Inula royleana
(Asteraceae/Compositae)

Common names: None
Height: 80cm (32 in)
Spread: 45cm (18in)
Aspect: Sun
Soil: Moist, well-drained, fertile
Hardiness: Zone 6
Propagation: Seed or division, both in spring or autumn

A hardy species from the Himalayas. Leaves ovate, hairy, toothed, veined, green. Flowers solitary, single, yellow, daisy-like, from midsummer to autumn.

Ipheion
'Alberto Castillo'
(Alliaceae/Liliaceae)

Common names: None
Height: 20cm (8in)
Spread: 5cm (2in)
Aspect: Sun
Soil: Moist, well-drained, humus-rich
Hardiness: Zone 6
Propagation: Offsets, in summer

Selected form of a bulbous Argentinian plant. Leaves straplike, narrow, blue-green. Flowers upward-facing, larger than the type, solitary, scented, white, in spring.

Ipheion uniflorum
(Alliaceae/Liliaceae)

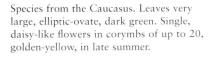

Common names: None
Height: 20cm (8in)
Spread: 5cm (2in)
Aspect: Sun
Soil: Moist, well-drained, humus-rich
Hardiness: Zone 6
Propagation: Offsets, in summer

A hardy bulbous perennial from Argentina. Leaves narrow, straplike, blue-green. Flowers solitary, upward-facing, perfumed, pale silvery blue stars, in spring.

Ipheion uniflorum
'Froyle Mill' A.G.M.
(Alliaceae/Liliaceae)

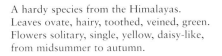

Common names: None
Height: 30cm (12in)
Spread: 5cm (2in)
Aspect: Sun
Soil: Moist, well-drained, humus-rich
Hardiness: Zone 6
Propagation: Offsets, in summer

Selected form of a bulbous hardy perennial from Argentina. Leaves narrow, straplike, blue-green. Flowers solitary, perfumed, dusky violet stars, in spring.

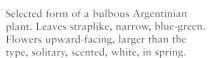

IRIS (Iridaceae)
Flag • Fleur de Lis • Sword lily

A genus of some 300 species from very diverse and scattered habitats in the northern hemisphere. They can be bulbous, rhizomatous, or fleshy-rooted, evergreen or deciduous, and vary widely in their cultural requirements. The classification by the Royal Horticultural Society (*see right*) will be used here. An iris flower has three outer and three inner tepals. The outer three bend back, and may also hang down, and so are called "falls"; they are usually the most colourfully marked part of the flower. The falls are especially large and colourful in the bearded irises, which have white or coloured hairs, like a beard, in the centre of each fall. Crested irises have a ridge, or crest, on each fall. The three inner tepals are called "standards," since they generally stand upright in the centre of the flower, but they may lie horizontal, as in *I. tectorum*; droop, as in *I. bucharica*; or be much reduced, as in *I. danfordiae*. Three modified styles called stigma flaps reach out over the falls from the middle of the flower and can form an important element. All parts of the plant are poisonous, and contact with the sap may cause skin irritation. Iris are low-allergen plants, however. The flowers and foliage are much used by flower-arrangers.

Iris 'Brighteyes' (Iridaceae)

Classification: Bearded iris
Height: 40cm (16in)
Spread: Indefinite
Aspect: Sun
Soil: Well-drained, fertile, acidic
Hardiness: Zone 6
Propagation: Division, in summer to autumn

An intermediate, rhizomatous iris. Leaves narrow, green. Pale yellow flowers with distinctive brown markings on the falls, hence its name.

Iris bucharica A.G.M. (Iridaceae)

Classification: Bulbous iris
Height: 40cm (16in)
Spread: 10cm (4in)
Aspect: Sun
Soil: Well-drained, neutral to alkaline
Hardiness: Zone 5
Propagation: Seed, in autumn or spring; division, in summer or autumn

A Juno iris from Central Asia. Leaves glossy, green. Flowers have standards below falls; standards yellow, falls white with a yellow spot.

Iris chrysographes (Iridaceae)

Classification: Beardless iris
Height: 50cm (20in)
Spread: Indefinite
Aspect: Sun or half shade
Soil: Well-drained, acidic
Hardiness: Zone 5
Propagation: Seed, in autumn or spring; division, in summer or autumn

A rhizomatous Siberian iris from China. Leaves linear, grey-green. Flowers perfumed, dark violet-red, with silver stripes on the falls.

Iris cristata (Iridaceae)

Classification: Crested iris
Height: 10cm (4in)
Spread: Indefinite
Aspect: Sun or half shade
Soil; Moist, humus-rich
Hardiness: Zone 4
Propagation: Seed, in autumn or spring; division, in summer or autumn

A crested iris species from eastern United States. Leaves lance-shaped, green. Flowers lilac-blue, with an orange patch on each fall, in late spring.

CLASSIFICATION of IRIS by the R.H.S.

Bearded species and cultivars, in various sizes from miniature dwarf to tall, form the most widely cultivated group of irises. They are rhizomatous, and prefer well-drained conditions.

Aril irises are a group of bearded irises that includes the Onocyclus, Regelia, Regeliocyclus and Arilbred types. These become dormant in summer after flowering, and should be kept dry while dormant.

Beardless irises generally have more flowers per stem than bearded types. They include Pacific Coast, Siberian, Spuria, Laevigatae, Louisiana and Unguiculares, and are rhizomatous. They prefer well-drained conditions, apart from the Laevigatae, which need damp soil.

Crested irises are rhizomatous and spread freely. They prefer moist soil.

Bulbous irises, grouped as Juno, Reticulata or Xiphium, are beardless and summer dormant. They prefer well-drained soil.

Iris danfordiae (Iridaceae)

Classification: Bulbous iris
Height: 15cm (6in)
Spread: 5cm (2in)
Aspect: Sun
Soil: Well-drained, alkaline
Hardiness: Zone 5
Propagation: Seed, in autumn or spring; division, in summer or autumn

A Reticulata species from Turkey. Leaves paired, narrow, green. Flowers have much-reduced standards. Falls bright yellow, speckled green.

Iris douglasiana A.G.M. (Iridaceae)

Classification: Beardless iris
Height: 70cm (28in)
Spread: Indefinite
Aspect: Sun or half shade
Soil: Well-drained, acidic
Hardiness: Zone 7
Propagation: Seed, in autumn or spring; division, in summer or autumn

A robust, evergreen Pacific Coast iris. Leaves stiff, glossy, green. Flowers lavender-blue, white or cream on branched stems, in late spring and early summer.

Iris ensata A.G.M. (Iridaceae)

Classification: Beardless iris
Height: 90cm (3ft)
Spread: Indefinite
Aspect: Sun
Soil: Moist to wet, deep, acidic, humus-rich
Hardiness: Zone 5
Propagation: Seed, in autumn or spring; division, in summer or autumn

A Laevigatae beardless iris. Leaves long straps, green. Flowers lilac, purple or red on branching stems, in midsummer. Marginal aquatic.

A beautiful display of Iris ensata *at Koichikawa Garden, in Tokyo.*

Iris ensata
'Freckled Geisha'
(Iridaceae)

Classification: Beardless iris
Height: 90cm (3ft)
Spread: Indefinite
Aspect: Sun
Soil: Moist to wet, deep, acidic, humus-rich
Hardiness: Zone 5
Propagation: Division, in summer or autumn

A hybrid, rhizomatous Laevigatae iris with very large flowers of lilac and white, with yellow bases on the falls. Marginal aquatic plant.

Iris ensata
'Galatea Marx'
(Iridaceae)

Classification: Beardless iris
Height: 90cm (3ft)
Spread: Indefinite
Aspect: Sun
Soil: Moist to wet, deep, acidic, humus-rich
Hardiness: Zone 5
Propagation: Division, in summer or autumn

A hybrid Laevigatae iris cultivar. Single, sometimes branched stems bear flowers with pale blue falls and purple standards. Marginal aquatic.

Iris ensata
'Moonlight Waves'
(Iridaceae)

Classification: Beardless iris
Height: 90cm (3ft)
Spread: Indefinite
Aspect: Sun
Soil: Moist to wet, deep, acidic, humus-rich
Hardiness: Zone 5
Propagation: Division, in summer or autumn

A hybrid Laevigatae iris cultivar, each stem bearing 3 or 4 large flowers of a rich, deep, purple-blue in midsummer. Marginal aquatic.

Iris graminea
A.G.M. (Iridaceae)

Classification: Beardless iris
Common name: Plum tart iris
Height: 40cm (16in)
Spread: Indefinite
Aspect: Sun or half shade
Soil: Well-drained, acidic
Hardiness: Zone 5
Propagation: Seed, in autumn or spring; division, in summer or autumn

A Spuria iris from Spain and across Europe to Russia. Leaves linear, flat, bright green. Flowers perfumed, of purple or violet colour, falls have white tips, veined violet.

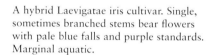

Iris
'Holden Clough' A.G.M.
(Iridaceae)

Classification: Beardless iris
Height: 90cm (3ft)
Spread: Indefinite
Aspect: Sun or half shade
Soil: Moist, deep, acidic, humus-rich
Hardiness: Zone 6
Propagation: Division, in summer or autumn

A hybrid Laevigatae iris. Leaves angled outwards, so plant takes up a lot of room; evergreen in warm areas. Flowers pale brown, veined purple. Marginal aquatic.

Iris innominata
(Iridaceae)

Classification: Beardless iris
Height: 20cm (8in)
Spread: Indefinite
Aspect: Sun or half shade
Soil: Well-drained, acidic
Hardiness: Zone 7
Propagation: Seed, in autumn or spring; division, in summer or autumn

An evergreen Pacific Coast iris, from the southwestern U.S.A. Leaves narrow, green. Flowers pale lavender-blue, purple, yellow or cream, in early summer.

Iris japonica
A.G.M. (Iridaceae)

Classification: Crested iris
Height: 45cm (18in)
Spread: Indefinite
Aspect: Sun or half shade
Soil: Moist, humus-rich
Hardiness: Zone 7
Propagation: Seed, in autumn or spring; division, in summer or autumn

Leaves glossy, strap-like. Flowers white or lavender, frilly; falls have orange crests and purple patches. Long-flowering. Rhizomes lie on soil surface and spread slowly.

Iris laevigata
A.G.M.
(Iridaceae)

Classification: Beardless iris
Height: 60cm (2ft)
Spread: Indefinite
Aspect: Sun or half shade
Soil: Moist to wet, deep, acidic, humus-rich
Hardiness: Zone 4
Propagation: Seed, in autumn or spring; division, in summer or autumn

A Laevigatae iris from Russia and the Far East. Leaves broad, green straps. Flowers purple-blue, with a yellow patch on the falls. Marginal aquatic.

Iris latifolia
A.G.M.
(Iridaceae)

Classification: Bulbous iris
Height: 60cm (2ft)
Spread: 20cm (8in)
Aspect: Sun
Soil: Well-drained, alkaline
Hardiness: Zone 5
Propagation: Seed, in autumn or spring; division, in summer or autumn

A Xiphium iris from Spain. Leaves narrow, green, lance-shaped. Flowers white, blue or violet, with a yellow spot on the falls, in early summer.

Iris missouriensis
(Iridaceae)

Classification: Beardless iris
Height: 50cm (20in)
Spread: Indefinite
Aspect: Sun or half shade
Soil: Well-drained, acidic
Hardiness: Zone 9
Propagation: Seed, in autumn or spring

Tender iris from western and central North America. Leaves narrow, taller than flowers, which have short, blue standards and larger blue falls, veined purple, in summer.

Iris pallida
'Argentea Variegata'
(Iridaceae)

Classification: Bearded iris
Height: 90cm (3ft)
Spread: Indefinite
Aspect: Sun
Soil: Well-drained, fertile, acidic
Hardiness: Zone 6
Propagation: Division, in summer or autumn

From Croatia. Leaves short, bright green, silver-striped, strap-like, evergreen. Tall spikes of scented flowers, blue with yellow beards, in late spring and early summer.

Iris pseudacorus
(Iridaceae)

Classification: Beardless iris
Height: 1.2m (4ft)
Spread: Indefinite
Aspect: Sun
Soil: Moist to wet, deep, acidic, humus-rich
Hardiness: Zone 6
Propagation: Seed, in autumn or spring; division, in summer or autumn

A robust Laevigatae iris from Europe, Asia and North Africa. Leaves ribbed, strap-like, grey-green. Flowers yellow, with brown markings on standards. Marginal aquatic.

Iris pumila
(Iridaceae)

Classification: Miniature dwarf bearded iris
Height: 15cm (4in)
Spread: Indefinite
Aspect: Sun
Soil: Well-drained, fertile, acidic
Hardiness: Zone 4
Propagation: Seed, in autumn or spring; division, in summer or autumn

A miniature dwarf bearded iris from Europe and the Urals. Leaves strap-like, green. Flowers solitary, perfumed, purple, blue or yellow, in spring.

Iris reticulata
A.G.M.
(Iridaceae)

Classification: Bulbous iris
Height: 15cm (6in)
Spread: 5cm (2in)
Aspect: Sun
Soil: Moist, well-drained, alkaline
Hardiness: Zone 5
Propagation: Seed, in autumn or spring; division, in summer or autumn

Reticulata from Turkey and the Caucasus. Leaves linear. Flowers solitary, scented, deep purple with yellow ridge on falls. Bulb may split into tiny, slow-to-flower bulbils.

Iris sibirica
A.G.M.
(Iridaceae)

Classification: Beardless iris
Height: 1m (3ft)
Spread: Indefinite
Aspect: Sun or half shade
Soil: Acid, moist
Hardiness: Zone 4
Propagation: Seed in autumn or spring; division in summer or autumn

From East Europe, Turkey, and Russia. Leaves grass-like, green. Flowers violet-blue, falls white next to the hafts, and darkly veined.

Iris sibirica
'Limeheart'
(Iridaceae)

Classification: Beardless iris
Height: 1.2m (4ft)
Spread: Indefinite
Aspect: Sun or half shade
Soil: Moist, acidic
Hardiness: Zone 4
Propagation: Division, in summer or autumn

A hybrid Siberian iris, one of a large number of cultivars from this species. Leaves are grass-like, flowers are white with greenish hafts.

Iris sibirica
'Wisley White' A.G.M.
(Iridaceae)

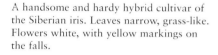

Classification: Beardless iris
Height: 1.2m (4ft)
Spread: Indefinite
Aspect: Sun or half shade
Soil: Moist, acidic
Hardiness: Zone 4
Propagation: Division, in summer or autumn

A handsome and hardy hybrid cultivar of the Siberian iris. Leaves narrow, grass-like. Flowers white, with yellow markings on the falls.

Iris spuria
'Destination'
(Iridaceae)

Classification: Beardless iris
Height: 1m (3ft)
Spread: Indefinite
Aspect: Sun or half shade
Soil: Well-drained, acidic
Hardiness: Zone 5
Propagation: Division, in summer or autumn

A rhizomatous, hybrid Spuria iris cultivar. The species originates in Eurasia. Leaves broad, tough, green. Flowers clear golden-yellow.

Iris
'Tinkerbell'
(Iridaceae)

Classification: Bearded iris
Height: 20cm (8in)
Spread: Indefinite
Aspect: Sun
Soil: Well-drained, fertile, acidic
Hardiness: Zone 6
Propagation: Division, in autumn or spring

A rhizomatous, standard dwarf bearded hybrid iris cultivar. Leaves lance-shaped, green. Flowers pale blue, with a darker blue centre.

Iris tenax
(Iridaceae)

Classification: Beardless iris
Height: 35cm (14in)
Spread: Indefinite
Aspect: Sun or half shade
Soil: Well-drained, acidic
Hardiness: Zone 7
Propagation: Seed, in autumn or spring; division, in summer or autumn

A Pacific Coast iris from the northwestern U.S.A. Leaves narrow, dark green. Flowers blue, white, cream, or yellow, from mid-spring to early summer.

Iris
'Three Cherries'
(Iridaceae)

Classification: Bearded iris
Height: 20cm (8in)
Spread: Indefinite
Aspect: Sun
Soil: Acid, well-drained
Hardiness: Zone 6
Propagation: Division, in summer or autumn

A rhizomatous, hybrid, miniature dwarf bearded iris with yellow flowers. The falls have bands of brown and cream towards the tip.

Iris tridentata
(Iridaceae)

Classification: Beardless iris
Height: 70cm (28in)
Spread: Indefinite
Aspect: Half shade
Soil: Moist, acidic
Hardiness: Zone 5
Propagation: Seed, in autumn or spring; division, in summer or autumn

A rhizomatous speacies from the eastern U.S.A. Leaves linear, dull green. Flowers purple-blue, with white basal spots, in early summer. Tricky to cultivate.

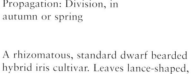

Iris uromovii
(Iridaceae)

Classification: Beardless iris
Height: 30cm (1ft)
Spread: Indefinite
Aspect: Sun or half shade
Soil: Well-drained, acidic
Hardiness: Zone 6
Propagation: Seed, in autumn or spring; division, in summer or autumn

A rhizomatous Spuria iris originating in Bulgaria. Leaves linear, sharp, green. Flowers strong violet-blue, with white falls veined violet-blue.

Isatis tinctoria
(Brassicaceae/Cruciferae)

Common name: Woad
Height: 1.2m (4ft)
Spread: 45cm (18in)
Aspect: Sun
Soil: Moist, well-drained
Hardiness: Zone 7
Propagation: Seed or division, both in spring

Short-lived, tap rooted plant from Europe. Leaves in basal rosettes, oblong to lance-shaped, grey-green. Flowers on branched stems, in panicles, yellow, in early summer.

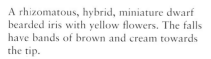

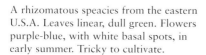

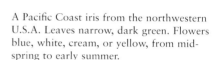

Jasione laevis
(Campanulaceae)

Common name: Sheep's bit scabious
Height: 30cm (12in)
Spread: 20cm (8in)
Aspect: Sun
Soil: Well-drained, gritty
Hardiness: Zone 5
Propagation: Seed, when ripe; division, in spring or autumn

A perennial from Europe, including Britain. Leaves in basal rosettes, narrow, oblong, green. Solitary, spherical heads of blue flowers, in summer.

Jeffersonia diphylla
(Berberidaceae)

Common name: Rheumatism root
Height: 20cm (8in)
Spread: 15cm (6in)
Aspect: Full or half shade
Soil: Moist, humus-rich
Hardiness: Zone 5
Propagation: Seed, when ripe; division, in spring

Choice woodlander from the U.S.A. Leaves kidney-shaped, cleft, grey-green, with glaucous undersides. Flowers cup-shaped, starry, white in late spring.

Juncus effusus
'Spiralis'
(Juncaceae)

Common name: Corkscrew rush
Height: 30cm (1ft)
Spread: Indefinite
Aspect: Sun or half shade
Soil: Moist, acidic
Hardiness: Zone 4
Propagation: Seed or division, both in spring

Invasive, leafless, marginal aquatic. Stems shiny, spiralled, dark green, forming a tangle. Flowers small, brown, on short stalks in cymes, all summer.

Kirengeshoma palmata
A.G.M. (Hydrangeaceae)

Common name: Yellow waxbells
Height: 1.2m (4ft)
Spread: 2m (6ft)
Aspect: Half shade
Soil: Moist, acidic, humus-rich
Hardiness: Zone 5
Propagation: Seed or division, both in spring

Distinctive rhizomatous woodlander. Leaves very large, broad, ovate, pale grey-green. Terminal cymes of 3 nodding flowers, broad yellow tubes, late summer to early autumn.

Knautia arvensis
(Dipsacaceae)

Common name: Field scabious
Height: 1.5m (5ft)
Spread: 45cm (18in)
Aspect: Sun
Soil: Well-drained, fertile
Hardiness: Zone 6
Propagation: Seed or basal cuttings, both in spring

Tap-rooted perennial from Eurasia. Leaves pinnatifid or simple, dull green. Flowers flat, lilac-blue, with involucral bracts, from midsummer to autumn.

Knautia macedonica
(Dipsacaceae)

Common name: Macedonian scabious
Height: 80cm (32in)
Spread: 45cm (18in)
Aspect: Sun
Soil: Well-drained, fertile
Hardiness: Zone 6
Propagation: Seed or basal cuttings, both in spring

Clump-forming perennial from Macedonia. Leaves basal and stem, pinnatifid, mid-green. Flowers purple-red, with involucral bracts, in mid- and late summer.

KNIPHOFIA (Asphodelaceae/Liliaceae)
Red Hot Poker

This genus contains some 70 or so species of rhizomatous perennials from Central and Southern Africa. Their native habitats are usually moist places, often along the banks of rivers or in grasslands on mountainsides. They will thrive in any soil as long as it is moisture-retentive, and they prefer sun but will take light shade, and vary from tender to fully hardy. Many will tolerate coastal conditions. Red hot pokers are mostly clump-forming, with arching, linear to strap-shaped leaves, and may be evergreen or deciduous; leaves of the deciduous types tend to be narrow, those of the evergreens both longer and broader. The flowers are cylindrical or tubular and usually pendent, but upright in some types. They are borne well above the leaves in spike-like racemes, usually dense. There are various colours, including green and toffee, but the most commonly seen are those that open red and then turn yellow, giving a characteristic, bicoloured inflorescence. Red hot pokers make good cut flowers, and are popular with flower-arrangers. Bees and butterflies are attracted to them, and they are low-allergen plants. Cultivars ranging in height from 50cm (20in) to 2m (6ft) are available; the taller varieties may require staking.

***Kniphofia* 'Atlanta' (Asphodelaceae/Liliaceae)**

Common name: Red hot poker
Height: 1.2m (4ft)
Spread: 80cm (32in)
Aspect: Sun or half shade
Soil: Moist, well-drained, humus-rich
Hardiness: Zone 5
Propagation: Division, in spring

Rhizomatous, evergreen hybrid. Leaves strap-shaped, grey-green. Flowers orange-red, in racemes, fading to yellow from base of spike, in late spring to early summer.

***Kniphofia* 'Bees Sunset' A.G.M. (Asphodelaceae/Liliaceae)**

Common name: Red hot poker
Height: 90cm (3ft)
Spread: 60cm (2ft)
Aspect: Sun or half shade
Soil: Moist, well-drained, humus-rich
Hardiness: Zone 5
Propagation: Division, in spring

A hardy, deciduous red hot poker. Leaves linear, toothed, mid-green. Flowers in racemes, yellow-orange, borne from early to late summer.

***Kniphofia caulescens* A.G.M. (Asphodelaceae/Liliaceae)**

Common name: Red hot poker
Height: 1.2m (4ft)
Spread: 60cm (2ft)
Aspect: Sun or half shade
Soil: Moist, well-drained, humus-rich
Hardiness: Zone 7
Propagation: Seed or division, both in spring

Evergreen hardy species. Leaves linear, arched, glaucous, toothed, keeled. Flowers in short racemes, coral-red fading to cream, from late summer to mid-autumn.

***Kniphofia* 'Fiery Fred' (Asphodelaceae/Liliaceae)**

Common name: Red hot poker
Height: 1.2m (4ft)
Spread: 60cm (2ft)
Aspect: Sun or half shade
Soil: Moist, well-drained, humus-rich, fertile
Hardiness: Zone 6
Propagation: Division, in spring

A hardy herbaceous perennial. Leaves linear, mid-green. Flowers in racemes, orange-red fading to light brown, from early to late summer.

***Kniphofia* 'Green Jade' (Asphodelaceae/Liliaceae)**

Common name: Red hot poker
Height: 1.5m (5ft)
Spread: 75cm (30in)
Aspect: Sun or half shade
Soil: Moist, well-drained, humus-rich, fertile
Hardiness: Zone 5
Propagation: Division, in spring

A hardy, evergreen perennial. Leaves linear, keeled, green. Flowers green fading to cream, in dense racemes in late summer and early autumn.

***Kniphofia* 'Shining Sceptre' (Asphodelaceae/Liliaceae)**

Common name: Red hot poker
Height: 1.2m (4ft)
Spread: 60cm (2ft)
Aspect: Sun or half shade
Soil: Moist, well-drained, humus-rich, fertile
Hardiness: Zone 5
Propagation: Division, in spring

A hardy, deciduous perennial. Leaves linear, mid-green. Flowers in racemes, opening clear yellow and fading to ivory, in summer.

***Kniphofia* 'Sunningdale Yellow' A.G.M. (Asphodelaceae/Liliaceae)**

Common name: Red hot poker
Height: 1.2m (4ft)
Spread: 60cm (2ft)
Aspect: Sun or half shade
Soil: Moist, well-drained, humus-rich, fertile
Hardiness: Zone 5
Propagation: Division, in spring

A hardy, deciduous perennial cultivar. Leaves linear, mid-green. Long-lasting flowers in racemes, clear yellow, in mid- and late summer.

***Kniphofia thompsonii* var. *snowdenii* (Asphodelaceae/Liliaceae)**

Common name: Red hot poker
Height: 90cm (36in)
Spread: 45cm (18in)
Aspect: Sun or half shade
Soil: Moist, well-drained, humus-rich, fertile
Hardiness: Zone 8
Propagation: Seed or division, both in spring

Rhizomatous species from Kenya and Uganda. Leaves linear, upright, mid-green. Flowers in very open few-flowered racemes, coral-pink, midsummer to late autumn.

Single-coloured Kniphofia, *such as 'Queen Victoria', make an elegant alternative to the bolder red and yellow types.*

Kniphofia triangularis
A.G.M.
(Asphodelaceae/Liliaceae)

Common name: Red hot poker
Height: 90cm (36in)
Spread: 45cm (18in)
Aspect: Sun or half shade
Soil: Moist, well-drained, humus-rich, fertile
Hardiness: Zone 6
Propagation: Seed or division, both in spring

A hardy species, known also as *K. galpinii*. Leaves grassy, arching, linear, green. Flowers in dense racemes, reddish-orange, in early and midsummer.

Lamium galeobdolon
(Labiatae/Lamiaceae)

Common name: Dead nettle
Height: 60cm (2ft)
Spread: Indefinite
Aspect: Half or full shade
Soil: Moist, well-drained
Hardiness: Zone 6
Propagation: Division, in spring or autumn

Highly invasive rhizomatous plant. Leaves ovate to heart-shaped, toothed, mid-green, may be silver-marked. Flowers 2-lipped, yellow, spotted brown, in spikes in summer.

Lamium galeobdolon
'Hermann's Pride'
(Labiatae/Lamiaceae)

Common name: Dead nettle
Height: 45cm (18in)
Spread: Indefinite
Aspect: Full or half shade
Soil: Moist, well-drained
Hardiness: Zone 6
Propagation: Division, in spring or autumn

More compact and marginally less invasive form of the species. Grown primarily for its small, ovate leaves, heavily streaked silver. Good ground cover in shade.

Lamium maculatum
(Labiatae/Lamiaceae)

Common names: Dead nettle
Height: 20cm (8in)
Spread: 1.2m (4ft)
Aspect: Half or full shade
Soil: Moist, well-drained
Hardiness: Zone 4
Propagation: Division, in spring or autumn

Rhizomatous, creeping plant. Leaves ovate, toothed, matt-green, often marked silver. Flowers in spikes, pink, purple or white, in early summer. Good ground cover.

Lamium maculatum
f. *album*
(Labiatae/Lamiaceae)

Common name: Dead nettle
Height: 20cm (8in)
Spread: 1.2m (4ft)
Aspect: Full or half shade
Soil: Moist, well-drained
Hardiness: Zone 4
Propagation: Division, in spring or autumn

White form of the species. Ovate, toothed leaves silver-grey, flowers pure white; a pleasing combination. A good ground cover plant for shady areas.

Lamium maculatum
'Aureum'
(Labiatae/Lamiaceae)

Common name: Dead nettle
Height: 20cm (8in)
Spread: 90cm (36in)
Aspect: Full or half shade
Soil: Moist, well-drained
Hardiness: Zone 4
Propagation: Division, in spring or autumn

A cultivar of the species with pink flowers that contrast with the yellow of the toothed, ovate leaves. Makes a colourful ground cover.

Lamium maculatum
'Ickwell Beauty'
(Labiatae/Lamiaceae)

Common name: Dead nettle
Height: 20cm (8in)
Spread: 90cm (36in)
Aspect: Full or half shade
Soil: Moist, well-drained
Hardiness: Zone 4
Propagation: Division, in spring or autumn

A form with toothed, ovate leaves that all have some variegation, but in differing degrees and in different colours. Unique ground cover.

Lamium orvala
(Labiatae/Lamiaceae)

Common names: Dead nettle
Height: 60cm (2ft)
Spread: 30cm (1ft)
Aspect: Full or half shade
Soil: Moist, well-drained
Hardiness: Zone 6
Propagation: Seed or division, spring or autumn.

A hardy perennial from Europe. Leaves large, broad, ovate, toothed, hairy, green. Flowers in spikes, purplish-pink, from late spring to summer. Non-invasive.

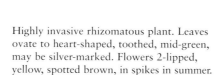

Lathyrus vernus
A.G.M.
(Leguminosae/Papilionaceae)

Common name: Spring vetchling
Height: 45cm (18in)
Spread: 45cm (18in)
Aspect: Sun or half shade
Soil: Well-drained, humus-rich, fertile
Hardiness: Zone 4
Propagation: Seed (after soaking) in spring

A hardy herbaceous plant. Leaves paired, ovate, pointed, mid-green. Flowers pea-like, in one-sided racemes, blue-purple, in spring, followed by purple seed pods.

Lavandula stoechas
A.G.M
(Labiatae/Lamiaceae)

Common name: French lavender
Height: 60cm (2ft)
Spread: 60cm (2ft)
Aspect: Sun
Soil: Well-drained, fertile
Hardiness: Zone 8
Propagation: Seed, in spring; semi-ripe cuttings, in summer

Evergreen Mediterranean subshrub. Leaves linear, aromatic, grey-green. Flowers purple, perfumed, in dense spikes topped by purple bracts, from late spring to summer.

Lavatera
'Barnsley' A.G.M.
(Malvaceae)

Common name: Mallow
Height: 2m (6ft)
Spread: 1.2m (4ft)
Aspect: Sun
Soil: Well-drained, fertile
Hardiness: Zone 7
Propagation: Softwood cuttings, in early summer

Robust, architectural, hybrid subshrub. Leaves palmate, grey-green. Flowers open funnels, white with a red eye, in racemes all summer long.

Lavatera
'Bredon Springs'
(Malvaceae)

Common name: Mallow
Height: 2m (6ft)
Spread: 1.2m (4ft)
Aspect: Sun
Soil: Well-drained, fertile
Hardiness: Zone 8
Propagation: Softwood cuttings, in early summer

Architectural, hybrid subshrub. Leaves palmate, 3- to 5-lobed, grey-green. Flowers in racemes, open funnels, dusky pink flushed mauve, all summer.

Lavatera
'Burgundy Wine'
(Malvaceae)

Common name: Mallow
Height: 1.2m (4ft)
Spread: 90cm (3ft)
Aspect: Sun
Soil: Well-drained, fertile
Hardiness: Zone 7
Propagation: Softwood cuttings, in summer

Robust, hybrid subshrub. Leaves palmate, 3- to 5-lobed, grey-green. Flowers deep pink, darker-veined, in racemes all summer. The best mallow for the small garden.

Lavatera
'Candy Floss'
(Malvaceae)

Common name: Mallow
Height: 2m (6ft)
Spread: 1.2m (4ft)
Aspect: Sun
Soil: Well-drained, fertile
Hardiness: Zone 8
Propagation: Softwood cuttings, in summer

Robust, architectural, hybrid subshrub. Leaves palmate, 3- to 5-lobed, grey-green. Flowers in racemes, open, pale pink funnels, all summer.

Leontopodium alpinum
(Asteraceae/Compositae)

Common name: Edelweiss
Height: 15cm (6in)
Spread: 15cm (6in)
Aspect: Sun
Soil: Sharply drained, alkaline
Hardiness: Zone 4
Propagation: Seed, in spring

Clump-forming alpine for a scree bed. Leaves linear to lance-shaped, basal, grey-green. Flowers white, surrounded by grey-white, woolly bracts, in spring.

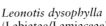

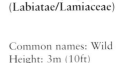

Leonotis dysophylla
(Labiatae/Lamiaceae)

Common names: Wild dagga
Height: 3m (10ft)
Spread: 1m (3ft)
Aspect: Sun
Soil: Well-drained, fertile
Hardiness: Zone 9
Propagation: Seed, in warmth in spring

A tall, tender, architectural perennial from South Africa. Leaves inversely lance-shaped, mid-green. Flowers in whorls, tubular, brilliant orange, in autumn.

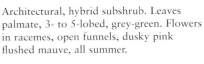

The intense colour of a drift of lavender is echoed by Eryngium *in the foreground in the Grey Walk at Hestercombe, in Somerset.*

Leonotis leonurus
(Labiatae/Lamiaceae)

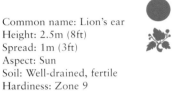

Common name: Lion's ear
Height: 2.5m (8ft)
Spread: 1m (3ft)
Aspect: Sun
Soil: Well-drained, fertile
Hardiness: Zone 9
Propagation: Seed, in warmth in spring

A tall, unusual, tender perennial from South Africa. Leaves are inversely lance-shaped, mid-green. Flowers in whorls, tubular, two-lipped, scarlet, in late autumn.

Leptinella dendyi
(Asteraceae/Compositae)

Common names: None
Height: 40cm (16in)
Spread: 10cm (4in)
Aspect: Sun
Soil: Sharply drained, gritty
Hardiness: Zone 8
Propagation: Seed, when ripe; division, in spring

Compact, cushion-forming scree plant from New Zealand. Leaves 2-pinnatifid, leathery, aromatic, grey-green. Flowers solitary, semi-double, cream, from late spring to summer.

Leucanthemopsis alpina
(Asteraceae/Compositae)

Common name: Alpine chrysanthemum
Height: 10cm (4in)
Spread: 15cm (6in)
Aspect: Sun
Soil: Sharply drained
Hardiness: Zone 6
Propagation: Seed, when ripe

Mat-forming, rhizomatous plant for a scree bed. Silver-grey leaves, from ovate- spoon-shaped to pinnatisect or pinnatifid. Flowers solitary, ray florets white, disc florets yellow.

Leucanthemum × *superbum*
'Aglaia' A.G.M.
(Asteraceae/Compositae)

Common name: Shasta daisy
Height: 60cm (2ft)
Spread: 60cm (2ft)
Aspect: Sun or half shade
Soil: Moist, well-drained, fertile
Hardiness: Zone 5
Propagation: Division, in spring or autumn

One of the very best shasta daisies, with inversely lance-shaped, glossy, dark green leaves. Flowers semi-double, white, shaggy, all summer.

LEUCANTHEMUM (Asteraceae/Compositae)
Shasta daisy

A genus of about 26 annual and perennial species from a range of habitats in temperate Asia and Europe, and previously included under *Chrysanthemum*. The plants in the genus that are of prime importance for perennial beds are *Leucanthemum* × *superbum*, the shasta daisy, a hybrid strain of garden origin, still also known as *Chrysanthemum maximum* of gardens. This group provides us with an invaluable set of robust, soundly perennial, easy-going plants, which will grow in sun or half shade in any good soil; in heavy clay soils they have a reputation for giving up the fight. They are inclined to be lax plants, and some form of support is required. The foliage is handsome, but it will be attacked by slugs as the plants break ground in spring, and will not reappear unless the plants are protected. The flowers are solitary and may be single or double. Although other species in the genus have yellow flowers, the flowers of these hybrids had been exclusively white, with yellow discs (which tend to be paler in double-flowered types), until the cultivar 'Sonnenschein' made its appearance; it has yellow buds that open to cream flowers. The flowers are excellent for cutting, and are liked by flower-arrangers.

Leucanthemum × *superbum*
'Beauté Nivelloise'
(Asteraceae/Compositae)

Common name: Shasta daisy
Height: 85cm (34in)
Spread: 60cm (2ft)
Aspect: Sun or half shade
Soil: Moist, well-drained, fertile
Hardiness: Zone 5
Propagation: Division, in spring or autumn

Leaves inversely lance-shaped, glossy, dark green. Flowers single, ray florets twisted and irregularly incurved or reflexed, white, disc florets yellow, all summer.

Leucanthemum × *superbum*
'Droitwich Beauty'
(Asteraceae/Compositae)

Common name: Shasta daisy
Height: 90cm (3ft)
Spread: 60cm (2ft)
Aspect: Sun or half shade
Soil: Moist, well-drained, fertile
Hardiness: Zone 5
Propagation: Division, in spring or autumn

Leaves inversely lance-shaped, shiny, dark green. Flowers semi-double, shaggy, with white ray florets and pale yellow disc florets, all summer.

Leucanthemum x *superbum* 'Phyllis Smith' (Asteraceae/Compositae)

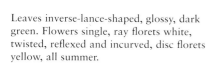

Common name: Shasta daisy
Height: 90cm (3ft)
Spread: 60cm (2ft)
Aspect: Sun or half shade
Soil: Moist, well-drained, fertile
Hardiness: Zone 5
Propagation: Division, in spring or autumn

Leaves inverse-lance-shaped, glossy, dark green. Flowers single, ray florets white, twisted, reflexed and incurved, disc florets yellow, all summer.

Leucanthemum x *superbum* 'Snowcap' (Asteraceae/Compositae)

Common name: Shasta daisy
Height: 45cm (18in)
Spread: 45cm (18in)
Aspect: Sun or half shade
Soil: Moist, well-drained, fertile
Hardiness: Zone 5
Propagation: Division, in spring or autumn

Leaves inversely lance-shaped, glossy, dark green. Flowers single, ray florets white, disc florets yellow, all summer. The best dwarf form, which may not need staking.

Leucanthemum x *superbum* 'Sonnenschein' (Asteraceae/Compositae)

Common name: Shasta daisy
Height: 90cm (3ft)
Spread: 60cm (2ft)
Aspect: Sun or half shade
Soil: Moist, well-drained, fertile
Hardiness: Zone 5
Propagation: Division, in spring or autumn

Very desirable shasta daisy. Leaves inversely lance-shaped, glossy, dark green. Flowers single, ray florets cream, disc florets yellow, all summer.

Leucanthemum x *superbum* 'White Iceberg' (Asteraceae/Compositae)

Common name: Shasta daisy
Height: 90cm (3ft)
Spread: 60cm (2ft)
Aspect: Sun or half shade
Soil: Moist, well-drained, fertile
Hardiness: Zone 5
Propagation: Division, in spring or autumn

Leaves inversely lance-shaped, glossy dark green. Flowers single, ray florets white, incurved and reflexed, disc florets yellow, all summer.

Leucanthemum x *superbum* 'Wirral Supreme' A.G.M. (Asteraceae/Compositae)

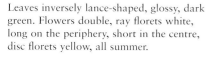

Common name: Shasta daisy
Height: 80cm (32in)
Spread: 60cm (24in)
Aspect: Sun or half shade
Soil: Moist, well-drained
Hardiness: Zone 5
Propagation: Division, in spring or autumn

Leaves inversely lance-shaped, glossy, dark green. Flowers double, ray florets white, long on the periphery, short in the centre, disc florets yellow, all summer.

Leucojum aestivum (Amaryllidaceae)

Common name: Summer snowflake
Height: 60cm (24in)
Spread: 10cm (4in)
Aspect: Sun
Soil: Moist to wet, humus-rich
Hardiness: Zone 4
Propagation: Offsets, after foliage dies down

Bulbous plant from Eurasia and the Near East. Leaves strap-shaped, dark glossy green. Up to 8 flowers per leafless stem, white bells with green tips, chocolate-scented, in spring.

Leucojum vernum A.G.M. (Amaryllidaceae)

Common name: Spring snowflake
Height: 30cm (12in)
Spread: 8cm (3in)
Aspect: Sun
Soil: Moist to wet, humus-rich
Hardiness: Zone 5
Propagation: Offsets, after foliage dies down

Bulbous plant from Europe. Leaves strap-shaped, glossy-green. Flowers 1 or 2 on each stem, white bells with green tips, in early spring.

Levisticum officinale (Apiaceae/Umbelliferae)

Common name: Lovage
Height: 2m (6ft)
Spread: 1m (3ft)
Aspect: Sun
Soil: Moist, well-drained, fertile
Hardiness: Zone 4
Propagation: Seed, when ripe; division, in spring

Vigorous Mediterranean herb. Dark green leaves in rosettes, 2- or 3-pinnate, lobes ovate, toothed. Flowers starry, in umbels, yellow, in summer; good seed heads.

Lewisia
Cotyledon Hybrids
(Portulacaceae)

Common names: None
Height: 30cm (1ft)
Spread: 40cm (16in)
Aspect: Half shade
Soil: Sharply drained, acidic, humus-rich, fertile
Hardiness: Zone 6
Propagation: Seed, in autumn; division, in early summer

Hybrid evergreen. Leaves in rosettes, dark green, fleshy. Flowers in compact panicles, funnel-shaped, pink, orange, yellow or magenta, spring to summer. Keep neck dry.

Liatris spicata
(Asteraceae/Compositae)

Common names: Blazing star; gayfeather
Height: 1.2m (4ft)
Spread: 45cm (18in)
Aspect: Sun
Soil: Moist, well-drained, fertile
Hardiness: Zone 3
Propagation: Seed in autumn; division in spring

Tuberous or cormous plant. Leaves basal, linear to lance-shaped, and stem, green. Flowers pink in dense spikes open from the top down, late summer and early autumn.

Liatris spicata 'Alba'
(Asteraceae/Compositae)

Common names: Blazing star; gayfeather
Height: 1.2m (4ft)
Spread: 45cm (18in)
Aspect: Sun
Soil: Moist, well-drained, fertile
Hardiness: Zone 3
Propagation: Seed, in autumn; division, in spring

White-flowered form of the species. Flowers in dense spikes, opening from the top downwards, white, in late summer to early autumn. Attracts bees.

Libertia formosa
(Iridaceae)

Common names: None
Height: 90cm (3ft)
Spread: 60cm (2ft)
Aspect: Sun
Soil: Moist, well-drained, humus-rich, fertile
Hardiness: Zone 8
Propagation: Seed, when ripe; division, in spring

Rhizomatous evergreen from Chile. Leaves linear, rigid, leathery, mid-green. Flowers in clustered panicles, white or cream from late spring to midsummer; good seed heads.

Libertia grandiflora
(Iridaceae)

Common names: None
Height: 90cm (3ft)
Spread: 60cm (2ft)
Aspect: Sun
Soil: Moist, well-drained, humus-rich, fertile
Hardiness: Zone 8
Propagation: Seed, when ripe; division, in spring

Rhizomatous evergreen from New Zealand. Leaves linear, leathery, dark green. Flowers in panicles, in clusters of up to 6, white, in late spring and early summer.

LIGULARIA (Asteraceae/Compositae)

A genus of some 150 species of perennials, mostly from Asia, with a few examples from Europe. Their natural habitats are moist areas, from the banks of mountain streams to damp grasslands and woodlands. As a consequence, they like a moisture-retaining or even a wet soil in the garden, and are not happy in dry climates unless the soil is kept reliably moist; their leaves droop obviously when they need to be watered. They prefer light shade, or at least shade from the midday sun, and are hardy. *Ligularia* are universally large and fairly coarse in appearance, and so are not for the very small garden; if you have the room for them, they will naturalize well in a moist wildflower garden, and make an impressive picture beside water. Despite being tall, they have stiff stems and do not need to be staked except in exposed areas. As with so many plants with daisy-like flowers, they are highly allergenic, and should be avoided by the allergic gardener; aside from this consideration, some of them do make good cut flowers. All are visited by bees. Unfortunately, the plants are also liked by slugs, which eat the emergent shoots in spring; the leaves will never recover fully from this, so as ever with slug control, take preventative measures early in the season, before growth begins.

Ligularia dentata
(Asteraceae/Compositae)

Common name: Golden groundsel
Height: 1.5m (5ft)
Spread: 1m (3ft)
Aspect: Half shade
Soil: Moist, deep, fertile, humus-rich
Hardiness: Zone 4
Propagation: Seed, in autumn or spring; division, in spring

Clump-forming plant. Leaves rounded, toothed, mid-green. Flowers orange-yellow with brown centres, in flat corymbs, from midsummer to early autumn.

Liatris spicata, *seen here in the dwarf cultivar 'Kobold' is unusual in opening from the top of the flowering spike downwards.*

Ligularia dentata
'Othello'
(Asteraceae/Compositae)

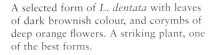

Common names: None
Height: 1m (3ft)
Spread: 60cm (2ft)
Aspect: Half shade
Soil: Moist, deep, fertile, humus-rich
Hardiness: Zone 4
Propagation: Division, in spring or autumn

A selected form of *L. dentata* with leaves of dark brownish colour, and corymbs of deep orange flowers. A striking plant, one of the best forms.

Ligularia × hessei
(Asteraceae/Compositae)

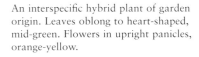

Common names: None
Height: 2m (6ft)
Spread: 1m (3ft)
Aspect: Half shade
Soil: Moist, humus-rich, deep, fertile
Hardiness: Zone 5
Propagation: Division, in spring or autumn

An interspecific hybrid plant of garden origin. Leaves oblong to heart-shaped, mid-green. Flowers in upright panicles, orange-yellow.

Ligularia hodgsonii
(Asteraceae/Compositae)

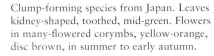

Common names: None
Height: 90cm (3ft)
Spread: 60cm (2ft)
Aspect: Half shade
Soil: Moist, humus-rich, deep, fertile
Hardiness: Zone 5
Propagation: Seed, in autumn or spring; division, in spring

Clump-forming species from Japan. Leaves kidney-shaped, toothed, mid-green. Flowers in many-flowered corymbs, yellow-orange, disc brown, in summer to early autumn.

Ligularia japonica
(Asteraceae/Compositae)

Common names: None
Height: 2m (6ft)
Spread: 1m (3ft)
Aspect: Half shade
Soil: Moist, humus-rich, deep, fertile
Hardiness: Zone 5
Propagation: Seed, in autumn or spring; division, in spring

Clump-forming species. Leaves basal, heart-shaped, lobed, toothed, mid-green. Flowers in racemes of 8 or more, orange-yellow, in early summer.

Ligularia przewalskii
(Asteraceae/Compositae)

Common names: None
Height: 2m (6ft)
Spread: 1m (3ft)
Aspect: Half shade
Soil: Moist, deep, humus-rich, fertile
Hardiness: Zone 5
Propagation: Seed, in spring; division, in spring or autumn

Species from China. Leaves palmate, lobed, deeply cut, toothed, mid-green. Flowers in dense, slender racemes, on purple stems, yellow, in mid- to late summer.

Ligularia
'The Rocket' A.G.M.
(Asteraceae/Compositae)

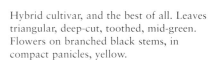

Common names: None
Height: 1.8m (6ft)
Spread: 1m (3ft)
Aspect: Half shade
Soil: Moist, deep, humus-rich, fertile
Hardiness: Zone 4
Propagation: Division, in spring or autumn

Hybrid cultivar, and the best of all. Leaves triangular, deep-cut, toothed, mid-green. Flowers on branched black stems, in compact panicles, yellow.

Ligularia
'Wiehenstephan'
(Asteraceae/Compositae)

Common names: None
Height: 1.8m (6ft)
Spread: 1m (3ft)
Aspect: Half shade
Soil: Moist, humus-rich, deep, fertile
Hardiness: Zone 5
Propagation: Division, in spring or autumn

A chance seedling in the Weihenstephan garden in Germany. Leaves triangular, deep-cut, toothed, mid-green. Flowers in dense racemes, bright yellow.

Lilium
'African Queen' (Div. 6)
(Liliaceae)

Common names: None
Height: 2m (6ft)
Spread: Nil
Aspect: Sun or half shade
Soil: Sharply-drained, moisture-retentive
Hardiness: Zone 8
Propagation: Scales, offsets, or bulbils in late summer

Hybrid strain. Leaves lance-shaped, glossy green. Flowers perfumed, large, in racemes of up to 12, outward-facing, outside purple-brown, inside apricot, mid- and late summer.

LILIUM (Liliaceae)
Lily

Genus of some 100 mostly bulbous species from the northern hemisphere, mostly Eurasia and North America, with a few from the Philippines. Many are beautiful and easily grown; as with most popular garden plants, there are many cultivars. The habitats of the genus vary, and so cultural requirements vary, but the great majority have one basic need: drainage. Most lilies will not thrive in heavy clay soil; raised beds or planters are the simple answer in such circumstances. Some, however, like moist soil, and some also prefer the soil to be slightly acidic. Moving and division are best done while the plants are still in active growth after flowering in summer, so that they have a spell of warm weather to settle before winter. Most lilies do not spread; plant the bulbs 3 times their own width apart. They may require staking. The flowers have six tepals, and may be bell-, bowl-, star-, trumpet-, Turk's-cap- or funnel-shaped; are classified as being small, medium or large; and may be upward- or outward-facing or pendent. They may be hardy or tender, fragrant or not, and of any colour except blue. They make excellent cut flowers, and are prized by flower-arrangers, but are highly allergenic, with sticky, staining pollen: florists often remove anthers as buds open.

Lilium bulbiferum
(Div. 9)
(Liliaceae)

Common name: Orange lily
Height: 1.5m(5ft)
Spread: Indefinite
Aspect: Sun or half shade
Soil: Sharply drained, moisture-retentive
Hardiness: Zone 7
Propagation: Scales, offsets or bulbils, all in late summer

Invasive species once satisfied. Leaves lance-shaped, hairy-edged, green. Flowers in umbels, of up to 5, bright orange-red bowls, in early to midsummer.

Lilium candidum
A.G.M. (Div. 9)
(Liliaceae)

Common name: Madonna lily
Height: 1.8m (6ft)
Spread: Nil
Aspect: Sun or half shade
Soil: Sharply drained, moisture-retentive
Hardiness: Zone 6
Propagation: Scales, offsets or bulbils, all in late summer

Leaves spirally-arranged, lance-shaped, mid-green. Flowers in racemes of up to 20, perfumed, trumpet-shaped, white with yellow bases, in summer.

Lilium formosanum
(Div. 9)
(Liliaceae)

Common name: Formosan lily
Height: 1.5m (5ft)
Spread: Nil
Aspect: Sun or half shade
Soil: Moist, acidic
Hardiness: Zone 5
Propagation: Scales, in late summer

Rhizomatous species. Leaves linear, dark green. Flowers scented, paired or solitary trumpets in umbels of up to 10, white flushed red-purple outside, in late summer.

Lilium formosanum
var. *pricei* A.G.M. (Div. 9)
(Liliaceae)

Common names: None
Height: 30cm (1ft)
Spread: Nil
Aspect: Sun or half shade
Soil: Moist, acidic
Hardiness: Zone
Propagation: Scales, in late summer

A very dwarf form of *Lilium formosanum*, making it suitable for rock gardens, the front of the border or containers. Flowers earlier and deeper flushed than the species.

Lilium grayi
(Div. 9)
(Liliaceae)

Common names: None
Height: 1.5m (5ft)
Spread: Nil
Aspect: Sun or half shade
Soil: Moist, acidic
Hardiness: Zone 5
Propagation: Scales, offsets, or bulbils, all in late summer

A species from the eastern U.S.A. Leaves lance-shaped, whorled, green. Flowers in umbels of up to 10, perfumed, funnel-shaped to tubular, red.

Classification according to the International Lily register, 1982, with amendments by the Royal Horticultural Society, 1992

Division 1 Asiatic hybrids, with racemes or umbels of usually unscented flowers.

Division 2 Martagon hybrids, with racemes of Turk's-cap, sometimes scented flowers.

Division 3 Candidum hybrids, with usually Turk's-cap, sometimes scented flowers, solitary or in umbels or racemes.

Division 4 American hybrids, with racemes of mostly Turk's-cap, sometimes scented flowers.

Division 5 Longiflorum hybrids, with umbels of large, often scented, trumpet- or funnel-shaped flowers.

Division 6 Trumpet and Aurelian hybrids, with racemes or umbels of usually scented flowers of various shapes.

Division 7 Oriental hybrids, with racemes or panicles of often scented flowers of various shapes.

Division 8 Other hybrids

Division 9 All true species

Lilium henryi
A.G.M. (Div. 9)
(Liliaceae)

Common names: None
Height: 3m (10ft)
Spread: Indefinite
Aspect: Sun or half shade
Soil: Well-drained, alkaline, humus-rich
Hardiness: Zone 5
Propagation: Scales, offsets or bulbils, all in late summer

Vigorous, easy species. Leaves lance-shaped to ovate. Flowers perfumed, Turk's-cap, orange, spotted black, in racemes of up to 10, in late summer. Good beginner's lily.

Lilium lancifolium
(Div. 9)
(Liliaceae)

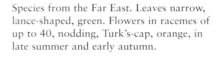

Common name: Tiger lily
Height: 1.5m (5ft)
Spread: Nil
Aspect: Sun or half shade
Soil: Moist, acidic
Hardiness: Zone 4
Propagation: Scales, offsets or bulbils, all in late summer

Species from the Far East. Leaves narrow, lance-shaped, green. Flowers in racemes of up to 40, nodding, Turk's-cap, orange, in late summer and early autumn.

Lilium martagon
(Div. 9)
(Liliaceae)

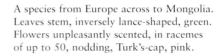

Common name: Turk's-cap lily
Height: 2m (6ft)
Spread: Nil
Aspect: Sun or half shade
Soil: Any, well-drained
Hardiness: Zone 4
Propagation: Scales, offsets or bulbils, all in late summer

A species from Europe across to Mongolia. Leaves stem, inversely lance-shaped, green. Flowers unpleasantly scented, in racemes of up to 50, nodding, Turk's-cap, pink.

Lilium martagon
var. *album* A.G.M. (Div. 9)
(Liliaceae)

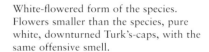

Common name: White turkscap lily
Height: 2m (6ft)
Spread: Nil
Aspect: Sun or half shade
Soil: Well-drained
Hardiness: Zone 4
Propagation: Scales, offsets or bulbils, all in late summer

White-flowered form of the species. Flowers smaller than the species, pure white, downturned Turk's-caps, with the same offensive smell.

Lilium monadelphum
A.G.M. (Div. 9)
(Liliaceae)

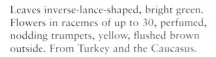

Common name: Caucasian lily
Height: 1.5m (5ft)
Spread: Nil
Aspect: Sun
Soil: Fertile
Hardiness: Zone 5
Propagation: Scales, offsets or bulbils, all in late summer

Leaves inverse-lance-shaped, bright green. Flowers in racemes of up to 30, perfumed, nodding trumpets, yellow, flushed brown outside. From Turkey and the Caucasus.

Lilium
Pink Perfection Group
A.G.M. (Div. 6) (Liliaceae)

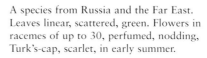

Common names: None
Height: 2m (6ft)
Spread: Nil
Aspect: Sun or half shade
Soil: Well-drained, moisture-retentive
Hardiness: Zone 7
Propagation: Seed, in warmth when ripe

A hybrid group derived from Asiatic species. Leaves linear, green. Flowers in racemes or umbels, perfumed, nodding trumpets, purple-pink, in summer.

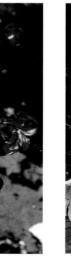

Lilium pumilum
A.G.M. (Div. 9)
(Liliaceae)

Common name: Coral lily
Height: 45cm (18in)
Spread: Nil
Aspect: Sun or half shade
Soil: Well-drained, acidic
Hardiness: Zone 5
Propagation: Scales, offsets or bulbils, all in late summer

A species from Russia and the Far East. Leaves linear, scattered, green. Flowers in racemes of up to 30, perfumed, nodding, Turk's-cap, scarlet, in early summer.

Lilium regale
A.G.M. (Div. 9)
(Liliaceae)

Common name: Regal lily
Height: 2m (6ft)
Spread: Nil
Aspect: Sun
Soil: Moist, well-drained
Hardiness: Zone 5
Propagation: Scales, offsets or bulbils, all in late summer

A species from China. Leaves linear, glossy, dark green. Flowers in umbels of up to 25, perfumed trumpets, white with yellow throats, in summer.

Lilium speciosum var. *album* (Div. 9) (Liliaceae)

Common names: None
Height: 1.5m (5ft)
Spread: Nil
Aspect: Half shade
Soil: Moist, acidic
Hardiness: Zone 8
Propagation: Scales, offsets or bulbils, all in late summer

A species from the Far East. Leaves lance-shaped, scattered, green. Racemes of up to 12, large, perfumed, pendent, white flowers, in late summer to early autumn.

Limonium latifolium (Plumbaginaceae)

Common names: Sea lavender; statice
Height: 90cm (36in)
Spread: 45cm (18in)
Aspect: Sun
Soil: Gritty, well-drained
Hardiness: Zone 5
Propagation: Seed, in spring

Evergreen seaside plant. Leaves in rosettes, dark green spoons. Flowers in open panicles, dense spikes of minute, blue-violet trumpets, in early summer.

Linaria purpurea (Scrophulariaceae)

Common name: Toadflax
Height: 90cm (3ft)
Spread: 30cm (1ft)
Aspect: Sun
Soil: Well-drained, gritty
Hardiness: Zone 6
Propagation: Seed or division, both in spring

Leaves linear, mid-green. Flowers in dense, slender racemes, pink, violet or purple, snapdragon-like, with curved spurs, from early summer to early autumn.

Linaria purpurea 'Canon Went' (Scrophulariaceae)

Common name: Toadflax
Height: 90cm (3ft)
Spread: 30cm (1ft)
Aspect: Sun
Soil: Well-drained, gritty
Hardiness: Zone 6
Propagation: Seed or division, both in spring

Selected form that comes true from seed. Leaves linear, mid-green. Slender, dense racemes of pink, snapdragon-like flowers, from early summer to early autumn.

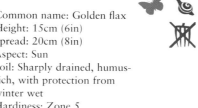

Linaria purpurea 'Springside White' (Scrophulariaceae)

Common name: Toadflax
Height: 90cm (3ft)
Spread: 30cm (1ft)
Aspect: Sun
Soil: Well-drained, gritty
Hardiness: Zone 6
Propagation: Seed or division, both in spring

A selected form of the species that comes true from seed, with white flowers appearing over a long period from early summer to early autumn.

Linaria triornithophora (Scrophulariaceae)

Common name: Three birds flying
Height: 1.2m (4ft)
Spread: 60cm (2ft)
Aspect: Sun
Soil: Well-drained, gritty
Hardiness: Zone 7
Propagation: Seed or division, both in spring

Invasive species. Leaves lance-shaped, mid-green, in whorls. Flowers in loose racemes, purple and yellow, snapdragon-like, in whorls of 3, from summer to autumn.

Linum flavum 'Compactum' (Linaceae)

Common name: Golden flax
Height: 15cm (6in)
Spread: 20cm (8in)
Aspect: Sun
Soil: Sharply drained, humus-rich, with protection from winter wet
Hardiness: Zone 5
Propagation: Seed, in spring or autumn

Compact form of a European plant. Leaves lance-shaped, deep green. Flowers many-branched cymes of upward-facing, golden cups, opening only in sun, in summer.

Linum monogynum (Linaceae)

Common name: Flax
Height: 60cm (2ft)
Spread: 30cm (1ft)
Aspect: Sun
Soil: Well-drained, gritty
Hardiness: Zone 8
Propagation: Seed, in spring or autumn

A perennial flax from New Zealand. Leaves narrow, grey-green. Flowers in corymbs, white, upward-facing, in terminal clusters.

In many of the red-flowered lobelias, such as this L. fulgens (*syn.* L. splendens), *the stems and leaves are purple-flushed, making a powerful impact in a border.*

Linum narbonense
(Linaceae)

Common name: Flax
Height: 60cm (24in)
Spread: 45cm (18in)
Aspect: Sun
Soil: Well-drained, gritty
Hardiness: Zone 5
Propagation: Seed, in spring or autumn

Short-lived Mediterranean species. Leaves narrow, lance-shaped, glaucous green. Few-flowered cymes of rich blue saucers with white eyes, in early to midsummer.

Linum perenne
(Linaceae)

Common name: Perennial flax
Height: 60cm (2ft)
Spread: 30cm (1ft)
Aspect: Sun
Soil: Well-drained, gritty
Hardiness: Zone 5
Propagation: Seed, in spring or autumn

Lax, straggly species. Leaves narrow, lance-shaped, glaucous. Flowers in terminal panicles, blue cups, fading over the day, over a long period in early to midsummer.

Liriope muscari
A.G.M.
(Convallariaceae/Liliaceae)

Common name: Lilyturf
Height: 30cm (1ft)
Spread: 45cm (18in)
Aspect: Full or half shade
Soil: Moist, well-drained, gritty, fertile
Hardiness: Zone 6
Propagation: Seed or division, both in spring

An evergreen, robust perennial from China. Leaves linear to straplike, dark green. Flowers in dense spikes, violet-mauve, from early to late autumn.

Lithodora diffusa
'Heavenly Blue' A.G.M.
(Boraginaceae)

Common names: None
Height: 15cm (6in)
Spread: 80cm (32in)
Aspect: Sun
Soil: Acidic, humus-rich
Hardiness: Zone 7
Propagation: Semi-ripe cuttings, in summer

Selected form of an evergreen subshrub from Europe. Leaves elliptic, deep green. Flowers in terminal cymes, blue, over a long period in late spring and early summer.

LOBELIA (Campanulaceae/Lobeliaceae)
Lobelia

A genus of some 370 species of annuals, perennials, and shrubs with a worldwide distribution, but from South, Central and North America in particular. They are found in a wide variety of habitats from marshlands to mountainsides, and range from hardy through half-hardy to tender. In general lobelias prefer a sunny position, but will tolerate light shade, and like moisture at the roots; some, indeed, are happiest as marginal aquatics, particularly if the soil is acid. The species vary widely in appearance, but all have alternate, simple leaves, and two-lipped, tubular flowers. The lips are divided into lobes: the upper lip into a pair of usually upright lobes, and the lower lip into three spreading lobes. The calyx tubes are sometimes swollen. In most species, the flowers are borne in terminal panicles or racemes, but in others they may be solitary. The foliage is handsome, and darkly coloured in some types. Their main drawback is that they are short-lived in the garden, and some need to be lifted and divided regularly to keep them at their best. Lobelias make good cut flowers, and are much used by flower-arrangers, but care should be taken in handling them, as contact with the sap may cause skin irritation.

Lobelia
'Butterfly Rose'
(Campanulaceae/Lobeliaceae)

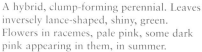

Common names: None
Height: 90cm (36in)
Spread: 30cm (12in)
Aspect: Sun or half shade
Soil: Moist, deep, humus-rich
Hardiness: Zone 7
Propagation: Seed, when ripe; division, in spring

A hybrid, clump-forming perennial. Leaves inversely lance-shaped, shiny, green. Flowers in racemes, pale pink, some dark pink appearing in them, in summer.

Lobelia cardinalis
A.G.M.
(Campanulaceae/Lobeliaceae)

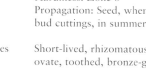

Common name: Cardinal flower
Height: 90cm (36in)
Spread: 30cm (12in)
Aspect: Sun or half shade
Soil: Moist, humus rich, fertile
Hardiness: Zone 3
Propagation: Seed, when ripe; bud cuttings, in summer

Short-lived, rhizomatous species. Leaves ovate, toothed, bronze-green. Flowers in racemes, tubular, scarlet; purplish bracts. Will grow in a bog or marginal aquatic site.

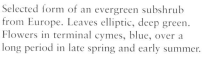

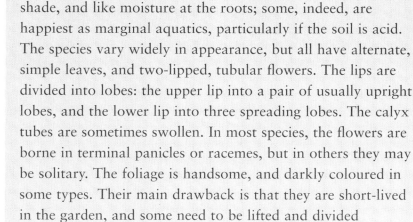

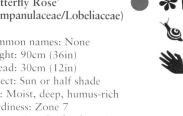

Lobelia
'Eulalia Berrige'
(Campanulaceae/Lobeliaceae)

Common names: None
Height: 75cm (30in)
Spread: 30cm (12in)
Aspect: Sun or half shade
Soil: Moist, deep, humus-rich
Hardiness: Zone 8
Propagation: Division, in spring

A hybrid perennial lobelia. Leaves ovate, mid-green. Flowers in open, upright racemes, cerise-mauve. Good for growing in a border.

Lobelia
'Fan Zinnoberrosa' A.G.M.
(Campanulaceae/Lobeliaceae)

Common names: None
Height: 60cm (24in)
Spread: 25cm (10in)
Aspect: Sun or half shade
Soil: Moist, deep, humus-rich
Hardiness: Zone 8
Propagation: Division, in spring

A reliable hybrid perennial lobelia. Leaves ovate, bronze-green. Flowers borne in dense, upright racemes, cinnabar rose, in summer.

Lobelia x *gerardii*
'Vedrariensis'
(Campanulaceae/Lobeliaceae)

Common names: None
Height: 1.2m (4ft)
Spread: 30cm (1ft)
Aspect: Sun or half shade
Soil: Moist, deep, humus-rich
Hardiness: Zone 7
Propagation: Division, in spring

A rhizomatous hybrid lobelia. Leaves basal, in rosettes, lance-shaped to elliptic, dark green. Flowers in racemes, tubular, violet, all summer.

Lobelia 'Kompliment Scharlach' A.G.M.
(Campanulaceae/Lobeliaceae)

Common names: None
Height: 90cm (36in)
Spread: 30cm (12in)
Aspect: Sun or half shade
Soil: Moist, deep, humus-rich
Hardiness: Zone 7
Propagation: Division in spring

A clump-forming, hybrid perennial lobelia. Leaves elliptic, dark green. Flowers in loose racemes, tubular, scarlet, borne in summer.

Lobelia siphilitica
(Campanulaceae/Lobeliaceae)

Common name: Blue cardinal flower
Height: 1.2m (4ft)
Spread: 30cm (1ft)
Aspect: Sun or half shade
Soil: Moist, deep, humus-rich
Hardiness: Zone 5
Propagation: Seed, when ripe; division, in spring

A hardy, clump-forming species. Leaves ovate, toothed, hairy, pale green. Flowers in dense racemes, bright blue, with leafy bracts, in late summer to autumn.

Lobelia siphilitica
'Alba'
(Campanulaceae/Lobeliaceae)

Common name: White cardinal flower
Height: 1.2m (4ft)
Spread: 30cm (1ft)
Aspect: Sun or half shade
Soil: Moist, deep, humus-rich
Hardiness: Zone 5
Propagation: Seed, when ripe; division, in spring

The white form of the species. Leaves ovate, toothed, hairy, light green. Flowers in dense racemes, white, from late summer to mid-autumn.

Lobelia tupa
(Campanulaceae/Lobeliaceae)

Common names: None
Height: 90cm (36in)
Spread: 30cm (12in)
Aspect: Sun or half shade
Soil: Moist, deep, humus-rich
Hardiness: Zone 8
Propagation: Seed, when ripe; division, in spring

A clump-forming perennial from Chile. Leaves ovate, downy green. Flowers in racemes, brick-red, with reddish-purple calyces, in late summer.

Lobelia 'Will Scarlet'
(Campanulaceae/Lobeliaceae)

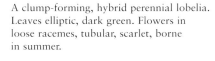

Common names: None
Height: 90cm (36in)
Spread: 30cm (12in)
Aspect: Sun or half shade
Soil: Moist, deep, humus-rich
Hardiness: Zone 7
Propagation: Division, in spring

A hybrid lobelia. Leaves ovate, greenish-blue or greenish-maroon. Flowers in racemes, bright red, from midsummer to early autumn.

Lotus corniculatus
(Leguminosae/Papilionaceae)

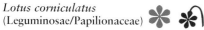

Common name: Bird's foot trefoil
Height: 30cm (12in)
Spread: 45cm (18in)
Aspect: Sun
Soil: Well-drained, fertile
Hardiness: Zone 5
Propagation: Seed, in autumn or spring

A spreading perennial of world wide distribution. Leaves pinnate, leaflets obovate, blue-green. Flowers in racemes, clear yellow.

Lotus maculatus
A.G.M.
(Leguminosae/papilionaceae)

Common name: Bird's foot trefoil
Height: 20cm (8in)
Spread: Indefinite
Aspect: Sun
Soil: Well-drained, fertile
Hardiness: Zone 10
Propagation: Seed, in warmth in spring

Creeping plant. Leaves palmate, leaflets linear, mid-green. "Lobster-claw" flowers, solitary or in small clusters, yellow, tipped orange or red, in spring and early summer.

Lunaria rediviva
(Cruciferae)

Common name: Perennial honesty
Height: 90cm (3ft)
Spread: 30cm (1ft)
Aspect: Sun or half shade
Soil: Moist, well-drained, fertile
Hardiness: Zone 8
Propagation: Seed, in spring

Perennial from Eurasia. Leaves dark green, large, triangular, toothed. Flowers scented, lilac-white, in racemes in late spring and early summer, followed by flat seed pods.

Lupinus 'Band of Nobles'
Series A.G.M.
(Leguminosae/Papilionaceae)

Common name: Lupin
Height: 1.5m (5ft)
Spread: 75cm (30in)
Aspect: Sun or half shade
Soil: Well-drained, gritty, acidic, fertile
Hardiness: Zone 5
Propagation: Seed, after soaking, in spring or autumn

Strain of hybrid lupins. Leaves basal, hairy, palmate, mid-green. Flowers in racemes, pea-like, perfumed, in colours from red, pink, yellow, white or blue to bicoloured.

LUPINUS (Leguminosae/Papilionaceae)
Lupin

A genus of some 200 species, including annuals, perennials, and both semi-evergreen and evergreen subshrubs or shrubs, from North Africa, southern Europe and the Americas. Their native habitats range from dry uplands to woodlands, riverbanks, and coastal situations. Lupins are an invaluable genus of repeat-flowering, handsome plants with attractive leaves for the border. The flowers are pea-like, and are borne in long, upright terminal racemes or spikes; they are scented, and attract bees. They are also, unfortunately, highly allergenic. There is a very large number of hybrids in cultivation, and many are derived from crosses with *Lupinus polyphyllus*, from western North America, as one parent; many hybrids have bicoloured flowers. Lupins will grow in sun or half shade, and tolerate a range of soils except alkaline or waterlogged ones. Their drawbacks are that they are prey to slugs and prone to powdery mildew. They are also short-lived, and resent disturbance, but they are easy to propagate. The seeds of lupins are poisonous, so children should be warned. The flowers last well in water provided that they are inverted and the hollow stem is filled with water and plugged with cotton wool before they are put in the vase.

Lupinus
'Chandelier'
(Leguminosae/Papilionaceae)

Common name: Lupin
Height: 90cm (36in)
Spread: 75cm (30in)
Aspect: Sun or half shade
Soil: Well-drained, gritty, acidic, fertile
Hardiness: Zone 5
Propagation: Basal cuttings, in mid-spring

A hybrid perennial lupin. Leaves basal, palmate, hairy, mid-green. Scented flowers in racemes, bright yellow, in early and midsummer.

Lupinus
'My Castle'
(Leguminosae/Papilionaceae)

Common name: Lupin
Height: 90cm (36in)
Spread: 75cm (30in)
Aspect: Sun or half shade
Soil: Well-drained, gritty, acidic, fertile
Hardiness: Zone 5
Propagation: Basal cuttings, in mid-spring

A hybrid, clump-forming perennial lupin. Leaves basal, palmate, hairy, mid-green. Flowers in racemes, deep pink, in early and midsummer.

Lupinus
'Noble Maiden'
(Leguminosae/Papilionaceae)

Common name: Lupin
Height: 90cm (36in)
Spread: 75cm (30in)
Aspect: Sun or half shade
Soil: Well-drained, gritty, acidic, fertile
Hardiness: Zone 5
Propagation: Basal cuttings, in mid-spring

A clump-forming, hybrid lupin cultivar. Leaves basal, palmate, hairy, mid-green. Flowers in racemes, creamy-white, in early and midsummer.

Lupinus
'The Chatelaine'
(Leguminosae/Papilionaceae)

Common name: Lupin
Height: 90cm (36in)
Spread: 75cm (30in)
Aspect: Sun or half shade
Soil: Well-drained, gritty, acidic, fertile
Hardiness: Zone 5
Propagation: Basal cuttings, in mid-spring

A clump-forming, hybrid lupin. Leaves basal, palmate, hairy, mid-green. Flowers in racemes, bicoloured, pink and white, in early and midsummer.

Lupinus
'The Governor'
(Leguminosae/Papilionaceae)

Common name: Lupin
Height: 90cm (36in)
Spread: 75cm (30in)
Aspect: Sun or half shade
Soil: Well-drained, gritty, fertile
Hardiness: Zone 5
Propagation: Basal cuttings, in mid-spring

A hybrid, clump-forming cultivar. Leaves basal, palmate, hairy, mid-green. Flowers in racemes, bicoloured, blue and white, in early and midsummer.

Lupinus
'The Page'
(Leguminosae/Papilionaceae)

Common name: Lupin
Height: 90cm (36in)
Spread: 75cm (30in)
Aspect: Sun or half shade
Soil: Well-drained, gritty, fertile
Hardiness: Zone 5
Propagation: Basal cuttings, in mid-spring

A hybrid, clump-forming lupin cultivar. Leaves basal, palmate, hairy, mid-green. Flowers in panicles, carmine red, in early and midsummer.

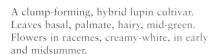

Luzula sylvatica
'Aurea'
(Juncaceae)

Common name: Woodrush
Height: 80cm (32in)
Spread: 45cm (18in)
Aspect: Full or half shade
Soil: Moist, well-drained, humus-rich, fertile
Hardiness: Zone 6
Propagation: Seed, in spring or autumn; division, in spring

A tufted, evergreen grass. Leaves linear, channelled, shiny yellow. Flowers in open panicles, small, chestnut-brown, from mid-spring to early summer.

LYCHNIS (Caryophyllaceae)
Campion • Catchfly

A genus of some 20 species of biennials and perennials from arctic and northern temperate regions; they are reliably hardy. Their natural habitats range from alpine conditions to damp woodlands and grasslands, and they will grow in sun or partial shade, and in any soil as long as it is well-drained and fertile. *Lychnis flos-cuculi* is even happy in bog conditions. *Lychnis* are upright, generally with branching stems, and bear tubular to salverform or star-shaped flowers in terminal cymes or panicles. The flowers come in a range of colours from purple through scarlet to pink or white, and some types make good cut flowers. The smaller, alpine types are most suitable for a rock or alpine garden, while the taller forms will do well in a sunny border or naturalised in a wildflower garden. Some species, most notably *L.* × *arkwrightii*, *L. coronaria* and *L.* × *haageana*, are short-lived, but the others are soundly perennial. The taller varieties need to be staked. *L. flos-jovis* and *L. chalcedonica* attract both bees and butterflies, while *L. flos-cuculi* is loved by bees. All are prone to damage by slugs in spring, so preventative action must be taken early. All seem to self-seed prolifically; deadhead after flowering to avoid this if it is not wanted.

Lychnis alpina
(Caryophyllaceae)

Common names: Alpine campion; alpine catchfly
Height: 15cm (6in)
Spread: 15cm (6in)
Aspect: Sun or half shade
Soil: Well-drained, fertile
Hardiness: Zone 5
Propagation: Seed, when ripe or in spring

A mountain perennial. Leaves in rosettes, lance-shaped, dark green. Flowers in terminal cymes of up to 20, pink, petals 2-lobed, frilled, in summer.

Lychnis x *arkwrightii* 'Vesuvius' (Caryophyllaceae)

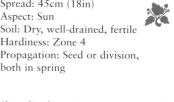

Common names: None
Height: 45cm (18in)
Spread: 30cm (12in)
Aspect: Sun or half shade
Soil: Well-drained, fertile
Hardiness: Zone 5
Propagation: Basal cuttings or division, both in spring

Short-lived, hybrid, clump-forming plant. Leaves lance-shaped, hairy, dark green-brown. Flowers in terminal cymes of up to 10, star-shaped, scarlet-orange, in summer.

Lychnis chalcedonica 'Flore Pleno' (Caryophyllacae)

Common names: Jerusalem cross; Maltese cross
Height: 1.2m (4ft)
Spread: 30cm (1ft)
Aspect: Sun or half shade
Soil: Moist, fertile
Hardiness: Zone 4
Propagation: Seed or division, both in spring

Leaves basal, ovate, mid-green. Flowers in terminal, rounded cymes, vermilion, petals deeply notched, double, in early and midsummer. From European Russia.

Lychnis chalcedonica 'Rosea' (Caryophyllaceae)

Common names: Pink Maltese cross; pink Jerusalem cross
Height: 1.2m (4ft)
Spread: 30cm (1ft)
Aspect: Sun or half shade
Soil: Moist, fertile
Hardiness: Zone 5
Propagation: Seed or division, both in spring

Single-flowered, pink form of the species. Leaves basal, ovate, mid-green. Flowers in terminal cymes, single, star-shaped, pink, in early and midsummer.

Lychnis coronaria (Caryophyllaceae)

Common names: Dusty miller; rose campion
Height: 80cm (32in)
Spread: 45cm (18in)
Aspect: Sun
Soil: Dry, well-drained, fertile
Hardiness: Zone 4
Propagation: Seed or division, both in spring

Short-lived species. Leaves ovate to lance-shaped, woolly silver-grey. Flowers in few-flowered, terminal racemes, single, scarlet or purple, over a long period in late summer.

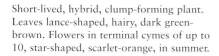

Lychnis coronaria 'Alba' A.G.M. (Caryophyllaceae)

Common names: White dusty miller; white rose campion
Height: 80cm (32in)
Spread: 45cm (18in)
Aspect: Sun
Soil: Dry, well-drained
Hardiness: Zone 4
Propagation: Seed or division, both in spring

White form of the species. Leaves ovate to lance-shaped, silver-grey, woolly. Flowers in few-flowered terminal cymes, single, white, over a long period in late summer.

Lychnis coronaria Oculata Group (Caryophyllaceae)

Common names: Dusty miller; rose campion
Height: 80cm (32in)
Spread: 45cm (18in)
Aspect: Sun
Soil: Dry, well-drained, fertile
Hardiness: Zone 4
Propagation: Seed or division, both in spring

A free-flowering cultivar. Leaves ovate to lance-shaped, silver-grey, woolly. Flowers in terminal cymes, white with a cherry-pink eye, over a long period in late summer.

Lychnis flos-cuculi var. *albiflora* (Caryophyllaceae)

Common names: White ragged robin
Height: 75cm (30in)
Spread: 90cm (36in)
Aspect: Sun or half shade
Soil: Moist, well-drained, fertile
Hardiness: Zone 6
Propagation: Seed or division, both in spring

White form of a rampant species. Leaves basal, inversely lance-shaped; stem, oblong, bluish-green. Flowers in terminal cymes, star-shaped, in late spring and early summer.

Lychnis flos-jovis (Caryophyllaceae)

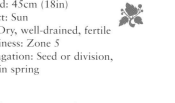

Common names: Flower of Jove; flower of Jupiter
Height: 60cm (24in)
Spread: 45cm (18in)
Aspect: Sun
Soil: Dry, well-drained, fertile
Hardiness: Zone 5
Propagation: Seed or division, both in spring

Mat-forming species from the Alps. Leaves basal and stem, spoon- to lance-shaped, grey-green. Flowers in loose cymes, single, pink, white or scarlet, early to late summer.

Lychnis miqueliana
(Caryophyllaceae)

Common names: None
Height: 60cm (2ft)
Spread: 30cm (1ft)
Aspect: Sun or half shade
Soil: Well-drained, fertile
Hardiness: Zone 6
Propagation: Seed or division, both in spring

A hardy species from Japan. Leaves oblong to ovate, mid-green. Flowers single, large, petals toothed, vermilion, in few-flowered cymes, in summer.

LYSIMACHIA (Primulaceae)
Loosestrife

A genus of some 150 species of evergreen and herbaceous perennials and shrubs from northern temperate and southern subtropical regions; they vary from hardy to half-hardy, as a consequence. Their natural habitats are damp woodlands and grasslands, often near water; in the garden, they prefer a soil which is moist, and moisture-retentive, especially in summer, but also like good drainage. If they are given the moist root run they enjoy, they can be invasive (except *Lysimachia ephemerum*), so they are best used as water marginals, or in a bog garden or wild or woodland garden. Many make large plants, and some of the taller types may require staking. Slugs also enjoy the moist conditions preferred by these plants, and measures to protect the foliage from attack should be taken early. Some species, however, are low-growing, and make good ground cover. They will grow in sun or part-shade. Leaf shapes and arrangements vary, although the leaves are generally simple. All bear 5-petalled flowers, ranging from cup- or saucer-shaped to star-shaped, which are either solitary and axillary or carried in terminal panicles or racemes. The flowers are usually yellow in colour, but there are also white-, pink- or purple-flowered types.

Lysimachia ciliata
(Primulaceae)

Common name: Loosestrife
Height: 1.2m (4ft)
Spread: 60cm (2ft)
Aspect: Sun or half shade
Soil: Moist, humus-rich
Hardiness: Zone 4
Propagation: Seed or division, both in spring

Invasive, rhizomatous species from North America. Leaves ovate to lance-shaped, mid-green. Flowers on slim stems, single or paired, pendent, yellow stars, in summer.

Lysimachia ciliata
'Firecracker' A.G.M.
(Primulaceae)

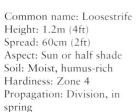

Common name: Loosestrife
Height: 1.2m (4ft)
Spread: 60cm (2ft)
Aspect: Sun or half shade
Soil: Moist, humus-rich
Hardiness: Zone 4
Propagation: Division, in spring

A form of the species with purple foliage, which contrasts well with the yellow flowers. This is also known as *Lysimachia ciliata* 'Purpurea'.

Lysimachia clethroides
A.G.M.
(Primulaceae)

Common name: Loosestrife
Height: 90cm (3ft)
Spread: 60cm (2ft)
Aspect: Sun or half shade
Soil: Moist, humus-rich
Hardiness: Zone 4
Propagation: Seed or division, both in spring

Invasive rhizomatous species. Leaves lance-shaped, pointed, mid-green, paler beneath. Flowers in dense, tapering, arching racemes, white, single, starry, mid- and late summer.

Lysimachia ephemerum
(Primulaceae)

Common name: Loosestrife
Height: 90cm (3ft)
Spread: 30cm (1ft)
Aspect: Sun or half shade
Soil: Moist, humus-rich
Hardiness: Zone 7
Propagation: Seed or division, both in spring

Non-spreading species. Leaves linear to lance-shaped, glaucous grey-green. Flowers white saucers, in dense, upright, terminal racemes, in early and midsummer.

Lysimachia nummularia
'Aurea' A.G.M.
(Primulaceae)

Common name: Golden creeping Jenny
Height: 5cm (2in)
Spread: Indefinite
Aspect: Sun or half shade
Soil: Moist, humus-rich
Hardiness: Zone 5
Propagation: Seed or division, both in spring

Golden form of a rampant, evergreen species from Europe. Leaves ovate to round, golden-yellow. Flowers solitary, single, cup-shaped, upturned, yellow.

A white-flowered loosestrife, such as this Lysimachia clethroides, *makes a cool statement on a pond margin.*

Lysimachia punctata
(Primulaceae)

Common name: Loosestrife
Height: 90cm (3ft)
Spread: 60cm (2ft)
Aspect: Sun or half shade
Soil: Moist, humus-rich
Hardiness: Zone 5
Propagation: Seed or division, both in spring

An invasive, rhizomatous species. Leaves elliptic- to lance-shaped, dark green. Yellow flowers in whorls from the leaf axils, in mid- and late summer.

Lysimachia punctata
'Alexander'
(Primulaceae)

Common names: Loosestrife
Height: 90cm (3ft)
Spread: 60cm (3ft)
Aspect: Sun or half shade
Soil: Moist, humus-rich
Hardiness: Zone 5
Propagation: Division, in spring

A selected cultivar of the species. Leaves elliptic- to lance-shaped, dark green edged cream or white. Flowers yellow, in whorls in the leaf axils, mid- and late summer.

Lythrum salicaria
(Lythraceae)

Common name: Purple loosestrife
Height: 1.2m (4ft)
Spread: 45cm (18in)
Aspect: Sun
Soil: Wet to marginal aquatic, fertile
Hardiness: Zone 3
Propagation: Seed, in warmth in spring; division, in spring

Clump-forming plant. Leaves lance-shaped, downy, green. Flowers bright purple-red stars in spiky racemes, midsummer to early autumn. Dead-head to prevent self-seeding.

Lythrum salicaria
'Blush'
(Lythraceae)

Common name: Purple loosestrife
Height: 1.2m (4ft)
Spread: 45cm (18in)
Aspect: Sun
Soil: Wet to marginal aquatic, fertile
Hardiness: Zone 3
Propagation: Division, in spring

Selected form of the species. Leaves lance-shaped, downy, green. Flowers blush-pink stars in spiky racemes, midsummer to early autumn. Dead-head to prevent self-seeding.

Lythrum salicaria
'Robert'
(Lythraceae)

Common name: Purple loosestrife
Height: 1.2m (4ft)
Spread: 45cm (18in)
Aspect: Sun
Soil: Wet to marginal aquatic, fertile
Hardiness: Zone 3
Propagation: Division, in spring

A selected form with bright pink, starry flowers in spiky racemes, midsummer to early autumn. Leaves lance-shaped, downy, green. Dead-head to prevent self-seeding.

Lythrum virgatum
'The Rocket'
(Lythraceae)

Common name: Purple loosestrife
Height: 90cm (36in)
Spread: 45cm (18in)
Aspect: Sun
Soil: Moist, fertile
Hardiness: Zone 4
Propagation: Seed or division, both in spring

A clump-forming perennial from Europe, Asia and China. Leaves linearly lance-shaped, mid-green. Flowers in slim, spiky racemes, deep pink, all summer.

Macleaya cordata
A.G.M.
(Papaveraceae)

Common name: Plume poppy
Height: 2.5m (8ft)
Spread: 90cm (3ft)
Aspect: Sun or half shade
Soil: Moist, well-drained, fertile
Hardiness: Zone 3
Propagation: Seed, in spring; division, in spring or autumn

Rhizomatous plant from the Far East. Leaves handsome, 5- to 7-lobed, grey-green, white-downy below. Flowers creamy-white, tubular, in panicles, mid- and late summer.

Maianthemum bifolium
(Convallariaceae/Liliaceae)

Common name: False lily-of-the-valley
Height: 15cm (6in)
Spread: Indefinite
Aspect: Full or half shade
Soil: Moist, well-drained, acidic, humus-rich
Hardiness: Zone 3
Propagation: Seed, when ripe; division of runners, in spring

Invasive ground cover. Leaves ovate to heart-shaped, glossy deep green. Flowers in racemes of up to 20, perfumed, white, in early summer, followed by small, red berries.

Malva moschata
(Malvaceae)

Common name: Musk mallow
Height: 90cm (3ft)
Spread: 60cm (2ft)
Aspect: Sun
Soil: Moist, well-drained, fertile
Hardiness: Zone 3
Propagation: Seed or basal cuttings, both in spring

A short-lived perennial from Africa. Leaves heart-shaped and pinnatisect, mid-green. Flowers in axillary clusters, pink saucers, early summer to early autumn.

Malva moschata f. *alba* A.G.M.
(Malvaceae)

Common name: White musk mallow
Height: 90cm (3ft)
Spread: 60cm (2ft)
Aspect: Sun
Soil: Moist, well-drained, fertile
Hardiness: Zone 3
Propagation: Seed or basal cuttings, both in spring

A white form of the species. Leaves heart-shaped and pinnatisect, mid-green, musk-scented. Flowers in axillary clusters, white saucers, early summer to early autumn.

Malva sylvestris
(Malvaceae)

Common names: Tall mallow; high mallow
Height: 1.2m (4ft)
Spread: 60cm (2ft)
Aspect: Sun
Soil: Moist, well-drained, fertile
Hardiness: Zone 5
Propagation: Seed or basal cuttings, both in spring

Leaves round to heart-shaped, light green. Flowers in axillary clusters, purplish-pink, with dark veins, from late spring to mid-autumn. From Eurasia and North Africa.

Malva sylvestris
'Primley Blue'
(Malvaceae)

Common name: Mallow
Height 20cm (8in)
Spread: 60cm (24in)
Aspect: Sun
Soil: Moist, well-drained, fertile
Hardiness: Zone 5
Propagation: Basal cuttings, in spring

Desirable, prostrate, hybrid. Leaves heart-shaped, mid-green. Flowers pale blue, with darker blue veining, in axillary clusters, from late spring to mid-autumn.

Malvastrum lateritium
(Malvaceae)

Common names: None
Height: 15cm (6in)
Spread: Indefinite
Aspect: Sun
Soil: Well-drained
Hardiness: Zone 8
Propagation: Seed or softwood cuttings, both in spring

A prostrate perennial from South America. Leaves rounded, lobed, rough, dark green. Flowers solitary, peach-coloured, yellow-centred, sporadically throughout summer.

Marrubium peregrinum
(Labiatae/Lamiaceae)

Common name: Horehound
Height: 60cm (2ft)
Spread: 30cm (1ft)
Aspect: Sun
Soil: Well-drained, poor
Hardiness: Zone 8
Propagation: Seed or softwood cuttings, both in spring

Leaves aromatic, obovate, hairy, crenate, dark green. Flowers tubular, 2-lipped, pale pink, in whorls, in early summer. Deadhead to prevent self-seeding. From Eurasia.

Matthiola
pink perennial
(Brassicaceae/Cruciferae)

Common name: Perennial stock
Height: 45cm (18in)
Spread: 30cm (12in)
Aspect: Sun
Soil: Moist, well-drained, fertile
Hardiness: Zone 7
Propagation: Seed, in spring or autumn

Short-lived plant, probably of garden origin. Leaves linear-ovate, grey-green. Flowers in terminal spikes, cruciform, pink, double, scented, over a long period in summer.

Matthiola
white perennial
(Brassicaceae/Cruciferae)

Common name: Perennial stock
Height: 45cm (18in)
Spread: 30cm (12in)
Aspect: Sun
Soil: Moist, well-drained, fertile
Hardiness: Zone 7
Propagation: Seed, in spring or autumn

Short-lived plant, of garden origin. Leaves linear-ovate, grey-green. Flowers in terminal spikes, perfumed, cruciform, white, over a long period in summer.

Mazus reptans
'Albus'
(Scrophulariaceae)

Common names: None
Height: 5cm (2in)
Spread: 45cm (18in)
Aspect: Sun
Soil: Moist, well-drained, fertile
Hardiness: Zone 3
Propagation: Seed or division, both in spring

Woodlander ground cover. Leaves lance-shaped, toothed, mid-green. Flowers in short racemes of up to 5, white, narrow, tubular, in late spring to summer.

MECONOPSIS (Papaveraceae)

Blue poppy • Himalayan poppy • Tibetan poppy

A genus of some 45 species of annuals, biennials and deciduous or evergreen, often monocarpic or short-lived perennials. Most originate in the Himalayas, Burma, and China. One, *Meconopsis cambrica*, is native to western Europe; this species will grow anywhere, and is exempt from the cultural guidance below, which applies to species from the Far East. *Meconopsis* have handsome foliage in basal rosettes, and striking seed heads, but it is for quality of flower that they are best loved. The flowers are single, open cups, usually pendent, and may be solitary (usually on leafless stems) or in short panicles or racemes (usually on leafy stems), which open from above. *M. cambrica* is yellow or orange, but the colouring of the blue species is quite exquisite, and worth any effort. These come from a range of habitats, from moist, shady woodlands to mountain screes and meadows; some are very hardy, others much less so. They like some degree of shade, and the soil should be acid, humus-rich to a degree, moist, but well-drained and never waterlogged; in dry summers they must be watered. They do best in cooler climates, especially those with cool, damp summers. They may need staking in exposed areas.

Meconopsis betonicifolia
A.G.M.
(Papaveraceae)

Common names: Himalayan blue poppy; Tibetan blue poppy
Height: 1.2m (4ft)
Spread: 45cm (18in)
Aspect: Half shade
Soil: Moist, well-drained, acidic, humus-rich
Hardiness: Zone 7
Propagation: Seed, when ripe

Deciduous, short-lived species. Leaves in basal rosettes, ovate, toothed, light blue-green. Flowers solitary, pendent or horizontal, blue saucers, in early summer.

Meconopsis betonicifolia var. alba
(Papaveraceae)

Common name: White Himalayan poppy
Height: 1.2m (4ft)
Spread: 45cm (18in)
Aspect: Half shade
Soil: Moist, well-drained, acidic, humus-rich
Hardiness: Zone 7
Propagation: Seed, when ripe

Leaves in basal rosettes, blue-green, rusty-hairy, ovate, toothed. Flowers single, white, pendent, in early summer. Prevent flowering for a year or two to improve longevity.

Meconopsis cambrica
(Papaveraceae)

Common name: Welsh poppy
Height: 45cm (18in)
Spread: 30cm (12in)
Aspect: Any
Soil: Any
Hardiness: Zone 6
Propagation: Seed, when ripe

Taprooted perennial from Europe. Leaves stem and basal, pinnatisect, fern-like, fresh green. Flowers solitary, single, yellow cups, from spring to autumn. Seeds prolifically.

Meconopsis cambrica var. *aurantiaca* 'Flore Pleno' (Papaveraceae)

Common name: Orange Welsh poppy
Height: 45cm (18in)
Spread: 30cm (12in)
Aspect: Any
Soil: Any
Hardiness: Zone 6
Propagation: Seed, when ripe

A double-flowered form of the orange variety of Welsh poppy. It does not self-seed prolifically, and so is not the nuisance that the single form can represent.

Meconopsis cambrica
'Flore Pleno'
(Papaveraceae)

Common name: Double Welsh poppy
Height: 45cm (18in)
Spread: 30cm (12in)
Aspect: Any
Soil: Any
Hardiness: Zone 6
Propagation: Division, in spring

The double yellow form of the Welsh poppy, perhaps less graceful than the single form, but having the virtue of not self-seeding everywhere.

Meconopsis chelidoniifolia
(Papaveraceae)

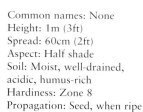

Common names: None
Height: 1m (3ft)
Spread: 60cm (2ft)
Aspect: Half shade
Soil: Moist, well-drained, acidic, humus-rich
Hardiness: Zone 8
Propagation: Seed, when ripe

A species from China. Leaves pinnatisect, lobes pinnatifid, hairy, pale green. Flowers on upper leaf stalks, single, pendent or horizontal, yellow.

Meconopsis grandis A.G.M.
(Papaveraceae)

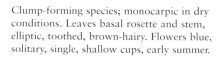

Common name: Himalayan blue poppy
Height: 1.2m (4ft)
Spread: 60cm (2ft)
Aspect: Half shade
Soil: Moist, well-drained, acidic, humus-rich
Hardiness: Zone 5
Propagation: Seed, when ripe

Clump-forming species; monocarpic in dry conditions. Leaves basal rosette and stem, elliptic, toothed, brown-hairy. Flowers blue, solitary, single, shallow cups, early summer.

Meconopsis napaulensis
(Papaveraceae)

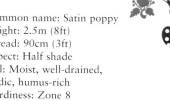

Common name: Satin poppy
Height: 2.5m (8ft)
Spread: 90cm (3ft)
Aspect: Half shade
Soil: Moist, well-drained, acidic, humus-rich
Hardiness: Zone 8
Propagation: Seed, when ripe

Monocarpic species. Leaves in rosettes, pinnatisect, yellow-green, red-hairy, lobes oblong. Flowers in racemes of up to 17, pendent bowls, late spring to midsummer.

Meconopsis paniculata
(Papaveraceae)

Common name: Himalayan poppy
Height: 2m (6ft)
Spread: 60cm (2ft)
Aspect: Half shade
Soil: Moist, well-drained, acidic, humus-rich
Hardiness: Zone 8
Propagation: Seed, when ripe

Monocarpic evergreen. Leaves in rosettes, pinnatisect, yellow-hairy, grey-green. Flowers in racemes, cup-shaped, pendent pale yellow, late spring to summer.

Meconopsis punicea
(Papaveraceae)

Common name: Himalayan poppy
Height: 75cm (30in)
Spread: 30cm (12in)
Aspect: Half shade
Soil: Moist, well-drained, acidic, humus-rich
Hardiness: Zone 7
Propagation: Seed, when ripe

Tap-rooted species. Leaves in rosettes, inverse lance-shaped, grey-hairy, mid-green. Flowers on scapes, pendent, crimson, petals flared, from summer to autumn.

Meconopsis quintuplinervia A.G.M.
(Papaveraceae)

Common name: Harebell poppy
Height: 45cm (18in)
Spread: 30cm (12in)
Aspect: Half shade
Soil: Moist, well-drained, acidic, humus-rich
Hardiness: Zone 8
Propagation: Seed, when ripe

Clump-forming species. Leaves in rosettes, lance-shaped, golden-hairy, mid-green. Flowers solitary, pendent, lavender cups, from early to late summer.

Meconopsis regia
(Papaveraceae)

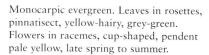

Common names: None
Height: 2m (6ft)
Spread: 1m (3ft)
Aspect: Half shade
Soil: Moist, well-drained, acidic, humus-rich
Hardiness: Zone 8
Propagation: Seed, when ripe

Monocarpic evergreen from Nepal. Leaves in rosettes, elliptic, silver-hairy, mid-green. Flowers outward-facing on branched stems, red cups, from late spring to midsummer.

Meconopsis × sheldonii A.G.M.
(Papaveraceae)

Common names: None
Height: 1.5m (5ft)
Spread: 60cm (2ft)
Aspect: Half shade
Soil: Moist, well-drained, acidic, humus-rich
Hardiness: Zone 6
Propagation: Division, after flowering

Hybrid perennial of garden origin. Leaves in rosettes, lance-shaped, hairy, dark green. Flowers solitary, cup-shaped, deep rich blue, in late spring and early summer.

Although they can be difficult, blue poppies such as Meconopsis × sheldonii *'Slieve Donard' add glamour to any garden.*

Meconopsis x *sheldonii* 'Slieve Donard' A.G.M.
(Papaveraceae)

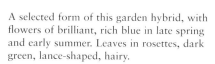

Common names: None
Height: 1.5m (5ft)
Spread: 60cm (2ft)
Aspect: Half shade
Soil: Moist, well-drained, acidic, humus-rich
Hardiness: Zone 6
Propagation: Division, after flowering

A selected form of this garden hybrid, with flowers of brilliant, rich blue in late spring and early summer. Leaves in rosettes, dark green, lance-shaped, hairy.

Megacarpaea polyandra
(Brassicaceae/Cruciferae)

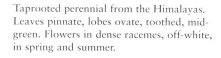

Common names: None
Height: 2m (6ft)
Spread: 60cm (2ft)
Aspect: Sun
Soil: Well-drained, fertile
Hardiness: Zone 7
Propagation: Seed, when ripe

Taprooted perennial from the Himalayas. Leaves pinnate, lobes ovate, toothed, mid-green. Flowers in dense racemes, off-white, in spring and summer.

Melianthus major A.G.M.
(Melianthaceae)

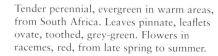

Common name: Honey bush
Height: 3m (10ft)
Spread: 3m (10ft)
Aspect: Sun
Soil: Well-drained, fertile
Hardiness: Zone 9
Propagation: Seed in warmth, suckers or softwood cuttings, all in spring

Tender perennial, evergreen in warm areas, from South Africa. Leaves pinnate, leaflets ovate, toothed, grey-green. Flowers in racemes, red, from late spring to summer.

Melissa officinalis 'Aurea'
(Labiatae/Lamiaceae)

Common names: Bee balm; lemon balm
Height: 1.2m (4ft)
Spread: 45cm (18in)
Aspect: Sun
Soil: Poor, well-drained
Hardiness: Zone 4
Propagation: Seed or division, both in spring

Bushy perennial. Leaves aromatic, ovate, wrinkled, dark green, splashed gold. Flowers small, in spikes, pale yellow, all summer. Liked by bees and butterflies.

Mellitis melissophyllum
(Labiatae/Lamiaceae)

Common name: Bastard balm
Height: 70cm (28in)
Spread: 50cm (20in)
Aspect: Half shade
Soil: Moist, well-drained, fertile
Hardiness: Zone 6
Propagation: Seed, when ripe; division, in spring

Woodlander. Leaves honey-scented, oval, scalloped, veined, hairy, wrinkled, green. Flowers in whorls, 2-lipped, tubular, white, pink-lipped, in spring and early summer.

Mentha x *gracilis* 'Variegata'
(Labiatae/Lamiaceae)

Common names: Ginger mint; red mint
Height: 45cm (18in)
Spread: Indefinite
Aspect: Sun
Soil: Moist, poor
Hardiness: Zone 7
Propagation: Division, in spring or autumn

A very invasive perennial from Europe. Leaves aromatic, ginger-flavoured, ovate, flecked or striped yellow. Flowers in whorls, lilac, in summer. Ground cover.

Mertensia pulmonariodes A.G.M.
(Boraginaceae)

Common name: Blue bells; Virginian cowslip
Height: 45cm (18in)
Spread: 25cm (10in)
Aspect: Half shade
Soil: Sharply drained, poor
Hardiness: Zone 3
Propagation: Seed or root cuttings, both in autumn; division, in spring

A clump-forming woodlander from North America. Leaves ovate, blue-green. Flowers in terminal cymes, tubular, blue, in mid- and late spring.

Mertensia simplicissima
(Boraginaceae)

Common names: None
Height: 90cm (3ft)
Spread: 30cm (1ft)
Aspect: Half shade
Soil: Sharply drained, poor
Hardiness: Zone 6
Propagation: Seed or root cuttings, both in autumn; division, in spring

Prostrate plant from Russia to the Far East. Leaves ovate, glaucous, blue-green. Flowers tubular, turquoise, in terminal cymes on prostrate stems, spring to early autumn.

Microseris ringens
(Asteraceae/Compositae)

Common names: None
Height: 60cm (2ft)
Spread: 30cm (1ft)
Aspect: Sun
Soil: Well-drained, humus-rich
Hardiness: Zone 8
Propagation: Seed, in spring or autumn

Australian perennial. Leaves ovate, hairy, rough, soft green. Flowers single, yellow, daisy-like, in large, flat-topped racemes in early summer and again in late summer.

Milium effusum
'Aureum'
(Graminae/Poaceae)

Common name: Bowles' golden grass
Height: 60cm (2ft)
Spread: 30cm (1ft)
Aspect: Half shade or sun
Soil: Moist, well-drained, humus-rich
Hardiness: Zone 6
Propagation: Seed, *in situ* in spring; division, in spring

A spreading grass from Eurasia and North America. Leaves flat, linear, yellow-green. Flowers in open panicles, single-flowered spikes from late spring to midsummer.

Mimulus
'Andean Nymph' A.G.M.
(Scrophulariaceae)

Common names: Monkey flower; musk
Height: 20cm (8in)
Spread: 30cm (12in)
Aspect: Wet, humus-rich, fertile
Soil: Sun or half shade
Hardiness: Zone 6
Propagation: Division, in spring; softwood cuttings, in early summer

Short-lived, rhizomatous hybrid aquatic marginal. Leaves ovate, hairy, toothed, light green. Flowers in racemes, white with pink throats, over a long period in summer.

Mimulus aurantiacus
A.G.M.
(Scrophulariaceae)

Common names: Monkey flower; musk
Height: 1m (3ft)
Spread: 1m (3ft)
Aspect: Sun or half shade
Soil: Moist, humus-rich, fertile
Hardiness: Zone 8
Propagation: Seed in autumn or spring; division in spring

Subshrub from the U.S.A. Leaves oblong, toothed, sticky, glossy green. Flowers in leafy racemes, red, orange or yellow trumpets, in late summer to autumn.

Mimulus cardinalis
A.G.M.
(Scrophulariaceae)

Common name: Scarlet monkey flower
Height: 90cm (36in)
Spread: 60cm (24in)
Aspect: Sun or half shade
Soil: Wet, humus-rich, fertile
Hardiness: Zone 7
Propagation: Seed, in autumn or spring; division, in spring

A creeping perennial from the western U.S.A. and Mexico. Leaves ovate, toothed, downy, green. Flowers on erect stems, solitary, tubular, scarlet, all summer long.

Mimulus luteus
(Scrophulariaceae)

Common names: Monkey musk; yellow monkey flower
Height: 30cm (1ft)
Spread: 60cm (2ft)
Aspect: Sun or half shade
Soil: Wet, humus-rich, fertile
Hardiness: Zone 7
Propagation: Seed, in spring or autumn; division, in spring

Invasive species from Chile. Leaves ovate-oblong, mid-green. Flowers on upright or decumbent stems, yellow, spotted red-purple, from late spring to summer.

Mirabilis jalapa
(Nyctaginaceae)

Common names: Four o'clock flower; marvel of Peru
Height: 60cm (2ft)
Spread: 60cm (2ft)
Aspect: Sun
Soil: Well-drained, fertile, protected from winter wet
Hardiness: Zone 8
Propagation: Seed, in warmth in spring; division, in spring

Tuberous perennial. Leaves ovate, mid-green. Flowers perfumed, pink, red, yellow, white, or magenta open in late afternoon, and die next morning. Blooms all summer.

Mitchella repens
(Rubiaceae)

Common names: Creeping box; partridge berry
Height: 5cm (2in)
Spread: 30cm (12in)
Aspect: Half shade
Soil: Moist, well-drained, acidic, humus-rich
Hardiness: Zone 3
Propagation: Seed, in autumn; division of runners, in spring

A creeping, evergreen perennial from the U.S.A. Leaves ovate, green. Flowers white, perfumed, in summer, followed by red berries.

MONARDA *(Labiatae/Lamiaceae)*
Bee balm • Bergamot

A genus of only some 15 species of annuals and rhizomatous, clump-forming, herbaceous perennials from North America, but one which has been hybridised extensively to produce many very garden-worthy, hardy herbaceous perennials. Most hybrids derive from *Monarda didyma* or *M. fistulosa*. They like sun, but will grow in dappled shade. Their natural habitats include both dry prairie and woodlands, so they vary in that some like drier soils whilst others prefer them moist, but the soil must be moisture-retentive for all; in dry spells they are very prone to mildew. The flowers are in whorls, sage-like, tubular, 2-lipped, with a hooded upper lip and a spreading lower lip, and often have coloured bracts. Bergamots are long-flowering, make excellent cut flowers, and are often used for flower arrangements, in both the fresh and dried state. Bees also like the flowers, but only bumblebees can gain direct access; honey bees can reach the pollen only after other insects have made holes. The stems are distinctive in that they are square; in the taller varieties they require staking. The foliage is unspectacular, but aromatic. Slugs attack the young growth in spring. Bergamots are low-allergen plants, so suit the allergic gardener.

Monarda
'Aquarius'
(Labiatae/Lamiaceae)

Common name: Bergamot
Height: 1m (36in)
Spread: 45cm (18in)
Aspect: Sun or half shade
Soil: Moist, well-drained, humus-rich, fertile
Hardiness: Zone 4
Propagation: Division or basal cuttings, both in spring

Rhizomatous hybrid. Leaves aromatic, ovate, toothed, dark green. Flowers 2-lipped, deep lilac-purple with purple-green bracts, from summer to autumn.

Monarda
'Balance'
(Labiatae/Lamiaceae)

Common name: Bergamot
Height: 1m (36in)
Spread: 45cm (18in)
Aspect: Sun or half shade
Soil: Moist, humus-rich, well-drained, fertile
Hardiness: Zone 4
Propagation: Division basal or cuttings in spring

A rhizomatous hybrid cultivar. Leaves aromatic, ovate, toothed, dark green. Flowers 2-lipped, brick-red, from summer to autumn.

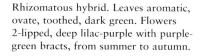

Monarda
'Cambridge Scarlet'
(Labiatae/Lamiaceae)

Common name: Bergamot
Height: 1m (36in)
Spread: 45cm (18in)
Aspect: Sun or half shade
Soil: Moist, well-drained, humus-rich, fertile
Hardiness: Zone 4
Propagation: Division or basal cuttings, both in spring

Hybrid, rhizomatous cultivar. Leaves aromatic, ovate, toothed, dark green. Flowers 2-lipped, scarlet with brown bracts, from summer to autumn.

Monarda
'Croftway Pink'
(Labiatae/Lamiaceae)

Common name: Bergamot
Height: 1m (36in)
Spread: 45cm (18in)
Aspect: Sun or half shade
Soil: Moist, well-drained, humus-rich, fertile
Hardiness: Zone 4
Propagation: Division or basal cuttings, both in spring

Rhizomatous, hybrid cultivar. Leaves aromatic, ovate, toothed, dark green. Flowers 2-lipped, pink with pink-tinged bracts, from summer to autumn.

Monarda didyma
(Labiatae/Lamiaceae)

Common names: Bee balm; bergamot
Height: 1m (36in)
Spread: 45cm (18in)
Aspect: Sun or half shade
Soil: Moist, well-drained, humus-rich, fertile
Hardiness: Zone 4
Propagation: Seed, in spring or autumn; division, in spring

Rhizomatous species from the eastern U.S.A. Leaves aromatic, ovate, toothed, dull green. Flowers pink with red-tinted bracts, from mid- to late summer.

Monarda fistulosa
(Labiatae/Lamiaceae)

Common name: Wild bergamot
Height: 1.2m (4ft)
Spread: 45cm (18in)
Aspect: Sun
Soil: Moist, well-drained, humus-rich, fertile
Hardiness: Zone 4
Propagation: Seed, in spring or autumn; division, in spring

A rhizomatous perennial. Leaves aromatic, ovate, toothed, dull green. Flowers sage-like, 2-lipped, pale pink with purple bracts, from summer to autumn.

Monarda
'Gardenview Scarlet'
(Labiatae/Lamiaceae)

Common name: Bergamot
Height: 1m (3ft)
Spread: 45cm (18in)
Aspect: Sun or half shade
Soil: Moist, well-drained, humus-rich, fertile
Hardiness: Zone 4
Propagation: Division or basal cuttings, both in spring

A hybrid, rhizomatous bergamot. Leaves aromatic, ovate, toothed, dark green. Flowers 2-lipped, scarlet with dark bracts, from summer to autumn.

Monarda
'Isla'
(Labiatae/Lamiaceae)

Common name: Bergamot
Height: 1m (3ft)
Spread: 45cm (18in)
Aspect: Sun or half shade
Soil: Moist, well-drained, humus-rich, fertile
Hardiness: Zone 4
Propagation: Division or basal cuttings, both in spring

A rhizomatous, hybrid cultivar. Leaves aromatic, ovate, toothed, dark green. Flowers sage-like, 2-lipped, pink with pinkish bracts, from summer to autumn.

Monarda
'Prärienacht'
(Labiatae/Lamiaceae)

Common name: Bergamot
Height: 1m (3ft)
Spread: 45cm (18in)
Aspect: Sun or half shade
Soil: Moist, well-drained, humus-rich, fertile
Hardiness: Zone 4
Propagation: Division or basal cuttings, both in spring

A rhizomatous, hybrid bergamot. Leaves aromatic, ovate, toothed, dark green. Flowers 2-lipped, purple-lilac with red-green bracts, from midsummer to autumn.

Monarda punctata
(Labiatae/Lamiaceae)

Common name: Spotted bee balm
Height: 1m (3ft)
Spread: 45cm (18in)
Aspect: Sun or half shade
Soil: Moist, well-drained, humus-rich, fertile
Hardiness: Zone 4
Propagation: Division or basal cuttings, both in spring; seed, in autumn

A species from the U.S.A. Leaves aromatic, toothed, pale green. Flowers in whorls, sage-like, 2-lipped, pink, spotted purple, bracts green, tinged pink, in summer.

Monarda
'Scorpion'
(Labiatae/Lamiaceae)

Common name: Bergamot
Height: 1m (3ft)
Spread: 45cm (18in)
Aspect: Sun or half shade
Soil: Moist, well-drained, humus-rich, fertile
Hardiness: Zone 4
Propagation: Division or basal cuttings, both in spring

A hybrid, rhizomatous cultivar. Leaves aromatic, ovate, toothed, dark green, Flowers in whorls, 2-lipped, hooded, deep pink, from summer to autumn.

Monarda
'Squaw'
(Labiatae/Lamiaceae)

Common name: Bergamot
Height: 1m (3ft)
Spread: 45cm (18in)
Aspect: Sun or half shade
Soil: Moist, well-drained, humus-rich, fertile
Hardiness: Zone 4
Propagation: Division or basal cuttings, both in spring

A rhizomatous, hybrid bergamot. Leaves aromatic, ovate, toothed, dark green. Flowers in whorls, sage-like, hooded, bright crimson, from summer to autumn.

Monarda
'Twins'
(Labiatae/Lamiaceae)

Common name: Bergamot
Height: 1m (3ft)
Spread: 45cm (18in)
Aspect: Sun or half shade
Soil: Moist, well-drained, humus-rich, fertile
Hardiness: Zone 4
Propagation: Division or basal cuttings, both in spring

A hybrid, rhizomatous bergamot. Leaves aromatic, toothed, dark green. Flowers in whorls, sage-like, hooded, lilac-pink, from summer to autumn.

Moraea spathulata
(Iridaceae)

Common names: None
Height: 90cm (3ft)
Spread: 8cm (3in)
Aspect: Sun
Soil: Well-drained, humus-rich, fertile
Hardiness: Zone 8
Propagation: Seed, in warmth in autumn; offsets, when dormant

A cormous perennial from Africa. Leaves basal, narrowly linear, flat, green. Flowers in succession, in clusters, each short-lived, iris-like, from spring to summer.

Morina longifolia
(Morinaceae)

Common name: Whorlflower
Height: 90cm (3ft)
Spread: 30cm (1ft)
Aspect: Sun
Soil: Sharply drained, humus-rich, protected from winter wet
Hardiness: Zone 6
Propagation: Seed, when ripe; root cuttings, in winter

Evergreen with leaves in a basal rosette, lance-shaped, spiny, dark green. Flowers in tiered whorls, with spiny bracts, white, becoming pink, then red, in summer.

Muscari armeniacum
A.G.M.
(Hyacinthaceae/Liliaceae)

Common name: Grape hyacinth
Height: 20cm (8in)
Spread: 5cm (2in)
Aspect: Sun
Soil: Moist, well-drained, fertile
Hardiness: Zone 4
Propagation: Offsets, in summer

A vigorous, bulbous perennial from the Caucasus. Leaves linear, mid-green, after the flowers. Flowers in dense racemes, bright blue with white mouths, in spring.

Muscari azureum
A.G.M.
(Hyacinthaceae/Liliaceae)

Common name: Grape hyacinth
Height: 10cm (4in)
Spread: 5cm (2in)
Aspect: Sun
Soil: Moist, well-drained, fertile
Hardiness: Zone 8
Propagation: Offsets, in summer

A bulbous perennial from Turkey. Leaves inverse lance-shaped, grey-green. Flowers in dense racemes, sky-blue bells with a dark stripe on each lobe, in spring.

Muscari comosum
'Plumosum'
(Hyacinthaceae/Liliaceae)

Common name: Tassel grape hyacinth
Height: 60cm (24in)
Spread: 5cm (2in)
Aspect: Sun
Soil: Moist, well-drained, fertile
Hardiness: Zone 4
Propagation: Offsets, in summer

Bulbous perennial from Europe and Turkey. Leaves linear, spreading, mid-green. Flowers are absent; heads are composed of sterile, purple threads.

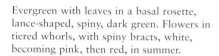

Muscari latifolium
(Hyacinthaceae/Liliaceae)

Common name: Grape hyacinth
Height: 20cm (8in)
Spread: 5cm (2in)
Aspect: Sun
Soil: Moist, well-drained, fertile
Hardiness: Zone 4
Propagation: Offsets, in summer

Bulbous perennial. Leaves mid-green, semi-erect, inverse lance-shaped. Dense racemes of purple-black, urn-shaped flowers are crowned by sterile, blue flowers.

Myosotidium hortensia
(Boraginaceae)

Common name: Chatham Island forget-me-not
Height: 60cm (2ft)
Spread: 90cm (3ft)
Aspect: Half shade
Soil: Moist, well-drained, gritty
Hardiness: Zone 8
Propagation: Seed, when ripe; division, in spring

Leaves large, ovate to heart-shaped, with conspicuous veins, glossy green. Flowers in cymes, blue bells with white margins, in early summer. Not for a hot, dry garden.

Myosotis scorpioides
(Boraginaceae)

Common names: Water forget-me-not
Height: 30cm (1ft)
Spread: 30cm (1ft)
Aspect: Sun or half shade
Soil: Marginal aquatic
Hardiness: Zone 5
Propagation: Seed or division, both in spring

A rampant, rhizomatous perennial from Eurasia and North America. Leaves ovate, mid-green. Flowers in open cymes, small, blue, salverform, in early summer.

Myrrhis odorata
(Apiaceae/Umbelliferae)

Common names: Garden myrrh; sweet cicely
Height: 2m (6ft)
Spread: 1.5m (5ft)
Aspect: Half shade
Soil: Moist, well-drained, fertile
Hardiness: Zone 5
Propagation: Seed, in spring; division, in spring or autumn

Aniseed-flavoured culinary herb. Leaves 2- or 3-pinnate, lobes lance-shaped, toothed, bright green. Flowers in compound umbels, small, star-shaped, white; fruits brown.

NARCISSUS (Amaryllidaceae)
Daffodil

A genus of some 50 species of bulbous perennials from varied habitats in Europe and North Africa; the genus has been hybridised extensively, and several thousand cultivars have been developed. The daffodil is an excellent garden plant, suitable for naturalizing, growing in a border, or planting in containers. They will grow in sun or half-shade, although the former is preferred. They like the soil to be moist during the growing season but dry during the dormant period, and so a humus-rich but sharply drained soil is best. The flowers are borne on leafless stems, which may carry anything from one to 20 blooms. The flower has a perianth and a corona: the perianth is made up of six petals, spreading or reflexed, and the corona may be any shape between a shallow cup and a long trumpet. The leaves are basal, and usually strap-shaped, sometimes cylindrical; they should be left to die down, not cut back, or flowering will be poorer the following year. Daffodils benefit from lifting and dividing every few years, and as this is best done during the summer dormancy, it is best to mark the positions of the clumps whilst the foliage is there to guide you. The bulbs are poisonous, and contact with the sap may cause skin irritation.

Narcissus
'Actaea' A.G.M. (Div. 9)
(Amaryllidaceae)

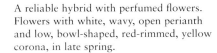

Common name: Daffodil
Height: 45cm (18in)
Spread: 15cm (6in)
Aspect: Sun or half shade
Soil: Well-drained, fertile, humus-rich
Hardiness: Zone 4
Propagation: Offsets, in summer or autumn

A reliable hybrid with perfumed flowers. Flowers with white, wavy, open perianth and low, bowl-shaped, red-rimmed, yellow corona, in late spring.

Narcissus
'Baby Moon' (Div. 7)
(Amaryllidaceae)

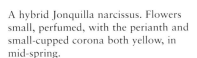

Common name: Daffodil
Height: 25cm (10in)
Spread: 8cm (3in)
Aspect: Sun or half shade
Soil: Well-drained, alkaline, humus-rich, fertile
Hardiness: Zone 4
Propagation: Offsets, in summer or autumn

A hybrid Jonquilla narcissus. Flowers small, perfumed, with the perianth and small-cupped corona both yellow, in mid-spring.

Narcissus
'Bantam' A.G.M. (Div. 2)
(Amaryllidaceae)

Common name: Daffodil
Height: 25cm (10in)
Spread: 15cm (6in)
Aspect: Sun or half shade
Soil: Well-drained, fertile, humus-rich
Hardiness: Zone 4
Propagation: Offsets, in summer or autumn

A good hybrid narcissus. Flowers with short, golden yellow perianth segments and short, flared, orange, cup-shaped, red-rimmed corona, in mid-spring.

Narcissus
'Bravoure' A.G.M. (Div. 1)
(Amaryllidaceae)

Common name: Daffodil
Height: 45cm (18in)
Spread: 15cm (6in)
Aspect: Sun or half shade
Soil: Moist, well-drained, humus-rich
Hardiness: Zone 4
Propagation: Offsets, in summer or autumn

A robust Trumpet daffodil. Flowers with pointed, overlapping, white perianth segments and a long, yellow, trumpet-shaped corona, in mid-spring.

Narcissus bulbocodium
(Div. 13)
(Amaryllidaceae)

Common name: Hoop-petticoat daffodil
Height: 15cm (6in)
Spread: 8cm (3in)
Aspect: Sun or half shade
Soil: Well-drained, acidic, humus-rich
Hardiness: Zone 6
Propagation: Seed, when ripe; offsets, in summer or autumn

A species from Europe and North Africa. Flowers small, yellow, with reduced, pointed perianth segments and an expanded, megaphone-shaped corona, in mid-spring.

Narcissus
'Canaliculatus' (Div. 8)
(Amaryllidaceae)

Common name: Daffodil
Height: 12cm (5in)
Spread: 16cm (6in)
Aspect: Sun or half shade
Soil: Well drained, alkaline, humus-rich
Hardiness: Zone 8
Propagation: Offsets, in summer or autumn

A perfumed, cluster-headed, Tazetta narcissus. Flower with reflexed, white perianth and a yellow, barrel-shaped corona, in mid-spring.

Narcissus cyclamineus
A.G.M. (Div. 13)
(Amaryllidaceae)

Common name: Daffodil
Height: 20cm (8in)
Spread: 8cm (3in)
Aspect: Sun or half shade
Soil: Well-drained, acidic, humus-rich
Hardiness: Zone 5
Propagation: Seed, when ripe; offsets, in summer or autumn

Species from Spain and Portugal. Leaves narrow, keeled, spreading. Flowers small, nodding, yellow. Perianth totally reflexed, corona long and narrow, in early spring.

Narcissus
'February Gold' A.G.M.
(Div. 6) (Amaryllidaceae)

Common name: Daffodil
Height: 30cm (12in)
Spread: 8cm (3in)
Aspect: Sun or half shade
Soil: Well-drained, acidic, humus-rich, fertile
Hardiness: Zone 6
Propagation: Offsets, in summer or autumn

A robust, hybrid, Cyclamineus narcissus. Flowers with golden-yellow, reflexed perianth and long, trumpet-shaped corona of deeper yellow, in early spring

Narcissus
'Hawera' A.G.M. (Div. 5)
(Amaryllidaceae)

Common name: Daffodil
Height: 18cm (7in)
Spread: 8cm (3in)
Aspect: Sun or half shade
Soil: Well-drained, acidic, humus-rich, fertile
Hardiness: Zone 4
Propagation: Offsets, in summer or autumn

A Triandrus hybrid with many flowers on each stem. Perianth segments reflexed, canary yellow; corona a shallow cup of paler yellow. Flowers in late spring.

Narcissus
'Ice Follies' A.G.M. (Div. 2)
(Amaryllidaceae)

Common name: Daffodil
Height: 40cm (16in)
Spread: 16cm (6in)
Aspect: Sun or half shade
Soil: Well-drained, fertile, humus-rich
Hardiness: Zone 6
Propagation: Offsets, in summer or autumn

A prolific daffodil, with large, cream perianth segments and a wide, frilly-edged, cup-shaped corona, lemon fading to almost white, in mid-spring.

DIVISIONS OF NARCISSUS by the R.H.S. (as revised 1977)

1) Trumpet

2) Large-cupped

3) Small-cupped

4) Double

5) Triandrus

6) Cyclamineus

7) Jonquilla

8) Tazetta

9) Poeticus

10) Species, wild forms, and hybrids

11) Split-corona

12) Miscellaneous

13) Species

Each daffodil illustrated will have a division number.

Narcissus
'Jack Snipe' A.G.M. (Div. 6)
(Amaryllidaceae)

Common name: Daffodil
Height: 20cm (8in)
Spread: 8cm (3in)
Aspect: Sun or half shade
Soil: Well-drained, acidic, humus-rich
Hardiness: Zone 6
Propagation: Offsets, in summer or autumn

A robust, hybrid, Cyclamineus daffodil. Flowers with reflexed, white perianth segments and a yellow, trumpet-shaped corona, in early to mid-spring.

Narcissus
'Jetfire' A.G.M. (Div. 6)
(Amaryllidacae)

Common name: Daffodil
Height: 20cm (8in)
Spread: 15cm (6in)
Aspect: Sun or half shade
Soil: Well-drained, acidic, humus-rich, fertile
Hardiness: Zone 6
Propagation: Offsets, in summer or autumn

A robust, hybrid, Cyclamineus daffodil. Flowers with reflexed, golden-yellow perianth and a long, orange, trumpet-shaped corona in early spring.

Narcissus jonquilla
A.G.M. (Div. 13)
(Amaryllidaceae)

Common name: Wild jonquil
Height: 30cm (12in)
Spread: 8cm (3in)
Aspect: Sun or half shade
Soil: Well-drained, acidic, humus-rich, fertile
Hardiness: Zone 4
Propagation: Seed, when ripe; offsets, in summer or autumn

A species from Spain. Leaves narrow, erect to spreading, mid-green. Flowers strongly scented, yellow; perianth segments pointed, corona a small, flat cup, in late spring.

Daffodils can range from robust, yellow trumpets to the cool grace of Narcissus triandrus *var.* albus, *the white form of the angel's tears daffodil.*

Narcissus
'Minnow' A.G.M. (Div. 8) (Amaryllidaceae)

Common name: Daffodil
Height: 18cm (7in)
Spread: 8cm (3in)
Aspect: Sun or half shade
Soil: Well-drained, acidic, humus-rich, fertile
Hardiness: Zone 8
Propagation: Offsets, in summer or autumn

A robust, hybrid Tazetta daffodil. Flowers with cream perianth segments fading to white and a yellow, cup-shaped corona, in mid-spring.

Narcissus obvallaris
A.G.M. (Div. 13) (Amaryllidaceae)

Common name: Tenby daffodil
Height: 30cm (12in)
Spread: 16cm (6in)
Aspect: Sun or half shade
Soil: Well-drained, humus-rich, fertile
Hardiness: Zone 4
Propagation: Seed, when ripe; offsets, in summer or autumn

A species found in South Wales and across W Europe. Leaves erect, glaucous green. Flowers golden-yellow, with spreading perianth segments and a long corona.

Narcissus
'Peeping Tom' A.G.M. (Div. 6) (Amaryllidaceae)

Common name: Daffodil
Height: 20cm (8in)
Spread: 8cm (3in)
Aspect: Sun or half shade
Soil: Well-drained, acidic, humus-rich, fertile
Hardiness: Zone 6
Propagation: Offsets, in summer or autumn

A robust, hybrid, Cyclamineus daffodil. Flowers yellow, with strongly reflexed perianth segments, and a long, trumpet-shaped corona, in mid-spring.

Narcissus
'Pipit' (Div. 7) (Amaryllidaceae)

Common name: Daffodil
Height: 25cm (10in)
Spread: 8cm (3in)
Aspect: Sun or half shade
Soil: Well-drained, acidic, humus-rich, fertile
Hardiness: Zone 4
Propagation: Offsets, in summer or autumn

A perfumed, hybrid, Jonquilla daffodil. Flowers with recurved, lemon perianth segments and a yellow, cup-shaped corona, in mid- to late spring.

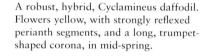

Narcissus
'Rippling Waters' A.G.M. (Div. 5) (Amaryllidaceae)

Common name: Daffodil
Height: 20cm (8in)
Spread: 8cm (3in)
Aspect: Sun or half shade
Soil: Well-drained, acidic, humus-rich, fertile
Hardiness: Zone 4
Propagation: Offsets, in summer or autumn

Hybrid with multiflowered stems. Flowers with large, reflexed, white perianth segments and a pale yellow, cup-shaped, shallow corona, in mid- and late spring.

Narcissus
'Rip van Winkle' (Div. 4) (Amaryllidaceae)

Common name: Daffodil
Height: 15cm (6in)
Spread: 15cm (6in)
Aspect: Sun or half shade
Soil: Well-drained, humus-rich, fertile
Hardiness: Zone 4
Propagation: Offsets, in summer or autumn

A hybrid with double flowers. Perianth segments narrow, pointed, cream. Corona divided, segments doubled into irregular central mass, yellow, in early spring.

Narcissus
'Salomé' (Div. 2) (Amaryllidaceae)

Common name: Daffodil
Height: 45cm (18in)
Spread: 15cm (6in)
Aspect: Sun or half shade
Soil: Well-drained, humus-rich, fertile
Hardiness: Zone 4
Propagation: Offsets, in summer or autumn

Large-cupped, hybrid daffodil. Flowers with pale cream perianth segments and a large, peach, cup-shaped, almost trumpet-shaped corona, in mid-spring.

Narcissus
'Sundial' (Div. 7) (Amaryllidaceae)

Common name: Daffodil
Height: 20cm (8in)
Spread: 8cm (3in)
Aspect: Sun or half shade
Soil: Well-drained, acidic, humus-rich, fertile
Hardiness: Zone 4
Propagation: Offsets, in summer or autumn

A small, hybrid Jonquilla daffodil. Flowers with perianth segments of cream, and a small, golden-yellow, cup-shaped corona, in mid-spring.

Narcissus
'Tête-à-tête' A.G.M. (Div. 12) (Amaryllidaceae)

Common name: Daffodil
Height: 15cm (6in)
Spread: 15cm (6in)
Aspect: Sun or half shade
Soil: Well-drained, humus-rich, fertile
Hardiness: Zone 4
Propagation: Offsets, in summer or autumn

A vigorous, Miscellaneous section daffodil. Flowers with golden-yellow, reflexed perianth segments and a yellow, cup-shaped corona, in early spring.

Narcissus
'Thalia' (Div. 5) (Amaryllidaceae)

Common name: Daffodil
Height: 35cm (14in)
Spread: 8cm (3in)
Aspect: Sun or half shade
Soil: Well-drained, acidic, humus-rich, fertile
Hardiness: Zone 4
Propagation: Offsets, in summer or autumn

A Triandrus daffodil. Flowers milk-white, in pairs, with twisted, reflexed, narrow perianth segments and an open, cup-shaped corona, in mid-spring.

Nectaroscordum siculum
(Alliaceae/Liliaceae)

Common name: Sicilian honey garlic
Height: 1.5m (5ft)
Spread: 10cm (4in)
Aspect: Sun or half shade
Soil: Well-drained, fertile
Hardiness: Zone 6
Propagation: Seed, in autumn or spring; offsets, in summer

A vigorous, bulbous plant from Italy and France. Leaves basal, linear, keeled, mid-green. Flowers in umbels of up to 30, open, pendulous, plum-coloured bells, in summer.

Nemesia denticulata
(Scrophulariaceae)

Common names: None
Height: 40cm (16in)
Spread: 20cm (8in)
Aspect: Sun
Soil: Moist, well-drained, acidic, fertile
Hardiness: Zone 8
Propagation: Seed, in warmth in spring or autumn

A neat, compact, mound-forming perennial from South Africa. Leaves lance-shaped, toothed. Flowers large, flattish, lilac, from spring to autumn.

Nepeta govaniana
(Labiatae/Lamiaceae)

Common name: Catmint
Height: 90cm (3ft)
Spread: 60cm (2ft)
Aspect: Sun or half shade
Soil: Well-drained
Hardiness: Zone 5
Propagation: Division, in spring or autumn; seed, in autumn

A clump-forming Himalayan plant. Leaves aromatic, ovate, hairy, pointed, scalloped, mid-green. Flowers in panicles, pale yellow, from midsummer to early autumn.

Nepeta sibirica
(Labiatae/Lamicaeae)

Common names: Catmint; catnip
Height: 90cm (36in)
Spread: 45cm (18in)
Aspect: Sun
Soil: Well-drained
Hardiness: Zone 3
Propagation: Division, in spring or autumn; seed, in autumn

Species from Russia and Asia. Leaves aromatic, lance-shaped, toothed, dark green. Flowers in whorled cymes, blue, in mid- and late summer.

Nepeta subsessilis
(Labiatae/Lamiaceae)

Common name: Catmint
Height: 90cm (3ft)
Spread: 30cm (1ft)
Aspect: Sun
Soil: Well-drained
Hardiness: Zone 7
Propagation: Division, in spring or autumn; seed, in autumn

A clump-forming perennial from Japan. Leaves aromatic, ovate, toothed, dark green. Flowers in upright, whorled cymes, from midsummer to early autumn.

Nerine bowdenii
A.G.M. (Amaryllidaceae)

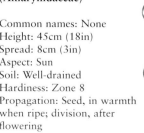

Common names: None
Height: 45cm (18in)
Spread: 8cm (3in)
Aspect: Sun
Soil: Well-drained
Hardiness: Zone 8
Propagation: Seed, in warmth when ripe; division, after flowering

A bulbous perennial from Africa. Leaves broad straps, mid-green. Flowers in open umbels of up to 7, perfumed, pink funnels with recurved tepals, in late autumn.

Nierembergia repens
(Solanaceae)

Common name: White cup flower
Height: 5cm (2in)
Spread: 45cm (18in)
Aspect: Sun
Soil: Moist, well-drained
Hardiness: Zone 8
Propagation: Seed or division, both in spring

A prostrate perennial from the Andes. Leaves spoon-shaped, bright green. Flowers open, upward-facing cups, white, over long periods in summer.

Nomocharis pardanthina
(Liliaceae)

Common names: None
Height: 90cm (36in)
Spread: 10cm (4in)
Aspect: Half shade, or sun in cool areas
Soil: Moist in summer, acidic, humus-rich
Hardiness: Zone 7
Propagation: Seed, in warmth in autumn or spring

A woodlander from China. Leaves lance-shaped, mid-green. Flowers in racemes of up to 6, nodding, saucer-shaped, pink, spotted purple, in early summer.

Nymphaea alba
(Nymphaeaceae)

Common name: White water lily
Height: Surface
Spread: 1.5m (5ft)
Aspect: Sun
Soil: Undisturbed water
Hardiness: Zone 5
Propagation: Seed, covered by an inch of water, in warmth when ripe

A rhizomatous, aquatic perennial from Eurasia and North Africa. Leaves round, deep green. Flowers perfumed, star-shaped, yellow-centred, in summer.

Nymphaea
'James Brydon' A.G.M.
(Nymphaeaceae)

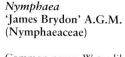

Common name: Water lily
Height: Surface
Spread: 1.2m (4ft)
Aspect: Sun
Soil: Still water
Hardiness: Zone 4
Propagation: Division of rhizomes or separated offsets, both in summer

A rhizomatous, hybrid, aquatic perennial. Leaves rounded, bronze-green. Flowers cup-shaped, vivid rose-red with yellow stamens, in summer.

Nymphoides peltata
(Menyanthaceae)

Common names: Waterfringe; yellow floating heart
Height: 8cm (3in)
Spread: Indefinite
Aspect: Sun
Soil: Still water
Hardiness: Zone 6
Propagation: Separated runners, in summer

A rhizomatous, herbaceous perennial from Eurasia. Leaves ovate, mottled, green. Flowers on long stems, yellow, funnel-shaped, in summer.

OENOTHERA (Onagraceae)
Evening primrose • Sundrops

A genus of some 125 species of annuals, biennials and perennials from North America in particular, but also distributed in Central and South America. The perennial members of the genus are mostly short-lived. Their natural habitats are often on mountainsides, and in the garden they prefer a position in sun in a well-drained soil; small types such as *Oenothera macrocarpa* are suitable for a rock garden. Some evening primroses are tap-rooted, and resent disturbance, so these should be sited carefully when they are first planted. The individual flowers are often short-lived, but they are borne in succession over a long period throughout the summer. The flowers are cup- or saucer-shaped, sometimes trumpet-shaped, white, yellow, or pink, and often perfumed. They are borne either singly in the axils or in terminal racemes. All are attractive to bees. The taller forms of evening primrose require staking. Many of them seed around to an unacceptable degree; dead-heading to prevent self-seeding is not easy in this genus, since ripened seed pods and unopened flower buds are found on the same stem, so naturalizing them in a wild garden may be a preferred option for these types.

Oenothera deltoides
(Onagraceae)

Common name: Desert evening primrose
Height: 30cm (12in)
Spread: 20cm (8in)
Aspect: Sun
Soil: Sharply drained
Hardiness: Zone 9
Propagation: Seed, in early spring

A perennial from Arizona, Baja California and Mexico. Leaves ovate, mid-green. Flowers solitary, white bowls, on erect and decumbent stems, in summer.

Oenothera fruticosa
(Onagraceae)

Common name: Sundrops
Height: 90cm (3ft)
Spread: 30cm (1ft)
Aspect: Sun
Soil: Sharply drained, fertile
Hardiness: Zone 4
Propagation: Seed, in early spring

A short-lived species from North America. Leaves ovate, toothed, mid-green. Flowers in racemes of up to 10, deep yellow cups, from late spring to late summer.

Oenothera fruticosa
'Fyrverkeri' A.G.M.
(Onagraceae)

Common name: Sundrops
Height: 90cm (3ft)
Spread: 30cm (1ft)
Aspect: Sun
Soil: Sharply drained, fertile
Hardiness: Zone 4
Propagation: Division, in early spring

A selected form of the species, with purple-brown-flushed leaves, and red buds opening to chrome-yellow flowers, from late spring for many weeks.

Oenothera macrocarpa
A.G.M.
(Onagraceae)

Common name: Ozark sundrops
Height: 15cm (6in)
Spread: 45cm (18in)
Aspect: Sun
Soil: Sharply drained
Hardiness: Zone 5
Propagation: Seed, in early spring

A robust perennial from the southern U.S.A. Leaves lance-shaped, toothed, mid-green. Flowers solitary, golden cups, over a long period from spring to autumn.

Oenothera nuttallii
(Onagraceae)

Common name: Sundrops
Height: 90cm (3ft)
Spread: 60cm (2ft)
Aspect: Sun
Soil: Sharply drained
Hardiness: Zone 5
Propagation: Seed, in early spring

North American species. Leaves oblong, dull green. Flowers on straggly stems, large, creamy-white, in summer. Long-lived. Very late to reappear, so mark position.

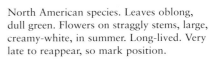

Oenothera rosea
(Onagraceae)

Common names: Rose of Mexico; sundrops
Height: 60cm (2ft)
Spread: 30cm (1ft)
Aspect: Sun
Soil: Sharply drained
Hardiness: Zone 6
Propagation: Seed, in early spring

A species from the Americas. Leaves oblong, mid-green. Flowers small, pink, diurnal cups. Not to be confused with *O. speciosa* 'Rosea', a superior plant.

Oenothera speciosa
(Onagraceae)

Common name: Evening primrose
Height: 30cm (1ft)
Spread: 30cm (1ft)
Aspect: Sun
Soil: Sharply drained
Hardiness: Zone 5
Propagation: Seed, in early spring

Species from the south-west U.S.A. Leaves basal, in rosettes, oblong, mid-green. Flowers solitary, single white cups, ageing to pink, over a long period in summer.

Oenothera speciosa
'Rosea'
(Onagraceae)

Common name: Evening primrose
Height: 30cm (1ft)
Spread: 30cm (1ft)
Aspect: Sun
Soil: Sharply drained
Hardiness: Zone 5
Propagation: Seed, in early spring

A form of the species with yellow-centred flowers that have white petals suffused pink towards the periphery. Long-flowering, but can be invasive.

Oenothera speciosa
'Siskiyou'
(Onagraceae)

Common name: Evening primrose
Height: 30cm (1ft)
Spread: 30cm (1ft)
Aspect: Sun
Soil: Sharply drained
Hardiness: Zone 5
Propagation: Division, in early spring

A selected form of the species with yellow-centred flowers that have white petals suffused pink around the perimeter. Can be invasive.

Oenothera macrocarpa *makes a long-flowering candidate for a scree bed similar to its natural habitat.*

Oenothera stubbei
(Onagraceae)

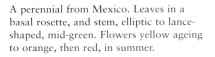

Common name: Evening primrose
Height: 1.2m (4ft)
Spread: 30cm (1ft)
Aspect: Sun
Soil: Sharply drained
Hardiness: Zone 8
Propagation: Seed, in early spring

A perennial from Mexico. Leaves in a basal rosette, and stem, elliptic to lance-shaped, mid-green. Flowers yellow ageing to orange, then red, in summer.

Olsynium douglasii album
(Iridaceae)

Common name: Grass widow
Height: 30cm (12in)
Spread: 10cm (4in)
Aspect: Half shade
Soil: Moist, humus-rich, fertile
Hardiness: Zone 9
Propagation: Seed, in autumn

A tender, clump-forming perennial from North America. Leaves linear, grey-green. Flowers nodding, bell-shaped, in spathes of up to 4, white, in early spring.

Omphalodes cappadocica
'Cherry Ingram' A.G.M.
(Boraginaceae)

Common name: Navelwort
Height: 30cm (1ft)
Spread: 30cm (1ft)
Aspect: Half shade
Soil: Moist, humus-rich, fertile
Hardiness: Zone 6
Propagation: Division, in early spring

An evergreen, clump-forming, woodland ground cover. Leaves basal, ovate, veined, pointed, dull green. Flowers deep blue, in racemes, in spring, intermittently thereafter.

Omphalodes cappadocica
'Starry Eyes'
(Boraginaceae)

Common name: Navelwort
Height: 30cm (12in)
Spread: 45cm (18in)
Aspect: Half shade
Soil: Moist, humus-rich, fertile
Hardiness: Zone 6
Propagation: Division, in early spring

Evergreen woodland ground cover. Leaves ovate, green. Flowers pale blue with a central white stripe on each petal, in loose racemes in spring, intermittently thereafter.

Onoclea sensibilis
A.G.M.
(Aspidiaceae)

Common name: Sensitive fern
Height: 60cm (2ft)
Spread: Indefinite
Aspect: Half shade
Soil: Moist, acidic, fertile, humus-rich
Hardiness: Zone 4
Propagation: Spores, in warmth when ripe; division, in spring

A deciduous fern from North America and Asia. Spring fronds sterile, pinnate, lobes lance-shaped, pale green. Autumn fronds fertile, erect, 2-pinnate; pinnate black lobes.

Onosma alborosea
(Boraginaceae)

Common names: None
Height: 25cm (10in)
Spread: 25cm (10in)
Aspect: Sun
Soil: Dry, sharply drained
Hardiness: Zone 7
Propagation: Seed in autumn

Clump-forming evergreen from Asia. Leaves obovate, white-hairy, grey-green. Flowers in terminal, congested cymes, narrow, white, tubular, tips turning pink with age.

Ophiopogon planiscapus
'Nigrescens' A.G.M.
(Convallariaceae/Liliaceae)

Common name: Lilyturf
Height: 20cm (8in)
Spread: 30cm (12in)
Aspect: Sun or half shade
Soil: Acidic, humus-rich, fertile
Hardiness: Zone 6
Propagation: Seed, when ripe; division, in spring

A stoloniferous, evergreen ground cover from Japan. Leaves near-black straps. Flowers in racemes, pinkish-white, in summer, followed by black berries.

Orchis mascula
(Orchidaceae)

Common name: Early purple orchid
Height: 30cm (12in)
Spread: 15cm (6in)
Aspect: Half shade
Soil: Sharply drained, humus-rich, fertile
Hardiness: Zone 5
Propagation: Offsets, in spring

A terrestrial orchid from Europe. Leaves long, pointed, purple-spotted, mid-green. Flowers in erect racemes, pale or dark purple, in spring and summer.

***Origanum amanum* A.G.M.**
(Labiatae/Lamiaceae)

Common names: Marjoram; oregano
Height: 20cm (8in)
Spread: 30cm (12in)
Aspect: Sun
Soil: Well-drained, alkaline, fertile
Hardiness: Zone 8
Propagation: Seed, division or basal cuttings, all in spring

Evergreen subshrub from Turkey. Leaves aromatic, ovate, bright green. Flowers in terminal whorls, pink surrounded by green bracts, in summer and autumn.

***Origanum* 'Buckland'**
(Labiatae/Laamiaceae)

Common names: Marjoram; oregano
Height: 20cm (8in)
Spread: 15cm (6in)
Aspect: Sun
Soil: Well-drained, alkaline, fertile
Hardiness: Zone 7
Propagation: Division or basal cuttings, both in spring

A hybrid marjoram. Leaves aromatic, rounded, hairy, grey-green. Flowers in whorls, pink, tubular, surrounded by pink bracts, in summer and autumn.

***Origanum laevigatum* A.G.M.**
(Labiatae/Lamiaceae)

Common names: Marjoram; oregano
Height: 60cm (24in)
Spread: 45cm (18in)
Aspect: Sun
Soil: Well-drained, alkaline, fertile
Hardiness: Zone 8
Propagation: Seed, division or basal cuttings, all in spring

A perennial from Turkey and Cyprus. Leaves aromatic, ovate, dark green. Flowers in whorls, tubular, purple-pink, from spring to autumn.

***Origanum laevigatum* 'Herrenhausen' A.G.M.**
(Labiatae/Lamiaceae)

Common names: Marjoram; oregano
Height: 45cm (18in)
Spread: 45cm (18in)
Aspect: Sun
Soil: Well-drained, alkaline, fertile
Hardiness: Zone 8
Propagation: Division or basal cuttings, both in spring

A hybrid evergreen perennial. Leaves aromatic, ovate, purple-green. Flowers in whorls, denser form than the species, deep pink, from spring to autumn.

***Origanum vulgare* 'Aureum' A.G.M.**
(Labiatae/Lamiaceae)

Common name: Golden marjoram
Height: 60cm (2ft)
Spread: 30cm (1ft)
Aspect: Sun
Soil: Well-drained, alkaline, fertile
Hardiness: Zone 5
Propagation: Division or basal cuttings, both in spring

A rhizomatous perennial from Europe. Leaves aromatic, ovate, golden. Flowers in whorls, tubular, pink, midsummer to early autumn. Less invasive than the species.

Ornithogalum arabicum
(Hyacinthaceae/Liliaceae)

Common name: Star of Bethlehem
Height: 80cm (32in)
Spread: 10cm (4in)
Aspect: Sun
Soil: Well-drained, fertile
Hardiness: Zone 9
Propagation: Seed, in autumn or spring; offsets, when dormant

Bulbous Mediterranean plant. Leaves dark green, linear, broad, arching. Flowers cup-shaped, in corymbs of up to 25, perfumed, white with a black ovary, in early summer.

Ornithogalum narbonense
(Hyacinthaceae/Liliaceae)

Common name: Star of Bethlehem
Height: 90cm (36in)
Spread: 20cm (8in)
Aspect: Sun
Soil: Well-drained, fertile
Hardiness: Zone 7
Propagation: Seed, in autumn or spring; offsets, when dormant

A bulbous perennial from Turkey and Iran. Leaves basal, linear, arching, grey-green. Flowers starry, white, in narrow, tapering racemes, in late spring and early summer.

***Ornithogalum nutans* A.G.M.**
(Hyacinthaceae/Liliaceae)

Common name: Star of Bethlehem
Height: 60cm (24in)
Spread: 5cm (2in)
Aspect: Sun
Soil: Well-drained, fertile
Hardiness: Zone 6
Propagation: Seed, autumn or spring; offsets, when dormant

Bulbous plant from Eurasia. Leaves semi-erect, strap-shaped, green with a central silver stripe. Flowers in one-sided racemes of up to 20, silver-white funnels, in spring.

Ornithogalum thyrsoides
(Hyacinthaceae/Liliaceae)

Common name: Chincherinchee
Height: 80cm (32in)
Spread: 10cm (4in)
Aspect: Sun
Soil: Well-drained, fertile
Hardiness: Zone 9
Propagation: Seed, in autumn or spring; offsets, when dormant

A bulbous plant from South Africa. Leaves basal, narrow, lance-shaped, mid-green, before the many-flowered, dense racemes of white cups, in spring and early summer.

Ornithogalum umbellatum
(Hyacinthaceae/Liliaceae)

Common name: Star of Bethlehem
Height: 30cm (12in)
Spread: 10cm (4in)
Aspect: Sun
Soil: Well-drained, fertile
Hardiness: Zone 5
Propagation: Seed, in autumn or spring; offsets, when dormant

A robust, bulbous perennial from Europe to the Middle East. Leaves basal, linear, veined silver, green. Flowers in racemes of up to 20, starry, white, in early summer.

Orthrosanthus chimboracensis
(Iridaceae)

Common names: None
Height: 60cm (24in)
Spread: 20cm (8in)
Aspect: Sun
Soil: Well-drained, fertile, humus-rich
Hardiness: Zone 9
Propagation: Seed, in warmth in spring; division, in spring

A tender, rhizomatous, evergreen perennial from Mexico to Peru. Leaves basal, linear, rough, green. Flowers in loose panicles, lavender bowls, in summer.

Osmunda cinnamomea
(Osmundaceae)

Common name: Cinnamon fern
Height: 90cm (3ft)
Spread: 60cm (2ft)
Aspect: Half shade
Soil: Moist, acidic, fertile, humus-rich
Hardiness: Zone 3
Propagation: Spores, in summer; division, in autumn or spring

Deciduous fern. Sterile, blue-green, ovate to lance-shaped, pinnate fronds, segments pinnatifid, surround erect, narrow, fertile fronds topped by cinnamon sporangia.

OSTEOSPERMUM (Asteraceae/Compositae)
Veldt daisy

A genus of some 70 species of annuals, perennials and evergreen subshrubs from mountainous, forest edge or grassland habitats in southern Africa and the Arabian Peninsula. They are mostly tender or half-hardy, but a few are reliably hardy, and hybrids are being produced from these which are also hardy. In frost-prone areas the more tender types can be treated as annuals. *Osteospermum* have three features that commend them to the gardener: they have a very long flowering season, stretching from late spring to autumn, they are evergreen, and they make excellent ground cover, so are worth taking some trouble over. Their daisy-like flowerheads have ray florets of pink, white or yellow, with a wider range of shades available in the cultivars, and often contrasting, darker disc florets. They require little more than a position in full sun (the flowers of many will close in shade or dull weather) and well-drained soil; a sunny bank is an ideal situation. Dead-heading will improve and prolong flowering. They make good cut flowers. Regrettably, like most daisy-like flowers, they are highly allergenic, so best avoided by the allergic gardener. They are prone to downy mildew in wet areas.

Osteospermum
'Buttermilk' A.G.M.
(Asteraceae/Compositae)

Common name: Veldt daisy
Height: 60cm (2ft)
Spread: 60cm (2ft)
Aspect: Sun
Soil: Well-drained, fertile
Hardiness: Zone 9
Propagation: Softwood cuttings, in spring; semi-ripe cuttings, in summer

Evergreen subshrub. Leaves inverse lance-shaped, mid-green. Flowers solitary, single, daisy-like, ray florets primrose, disc florets mauve, from late spring to autumn.

Osteospermum caulescens
syn. *O.* 'White Pim' A.G.M.
(Asteraceae/Compositae)

Common name: Veldt daisy
Height: 10cm (4in)
Spread: 60cm (24in)
Aspect: Sun
Soil: Well-drained, fertile
Hardiness: Zone 8
Propagation: Seed, in warmth in spring

Subshrub from South Africa. Leaves inverse lance-shaped, toothed, mid-green. Flowers solitary, single, ray florets white, disc florets blue, from late spring to autumn.

Osteospermum jucundum
A.G.M.
(Asteraceae/Compositae)

Common name: Veldt daisy
Height: 50cm (20in)
Spread: 90cm (36in)
Aspect: Sun
Soil: Well-drained, fertile
Hardiness: Zone 7
Propagation: Seed, in warmth in spring

Rhizomatous subshrub. Leaves inverse lance-shaped, greyish-green. Flowers single, solitary, ray florets mauve, disc florets purple, from late spring to autumn.

Osteospermum
'Nairobi Purple'
(Asteraceae/Compositae)

Common name: Veldt daisy
Height: 15cm (6in)
Spread: 90cm (36in)
Aspect: Sun
Soil: Well-drained, fertile
Hardiness: Zone 9
Propagation: Softwood cuttings, in spring; semi-ripe cuttings, in summer

Tender, evergreen hybrid subshrub. Leaves ovate to spoon-shaped, bright green. Flowers solitary, single, ray florets purple, disc florets black, from late spring to autumn.

Osteospermum
'Silver Sparkler' A.G.M.
(Asteraceae/Compositae)

Common names: Veldt daisy
Height: 45cm (18in)
Spread: 90cm (36in)
Aspect: Sun
Soil: Well-drained, fertile
Hardiness: Zone 8
Propagation: Softwood cuttings, in spring; semi-ripe cuttings, in summer

Evergreen subshrub. Leaves inverse lance-shaped, grey-green, edged white. Flowers solitary, single, ray florets steely-white, disc florets brown, late spring to autumn.

Osteospermum
'Sirius'
(Asteraceae/Compositae)

Common name: Veldt daisy
Height: 30cm (1ft)
Spread: 30cm (1ft)
Aspect: Sun
Soil: Well-drained, fertile
Hardiness: Zone 8
Propagation: Softwood cuttings, in spring; semi-ripe cuttings, in summer

Hybrid, evergreen subshrub. Leaves ovate to spoon-shaped, dull green. Flowers single, solitary, ray florets cerise, ageing to pink, disc florets green, late spring to autumn.

Osteospermum
'Sunny Alex'
(Asteraceae/Compositae)

Common name: Veldt daisy
Height: 30cm (1ft)
Spread: 30cm (1ft)
Aspect: Sun
Soil: Well-drained, fertile
Hardiness: Zone 8
Propagation: Softwood cuttings, in spring; semi-ripe cuttings, in summer

Evergreen subshrub. Leaves inverse lance-shaped, toothed, dull green. Flowers single, solitary, ray florets bright yellow, disc florets orange, from late spring to autumn.

Ostrowskia magnifica
(Campanulaceae)

Common name: Giant bellflower
Height: 1.5m (5ft)
Spread: 45cm (18in)
Aspect: Sun
Soil: Moist, well-drained, deep, fertile
Hardiness: Zone 7
Propagation: Seed, when ripe

Leaves in whorls, ovate, toothed. Flowers in racemes, outward-facing, milky-blue or white, open bells, in early and midsummer. Taproot is easily damaged; avoid moving it.

Othonna cheirifolia
(Asteraceae/Compositae)

Common names: None
Height: 30cm (12in)
Spread: 45cm (18in)
Aspect: Sun
Soil: Sharply drained, fertile
Hardiness: Zone 8
Propagation: Seed, in warmth in spring; basal cuttings, in summer

An evergreen, spreading subshrub from North Africa. Leaves spoon-shaped, fleshy, grey-green. Flowers in corymbs, daisy-like, yellow, in late autumn and early winter.

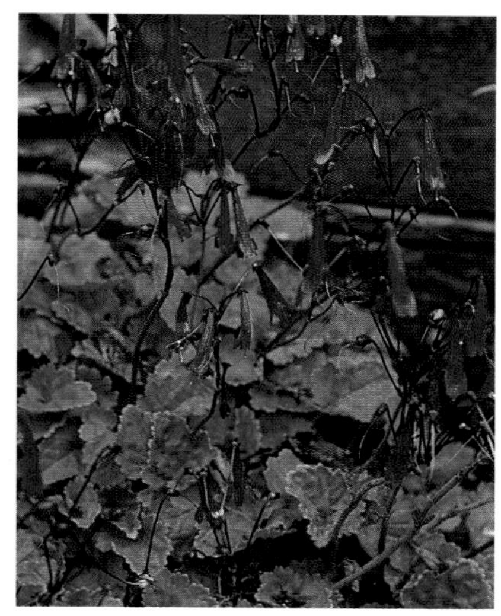

Ourisia coccinea
(Scrophulariaceae)

Common names: None
Height: 20cm (8in)
Spread: 40cm (16in)
Aspect: Half shade
Soil: Moist, humus-rich, fertile
Hardiness: Zone 7
Propagation: Seed, when ripe or in spring

Mat-forming evergreen from the Andes. Leaves in rosettes, oblong, veined, toothed, pale green. Flowers tubular, 2-lipped, pendent, scarlet, in racemes, all summer.

Oxalis acetosella
(Oxalidaceae)

Common names: Shamrock; sorrel
Height: 5cm (2in)
Spread: Indefinite
Aspect: Full or half shade
Soil: Moist, humus-rich, fertile
Hardiness: Zone 3
Propagation: Division, in spring

Hardy, highly invasive woodland plant. Leaves 3-lobed, leaflets inverse heart-shaped, pale green. Flowers solitary, dark-veined pink cups, in spring.

Oxalis hedysariodes
(Oxalidaceae)

Common names: Shamrock; sorrel
Height: 1m (36in)
Spread: 45cm (18in)
Aspect: Full or half shade
Soil: Sharply-drained, fertile
Hardiness: Zone 9
Propagation: Seed, in warmth in late winter to spring

A tender subshrub from Central America. Leaves 3-lobed, leaflets ovate, light green. Flowers in axillary cymes, funnel-shaped, yellow, in summer.

Oxalis pes-caprae
(Oxalidaceae)

Common name: Bermuda buttercup
Height: 12cm (5in)
Spread: Indefinite
Aspect: Shade
Soil: Moist, humus-rich
Hardiness: Zone 9
Propagation: Seed, in warmth in late winter to spring

Rampant, bulbous plant. Leaves 3-lobed, leaflets inverse heart-shaped, bright green. Flowers in umbellate cymes, solitary, deep golden-yellow, in spring and early summer.

Oxalis tetraphylla
'Iron Cross'
(Oxalidaceae)

Common name: Lucky clover
Height: 15cm (6in)
Spread: 15cm (6in)
Aspect: Full or half shade
Soil: Moist, humus-rich, fertile
Hardiness: Zone 8
Propagation: Seed or offsets, both in spring

Invasive, bulbous plant. Leaves 4-lobed, each leaflet inversely triangular, mid-green, with a purple basal band. Flowers in cymes of up to 12, funnel-shaped, pink, in summer.

Pachyphragma macrophyllum
(Brassicaceae/Cruciferae)

Common names: None
Height: 40cm (16in)
Spread: 90cm (36in)
Aspect: Half shade
Soil: Humus-rich, fertile
Hardiness: Zone 7
Propagation: Seed, in autumn; division, in spring

Woodland plant. Leaves large, basal, rounded, scalloped, some overwintering. Flowers in flat corymbs, cruciform, white, malodorous, in spring, followed by berries.

PAEONIA (PAEONIACEAE)
Peony

A genus of some 30 or so species from rocky scrubland and meadows across Eurasia and western North America. There are two types of plant in the genus: the herbaceous, tuberous perennials, and the shrubs that are known as tree peonies; only one of the latter will be included here. The perennial peonies are long-lived and easy to grow in sun or part-shade, and in any soil provided that it is not waterlogged. They do not take kindly to root disturbance, so site them carefully when first planting them; they can become large in time, so leave them plenty of room. Most peonies flower in early summer. The flowers are large, often brightly coloured, showy, and sometimes perfumed; they may be single, semi-double, double or anemone-form, and are followed by attractive, lobed seed pods containing red or black seeds. The foliage is dissected and handsome. Some species are invasive, notably *P. mascula* subsp. *arietina* (Zone 8), *P. mollis* (Zone 6), *P. officinalis*, *P. peregrina* (Zone 8) and *P. tenuifolia*, but the rest are well-behaved. They may require staking in exposed areas, especially those with large and double flowers. They are low-allergen, and suit the allergic gardener. All parts of the plants are poisonous, however.

Paeonia lactiflora
'Bowl of Beauty' A.G.M.
(Paeoniaceae)

Common name: Peony
Height: 1m (3ft)
Spread: 1m (3ft)
Aspect: Sun or half shade
Soil: Moist, well-drained, fertile, humus-rich
Hardiness: Zone 6
Propagation: Division, in spring or autumn

A herbaceous perennial. Leaves 2-ternate, lobes obovate, mid-green. Flowers large, anemone-form, carmine red with a cream centre, in early summer.

The clump-forming Oxalis adenophylla *covers itself with purplish-pink flushed flowers in late spring.*

Paeonia broteroi
(Paeoniaceae)

Common name: Peony
Height: 50cm (20in)
Spread: 50cm (20in)
Aspect: Sun or half shade
Soil: Moist, well-drained, fertile, humus-rich
Hardiness: Zone 7
Propagation: Seed, in autumn to early winter

A herbaceous perennial from Spain and Portugal. Leaves divided, glossy, mid-green. Flowers single, pink cups, in late spring and early summer.

Paeonia delavayi
A.G.M.
(Paeoniaceae)

Common name: Tree peony
Height: 2m (6ft)
Spread: 1.2m (4ft)
Aspect: Sun or half shade
Soil: Moist, well-drained, fertile, humus-rich
Hardiness: Zone 6
Propagation: Seed, in autumn or spring; semi-ripe cuttings, in summer

A robust tree peony from China. Leaves 2-pinnate, lobes deeply cut, dark green. Flowers single, cup-shaped, rich, dark red, in early summer.

Paeonia lactiflora
'Lady Alexandra Duff'
A.G.M. (Paeoniaceae)

Common name: Peony
Height: 70cm (28in)
Spread: 70cm (28in)
Aspect: Sun or half shade
Soil: Moist, well-drained, fertile, humus-rich
Hardiness: Zone 6
Propagation: Division, in spring or autumn

One of many cultivars of this species. Leaves divided, leaflets elliptic to lance-shaped. Flowers double, pale pink, in midsummer.

Paeonia mascula
subsp. *arietina*
(Paeoniaceae)

Common name: Peony
Height: 1m (3ft)
Spread: 1m (3ft)
Aspect: Sun or half shade
Soil: Moist, well-drained, fertile, humus-rich
Hardiness: Zone 8
Propagation: Seed in autumn or winter; division, in spring or autumn

A herbaceous perennial. Leaves divided into 9 ovate leaflets, bluish-green. Flowers single, rose-pink cups with yellow stamens, in early summer.

Paeonia mascula
subsp. *russii*
(Paeoniaceae)

Common name: Peony
Height: 45cm (18in)
Spread: 45cm (18in)
Aspect: Sun or half shade
Soil: Moist, well-drained, fertile, humus-rich
Hardiness: Zone 8
Propagation: Seed, in autumn or winter; division, in spring or autumn

A very compact form of the species, found in Greece, Corsica, Sicily and Sardinia. Leaves tinged purple. Flowers single, rose-pink with yellow stamens, in early summer.

Paeonia mascula
subsp. *triternata*
(Paeoniaceae)

Common name: Peony
Height: 45cm (18in)
Spread: 45cm (18in)
Aspect: Sun or half shade
Soil: Moist, well-drained, fertile, humus-rich
Hardiness: Zone 8
Propagation: Seed, in autumn or winter; division, in spring or autumn

A form of the species from Asia Minor and the Balkans. Flowers single, pink; the bright red seed heads found in this and many other peonies are shown here.

Paeonia mlokosewitschii
A.G.M.
(Paeoniaceae)

Common name: Peony
Height: 90cm (3ft)
Spread: 90cm (3ft)
Aspect: Sun or half shade
Soil: Moist, well-drained, fertile, humus-rich
Hardiness: Zone 6
Propagation: Seed, in autumn or early winter; division, in spring or autumn

Leaves divided into 9 ovate leaflets, bluish-green. Flowers short-lived, single, bowl-shaped, petals broad, lemon-yellow, in late spring and early summer.

Paeonia obovata
var. *alba* A.G.M.
(Paeoniaceae)

Common name: Peony
Height: 70cm (28in)
Spread: 70cm (28in)
Aspect: Sun or half shade
Soil: Moist, well-drained, fertile, humus-rich
Hardiness: Zone 7
Propagation: Seed, in autumn or early winter; division, in spring or autumn

Peony from China. Leaves divided into 9 leaflets, with elliptic lobes, dark green. Flowers single, cup-shaped, white, with yellow anthers and purple filaments.

Paeonia officinalis
(Paeoniaceae)

Common name: Common peony
Height: 70cm (28in)
Spread: 70cm (28in)
Aspect: Sun or half shade
Soil: Moist, well-drained, humus-rich, fertile
Hardiness: Zone 8
Propagation: Seed, in autumn or early winter; division, in spring or autumn

A species from Europe. Leaves divided into 9 leaflets, with oblong lobes, dark green. Flowers single, cup-shaped, rose-pink with yellow stamens, in early to midsummer.

Paeonia officinalis
'Anemoniflora Rosea' A.G.M. (Paeoniaceae)

Common name: Anemone-flowered peony
Height: 70cm (28in)
Spread: 70cm (28in)
Aspect: Sun or half shade
Soil: Moist, well-drained, humus-rich, fertile
Hardiness: Zone 8
Propagation: Seed, in autumn or early winter; division, in spring or autumn

A form of the European common peony with anemone-centred flowers of pale pink. Leaves dark green, divided into 9 leaflets with oblong lobes.

Paeonia tenuifolia
(Paeoniaceae)

Common name: Peony
Height: 70cm (28in)
Spread: 70cm (28in)
Aspect: Sun or half shade
Soil: Moist, well-drained, humus-rich, fertile
Hardiness: Zone 8
Propagation: Seed, in autumn or early winter; division, in spring or autumn

Leaves many-segmented, segments linear, dark green. Flowers single, cup-shaped, deep red with yellow stamens, late spring to early summer. From Europe and Russia.

Paeonia lactiflora
'White Wings' (Paeoniaceae)

Common name: Peony
Height: 85cm (35in)
Spread: 85cm (35in)
Aspect: Sun or half shade
Soil: Moist, well-drained, humus-rich, fertile
Hardiness: Zone 7
Propagation: Seed, in autumn or early winter; division, in spring or autumn

A hardy perennial cultivar. Leaves dark, glossy green. Flowers single, cup-shaped, perfumed, white, with ruffled petals, in early summer.

PAPAVER (Papaveraceae)
Poppy

A genus of some 70 species of annuals, biennials and perennials from many parts of the world, including Europe, Asia, South Africa, North America, Australia and some subarctic areas. The perennial members of the genus are easy to grow. All are sun-lovers, and will grow well so long as they are in sun and their soil is not waterlogged; they do best in poor but deeply cultivated, well-drained soil, or even sharply drained in the case of the *Papaver alpinum* and its forms. Poppies are tap-rooted and do not transplant well, so should be sited carefully when they are first planted. The flowers are short-lived but beautiful, being brightly coloured and silky, and are followed by decorative, distinctively shaped "pepper-pot" seed capsules. These are best removed if abundant self-seeding is not desired, but if seed is wanted they must ripen on the plant. The flowers are low-allergen. They are good for arrangements, but they need to be picked at night before the bud opens, and the bottom of the stem dipped in very hot water, kept cool overnight, then arranged in the morning. The seed pods are also good, either fresh or dried. The only drawbacks of poppies are that they often need to be staked, and they are prone to downy mildew.

Papaver anomalum album
(Papaveraceae)

Common names: None
Height: 40cm (16in)
Spread: 15cm (6in)
Aspect: Sun
Soil: Well-drained, deep, fertile
Hardiness: Zone 7
Propagation: Seed, in spring

A perennial poppy from China. Leaves basal, 2-pinnatisect, glabrous, blue-green. Flowers solitary, single, white (yellow in type) with yellow centres, in late spring.

Papaver atlanticum
(Papaveraceae)

Common names: None
Height: 30cm (12in)
Spread: 15cm (6in)
Aspect: Sun
Soil: Well-drained, deep, fertile
Hardiness: Zone 6
Propagation: Seed, in spring

A short-lived, clump-forming perennial from Morocco. Leaves oblong, toothed, mid-green. Flowers solitary, single, orange saucers, in summer.

Papaver nudicaule
(Papaveraceae)

Common names: Arctic poppy; Icelandic poppy
Height: 30cm (12in)
Spread: 15cm (6in)
Aspect: Sun
Soil: Well-drained, deep, fertile
Hardiness: Zone 3
Propagation: Seed, in spring

A hardy plant derived from the sub-arctic *P. croceum*. Dense tuft of oval, pinnatisect, hairy, grey-green leaves. Flowers scented, in all colours, solitary, single bowls, summer.

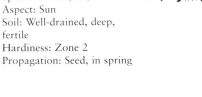

Papaver fauriei
(Papaveraceae)

Common names: None
Height: 10cm (4in)
Spread: 10cm (4in)
Aspect: Sun
Soil: Well-drained, deep, fertile
Hardiness: Zone 2
Propagation: Seed, in spring

A hardy, mound-forming, short-lived plant from Japan and Russia. Leaves pinnate, lobes lance-shaped, deep-cut, grey-green. Flowers solitary, single yellow in summer.

Papaver
'Fireball'
(Papaveraceae)

Common names: None
Height: 30cm (1ft)
Spread: Indefinite
Aspect: Sun
Soil: Well-drained, deep, fertile
Hardiness: Zone 7
Propagation: Seed, in spring

An invasive perennial of uncertain origin. Leaves lance-shaped, toothed, mid-green. Flowers semi-double, solitary, scarlet-orange, from late spring to summer.

Papaver orientale
'Allegro'
(Papaveraceae)

Common name: Oriental poppy
Height: 90cm (36in)
Spread: 75cm (30in)
Aspect: Sun
Soil: Well-drained
Hardiness: Zone 3
Propagation: Division, in spring

Spreading, clump-forming cultivar. Leaves pinnatisect, leaflets lance-shaped, toothed. Flowers solitary cups, scarlet-orange with black basal spots, late spring to midsummer.

Papaver orientale
'Beauty of Livermere'
A.G.M. (Papaveraceae)

Common name: Oriental poppy
Height: 1.2m (4ft)
Spread: 90cm (3ft)
Aspect: Sun
Soil: Well-drained, deep, fertile
Hardiness: Zone 3
Propagation: Division, in spring

Clump-forming, spreading cultivar. Leaves pinnatisect, leaflets lance-shaped, toothed. Flowers solitary, single cups, scarlet with black basal marks, spring to midsummer.

Papaver orientale
'Black and White' A.G.M.
(Papaveraceae)

Common name: Oriental poppy
Height: 90cm (3ft)
Spread: 90cm (3ft)
Aspect: Sun
Soil: Well-drained, deep, fertile
Hardiness: Zone 3
Propagation: Division, in spring

Clump-forming cultivar. Leaves pinnatisect, leaflets lance-shaped, toothed, mid-green. Flowers solitary, single cups, white with red or black basal marks, spring to midsummer.

Papaver orientale
'Charming'
(Papaveraceae)

Common name: Oriental poppy
Height: 90cm (3ft)
Spread: 90cm (3ft)
Aspect: Sun
Soil: Well-drained, deep, fertile
Hardiness: Zone 3
Propagation: Division, in spring

Leaves pinnatisect, leaflets lance-shaped, toothed, mid-green. Flowers solitary, single cups, blush pink with plum-coloured basal marks, late spring to midsummer.

Papaver orientale
'Harvest Moon'
(Papaveraceae)

Common name: Oriental poppy
Height: 90cm (3ft)
Spread: 90cm (3ft)
Aspect: Sun
Soil: Well-drained, deep, fertile
Hardiness: Zone 3
Propagation: Division, in spring

Hybrid oriental poppy. Leaves pinnatisect, leaflets lance-shaped, toothed, mid-green. Flowers solitary, single cups, burnt orange, from late spring to midsummer.

Papaver orientale
'Patty's Plum'
(Papaveraceae)

Common name: Oriental poppy
Height: 90cm (3ft)
Spread: 90cm (3ft)
Aspect: Sun
Soil: Well-drained, deep, fertile
Hardiness: Zone 3
Propagation: Division, in spring

Hybrid oriental poppy. Leaves pinnatisect, leaflets lance-shaped, toothed, mid-green. Flowers solitary, single, plum-coloured cups, from late spring to midsummer.

Papaver rupifragum
(Papaveraceae)

Common names: None
Height: 45cm (18in)
Spread: 20cm (8in)
Aspect: Sun
Soil: Well-drained, deep, fertile
Hardiness: Zone 7
Propagation: Seed, in spring

A short-lived perennial species from Spain. Leaves obovate, toothed, mid-green. Flowers solitary, single, dark orange bowls, in summer.

Papaver spicatum
(Papaveraceae)

Common name: Spicate poppy
Height: 60cm (24in)
Spread: 15cm (6in)
Aspect: Sun
Soil: Well-drained, deep, fertile
Hardiness: Zone 8
Propagation: Seed in spring

A species from Turkey. Leaves in a basal rosette, oblong-elliptic, toothed, pale green. Flowers pale orange, outward-facing, in a slender raceme, in succession, in summer.

Paradisea liliastrum
A.G.M.
(Asphodelaceae/Liliaceae)

Common names: Paradise lily; St Bruno's lily
Height: 60cm (2ft)
Spread: 30cm (1ft)
Aspect: Sun or half shade
Soil: Moist, well-drained, fertile
Hardiness: Zone 7
Propagation: Seed, when ripe or in spring; division, in spring

A rhizomatous, clump-forming perennial. Leaves grassy. Flowers white with large yellow anthers, strongly scented, in one-sided racemes, late spring or early summer.

Paradisea lusitanicum
(Asphodelaceae/Liliaceae)

Common names: Paradise lily; St. Bruno's lily
Height: 1.2m (4ft)
Spread: 40cm (16in)
Aspect: Sun or half shade
Soil: Moist, well-drained, fertile
Hardiness: Zone 8
Propagation: Seed, when ripe or in spring; division, in spring

A rhizomatous perennial from Spain and Portugal. Leaves in basal rosettes, linear, green. Flowers in racemes of up to 25, white, perfumed trumpets, in summer.

Parahebe perfoliata
A.G.M.
(Scrophulariaceae)

Common name: Digger's speedwell
Height: 80cm (32in)
Spread: 45cm (18in)
Aspect: Sun
Soil: Well-drained, fertile
Hardiness: Zone 9
Propagation: Seed, when ripe or in spring

Tender, evergreen perennial from Australia. Leaves in perfoliate pairs, toothed, leathery, glaucous, blue-green. Flowers in racemes, blue saucers, in late summer.

Paraquilegia anemonoides
(Scrophulariaceae)

Common names: None
Height: 10cm (4in)
Spread: 10cm (4in)
Aspect: Sun
Soil: Sharply drained, alkaline, poor, protected from winter wet
Hardiness: Zone 5
Propagation: Seed, when ripe

A perennial from Asia. Leaves ferny, 2- or 3-ternate, segments blue-green, deeply lobed. Flowers nodding, lilac, in late spring. For cool summers; best in a raised bed.

Paris polyphylla
(Trilliaceae)

Common name: Herb Paris
Height: 90cm (3ft)
Spread: 30cm (1ft)
Aspect: Full or half shade
Soil: Moist, humus-rich
Hardiness: Zone 7
Propagation: Seed, in autumn; division, after foliage dies down

Rhizomatous woodlander. Bare stems topped with whorls of oval, green leaves, then of greenish sepals, then of greenish-yellow petals. Violet stigma.

Parnassia nubicola
(Parnassiaceae/Saxifragaceae)

Common names: Bog star; grass of Parnassus
Height: 30cm (12in)
Spread: 15cm (6in)
Aspect: Sun
Soil: Wet, humus-rich, fertile
Hardiness: Zone 4
Propagation: Seed, in autumn; division, in spring or autumn

A hardy, waterside perennial from the Himalayas. Leaves elliptic, matt green. Flowers open saucers, white with yellow staminodes, in late summer.

Pelargonium crispum
'Variegatum' A.G.M.
(Geraniaceae)

Common names: Lemon geranium; lemon pelargonium
Height: 45cm (18in)
Spread: 15cm (6in)
Aspect: Sun
Soil: Well-drained, fertile
Hardiness: Zone 10
Propagation: Softwood cuttings, in spring, summer or autumn

An upright, tender perennial subshrub from South Africa. Leaves pale green, margined cream, aromatic. Flowers pale mauve, in spring and summer.

Pelargonium endlicherianum
(Geraniaceae)

Common names: None
Height: 25cm (10in)
Spread: 15cm (6in)
Aspect: Sun
Soil: Sharply-drained, alkaline, fertile, protected from winter wet
Hardiness: Zone 7
Propagation: Seed, in spring

A hardy perennial from Asia Minor, Syria and Armenia. Leaves basal, rounded, crenate, hairy, dark green. Flowers deep pink, veined purple, in scapes, in summer.

Pelargonium peltatum
hybrids
(Geraniaceae)

Common names: Ivy-leaved geraniums; ivy-leaved pelargoniums
Height: 20cm (8in)
Spread: 45cm (18in)
Aspect: Sun
Soil: Well-drained, fertile
Hardiness: Zone 10
Propagation: Softwood cuttings, in spring, summer or autumn

Tender, trailing evergreens. Leaves peltate, fleshy, bright green. Flowers purple, pink, red, white or mauve, single or double, over a very long period in spring and summer.

Pelargonium zonale
hybrids
(Geraniaceae)

Common names: Zonal geraniums; zonal pelargoniums
Height: 60cm (2ft)
Spread: 30cm (1ft)
Aspect: Sun or half shade
Soil: Well-drained, fertile
Hardiness: Zone 10
Propagation: Softwood cuttings, in spring, summer, or autumn

Bushy evergreens. Leaves rounded, green, edged or zoned maroon or bronze. Flowers single or double, red, purple, pink or orange, over a long period in spring and summer.

PENSTEMON (Scrophulariaceae)
Penstemon

A genus of about 250 species of evergreen to deciduous perennials and subshrubs from North and Central America, and one which has been hybridised comprehensively. They come from a wide range of habitats, from mountain areas to plains, and as a result the genus varies in hardiness. The majority of species are half-hardy, with just a few tender or reliably hardy types. They are most likely to remain evergreen in mild areas. Penstemons prefer a sunny position, but they will tolerate light shade. The soil should be well-drained, and not too fertile, otherwise they become lush, flower less freely, and are less likely to survive the winter. A dry winter mulch is advisable in frost-prone areas. They are long-flowering, with a season lasting from early summer until well into autumn if dead-headed. The flowers are tubular, funnel-shaped or bell-shaped, and 2-lipped, the upper lip usually 2-lobed and the lower lip usually 3-lobed. They are borne in upright panicles or racemes, and the colours range from deep purple through reds and pinks to white, with rare yellows. Penstemons are low-allergen plants. Their drawbacks are that they are prey to slugs and susceptible to powdery mildew. Some of the taller varieties need to be staked.

Penstemon 'Andenken an Friedrich Hahn' A.G.M.
(Scrophulariaceae)

Common names: None
Height: 75cm (30in)
Spread: 60cm (24in)
Aspect: Sun or half shade
Soil: Well-drained, fertile
Hardiness: Zone 7
Propagation: Division, in spring

Hybrid cultivar. Leaves linear to lance-shaped, mid-green. Flowers tubular, deep wine red, in racemes, from midsummer to mid-autumn. Has also been called 'Garnet'.

The open spires of flowers on Penstemon hartwegii *'Scarlet and White' make a long-lasting contribution to borders or bedding.*

Penstemon barbatus
(Scrophulariaceae)

Common name: Beardlip penstemon
Height: 1.8m (6ft)
Spread: 50cm (20in)
Aspect: Sun or half shade
Soil: Well-drained, fertile
Hardiness: Zone 3
Propagation: Seed, in late winter or spring; division, in spring

A tall penstemon species. Leaves in basal rosettes, lance-shaped, mid-green. Flowers in panicles, pendent, tubular, red, from early summer to early autumn.

Penstemon cardwellii f. *albus*
(Scrophulariaceae)

Common names: None
Height: 20cm (8in)
Spread: 30cm (12in)
Aspect: Sun or half shade
Soil: Well-drained, fertile
Hardiness: Zone 8
Propagation: Seed, in late winter or spring; division, in spring

A dwarf, evergreen subshrub. Leaves elliptic, toothed, mid-green. Flowers in few-flowered panicles, tubular, white, (deep purple in type) in early summer.

Penstemon
'Charles Rudd'
(Scrophulariaceae)

Common names: None
Height: 60cm (24in)
Spread: 45cm (18in)
Aspect: Sun or half shade
Soil: Well-drained, fertile
Hardiness: Zone 7
Propagation: Division, in spring

A hybrid penstemon. Leaves lance-shaped to linear, mid-green. Flowers in racemes, small, tubular, magenta with a white throat, from midsummer to mid-autumn.

Penstemon
'Cherry Ripe' A.G.M.
(Scrophulariaceae)

Common names: None
Height: 1m (36in)
Spread: 45cm (18in)
Aspect: Sun or half shade
Soil: Well-drained, fertile
Hardiness: Zone 7
Propagation: Division, in spring

Short-lived cultivar. Leaves linear to lance-shaped, bluish-green. Flowers rose-pink with a white throat, nodding, tubular, in open panicles, midsummer to autumn.

Penstemon
'Chester Scarlet' A.G.M.
(Scrophulariaceae)

Common names: None
Height: 60cm (24in)
Spread: 45cm (18in)
Aspect: Sun or half shade
Soil: Well-drained, fertile
Hardiness: Zone 7
Propagation: Division, in spring

A hybrid penstemon. Leaves elliptic, mid-green. Flowers in panicles, large, tubular to bell-shaped, scarlet, with a white throat, from midsummer to mid-autumn.

Penstemon digitalis
(Scrophulariaceae)

Common names: None
Height: 1m (36in)
Spread: 45cm (18in)
Aspect: Sun or half shade
Soil: Well-drained, fertile
Hardiness: Zone 3
Propagation: Seed, in late winter or spring; division, in spring

Hardy species. Leaves in basal rosettes, inverse lance-shaped, mid-green. Flowers in panicles, tubular to bell-shaped, white, interior striped purple, all summer.

Penstemon digitalis
'Husker's Red'
(Scrophulariaceae)

Common names: None
Height: 75cm (30in)
Spread: 30cm (12in)
Aspect: Sun or half shade
Soil: Well-drained, fertile
Hardiness: Zone 3
Propagation: Division, in spring

A selected form of the species. Leaves in basal rosettes, inverse lance-shaped, maroon-red. Flowers white, tinted pink, from early to late summer.

Penstemon
'Drinkstone'
(Scrophulariaceae)

Common names: None
Height: 80cm (32in)
Spread: 45cm (18in)
Aspect: Sun or half shade
Soil: Well-drained, fertile
Hardiness: Zone 7
Propagation: Division, in spring

Also called 'Drinkstone Red'. Leaves ovate-elliptic, mid-green. Flowers tubular to bell-shaped, scarlet-vermilion, streaked magenta inside, early to late summer.

Penstemon heterophyllus
(Scrophulariaceae)

Common name: Foothill penstemon
Height: 50cm (20in)
Spread: 50cm (20in)
Aspect: Sun or half shade
Soil: Well-drained, fertile
Hardiness: Zone 8
Propagation: Seed, in late winter to early spring; division, in spring

An evergreen subshrub from California. Leaves linear to lance-shaped, mid-green. Flowers in racemes, tubular to bell-shaped, blue, lobes lilac, in summer.

Penstemon
'Modesty'
(Scrophulariaceae)

Common names: None
Height: 80cm (32in)
Spread: 45cm (18in)
Aspect: Sun or half shade
Soil: Well-drained, fertile
Hardiness: Zone 7
Propagation: Division, in spring

A hybrid penstemon. Leaves lance-shaped to linear, mid-green. Flowers in racemes, tubular to bell-shaped, pink with a white throat, from summer to autumn.

Penstemon
'Osprey' A.G.M.
(Scrophulariaceae)

Common names: None
Height: 1m (36in)
Spread: 45cm (18in)
Aspect: Sun or half shade
Soil: Well-drained, fertile
Hardiness: Zone 7
Propagation: Division, in spring

Tall hybrid. Leaves linear to lance-shaped, mid-green. Flowers in racemes, tubular to bell-shaped, rose-carmine, throat white, in summer to autumn.

Penstemon
'Peace'
(Scrophulariaceae)

Common names: None
Height: 60cm (24in)
Spread: 45cm (18in)
Aspect: Sun or half shade
Soil: Moist, well-drained
Hardiness: Zone 7
Propagation: Division, in spring

A hybrid cultivar. Leaves linear to lance-shaped, mid-green. Flowers in racemes, tubular to bell-shaped, white with pink margins to the lobes, summer to autumn.

Penstemon
'Pennington Gem' A.G.M.
(Scrophulariaceae)

Common names: None
Height: 75cm (30in)
Spread: 45cm (18in)
Aspect: Sun or half shade
Soil: Well-drained, fertile
Hardiness: Zone 7
Propagation: Division, in spring

A hybrid penstemon. Leaves lance-shaped to linear, mid-green. Flowers in racemes, tubular to bell-shaped, pink with white throats, from midsummer to mid-autumn.

Penstemon pinifolius
A.G.M.
(Scrophulariaceae)

Common names: None
Height: 40cm (16in)
Spread: 25cm (10in)
Aspect: Sun or half shade
Soil: Moist, well-drained
Hardiness: Zone 8
Propagation: Seed, in late winter to spring; division, in spring

An evergreen species from Mexico and the southern U.S.A. Leaves needle-like, mid-green. Flowers in terminal racemes, tubular, scarlet, in summer.

Penstemon pinifolius
'Mersea Yellow'
(Scrophulariaceae)

Common names: None
Height: 40cm (16in)
Spread: 25cm (10in)
Aspect: Sun or half shade
Soil: Well-drained, fertile
Hardiness: Zone 8
Propagation: Seed, in late winter to spring; division, in spring

A yellow-flowered form of the species. Leaves needle-like, pale green. Flowers in racemes, tubular, yellow, in summer. The best of the yellow penstemons.

Penstemon
'Pershore Pink Necklace'
(Scrophulariaceae)

Common names: None
Height: 1m (3ft)
Spread: 45cm (18in)
Aspect: Sun or half shade
Soil: Moist, well-drained
Hardiness: Zone 7
Propagation: Division, in spring

Leaves lance-shaped to linear, mid-green. Flowers in racemes, pink with white throat and carmine band at base of lower lobes, tubular to bell-shaped, in summer.

***Penstemon* 'Port Wine' A.G.M. (Scrophulariaceae)**

Common names: None
Height: 90cm (36in)
Spread: 45cm (18in)
Aspect: Sun or half shade
Soil: Well-drained, fertile
Hardiness: Zone 7
Propagation: Division, in spring

A hybrid penstemon. Leaves linear to lance-shaped, mid-green. Flowers in racemes, tubular to bell-shaped, claret with white throat, from early to late summer.

***Penstemon* 'Red Emperor' (Scrophulariaceae)**

Common names: None
Height: 90cm (36in)
Spread: 45cm (18in)
Aspect: Sun or half shade
Soil: Well-drained, fertile
Hardiness: Zone 7
Propagation: Division, in spring

A hybrid cultivar. Leaves linear to lance-shaped, mid-green. Flowers in racemes, tubular to bell-shaped, deep red with a white ring around mouth, in summer.

***Penstemon* 'Rubicundus' A.G.M. (Scrophulariaceae)**

Common names: None
Height: 1.2m (4ft)
Spread: 45cm (18in)
Aspect: Sun or half shade
Soil: Well-drained, fertile
Hardiness: Zone 7
Propagation: Division, in spring

Short-lived hybrid. Leaves lance-shaped to linear, light green. Flowers in racemes, tubular to bell-shaped, red, mouth white, streaked red, in summer to autumn.

***Penstemon rupicola* 'Diamond Lake' (Scrophulariaceae)**

Common names: None
Height: 20cm (8in)
Spread: 45cm (18in)
Aspect: Sun or half shade
Soil: Moist, well-drained
Hardiness: Zone 8
Propagation: Division in spring

Selected form of evergreen species. Leaves elliptic-round, toothed, thick, blue-green. Flowers pink with white mouths, tubular to funnel-shaped, in racemes, early summer.

***Penstemon* 'Sour Grapes' (Scrophulariaceae)**

Common names: None
Height: 60cm (24in)
Spread: 45cm (18in)
Aspect: Sun or half shade
Soil: Well-drained, fertile
Hardiness: Zone 8
Propagation: Division, in spring

A hybrid penstemon. Leaves elliptic-ovate, mid-green. Flowers in racemes, tubular to bell-shaped, dull lilac-blue, with white throats, from midsummer to mid-autumn.

***Penstemon* 'White Bedder' A.G.M. (Scrophulariaceae)**

Common names: None
Height: 70cm (28in)
Spread: 30cm (12in)
Aspect: Sun or half shade
Soil: Well-drained, fertile
Hardiness: Zone 7
Propagation: Division, in spring

A hybrid penstemon. Leaves elliptic-ovate, bright green. Flowers tubular to bell-shaped, pure white, in racemes, from midsummer to early autumn.

***Penstemon* 'Whitethroat' (Scrophulariaceae)**

Common names: None
Height: 90cm (36in)
Spread: 45cm (18in)
Aspect: Sun or half shade
Soil: Well-drained, fertile
Hardiness: Zone 7
Propagation: Division, in spring

A hybrid penstemon. Leaves lance-shaped to linear, mid-green. Flowers in racemes, tubular to bell-shaped, cerise, throat pure white, from summer to autumn.

***Pentaglottis sempervirens* (Boraginaceae)**

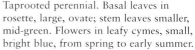

Common name: Green alkanet
Height: 1m (3ft)
Spread: 1m (3ft)
Aspect: Full or half shade
Soil: Moist, humus-rich
Hardiness: Zone 7
Propagation: Seed, when ripe or in spring; division, in spring

Taprooted perennial. Basal leaves in rosette, large, ovate; stem leaves smaller, mid-green. Flowers in leafy cymes, small, bright blue, from spring to early summer.

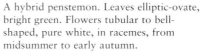

Pentas lanceolata
(Rubiaceae)

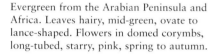

Common name: Star cluster
Height: 2m (6ft)
Spread: 1m (3ft)
Aspect: Sun
Soil: Well-drained, fertile
Hardiness: Zone 10
Propagation: Seed, in warmth in spring; softwood cuttings, at any time

Evergreen from the Arabian Peninsula and Africa. Leaves hairy, mid-green, ovate to lance-shaped. Flowers in domed corymbs, long-tubed, starry, pink, spring to autumn.

Perovskia atriplicifolia
(Labiatae/Lamiaceae)

Common names: None
Height: 1.2m (4ft)
Spread: 1m (3ft)
Aspect: Sun
Soil: Well-drained, fertile
Hardiness: Zone 6
Propagation: Softwood cuttings, in late spring; semi-ripe cuttings, in summer

A subshrub from Afghanistan. Leaves ovate, deeply cut, grey-green. Flowers in tall panicles, small, tubular, lilac-blue, from late summer to early autumn.

Perovskia
'Blue Spire' A.G.M.
(Labiatae/Lamiaceae)

Common names: None
Height: 1.2m (4ft)
Spread: 1m (3ft)
Aspect: Sun
Soil: Well-drained, fertile
Hardiness: Zone 6
Propagation: Softwood cuttings, in late spring; semi-ripe cuttings, in summer

An upright subshrub, with ovate, deeply divided, silver-grey leaves. Flowers in panicles, tubular, violet-blue, in late summer and early autumn.

Persicaria affinis
(Polygonaceae)

Common names: None
Height: 25cm (10in)
Spread: Indefinite
Aspect: Sun or half shade
Soil: Moist
Hardiness: Zone 3
Propagation: Division, in spring or autumn

A vigorous, evergreen ground cover. Leaves dark green, lance-shaped to elliptic. Flowers in spikes, bright rose-red cups, fading to pink, then brown, midsummer to autumn.

PERSICARIA (Polygonaceae)
Bistort

A genus of around 80 species of annuals, stoloniferous or rhizomatous perennials and a few subshrubs, from very varied habitats worldwide. They may be hardy or half-hardy, and deciduous to evergreen. *Persicaria* like growing in sun, as long as they are in a moisture-retentive soil, but tolerate light shade; some species, such as *P. bistorta,* will even tolerate dry soil. Some members of the genus, most notably *P. affinis*, *P. cuspidatum* (Zone 4) and *P. sachalinense* (Zone 4), are rampant invaders, and best avoided in a small garden. Most species are undemanding, easy-going plants, however, and make excellent ground cover, or can be naturalised in a wild garden. Some have a long flowering season. They bear small, cup-, bell- or funnel-shaped flowers, in densely packed spikes or racemes. The flowers are usually long-lasting and may be red, pink or white; they are followed by distinctive, ovoid or 3-angled fruits, usually brownish in colour. Many of the members of the genus were, until very recently, classified under *Polygonum*, and may still be found under that name in old catalogues and books. The main drawbacks of these plants are that all members of the genus are highly allergenic, poisonous, and skin-irritant.

Persicaria amplexicaulis
(Polygonaceae)

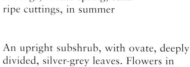

Common name: Bistort
Height: 1.2m (4ft)
Spread: 1.2m (4ft)
Aspect: Sun or half shade
Soil: Moist
Hardiness: Zone 5
Propagation: Division, in spring or autumn

Vigorous, clump-forming perennial. Leaves lance-shaped to ovate, pointed, mid-green. Flowers in narrow spikes, bright red bells, from midsummer to early autumn.

Persicaria amplexicaulis
'Firetail' A.G.M.
(Polygonaceae)

Common name: Bistort
Height: 1.2m (4ft)
Spread: 1.2m (4ft)
Aspect: Sun or half shade
Soil: Moist
Hardiness: Zone 5
Propagation: Division, in spring or autumn

A selected form of the species, with flowers of larger size and brighter red, from midsummer to early autumn. Leaves ovate to lance-shaped, pointed, mid-green.

Persicaria bistorta *'Superba' gives excellent value in a garden, with abundant pink flowers throughout summer and attractive fruits in autumn.*

Persicaria amplexicaulis var. *pendula* (Polygonaceae)

Common names: None
Height: 1.2m (4ft)
Spread: 1.2m (4ft)
Aspect: Sun or half shade
Soil: Moist
Hardiness: Zone 6
Propagation: Division, in spring or autumn

A form of this vigorous, clump-forming species, with narrow, arching spikes of red flowers, and pale green, ovate to lance-shaped, pointed leaves.

Persicaria bistorta subsp. *carnea* (Polygonaceae)

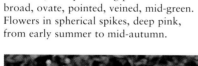

Common name: Bistort
Height: 70cm (28in)
Spread: 45cm (18in)
Aspect: Sun or half shade
Soil: Moist
Hardiness: Zone 4
Propagation: Division, in spring or autumn

A robust, clump-forming perennial. Leaves broad, ovate, pointed, veined, mid-green. Flowers in spherical spikes, deep pink, from early summer to mid-autumn.

Persicaria bistorta 'Superba' A.G.M. (Polygonaceae)

Common name: Bistort
Height: 90cm (3ft)
Spread: 90cm (3ft)
Aspect: Sun or half shade
Soil: Moist
Hardiness: Zone 4
Propagation: Division, in spring or autumn

A robust perennial from Eurasia. Leaves broad, ovate, pointed, veined, mid-green. Flowers in dense, cylindrical spikes, pink bells, over a long period in summer.

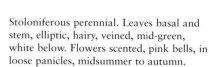

Persicaria campanulata (Polygonaceae)

Common names: None
Height: 90cm (3ft)
Spread: 90cm (3ft)
Aspect: Sun or half shade
Soil: Moist
Hardiness: Zone 8
Propagation: Division, in spring or autumn

Stoloniferous perennial. Leaves basal and stem, elliptic, hairy, veined, mid-green, white below. Flowers scented, pink bells, in loose panicles, midsummer to autumn.

Persicaria campanulata 'Rosenrot' (Polygonaceae)

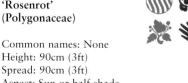

Common names: None
Height: 90cm (3ft)
Spread: 90cm (3ft)
Aspect: Sun or half shade
Soil: Moist
Hardiness: Zone 8
Propagation: Division, in spring

Selected form of the species with rosy red flowers, in loose panicles, midsummer to autumn. Leaves basal and stem, elliptic, hairy, veined, mid-green, white below.

Persicaria capitata (Polygonaceae)

Common names: None
Height: 8cm (3in)
Spread: Indefinite
Aspect: Sun or half shade
Soil: Moist
Hardiness: Zone 8
Propagation: Division, in spring or autumn

Creeping, stem-rooting ground cover from the Himalayas. Leaves ovate, dark green, with a purple 'V'. Flowers pink bells, in short-stemmed, dense panicles, in summer.

Persicaria virginiana 'Painter's Palette' (Polygonaceae)

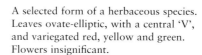

Common names: None
Height: 1.2m (4ft)
Spread: 1.2m (4ft)
Aspect: Sun or half shade
Soil: Moist
Hardiness: Zone 5
Propagation: Division, in spring or autumn

A selected form of a herbaceous species. Leaves ovate-elliptic, with a central 'V', and variegated red, yellow and green. Flowers insignificant.

Petasites japonicus var. *giganteus* 'Variegatus' (Asteraceae/Compositae)

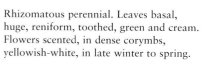

Common names: Butterbur; sweet coltsfoot
Height: 1.2m (4ft)
Spread: 1.5m (5ft)
Aspect: Full or half shade
Soil: Moist, humus-rich, fertile, deep
Hardiness: Zone 5
Propagation: Division, in spring or autumn

Rhizomatous perennial. Leaves basal, huge, reniform, toothed, green and cream. Flowers scented, in dense corymbs, yellowish-white, in late winter to spring.

Phaenosperma globosa
(Poaceae)

Common names: None
Height: 1.5m (5ft)
Spread: 60cm (2ft)
Aspect: Sun
Soil: Well-drained
Hardiness: Zone 7
Propagation: Seed, in autumn or spring

A deciduous grass. Leaves broad, linear, long, light green with darker ribs. Flower stems tall, with pyramidal panicles of pale brown flowers.

Phlomis fruticosa
AG.M.
(Labiatae/Lamiaceae)

Common name: Jerusalem sage
Height: 1m (3ft)
Spread: 1.5m (5ft)
Aspect: Sun
Soil: Well-drained, fertile
Hardiness: Zone 7
Propagation: Seed, in warmth in spring; softwood cuttings, in summer

Evergreen, Mediterranean subshrub. Leaves ovate to lance-shaped, sage-like, grey-green, wrinkled. Flowers in whorls, dead-nettle-like, yellow, in early and midsummer.

Phlomis italica
(Labiatae/Lamiaceae)

Common names: None
Height: 30cm (1ft)
Spread: 60cm (2ft)
Aspect: Sun
Soil: Well-drained, fertile
Hardiness: Zone 8
Propagation: Seed, in warmth in spring; softwood cuttings, in summer

An evergreen subshrub from the Balearic islands. Leaves lance-shaped to oblong, grey-woolly. Flowers in whorls, tubular, dead-nettle-like, lilac, in summer.

Phlox adsurgens
'Wagon Wheel'
(Polemoniaceae)

Common names: None
Height: 30cm (1ft)
Spread: 30cm (1ft)
Aspect: Half shade
Soil: Moist, well-drained, fertile, humus-rich
Hardiness: Zone 6
Propagation: Softwood cuttings of blind shoots, in spring

A prostrate woodlander from the U.S.A. Leaves ovate, mid-green. Flowers salmon-pink, salverform, narrow-petalled, in open cymes, in late spring and early summer.

PHLOX (Polemoniaceae)
Phlox

A genus of over 60 species, all North American except one from Siberia. They come from three types of habitat: alpine phloxes need a sharply drained soil and sun; woodlanders, represented by *Phlox divaricata* and its cultivars, require a humus-rich soil in part shade; waterside species, most notably *P. paniculata*, have given us the modern, hybrid, border phloxes, which need a moist, fertile soil, in sun or half shade. This group has been hybridised extensively; some of the hybrids have large, colourful flowers, but are shorter-lived than one might hope, given that *P. paniculata* is soundly perennial; their survival depends on their having moisture and nutrients at the roots at all times, so they require annual top-dressing, but they dislike waterlogged soil. They have a rich fragrance and attract bees and butterflies. Phlox are low-allergen plants. They benefit from being lifted and divided every few years, keeping the young growths and discarding the woody centre. Some taller varieties may need staking. All can be devoured by slugs in spring, especially the woodland types, so one must take action early. All are also prone to powdery mildew in some degree; border phloxes must never be allowed to dry out, or be enclosed closely by other plants.

Phlox
'Chattahoochee' A.G.M.
(Polemoniaceae)

Common names: None
Height: 15cm (6in)
Spread: 30cm (12in)
Aspect: Half shade
Soil: Moist, well-drained, fertile, humus-rich
Hardiness: Zone 4
Propagation: Softwood cuttings of blind shoots, in spring

Short-lived, prostrate hybrid. Leaves lance-shaped, purple becoming mid-green. Flowers in cymes, salverform, lavender-blue with a red eye, long periods in summer to autumn.

Phlox divaricata
'Blue Dreams'
(Polemoniaceae)

Common name: Wild sweet William
Height: 35cm (14in)
Spread: 50cm (20in)
Aspect: Half shade
Soil: Moist, well-drained, humus-rich, fertile
Hardiness: Zone 4
Propagation: Softwood cuttings of blind shoots, in spring

A spreading, hybrid perennial. Leaves ovate, hairy, mid-green. Flowers in open cymes salverform, lavender-blue with a dark eye, in early summer.

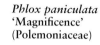

Phlox maculata
(Polemoniaceae)

Common name: Meadow phlox
Height: 1m (36in)
Spread: 45cm (18in)
Aspect: Sun or half shade
Soil: Moist, fertile
Hardiness: Zone 5
Propagation: Division, in spring or autumn

A herbaceous perennial from the eastern U.S.A. Leaves linear, mid-green. Flowers in cymes, perfumed, salverform, violet, white or pink, in early and midsummer.

Phlox paniculata
'Fujiyama' A.G.M.
(Polemoniaceae)

Common names: None
Height: 75cm (30in)
Spread: 90cm (36in)
Aspect: Sun or half shade
Soil: Moist, fertile
Hardiness: Zone 4
Propagation: Division, in spring or autumn

A hybrid perennial. Leaves thin, ovate, toothed, mid-green. Flowers white, perfumed, salverform, in cymes, from summer to mid-autumn.

Phlox paniculata
'Harlequin'
(Polemoniaceae)

Common names: None
Height: 1m (3ft)
Spread: 1m (3ft)
Aspect: Sun or half shade
Soil: Moist, fertile
Hardiness: Zone 4
Propagation: Division, in spring or autumn

A hybrid perennial. Leaves thin, ovate, toothed, pale green, margined ivory. Flowers in cymes, perfumed, red-purple, from summer to early autumn.

Phlox paniculata
'Magnificence'
(Polemoniaceae)

Common names: None
Height: 1m (3ft)
Spread: 1m (3ft)
Aspect: Sun or half shade
Soil: Moist, fertile
Hardiness: Zone 4
Propagation: Division, in spring or autumn

A hybrid perennial. Leaves thin, ovate, toothed, mid-green. Flowers in cymes, scented, salverform, bright, clear pink, from summer to autumn.

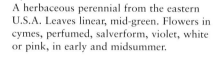

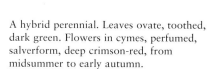

Phlox paniculata
'Norah Leigh'
(Polemoniaceae)

Common names: None
Height: 1m (3ft)
Spread: 1m (3ft)
Aspect: Sun or half shade
Soil: Moist, fertile
Hardiness: Zone 4
Propagation: Division, in spring or autumn

A hybrid perennial. Leaves thin, ovate, toothed, variegated pale green and cream. Flowers in small cymes, perfumed, pale lilac, from summer to autumn.

Phlox paniculata
'Otley Choice'
(Polemoniaceae)

Common names: None
Height: 1m (3ft)
Spread: 1m (3ft)
Aspect: Sun or half shade
Soil: Moist, fertile
Hardiness: Zone 4
Propagation: Division, in spring or autumn

A hybrid perennial. Leaves thin, ovate, toothed, mid-green. Flowers in cymes, scented, salverform, cerise, from midsummer to autumn.

Phlox paniculata
'Starfire'
(Polygonaceae)

Common names: None
Height: 1.2m (4ft)
Spread: 90cm (3ft)
Aspect: Sun or half shade
Soil: Moist, fertile
Hardiness: Zone 4
Propagation: Division in spring or autumn

A hybrid perennial. Leaves ovate, toothed, dark green. Flowers in cymes, perfumed, salverform, deep crimson-red, from midsummer to early autumn.

Phormium cookianum
'Jester'
(Agavaceae/Phormiaceae)

Common name: Mountain flax
Height: 2m (6ft)
Spread: 3m (10ft)
Aspect: Sun
Soil: Moist, well-drained
Hardiness: Zone 8
Propagation: Division, in spring

Hybrid evergreen. Leaves linear, keeled, arching to erect, bronze and green. Flowers in panicles, tubular, green, in summer. Foliage very good for flower arrangements.

Phormium
'Sundowner' A.G.M.
(Agavaceae/Phormiaceae)

Common name: Mountain flax
Height: 2m (6ft)
Spread: 3m (10ft)
Aspect: Sun
Soil: Moist, well-drained
Hardiness: Zone 8
Propagation: Division, in spring

Evergreen hybrid. Leaves linear, keeled, arching to erect, long, bronze-green with pink margins. Flowers green-yellow, in tall panicles, in summer; good seed heads.

Phormium tenax
A.G.M.
(Agavaceae/Phormiaceae)

Common name: New Zealand flax
Height: 4m (12ft)
Spread: 2m (6ft)
Aspect: Sun
Soil: Moist, well-drained
Hardiness: Zone 8
Propagation: Seed or division, both in spring

A tall, evergreen perennial from New Zealand. Leaves stiff, linear, dark green above, blue-green below. Flowers in tall panicles, dull red, in summer.

Phuopsis stylosa
(Rubiaceae)

Common names: None
Height: 15cm (6in)
Spread: 75cm (30in)
Aspect: Sun or half shade
Soil: Moist, sharply drained, fertile
Hardiness: Zone 7
Propagation: Seed, in autumn; division, in spring

Trailing, mat-forming perennial. Leaves in whorls, musk-scented, pale green, elliptic, pointed. Flowers in globular heads, tubular, small, pink, over a long period in summer.

Phygelius aequalis
(Scrophulariaceae)

Common names: None
Height: 1m (3ft)
Spread: 1m (3ft)
Aspect: Sun
Soil: Moist, well-drained, fertile
Hardiness: Zone 8
Propagation: Seed, softwood cuttings or separated suckers, all in spring

A subshrub from South Africa. Leaves ovate, dark green. Flowers in panicles, long, pendent, dusky pink with yellow throats, in summer.

Phygelius aequalis
'Yellow Trumpet' A.G.M.
(Scrophulariaceae)

Common names: None
Height: 1m (3ft)
Spread: 1m (3ft)
Aspect: Sun
Soil: Moist, well-drained, fertile
Hardiness: Zone 8
Propagation: Softwood cuttings or separated suckers, both in spring

A yellow sport of the species; suckering subshrub with a long flowering season in summer. Flowers creamy-yellow, leaves pale green.

Phygelius x *rectus*
'Moonraker'
(Scrophulariaceae)

Common names: None
Height: 1.5m (5ft)
Spread: 1.5m (5ft)
Aspect: Sun
Soil: Moist, well-drained, fertile
Hardiness: Zone 8
Propagation: Softwood cuttings or separated suckers, both in spring

An evergreen, suckering subshrub of garden origin. Leaves ovate, dark green. Flowers in panicles, tubular, curved, pale yellow, over a long period in summer.

Phygelius x *rectus*
'Salmon Leap'
(Scrophulariaceae)

Common names: None
Height: 1.2m (4ft)
Spread: 1.5m (5ft)
Aspect: Sun
Soil: Moist, well-drained, fertile
Hardiness: Zone 8
Propagation: Softwood cuttings or separated suckers, both in spring

Evergreen, suckering subshrub of garden origin. Leaves ovate, dark green. Flowers in panicles, tubular, curved, deeply lobed, orange, over a long period in summer.

Phygelius x *rectus*
'Winchester Fanfare'
(Scrophulariaceae)

Common names: None
Height: 1.5m (5ft)
Spread: 1.5m (5ft)
Aspect: Sun
Soil: Moist, well-drained, fertile
Hardiness: Zone 8
Propagation: Softwood cuttings or separated suckers, both in spring

An evergreen, suckering subshrub of garden origin. Leaves ovate, dark green. Flowers in panicles, pendent, tubular, dusky pink, over a long period in summer.

***Physalis alkekengi* var. *franchettii* (Solanaceae)**

Common names: Chinese lantern; Japanese lantern
Height: 75cm (30in)
Spread: Indefinite
Aspect: Sun or half shade
Soil: Well-drained
Hardiness: Zone 6
Propagation: Seed or division, both in spring

Rhizomatous perennial from Europe and Asia. Leaves broad, ovate, bright green. Flowers solitary, white, in summer, then orange berries inside papery, red calyces.

***Physostegia virginiana* (Labiatae/Lamiaceae)**

Common name: Obedient plant
Height: 1.2m (4ft)
Spread: Indefinite
Aspect: Sun or half shade
Soil: Moist, humus-rich, fertile
Hardiness: Zone 4
Propagation: Seed, in autumn; division, in early spring

Invasive rhizomatous ground cover. Leaves ovate to lance-shaped, toothed, mid-green. Flowers in racemes, bright pink, from midsummer to early autumn.

***Physostegia virginiana* 'Alba' (Labiatae/Lamiaceae)**

Common names: Virginia plant
Height: 1.2m (4ft)
Spread: Indefinite
Aspect: Sun or half shade
Soil: Moist, humus-rich, fertile
Hardiness: Zone 4
Propagation: Seed, in autumn; division, in early spring

White-flowered form of the species; invasive ground cover. Leaves ovate, toothed, mid-green. Flowers in racemes, white, from midsummer to early autumn.

***Physostegia virginiana* subsp. *speciosa* 'Bouquet Rose' (Labiatae/Lamiaceae)**

Common name: Obedient plant
Height: 1.2m (4ft)
Spread: Indefinite
Aspect: Sun or half shade
Soil: Moist, humus-rich, fertile
Hardiness: Zone 4
Propagation: Division, in early spring

A selected form of the species, with racemes of pale lilac-pink flowers from midsummer to early autumn. Leaves ovate, toothed, mid-green. Good ground cover.

***Physostegia virginiana* 'Summer Snow' (Labiatae/Lamiaceae)**

Common name: Obedient plant
Height: 1.2m (4ft)
Spread: Indefinite
Aspect: Sun or half shade
Soil: Moist, well-drained, fertile
Hardiness: Zone 4
Propagation: Division, in early spring

A selected form; invasive ground cover. Leaves ovate, toothed, mid-green. Flowers white with green calyces, in racemes, midsummer to early autumn.

***Physostegia virginiana* subsp. *speciosa* 'Variegata' (Labiatae/Lamiaceae)**

Common name: Obedient plant
Height: 1.2m (4ft)
Spread: Indefinite
Aspect: Sun or half shade
Soil: Moist, well-drained, fertile
Hardiness: Zone 4
Propagation: Division, in early spring

Invasive ground cover. Grown for its ovate, toothed, greyish-green, white-margined leaves. Racemes of purple flowers from midsummer to early autumn.

***Phyteuma orbiculare* (Campanulaceae)**

Common name: Round-headed rampion
Height: 50cm (20in)
Spread: 45cm (18in)
Aspect: Sun
Soil: Well-drained, fertile
Hardiness: Zone 6
Propagation: Seed, in autumn

A perennial from Eurasia. Leaves elliptic to lance-shaped, toothed, mid-green. Flowers in terminal dense spherical clusters, blue, with acuminate bracts, in summer.

***Phytolacca americana* (Phytolaccaceae)**

Common names: Pokeweed; red ink plant
Height: 4m (12ft)
Spread: 1m (3ft)
Aspect: Sun or half shade
Soil: Moist, fertile
Hardiness: Zone 4
Propagation: Seed, in warmth in early spring

A foul-smelling North American perennial. Leaves ovate, mid-green. Flowers white or pink, in racemes, from midsummer to early autumn; maroon berries extremely toxic.

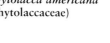

Phytolacca polyandra
(Phytolaccaceae)

Common names: None
Height: 2m (6ft)
Spread: 60cm (2ft)
Aspect: Sun or half shade
Soil: Moist, fertile
Hardiness: Zone 6
Propagation: Seed, in warmth in early spring

Perennial from China. Leaves elliptic-ovate, mid-green, yellow in autumn. Pink flowers in compact racemes on red stems in late summer, followed by toxic, black berries.

Pilosella aurantiaca
(Asteraceae/Compositae)

Common names: Fox and cubs; orange hawkweed
Height: 30cm (12in)
Spread: 75cm (30in)
Aspect: Sun or half shade
Soil: Sharply drained, fertile
Hardiness: Zone 5
Propagation: Seed or division, in autumn or spring

A stoloniferous perennial. Leaves in basal rosettes, lance-shaped to elliptic, bluish-green. Flowers in clusters of up to 10, orange-red, daisy-like, in summer.

Pimpinella major
'Rosea'
(Apiaceae/Umbelliferae)

Common name: Greater burnet saxifrage
Height: 90cm (3ft)
Spread: 60cm (2ft)
Aspect: Sun or half shade
Soil: Moist, fertile
Hardiness: Zone 5
Propagation: Seed, when ripe

A tap-rooted perennial from Eurasia. Leaves basal and stem, pinnate, leaflets ovate, mid-green. Flowers small, pink, in compound, flat umbels, in spring.

Plantago major
'Rosularis'
(Plantaginaceae)

Common name: Rose plantain
Height: 30cm (1ft)
Spread: 30cm (1ft)
Aspect: Sun
Soil: Sharply-drained, acidic, fertile
Hardiness: Zone 5
Propagation: Division, in spring

Invasive perennial from Europe. Leaves in basal rosettes, ovate, light green. Flowering spike a scape reduced to a rosette of green leaves, said to resemble a rose flower.

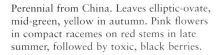

Plantago major
'Rubrifolia'
(Plantaginaceae)

Common name: Plantain
Height: 30cm (1ft)
Spread: 30cm (1ft)
Aspect: Sun
Soil: Sharply drained, acidic, fertile
Hardiness: Zone 5
Propagation: Seed, in autumn; division, in spring

A hardy European perennial, a weed of lawns. Leaves in basal rosettes, ovate, purple and green. Flowers in slender spikes, brownish-green, in summer.

Platycodon grandiflorus
A.G.M.
(Campanulaceae)

Common name: Balloon flower
Height: 60cm (2ft)
Spread: 30cm (1ft)
Aspect: Sun or half shade
Soil: Moist, well-drained, humus-rich, fertile
Hardiness: Zone 4
Propagation: Seed, *in situ* in spring; division or separation, in summer

Perennial from Asia. Leaves ovate, toothed, bluish-green. Flowers in clusters, open, purple-blue, 5-petalled saucers, in late summer. Late to appear, so mark position.

Platycodon grandiflorus
f. *albus*
(Campanulaceae)

Common name: Balloon flower
Height: 60cm (2ft)
Spread: 30cm (1ft)
Aspect: Sun or half shade
Soil: Moist, well-drained, humus-rich, fertile
Hardiness: Zone 4
Propagation: Seed, *in situ* in spring; division or separation, in summer

White-flowered form. Leaves ovate, toothed, bluish-green. Flowers pure white saucers, in late summer. Late to reappear in spring, so mark the position.

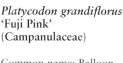

Platycodon grandiflorus
'Fuji Pink'
(Campanulaceae)

Common name: Balloon flower
Height: 60cm (2ft)
Spread: 30cm (1ft)
Aspect: Sun or half shade
Soil: Moist, well-drained, humus-rich, fertile
Hardiness: Zone 4
Propagation: Division or separation of rooted basal shoots, both in summer

A form of the species with flowers of lilac-pink, in late summer. Leaves ovate, toothed, bluish-green. Is late to emerge in spring, so mark its position.

The sole species in the genus, Platycodon grandiflorus *has given rise to many garden-worthy cultivars.*

Plectranthus ciliatus
(Labiatae/Lamiaceae)

Common names: None
Height: 45cm (18in)
Spread: Indefinite
Aspect: Full or half shade
Soil: Any
Hardiness: Zone 9
Propagation: Seed, when ripe; division, in spring

A tender, invasive, evergreen ground cover from South Africa. Leaves ovate, toothed, bright green. Flowers in short sprays, starry, mauve, in summer to autumn.

Pleione formosana
A.G.M.
(Orchidaceae)

Common name: Indian crocus
Height: 15cm (6in)
Spread: 30cm (12in)
Aspect: Half shade
Soil: Sharply drained, humus-rich, fertile
Hardiness: Zone 8
Propagation: Division, in spring

Terrestrial or lithophytic orchid. Single, mid-green, lance-shaped to elliptic, folded leaf from each pseudobulb. Flowers pale pink, white lips spotted brown, solitary, spring.

Pleione speciosa
(Orchidaceae)

Common names: Indian crocus
Height: 7cm (3in)
Spread: 10cm (4in)
Aspect: Half shade
Soil: Sharply drained, humus-rich, fertile
Hardiness: Zone 8
Propagation: Division, in spring

Terrestrial or lithophytic orchid. Single leaf from each pseudobulb, lance-shaped, mid-green. Flowers solitary, bright magenta with peach-blotched lip, in spring.

Podophyllumm hexandrum
(Berberidaceae)

Common name: Himalayan mandrake
Height: 45cm (18in)
Spread: 30cm (12in)
Aspect: Full or half shade
Soil: Moist, humus-rich, fertile
Hardiness: Zone 6
Propagation: Seed, when ripe; division, in spring or autumn

Leaves 3- to 5-lobed, purple-blotched, toothed. Flower solitary, single, open cups, white with yellow anthers, in spring to summer; edible red fruit. Plant poisonous.

Polemonium caeruleum
(Polemoniaceae)

Common names: Greek valerian; Jacob's ladder
Height: 90cm (3ft)
Spread: 30cm (1ft)
Aspect: Sun or half shade
Soil: Moist, well-drained, fertile
Hardiness: Zone 2
Propagation: Seed or division, both in spring

A clump-forming perennial from Eurasia and North America. Leaves 2-pinnate, with up to 27 oblong leaflets, mid-green. Flowers in cymes, open, blue bells, in early summer.

Polemonium caeruleum
subsp. *caeruleaum*
var. *album* (Polemoniaceae)

Common names: Greek valerian; Jacob's ladder
Height: 90cm (3ft)
Spread: 30cm (1ft)
Aspect: Sun or half shade
Soil: Moist, well-drained, fertile
Hardiness: Zone 2
Propagation: Seed or division, both in spring

White form of a good low-allergen plant. Flowers in cymes, open white bells in early summer. Leaves 2-pinnate, with up to 27 oblong leaflets, mid-green.

Polemonium caeruleum
'Brise d'Anjou'
(Polemoniaceae)

Common names: Jacob's ladder
Height: 75cm (30in)
Spread: 30cm (12in)
Aspect: Sun or half shade
Soil: Moist, well-drained, fertile
Hardiness: Zone 2
Propagation: Division, in spring or autumn

A form of Jacob's ladder with mid-green, cream-margined, 2-pinnate leaves with up to 27 oblong leaflets. Flowers pink, in cymes, in early summer.

Polemonium carneum
(Polemoniaceae)

Common names: None
Height: 40cm (16in)
Spread: 20cm (8in)
Aspect: Sun or half shade
Soil: Moist, well-drained, fertile
Hardiness: Zone 6
Propagation: Seed, in autumn or spring; division, in spring

A hardy, clump-forming perennial from the western U.S.A. Leaves pinnate, leaflets ovate-elliptic, mid-green. Flowers in cymes, pale pink saucers, in early summer.

Polemonium carneum
'Apricot Delight'
(Polemoniaceae)

Common names: None
Height: 40cm (16in)
Spread: 20cm (8in)
Aspect: Sun or half shade
Soil: Moist, well-drained, fertile
Hardiness: Zone 6
Propagation: Division, in spring

A selected form of the species. Leaves pinnate, leaflets elliptic-ovate. Flowers large, apricot, borne over a rather longer season than the type.

Polygala chamaebuxus
A.G.M.
(Polygalaceae)

Common names: None
Height: 15cm (6in)
Spread: 30cm (12in)
Aspect: Sun or half shade
Soil: Sharply drained, fertile, humus-rich
Hardiness: Zone 6
Propagation: Seed, in autumn; softwood cuttings, in early summer

Dwarf, evergreen subshrub. Leaves leathery, lance-shaped, dark green. Flowers with yellow lips and wings, yellow keel ageing to purple, in late spring and early summer.

Polygonatum × *hybridum*
A.G.M.
(Convallariaceae/Liliaceae)

Common name: Common Solomon's seal
Height: 1.5m (5ft)
Spread: 30cm (1ft)
Aspect: Sun or half shade
Soil: Moist, well-drained, fertile, humus-rich
Hardiness: Zone 6
Propagation: Seed, in autumn; division, in spring

Rhizomatous woodlander. Leaves ovate to lance-shaped, mid-green. Flowers pendent, tubular, creamy-white, axillary, in late spring. May bear berries. All parts toxic.

Polygonatum × *hybridum*
'Striatum'
(Convallariaceae/Liliaceae)

Common name: Common Solomon's seal
Height: 1.5m (5ft)
Spread: 30cm (1ft)
Aspect: Sun or half shade
Soil: Moist, well-drained, fertile, humus-rich
Hardiness: Zone 6
Propagation: Division, in spring

Form of Solomon's seal with leaves striped green and creamy-white. Flowers pendent, tubular, creamy-white, axillary, in late spring. May bear berries. All parts toxic.

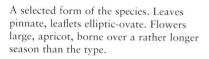

Polygonatum stewartianum
(Convallariaceae/Liliaceae)

Common names: None
Height: 90cm (36in)
Spread: 25cm (10in)
Aspect: Sun or half shade
Soil: Moist, well-drained, humus-rich, fertile
Hardiness: Zone 6
Propagation: Seed, in autumn; division, in spring

A rhizomatous perennial. Leaves in whorls, linear to lance-shaped, mid-green. Flowers in clusters, pendent, tubular, pink, spring to midsummer. May have red berries.

POLYPODIUM (Polypodaceae)
Polypody

A genus of some 75 species of evergreen and decidous ferns. They originate mainly in the tropical areas of North, Central and South America, with a few distributed in more temperate regions, in Africa and in western Europe, including Britain with *P. cambricum*, the Welsh polypody. The majority of the species are evergreen. They vary from tender to hardy; the hardier types are terrestrial, but the more numerous tropical types are epiphytic. In moist, frost-free areas, they can be found growing on trees and damp walls, and at the other extreme on sand dunes. Terrestrial types are good colonisers, spreading by creeping rhizomes, often on the surface of the soil. This makes them excellent ground cover plants, especially in dry positions in sun or dappled shade, where they will provide greenery through the winter; they are also suitable for growing in mixed borders or rock gardens. Polypody ferns like a sharply drained but moisture-retentive soil. They are good architectural plants, with simple to pinnatifid or pinnate, occasionally more divided, fronds, with the sori arranged in rows either side of the midrib of each frond or pinna. They are borne along the rhizomes in double rows, seemingly at random.

Polypodium cambricum
'Omnilacerum Oxford'
(Polypodiaceae)

Common names: Southern polypody; Welsh polypody
Height: 60cm (2ft)
Spread: Indefinite
Aspect: Sun or half shade
Soil: Sharply drained, alkaline, humus-rich, fertile
Hardiness: Zone 6
Propagation: Spores, in warmth when ripe; division, in spring or autumn

A deciduous, terrestrial fern from Europe. Fronds tall, erect, lance-shaped to oblong, pinnate, pinnae lance-shaped, deeply cut, mid-green. Sori yellow in winter.

Polypodium vulgare
'Cornubiense'
(Polypodiaceae)

Common name: Common polypody
Height: 40cm (16in)
Spread: Indefinite
Aspect: Sun or half shade
Soil: Sharply drained, humus-rich, fertile
Hardiness: Zone 3
Propagation: Spores, in warmth when ripe; division, in autumn or spring

An evergreen, terrestrial or epiphytic fern from Eurasia and Africa. Fronds thin, leathery, 3-pinnate, pinnae oblong to linear, dark green.

POLYSTICHUM (Dryopteridaceae)
Holly fern • Shield fern

A genus of some 200 or so terrestrial, usually evergreen, rhizomatous ferns from many and varied habitats all over the world. Shield ferns are generally regarded as some of the most desirable and garden-worthy ferns in cultivation. They are easy to grow and remarkably trouble-free plants, provided that their simple needs are met; they require good drainage and a moisture-retentive, fertile soil that is preferably neutral or acid, although they will tolerate slightly alkaline conditions. Due to their diverse natural ranges, they vary from hardy to tender. They are mostly shade-lovers (although *P. setiferum* 'Acutilobum' will grow in sun, and almost anywhere); they are even tolerant of dry conditions, making them a good choice for the notoriously difficult areas of dry shade under trees. Shield ferns are excellent subjects for a fernery, and also suit a mixed border. They bear handsome, often lance-shaped fronds, which are pinnate to 3-pinnate. The pinnae are holly-like, often with pointed lobes, giving rise to one of the common names. The old foliage should be removed in late spring as the new growth is about to unfold, to give the fronds space to develop when they appear in early summer.

Polystichum setiferum
A.G.M.
(Aspidaceae/Dryopteridaceae)

Common name: Soft shield fern
Height: 1.2m (4ft)
Spread: 90cm (3ft)
Aspect: Full or half shade
Soil: Well-drained, humus-rich, fertile
Hardiness: Zone 7
Propagation: Spores, when ripe; division, in spring; offsets, in autumn

A rhizomatous, terrestrial European fern. Fronds in "shuttlecocks", 2-pinnate, lance-shaped, mid-green. Lobes of pinnae ovate, toothed, angled obtusely from midrib.

Polystichum setiferum
'Pulcherrimum Bevis' A.G.M.
(Aspidaceae/Dryopteridaceae)

Common name: Soft shield fern
Height: 45cm (18in)
Spread: 90cm (36in)
Aspect: Full or half shade
Soil: Well-drained, humus-rich, fertile
Hardiness: Zone 4
Propagation: Spores, when ripe; division, in spring; offsets, in autumn

Rhizomatous fern from North America. Fronds in a "shuttlecock", narrow, lance-shaped, pinnate, pinnae like holly, dark green. Fertile fronds narrow sharply to tip.

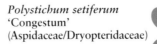

Polystichum setiferum
'Congestum'
(Aspidaceae/Dryopteridaceae)

Common name: Soft shield fern
Height: 50cm (20in)
Spread: 60cm (24in)
Aspect: Full or half shade
Soil: Well-drained, humus-rich, fertile
Hardiness: Zone 7
Propagation: Spores, when ripe; division, in spring; offsets, in autumn

Evergreen, rhizomatous, hardy fern. A very compact, congested form of the species; the congestion of the fronds is often combined with cresting.

Pontederia cordata
A.G.M.
(Pontederiaceae)

Common name: Pickerel weed
Height: 1.2m (4ft)
Spread: 80cm (32in)
Aspect: Sun
Soil: Marginal aquatic
Hardiness: Zone 3
Propagation: Seed, when ripe; division, in late spring

A marginal aquatic from the Americas. Leaves broadly ovate, erect, floating and submerged, glossy-green. Flowers in closely packed spikes, tubular, blue, late summer.

Potentilla
'Blazeaway'
(Rosaceae)

Common name: Cinquefoil
Height: 45cm (18in)
Spread: 60cm (24in)
Aspect: Sun
Soil: Well-drained, poor
Hardiness: Zone 5
Propagation: Division, in autumn or spring

Hybrid cultivar. Leaves pinnate; 5 to 7 mid-green, oblong leaflets. Flowers large, single, orange with a red band around a dark centre, in cymes, early to late summer.

POTENTILLA (Rosaceae)
Cinquefoil

A genus of some 500 species of shrubs and clump-forming subshrubs, as well as a few annuals and biennials. They come from habitats across the northern hemisphere, ranging from mountain to grassland. Cinquefoils have 3- to 7-palmate or pinnate leaves, and saucer- or cup-shaped flowers in colours from yellow to red, as well as some in white or pink. The shrubby types, derived from *Potentilla fruticosa*, make good low hedging. The clump-forming subshrubs are used extensively in beds and borders because of their long flowering season, and are hybrids derived from *P. nepalensis* and *P. atrosanguinea* (Zone 5). They have attractive, 5-palmate leaves, which closely resemble the leaves of strawberry plants. The flowers are the typical saucer- or cup-shape, and are borne in panicles or cymes over a long period from spring to autumn, in a range of colours. They like a position in sun. The soil should be well-drained, and poor to moderately fertile; if it is too rich, the plants will produce foliage at the expense of flowers. They benefit from being cut back hard in autumn. *P. anserina* is very invasive, and should be avoided in the garden. Cinquefoils are low-allergen plants; the flowers attract bees and are good for cutting.

***Potentilla* 'Flamenco' (Rosaceae)**

Common name: Cinquefoil
Height: 45cm (18in)
Spread: 60cm (24in)
Aspect: Sun
Soil: Well-drained, poor
Hardiness: Zone 5
Propagation: Division, in spring or autumn

A clump-forming hybrid. Leaves palmate, leaflets narrow, elliptic, mid-green. Flowers in cymes, single, bright scarlet with a black centre, from late spring to midsummer.

***Potentilla fruticosa* (Rosaceae)**

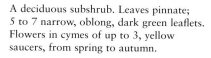

Common name: Cinquefoil
Height: 1m (3ft)
Spread: 1.5m (5ft)
Aspect: Sun
Soil: Well-drained, poor
Hardiness: Zone 2
Propagation: Seed, in spring or autumn; greenwood cuttings, in early summer

A deciduous subshrub. Leaves pinnate; 5 to 7 narrow, oblong, dark green leaflets. Flowers in cymes of up to 3, yellow saucers, from spring to autumn.

***Potentilla fruticosa* 'Abbotswood Silver' (Rosaceae)**

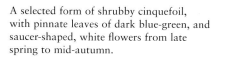

Common name: Cinquefoil
Height: 1m (3ft)
Spread: 1.5m (5ft)
Aspect: Sun
Soil: Well-drained, poor
Hardiness: Zone 2
Propagation: Greenwood cuttings, in early summer

A selected form of shrubby cinquefoil, with pinnate leaves of dark blue-green, and saucer-shaped, white flowers from late spring to mid-autumn.

***Potentilla nepalensis* 'Miss Willmott' A.G.M. (Rosaceae)**

Common name: Cinquefoil
Height: 45cm (18in)
Spread: 60cm (24in)
Aspect: Sun
Soil: Well-drained, poor
Hardiness: Zone 5
Propagation: Division, in autumn or spring

Hybrid cultivar. Leaves 5-palmate, leaflets obovate, hairy, toothed, mid-green. Flowers in loose cymes, cherry with darker pink centre, all summer.

***Potentilla recta* 'Warrenii' (Rosaceae)**

Common name: Cinquefoil
Height: 60cm (24in)
Spread: 45cm (18in)
Aspect: Sun
Soil: Well-drained, poor
Hardiness: Zone 4
Propagation: Division, in spring or autumn

A selected form of the species. Leaves 5- to 7-palmate, leaflets oblong, toothed, mid-green. Flowers in loose cymes, canary yellow, from early to late summer.

***Potentilla* x *tonguei* (Rosaceae)**

Common name: Cinquefoil
Height: 10cm (4in)
Spread: 30cm (12in)
Aspect: Sun
Soil: Well-drained, poor
Hardiness: Zone 5
Propagation: Division, in spring or autumn

Clump-forming garden hybrid. Leaves 3- to 5-palmate, leaflets obovate, dark green. Flowers solitary or in cymes, flat, apricot saucers with a red eye, in summer.

Pratia pedunculata
'County Park'
(Campanulaceae)

Common names: None
Height: 3cm (1in)
Spread: Indefinite
Aspect: Full or deep shade
Soil: Humus-rich, fertile
Hardiness: Zone 7
Propagation: Division, at any time

Creeping, mat-forming perennial from Australia. Leaves ovate, mid-green. Flowers almost stemless, small, deep blue stars, in summer. Excellent ground cover.

PRIMULA (Primulaceae)
Primula

A large genus of over 400 species of perennials, mostly herbaceous but some evergreen and woody. A few species are from the southern hemisphere, but the majority of them originate in the northern hemisphere; nearly half of those from the northern hemisphere are native to the Himalayas. Their range of habitats is very wide, from mountains to marshes, and their botanical classification is complex: the species have given rise to an abundance of cultivars. Of the large number of botanical groups, some are good rock-garden plants and a few have value as border plants; others require alpine house conditions, or a warm greenhouse or conservatory, and some are so difficult to cultivate that they are for the enthusiast only. All have basal rosettes of leaves that range from linear to ovate in shape. The flowers are usually salverform, but may be bell- or funnel-shaped or even tubular, and may be borne among the leaves or in whorls, umbels or racemes on upright stalks. The colour range in species includes yellow, orange, white, and shades of pink and purple; cultivars are often intensely coloured or boldly patterned. Many members of the genus are highly allergenic, and contact with the foliage may cause skin irritation.

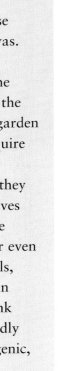

***Primula auricula* hort.**
(B) A.G.M.
(Primulaceae)

Common name: Auricula
Height: 20cm (8in)
Spread: 20cm (8in)
Aspect: Sun or half shade
Soil: Moist, well-drained, humus-rich, fertile
Hardiness: Zone 3
Propagation: Seed, when ripe or in spring; division, over winter

Evergreen hybrid. Leaves obovate, shiny, grey-green, white-mealy sometimes. Flowers in arched umbels, large, salverform, purple with a cream centre, in spring.

Primula bulleyana
(4) A.G.M.
(Primulaceae)

Common name: Candelabra primula
Height: 60cm (2ft)
Spread: 60cm (2ft)
Aspect: Half shade
Soil: Moist, acidic, deep, humus-rich
Hardiness: Zone 6
Propagation: Seed, when ripe or late winter to spring; division, in autumn or spring

Candelabra primula from China. Leaves ovate, toothed, mid-green. Flowers in whorls, salverform, red, ageing quickly to orange, in summer.

Primula capitata
(5)
(Primulaceae)

Common names: None
Height: 40cm (16in)
Spread: 20cm (8in)
Aspect: Half shade
Soil: Moist, acidic, deep, humus-rich
Hardiness: Zone 5
Propagation: Seed, when ripe or in late winter to spring; division, in autumn or spring

Short-lived perennial from India, Tibet and Bhutan. Leaves lance-shaped, toothed, mealy, pale green. Flowers in flat racemes, tubular, dark purple, early to late summer.

Primula denticulata
(9) A.G.M.
(Primulaceae)

Common name: Drumstick primula
Height: 45cm (18in)
Spread: 45cm (18in)
Aspect: Sun or half shade
Soil: Moist, acidic, deep, humus-rich
Hardiness: Zone 5
Propagation: Seed when ripe, or late winter to spring; division, in autumn or spring

Vigorous primula from the Himalayas. Leaves spoon-shaped, white-mealy below. Flowers open bells, purple, yellow-eyed, in tight, globular umbels, in early summer.

Primula denticulata
var. *alba* (9)
(Primulaceae)

Common name: White drumstick primula
Height: 45cm (18in)
Spread: 45cm (18in)
Aspect: Sun or half shade
Soil: Moist, well-drained, acidic, deep, humus-rich
Hardiness: Zone 5
Propagation: Seed when ripe, or late winter to spring; division, in autumn or spring

Pure white-flowered form of the species. Tight, globular umbels of flowers in early summer. An excellent plant for lighting up a semi-shady corner.

***Primula* 'Inverewe' (4) A.G.M.**
(Primulaceae)

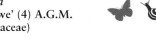

Common name: Candelabra primula
Height: 75cm (30in)
Spread: 60cm (24in)
Aspect: Half shade
Soil: Moist, acidic, deep, humus-rich
Hardiness: Zone 6
Propagation: Division, in autumn or spring

A hybrid candelabra primula. Leaves oval to lance-shaped, toothed, coarse, mid-green. Flowers in whorls, salverform, scarlet, in summer.

***Primula japonica* (4) A.G.M.**
(Primulaceae)

Common name: Japanese primrose
Height: 45cm (18in)
Spread: 45cm (18in)
Aspect: Half shade
Soil: Moist, acidic, deep, humus-rich
Hardiness: Zone 5
Propagation: Seed, when ripe or late winter to early spring; division, in autumn or spring

Vigorous perennial from Japan. Leaves obovate, toothed, mid-green. Flowers in whorls of up to 25, salverform, pink and purple, in late spring and early summer.

***Primula japonica* 'Alba' (4)**
(Primulaceae)

Common name: White Japanese primrose
Height: 45cm (18in)
Spread: 45cm (18in)
Aspect: Half shade
Soil: Moist, acidic, deep, humus-rich
Hardiness: Zone 5
Propagation: Seed, when ripe or late winter to early spring; division, in autumn or spring

Flowers in whorls of up to 25, salverform, white, in late spring and early summer. Excellent for lighting up a semi-shady corner, but must have moisture at all times.

***Primula juliae* (30)**
(Primulaceae)

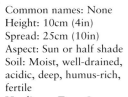

Common names: None
Height: 10cm (4in)
Spread: 25cm (10in)
Aspect: Sun or half shade
Soil: Moist, well-drained, acidic, deep, humus-rich, fertile
Hardiness: Zone 5
Propagation: Seed, when ripe or late winter to early spring; division, in autumn or spring

A primula from the Caucasus. Leaves in basal rosettes, round, scalloped, dark green. Flowers solitary, magenta saucers, on long stems, in spring and summer.

***Primula marginata* (2) A.G.M.**
(Primulaceae)

Common names: None
Height: 15cm (6in)
Spread: 30cm (12in)
Aspect: Sun or half shade, shaded from midday sun
Soil: Moist, sharply drained, alkaline
Hardiness: Zone 7
Propagation: Seed, when ripe or in late winter to early spring

An auricula primula from the Alps. Leaves obovate, toothed, mid-green. Flowers in umbels, of up to 20, perfumed, lavender-blue cups, with white-mealy eyes.

***Primula prolifera* (4) A.G.M.**
(Primulaceae)

Common name: Candelabra primula
Height: 60cm (2ft)
Spread: 60cm (2ft)
Aspect: Half shade
Soil: Moist, acidic, deep, humus-rich
Hardiness: Zone 6
Propagation: Seed, when ripe or late winter to early spring; division, in autumn or spring

Primula from India, Myanmar, China and Indonesia. Leaves dark green, toothed, spoon-shaped. Flowers in whorls, scented, white-mealy, yellow, in early summer.

CLASSIFICATION OF PRIMULA by Smith and Forrest (1928), modified by Smith and Fletcher (1941–49)

Of most interest as garden perennials are 2, 4, 5, 9, 17, 26, 30, and B.

Group 1 Amethystina
Group 2 Auricula
Group 3 Bullatae
Group 4 Candelabra
Group 5 Capitatae
Group 6 Carolinella
Group 7 Cortusoides
Group 8 Cuneifolia
Group 9 Denticulata
Group 10 Dryadifolia
Group 11 Farinosae
Group 12 Floribundae
Group 13 Grandis
Group 14 Malacoides
Group 15 Malvaceae
Group 16 Minutissimae
Group 17 Muscarioides
Group 18 Nivales
Group 19 Obconica
Group 20 Parryi
Group 21 Petiolares
Group 22 Pinnatae
Group 23 Pycnoloba
Group 24 Reinii
Group 25 Rotundifolia
Group 26 Sikkimensis
Group 27 Sinenses
Group 28 Soldanelloideae
Group 29 Souliei
Group 30 Vernales
Group A Alpine Auricula
Group B Border Auricula
Group D Double
Group Poly Polyanthus
Group Prim Primrose
Group S Show auricula

Once a common flower in meadows, Primula veris *can be naturalised in a reliably moist, fertile soil.*

Primula pulverulenta
(4) A.G.M.
(Primulaceae)

Common name: Candelabra primula
Height: 90cm (3ft)
Spread: 60cm (2ft)
Aspect: Half shade
Soil: Moist, acidic, humus-rich, deep
Hardiness: Zone 6
Propagation: Seed, when ripe or late winter to early spring; division, in autumn or spring

A primula from wet areas of China. Leaves obovate, toothed, mid-green. Flowers in whorls, tubular, deep red with dark eyes, in late spring and early summer.

Primula rosea
(11) A.G.M.
(Primulaceae)

Common names: None
Height: 20cm (8in)
Spread: 20cm (8in)
Aspect: Half shade
Soil: Moist, acidic, deep, humus-rich
Hardiness: Zone 6
Propagation: Seed, when ripe or in late winter to early spring; division, in autumn or spring

Perennial from wet Himalayan meadows. Leaves obovate, toothed, bronze turning mid-green. Flowers in umbels of up to 12, pinkish-red with a yellow eye, in spring.

Primula sikkimensis
(26)
(Primulaceae)

Common name: Himalayan cowslip
Height: 90cm (3ft)
Spread: 60cm (2ft)
Aspect: Half shade
Soil: Moist, acidic, deep, humus-rich
Hardiness: Zone 6
Propagation: Seed, when ripe or late winter to early spring; division, in autumn or spring

Perennial from wet Himalayan meadows. Leaves oblong, toothed, shiny green. Flowers in umbels, pendent, funnel-shaped, yellow, white-mealy, late spring and early summer.

Primula veris
(30) A.G.M.
(Primulaceae)

Common name: Cowslip
Height: 25cm (10in)
Spread: 25cm (10in)
Aspect: Sun or half shade
Soil: Moist, well-drained, acidic, humus-rich
Hardiness: Zone 5
Propagation: Seed, when ripe or late winter to early spring; division, in autumn or spring

A perennial from Eurasia, including Britain. Leaves ovate, mid-green. Flowers in umbels, perfumed, pendent, salverform, deep yellow, in mid- to late spring.

Primula vialii
(17) A.G.M.
(Primulaceae)

Common names: None
Height: 60cm (2ft)
Spread: 30cm (1ft)
Aspect: Half shade
Soil: Moist, acidic, deep, humus-rich
Hardiness: Zone 7
Propagation: Seed, when ripe or in late winter to early spring; division, in autumn or spring

Perennial from wetlands in China. Leaves broad, lance-shaped, toothed, mid-green. Spikes of many, pendent, tubular flowers, violet opening from red buds, in summer.

Primula vulgaris
(30)
(Primulaceae)

Common name: Primrose
Height: 20cm (8in)
Spread: 30cm (12in)
Aspect: Half shade
Soil: Moist, acidic, deep, humus-rich
Hardiness: Zone 6
Propagation: Seed, when ripe or in late winter to early spring; division, in autumn or spring

Perennial from Europe and Turkey. Leaves evergreen in mild areas, obovate, toothed, veined, bright green. Clusters of pale yellow, scented, saucer flowers, early to late spring.

Prunella grandiflora
(Labiatae/Lamiaceae)

Common name: Large self-heal
Height: 15cm (6in)
Spread: 1.2m (4ft)
Aspect: Sun or half shade
Soil: Any
Hardiness: Zone 5
Propagation: Seed, in spring; division, in spring or autumn

An invasive, ground-covering perennial from Europe. Leaves ovate, toothed, dark green. Flowers in whorls, on upright leafy spikes, purple, in summer.

Prunella grandiflora
'Pink Loveliness'
(Labiatae/Lamiaceae)

Common name: Large self-heal
Height: 15cm (6in)
Spread: 1.2m (4ft)
Aspect: Sun or half shade
Soil: Any
Hardiness: Zone 5
Propagation: Seed, in spring; division, in spring or autumn

Form of the species with clear pink flowers in whorls on upright leafy spikes, in summer. Invasive ground cover, only for a wild or woodland garden.

Pulmonaria angustifolia
A.G.M.
(Boraginaceae)

Common name: Blue cowslip
Height: 30cm (12in)
Spread: 45cm (18in)
Aspect: Full or half shade
Soil: Moist, humus-rich, fertile
Hardiness: Zone 3
Propagation: Seed, when ripe; division, after flowering or in autumn

Rhizomatous European perennial; excellent ground cover in shade. Leaves lance-shaped, mid-green. Flowers on erect stems, blue, funnel-shaped, from early to late spring.

Pulmonaria officinalis
(Boraginaceae)

Common names: Lungwort; soldiers and sailors
Height: 25cm (10in)
Spread: 60cm (24in)
Aspect: Full or half shade
Soil: Moist, humus-rich, fertile
Hardiness: Zone 6
Propagation: Seed, when ripe; division, after flowering or in autumn

Rhizomatous, evergreen ground cover. Leaves ovate, mid-green, spotted white. Flowers tubular, pink, turning violet, then blue, in terminal cymes, early to late spring.

Pulmonaria rubra
'Bowles' Red'
(Boraginaceae)

Common name: Lungwort
Height: 40cm (16in)
Spread: 90cm (36in)
Aspect: Full or partial shade
Soil: Moist, humus-rich, fertile
Hardiness: Zone 5
Propagation: Seed, when ripe; division, after flowering or in autumn

Rhizomatous, evergreen ground cover. Leaves elliptic, bright green with pale green spots. Flowers in cymes, coral-red, funnel-shaped, from late winter to mid-spring.

Pulmonaria saccharata
(Boraginaceae)

Common name: Jerusalem sage
Height 30cm (1ft)
Spread: 60cm (2ft)
Aspect: Full or half shade
Soil: Moist, humus-rich, fertile
Hardiness: Zone 3
Propagation: Seed, when ripe; division, after flowering or in autumn

Rhizomatous, evergreen ground cover from Italy and France. Leaves elliptic, spotted white. Flowers pink turning blue, funnel-shaped, in cymes, late winter to late spring.

Pulsatilla alpina
subsp. *apiifolia* A.G.M.
(Ranunculaceae)

Common name: Alpine pasque flower
Height: 30cm (12in)
Spread: 20cm (8in)
Aspect: Sun
Soil: Sharply drained, acidic, humus-rich,
Hardiness: Zone 5
Propagation: Seed, as soon as ripe; root cuttings, in winter

A clump-forming perennial. Leaves 2-pinnate, hairy, mid-green. Flowers pale yellow cups, petals silky-hairy, in spring, followed by attractive seed heads.

Pulsatilla vulgaris
A.G.M.
(Ranunculaceae)

Common name: Pasque flower
Height: 20cm (8in)
Spread: 20cm (8in)
Aspect: Sun
Soil: Sharply drained, fertile
Hardiness: Zone 5
Propagation: Seed, as soon as ripe; root cuttings, in winter

A clump-forming perennial. Leaves pinnate, leaflets pinnatisect, lobes linear, light green. Flowers solitary, cup-shaped, silky-hairy, purple, in spring. Dislikes transplantation.

Pulsatilla vulgaris
'Alba' A.G.M.
(Ranunculaceae)

Common name: White pasque flower
Height: 20cm (8in)
Spread: 20cm (8in)
Aspect: Sun
Soil: Sharply drained, fertile
Hardiness: Zone 5
Propagation: Seed, as soon as ripe

Differs from the species in its white, silky-hairy, cup-shaped flowers. Leaves pinnate, leaflets pinnatisect, lobes linear, light green. Dislikes transplantation.

Pulsatilla vulgaris rosea
(Ranunculaceae)

Common name: Pink pasque flower
Height: 20cm (8in)
Spread: 20cm (8in)
Aspect: Sun
Soil: Sharply drained, fertile
Hardiness: Zone 5
Propagation: Seed, as soon as ripe; root cuutings, in winter

Pink form of the pasque flower with silky-hairy, cup-shaped flowers. Very handsome leaves, pinnate, leaflets pinnatisect, lobes linear, light green. Dislikes transplantation.

Pulsatilla vulgaris
var. *rubra*
(Ranunculaceae)

Common name: Red pasque flower
Height: 20cm (8in)
Spread: 20cm (8in)
Aspect: Sun
Soil: Sharply drained, fertile
Hardiness: Zone 5
Propagation: Seed, as soon as ripe; root cuttings, in winter

Red form of the species. Leaves pinnate, leaflets pinnatisect, lobes linear, light green. Flowers solitary, cup-shaped, silky-hairy, in spring. Dislikes transplantation.

Puschkinia scilloides
var. *libanotica*
(Hyacinthaceae/Liliaceae)

Common names: None
Height: 20cm (8in)
Spread: 5cm (2in)
Aspect: Sun or half shade
Soil: Well-drained
Hardiness: Zone 5
Propagation: Offsets, in summer after foliage dies down

Bulbous plant from the Lebanon and Turkey. Leaves basal, paired, semi-erect, linear, mid-green. Flowers open bell-shaped, in dense racemes of up to 10, white, spring.

Ramonda myconi
A.G.M.
(Gesneriaceae)

Common names: None
Height: 10cm (4in)
Spread: 15cm (6in)
Aspect: Half shade
Soil: Moist, well-drained, humus-rich, fertile
Hardiness: Zone 6
Propagation: Seed, as soon as ripe; rooted rosettes, in summer; leaf cuttings, in autumn

Slow-growing, rosette-forming evergreen. Leaves spoon-shaped, crinkled, hairy, dark green. Flowers in cymes or solitary, lilac-blue, in late spring and early summer.

Ranunculus acris
'Flore Pleno'
(Ranunculaceae)

Common name: Bethlehem buttercup
Height: 90cm (36in)
Spread: 25cm (10in)
Aspect: Sun
Soil: Moist, well-drained, humus-rich
Hardiness: Zone 5
Propagation: Seed, when ripe; division, in spring or autumn

Leaves ovate, palmately 3- to 7-lobed, toothed. Flowers in panicles, double, dazzling yellow, in early and midsummer. Unlike the single form, this is not invasive.

RANUNCULUS (Ranunculaceae)
Buttercup • Crowfoot

A genus of some 400 species of annuals, biennials and perennials from temperate regions of both hemispheres. They come from very varied habitats, such that it is not possible to generalise about their cultural requirements. They are variably hardy, and may be evergreen or deciduous. The root system can be fibrous, tuberous, rhizomatous or fleshy and suckering. Some are bog plants, some originate in high alpine conditions, some are woodlanders and some can only be kept in an alpine house in wet countries because they need a dry summer dormancy. A good number, however, are reliably hardy, easy to cultivate and suitable for a mixed border. Their foliage may be basal or stem, and the leaf shape varies widely. They are grown for their 5-petalled, cup-, bowl-, or saucer-shaped flowers, which are usually yellow but also orange, red, pink or white, and borne in spring or summer, or sometimes in autumn. *R. acris* (Zone 5), *R. ficaria* and *R. repens* are invasive weeds, and best kept out of beds or borders, and reserved for the wild or woodland garden. Some species are skin-irritant, whilst others are poisonous, and all appear to be highly allergenic, so allergic gardeners should treat them with caution.

Ranunculus aquatilis
(Ranunculaceae)

Common name: Water crowfoot
Height: Nil
Spread: Indefinite
Aspect: Sun
Soil: Marginal aquatic
Hardiness: Zone 5
Propagation: Seed, when ripe; division, in spring or autumn

Spreading, evergreen, aquatic plant. Leaves floating and submerged, round to reniform, deeply divided, mid-green. Flowers solitary white saucers, surface-borne, in summer.

Ranunculus bulbosus
'F.M. Burton'
(Ranunculaceae)

Common name: Bulbous buttercup
Height: 75cm (30in)
Spread: 30cm (12in)
Aspect: Sun or half shade
Soil: Moist, well-drained, fertile
Hardiness: Zone 7
Propagation: Offsets, in spring or autumn

Selected form of a bulbous species. Leaves basal and stem, ovate, trilobed, dark green. Flowers in panicles of a few glossy, pale cream saucers, late spring and early summer.

Ranunculus cortusifolius
(Ranunculaceae)

Common names: None
Height: 1.2m (4ft)
Spread: 60cm (2ft)
Aspect: Sun
Soil: Moist, well-drained, fertile
Hardiness: Zone 9
Propagation: Seed, when ripe; division, in spring or autumn

Tender perennial from the Canary Islands, the Azores and Madeira. Leaves basal, leathery, rounded, toothed, mid-green. Flowers in corymbs, scented, yellow.

Ranunculus creticus
(Ranunculaceae)

Common names: None
Height: 30cm (12in)
Spread: 15cm (6in)
Aspect: Half shade
Soil: Moist, well-drained, fertile
Hardiness: Zone 8
Propagation: Seed, when ripe; division, in spring or autumn

Pubescent perennial from Crete. Basal leaves rounded, hairy, 5-lobed, stem leaves mid-green. Flowers large, several to a stem, yellow, in spring.

Ranunculus ficaria
(Ranunculaceae)

Common names: Lesser celandine; pilewort
Height: 5cm (2in)
Spread: 45cm (18in)
Aspect: Full or half shade
Soil: Moist, humus-rich
Hardiness: Zone 5
Propagation: Seed, when ripe; division, in spring or autumn

A tuberous perennial with axillary bulbils; highly invasive. Leaves broad, heart-shaped, scalloped, dark green. Flowers solitary, yellow or orange cups, in spring.

Ranunculus gramineus A.G.M.
(Ranunculaceae)

Common names: None
Height: 30cm (12in)
Spread: 20cm (8in)
Aspect: Sun or half shade
Soil: Moist, well-drained, fertile
Hardiness: Zone 7
Propagation: Seed, when ripe; division, in spring or autumn

A clump-forming perennial. Leaves basal, grassy, linear, glaucous green. Flowers on branched stems, up to 3 on a stem, lemon-yellow, in late spring and early summer.

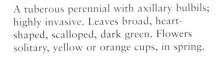

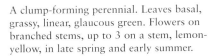

Ranunculus lingua
(Ranunculaceae)

Common name: Greater spearwort
Height: 1.2m (4ft)
Spread: 2m (6ft)
Aspect: Sun
Soil: Marginal aquatic
Hardiness: Zone 4
Propagation: Seed, when ripe; division, in spring or autumn

A large aquatic marginal. Leaves on non-flowering stems heart-shaped, on flowering stems linear. Flowers yellow, solitary or in few-flowered panicles, in early summer.

Ranunculus lyalii
(Ranunculaceae)

Common names: Giant buttercup; Mount Cook lily
Height: 1m (36in)
Spread: 35cm (14in)
Aspect: Sun or half shade
Soil: Moist, well-drained, fertile
Hardiness: Zone 6
Propagation: Seed, when ripe; division, in spring or autumn

Rhizomatous perennial from New Zealand. Leaves basal, rounded, leathery, peltate, dark green, evergreen in mild areas. Flowers in panicles, white cups, in summer.

Ranunculus psilostachys
(Ranunculaceae)

Common names: None
Height: 30cm (12in)
Spread: 20cm (8in)
Aspect: Sun
Soil: Moist, well-drained, fertile
Hardiness: Zone 6
Propagation: Seed, when ripe; division, after flowering

Tuberous, spreading plant from Turkey and the Balkans. Leaves basal, 3-lobed, segments obovate, toothed, hairy below. Flowers upward-facing, yellow, early summer.

Ratibida columnifera
(Asteraceae/Compositae)

Common names: Mexican hat; prairie cone flower
Height: 90cm (3ft)
Spread: 30cm (1ft)
Aspect: Sun
Soil: Dry, well-drained, fertile
Hardiness: Zone 3
Propagation: Seed, in early spring; division, in spring, when young

Perennial from North America and Mexico. Leaves pinnate, hairy, grey-green. Flowers daisy-like, rays reflexed, yellow, disc brown, columnar, early summer to early autumn.

There are many non-invasive buttercups, such as Ranunculus gramineus, *that make a miniature meadow possible in any garden.*

Rehmannia elata
(Scrophulariaceae)

Common name: Chinese foxglove
Height: 1.2m (4ft)
Spread: 50cm (20in)
Aspect: Sun
Soil: Well-drained, humus-rich, fertile
Hardiness: Zone 9
Propagation: Seed, in warmth in late winter; separated runners, in spring

Rosette-forming perennial. Leaves obovate, toothed, veined, hairy. Flowers in leafy racemes, tubular, semi-pendent, pink with spotted throats, from summer to autumn.

Rehmannia glutinosa A.G.M.
(Scrophulariaceae)

Common names: None
Height: 30cm (1ft)
Spread: 30cm (1ft)
Aspect: Sun
Soil: Well-drained, humus-rich, fertile
Hardiness: Zone 9
Propagation: Seed, in warmth in late winter; separated runners, in spring

Leaves in rosettes, obovate, scalloped, veined. Flowers pendent, tubular, reddish-brown with purple veins and pale brown lips, in racemes, mid-spring to summer.

Reineckea carnea
(Convallariaceae/Liliaceae)

Common names: None
Height: 20cm (8in)
Spread: 60cm (24in)
Aspect: Half shade
Soil: Moist, well-drained, acidic, humus-rich
Hardiness: Zone 7
Propagation: Seed, when ripe; division, in spring

Rhizomatous evergreen. Leaves arching, linear, glossy, bright green. Flowers shallow pink cups fading to white, in dense spikes, in late spring. Red berries in warm areas.

Rheum 'Ace of Hearts'
(Polygonaceae)

Common name: Rhubarb
Height: 1.2m (4ft)
Spread: 1.2m (4ft)
Aspect: Sun or half shade
Soil: Moist, deep, humus-rich
Hardiness: Zone 7
Propagation: Seed, in autumn; division, in early spring

A rhizomatous, hybrid perennial. Leaves large, heart-shaped, dark green, veined red. Flowers in panicles, tiny, pink stars, in mid- and late summer.

Rheum palmatum var. _tanguticum_
(Polygonaceae)

Common name: Rhubarb
Height: 2m (6ft)
Spread: 2m (6ft)
Aspect: Sun or half shade
Soil: Moist, humus-rich, fertile
Hardiness: Zone 7
Propagation: Seed, in autumn; division, in early spring

Rhizomatous perennial. Leaves large, jagged, reddish-green turning dark green and purple. Flowers in huge many-flowered panicles, white, red or pink, in early summer.

Rhodanthemum gayanum
(Asteraceae/Compositae)

Common names: None
Height: 30cm (1ft)
Spread: 30cm (1ft)
Aspect: Sun
Soil: Sharply drained, fertile
Hardiness: Zone 8
Propagation: Seed, in spring; softwood cuttings, in early summer

Leaves deeply 3-lobed, hairy, grey-green. Flowers solitary, daisy-like, ray florets pale pink or white, disc florets brown, in summer. From Algeria and Morocco.

Rhodanthemum hosmariense A.G.M.
(Asteraceae/Compositae)

Common names: None
Height: 30cm (1ft)
Spread: 30cm (1ft)
Aspect: Sun
Soil: Sharply drained, fertile
Hardiness: Zone 8
Propagation: Seed, in spring; softwood cuttings, in early summer

Spreading subshrub from Morocco. Leaves deeply 3-lobed, hairy, silver. Flowers single, solitary, white, daisy-like with yellow centres, and surrounded by silver bracts.

Rhodiola wallichiana
(Crassulaceae)

Common names: None
Height: 40cm (16in)
Spread: 30cm (12in)
Aspect: Sun
Soil: Fertile
Hardiness: Zone 6
Propagation: Seed, in spring or autumn; division, in spring or early summer

Rhizomatous Himalayan perennial. Leaves linear to lance-shaped, toothed, mid-green. Flowers in dense terminal corymbs, pale or greenish-yellow stars, in early summer.

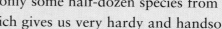

Rhodohypoxis baurii **A.G.M.**
(Hypoxidaceae)

Common names: None
Height: 10cm (4in)
Spread: 10cm (4in)
Aspect: Sun
Soil: Well-drained, humus-rich, fertile
Hardiness: Zone 8
Propagation: Seed, in warmth when ripe; offsets, in late autumn

A cormous perennial from South Africa. Leaves narrow, lance-shaped, keeled, greyish-green. Flowers solitary, flat, reddish-pink or white, all summer.

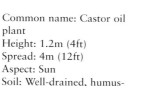

Ricinus communis **'Impala'**
(Euphorbiaceae)

Common name: Castor oil plant
Height: 1.2m (4ft)
Spread: 4m (12ft)
Aspect: Sun
Soil: Well-drained, humus-rich, fertile
Hardiness: Zone 9
Propagation: Seed, after soaking in late spring

Tender subshrub, good in mixed plantings. Leaves large, broad, ovate, toothed, glossy, reddish-purple. Flowers in spikes, females with red stigma, males yellow, in summer.

RODGERSIA (Saxifragaceae)

A genus of only some half-dozen species from the Far East, but one which gives us very hardy and handsome architectural plants for our gardens. They originate in the mountains of Burma, Korea, China, and Japan, growing along streams in scrub and woodlands. They are naturally moisture-lovers, but do not do well in waterlogged soil, and will grow in sun or half shade; they will tolerate drier soil in a partially shaded position better than they will in a sunny site. *Rodgersia* are large plants, and not really suitable for the very small garden, but do not usually require staking. Their large, palmate or pinnate leaves are handsome, although deciduous; some species have good autumn colour. The flowers are petalless and star-shaped, borne in summer in upright, pyramidal panicles on tall stems, and are followed by attractive, dark red or brown seed capsules. *Rodgersia* will build up into quite large clumps requiring lots of room, and to prevent this, the roots should be divided in a circle around the plant. They are low-allergen plants and suit the allergic gardener. The young leaves may be damaged by slugs, and since they are grown as much for their foliage as their flowers, preventative measures must be taken early or the plant will look untidy all season.

Rodgersia aesculifolia **A.G.M.**
(Saxifragaceae)

Common names: None
Height: 2m (6ft)
Spread: 1m (3ft)
Aspect: Sun or half shade
Soil: Moist, humus-rich
Hardiness: Zone 5
Propagation: Seed or division, both in spring

Rhizomatous plant. Leaves basal, palmate, 5- to 9-lobed, leaflets obovate, toothed, mid-green, red-veined. Tall panicles of many small, starry, pink or white flowers, summer.

Rodgersia pinnata **'Alba'**
(Saxifragaceae)

Common names: None
Height: 90cm (3ft)
Spread: 1.2m (4ft)
Aspect: Sun or half shade
Soil: Moist, humus-rich
Hardiness: Zone 5
Propagation: Seed or division, both in spring

Clump-forming, rhizomatous plant. Leaves large, palmate, 5- to 9-lobed, obovate, glossy leaflets. Flowers small, starry, white, in fluffy panicles, in mid- and late summer.

Rodgersia pinnata **'Elegans'**
(Saxifragaceae)

Common names: None
Height: 90cm (3ft)
Spread: 1.2m (4ft)
Aspect: Sun or half shade
Soil: Moist, humus-rich
Hardiness: Zone 5
Propagation: Seed or division, both in spring

Cultivar with starry, pink flowers, tinted cream. Leaves large, palmate, 5- to 9-lobed, obovate, glossy leaflets. Lovely seed heads after flowering.

Rodgersia pinnata **'Superba' A.G.M.**
(Saxifragaceae)

Common names: None
Height: 1.2m (4ft)
Spread: 75cm (30in)
Aspect: Sun or half shade
Soil: Moist, humus-rich
Hardiness: Zone 5
Propagation: Seed or division, both in spring

Tall selected form; may be a separate species. Leaves very large, palmate, lobes fewer than in type, glossy, veined, bronze-tinted. Large panicle of salmon-pink flowers.

Rodgersia podophylla
A.G.M.
(Saxifragaceae)

Common names: None
Height: 1.5m (5ft)
Spread: 1.8m (6ft)
Aspect: Sun or half shade
Soil: Moist, humus-rich
Hardiness: Zone 5
Propagation: Seed or division, both in spring

Rhizomatous plant from Japan and Korea. Leaves huge, palmate, with 5 jagged, glossy mid-green, obovate leaflets. Creamy-green flowers (not open here) in panicles, summer.

Romneya coulteri
A.G.M.
(Papaveraceae)

Common names: Matilija poppy; tree poppy
Height: 2.5m (8ft)
Spread: Indefinite
Aspect: Sun
Soil: Well-drained, fertile
Hardiness: Zone 7
Propagation: Seed or basal cuttings, both in spring; root cuttings, in winter

Suckering subshrub. Leaves glaucous grey-green, rounded-pinnatifid, lobes ovate to lance-shaped. Flowers solitary, scented, large, yellow-centred white cups, summer.

Romulea bulbocodium
(Iridaceae)

Common names: None
Height: 10cm (4in)
Spread: 5cm (2in)
Aspect: Sun
Soil: Well-drained, fertile
Hardiness: Zone 7
Propagation: Seed, in autumn; offsets, when dormant

Cormous perennial from the Mediterranean and Africa. Leaves basal, linear, channelled, arched. Up to 5 flowers per stem, lilac funnels with white centres, in spring.

Roscoea auriculata
(Zingiberaceae)

Common names: None
Height: 60cm (24in)
Spread: 20cm (8in)
Aspect: Half shade
Soil: Moist, well-drained, humus-rich, fertile
Hardiness: Zone 6
Propagation: Seed, when ripe; division, in spring

Tuberous perennial from Nepal and India. Leaves linear to lance-shaped, dark green. Flowers axillary, hooded, lips large, bracts overlapping, purple, late summer to autumn.

Roscoea
'Beesiana'
(Zingiberaceae)

Common names: None
Height: 45cm (18in)
Spread: 30cm (12in)
Aspect: Half shade
Soil: Moist, well-drained, humus-rich, fertile
Hardiness: Zone 6
Propagation: Seed, when ripe; division, in spring

Hybrid perennial. Leaves lance-shaped, arching, dark green. Flowers hooded, with overlapping bracts, yellow, striped mauve sometimes, in late summer to autumn.

Roscoea cautleyoides
A.G.M.
(Zingiberaceae)

Common names: None
Height: 60cm (24in)
Spread: 20cm (8in)
Aspect: Half shade
Soil: Moist, well-drained, humus-rich, fertile
Hardiness: Zone 6
Propagation: Seed, when ripe; division, in spring

Tuberous perennial from China. Leaves linear, mid-green. Flowers hooded, with overlapping bracts, on leafy stalks, yellow, purple or white, late summer to autumn.

Roscoea purpurea
(Zingiberaceae)

Common names: None
Height: 60cm (2ft)
Spread: 30cm (1ft)
Aspect: Half shade
Soil: Moist, well-drained, humus-rich, fertile
Hardiness: Zone 6
Propagation: Seed, when ripe; division, in spring

A tuberous perennial from the Himalayas. Leaves lance-shaped, dark green. Flowers hooded, purple, in late summer to early autumn. Appears late, so mark position.

Rosmarinus officinalis
'Severn Sea' A.G.M.
(Labiatae/Lamiaceae)

Common names: Rosemary
Height: 90cm (3ft)
Spread: 1.5m (5ft)
Aspect: Sun
Soil: Well-drained, fertile
Hardiness: Zone 6
Propagation: Semi-ripe cuttings in summer

An aromatic, evergreen subshrub from the Mediterranean. Leaves linear, dark green, white-woolly below. Flowers in axillary whorls, blue, in late spring to summer.

Rosularia sedoides
(Crassulaceae)

Common name: Himalayan houseleek
Height: 5cm (2in)
Spread: 20cm (8in)
Aspect: Sun
Soil: Sharply drained, humus-rich
Hardiness: Zone 7
Propagation: Separated offsets, in spring

Succulent, stoloniferous evergreen from the Himalayas. Leaves ovoid, hairy, green, red in sun, in rosettes like a houseleek. Flowers star-shaped, white, late summer to autumn.

***Rudbeckia fulgida* var. *sullivantii* 'Goldsturm' A.G.M.**
(Asteraceae/Compositae)

Common name: Coneflower
Height: 60cm (24in)
Spread: 45cm (18in)
Aspect: Sun or half shade
Soil: Well-drained, humus-rich, fertile
Hardiness: Zone 4
Propagation: Division, in autumn or spring

Cultivar of a rhizomatous plant from the U.S.A. Leaves basal and stem, lance-shaped, mid-green. Flowers solitary, single, golden-yellow, daisy-like, late summer to autumn.

***Rudbeckia* 'Herbstonne'**
(Asteraceae/Compositae)

Common name: Coneflower
Height: 1.8m (6ft)
Spread: 90cm (3ft)
Aspect: Sun or half shade
Soil: Well-drained, humus-rich, fertile
Hardiness: Zone 3
Propagation: Division, in spring or autumn

Hardy, rhizomatous, clump-forming, short-lived hybrid. Leaves ovate, toothed, glossy green. Flowers solitary, yellow, with a high, green boss, summer to early autumn.

Rudbeckia hirta
(Asteraceae/Compositae)

Common name: Black-eyed Susan
Height: 90cm (36in)
Spread: 45cm (18in)
Aspect: Sun or half shade
Soil: Well-drained, humus-rich, fertile
Hardiness: Zone 4
Propagation: Seed, in spring; division, in spring or autumn

Rhizomatous, short-lived perennial. Leaves basal and stem, ovate, mid-green. Solitary, large, yellow, daisy-like flowers with black, domed centres, summer to early autumn.

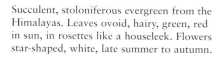

Rudbeckia subtomentosa
(Asteraceae/Compositae)

Common name: Sweet coneflower
Height: 70cm (28in)
Spread: 60cm (24in)
Aspect: Sun or half shade
Soil: Well-drained, humus-rich, fertile
Hardiness: Zone 5
Propagation: Seed, in spring; division, in spring or autumn.

A short-lived perennial from the central U.S.A. Leaves ovate, mid-green. Flowers solitary, single, daisy-like, yellow with dark purple-brown centres, in autumn.

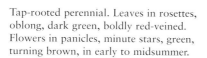

Rumex sanguineus
(Polygonaceae)

Common names: Bloody dock; red-veined dock
Height: 80cm (32in)
Spread: 30cm (12in)
Aspect: Sun
Soil: Well-drained, fertile
Hardiness: Zone 6
Propagation: Seed, sown *in situ* in spring

Tap-rooted perennial. Leaves in rosettes, oblong, dark green, boldly red-veined. Flowers in panicles, minute stars, green, turning brown, in early to midsummer.

Ruta graveolens
(Rutaceae)

Common name: Rue
Height: 90cm (36in)
Spread: 80cm (32in)
Aspect: Sun or half shade
Soil: Sharply drained, fertile
Hardiness: Zone 5
Propagation: Seed, in spring; semi-ripe cuttings, in summer

Evergreen subshrub. Leaves 2-pinnatisect, ovate, lobes obovate, glaucous blue-green, aromatic. Flowers in cymes, yellow cups, in summer. Irritant; poisonous in quantity.

Sagittaria latifolia
(Alismataceae)

Common names: Duck potato; wapato
Height: 1.2m (4ft)
Spread: 90cm (3ft)
Aspect: Sun
Soil: Marginal aquatic
Hardiness: Zone 7
Propagation: Seed, as soon as ripe; division or separated runners, both in spring

A tuberous, aquatic marginal perennial from the U.S.A. Leaves aerial, arrow-shaped. Flowers in whorled racemes, white, in summer.

Sagittaria sagittifolia
(Alismataceae)

Common name: Japanese arrowhead
Height: 90cm (3ft)
Spread: Indefinite
Aspect: Sun
Soil: Marginal aquatic
Hardiness: Zone 7
Propagation: Seed, as soon as ripe; division or separated runners, both in spring

Spreading, tuberous plant from Eurasia. Leaves arrow-shaped, mid-green, aerial. Flowers in racemes, white with a purple spot at the base of each petal, in summer.

SALVIA (Labiatae/Lamiaceae)
Sage

A very large and varied genus of about 900 species of annuals, biennials, perennials and shrubs from grassland, scrub, or woodland habitats in tropical and temperate regions the world over. The perennials may be rhizomatous, tuberous or fibrous-rooted, and evergreen or herbaceous, and they vary widely in hardiness from fully hardy to tender. The foliage is aromatic in many, hairy in some, and silvery in others. *Salvia* species all prefer light, alkaline soils that are well drained and moisture retentive. Almost all require full sun, especially the low-growing types with woolly or densely hairy leaves, but a few will tolerate light shade. The leaves are both basal and stem, and the two types often differ in form. The flowers are two-lipped; the upper petal arches forward to form a hood, and the lower petal is two-toothed. They are borne in panicles or in axillary whorls on upright stems. Many types attract bees, and some have culinary or medicinal use: *S. officinalis* is the common culinary sage. All sages are low-allergen, and suitable for the allergic gardener. Some of the taller varieties may need to be staked. The silvery-woolly types dislike winter wet and cold, drying winds, so should be either lifted and brought in or covered with a cloche.

Salvia africana-lutea
(Labiatae/Lamiaceae)

Common names: None
Height: 90cm (3ft)
Spread: 90cm (3ft)
Aspect: Sun
Soil: Moist, well-drained, humus-rich, fertile
Hardiness: Zone 9
Propagation: Basal or softwood cuttings, both in spring; semi-ripe cuttings, in autumn

A tender, evergreen subshrub from Africa. Leaves rounded, aromatic, hairy, white-woolly. Flowers in terminal racemes, red-brown, from summer to late autumn.

Salvia argentea
A.G.M.
(Labiatae/Lamiaceae)

Common names: None
Height: 90cm (3ft)
Spread: 60cm (2ft)
Aspect: Sun
Soil: Moist, well-drained, humus-rich, fertile
Hardiness: Zone 5
Propagation: Seed or division, both in spring

Short-lived perennial. Leaves large, in basal rosette, silky, silver-hairy. Flowers white or pale pink, in branched panicles, in summer; if cut down, will flower again in autumn.

Salvia azurea
(Labiatae/Lamiaceae)

Common names: None
Height: 1.2m (4ft)
Spread: 90cm (3ft)
Aspect: Sun or half shade
Soil: Moist, well-drained, humus-rich, fertile
Hardiness: Zone 4
Propagation: Basal or softwood cuttings, both in spring; semi-ripe cuttings, in late summer

A straggly perennial from the U.S.A. Leaves lance-shaped, softly hairy, mid-green. Flowers in dense terminal racemes, blue or white, from autumn to winter.

Salvia buchananii
A.G.M.
(Labiatae/Lamiaceae)

Common names: None
Height: 30cm (1ft)
Spread: 30cm (1ft)
Aspect: Sun or half shade
Soil: Moist, well-drained, humus-rich, fertile
Hardiness: Zone 9
Propagation: Basal or softwood cuttings, both in spring; semi-ripe cuttings, in late summer

Spreading evergreen. Leaves ovate, toothed, leathery, glossy green. Flowers in terminal racemes, red with brown-purple calyces, from midsummer to mid-autumn.

Salvia cacaliifolia
A.G.M.
(Labiatae/Lamiaceae)

Common names: None
Height: 1.2m (4ft)
Spread: 30cm (1ft)
Aspect: Sun or half shade
Soil: Moist, well-drained, humus-rich, fertile
Hardiness: Zone 9
Propagation: Basal or softwood cuttings, both in spring; semi-ripe cuttings, in late summer

A tender perennial from Mexico and Guatemala. Leaves triangular, mid-green. Flowers in terminal panicles, in pairs, deep blue, all summer and into autumn.

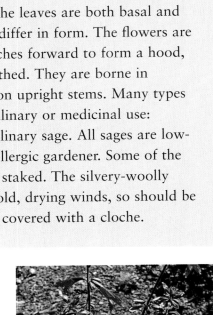

Salvia farinacea *'Victoria' is a particularly densely branching cultivar; it is tender, and usually treated as an annual.*

Salvia coccinea
(Labiatae/Lamiaceae)

Common name: Red Texas sage
Height: 75cm (30in)
Spread: 30cm (12in)
Aspect: Sun or half shade
Soil: Moist, well-drained, humus-rich, fertile
Hardiness: Zone 8
Propagation: Seed, in spring

A short-lived perennial from the Americas. Leaves oval, hairy, toothed, dark green. Flowers cherry-red, in open spikes, from summer to autumn.

Salvia coccinea
'Coral Nymph'
(Labiatae/Lamiaceae)

Common names: None
Height: 75cm (30in)
Spread: 30cm (12in)
Aspect: Sun or half shade
Soil: Moist, well-drained, humus-rich, fertile
Hardiness: Zone 8
Propagation: Division, in spring

A selected form of the species, with flowers having an upper lip of salmon-pink, and a lower lip of pale pink. Leaves oval, hairy, toothed, dark green.

Salvia confertiflora
(Labiatae/Lamiaceae)

Common names: None
Height: 1.2m (4ft)
Spread: 60cm (2ft)
Aspect: Sun or half shade
Soil: Moist, well-drained, humus-rich, fertile
Hardiness: Zone 9
Propagation: Basal or softwood cuttings, both in spring; semi-ripe cuttings, in late summer

Leaves ovate, scalloped, green-yellow, woolly below, pungent. Flowers in terminal spikes, indigo-black with hairy, brown calyces, in late summer to mid-autumn.

Salvia darcyi
(Labiatae/Lamiaceae)

Common names: None
Height: 1m (3ft)
Spread: 60cm (2ft)
Aspect: Sun or half shade
Soil: Moist, well-drained, humus-rich, fertile
Hardiness: Zone 8
Propagation: Basal or softwood cuttings, both in spring; semi-ripe cuttings, in late summer

Subshrub from Mexico. Leaves triangular, hairy, crenate, mid-green. Flowers in whorls of up to 6 on unbranched spikes, red, from summer to late autumn.

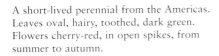

Salvia farinacea
(Labiatae/Lamiaceae)

Common name: Mealy sage
Height: 60cm (2ft)
Spread: 30cm (1ft)
Aspect: Sun or half shade
Soil: Moist, well-drained, humus-rich, fertile
Hardiness: Zone 9
Propagation: Seed, in spring

Bushy perennial from Mexico and the U.S.A. Leaves ovate, thin, glossy, mid-green, white below. Flowers in whorls of up to 16, in spikes, lavender-blue, summer to autumn.

Salvia forsskaolii
(Labiatae/Lamiaceae)

Common names: None
Height: 90cm (36in)
Spread: 45cm (18in)
Aspect: Sun or half shade
Soil: Moist, well-drained, humus-rich, fertile
Hardiness: Zone 7
Propagation: Seed, in spring

Perennial from the Black Sea coast. Leaves basal, broad, ovate, toothed, mid-green. Flowers in spikes, tubes white, lips violet, lower lip marked yellow, all summer.

Salvia fulgens
A.G.M.
(Labiatae/Lamiaceae)

Common names: None
Height: 1m (3ft)
Spread: 1m (3ft)
Aspect: Sun or half shade
Soil: Moist, well-drained, humus-rich, fertile
Hardiness: Zone 9
Propagation: Basal or softwood cuttings, both in spring; semi-ripe cuttings, in late summer

Tender, evergreen perennial from Mexico. Leaves ovate, toothed, bright green, white-woolly below. Flowers in terminal racemes, red, lower lip downy, in summer.

Salvia glutinosa
(Labiatae/Lamiaceae)

Common name: Jupiter's distaff
Height: 90cm (3ft)
Spread: 60cm (2ft)
Aspect: Half shade
Soil: Moist, humus-rich, fertile
Hardiness: Zone 5
Propagation: Seed, in spring

Eurasian perennial. Leaves heart-shaped, hairy, toothed. Flowers sticky, in loose terminal racemes, pale yellow, spotted maroon, from midsummer to mid-autumn.

Salvia greggii
(Labiatae/Lamiaceae)

Common name: Autumn sage
Height: 75cm (30in)
Spread: 75cm (30in)
Aspect: Sun or half shade
Soil: Moist, well-drained, humus-rich, fertile
Hardiness: Zone 9
Propagation: Basal or softwood cuttings, both in spring; semi-ripe cuttings, in late summer

Evergreen from Texas and Mexico. Leaves elliptic, small, leathery. Flowers in pairs in terminal racemes, mauvish-red, pink, yellow or violet, late summer to autumn

Salvia greggii
'Peach' A.G.M.
(Labiatae/Lamiaceae)

Common name: Autumn sage
Height: 75cm (30in)
Spread: 75cm (30in)
Aspect: Sun or half shade
Soil: Moist, well-drained, humus-rich, fertile
Hardiness: Zone 9
Propagation: Basal or softwood cuttings, both in spring; semi-ripe cuttings, in late summer

A selected form of the species, with flowers in pairs, of a strong peach colour, from late summer to autumn. Leaves elliptic, small, leathery, mid-green.

Salvia hians
(Labiatae/Lamiaceae)

Common names: None
Height: 60cm (2ft)
Spread: 60cm (2ft)
Aspect: Sun or half shade
Soil: Moist, well-drained, humus-rich, fertile
Hardiness: Zone 6
Propagation: Seed or division, both in spring

Short-lived perennial from the Himalayas. Leaves ovate, toothed, veined, wrinkled, dark green. Flowers in terminal spikes, purplish-blue, lower lip white, all summer.

Salvia involucrata
'Bethellii'
(Labiatae/Lamiaceae)

Common names: None
Height: 1.5m (5ft)
Spread: 90cm (3ft)
Aspect: Sun or half shade
Soil: Moist, well-drained, humus-rich, fertile
Hardiness: Zone 9
Propagation: Basal or softwood cuttings, both in spring; semi-ripe cuttings, in late summer

Selected form of a perennial from Mexico. Leaves ovate, hairy, bright green. Flowers in dense, terminal racemes, purplish-crimson, bracts pink, late summer to mid-autumn.

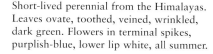

Salvia involucrata
'Boutin' A.G.M.
(Labiatae/Lamiaceae)

Common names: None
Height: 1.5m (5ft)
Spread: 90cm (3ft)
Aspect: Sun or half shade
Soil: Moist, well-drained, humus-rich, fertile
Hardiness: Zone 9
Propagation: Basal or softwood cuttings, both in spring; semi-ripe cuttings, in late summer

Selected form of the species with flowers in dense, terminal racemes, dark pink with dark pink bracts, from late summer to mid-autumn. Leaves ovate, hairy.

Salvia leucantha
A.G.M.
(Labiatae/Lamiaceae)

Common name: Mexican bush
Height: 90cm (3ft)
Spread: 90cm (3ft)
Aspect: Sun or half shade
Soil: Moist, well-drained, humus-rich, fertile
Hardiness: Zone 10
Propagation: Basal or softwood cuttings, both in spring; semi-ripe cuttings, in late summer

Evergreen subshrub. Leaves ovate, hairy, grey, white-tomentose below. Flowers in terminal racemes, white with bell-shaped, lavender calyces, in autumn to winter.

Salvia microphylla
(Labiatae/Lamiaceae)

Common name: Myrtle sage
Height: 1.2m (4ft)
Spread: 1.2m (4ft)
Aspect: Sun or half shade
Soil: Moist, well-drained, humus-rich, fertile
Hardiness: Zone 9
Propagation: Basal or softwood cuttings, both in spring; semi-ripe cuttings, in late summer

Evergreen perennial. Leaves small, ovate, hairy, toothed, mid-green. Flowers paired or whorled in terminal racemes, crimson, in late summer and autumn.

Salvia microphylla
var. *neurepia*
(Labiatae/Lamiaceae)

Common names: Myrtle sage
Height: 1.2m (4ft)
Spread: 1.2m (4ft)
Aspect: Sun or half shade
Soil: Moist, well-drained, humus-rich, fertile
Hardiness: Zone 9
Propagation: Basal or softwood cuttings, both in spring; semi-ripe cuttings, in late summer

A form of the species with shiny, glabrous leaves of pale green, and red flowers paired or whorled in terminal racemes, from late summer to autumn.

Salvia nemorosa
'Ostfriesland' A.G.M.
(Labiatae/Lamiaceae)

Common names: None
Height: 1m (3ft)
Spread: 60cm (2ft)
Aspect: Sun or half shade
Soil: Moist, well-drained, humus-rich, fertile
Hardiness: Zone 5
Propagation: Basal or softwood cuttings, both in spring; semi-ripe cuttings, in late summer

A selected form of a species from Eurasia. Leaves ovate, crenulate, mid-green. Flowers in very dense, terminal racemes, deep violet-blue, from summer to autumn.

Salvia officinalis
(Labiatae/Lamiaceae)

Common name: Common sage
Height: 45cm (18in)
Spread: 45cm (18in)
Aspect: Sun or half shade
Soil: Moist, well-drained, humus-rich, fertile
Hardiness: Zone 5
Propagation: Seed or cuttings, both in spring

An evergreen, Mediterranean culinary herb. Leaves aromatic, oblong, woolly, grey-green. Flowers in racemes, lilac, in early to midsummer.

Salvia officinalis
'Kew Gold' A.G.M.
(Labiatae/Lamiaceae)

Common name: Common sage
Height: 30cm (1ft)
Spread: 30cm (1ft)
Aspect: Sun or half shade
Soil: Moist, well-drained, humus-rich, fertile
Hardiness: Zone 5
Propagation: Division, in spring

A form of the common sage with oblong, woolly, aromatic leaves of pale green splashed with gold. Flowers in racemes, lilac, in early to midsummer.

Salvia officinalis
'Tricolor' A.G.M.
(Labiatae/Lamiaceae)

Common name: Common sage
Height: 30cm (12in)
Spread: 45cm (18in)
Aspect: Sun or half shade
Soil: Moist, well-drained, humus-rich, fertile
Hardiness: Zone 5
Propagation: Division, in spring

Form of the common sage with grey-green leaves margined cream and pink; young leaves have more pink than cream. Flowers in racemes, lilac, in early to midsummer.

Salvia patens
A.G.M.
(Labiatae/Lamiaceae)

Common names: None
Height: 60cm (24in)
Spread: 45cm (18in)
Aspect: Sun or half shade
Soil: Moist, well-drained, humus-rich, fertile
Hardiness: Zone 8
Propagation: Seed or division, both in spring

A tuberous perennial from Mexico. Leaves ovate, hairy, toothed, mid-green. Flowers in few-flowered racemes, deep blue, from midsummer to mid-autumn.

Salvia patens
'Cambridge Blue' A.G.M.
(Labiatae/Lamiaceae)

Common names: None
Height: 60cm (24in)
Spread: 45cm (18in)
Aspect: Sun or half shade
Soil: Moist, well-drained, humus-rich, fertile
Hardiness: Zone 8
Propagation: Division, in spring

A form of the species with flowers of pale blue in few-flowered racemes, from midsummer to mid-autumn. Leaves ovate, hairy, toothed, mid-green.

Salvia patens
'White Trophy'
(Labiatae/Lamiaceae)

Common names: None
Height: 60cm (24in)
Spread: 45cm (18in)
Aspect: Sun or half shade
Soil: Moist, well-drained, fertile, humus-rich
Hardiness: Zone 8
Propagation: Division, in spring

A white-flowered form of the species, bearing few-flowered racemes from midsummer to mid-autumn. Leaves ovate, hairy, toothed, mid-green.

Salvia pratensis
Haematodes Group A.G.M.
(Labiatae/Lamiaceae)

Common name: Meadow clary
Height: 1m (3ft)
Spread: 30cm (1ft)
Aspect: Sun or half shade
Soil: Moist, well-drained, humus-rich, fertile
Hardiness: Zone 3
Propagation: Seed, in spring

Also called *S. haematodes*. Leaves in basal rosettes, large, ovate, dark green. Flowers in panicles, bluish-violet with pale throats, from early to mid-summer. Short-lived.

Salvia purpurea
(Labiatae/Lamiaceae)

Common names: None
Height: 1.8m (6ft)
Spread: 90cm (3ft)
Aspect: Sun
Soil: Moist, well-drained, humus-rich, fertile
Hardiness: Zone 9
Propagation: Basal or softwood cuttings, both in spring; semi-ripe cuttings, in late summer

A tender perennial from Central America. Leaves ovate, toothed, mid-green. Flowers in short racemes, pinkish-lilac, upper lip densely hairy, from winter to spring.

Salvia roemeriana
A.G.M.
(Labiatae/Lamiaceae)

Common name: Cedar sage
Height: 30cm (1ft)
Spread: 30cm (1ft)
Aspect: Sun or half shade
Soil: Moist, well-drained, humus-rich, fertile
Hardiness: Zone 8
Propagation: Seed or basal or softwood cuttings, all in spring

A small perennial from Texas, Arizona, and Mexico. Leaves rounded, toothed, bright green. Flowers in loose racemes, scarlet, from midsummer to mid-autumn.

Salvia sclarea var. *turkestanica* hort.
(Labiatae/Lamiaceae)

Common name: Biennial clary
Height: 1m (3ft)
Spread: 30cm (1ft)
Aspect: Sun or half shade
Soil: Moist, well-drained, humus-rich, fertile
Hardiness: Zone 5
Propagation: Basal or softwood cuttings, both in spring; semi-ripe cuttings, in late summer

Unpleasant-smelling perennial. Leaves in basal rosette, ovate, toothed, wrinkled, mid-green. Flowers in terminal panicles, white, edged pink, from spring to summer.

Salvia spathacea
A.G.M.
(Labiatae/Lamiaceae)

Common names: Humming-bird sage; pitcher sage
Height: 30cm (1ft)
Spread: 90cm (3ft)
Aspect: Half shade
Soil: Moist, well-drained, humus-rich, fertile
Hardiness: Zone 8
Propagation: Seed or basal cuttings, both in spring

A rhizomatous, spreading perennial from California. Leaves oblong, sticky-hairy, light green. Flowers in whorls, deep pink, surrounded by bracts, in summer.

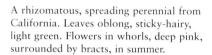

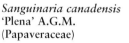

Salvia uliginosa
A.G.M.
(Labiatae/Lamiaceae)

Common name: Bog sage
Height: 1.5m (5ft)
Spread: 1m (3ft)
Aspect: Sun
Soil: Wet, humus-rich, fertile
Hardiness: Zone 9
Propagation: Basal or softwood cuttings, both in spring; semi-ripe cuttings, in late summer

Rhizomatous perennial from swampy areas of South America. Leaves oblong, toothed, mid-green. Flowers in terminal racemes, clear blue, late summer to mid-autumn.

Salvia verticillata
(Labiatae/Lamiaceae)

Common names: None
Height: 80cm (32in)
Spread: 50cm (20in)
Aspect: Sun or half shade
Soil: Moist, well-drained, humus-rich, fertile
Hardiness: Zone 6
Propagation: Basal or softwood cuttings, both in spring; semi-ripe cuttings, in late summer

A herbaceous perennial from Europe. Leaves ovate, hairy, mid-green. Flowers on branched stems, whorled, in racemes, lilac, all summer.

Salvia verticillata
'Alba'
(Labiatae/Lamiaceae)

Common names: None
Height: 80cm (32in)
Spread: 50cm (20in)
Aspect: Sun or half shade
Soil: Moist, well-drained, humus-rich, fertile
Hardiness: Zone 6
Propagation: Basal or softwood cuttings, both in spring; semi-ripe cuttings, in late summer

The white-flowered form of the species. Flowers borne in whorled racemes, on branched stems, all summer. Leaves ovate, hairy, mid-green.

Sanguinaria canadensis
'Plena' A.G.M.
(Papaveraceae)

Common names: Bloodroot; red puccoon
Height: 15cm (6in)
Spread: 30cm (12in)
Aspect: Full or deep shade
Soil: Moist, well-drained, humus-rich, fertile
Hardiness: Zone 3
Propagation: Seed, in autumn; division, just after flowering

Hardy rhizomatous woodlander. Leaves heart- or kidney-shaped, blue-green. Flowers solitary, white, double, very brief period in spring. Leaves also vanish; mark position.

The robust, reliable Salvia patens *is one of the best blue-flowered forms for the garden.*

Sanguisorba albiflora
(Rosaceae)

Common name: Burnet
Height: 60cm (2ft)
Spread: 60cm (2ft)
Aspect: Sun or half shade
Soil: Moist, well-drained, humus-rich, fertile
Hardiness: Zone 5
Propagation: Seed or division, both in spring or autumn

Short-lived, rhizomatous perennial. Leaves pinnate, leaflets ovate, grey-green. Flowers in arching, bottle-brush spikes, small, fluffy, white, summer to early autumn.

Sanguisorba canadensis
(Rosaceae)

Common name: Canadian burnet
Height: 2m (6ft)
Spread: 1m (3ft)
Aspect: Sun or half shade
Soil: Moist, well-drained, humus-rich, fertile
Hardiness: Zone 4
Propagation: Seed or division, both in spring or autumn

Rhizomatous, invasive perennial. Leaves pinnate, leaflets oblong, grey-green. Flowers in bottle-brush spikes, small, white, fluffy, from midsummer to mid-autumn.

Sanguisorba menziesii
(Rosaceae)

Common name: Burnet
Height: 60cm (2ft)
Spread: 30cm (1ft)
Aspect: Sun
Soil: Moist, well-drained, humus-rich, fertile
Hardiness: Zone 5
Propagation: Seed or division, both in spring or autumn

A dwarf perennial. Leaves pinnate, leaflets obovate, toothed, light green. Flowers in bottle-brush spikes, small, maroon, over a few weeks in summer.

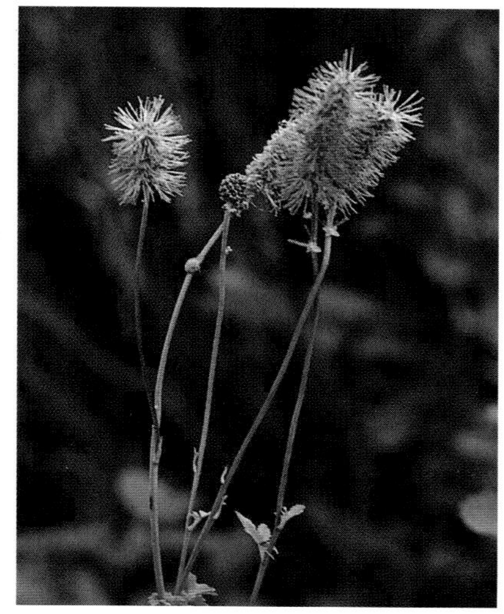

Sanguisorba obtusa
(Rosaceae)

Common name: Burnet
Height: 60cm (2ft)
Spread: 60cm (2ft)
Aspect: Sun or half shade
Soil: Moist, well-drained, humus-rich, fertile
Hardiness: Zone 5
Propagation: Seed or division, both in spring or autumn

Rhizomatous, spreading perennial from Japan. Leaves pinnate, leaflets oblong, grey-green. Flowers in bottle-brush spikes, small, fluffy, pink, summer to early autumn.

Sanguisorba officinalis 'Tanna'
(Rosaceae)

Common name: Greater burnet
Height: 25cm (10in)
Spread: 60cm (24in)
Aspect: Sun or half shade
Soil: Moist, well-drained, humus-rich, fertile
Hardiness: Zone 4
Propagation: Division, in spring or autumn

Form of a rhizomatous, dwarf plant. Leaves basal, pinnate, leaflets elliptic, mid-green. Flowers maroon-purple, in short, bottle-brush spikes, late summer to early autumn.

Sanguisorba tenuifolia 'Rosea'
(Rosaceae)

Common name: Burnet
Height: 1.2m (4ft)
Spread: 60cm (2ft)
Aspect: Sun or half shade
Soil: Wet, humus-rich, fertile
Hardiness: Zone 4
Propagation: Seed or division, both in spring or autumn

Rhizomatous perennial from the Far East. Leaves basal, large, pinnate, leaflets deeply divided, feathery. Flowers pink, in arching bottle-brushes, late summer to early autumn.

Santolina chamaecyparissus A.G.M.
(Asteraceae/Compositae)

Common name: Cotton lavender
Height 45cm (18in)
Spread: 1m (36in)
Aspect: Sun
Soil: Well-drained, fertile
Hardiness: Zone 7
Propagation: Seed, in autumn or spring

Evergreen Mediterrenean subshrub. Leaves aromatic, pinnatisect, leaflets toothed, grey-white, deeply dissected. Flowers bright yellow buttons, in mid- to late summer.

Santolina pinnata subsp. *neapolitana* 'Edward Bowles'
(Asteraceae/Compositae)

Common name: Cotton lavender
Height: 75cm (30in)
Spread: 1m (36in)
Aspect: Sun
Soil: Well-drained, fertile
Hardiness: Zone 7
Propagation: Seed, in autumn or spring

An evergreen subshrub from Italy. Leaves aromatic, pinnate, leaflets cylindrical, grey-green. Flowers on long stems, creamy-white buttons, in summer.

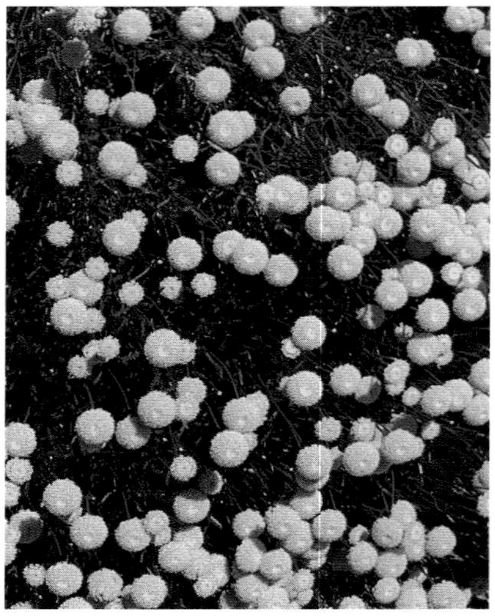

Santolina rosmarinifolia* subsp. *rosmarinifolia
(Asteraceae/Compositae)

Common name: Holy flax
Height: 60cm (2ft)
Spread: 1m (3ft)
Aspect: Sun
Soil: Well-drained, fertile
Hardiness: Zone 7
Propagation: Seed, in spring or autumn

Evergreen subshrub from Europe. Leaves aromatic, pinnate, leaflets narrowly linear, toothed, bright green. Flowers on slim stems, pale yellow buttons, in midsummer.

Saponaria ocymoides
A.G.M.
(Caryophyllaceae)

Common name: Tumbling Ted
Height: 10cm (4in)
Spread: 45cm (18in)
Aspect: Sun
Soil: Well-drained, fertile, alkaline
Hardiness: Zone 4
Propagation: Seed, in autumn or spring

A creeping, mat-forming perennial. Leaves ovate, hairy, bright green. Flowers in loose cymes, pink, in summer. Cut to the ground after flowering to keep compact.

Saponaria officinalis
(Caryophyllaceae)

Common names: Bouncing Bet; soapwort
Height: 60cm (24in)
Spread: 45cm (18in)
Aspect: Sun
Soil: Well-drained, fertile
Hardiness: Zone 4
Propagation: Seed or division, both in autumn or spring

Untidy, extremely invasive, rhizomatous perennial. Leaves ovate, veined, rough, mid-green. Flowers in cymes, scented, pink, white or red from summer to autumn.

Sarracenia* × *catesbyi
A.G.M.
(Sarraceniaceae)

Common name: Pitcher plant
Height: 75cm (30in)
Spread: 1m (36in)
Aspect: Sun
Soil: Moist, sharply drained, acidic, humus-rich
Hardiness: Zone 5
Propagation: Seed or division, both in spring

Carnivorous, natural hybrid. Leaves form vases, or "pitchers", which secrete nectar and trap insects. Pitcher erect, red. Flowers (not shown) large, red, in spring.

Sarracenia flava
A.G.M.
(Sarraceniaceae)

Common name: Yellow trumpet
Height: 1m (3ft)
Spread: 1m (3ft)
Aspect: Sun
Soil: Moist, well-drained, acidic, humus-rich
Hardiness: Zone 7
Propagation: Seed or division, both in spring

Carnivorous perennial. Leaves form vases, or "pitchers", which secrete nectar and trap insects. Pitchers yellow-green. Flowers (not shown) yellow, in spring.

Sauromatum venosum
(Araceae)

Common names: Monarch of the East; voodoo lily
Height: 45cm (18in)
Spread: 20cm (8in)
Aspect: Half shade
Soil: Well-drained, acidic, humus-rich, fertile
Hardiness: Zone 10
Propagation: Offsets, in winter when dormant

Tuberous perennial. Spathe green, spotted black, spadix long, arched, foul-smelling, in spring to summer, then a single leaf stem with a crown of lance-shaped segments.

Saururus cernuus
(Saururaceae)

Common names: Lizard's tail; swamp lily
Height: 1.2m (4ft)
Spread: 60cm (2ft)
Aspect: Sun
Soil: Wet
Hardiness: Zone 5
Propagation: Seed, when ripe

A rhizomatous perennial from the U.S.A. Leaves heart-shaped, pointed, mid-green. Flowers small, in arching spikes, white, in early summer.

Saxifraga fortunei
A.G.M. (4)
(Saxifragaceae)

Common name: Saxifrage
Height: 30cm (1ft)
Spread: 30cm (1ft)
Aspect: Full or half shade
Soil: Moist, well-drained, humus-rich
Hardiness: Zone 7
Propagation: Seed, in autumn; division, in spring

Clump-forming perennial. Leaves rounded, scalloped, 7-lobed, mid-green, red beneath. Flowers in large, wide panicles, small, starry, white, from early autumn to early winter.

SAXIFRAGA (Saxifragaceae)
Saxifrage

A genus of over 400 species of perennials, biennials, and a few annuals, found in mountain habitats, principally in the northern hemisphere. The great majority of species are cushion-forming or mat-forming alpine plants that are more suited to the rock garden than the herbaceous border, but some make good ground cover; *Saxifraga* x *urbium* is excellent for this, even in the poorest of soils. The genus is a complex one botanically, subdivided into sections as outlined below. The species vary greatly in both their habit and their leaf form, but the leaves of all are in rosettes, and many are evergreen. In a monocarpic saxifrage, only the flowering rosette dies, not the plant; new rosettes will replace the old. The flowers are small, cup-shaped or star-shaped, and may be borne singly or in racemes, cymes or panicles; they are generally pink, white, or yellow. Saxifrages are low-allergen plants. Many species are difficult to cultivate in the open garden, as they must be completely protected from winter wet, so must be given overhead cover. These types are really only suitable for growing in an alpine house, and are therefore not covered here. Slugs are the most common problem with the saxifrages that can be grown outside.

Saxifraga 'Flore Pleno' (*granulata*) (11) (Saxifragaceae)

Common names: Fair maids of France; meadow saxifrage
Height: 35cm (14in)
Spread: 30cm (12in)
Aspect: Sun or light shade
Soil: Moist, sharply drained, humus-rich
Hardiness: Zone 5
Propagation: Seed, in autumn; division, in spring

Bulbous perennial. Leaves in loose rosettes, kidney-shaped, toothed, mid-green. Flowers in panicles, on sticky stems, double white, in late spring; summer dormant.

Saxifraga 'Southside Seedling' A.G.M. (7) (Saxifragaceae)

Common names: None
Height: 30cm (1ft)
Spread: 30cm (1ft)
Aspect: Sun or half shade; shaded from midday sun
Soil: Moist, sharply drained, humus-rich
Hardiness: Zone 7
Propagation: Division, in spring

A hybrid saxifrage. Leaves in rosettes, spoon-shaped, light green. Flowers in arched panicles, cup-shaped, white, spotted red, in late spring and early summer.

Saxifraga stolonifera A.G.M. (4) (Saxifragaceae)

Common name: Mother of thousands
Height: 30cm (1ft)
Spread: 30cm (1ft)
Aspect: Full or half shade
Soil: Moist, well-drained, humus-rich
Hardiness: Zone 6
Propagation: Seed, in autumn; division, in spring

A stoloniferous perennial from Japan and China. Leaves in rosettes or tufts, rounded, mid-green. Flowers in loose panicles, tiny, white, spotted red or yellow, in summer.

Saxifraga 'Tumbling Waters' A.G.M. (7) (Saxifragaceae)

Common name: Saxifrage
Height: 45cm (18in)
Spread: 30cm (12in)
Aspect: Sun
Soil: Sharply drained, fertile
Hardiness: Zone 7
Propagation: Division, in spring

Hybrid perennial. Leaves in large, tight rosettes, linear, silver-green, lime-encrusted. Flowers only after a few years, small, white cups, in dense, arched panicles, in spring.

Saxifraga x *urbium* A.G.M. (3) (Saxifragaceae)

Common name: London pride
Height: 30cm (1ft)
Spread: Indefinite
Aspect: Full or half shade
Soil: Moist, well-drained, humus-rich
Hardiness: Zone 6
Propagation: Seed, in autumn; division, in spring

Rampant ground cover. Leaves in large rosettes, leathery, toothed, mid-green spoons. Flowers in upright, loose panicles, small, white stars, flushed pink, in summer.

CLASSIFICATION of SAXIFRAGE by G. Hegi, 1975

Classes 3, 4, 7, 8, 11 and 12 are of general horticultural interest.

Class 1 Micranthes

Class 2 Hirculus

Class 3 Gymnopera

Class 4 Diptera

Class 5 Trachyphyllum

Class 6 Xanthizoon

Class 7 Aizoonia

Class 8 Porophyllum

Class 9 Porophyrion

Class 10 Miscopetalum

Class 11 Saxifraga

Class 12 Trachyphylloides

Class 13 Cymbalaria

Class 14 Discogyne

Saxifraga veitchiana
(4)
(Saxifragaceae)

Common name: Saxifrage
Height: 30cm (1ft)
Spread: Indefinite
Aspect: Full or half shade
Soil: Moist, well-drained, humus-rich
Hardiness: Zone 7
Propagation: Seed, in autumn; division, in spring

Stoloniferous, evergreen ground cover from China. Leaves rounded, crenate, matt green, red-brown below. Flowers in loose panicles, tiny, white, in late spring and early summer.

Scabiosa atropurpurea
(Dipsacaceae)

Common names: Pincushion flower; sweet scabious
Height: 90cm (36in)
Spread: 25cm (10in)
Aspect: Sun
Soil: Well-drained, fertile
Hardiness: Zone 7
Propagation: Seed, when ripe or in spring; division, in spring

A short-lived perennial from S Europe. Leaves basal, spoon-shaped, and stem, pinnatifid, mid-green. Flowers solitary, perfumed, dark purple, in summer.

Scabiosa caucasica
'Clive Greaves' A.G.M.
(Dipsacaceae)

Common names: Pincushion flower; scabious
Height: 60cm (2ft)
Spread: 60cm (2ft)
Aspect: Sun
Soil: Well-drained, fertile
Hardiness: Zone 4
Propagation: Seed, when ripe or in spring; division, in spring

A selected form of a hardy, clump-forming perennial from the Caucasus. Leaves lance-shaped, grey-green. Flowers solitary, domed, double, lavender, all summer if dead-headed.

Scabiosa columbaria
var. *ochroleuca*
(Dipsacaceae)

Common name: Small scabious
Height: 75cm (30in)
Spread: 90cm (36in)
Aspect: Sun
Soil: Well-drained, fertile
Hardiness: Zone 6
Propagation: Seed, when ripe or in spring; division, in spring

Perennial from Eurasia. Leaves basal, and stem, pinnatifid, greyish-green. Flowers solitary, lemon-yellow, from summer to early autumn. Superb for flower-arranging.

***Schoenoplectus lacustris* subsp. *tabernaemontani* 'Zebrinus'**

Common name: Club rush
Height: 1m (3ft)
Spread: 60cm (2ft)
Aspect: Sun
Soil: Wet, or marginal aquatic
Hardiness: Zone 7
Propagation: Division, from spring to summer

Rhizomatous perennial. Stems from rhizome leafless, grey-green, banded creamy-white. Flowers brown, spikelets, in clusters, from early to late summer.

Schizostylis coccinea
f. *alba*
(Iridaceae)

Common name: Kaffir lily
Height: 60cm (2ft)
Spread: 30cm (1ft)
Aspect: Sun
Soil: Moist to wet, well-drained, fertile
Hardiness: Zone 6
Propagation: Seed or division, both in spring

Rhizomatous evergreen from southern Africa. Leaves erect, narrow-linear, pointed, mid-green. Flowers in spikes, open cups, white, in autumn. Soon becomes congested.

Schizostylis coccinea
'Major' A.G.M.
(Iridaceae)

Common name: Kaffir lily
Height: 60cm (2ft)
Spread: 30cm (1ft)
Aspect: Sun
Soil: Moist to wet, well-drained, fertile
Hardiness: Zone 6
Propagation: Seed or division, both in spring

Rhizomatous evergreen from southern Africa. Leaves erect, sword-shaped, mid-green. Flowers in spikes, open cups, red, in autumn. Becomes congested rapidly.

Schizostylis coccinea
'Professor Barnard'
(Iridaceae)

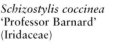

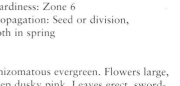

Common name: Kaffir lily
Height: 60cm (2ft)
Spread: 30cm (1ft)
Aspect: Sun
Soil: Moist to wet, well-drained, fertile
Hardiness: Zone 6
Propagation: Seed or division, both in spring

Rhizomatous evergreen. Flowers large, deep dusky pink. Leaves erect, sword-shaped, mid-green. Rapidly becomes overcrowded; lift and divide regularly.

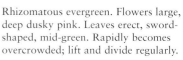

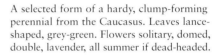

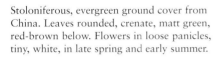

Saxifrages such as 'Southside Seedling' *need sharply drained soil; their low clumps of rosetted leaves suit a stone trough or a rock garden.*

Schizostylis coccinea 'Sunrise' A.G.M. (Iridaceae)

Common name: Kaffir lily
Height: 60cm (2ft)
Spread: 30cm (1ft)
Aspect: Sun
Soil: Moist to wet, well-drained, fertile
Hardiness: Zone 6
Propagation: Division, in spring

Selected form of rhizomatous evergreen, with large, salmon-pink flowers in autumn. Leaves evergreen, erect, pointed, mid-green. Rapidly becomes congested.

Scilla natalensis (Hyacinthaceae/Liliaceae)

Common names: None
Height: 1.2m (4ft)
Spread: 10cm (4in)
Aspect: Sun or half shade
Soil: Well-drained, fertile, humus-rich
Hardiness: Zone 9
Propagation: Seed, when ripe; offsets, when dormant

Bulbous perennial from South Africa. Leaves basal, lance-shaped, mid-green. Bears tall racemes of up to 100 small, flat, lilac-blue, pink or white flowers, in summer.

Scilla peruviana (Hyacinthaceae/Liliaceae)

Common names: None
Height: 45cm (18in)
Spread: 30cm (12in)
Aspect: Sun or half shade
Soil: Well-drained, fertile, humus-rich
Hardiness: Zone 8
Propagation: Seed, when ripe; offsets, when dormant

Bulbous Mediterranean plant; named for the ship it came to Britain on, the *Peru*. Leaves in basal clusters, lance-shaped. Flowers deep blue stars in conical racemes.

Scopolia carniolica (Solanaceae)

Common names: None
Height: 45cm (18in)
Spread: 60cm (24in)
Aspect: Half shade
Soil: Moist, well-drained, humus-rich
Hardiness: Zone 5
Propagation: Seed, in autumn or spring; division, in spring

A poisonous, rhizomatous perennial from Europe and the Caucasus. Leaves ovate, veined, wrinkled, mid-green. Flowers solitary, pendent, brown-purple bells, spring.

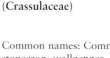

Scrophularia auriculata 'Variegata' (Scrophulariaceae)

Common name: Figwort
Height: 75cm (30in)
Spread: 60cm (24in)
Aspect: Half shade
Soil: Moist to wet or marginal aquatic
Hardiness: Zone 5
Propagation: Division, in spring

Perennial from Europe. Leaves large, ovate, wrinkled, toothed, pale green, marked pink and cream. Flowers insignificant, in cymes, yellowish-green, in summer to autumn.

Scutellaria incana (Labiatae/Lamiaceae)

Common names: Helmet flower; skullcap
Height: 1.2m (4ft)
Spread: 60cm (2ft)
Aspect: Sun or half shade
Soil: Sharply drained, alkaline, fertile
Hardiness: Zone 5
Propagation: Seed, in spring; division, in spring or autumn

A perennial from the U.S.A. Leaves ovate, toothed, hairy, crenate, sage-grey. Flowers in corymbs, tubular, 2-lipped, blue, in summer, and again later if dead-headed.

Scutellaria integrifolia (Labiatae/Lamiaceae)

Common name: Lyre-leaved sage
Height: 60cm (2ft)
Spread: 30cm (1ft)
Aspect: Sun or half shade
Soil: Sharply drained, alkaline, fertile
Hardiness: Zone 5
Propagation: Seed, in spring; division, in spring or autumn

A perennial from the eastern U.S.A. Leaves ovate, hairy, mid-green. Flowers tubular, 2-lipped, lilac-blue, in racemes, in late spring to early summer.

Sedum acre (Crassulaceae)

Common names: Common stonecrop; wallpepper
Height: 5cm (2in)
Spread: 80cm (32in)
Aspect: Sun
Soil: Sharply drained, alkaline, fertile
Hardiness: Zone 5
Propagation: Seed, in autumn; softwood cuttings of blind shoots, in early summer

Creeping, evergreen perennial from Turkey, North Africa and Europe. Leaves triangular, light green. Flowers in cymes, yellow-green stars, over a long period in summer.

SEDUM (Crassulaceae)
Stonecrop

A wide genus of some 400 species, encompassing annuals, biennials, deciduous, semi-evergreen and evergreen perennials, subshrubs and shrubs from both hemispheres. Their habitats in the wild vary from mountainous areas, where most are found, to arid regions of South America. As a result, they vary widely from dwarf, rock-garden plants (the predominant type) to fairly tall plants, eminently suitable for beds or borders. Some of the smaller species can be quite invasive. Stonecrops prefer sun, but some will tolerate light shade. They are drought-tolerant, and prefer light, well-drained soils; the border types will grow in almost all soils, but become lush and need to be staked if grown in over-fertile conditions. The foliage of stonecrops is of a thick, fleshy, succulent nature, although the arrangement and form of the leaves is very variable. The flowers appear in summer and autumn. They are mostly 5-petalled and star-shaped, and borne in usually terminal corymbs, panicles or cymes. The flowers are beloved of butterflies, especially those of *Sedum spectabile*. Unfortunately, slugs and snails are also fond of the leaves. All parts of the plants are poisonous, and contact with the sap may cause skin irritation.

Sedum acre
'Aureum'
(Crassulaceae)

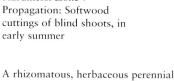

Common names: Common stonecrop; wallpepper
Height: 10cm (4in)
Spread: 20cm (8in)
Aspect: Sun
Soil: Well-drained, alkaline, fertile
Hardiness: Zone 5
Propagation: Softwood cuttings of blind shoots, in early summer

A form of the species in which the leaves and flowers are bright yellow. Very good for a scree garden or the front of a border, and a superb backdrop for butterflies.

Sedum aizoon
'Euphorbioides'
(Crassulaceae)

Common name: Stonecrop
Height: 35cm (14in)
Spread: 30cm (12in)
Aspect: Sun
Soil: Well-drained, alkaline
Hardiness: Zone 7
Propagation: Softwood cuttings of blind shoots, in early summer

A rhizomatous, herbaceous perennial from Japan and China. Leaves ovate, toothed, dark green. Flowers in terminal clusters, star-shaped, orange-yellow, in summer.

Sedum alboroseum
'Mediovariegatum'
(Crassulaceae)

Common name: Stonecrop
Height: 45cm (18in)
Spread: 30cm (12in)
Aspect: Sun
Soil: Well-drained, alkaline
Hardiness: Zone 4
Propagation: Softwood cuttings of blind shoots, in early summer

Also known as *S. erythrostictum*; from Asia. Leaves ovate, cream, margined green. Flowers in terminal clusters, greenish-white stars, in late summer.

Sedum populifolium
(Crassulaceae)

Common name: Stonecrop
Height: 30cm (12in)
Spread: 45cm (18in)
Aspect: Sun
Soil: Well-drained, alkaline
Hardiness: Zone 4
Propagation: Softwood cuttings of blind shoots, in early summer

A deciduous perennial from Siberia. Leaves ovate, toothed, pale green. Flowers scented, in many-flowered cymes, pinkish-white, star-shaped, in late summer and early autumn.

Sedum
'Ruby Glow' A.G.M.
(Crassulaceae)

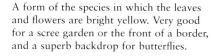

Common name: Stonecrop
Height: 30cm (12in)
Spread: 45cm (18in)
Aspect: Sun
Soil: Well-drained, alkaline
Hardiness: Zone 7
Propagation: Softwood cuttings of blind shoots, in early summer

Hybrid perennial. Leaves elliptic, toothed, purple-green. Flowers star-shaped, ruby-coloured, in loose, many-flowered cymes, from summer to early autumn.

Sedum rupestre
(Crassulaceae)

Common name: Stone orpine
Height: 15cm (6in)
Spread: 60cm (24in)
Aspect: Sun
Soil: Well-drained, alkaline
Hardiness: Zone 4
Propagation: Softwood cuttings of blind shoots, in early summer

An evergreen, mat-forming ground cover from the mountains of Europe. Leaves linear, grey-green. Flowers in terminal cymes, star-shaped, yellow, in summer.

Sedum spectabile
A.G.M.
(Crassulaceae)

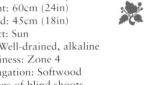

Common name: Ice plant
Height: 45cm (18in)
Spread: 45cm (18in)
Aspect: Sun
Soil: Well-drained, alkaline
Hardiness: Zone 4
Propagation: Softwood cuttings of blind shoots, in early summer

Clump-forming perennial from Japan and China. Leaves fleshy, ovate, toothed, light green. Flowers in dense, flat-topped cymes, star-shaped, pink, late summer to autumn.

Sedum telephium
'Abbeydore'
(Crassulaceae)

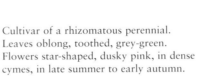

Common name: Orpine
Height: 60cm (2ft)
Spread: 30cm (1ft)
Aspect: Sun
Soil: Well-drained, alkaline
Hardiness: Zone 4
Propagation: Softwood cuttings of blind shoots, in early summer

Cultivar of a rhizomatous perennial. Leaves oblong, toothed, grey-green. Flowers star-shaped, dusky pink, in dense cymes, in late summer to early autumn.

Sedum telephium
'Arthur Branch'
(Crassulaceae)

Common name: Orpine
Height: 60cm (2ft)
Spread: 30cm (1ft)
Aspect: Sun
Soil: Well-drained, alkaline
Hardiness: Zone 4
Propagation: Softwood cuttings of blind shoots, in early summer

Cultivar of a rhizomatous perennial from Eurasia and the Far East. Leaves oblong, toothed, light green. Flowers dusky red, in dense cymes, late summer to early autumn.

***Sedum telephium* subsp. *maximum* 'Atropurpureum' A.G.M.** (Crassulaceae)

Common name: Orpine
Height: 60cm (24in)
Spread: 45cm (18in)
Aspect: Sun
Soil: Well-drained, alkaline
Hardiness: Zone 4
Propagation: Softwood cuttings of blind shoots, in early summer

A form of the species with dark purple stems and glaucous, dark purple leaves. Flowers in cymes, star-shaped, purple-red, in late summer and early autumn.

Sedum telephium
subsp. *ruprechtii*
(Crassulaceae)

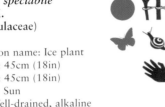

Common name: Orpine
Height: 60cm (24in)
Spread: 45cm (18in)
Aspect: Sun
Soil: Well-drained, alkaline
Hardiness: Zone 4
Propagation: Softwood cuttings of blind shoots, in early summer

A naturally occurring form of the orpine with glaucous, blue-green leaves and creamy-pink, star-shaped flowers, in late summer and early autumn.

Selaginella kraussiana
A.G.M.
(Selaginellaceae)

Common name: Krauss's spikemoss
Height: 2.5cm (1in)
Spread: Indefinite
Aspect: Half shade
Soil: Well-drained, acidic, humus-rich, fertile
Hardiness: Zone 9
Propagation: Spores, in warmth as soon as ripe; division, in spring

A tender, evergreen, mat-forming perennial from the Azores and southern Africa. Stems covered in pinnatisect foliage of bright green.

Semiaquilegia ecalcarata
(Ranunculaceae)

Common names: None
Height: 30cm (12in)
Spread: 20cm (8in)
Aspect: Sun or half shade
Soil: Well-drained, acidic, humus-rich
Hardiness: Zone 6
Propagation: Seed, when ripe

A short-lived perennial from China. Leaves 2-ternate, mid-green, purple below. Flowers in loose panicles, pendent, pink bells, in early summer.

Sempervivum
arachnoideum
A.G.M. (Crassulaceae)

Common name: Cobweb houseleek
Height: 10cm (4in)
Spread: 30cm (12in)
Aspect: Sun
Soil: Very sharply drained, humus-rich
Hardiness: Zone 5
Propagation: Seed, in spring; offsets, in spring to early summer

Evergreen, rosette-forming succulent from the Alps. Leaves fleshy, obovate, green or red, in cobwebbed rosettes. Flowers in flat cymes, on leafy stems, pink, in summer.

Senecio cineraria
(Asteraceae/Compositae)

Common names: None
Height: 60cm (2ft)
Spread: 60cm (2ft)
Aspect: Sun
Soil: Well-drained, fertile
Hardiness: Zone 8
Propagation: Seed, in spring; semi-ripe cuttings, in summer

An evergreen, Mediterranean subshrub. Leaves ovate, pinnatisect, felted, silver-grey. Flowers in loose corymbs, mustard yellow, in summer.

Senecio pulcher
(Asteraceae/Compositae)

Common names: None
Height: 60cm (24in)
Spread: 45cm (18in)
Aspect: Sun
Soil: Well-drained, fertile
Hardiness: Zone 8
Propagation: Seed, in spring; semi-ripe cuttings, in summer

Perennial from Argentina, Uruguay and Brazil. Leaves basal, elliptic, and stem, lance-shaped, toothed. Flowers in solitary corymbs, carmine-purple, in late autumn.

Senecio viravira
A.G.M.
(Asteraceae/Compositae)

Common names: None
Height: 60cm (2ft)
Spread: 90cm (3ft)
Aspect: Sun
Soil: Well-drained, fertile
Hardiness: Zone 8
Propagation: Seed, in spring; semi-ripe cuttings, in summer

Evergreen subshrub from Argentina. Leaves deeply pinnatisect, with 5 to 9 silver-white leaflets. Flowers of disc florets only, in loose corymbs, off-white, summer to autumn.

Serratula seoanei
(Asteraceae/Compositae)

Common name: Saw-wort
Height: 30cm (12in)
Spread: 20cm (8in)
Aspect: Sun
Soil: Well-drained
Hardiness: Zone 7
Propagation: Seed, in autumn or spring; offsets, in spring

Perennial from Europe. Leaves pinnate, toothed, mid-green. Flowers purple-pink, cornflower-like, on branched stems, solitary or in panicles, in autumn to winter.

Seseli gummiferum
(Apiaceae/Umbelliferae)

Common name: Moon carrot
Height: 1m (3ft)
Spread: 60cm (2ft)
Aspect: Sun
Soil: Well-drained, fertile
Hardiness: Zone 6
Propagation: Seed or division, both in autumn or spring

From the Crimea and Aegean. Leaves 2- or 3-pinnatisect, segments wedge-shaped, hairy, glaucous-green. Flowers in umbels of up to 60, pinkish-white or red, in summer.

Sesleria glauca
(Graminae/Poaceae)

Common name: Moor grass
Height: 30cm (12in)
Spread: 20cm (8in)
Aspect: Sun or half shade
Soil: Well-drained, fertile
Hardiness: Zone 6
Propagation: Seed, in spring or autumn; division, in spring

An evergreen, perennial grass from Eurasia. Leaves narrow, linear, glaucous green. Flowers in dense, cylindrical panicles, greenish-white.

Sidalcea
'Croftway Red'
(Malvaceae)

Common names: False mallow; prairie mallow
Height: 90cm (36in)
Spread: 45cm (18in)
Aspect: Sun
Soil: Moist, well-drained, acidic, fertile
Hardiness: Zone 6
Propagation: Division, in spring or autumn

A hybrid perennial. Leaves round, lobed, mid-green. Flowers in racemes, rich pinkish-red, in early and midsummer. Good for flower arrangements.

Sidalcea
'Elsie Heugh'
(Malvaceae)

Common names: False mallow; prairie mallow
Height: 90cm (36in)
Spread: 45cm (18in)
Aspect: Sun
Soil: Moist, well-drained, acidic, fertile
Hardiness: Zone 6
Propagation: Division, in spring or autumn

Hybrid perennial. Leaves round, shallowly lobed, mid-green. Flowers in racemes, large, satiny, lilac-pink, with frilled petals, in early and midsummer.

Sidalcea
'William Smith' A.G.M.
(Malvaceae)

Common names: False mallow; prairie mallow
Height: 90cm (36in)
Spread: 45cm (18in)
Aspect: Sun
Soil: Moist, well-drained, acidic, fertile
Hardiness: Zone 6
Propagation: Division, in spring or autumn

A hybrid perennial. Leaves round, shallowly lobed, mid-green. Flowers borne in upright racemes, deep pink, in early and midsummer.

Silene dioica
(Caryophyllaceae)

Common name: Red campion
Height: 75cm (30in)
Spread: 45cm (18in)
Aspect: Sun or half shade
Soil: Well-drained, alkaline, fertile
Hardiness: Zone 6
Propagation: Seed, in autumn; basal cuttings, in spring

Clump-forming European perennial. Leaves obovate, dark green. Flowers in branched cymes, round, deep pink with white base and notched petals, in spring and summer.

Silene dioica
'Thelma Kay'
(Caryophyllaceae)

Common name: Red campion
Height: 80cm (32in)
Spread: 45cm (18in)
Aspect: Sun or half shade
Soil: Well-drained, alkaline, fertile
Hardiness: Zone 6
Propagation: Rooted offshoots, from midsummer to autumn

Cultivar of the red campion with variegated foliage and double flowers in late spring to midsummer. Does not self-seed as much as the single form.

Silene uniflora
'Druett's Variegated'
(Caryophyllaceae)

Common names: Bladder campion; sea campion
Height: 20cm (8in)
Spread: 20cm (8in)
Aspect: Sun
Soil: Well-drained, alkaline, fertile
Hardiness: Zone 3
Propagation: Rooted offshoots, from midsummer to autumn

Cultivar of a creeping, semi-evergreen, coastal plant. Leaves lance-shaped, fleshy, cream and green. Flowers white, solitary or in clusters, petals deeply cut, in summer.

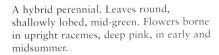

Silene uniflora
'Robin Whitebreast'
(Caryophyllaceae)

Common names: Bladder campion; sea campion
Height: 20cm (8in)
Spread: 30cm (12in)
Aspect: Sun
Soil: Well-drained, alkaline, fertile
Hardiness: Zone 3
Propagation: Rooted offshoots, from midsummer to autumn

A sprawling, hybrid perennial. Leaves lance-shaped, fleshy, green. Flowers solitary or in clusters, white with a green calyx, in summer.

Silphium laciniatum
(Asteraceae/Compositae)

Common names: Compass plant; pilot plant; polar plant
Height: 3m (10ft)
Spread: 60cm (2ft)
Aspect: Sun or half shade
Soil: Moist, fertile, deep, heavy
Hardiness: Zone 4
Propagation: Seed, when ripe; division, in spring

Ovate, bristly, toothed, mid-green leaves, pointing north-south to minimise exposure to sun. Terminal corymbs of dark-centred, yellow daisies, midsummer to early autumn.

Sisyrinchium angustifolium
(Iridaceae)

Common name: Blue-eyed grass
Height: 50cm (20in)
Spread: 15cm (6in)
Aspect: Sun
Soil: Well-drained, alkaline, fertile
Hardiness: Zone 3
Propagation: Seed, in spring; division, in spring or autumn

A clump-forming perennial from North America. Leaves linear, mid-green. Flowers solitary, single, blue with a yellow throat, in summer.

Sisyrinchium
'Californian Skies'
(Iridaceae)

Common name: Blue-eyed grass
Height: 15cm (6in)
Spread: 10cm (4in)
Aspect: Sun
Soil: Well-drained, alkaline, fertile
Hardiness: Zone 8
Propagation: Division, in spring or autumn

Short-lived, rhizomatous hybrid. Leaves basal, sword-shaped, grey-green. Flowers large, flat, blue, dark-centred, in clusters, surrounded by bracts, spring and summer.

Sisyrinchium californicum
Brachypus Group
(Iridaceae)

Common name: Yellow-eyed grass
Height: 60cm (24in)
Spread: 15cm (6in)
Aspect: Sun
Soil: Well-drained, alkaline, fertile
Hardiness: Zone 8
Propagation: Seed, in spring; division, in spring or autumn

A rhizomatous perennial from North America. Leaves sword-shaped, grey-green. Flowers small, solitary stars, yellow with dark veins, in succession, in summer.

Sisyrinchium idahoense
'Album'
(Iridaceae)

Common names: None
Height: 15cm (6in)
Spread: 15cm (6in)
Aspect: Sun
Soil: Well-drained, alkaline, fertile
Hardiness: Zone 3
Propagation: Seed, in spring; division, in spring or autumn

A rhizomatous perennial from the U.S.A. Leaves narrowly linear, mid-green. Flowers star-shaped, white with yellow throats, in summer.

Sisyrinchium
'Quaint and Queer'
(Iridaceae)

Common name: Blue-eyed grass
Height: 20cm (8in)
Spread: 20cm (8in)
Aspect: Sun
Soil: Well-drained, alkaline, fertile
Hardiness: Zone 7
Propagation: Division, in spring or autumn

A hybrid, rhizomatous perennial. Leaves basal, narrowly linear, mid-green. Flowers small, star-shaped, yellow, brown and purple, in summer.

Sisyrinchium striatum
(Iridaceae)

Common names: None
Height: 90cm (3ft)
Spread: 30cm (1ft)
Aspect: Sun
Soil: Well-drained, alkaline, fertile
Hardiness: Zone 8
Propagation: Seed, in spring; division, in spring or autumn

Rhizomatous evergreen from Argentina and Chile. Leaves basal, linear, stiff, grey-green. Flowers in clusters, stemless, pale yellow cups, early to midsummer. Black seed heads.

Sisyrinchium striatum
'Aunt May'
(Iridaceae)

Common names: None
Height: 90cm (3ft)
Spread: 30cm (1ft)
Aspect: Sun
Soil: Well-drained, alkaline, fertile
Hardiness: Zone 8
Propagation: Division, in spring or autumn

A form of the species with leaves striped green and cream. Yellow, stemless flowers in clusters in early to midsummer, followed by attractive seed heads.

Smilacina racemosa
A.G.M.
(Convallariaceae/Liliaceae)

Common name: False Solomon's seal
Height: 1m (3ft)
Spread: 60cm (2ft)
Aspect: Full or half shade
Soil: Moist, well-drained, acidic, humus-rich, fertile
Hardiness: Zone 4
Propagation: Seed, in autumn; division, in spring

Rhizomatous woodlander. Leaves ovate to lance-shaped, mid-green. Flowers scented, creamy-white stars, in terminal racemes, in spring, sometimes followed by red berries.

Solenopsis axillaris
(Campanulaceae)

Common names: None
Height: 30cm (1ft)
Spread: 30cm (1ft)
Aspect: Sun
Soil: Well-drained, fertile
Hardiness: Zone 9
Propagation: Seed, in warmth in spring; softwood cuttings, in summer

A tender perennial from Australia. Leaves ovate, pinnatisect, leaflets narrow, mid-green. Flowers small, star-shaped, pale blue, abundant, from spring to autumn.

Solidago
'Goldenmosa' A.G.M.
(Asteraceae/Compositae)

Common name: Golden rod
Height: 80cm (32in)
Spread: 45cm (18in)
Aspect: Sun
Soil: Sharply drained, fertile
Hardiness: Zone 4
Propagation: Division, in autumn or spring

Woody hybrid. Leaves wrinkled, mid-green, lance-shaped. Flowers tiny, yellow, in one-sided, conical panicles, late summer and autumn. Dead-head to prevent self-seeding.

Golden rods such as Solidago elongata *are impressive in gardens that can accommodate their tendency to abundant self-seeding.*

× Solidaster luteus
(Asteraceae/Compositae)

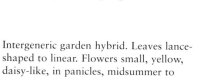

Common names: None
Height: 1m (3ft)
Spread: 30cm (1ft)
Aspect: Sun
Soil: Well-drained, fertile
Hardiness: Zone 6
Propagation: Basal cuttings or division, both in spring

Intergeneric garden hybrid. Leaves lance-shaped to linear. Flowers small, yellow, daisy-like, in panicles, midsummer to autumn. Dead-head to prevent self-seeding.

× Solidaster luteus
'Lemore' A.G.M.
(Asteraceae/Compositae)

Common names: None
Height: 80cm (32in)
Spread: 30cm (12in)
Aspect: Sun
Soil: Well-drained, fertile
Hardiness: Zone 6
Propagation: Division, in spring

Selected form of intergeneric garden hybrid, with panicles of small, daisy-like flowers of pale lemon. Leaves lance-shaped to linear. Dead-head to prevent self-seeding.

Sparaxis elegans
(Iridaceae)

Common name: Harlequin flower
Height: 45cm (18in)
Spread: 10cm (4in)
Aspect: Sun
Soil: Well-drained, fertile
Hardiness: Zone 9
Propagation: Seed, when ripe; offsets, when dormant

Cormous perennial from South Africa. Leaves basal, in fans, sword-shaped, bright green. Flowers in spikes, wide funnels, red, orange or white, in spring and summer.

Sphaeralcea fendleri
(Malvaceae)

Common names: False mallow; globe mallow
Height: 80cm (32in)
Spread: 60cm (24in)
Aspect: Sun
Soil: Sharply drained, fertile
Hardiness: Zone 8
Propagation: Seed, in spring; softwood cuttings, in summer

Sprawling subshrub from the U.S.A. Leaves ovate, 3-lobed, toothed, grey-green. Flowers in axillary panicles, pink saucers, in summer. Prune to keep compact.

Sphaeralcea munroana
(Malvaceae)

Common names: False mallow; globe mallow
Height: 80cm (32in)
Spread: 90cm (36in)
Aspect: Sun
Soil: Well-drained, fertile
Hardiness: Zone 8
Propagation: Seed, in spring; softwood cuttings, in summer

Sprawling perennial. Leaves ovate to diamond-shaped, 3- to 5-lobed, grey-green. Flowers in axillary panicles, salmon-pink saucers, over a very long period in summer.

Spiranthes gracilis
(Orchidaceae)

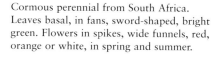

Common name: Nodding ladies' tresses
Height: 75cm (30in)
Spread: 10cm (4in)
Aspect: Half shade
Soil: Moist, well-drained, humus-rich, fertile
Hardiness: Zone 3
Propagation: Division, when dormant

A hardy, tuberous, terrestrial orchid from North America. Leaves basal, ovate, mid-green. Flowers in spiral racemes, small, white, perfumed, in autumn.

Stachys byzantina
(Labiatae/Lamiaceae)

Common name: Lamb's ears
Height: 45cm (18in)
Spread: 60cm (24in)
Aspect: Sun
Soil: Well-drained, fertile
Hardiness: Zone 5
Propagation: Seed, in autumn or spring; division, in spring

Mat-forming perennial. Leaves in basal rosettes, oblong, veined, densely white-woolly. Flowers in spikes, pink-purple, woolly, from early summer to autumn

Stachys macrantha
(Labiatae/Lamiaceae)

Common names: None
Height: 60cm (2ft)
Spread: 30cm (1ft)
Aspect: Sun or half shade
Soil: Well-drained, fertile
Hardiness: Zone 5
Propagation: Seed, in autumn or spring; division, in spring

Leaves ovate, scalloped, veined, wrinkled, deep green. Flowers in dense spikes, hooded, purplish-pink, from early summer to early autumn.

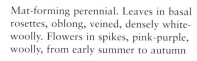

Stachys macrantha
'Superba'
(Labiatae/Lamiaceae)

Common names: None
Height: 60cm (2ft)
Spread: 30cm (1ft)
Aspect: Sun or half shade
Soil: Well-drained, fertile
Hardiness: Zone 5
Propagation: Seed, in autumn or spring; division, in spring

A form of the species with dense spikes of purplish, hooded flowers. Leaves ovate, scalloped, veined, wrinkled, deep green. Top-heavy, especially in rain; needs staking.

Stachys monieri
(Labiatae/Lamiaceae)

Common names: None
Height: 50cm (20in)
Spread: 45cm (18in)
Aspect: Sun
Soil: Well-drained, fertile
Hardiness: Zone 5
Propagation: Seed, in autumn or spring; division, in spring

A perennial from the Alps and Pyrenees. Leaves in basal rosette, ovate, crinkled, glossy, dark green. Flowers in spikes, pale pink, white or deep pink, in late summer.

Stachys officinalis
(Labiatae/Lamiaceae)

Common names: Bishop's wort; wood betony
Height: 60cm (2ft)
Spread: 30cm (1ft)
Aspect: Sun or half shade
Soil: Well-drained, fertile
Hardiness: Zone 5
Propagation: Seed, in autumn or spring; division, in spring

Perennial from Europe. Leaves in rosettes, ovate, veined, wrinkled, scalloped, mid-green. Flowers in dense spikes, purplish-red, white or pink, all summer.

Stipa gigantea
A.G.M.
(Graminae/Poaceae)

Common names: Giant feather grass; golden oats
Height: 2.5m (8ft)
Spread: 1.2m (4ft)
Aspect: Sun
Soil: Well-drained, fertile, light
Hardiness: Zone 8
Propagation: Seed or division, both in spring

Evergreen grass from the Iberian peninsula. Leaves long, linear, inrolled, mid-green. Flowers silvery, green-purple spikes, turning gold, in panicles in summer.

Stokesia laevis
(Asteraceae/Compositae)

Common name: Stokes' aster
Height: 60cm (24in)
Spread: 45cm (18in)
Aspect: Sun
Soil: Moist, well-drained, acidic, light, fertile
Hardiness: Zone 5
Propagation: Seed, in autumn; division, in spring

Rosette-forming evergreen. Leaves basal, lance-shaped, spiny, with white midribs. Flowers solitary, cornflower-like, purplish-pink, centre paler, midsummer to autumn.

Stokesia laevis
'Alba'
(Asteraceae/Compositae)

Common name: White Stokes' aster
Height: 60cm (24in)
Spread: 45cm (18in)
Aspect: Sun
Soil: Moist, well-drained, acidic, light, fertile
Hardiness: Zone 5
Propagation: Seed, in autumn; division, in spring

Form of the species with cornflower-like, solitary, white flowers from midsummer to autumn. Leaves in basal rosette, evergreen, lance-shaped, spiny, with white midribs.

Strelitzia reginae
A.G.M.
(Musaceae/Strelitziaceae)

Common name: Bird of paradise
Height: 1.8m (6ft)
Spread: 90cm (3ft)
Aspect: Sun or half shade
Soil: Moist, well-drained, humus-rich, fertile
Hardiness: Zone 9
Propagation: Seed or division, both in spring

Evergreen from South Africa. Leaves oblong to lance-shaped, mid-green. Flowers have green spathes, flushed purple-red, yellow calyces, blue corollas, in winter to spring.

Strobilanthes atropurpureus
(Acanthaceae)

Common names: None
Height: 1.2m (4ft)
Spread: 90cm (3ft)
Aspect: Sun or half shade
Soil: Sharply drained, fertile
Hardiness: Zone 5
Propagation: Seed or basal or softwood cuttings, all in warmth in spring

A perennial from N India. Leaves large, ovate, toothed, dark green. Flowers tubular, indigo-blue, borne in dense spikes, in summer.

Stylophorum diphyllum
(Papaveraceae)

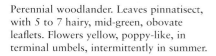

Common name: Celandine poppy
Height: 30cm (1ft)
Spread: 30cm (1ft)
Aspect: Full or half shade
Soil: Moist, humus-rich, fertile
Hardiness: Zone 7
Propagation: Seed, in autumn; division, in spring

Perennial woodlander. Leaves pinnatisect, with 5 to 7 hairy, mid-green, obovate leaflets. Flowers yellow, poppy-like, in terminal umbels, intermittently in summer.

Stylophorum lasiocarpum
(Papaveraceae)

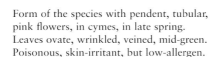

Common names: None
Height: 45cm (18in)
Spread: 30cm (12in)
Aspect: Full or half shade
Soil: Moist, humus-rich, fertile
Hardiness: Zone 7
Propagation: Seed, in autumn; division, in spring

Perennial woodlander from China. Leaves pinnatifid, with 4 to 7 oblong, toothed lobes, mid-green. Flowers in terminal clusters, yellow, poppy-like, in summer.

Symphyandra armena
(Campanulaceae)

Common name: Ring bellflower
Height: 45cm (18in)
Spread: 30cm (12in)
Aspect: Sun or half shade
Soil: Well-drained, fertile
Hardiness: Zone 7
Propagation: Seed, when ripe or in spring

Rhizomatous plant from Turkey and Iran. Leaves heart-shaped, velvety-hairy, toothed, mid-green. Flowers in corymbs, pendent, tubular, pale blue, long period in summer.

Symphytum
'Goldsmith'
(Boraginaceae)

Common name: Comfrey
Height: 30cm (1ft)
Spread: 30cm (1ft)
Aspect: Sun or half shade
Soil: Moist, fertile
Hardiness: Zone 5
Propagation: Division, in spring; root cuttings, in early winter

Rhizomatous ground cover. Leaves ovate to lance-shaped, dark green, variegated cream and gold. Flowers in cymes, pale blue, mid- and late spring. Toxic and skin-irritant.

Symphytum ibericum
(Boraginaceae)

Common name: Comfrey
Height: 40cm (16in)
Spread: Indefinite
Aspect: Sun or half shade
Soil: Moist, fertile
Hardiness: Zone 5
Propagation: Seed, in autumn or spring; division, in spring

Invasive, rhizomatous plant. Leaves ovate, wrinkled, veined, mid-green. Flowers tubular, pendent, white or pale yellow, in cymes, in late spring. Toxic and irritant.

Symphytum ibericum
'Langthornes Pink'
(Boraginaceae)

Common name: Comfrey
Height: 40cm (16in)
Spread: 45cm (18in)
Aspect: Sun or half shade
Soil: Moist, fertile
Hardiness: Zone 5
Propagation: Division, in spring; root cuttings, in early winter

Form of the species with pendent, tubular, pink flowers, in cymes, in late spring. Leaves ovate, wrinkled, veined, mid-green. Poisonous, skin-irritant, but low-allergen.

Symphytum
'Lambrook Sunrise'
(Boraginaceae)

Common name: Comfrey
Height: 55cm (22in)
Spread: 30cm (12in)
Aspect: Sun or half shade
Soil: Moist, fertile
Hardiness: Zone 5
Propagation: Division, in spring; root cuttings, in early winter

A form which is non-invasive, and has leaves of acid yellow. Flowers in cymes, tubular, blue, in spring, making a lovely contrast to the foliage. Toxic and irritant.

Symphytum orientale
(Boraginaceae)

Common names: Comfrey
Height: 70cm (28in)
Spread: 45cm (18in)
Aspect: Sun or half shade
Soil: Moist, fertile
Hardiness: Zone 5
Propagation: Seed, in autumn or spring; division, in spring

Rhizomatous perennial from Europe. Leaves ovate-oblong, densely hairy, mid-green. Flowers in many-flowered cymes, pendent, tubular, white, in summer. Toxic, irritant.

Symphytum x *uplandicum*
(Boraginaceae)

Common names: None
Height: 1.8m (6ft)
Spread: 1.2m (4ft)
Aspect: Sun or half shade
Soil: Moist, fertile
Hardiness: Zone 5
Propagation: Seed, in autumn or spring; division, in spring

A rhizomatous hybrid of garden origin. Leaves basal, elliptic to lance-shaped, mid-green. Flowers in cymes, lilac-blue, from late spring to late summer.

Symphytum x *uplandicum*
'Axminster Gold'
(Boraginaceae)

Common names: None
Height: 1.8m (6ft)
Spread: 1.2m (4ft)
Aspect: Sun or half shade
Soil: Moist, well-drained
Hardiness: Zone 5
Propagation: Division, in spring; root cuttings, in early winter

A variegated and non-invasive form of this garden hybrid, with elliptic to lance-shaped leaves margined pale gold. Flowers white, in cymes, from late spring to late summer.

Symphytum x *uplandicum*
'Variegatum' A.G.M.
(Boraginaceae)

Common names: None
Height: 1.8m (6ft)
Spread: 1.2m (4ft)
Aspect: Sun or half shade
Soil: Moist, fertile
Hardiness: Zone 5
Propagation: Division, in spring; root cuttings, in early winter

A non-invasive cultivar of this hybrid, with elliptic to lance-shaped leaves variegated heavily in yellow. Flowers in cymes, lilac, from late spring to late summer.

Tanacetum coccineum
'Brenda' A.G.M.
(Asteraceae/Compositae)

Common names: Painted daisy; pyrethrum
Height: 75cm (30in)
Spread: 45cm (18in)
Aspect: Sun
Soil: Sharply drained
Hardiness: Zone 5
Propagation: Division or basal cuttings, both in spring

Clump-forming. Leaves basal, 2-pinnatisect, 10–14 lance-shaped, toothed leaflets. Single, solitary, yellow-centred, cerise daisies, early summer, again if dead-headed. Skin irritant.

Tanacetum coccineum
'Eileen May Robinson' A.G.M.
(Asteraceae/Compositae)

Common names: Painted daisy; pyrethrum
Height: 75cm (30in)
Spread: 45cm (18in)
Aspect: Sun
Soil: Sharply drained
Hardiness: Zone 5
Propagation: Division or basal cuttings, both in spring

Clump-forming. Leaves pinnatisect, 10–14 lance-shaped, toothed segments. Solitary, single daisies, rich pink, yellow discs, early summer, again if dead-headed. Skin irritant.

Tanacetum coccineum
'James Kelway' A.G.M.
(Asteraceae/Compositae)

Common names: Painted daisy; pyrethrum
Height: 75cm (30in)
Spread: 45cm (18in)
Aspect: Sun
Soil: Sharply drained
Hardiness: Zone 5
Propagation: Division or basal cuttings, both in spring

Short-lived. Leaves pinnatisect, 10–14 lance-shaped, toothed segments. Solitary, single daisies, deep crimson, yellow discs, in early summer, again if dead-headed. Skin irritant.

Tanacetum coccineum
'Snow Cloud'
(Asteraceae/Compositae)

Common names: Painted daisy; pyrethrum
Height: 60cm (24in)
Spread: 45cm (18in)
Aspect: Sun
Soil: Sharply drained
Hardiness: Zone 5
Propagation: Division or basal cuttings, both in spring

Short-lived. Leaves pinnatisect, 10–14 lance-shaped, toothed segments. Solitary, single white daisies, yellow centres, in early summer, again if dead-headed. Skin irritant.

Tanacetum parthenium
'Aureum'
(Asteraceae/Compositae)

Common name: Feverfew
Height: 60cm (2ft)
Spread: 30cm (1ft)
Aspect: Sun
Soil: Sharply drained
Hardiness: Zone 6
Propagation: Seed or division, both in spring

Aromatic herb. Leaves basal and stem, hairy, ovate, pinnatisect, golden-yellow. Flowers in dense corymbs, small, single, white, daisy-like, with yellow discs, summer.

Tanacetum vulgare
(Asteraceae/Compositae)

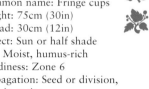

Common name: Tansy
Height: 90cm (36in)
Spread: 45cm (18in)
Aspect: Sun
Soil: Sharply drained
Hardiness: Zone 4
Propagation: Seed or division, both in spring

Invasive perennial from Europe. Leaves aromatic, pinnate, up to 12 lance-shaped, toothed leaflets, mid-green. Flowers in flat corymbs, bright yellow buttons, in summer.

Telekia speciosa
(Asteraceae/Compositae)

Common names: None
Height: 1.8m (6ft)
Spread: 90cm (3ft)
Aspect: Half shade
Soil: Moist
Hardiness: Zone 6
Propagation: Seed, when ripe; division, in spring

Woodlander. Leaves ovate, toothed, mid-green, aromatic. Flowers in branched sprays, single, with bracts, ray florets narrow, yellow, late summer and early autumn.

Tellima grandiflora
(Saxifragaceae)

Common name: Fringe cups
Height: 75cm (30in)
Spread: 30cm (12in)
Aspect: Sun or half shade
Soil: Moist, humus-rich
Hardiness: Zone 6
Propagation: Seed or division, both in spring

Rosette-forming ground cover for shade. Leaves heart-shaped, hairy, lobed, scalloped. Flowers greenish-white, in terminal racemes on hairy stems, late spring to midsummer.

Teucrium × *lucidrys*
(Labiatae/Lamiaceae)

Common name: Wall germander
Height: 50cm (20in)
Spread: 30cm (12in)
Aspect: Sun
Soil: Well-drained, alkaline, poor
Hardiness: Zone 5
Propagation: Seed, when ripe; softwood or semi-ripe cuttings, in summer

Subshrub from Eurasia and North Africa. Leaves aromatic, ovate-obovate, toothed, dark green. Flowers in racemes, in whorls, tubular, purplish-pink, summer to autumn.

Teucrium × *lucidrys*
'Variegata'
(Labiatae/Lamiaceae)

Common name: Variegated wall germander
Height: 50cm (20in)
Spread: 30cm (12in)
Aspect: Sun
Soil: Well-drained, alkaline, poor
Hardiness: Zone 5
Propagation: Softwood or semi-ripe cuttings, both in summer

Subshrub cultivar with aromatic, ovate-obovate, toothed, cream and green leaves. Flowers tubular, purplish-pink, in whorled racemes. Excellent ground cover.

Thalictrum aquilegiifolium
'White Cloud'
(Ranunculaceae)

Common name: Meadow rue
Height: 1m (3ft)
Spread: 45cm (18in)
Aspect: Half shade
Soil: Moist, humus-rich
Hardiness: Zone 6
Propagation: Seed, when ripe; division, in spring

Architectural, rhizomatous perennial. Leaves columbine-like, 2-pinnate, leaflets obovate, mid-green. Flowers in flat-topped panicles, in clusters, white, fluffy, in early summer.

Thalictrum delavayi
A.G.M.
(Ranunculaceae)

Common name: Meadow rue
Height: 1.5m (5ft)
Spread: 60cm (2ft)
Aspect: Half shade
Soil: Moist, humus-rich
Hardiness: Zone 6
Propagation: Seed, when ripe or in spring

Rhizomatous perennial from Tibet to China. Leaves 2- or 3-pinnate, lobes 3-lobed. Pink, fluffy flowers on widely branching stems, in panicles, midsummer to early autumn.

Thalictrum delavayi
'Album'
(Ranunculaceae)

Common name: Meadow rue
Height: 1.5m (5ft)
Spread: 60cm (2ft)
Aspect: Half shade
Soil: Moist, humus-rich
Hardiness: Zone 6
Propagation: Division, in spring

Form of the species with white, fluffy flowers in panicles on widely branching stems, midsummer to early autumn. Leaves 2- or 3-pinnate.

Planted in paving crevices, mat-forming thyme cultivars such as 'Doone Valley' will release their scent when they are stepped upon.

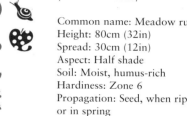

***Thalictrum delavayi* 'Hewitt's Double' A.G.M. (Ranunculaceae)**

Common name: Meadow rue
Height: 1.5m (5ft)
Spread: 60cm (2ft)
Aspect: Half shade
Soil: Moist, humus-rich
Hardiness: Zone 6
Propagation: Division, in spring

Sterile form with flowers that lack stamens but have many sepals, making the flower a rounded pompon, rich mauve in colour, from midsummer to early autumn.

***Thalictrum flavum* (Ranunculaceae)**

Common name: Yellow meadow rue
Height: 90cm (36in)
Spread: 45cm (18in)
Aspect: Half shade
Soil: Moist, humus-rich
Hardiness: Zone 6
Propagation: Seed, when ripe or in spring

Rhizomatous perennial from Eurasia. Leaves 2- or 3-pinnate, leaflets obovate, mid-green. Flowers scented, in panicles, with yellow sepals and stamens, in summer.

***Thalictrum flavum* subsp. *glaucum* A.G.M. (Ranunculaceae)**

Common name: Yellow meadow rue
Height: 1m (3ft)
Spread: 60cm (2ft)
Aspect: Sun
Soil: Humus-rich
Hardiness: Zone 6
Propagation: Seed, when ripe or in spring

Subspecies with 2- or 3-pinnate, glaucous foliage. Bears large panicles of pale lemon-yellow flowers in summer. An excellent flower for cutting.

***Thalictrum minus adiantifolium* (Ranunculaceae)**

Common name: Meadow rue
Height: 80cm (32in)
Spread: 30cm (12in)
Aspect: Half shade
Soil: Moist, humus-rich
Hardiness: Zone 6
Propagation: Seed, when ripe or in spring

Rhizomatous plant. Leaves 3- or 4-pinnate, leaflets ovate, lobed, glaucous, mid-green. Flowers in panicles, insignificant, yellow, in summer. Grown for its fern-like foliage.

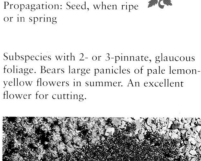

***Thermopsis lanceolata* (Leguminosae/Papilionaceae)**

Common names: None
Height: 80cm (32in)
Spread: 30cm (12in)
Aspect: Sun or half shade
Soil: Well-drained, humus-rich, fertile
Hardiness: Zone 3
Propagation: Seed, in spring

Rhizomatous perennial from Siberia to Japan. Leaves 3-palmate, leaflets ovate, light green. Flowers in racemes, lupin-like, yellow, from spring to midsummer.

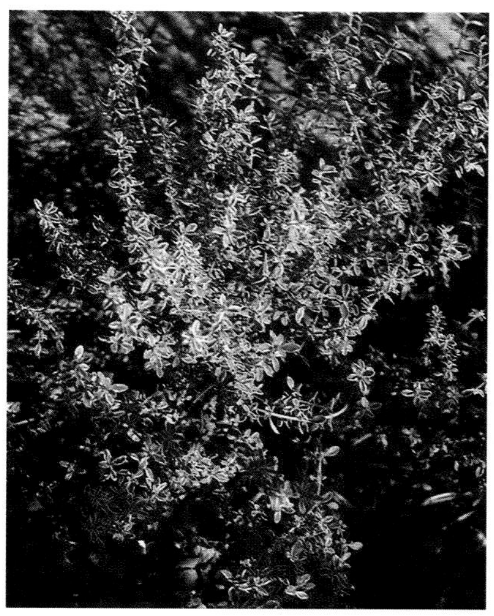

***Thymus* x *citriodorus* 'Silver Queen' A.G.M. (Labiatae/Lamiaceae)**

Common name: Lemon-scented thyme
Height: 30cm (12in)
Spread: 45cm (18in)
Aspect: Sun
Soil: Well-drained, alkaline
Hardiness: Zone 7
Propagation: Division, in spring

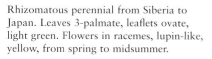

Evergreen subshrub of garden origin. Leaves lance-shaped, lemon-scented when bruised, mid-green, variegated cream. Flowers in irregular heads, pale pink, in summer.

***Thymus serpyllum* var. *coccineus* A.G.M. (Labiatae/Lamiaceae)**

Common name: Wild thyme
Height: 10cm (4in)
Spread: 30cm (12in)
Aspect: Sun
Soil: Well-drained, alkaline
Hardiness: Zone 5
Propagation: Division, in spring

Aromatic, evergreen subshrub from Europe. Leaves aromatic, linear-elliptic, dark green. Flowers crimson-red, in summer. Excellent in a scree or a raised bed.

***Tiarella cordifolia* A.G.M. (Saxifragaceae)**

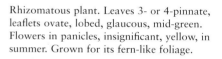

Common name: Foam flower
Height: 30cm (1ft)
Spread: 60cm (2ft)
Aspect: Full or half shade
Soil: Any protected from winter wet, but prefers moist, humus-rich
Hardiness: Zone 3
Propagation: Seed, when ripe or in spring; division, in spring

Rhizomatous, woodland perennial from North America. Leaves ovate, light green. Flowers in racemes, fluffy, white, in summer. Spreads by stolons.

Tiarella wherryi
A.G.M.
(Saxifragaceae)

Common name: Foam flower
Height: 20cm (8in)
Spread: 20cm (8in)
Aspect: Full or half shade
Soil: Any, but prefers moist, humus-rich
Hardiness: Zone 6
Propagation: Seed, when ripe or in spring; division, in spring

Rhizomatous perennial from the U.S.A. Leaves ovate, hairy, 3-lobed, light green. Flowers in racemes, white, tinged pink, in late spring and early summer.

Tolmeia menziesii
A.G.M.
(Saxifragaceae)

Common names: Pick-a-back plant; thousand mothers; youth on age
Height: 60cm (2ft)
Spread: 2m (6ft)
Aspect: Full shade
Soil: Moist, humus-rich
Hardiness: Zone 7
Propagation: Seed, in autumn; division, in spring

Rhizomatous ground cover. Leaves reniform, lobed, veined, toothed, light green. Flowers small, purple-brown, scented, in one-sided racemes, late spring and early summer.

TRADESCANTIA (Commelinaceae)
Spider lily • Spider wort

A genus of some 60 or so species, all perennial, from North, Central, and South America. The genus is well-known for the tender species, often grown as house- or conservatory plants, but there are also hardy types suitable for borders. Their natural habitats are scrub or woodland, so they are fairly tolerant of any soil as long as it is not waterlogged, and will do well in sun or partial shade. The varieties in cultivation are hybrids, and go by the name *Tradescantia* x *andersoniana*. Their leaves are green, often flushed with purple, narrowly lance-shaped and slightly fleshy, and they bear flowers in white and shades of pink, blue, and purple. *Tradescantia* flowers are 3-petalled and saucer-shaped. They are individually short-lived, but are borne in succession over a long season from summer to autumn, especially if dead-headed. They can be disappointing if not carefully positioned, because the flowers nestle down in the leaves, and may not be seen to their best advantage from any great distance. Despite being quite dwarf, *Tradescantia* sometimes need to be staked. They are fairly long-lived and become large in time, and so benefit from regular division. They are low-allergen plants, but contact with the sap may irritate the skin.

Tradescantia x *andersoniana*
'Isis' A.G.M.
(Commelinaceae)

Common names: Spider lily; spider wort
Height: 60cm (2ft)
Spread: 60cm (2ft)
Aspect: Sun or half shade
Soil: Moist, fertile
Hardiness: Zone 5
Propagation: Division, in spring or autumn

Clump-forming hybrid. Leaves narrow, lance-shaped, pointed, mid-green. Flowers 3-petalled, dark blue, in paired, terminal cymes, early summer to early autumn.

Tradescantia x *andersoniana*
'Karminglut'
(Commelinaceae)

Common names: Spider lily; spider wort
Height: 60cm (2ft)
Spread: 60cm (2ft)
Aspect: Sun or half shade
Soil: Moist, fertile
Hardiness: Zone 5
Propagation: Division, in spring or autumn

Clump-forming hybrid. Leaves narrow, pointed, lance-shaped, mid-green. Flowers 3-petalled, carmine-red, in paired, terminal cymes, early summer to early autumn.

Tradescantia x *andersoniana*
'Osprey' A.G.M.
(Commelinaceae)

Common names: Spider lily; spider wort
Height: 60cm (2ft)
Spread: 60cm (2ft)
Aspect: Sun or half shade
Soil: Moist, fertile
Hardiness: Zone 5
Propagation: Division, in spring or autumn

A hybrid, clump-forming perennial. Leaves narrow, pointed, lance-shaped, mid-green. Flowers in paired, terminal cymes, large, white, from early summer to early autumn.

Tradescantia x *andersoniana*
'Purewell Giant'
(Commelinaceae)

Common names: Spider lily; spider wort
Height: 60cm (2ft)
Spread: 60cm (2ft)
Aspect: Sun or half shade
Soil: Moist, fertile
Hardiness: Zone 5
Propagation: Division, in spring or autumn

Clump-forming hybrid. Leaves narrow, lance-shaped, pointed, mid-green. Flowers in paired, terminal cymes, large, 3-petalled, purple-red, from early summer to early autumn.

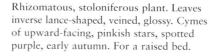

Tradescantia × *andersoniana* **'Zwanenburg Blue'** (Commelinaceae)

Common names: Spider lily; spider wort
Height: 60cm (2ft)
Spread: 60cm (2ft)
Aspect: Sun or half shade
Soil: Moist, fertile
Hardiness: Zone 5
Propagation: Division, in spring or autumn

Clump-forming hybrid. Leaves narrow, pointed, lance-shaped, mid-green. Flowers in paired, terminal cymes, 3-petalled, large, dark blue, early summer to early autumn.

Tradescantia ohiensis (Commelinaceae)

Common name: Ohio spiderwort
Height: 90cm (3ft)
Spread 60cm (2ft)
Aspect: Sun or half shade
Soil: Moist, fertile
Hardiness: Zone 7
Propagation: Seed, when ripe; division, in autumn or spring

A perennial species from the U.S.A. Leaves narrow, lance-shaped, mid-green. Flowers in pairs in terminal cymes, blue, white, purple or pink, in spring.

Tricyrtis formosana A.G.M. (Convallariaceae/Liliaceae)

Common name: Toad lily
Height: 75cm (30in)
Spread: 45cm (18in)
Aspect: Sun or half shade
Soil: Moist, well-drained, humus-rich
Hardiness: Zone 7
Propagation: Seed, when ripe; division, in early spring

Rhizomatous, stoloniferous plant. Leaves inverse lance-shaped, veined, glossy. Cymes of upward-facing, pinkish stars, spotted purple, early autumn. For a raised bed.

Tricyrtis hirta (Convallariaceae/Liliaceae)

Common name: Japanese toad lily
Height: 75cm (30in)
Spread: 60cm (24in)
Aspect: Sun or half shade
Soil: Moist, well-drained, humus-rich
Hardiness: Zone 5
Propagation: Seed, when ripe; division, in early spring

Rhizomatous plant. Leaves lance-shaped, hairy, veined, light green. Flowers white, purple-spotted stars, late summer to mid-autumn. Seen at best in a raised site.

Tricyrtis latifolia (Convallariaceae/Liliaceae)

Common name: Toad lily
Height: 75cm (30in)
Spread: 90cm (36in)
Aspect: Sun or half shade
Soil: Moist, well-drained, humus-rich
Hardiness: Zone 5
Propagation: Seed, when ripe; division, in spring or autumn

Rhizomatous, clump-forming plant. Leaves ovate, veined, glossy green. Branched cymes of yellow stars, spotted brown, in early to mid-summer. Seen best in a raised site.

Tricyrtis ohsumiensis (Convallariaceae/Liliaceae)

Common name: Toad lily
Height: 20cm (8in)
Spread: 30cm (12in)
Aspect: Half or full shade, protected from midday sun
Soil: Moist, well-drained, humus-rich
Hardiness: Zone 5
Propagation: Seed, when ripe; division, in spring or autumn

Rhizomatous, clump-forming plant. Leaves lance-shaped, veined, glossy, light green, scorched by hot sun. Flowers yellow saucers, spotted brown, in early autumn.

Trifolium pannonicum (Leguminosae/Papilionaceae)

Common name: Hungarian clover
Height: 90cm (3ft)
Spread: 90cm (3ft)
Aspect: Sun
Soil: Moist, well-drained, fertile
Hardiness: Zone 5
Propagation: Seed, division or separation of plantlets, all in spring

Perennial from E Europe. Leaves palmate, basal leaves obovate, stem leaves inverse lance-shaped, mid-green. Flowers clover-like, creamy-yellow, in summer.

Trifolium repens (Leguminosae/Papilionaceae)

Common names: Shamrock; white clover
Height: 30cm (12in)
Spread: 50cm (20in)
Aspect: Sun
Soil: Moist, well-drained, fertile
Hardiness: Zone 4
Propagation: Seed, division or separation of plantlets, all in spring

Selected form of the lawn weed, and equally invasive. Leaves 3-foliate, leaflets toothed, mid-green. Flowers clover-like, perfumed, pink, from spring to autumn.

TRILLIUM (Liliaceae/Ttrilliaceae)
Trinity flower • Wake robin • Wood lily

A genus of some 30 species of rhizomatous woodland plants, the majority of them originating in North America, but some native to the Himalayas and north-east Asia. They bloom in the spring, and bear their leaves, tepals and petals in threes, hence the name. The leaves, borne in an apical whorl, range from lance- to diamond-shaped, and are veined and often marbled with purple or silver. The flowers are cup- or funnel-shaped and often stalkless, growing directly above the leaves. All species like some degree of shade and an acidic soil, except for *Trillium rivale*, which prefers a sunny position and alkaline soil. All like a moisture-retentive, humus-rich, woodland type of soil, and should be mulched annually with leaf mould. They are extremely resentful of disturbance or damage to the roots, so site them carefully on first planting, and avoid digging around them. They require some patience: divisions may be slow to establish, and plants grown from seed take several years to reach flowering size. In all, these can be demanding plants, but the rewards are generous. They are soundly perennial, and would make good cut flowers, except that one has perforce to cut the leaves at the same time, and this is harmful to the plants, so best avoided.

Trillium chloropetalum var. giganteum A.G.M. (Liliaceae/Trilliaceae)

Common name: Giant trillium
Height: 40cm (16in)
Spread: 20cm (8in)
Aspect: Full or half shade
Soil: Moist, well-drained, deep, acidic, humus-rich
Hardiness: Zone 6
Propagation: Seed, as soon as ripe; division, after flowering

A rhizomatous perennial. Leaves ovate to diamond-shaped, dark green, marbled grey or maroon. Flowers scented, brown-purple, among or above the leaves, in spring.

Trillium chloropetalum var. giganteum A.G.M. (Liliaceae/Trilliaceae)

Common names: Giant trillium
Height: 40cm (16in)
Spread: 20cm (8in)
Aspect: Full or half shade
Soil: Moist, well-drained, deep, acidic, humus-rich
Hardiness: Zone 6
Propagation: Seed, as soon as ripe; division, after flowering

This rhizomatous plant has a both a purple form (left) and this white form. Leaves ovate to diamond-shaped, dark green, marbled grey or maroon.

Trillium cuneatum (Liliaceae/Trilliaceae)

Common names: Toadshade; whippoorwill flower
Height: 60cm (2ft)
Spread: 30cm (1ft)
Aspect: Full or half shade
Soil: Moist, well-drained, deep, acidic, humus-rich
Hardiness: Zone 6
Propagation: Seed, as soon as ripe; division, after flowering

Rhizomatous perennial from the south-east U.S.A. Leaves rounded, mid-green, marked silver. Flowers scented, maroon, borne above the leaves in spring.

Trillium erectum A.G.M. (Liliaceae/Trilliaceae)

Common names: Birthroot; red trillium; stinking Benjamin
Height: 50cm (20in)
Spread: 30cm (12in)
Aspect: Full or half shade
Soil: Moist, well-drained, deep, acidic, humus-rich
Hardiness: Zone 4
Propagation: Seed, as soon as ripe; division, after flowering

A rhizomatous perennial from E North America. Leaves ovate, mid-green. Flowers deep red-purple, borne above the leaves in spring. Smell described as like a wet dog.

Trillium grandiflorum A.G.M. (Liliaceae/Trilliaceae)

Common names: White trillium; white wake-robin
Height: 40cm (16in)
Spread: 45cm (18in)
Aspect: Full or half shade
Soil: Moist, well-drained, deep, acidic, humus-rich
Hardiness: Zone 5
Propagation: Seed, as soon as ripe; division, after flowering

Rhizomatous perennial from E North America. Leaves ovate, dark green. Flowers pure white, fading to pink, borne above the leaves in spring and summer.

Trillium luteum A.G.M. (Liliaceae/Trilliaceae)

Common names: Yellow trillium; yellow toadshade
Height: 40cm (16in)
Spread: 30cm (12in)
Aspect: Full or half shade
Soil: Moist, well-drained, deep, acidic, humus-rich
Hardiness: Zone 5
Propagation: Seed, as soon as ripe; division, after flowering

Rhizomatous perennial from the south-east U.S.A. Leaves ovate, mid-green. Flowers lemon-scented, upright, yellow, borne above the leaves in spring.

Once established, Trillium chloropetalum *makes a superb display in a moist, shady woodland setting.*

Trillium ovatum
(Liliaceae/Trilliaceae)

Common name: Western white trillium
Height: 50cm (20in)
Spread: 20cm (8in)
Aspect: Full or half shade
Soil: Moist, well-drained, deep, acidic, humus-rich
Hardiness: Zone 5
Propagation: Seed, as soon as ripe; division, after flowering

Rhizomatous plant from western North America. Leaves diamond-shaped, deep green. Flowers upright, pure white, petals ovate, borne above the leaves in spring.

Trillium pusillum
(Liliaceae/Trilliaceae)

Common names: Dwarf trillium; least trillium
Height: 15cm (6in)
Spread: 10cm (4in)
Aspect: Full or half shade
Soil: Moist, well-drained, deep, acidic, humus-rich
Hardiness: Zone 6
Propagation: Seed, as soon as ripe; division, after flowering

Rhizomatous perennial from eastern North America. Leaves lance-shaped, dark green. Flowers small, white, borne amongst the leaves, in spring.

Trillium sessile
(Liliaceae/Trilliaceae)

Common names: Toadshade; sessile trillium; wake robin
Height: 30cm (12in)
Spread: 20cm (8in)
Aspect: Full or half shade
Soil: Moist, well-drained, deep, acidic, humus-rich
Hardiness: Zone 4
Propagation: Seed, as soon as ripe; division, after flowering

Rhizomatous plant from the U.S.A. Leaves rounded, dark green, marbled grey, silver and maroon. Flowers upright, maroon-red, petals lance-shaped, above the leaves, spring.

Trillium vaseyi
(Liliaceae/Trilliaceae)

Common name: Vasey's trillium
Height: 65cm (26in)
Spread: 30cm (12in)
Aspect: Full or half shade
Soil: Moist, well-drained, deep, acidic, humus-rich
Hardiness: Zone 6
Propagation: Seed, as soon as ripe; division, after flowering

A rhizomatous perennial from the south-east U.S.A. Leaves rhombic, dark green. Flowers held horizontally, perfumed, dark red-purple, in spring.

Tritonia disticha* subsp. *rubrolucens
(Iridaceae)

Common names: None
Height: 90cm (36in)
Spread 15cm (6in)
Aspect: Sun
Soil: Sharply drained
Hardiness: Zone 9
Propagation: Seed, in warmth when ripe; offsets, when dormant

Cormous perennial from southern Africa. Leaves basal, linear, erect, lance-shaped, mid-green. Flowers open, pink funnels in one-sided spikes, from mid- to late summer.

Trollius acaulis
(Ranunculaceae)

Common name: Globeflower
Height: 30cm (12in)
Spread: 15cm (6in)
Aspect: Sun or half shade
Soil: Moist or wet, deep, humus-rich, fertile
Hardiness: Zone 6
Propagation: Seed, as soon as ripe or in spring; division, after flowering

Clump-forming waterside perennial. Leaves 5- to 7-palmate, leaflets 3-lobed, toothed, mid-green. Flowers solitary, single, yellow saucers, in spring. Poisonous.

Trollius chinensis
'Imperial Orange'
(Ranunculaceae)

Common name: Globeflower
Height: 90cm (36in)
Spread: 45cm (18in)
Aspect: Sun or half shade
Soil: Moist or wet, deep, humus-rich, fertile
Hardiness: Zone 5
Propagation: Seed, as soon as ripe or in spring; division, after flowering

Cultivar of a clump-forming bog plant. Leaves basal, large, 5 lance-shaped, toothed lobes, and smaller stem. Flowers solitary, bowl-shaped, orange, in summer. Poisonous.

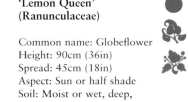

Trollius x *cultorum*
'Lemon Queen'
(Ranunculaceae)

Common name: Globeflower
Height: 90cm (36in)
Spread: 45cm (18in)
Aspect: Sun or half shade
Soil: Moist or wet, deep, humus-rich, fertile
Hardiness: Zone 5
Propagation: Seed, as soon as ripe or in spring; division, after flowering

Hybrid cultivar. Leaves basal, large, 5-lobed, lobes lance-shaped, toothed; smaller stem leaves. Flowers large, solitary, pale yellow, globular, mid-spring to midsummer. Toxic.

Trollius × *cultorum* 'Orange Princess' A.G.M. (Ranunculaceae)

Common name: Globeflower
Height: 90cm (36in)
Spread: 45cm (18in)
Aspect: Sun or half shade
Soil: Moist or wet, deep, humus-rich, fertile
Hardiness: Zone 5
Propagation: Seed, as soon as ripe or in spring; division, after flowering

Clump-forming hybrid. Leaves large basal, smaller stem, 5-lobed, lobes lance-shaped, toothed, glossy. Flowers solitary, orange bowls, mid-spring to midsummer. Poisonous.

Trollius europaeus (Ranunculaceae)

Common name: Common European globeflower
Height: 90cm (36in)
Spread: 45cm (18in)
Aspect: Sun or half shade
Soil: Moist or wet, deep, humus-rich, fertile
Hardiness: Zone 5
Propagation: Seed, as soon as ripe or in spring; division, after flowering

Clump-forming species. Leaves 5-lobed, segments wedge-shaped, toothed, mid-green. Flowers solitary, spherical, yellow, early to midsummer. Poisonous.

Trollius yunnanensis (Ranunculaceae)

Common name: Globeflower
Height: 70cm (28in)
Spread: 30cm (12in)
Aspect: Sun or half shade
Soil: Moist or wet, deep, humus-rich, fertile
Hardiness: Zone 5
Propagation: Seed, as soon as ripe or in spring; division, after flowering

A clump-forming bog plant. Leaves 3- to 5-lobed, segments ovate, toothed, glossy. Flowers solitary, yellow saucers, from late spring to early summer. Poisonous.

Tropaeolum polyphyllum (Tropaeolaceae)

Common names: Canary bird flower; Indian cress
Height: 10cm (4in)
Spread: 1.2m (4ft)
Aspect: Sun
Soil: Well-drained, humus-rich
Hardiness: Zone 8
Propagation: Division, in early spring; basal or stem cuttings, in spring or early summer

Trailing, rhizomatous, herbaceous plant for a sunny wall. Leaves up to 9 lobes, glaucous. Flowers yellow, over a long period in summer. Spreads a long way underground.

Tuberaria lignosa (Cistaceae)

Common names: None
Height: 30cm (1ft)
Spread: 90cm (3ft)
Aspect: Sun
Soil: Well-drained
Hardiness: Zone 8
Propagation: Seed, in early spring

A spreading, rosette-forming perennial from the Mediterranean. Leaves ovate, hairy, dull green. Flowers in loose cymes, bright yellow, all summer.

Tulbaghia cepacea (Alliaceae/Liliaceae)

Common names: None
Height: 60cm (24in)
Spread: 20cm (8in)
Aspect: Sun
Soil: Well-drained, humus-rich, fertile
Hardiness: Zone 8
Propagation: Seed, when ripe or in spring; division, in spring

Rhizomatous plant from southern Africa. Leaves narrow, linear, greyish-green. Flowers soft purple-pink, night-scented, tubular, in umbels, from late spring to summer.

Tulbaghia cominsii (Alliaceae/Liliaceae)

Common names: None
Height: 25cm (10in)
Spread: 10cm (4in)
Aspect: Sun
Soil: Well-drained, humus-rich, fertile
Hardiness: Zone 8
Propagation: Seed, when ripe or in spring; division, in spring

Rhizomatous perennial from South Africa. Leaves narrowly linear, glaucous, mid-green. Flowers in terminal scapes, white, night-scented, in spring to summer.

Tulbaghia violacea (Alliaceae/Liliaceae)

Common names: None
Height: 60cm (2ft)
Spread: 30cm (1ft)
Aspect: Sun
Soil: Well-drained, humus-rich, fertile
Hardiness: Zone 7
Propagation: Seed, when ripe or in spring; division, in spring

Rhizomatous perennial from South Africa. Leaves narrow, linear, greyish-green. Flowers in terminal umbels, scented, from summer to autumn.

TULIPA (Liliaceae)
Tulip

A genus of some 100 species from Europe, Asia and the Middle East, especially Central Asia. All are hardy, bulbous perennials. They prefer sun but will take light shade, and must have a well-drained soil but seem to prefer heavy soils to light ones. Tulips are grown for their showy flowers, which are usually terminal and upright, with six tepals. They vary from cup- or bowl-shaped to goblet-shaped, some with long, very narrow tepals, or lily-like or star-shaped; some are fringed. There is a wide range of colours and bicolours. The leaves are usually basal, broadly ovate, and sometimes wavy-edged or channelled. The bulbs should be planted 15cm (6in) deep in the autumn. Cultivars benefit from being lifted and ripened every year once the leaves have died down. The Greigii and Kaufmanniana groups and the species can be left in the ground all year; mark the position to avoid damaging the bulbs by infill planting. These also benefit from being lifted and divided every few years, and this should be done as soon as the foliage dies down; mice love tulip bulbs, so store lifted bulbs out of their reach and protect newly planted bulbs from disturbance. Contact with any part may cause skin irritation, and all parts are mildly poisonous if ingested.

Tulipa
'Apeldoorn' (4)
(Liliaceae)

Common names: None
Height: 60cm (2ft)
Spread: Nil
Aspect: Sun
Soil: Well-drained, fertile
Hardiness: Zone 5
Propagation: Offsets, after flowering

A Darwin hybrid tulip with flowers of cherry-red outside, signal-red with yellow-edged black marks inside, and with black anthers, in mid-spring.

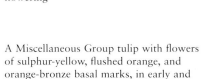

Tulipa
'Bright Gem' (15)
(Liliaceae)

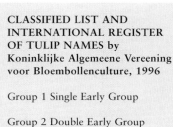

Common names: None
Height: 35cm (14in)
Spread: Nil
Aspect: Sun
Soil: Well-drained
Hardiness: Zone 5
Propagation: Offsets, after flowering

A Miscellaneous Group tulip with flowers of sulphur-yellow, flushed orange, and orange-bronze basal marks, in early and mid-spring.

Tulipa clusiana var. *chrysantha* A.G.M (15)
(Liliaceae)

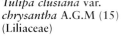

Common names: Lady tulip
Height: 30cm (1ft)
Spread: Nil
Aspect: Sun
Soil: Well-drained, fertile
Hardiness: Zone 6
Propagation: Seed, in autumn; offsets, after flowering

A species from Iran to the Himalayas. Leaves linear, glaucous, grey-green. Flowers bowl-shaped, yellow, tinged red-brown outside, in early and mid-spring.

Tulipa
'Keizerskroon' A.G.M. (1)
(Liliaceae)

Common names: None
Height: 30cm (1ft)
Spread: Nil
Aspect: Sun
Soil: Well-drained, fertile
Hardiness: Zone 5
Propagation: Offsets, after flowering

A Single Early Group tulip with cup-shaped, scarlet flowers with broad margins of bright yellow, in mid-spring. Leaves broadly ovate, mid-green.

Tulipa
'Fantasy' A.G.M. (10)
(Liliaceae)

Common names: None
Height: 55cm (22in)
Spread: Nil
Aspect: Sun
Soil: Well-drained, fertile
Hardiness: Zone 5
Propagation: Offsets, after flowering

A Parrot Group tulip. Flowers cup-shaped, salmon-pink streaked green, with fringed edges, in late spring. Excellent border plant and a good cut flower.

CLASSIFIED LIST AND INTERNATIONAL REGISTER OF TULIP NAMES by Koninklijke Algemeene Vereening voor Bloembollenculture, 1996

Group 1 Single Early Group

Group 2 Double Early Group

Group 3 Triumph Group

Group 4 Darwin hybrid Group

Group 5 Single late, including Darwin Group and Cottage Group

Group 6 Lily-Flowered Group

Group 7 Fringed Group

Group 8 Viridiflora Group

Group 9 Rembrandt Group

Group 10 Parrot Group

Group 11 Double Late Group

Group 12 Kaufmanniana Group

Group 13 Fosteriana Group

Group 14 Greigii Group

Group 15 Miscellaneous

The flowers of Tulipa sylvestris *are unusual in that they are scented, and also in being pendent in bud, turning upwards as they open.*

Tulipa linifolia
A.G.M (15)
(Liliaceae)

Common names: None
Height: 20cm (8in)
Spread: Nil
Aspect: Sun
Soil: Well-drained, fertile
Hardiness: Zone 5
Propagation: Seed, in autumn; offsets, after flowering

Species from Afghanistan, Uzbekistan, and Iran. Leaves linear, sickle-shaped, grey-green. Flowers red with black-purple bases, bowl-shaped, in early and mid-spring.

Tulipa
'Monte Carlo' (2)
(Liliaceae)

Common names: None
Height: 30cm (1ft)
Spread: Nil
Aspect: Sun
Soil: Well-drained, fertile
Hardiness: Zone 5
Propagation: Offsets, after flowering

A Double Early Group tulip with bowl-shaped flowers of sulphur-yellow, with small "feather" markings of red at the tips of the tepals, in mid-spring.

Tulipa
'Oranje Nassau' A.G.M. (2)
(Liliaceae)

Common names: None
Height: 30cm (1ft)
Spread: Nil
Aspect: Sun
Soil: Well-drained, fertile
Hardiness: Zone 5
Propagation: Offsets, after flowering

A Double Early Group tulip with open, bowl-shaped flowers of blood-red, flushed fiery-red, in mid-spring. Good for growing in a container.

Tulipa praestans
'Fusilier' A.G.M. (15)
(Liliaceae)

Common names: None
Height: 30cm (1ft)
Spread: Nil
Aspect: Sun
Soil: Well-drained, fertile
Hardiness: Zone 5
Propagation: Offsets, after flowering

Selected form of a species from Kazakhstan and Tajikistan. Leaves lance-shaped, keeled, downy grey-green. Flowers in clusters, bright red, in early to mid-spring.

Tulipa
'Red Riding Hood' A.G.M.
(14) (Liliaceae)

Common names: None
Height: 20cm (8in)
Spread: Nil
Aspect: Sun
Soil: Well-drained, fertile
Hardiness: Zone 5
Propagation: Offsets, after flowering

A Greigii Group tulip. Leaves broad, grey-green, spotted maroon-blue. Flowers carmine red outside, scarlet-red inside, with black bases, in early spring.

Tulipa saxatilis
Bakeri Group (15)
(Liliaceae)

Common names: None
Height: 35cm (14in)
Spread: Nil
Aspect: Sun
Soil: Well-drained, fertile
Hardiness: Zone 6
Propagation: Offsets, after flowering

Selection of a Mediterranean tulip. Leaves linear, shiny, mid-green. Flowers pink with yellow bases, margined white, fragrant, mid- and late spring. Spreads by runners.

Tulipa sprengeri
A.G.M. (15)
(Liliaceae)

Common names: None
Height: 50cm (20in)
Spread: Nil
Aspect: Sun or half shade
Soil: Well-drained
Hardiness: Zone 5
Propagation: Seed, in autumn; offsets, after flowering

Species from Turkey, but extinct in the wild. Leaves linear, shiny, mid-green. Flowers red or orange, in early summer. Will naturalise, and has attractive seed pods, shown here.

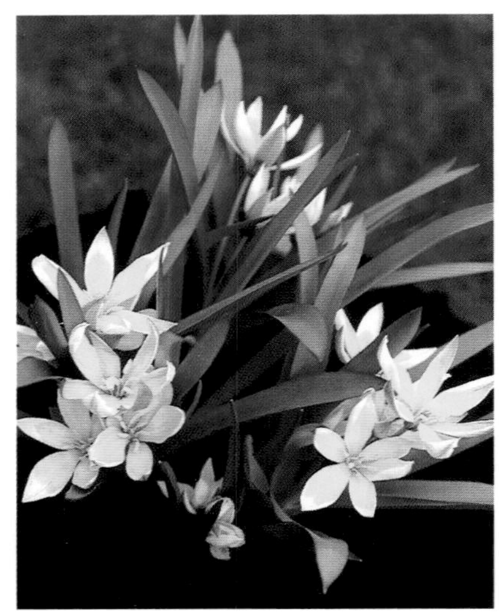

Tulipa tarda
A.G.M. (15)
(Liliaceae)

Common names: None
Height: 15cm (6in)
Spread: Nil
Aspect: Sun
Soil: Well-drained, fertile
Hardiness: Zone 5
Propagation: Seed, in autumn; offsets, after flowering

A species from Central Asia. Leaves lance-shaped, arching, shiny, bright green. Flowers in clusters, perfumed, white, with yellow bases, in early and mid-spring.

Tulipa
'Toronto' A.G.M. (14)
(Liliaceae)

Common names: None
Height: 20cm (8in)
Spread: Nil
Aspect: Sun
Soil: Well-drained, fertile
Hardiness: Zone 5
Propagation: Offsets, after flowering

A Greigii Group tulip with broad, ovate leaves, marked bluish-maroon. Flowers pinkish-red, tinged vermilion outside and tangerine inside, in mid-spring.

Tulipa turkestanica
A.G.M. (15)
(Liliaceae)

Common names: None
Height: 30cm (1ft)
Spread: Nil
Aspect: Sun
Soil: Well-drained, fertile
Hardiness: Zone 5
Propagation: Seed, in autumn; offsets, after flowering

A species from Central Asia and China. Leaves linear, grey-green. Flowers star-shaped, white with yellow centres, in early to mid-spring.

Tulipa urumiensis
A.G.M. (15)
(Liliaceae)

Common names: None
Height: 15cm (6in)
Spread: Nil
Aspect: Sun
Soil: Well-drained, fertile
Hardiness: Zone 5
Propagation: Seed, in autumn; offsets, after flowering

A Miscellanous Group tulip from Iran. Leaves linear, mid-green. Flowers star-shaped, yellow, flushed lilac or brown outside, in pairs or solitary, in early spring.

Tweedia caerulea
A.G.M.
(Asclepiadaceae)

Common names: None
Height: 1m (36in)
Spread: 20cm (8in)
Aspect: Sun
Soil: Moist, well-drained, fertile
Hardiness: Zone 10
Propagation: Seed, in spring; softwood cuttings, in summer

A twining, evergreen subshrub from Brazil. Leaves oblong, downy, pale green. Flowers in 3- or 4-flowered cymes, sky-blue ageing to purple, from summer to early autumn.

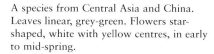

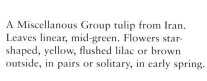

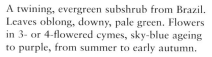

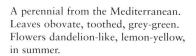

Umbilicus rupestris
(Crassulaceae)

Common names: Navelwort; pennywort
Height: 40cm (16in)
Spread: 15cm (6in)
Aspect: Sun or half shade
Soil: Sharply drained
Hardiness: Zone 7
Propagation: Seed, in spring or autumn

A perennial from Europe. Leaves rounded, succulent, depressed in centre, mid-green. Flowers in spikes, small, tubular, greenish-white, in summer. Good wall plant.

Uncinia rubra
(Cyperaceae)

Common name: Hook sedge
Height: 30cm (12in)
Spread: 40cm (16in)
Aspect: Sun or half shade
Soil: Moist, well-drained, fertile
Hardiness: Zone 8
Propagation: Seed, in spring; division, in early summer

An evergreen grass from New Zealand. Leaves flat, linear, pointed, rich red. Flowers dark brown to black, in spikes, in mid- to late summer.

Urospermum delachampii
(Asteraceae/Compositae)

Common names: None
Height: 40 cm (16in)
Spread: 60cm (24in)
Aspect: Sun
Soil: Sharply drained, fertile
Hardiness: Zone 6
Propagation: Seed, in spring or autumn; division, in spring

A perennial from the Mediterranean. Leaves obovate, toothed, grey-green. Flowers dandelion-like, lemon-yellow, in summer.

Uvularia grandiflora
A.G.M.
(Convallariaceae/Liliaceae)

Common name: Merrybells
Height: 80cm (32in)
Spread: 60cm (24in)
Aspect: Full or half shade
Soil: Moist, well-drained, humus-rich, fertile
Hardiness: Zone 4
Propagation: Seed, when ripe; division, in spring

Rhizomatous, spreading woodlander. Ovate, perfoliate, leaves. Flowers yellow, tubular, pendent, solitary or paired, on arching stems, mid and late spring. Red berries.

Valeriana officinalis* subsp. *sambucifolia
(Valerianaceae)

Common names: All heal; common valerian
Height: 2m (6ft)
Spread: 75cm (30in)
Aspect: Sun or half shade
Soil: Moist
Hardiness: Zone 4
Propagation: Seed, division or basal cuttings, all in spring

Rhizomatous plant from Europe. Leaves aromatic, pinnate; up to 9 pairs of lance-shaped, toothed, leaflets. Flowers white, salverform, in rounded cymes, all summer.

***Valeriana phu* 'Aurea'**
(Valerianaceae)

Common name: Valerian
Height: 1.5m (5ft)
Spread: 60cm (2ft)
Aspect: Sun or half shade
Soil: Moist
Hardiness: Zone 6
Propagation: Seed, division or basal cuttings, all in spring

Rhizomatous perennial from the Caucasus. Leaves aromatic, simple or pinnatifid, first yellow, then lime- then mid-green. Flowers in corymbs, white, salverform, in spring.

Valeriana montana
(Valerianaceae)

Common name: Dwarf valerian
Height: 40cm (16in)
Spread: 20cm (8in)
Aspect: Sun or half shade
Soil: Moist, alkaline, fertile
Hardiness: Zone 5
Propagation: Seed, division or basal cuttings, all in spring

Rhizomatous perennial from the mountains of Europe. Leaves basal, entire, elliptic, and stem, ovate. Flowers in corymbs, white, salverform, late spring or early summer.

Veratrum album
(Liliaceae/Melianthiaceae)

Common names: False hellebore; white hellebore
Height: 2m (6ft)
Spread: 60cm (2ft)
Aspect: Sun or half shade
Soil: Moist, well-drained, deep, fertile
Hardiness: Zone 5
Propagation: Seed, when ripe; division, in autumn or spring

Rhizomatous plant. Leaves broad, elliptic, pleated, shiny. Flowers in many-branched panicles, white stars, early and midsummer. Very poisonous. Slugs can decimate it.

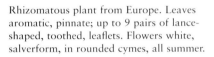

***Veratrum nigrum* A.G.M.**
(Liliaceae/Melianthiaceae)

Common names: None
Height: 1.2m (4ft)
Spread: 60cm (2ft)
Aspect: Sun or half shade
Soil: Moist, well-drained, deep, fertile
Hardiness: Zone 6
Propagation: Seed, when ripe; division, in autumn or spring

Rhizomatous plant. Leaves broad, elliptic, pleated, shiny, light green. Flowers offensive-smelling, small, brown-black, in panicles. Very toxic, highly allergenic and irritant.

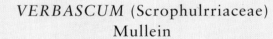

VERBASCUM (Scrophulrriaceae)
Mullein

A genus of over 350 species, from Europe, Asia and North Africa. Most of the species are biennial, but there are also annuals, perennials and some subshrubs; the perennial members are short-lived, often dying after flowering. Some are evergreen, but most are not. They grow for the most part in open scrubland or on dry hillsides, but a few are found in open woods. They like a sunny position and sharp drainage. They generally form a basal clump or rosette of large, soft, leaves, which may be simple, lobed or toothed, and produce one or more dense spikes of saucer-shaped flowers. The flowers are individually short-lived, but they are borne in succession over a long season. The flowers of hybrid cultivars tend to be larger and more showy than those of species. Many mulleins are quite tall, and they may need to be staked. All self-sow freely, and the seedlings of the named varieties will not come true, so they should be dead-headed. The larger species can be left to naturalise in gravel or in wild gardens, where they make impressive architectural plants and benefit from the support of other plants. The smaller types are good for rock gardens, screes, or even walls. All mulleins are unfortunately prone to powdery mildew.

***Verbascum bombyciferum* A.G.M.**
(Scrophulariaceae)

Common name: Mullein
Height: 1.8m (6ft)
Spread: 90cm (3ft)
Aspect: Sun
Soil: Sharply drained, alkaline, poor
Hardiness: Zone 6
Propagation: Seed or division, both in spring; root cuttings, in winter

Short-lived evergreen from Turkey. Leaves basal, densely white-woolly, silky-hairy. Flowers sulphur-yellow, saucer-shaped, in spikes, in clusters, in summer.

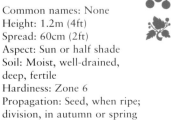

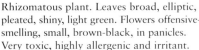

Verbascum chaixii
(Scrophulariaceae)

Common name: Nettle-leaved mullein
Height: 90cm (36in)
Spread: 45cm (18in)
Aspect: Sun
Soil: Sharply drained, alkaline, poor
Hardiness: Zone 5
Propagation: Seed or division, both in spring; root cuttings, in winter

Species from Europe. Leaves basal, ovate, hairy, and stem, rounded. Flowers in slim panicles on white-woolly stems, pale yellow saucers, from mid- to late summer.

Verbascum chaixii
'Album' (Scrophulariaceae)

Common name: White netttle-leaved mullein
Height: 90cm (3ft)
Spread: 60cm (2ft)
Aspect: Sun
Soil: Sharply drained, alkaline, poor
Hardiness: Zone 5
Propagation: Seed or division, both in spring; root cuttings, in winter

Leaves basal, ovate, hairy, mid-green, and stem, rounded. Flowers on white-woolly stems, in slim panicles, white saucers with mauve centres, from mid- to late summer.

Verbascum dumulosum
A.G.M.
(Scrophulariaceae)

Common name: Mullein
Height: 25cm (10in)
Spread: 40cm (16in)
Aspect: Sun
Soil: Sharply drained, alkaline, poor
Hardiness: Zone 8
Propagation: Seed or division, both in spring; root cuttings, in winter

Evergreen subshrub from Turkey. Leaves elliptic, hairy-felted, grey-green. Flowers on white-downy stems, in short racemes, yellow saucers, late spring to early summer.

Verbascum chaixii
'Gainsborough' A.G.M.
(Scrophulariaceae)

Common name: Mullein
Height: 1.2m (4ft)
Spread: 30cm (1ft)
Aspect: Sun
Soil: Sharply drained, alkaline, poor
Hardiness: Zone 6
Propagation: Division, in spring; root cuttings, in winter

A hybrid mullein. Leaves in basal rosettes, ovate, wrinkled, grey-green. Flowers in long panicles, soft yellow saucers, from early to late summer.

Verbascum
'Helen Johnson' A.G.M.
(Scrophulariaceae)

Common name: Mullein
Height: 90cm (3ft)
Spread: 30cm (1ft)
Aspect: Sun
Soil: Sharply drained, alkaline, poor
Hardiness: Zone 7
Propagation: Division, in spring; root cuttings, in winter

Evergreen, hybrid mullein. Leaves ovate, wrinkled, downy, grey-green. Flowers in erect spikes, pinkish-brown saucers, from early to late summer.

Verbascum
'Jackie'
(Scrophulariaceae)

Common name: Mullein
Height: 90cm (36in)
Spread: 45cm (18in)
Aspect: Sun
Soil: Sharply drained, alkaline, poor
Hardiness: Zone 6
Propagation: Division, in spring; root cuttings, in winter

Rosette-forming, hybrid mullein. Leaves ovate, downy, grey-green. Flowers in erect spikes, buff-pink saucers with a purple eye, in summer.

Verbascum nigrum
(Scrophulariaceae)

Common name: Dark mullein
Height: 90cm (3ft)
Spread: 60cm (2ft)
Aspect: Sun
Soil: Sharply drained, alkaline, poor
Hardiness: Zone5
Propagation: Seed or division, both in spring; root cuttings, in winter

Rosette-forming species. Leaves basal, ovate, and stem, rounded, mid- to dark-green. Slim racemes of clustered flowers, dark yellow saucers, midsummer to early autumn.

Verbascum olympicum
(Scrophulariaceae)

Common name: Mullein
Height: 2m (6ft)
Spread: 60cm (2ft)
Aspect: Sun
Soil: Sharply drained, alkaline, poor
Hardiness: Zone 6
Propagation: Seed or division, both in spring; root cuttings, in winter

Rosette-forming species. Leaves broad, lance-shaped, grey-white woolly. Flowers in panicles, clustered, golden-yellow saucers, from early to late summer. May then die.

Native to Europe, Turkey, and Central Asia, Veronica spicata *is excellent for rock or gravel gardens.*

Verbena bonariensis
(Verbenaceae)

Common names: None
Height: 2m (6ft)
Spread: 75cm (30in)
Aspect: Sun
Soil: Moist, well-drained, fertile
Hardiness: Zone 8
Propagation: Seed or division, both in spring

Clump-forming plant. Leaves few, oblong, wrinkled, stem-clasping, mid-green. Flowers in cymes, purple-lilac salvers, midsummer to early autumn. Excellent butterfly plant.

Verbena hastata
'Alba'
(Verbenaceae)

Common name: White blue vervain
Height: 1.2m (4ft)
Spread: 60cm (2ft)
Aspect: Sun
Soil: Moist, well-drained, fertile
Hardiness: Zone 3
Propagation: Seed or division, both in spring

Clump-forming plant from North America. Leaves lance-shaped, toothed, pointed, mid-green. Flowers in stiff panicles, white, salverform, early summer to early autumn.

Verbena
'Homestead Purple'
(Verbenaceae)

Common names: Hybrid verbena
Height: 45cm (18in)
Spread: 50cm (20in)
Aspect: Sun
Soil: Moist, well-drained, fertile
Hardiness: Zone 8
Propagation: Division in spring or autumn; stem-tip cuttings, in late summer

Hybrid cultivar. Leaves ovate, toothed, rough, dark green. Flowers in tight panicles, tiny, salverform, purple, all summer to autumn.

Verbena
'Sissinghurst' A.G.M.
(Verbenaceae)

Common name: Hybrid verbena
Height: 45cm (18in)
Spread: 50cm (20in)
Aspect: Sun
Soil: Moist, well-drained, fertile
Hardiness: Zone 8
Propagation: Division, in autumn or spring; stem-tip cuttings, in late summer

A hybrid cultivar. Leaves ovate, toothed, rough, mid-green. Flowers tiny, salverform, cherry-red, in tight panicles, from summer to autumn.

Veronica
'Blue Spire'
(Scrophulariaceae)

Common names: None
Height: 90cm (3ft)
Spread: 60cm (2ft)
Aspect: Sun or half shade
Soil: Moist, well-drained, humus-rich, fertile
Hardiness: Zone 6
Propagation: Division, in autumn or spring

A hybrid perennial. Leaves lance-shaped, toothed, pointed, mid-green. Flowers in dense, erect racemes, tubular, deep blue, in late summer and early autumn.

Veronica gentianoides
A.G.M.
(Scrophulariaceae)

Common names: None
Height: 45cm (18in)
Spread: 45cm (18in)
Aspect: Sun or half shade
Soil: Moist, well-drained, humus-rich, fertile
Hardiness: Zone 4
Propagation: Seed, in autumn; division, in autumn or spring

Rosette-forming perennial from Turkey and the Ukraine. Leaves broad, lance-shaped, thick, dark green. Flowers pale blue cups, in erect racemes, in early summer.

Veronica
'Ray of Fire'
(Scrophulariaceae)

Common names: None
Height: 75cm (30in)
Spread: 60cm (24in)
Aspect: Sun or half shade
Soil: Moist, well-drained, humus-rich, fertile
Hardiness: Zone 5
Propagation: Division, in autumn or spring

A hybrid, mat-forming perennial. Leaves lance-shaped, pointed, mid-green. Flowers in dense, terminal panicles, pinkish-red, tubular, in late summer and autumn.

Veronica spicata
subsp. *incana* A.G.M.
(Scrophulariaceae)

Common names: None
Height: 30cm (1ft)
Spread: 30cm (1ft)
Aspect: Sun or half shade
Soil: Moist, well-drained, humus-rich, fertile
Hardiness: Zone 3
Propagation: Seed, in autumn; division, in autumn or spring

A mat-forming perennial from Eurasia and Turkey. Leaves linear, toothed, silver-hairy. Flowers in dense, terminal racemes, bright blue stars, from early to late summer.

Veronica spicata
'Rotfuchs'
(Scrophulariaceae)

Common names: None
Height: 30cm (1ft)
Spread: 30cm (1ft)
Aspect: Sun or half shade
Soil: Moist, well-drained, humus-rich, fertile
Hardiness: Zone 3
Propagation: Division, in spring or autumn; stem-tip cuttings, in summer

A hybrid, mat-forming perennial. Leaves linear, toothed, mid-green. Flowers in dense, terminal racemes, deep pink stars, from early to late summer.

Veronicastrum virginicum
f. *album*
(Scrophulariaceae)

Common name: Culver's root
Height: 2m (6ft)
Spread: 45cm (18in)
Aspect: Sun or half shade
Soil: Moist, humus-rich, fertile
Hardiness: Zone3
Propagation: Seed, in autumn; division, in spring

Perennial from North America. Leaves lance-shaped, toothed, pointed, dark green. Flowers white, tubular, in slim, dense racemes, from midsummer to early autumn.

Veronicastrum virginicum
'Pink Glow'
(Scrophulariaceae)

Common name: Culver's root
Height: 2m (6ft)
Spread: 45cm (18in)
Aspect: Sun or half shade
Soil: Moist, humus-rich, fertile
Hardiness: Zone 3
Propagation: Division, in spring

Selected form of the species. Leaves lance-shaped, toothed, pointed, dark green. Soft pink, tubular flowers, in dense racemes, from midsummer to early autumn.

Vinca major
(Apocynaceae)

Common name: Greater periwinkle
Height: 45cm (18in)
Spread: Indefinite
Aspect: Sun or half shade
Soil: Moisture-retentive
Hardiness: Zone 7
Propagation: Division, from autumn to spring

Evergreen, trailing, Mediterranean ground-cover subshrub. Leaves ovate, shiny, dark green. Flowers starry, violet-blue, over long period from mid-spring to autumn. Toxic.

Vinca major
'Variegata' A.G.M.
(Apocynaceae)

Common name: Variegated greater periwinkle
Height: 45cm (18in)
Spread: Indefinite
Aspect: Sun or half shade
Soil: Moisture-retentive
Hardiness: Zone 7
Propagation: Division, from autumn to spring

Evergreen, trailing, Mediterranean ground cover subshrub. Leaves ovate, dark green margined cream; good for cutting. Flowers lilac-blue, starry, from spring to autumn.

Vinca minor
(Apocynaceae)

Common name: Lesser periwinkle
Height: 20cm (8in)
Spread: Indefinite
Aspect: Sun or half shade
Soil: Moisture-retentive
Hardiness: Zone 4
Propagation: Division, from autumn to spring

Trailing, evergreen subshrub from Eurasia, not invasive like *V. major*. Leaves ovate, dark green. Flowers reddish-purple, blue or white, all summer long.

VIOLA (Violaceae)
Viola • Pansy • Violetta

A genus of some 500 species from habitats the world over. The genus has given rise, by interbreeding, to three main types of plant: garden pansies, violas and violettas. The garden pansies, *Viola* x *wittrockiana*, have arisen from the crossing of several species. They are biennial or at best a very short-lived perennial, with unscented or only faintly scented flowers with a "face", and single-stemmed roots. The violas or tufted pansies are perennial, with rounded, usually scented flowers with rays of a contrasting, often deeper colour, and multiple-stemmed roots. The violettas are perennial, sweetly scented, with oval flowers with a yellow centre but no rays, and a multi-stemmed root system. Other forms include South American species that have rosettes of leaves like those of a sempervivum; these are very difficult in cultivation, and best left to the enthusiast. There are ten subdivisions in all, but only the violas (Va) and violettas (Vtta) are of interest and covered here. All forms of *Viola* like full sun or partial shade, and moist, well-drained but moisture-retentive soil. They all have a long flowering season, and can be made even more prolific by dead-heading. Many of the species violas are unfortunately short-lived.

Viola biflora
(Va)
(Violaceae)

Common name: Twin-flowered violet
Height: 8cm (3in)
Spread: 20cm (8in)
Aspect: Half shade
Soil: Moist, humus-rich, fertile
Hardiness: Zone 4
Propagation: Seed, as soon as ripe or in spring

Dwarf, creeping, rhizomatous species from Eurasia and North America. Leaves heart-shaped, toothed, pale green. Flowers pale yellow, dark-veined, late spring and summer.

Viola cornuta
A.G.M. (Va)
(Violaceae)

Common name: Horned violet
Height: 15cm (6in)
Spread: 40cm (16in)
Aspect: Sun or half shade
Soil: Moist, humus-rich, fertile
Hardiness: Zone 7
Propagation: Division or stem-tip cuttings, both in spring or autumn

A rhizomatous, evergreen species. Leaves ovate, toothed, mid-green. Flowers scented, lilac-blue, lower petals marked white, from spring to summer, twice if sheared over.

Viola cornuta
Alba Group A.G.M. (Va)
(Violaceae)

Common name: White horned violet
Height: 15cm (6in)
Spread: 45cm (18in)
Aspect: Sun or half shade
Soil: Moist, humus-rich, fertile
Hardiness: Zone 7
Propagation: Division or stem-tip cuttings, both in spring or autumn

White form of evergreen, rhizomatous species, flowering in spring and summer, twice if sheared over. Flowers pure white. Leaves ovate, toothed, mid-green.

Viola
'Columbine' (Va)
(Violaceae)

Common names: None
Height: 20cm (8in)
Spread: 30cm (12in)
Aspect: Sun or half shade
Soil: Moist, well-drained, fertile
Hardiness: Zone 7
Propagation: Division or stem-tip cuttings, both in spring or autumn

A compact, hybrid viola. Leaves ovate, toothed, mid-green. Flowers lilac and white, streaked purple, held high above the foliage, in spring and summer.

Viola
'Jackanapes' A.G.M. (Va)
(Violaceae)

Common names: None
Height: 20cm (8in)
Spread: 45cm (18in)
Aspect: Sun or half shade
Soil: Moist, well-drained, fertile
Hardiness: Zone 7
Propagation: Division or stem-tip cuttings, both in spring or autumn

Vigorous, evergreen hybrid. Leaves ovate, toothed, mid-green. Flowers have upper 3 petals chocolate-coloured, lower 3 yellow, streaked purple, in spring and summer.

Viola
'Jeannie Bellew' (Va)
(Violaceae)

Common names: None
Height: 20cm (8in)
Spread: 45cm (18in)
Aspect: Sun or half shade
Soil: Moist, well-drained, fertile
Hardiness: Zone 7
Propagation: Division or stem-tip cuttings, both in spring or autumn

A hybrid viola cultivar. Leaves ovate, toothed, mid-green. Flowers of pale yellow are borne among the leaves in spring and summer.

Viola
'Maggie Mott' A.G.M. (Va)
(Violaceae)

Common names: None
Height: 30cm (1ft)
Spread: 30cm (1ft)
Aspect: Sun or half shade
Soil: Moist, well-drained, fertile
Hardiness: Zone 7
Propagation: Division or stem-tip cuttings, both in spring or autumn

Hybrid viola. Leaves ovate, toothed, mid-green. Flowers perfumed, soft silvery-mauve, with a pale cream centre, in spring and summer. A very popular old variety.

Viola
'Rebecca' (Vtta)
(Violaceae)

Common names: None
Height: 15cm (6in)
Spread: 20cm (8in)
Aspect: Sun or half shade
Soil: Moist, well-drained, fertile
Hardiness: Zone 7
Propagation: Division or stem-tip cuttings, both in spring or autumn

A hybrid violetta. Leaves ovate, toothed, mid-green. Flowers scented, creamy-white, flecked and streaked with violet around the edges, in spring and summer.

Given its favoured conditions in a rock garden or wall, Zauschneria californica *will bear abundant flowers from late summer into early autumn.*

Viola tricolor (Va)
(Violaceae)

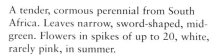

Common names: Heartsease; love-in-idleness; wild pansy
Height: 12cm (5in)
Spread: 15cm (6in)
Aspect: Sun or half shade
Soil: Moist, well-drained, fertile
Hardiness: Zone 4
Propagation: Seed, as soon as ripe or in spring

Short-lived, evergreen species. Leaves ovate, toothed, mid-green. Flowers have dark purple upper petals and yellow, streaked lower petals. Self-seeds plentifully.

Viola
'Zoe' (Vtta)
(Violaceae)

Common names: None
Height: 15cm (6in)
Spread: 20cm (8in)
Aspect: Sun or half shade
Soil: Moist, well-drained, fertile
Hardiness: Zone 7
Propagation: Division or stem-tip cuttings, both in spring or autumn

A hybrid violetta cultivar. Leaves ovate, toothed, mid-green. Flowers perfumed, mauve and white with a yellow eye, in spring and summer.

Wachendorfia paniculata
(Haemodoraceae)

Common name: Red root
Height: 1.8m (6ft)
Spread: 45cm (18in)
Aspect: Sun or half shade
Soil: Moist, well-drained, humus-rich fertile
Hardiness: Zone 8
Propagation: Seed in warmth or separated tubers, both in spring

Tuberous, evergreen perennial from South Africa. Leaves basal, broad, linear, veined, mid-green. Flowers in dense panicles, yellow, starry, in early summer.

Watsonia borbonica
subsp. *ardernei*
(Iridaceae)

Common names: None
Height: 1.5m (5ft)
Spread: 10cm (4in)
Aspect: Sun
Soil: Well-drained, humus-rich, fertile
Hardiness: Zone 9
Propagation: Seed, in warmth in autumn; division, in spring

A tender, cormous perennial from South Africa. Leaves narrow, sword-shaped, mid-green. Flowers in spikes of up to 20, white, rarely pink, in summer.

Watsonia densiflora
(Iridaceae)

Common names: None
Height: 1.5m (5ft)
Spread: 10cm (4in)
Aspect: Sun
Soil: Well-drained, humus-rich, fertile
Hardiness: Zone 9
Propagation: Seed, in warmth in autumn; division, in spring

A tender, cormous perennial from South Africa. Leaves narrow, sword-shaped, mid-green. Flowers in spikes of up to 30, red or orange-red, in summer.

Watsonia marginata
(Iridaceae)

Common names: None
Height: 2m (6ft)
Spread: 15cm (6in)
Aspect: Sun
Soil: Well-drained, humus-rich, fertile
Hardiness: Zone 9
Propagation: Seed, in warmth in autumn; division, in spring

A tender, cormous perennial from South Africa. Leaves sword-shaped, mid-green. Flowers in spikes, tubular, mauve-pink, in spring and early summer.

Woodsia polystichoides
A.G.M.
(Aspidiaceae/Dryopteridaceae)

Common name: Holly-fern woodsia
Height: 30cm (12in)
Spread: 40cm (16in)
Aspect: Half shade
Soil: Moist, sharply drained, fertile
Hardiness: Zone 4
Propagation: Spores, in warmth when ripe; division, when dormant

A deciduous, rhizomatous, terrestrial fern from high regions of East Asia. Fronds lance-shaped, pinnate, with 15–30 pairs of oblong pinnae, pale green.

Woodwardia radicans
A.G.M
(Blechnaceae)

Common name: European chain fern
Height: 1.8m (6ft)
Spread: 3m (10ft)
Aspect: Half shade
Soil: Wet, fertile
Hardiness: Zone 8
Propagation: Bulbils or spores, in warmth in early autumn; division, in spring

Evergreen fern from Europe and islands of the Atlantic. Fronds pinnate, lance-shaped, dark green; pinnae ovate, pinnatifid, with lance-shaped, toothed segments.

Yucca filamentosa
A.G.M
(Agavaceae)

Common names: Adam's needle; Spanish bayonet
Height: 75cm (30in)
Spread: 1.5m (5ft)
Aspect: Sun
Soil: Well-drained
Hardiness: Zone 7
Propagation: Seed in warmth or rooted suckers, both in spring; root cuttings, in winter

Evergreen shrub. Leaves in basal rosettes, inverse lance-shaped, fringed, dark green. Flowers in short-stemmed, upright panicles, nodding, white bells, mid- to late summer.

Yucca flaccida
'Ivory' A.G.M.
(Agavaceae)

Common name: Spanish bayonet
Height: 60cm (2ft)
Spread: 1.5m (5ft)
Aspect: Sun
Soil: Well-drained
Hardiness: Zone 7
Propagation: Seed in warmth or rooted suckers, both in spring; root cuttings, in winter

Evergreen shrub. Leaves in basal rosettes, lance-shaped, dark blue-green, fringed. Flowers in panicles, nodding creamy-white bells, in mid and late summer.

Yucca gloriosa
'Variegata' A.G.M.
(Agavaceae)

Common names: Spanish bayonet; Spanish dagger
Height: 2m (6ft)
Spread: 2m (6ft)
Aspect: Sun
Soil: Well-drained
Hardiness: Zone 7
Propagation: Seed in warmth or rooted suckers, both in spring; root cuttings, in winter

Evergreen shrub. Leaves in basal rosettes, arching, lance-shaped, pointed, green, edged yellow. Flowers in panicles, white pendent bells, from late summer to autumn.

Zantedeschia aethiopica
A.G.M.
(Araceae)

Common name: Arum lily
Height: 90cm (3ft)
Spread: 60cm (2ft)
Aspect: Sun
Soil: Moist or marginal aquatic, humus-rich
Hardiness: Zone 8
Propagation: Seed, in warmth when ripe; division, in spring

A rhizomatous perennial from southern Africa. Leaves arrow-shaped, glossy-green. Bears large, pure white spathes with yellow spadices from late spring to mid-summer.

Zantedeschia elliottiana
A.G.M.
(Araceae)

Common name: Golden arum lily
Height: 90cm (36in)
Spread: 25cm (10in)
Aspect: Sun
Soil: Moist, humus-rich
Hardiness: Zone 9
Propagation: Seed, in warmth when ripe; division, in spring

Tender rhizomatous perennial of unknown source. Leaves basal, heart-shaped, dark green, spotted white. Spathes and spadices golden yellow, in summer.

Zantedeschia
Elliottiana hybrids
(Araceae)

Common name: Golden arum lily
Height: 60cm (2ft)
Spread: 20cm (8in)
Aspect: Sun
Soil: Moist, humus-rich
Hardiness: Zone 9
Propagation: Division, in spring

Tender, rhizomatous perennial hybrids from *Z. elliottiana*. Leaves basal, heart-shaped, dark green, unspotted. Spathes in a variety of shades of red, orange and yellow.

Zantedeschia rehmannii
A.G.M.
(Araceae)

Common name: Pink arum
Height: 40cm (16in)
Spread: 28cm (11in)
Aspect: Sun
Soil: Moist, humus-rich
Hardiness: Zone 9
Propagation: Seed, in warmth when ripe; division, in spring

A tender, rhizomatous perennial from southern Africa. Leaves basal, lance-shaped, dark green. Spathe pink, spadix yellow, in summer.

Zauschneria californica
(Onagraceae)

Common name: Californian fuchsia
Height: 30cm (12in)
Spread: 50cm (20in)
Aspect: Sun
Soil: Well-drained, fertile
Hardiness: Zone 8
Propagation: Seed or basal cuttings, both in spring

Rhizomatous evergreen from California. Leaves lance-shaped, hairy, grey-green. Flowers in racemes, tubular, scarlet, long periods in late summer and early autumn.

Zauschneria californica **subsp.** *cana*
(Onagraceae)

Common name: Californian fuchsia
Height: 60cm (24in)
Spread: 45cm (18in)
Aspect: Sun
Soil: Well-drained, fertile
Hardiness: Zone 8
Propagation: Seed or basal cuttings, both in spring

Deciduous, rhizomatous perennial from California. Leaves linear, grey woolly-hairy. Flowers in racemes, tubular, vermilion; long period from late summer to early autumn.

Zephyranthes candida
(Amaryllidaceae)

Common names: Rain flower; windflower
Height: 20cm (8in)
Spread: 8cm (3in)
Aspect: Sun
Soil: Moist, well-drained
Hardiness: Zone 9
Propagation: Seed, in warmth when ripe; offsets, in spring

Tender, bulbous perennial from Argentina. Leaves basal, grassy, upright, mid-green. Flowers solitary, crocus-like, white, over a long period from summer to early autumn.

Zephyranthes flavissima
(Amaryllidaceae)

Common names: Rain flower; windflower
Height: 20cm (8in)
Spread: 8cm (3in)
Aspect: Sun
Soil: Moist, well-drained
Hardiness: Zone 8
Propagation: Seed, in warmth when ripe; offsets, in spring

A bulbous perennial from South America. Leaves grassy, linear, mid-green. Flowers solitary, crocus-like, yellow goblets, from summer to autumn.

Zigadenus elegans
(Liliaceae/Melianthaceae)

Common names: None
Height: 70cm (28in)
Spread: 20cm (8in)
Aspect: Sun or half shade
Soil: Moist, well-drained deep, fertile
Hardiness: Zone 3
Propagation: Seed, in warmth when ripe; offsets, in spring

A bulbous perennial from North America. Leaves basal, grassy, grey-green. Flowers in many-flowered spikes, small, greenish-white, starry, in mid- and late summer.

APPENDICES

THE APPENDICES BELOW list genera and species of perennials that share certain characteristics. These lists provide instant reference for the gardener looking for plants to suit specific growing conditions or plants with desirable attributes such as a long flowering season, perfumed flowers or attractive seed heads. The selections also list plants to avoid if, for example, a child-friendly garden is required, free from poisonous plants, or if a household member is prone to allergies and therefore favours low-allergen plants. Detailed information on the plants in these appendices can be found by referring to the individual entry in the Plant Directory on pages 26–289.

Long-flowering perennials

Acanthus
Achillea
Aeonium
Alcea
Alchemilla
Alstroemeria
Althaea
Anchusa
Anemone × *hybrida*
Anemone multifida
Anisodontea capensis
Anthemis
Arctotis
Argyranthemum
Aster × *frikartii* 'Monch'
Astrantia
Begonia grandis
Bellis
Calceolaria
Campanula
Canna
Catananche
Centranthus
Chrysogonum virginianum
Commelina coelestis
Coreopsis
Corydalis ochroleuca
Cosmos atrpsanguineus
Crepis incana
Crocosmia
Dahlia
Dianthus deltoides
Diascia
Dicentra
Epilobium
Eremurus
Erigeron
Erodium
Erysimum
Eucomis
Fragaria
Fuchsia
Gaillardia
Gaura
Gazania
Geranium
Geum
Helenium
Helianthemum
Helichrysum italicum
Hieracium
Hemerocallis
Hosta
Iris japonica
Lavatera
Leucanthemum × *superbum*
Linaria purpurea
Linum perenne
Liriope
Lychnis coronaria
Lysimachia punctata
Lythrum
Malva moschata
Meconopsis cambrica
Melissa officinalis
Mertensia
Mimulus
Mirabilis jalapa
Monarda
Neirembergia
Nemesia denticulata
Nepeta
Nerine
Oenothera
Omphalodes
Origanum
Osteospermum
Pelargonium
Penstemon
Phlox 'Chattahoochee'
Phuopsis
Phygelius
Potentilla
Pratia
Pulmonaria
Rhodanthemum
Rhodohypoxis
Romneya
Roscoea
Rudbeckia
Salvia
Scabiosa
Senecio viravira
Solenopsis axillaris
Sphaeralcea
Stachys
Symphyandra
Symphytum armena
Teucrium
Tradescantia × *andersoniana*
Tuberaria lignosa
Tulbaghia
Verbascum
Verbena
Viola
Zauschneria

Evergreen perennials

Achillea (some)
Aciphylla
Agapanthus (some)
Agave
Alchemilla
Alyssum saxatile
Anthemis
Arabis
Armeria
Asarum
Asplenium
Astilbe glaberrima
Aubrieta
Bergenia
Blechnum
Campanla porschkiana
Carex
Celmisia
Cerastium
Chrysogonum virginianum
Cortaderia
Dianella
Dianthus
Dicksonia
Dierama
Draba
Dryopteris (some)
Epimedium (some)
Erigeron glaucus
Eryngium (some)
Erysimum
Euphorbia (most)
Fascicularia
Festuca (some)
Gazania
Geum
Helleborus
Heuchera (most)
× *Heucherella*
Iris douglasiana
Iris 'Holden Clough'
Iris innominata
Iris japonica
Iris pallida
Juncus
Kniphofia (some)
Lavandula
Lewisia
Libertia
Limonium
Liriope
Luzula
Mitchella repens
Moraea
Morina
Orthrosanthus
Parahebe
Pelargonium
Phlomis
Phormium
Plectranthus ciliatus
Polygala chamaebuxus
Polypodium (some)
Polystichium (some)
Pulmonaria (most)
Reineckia
Salvia africana-lutea
Salvia leucantha
Santolina chamaecyparissus
Saxifraga stolonifera
Saxifraga veitchiana
Sedum acre
Sedum rupestre
Selaginella
Sempervivum arachnoideum
Sesleria
Sisyrinchium
Stachys
Stipa gigantea
Strelitzia reginae
Tanacetum
Tellima
Tulbaghia
Tweedia caerulea
Uncinia
Valeriana
Vinca
Woodsia (some)
Woodwardia some
Yucca

Shade-loving perennials

Actaea
Ajuga
Alchemilla
Anemone × *hybrida*
Anemone nemorosa
Aquilegia
Arum italicum
Aruncus
Asplenium scolopodendrium
Aster macrophyllus
Astilbe
Athyrium filix-femina
Begonia grandis
Bergenia
Blechnum
Brunnera
Campanula latifolia
Cardamine
Cardiocrinum
Carex
Chaerophyllum
Chelidonium
Chrysogonum
Cicerbita
Cimicifuga

Clintonia
Codonopsis
Convallaria
Cortusa
Corydalis
Cyclamen
Cypripedium
Dactylorhiza
Davallia
Dicentra
Dicksonia
Digitalis
Diphylleia
Disporum
Dodecatheon
Doronicum
Dryopteris
Eomecon
Epimedium
Epipactis
Eupatorium
Euphorbia some
Gentiana aslepiadea
Geranium some
Helleborus
× *Heucherella*
Hosta
Hyacinthoides
Hylomecon
Iris foetidissima
Kirengeshoma palmata
Lamium
Leucojum
Lilium martagon
Liriope
Lunaria
Luzula
Meconopsis
Milium
Mitchella
Myrrhis
Nomocharis
Osmunda
Ourisia
Paeonia (some)
Paris
Podophyllum
Polygonatum
Polygonum
Polypodium
Polystichium
Primula
Pulmonaria
Saxifraga some
Scopolia
Selaginella
Sesleria
Smilacina
Spiranthes
Stipa
Stylophorum
Symphytum
Tellima
Tiarella
Trillium
Uvularia
Vinca

Drought-tolerant perennials

Acanthus
Achillea
Agapanthus
Agave
Aloe
Anemone nemorosa
Anisodontea
Anomatheca
Anthericum
Aristaea
Artemesia
Arthropodium
Arum
Asarina
Asphodelus
Asteriscus
Ballota
Begonia grandis
Buglossoides
Buphthalmum
Bupleurum
Camassia
Carex
Catananche
Centaurea
Chiastophyllum
Claytonia
Commelina
Convolvulus
Crambe
Crepis
Cynara
Dicentra
Dichelostemma
Digitalis
Diplarrhena
Dracunculus
Echinops
Echium
Elsholtzia
Elymus
Eranthis
Eremurus
Eriophyllum
Erodium
Eucomis
Francoa
Fritillaria
Galanthus
Galega
Galtonia
Geranium (most)
Gladiolus
Glaucium
Grindelia
Hedysarum
Hieracium
Hyacinthus
Ipheion
Iris (some)
Ixia
Knautia
Lamium
Lathyrus
Lavandula
Lavatera
Leonotis
Leptinella
Lewisia
Lilium (some)
Limonium
Linaria
Linum
Lotus
Luzula
Lychnis
Malvastrum
Marrubium
Megacarpaea
Melianthus
Melissa
Nepeta
Nerine
Oenothera (some)
Onosma
Ophiopogon
Origanum
Ornithogalum
Othonna
Oxalis
Papaver
Pentas
Perovskia
Phaenosperma
Phlomis
Phyteuma
Pilosella
Plantago
Polypodium
Polystichium
Pulsatilla
Puschkinia
Rehmannia
Reineckia
Rhodanthemum
Rhodiola
Rhodohypoxis
Rosularia
Scabiosa
Scilla
Sedum
Silene
Stachys
Stipa
Stokesia
Symphytum (some)
Thalictrum
Tiarella
Trifolium
Tritonia
Tulbaghia
Umbilicus
Verbascum
Verbena
Wachendorfia

Perennials for acid soils

Anemonopsis macrophylla
Blechnum
Celmisia
Cornus canadensis
Cypripedium
Dianella
Dodecatheon
Erythronium
Galax urceolata
Gentiana (autumn-flowering)
Hacquetia
Hylomecon
Iris 'Brighteyes'
Iris chrysographes
Iris douglasiana
Iris ensata
Iris graminea
Iris innominata
Iris laevigata
Iris missouriensis
Iris pallida
Iris pumila
Iris sibirica
Iris spuria
Iris tenax
Iris tridentata
Iris uromovii
Kirengeshoma palmata
Lilium formosanum
Lilium grayi
Lilium lancifolium
Lilium pumilum
Lilium speciosum
Lithodora diffusa
Maianthemum bifolium
Meconopsis betonicifolia
Meconopsis chelidoniifolia
Meconopsis grandis
Meconopsis napaulensis
Meconopsis punicea
Meconopsis regia
Meconopsis × *sheldonii*
Mitchella
Narcissus (some)
Ophiopogon
Osmunda
Plantago
Podophyllum
Primula bulleyana
Primula capitata
Primula denticulata
Primula japonica
Primula juliae
Primula prolifera
Primula pulverulenta
Primula rosea
Primula veris
Primula vialii
Reineckia carnea
Sarracenia
Sidalcea
Smilacina racemosa
Trillium
Uvularia
Viola pedata

Perennials for cut flowers

Achillea
Aconitum
Agapanthus
Anaphalis
Anchusa
Anemone × *hybrida*
Aquilegia
Aster novae-angliae
Aster novae-belgii
Astilbe
Astrantia major
Bergenia
Campanula
Catananche
Convallaria
Crocosmia
Delphinium
Dianthus
Dicentra
Digitalis
Doronicum
Echinacea
Echinops ritro
Gaillardia
Galanthus
Gentiana
Gypsophila
Helianthus
Helleborus
Iris
Leucanthemum
Liatris
Lilium
Monarda
Narcissus
Paeonia officinalis
Paradisea
Phlox paniculata
Platycodon
Polemonium
Polygonatum × *hybridum*
Ranunculus
Rudbeckia
Schizostylis
Solidago
Stachys
Strelitzia
Tanacetum
Tulipa
Viola odorata
Zantedeschia

Perennials with perfumed flowers

Asphodeline lutea
Begonia grandis
Cardiocrinum giganteum
Clematis heracleifolia
Convallaria majalis
Cosmos atrosanguineus
Crambe
Crinum × *powellii*
Cyclamen
Dianthus
Dictamnus
Erysimum
Filipendula
Galanthus
Galtonia candicans
Hedychium
Hemerocallis (some)
Hesperis matrionalis
Hosta 'Honeybells'
Hosta plantaginea
Hosta 'Sweet Susan'
Hyacinthoides non-scripta
Hyacinthus orientalis
Ipheion
Iris chrysographes
Iris graminea
Iris pallida
Iris reticulata
Lathyrus odoatus
Lilium 'African Queen'
Lilium candidum
Lilium formosanum
Lilium grayi
Lilium henryi
Lilium monadelphum
Lilium Pink Perfection Group
Lilium pumilum
Lilium regale
Lunaria rediviva
Mirabilis jalapa
Muscari armeniacum
Narcissus jonquilla
Nymphaea
Ornithogalum arabicum
Paeonia lactiflora
Paradisea
Phlox maculata
Phlox paniculata (some)
Primula auricula
Primula vulgaris
Romneya coulteri
Sedum populifolium
Spiranthes
Tulbaghia
Tulipa sylvestris
Verbena bonariensis
Verbena × *hybrida*
Viola odorata

Aquatic and marginal perennials

Alisma plantago-aquatica
Butomus umbellatus
Caltha palustris
Carex
Cyperus
Houttuynia
Iris ensata
Iris 'Holden Clough'
Iris laevigata
Iris pseudacorus
Iris sibirica
Juncus spiralis
Lobelia cardinalis
Lythrum salicaria
Mimulus
Myosotis scorpiodes
Nymphaea
Nymphoides
Peltiphyllum peltatum
Phormium tenax
Pontederia cordata
Ranunculus aquatilis
Ranunculus lingua
Sagittaria
Saururus cernuus
Schoenoplectus lacustris
Scirpus
Scrophularia auriculata
Zantedeschia

Bog garden perennials

Aruncus dioicus
Astilbe
Caltha
Cardamine
Cardiocrinum
Cimicifuga simplex
Eupatorium
Filipendula
Fritillaria meleagris
Geum rivale
Glyceria
Gunnera
Hemerocallis
Hosta
Houttuynia
Iris ensata
Iris laevigata
Iris pseudacorus
Iris sibirica
Kirengeshoma
Leucojum
Ligularia
Lobelia cardinalis
Lychnis flos-cuculi
Lysimachia
Lythrum
Mimulus
Monarda
Onoclea
Osmunda
Parnassia
Polygonum
Primula (many)
Ranunculus aconitifolius
Ranunculus lingua
Rheum
Rodgersia
Sanguisorba obtusa
Sarracenia
Schizostylis
Symphytum × *uplandicum*
Trollius
Uvularia
Woodsia
Woodwardia

Perennials with attractive seed heads

Acanthus
Achillea
Aconitum
Agapanthus
Alchemilla
Allium
Alstroemeria
Althaea
Anaphalis
Anemone × *hybrida*
Artemesia
Asphodeline
Asphodelus
Astilbe
Baptisia
Cardiocrinum
Catananche
Cautleya
Centaurea
Cimicifuga simplex
Clematis (some)
Crambe maritima
Dierama
Diplarrhena
Echinops
Eremurus
Eryngium
Eupatorium
Euphorbia some
Filipendula
Galtonia
Gillenia
Glaucium
Gypsophila
Hyacinthoides
Incarvillea
Iris (some)
Lathyrus vernus
Lychnis (some)
Malva
Monarda
Moraea
Morina
Nectaroscordum siculum
Paeonia (some)
Papaver orientale
Paradisea
Paris
Phlomis
Phormium
Pulsatilla
Rheum
Rodgersia
Rumex
Scabiosa (some)
Sedum (some)
Sisyrinchium striatum
Stokesia
Thalictrum
Veratrum
Veronicastrum

Perennials for ground cover

Acaena
Acanthus
Achillea
Adiantium
Aegopodium podagraria
Ajuga
Alchemilla
Alyssum
Anaphalis
Anemone × *hybrida*
Antennaria
Anthemis
Anthericum
Arabis
Arenaria
Arisarum
Armeria
Artemesia
Aruncus
Aster macrophyllus
Astilbe
Astrantia
Aubrieta
Ballota
Bergenia
Blechnum
Brunnera
Buphthalmum
Calamintha
Campanula carpatica
Campanula latiloba
Centaurea
Cerastium tomentosum
Chiastophyllum oppositifolium
Chrysanthemum yezoense
Claytonia sibirica
Convallaria
Corydalis
Crambe
Crocosmia
Cyclamen
Darmera
Dianthus
Dicentra
Dryopteris filix-mas
Epimedium
Erigeron glaucus
Eriogonum umbellatum
Eriophyllum lanatum
Erodium carviflorum
Erodium manescauii
Euphorbia polychroma
Euphorbia griffithii
Filipendula
Fragaria
Geranium (most)
Geum
Gypsophila
Helianthemum
Helleborus
Hemerocallis
Heuchera
× *Heucherella*
Hosta (all)
Houttuynia
Hypericum
Iberis
Iris (some)
Lamium
Limonium
Liriope
Lithodora diffusa
Lysimachia nummularia
Maianthemum
Mentha
Mitella
Nepeta
Omphalodes
Onoclea sensibilis
Ophiopogon
Osmunda
Othonna
Ourisia
Oxalis acetosella
Persicaria
Phlomis
Physalis
Polygonatum
Polygonum
Potentilla
Prunella grandiflora
Pulmonaria
Ranunculus aconitifolus
Rheum
Rodgersia

Saponaria
Saxifraga stolonifera
Saxifraga × *urbium*
Sedum
Smilacina
Stachys macrantha
Symphytum ibericum
Tellima
Teucrium × *lucidrys*
Thymus
Tiarella
Tolmiea
Trollius
Veronica
Vinca
Viola
Zauschneria

Perennials with aromatic foliage

Achillea filipendula
Achillea millefolium
Artemesia
Cedronella canariensis
Chamaemelum nobile
Dictamnus albus
Elsholtzia stauntonii
Filipendula ulmaria
Foeniculum vulgare
Geranium incanum
Geranium macorrhizum
Helichrysum italicum
Houttuynia cordata
Hyssopus officinalis
Lavandula
Leptinella dendyi
Malva moschata
Melissa officinalis
Mellitis melissophyllum
Mentha × *gracilis*
Monarda (all)
Morina longifolia
Myrrhis odorata
Nepeta
Origanum vulgare
Perovskia
Phuopsis stylosa
Rosmarinus
Ruta graveolens
Salvia oficinalis
Santolina chamaecyparissus
Tanacetum parthenium
Tanacetum vulgare
Teucrium × *lucidrys*
Thymus

Architectural perennials

Acanthus
Aciphylla
Aeonium
Amicia
Angelica archangelica
Cortaderia selloana
Crambe cordifolia
Cynara cardunculus
Darmera peltata
Dierama
Echinops
Echium
Eremurus
Eupatorium
Ferula
Hedychium
Helianthus
Heliopsis
Inula magnifica
Kniphofia
Leonotis
Ligularia
Macleaya
Meconopsis grandis
Meconopsis napaulensis
Meconopsis paniculata
Melianthus major
Nectaroscordum siculum
Ostrowskia magnifica
Paeonia (some)
Phormium tenax
Phygelius
Rheum
Ricinus
Rodgersia
Strelitzia
Telekia speciosa
Thalictrum

Perennials which have berries after flowering

Actaea alba
Actaea rubra
Arisaema ssp.
Arum italicum
Clintonia umbellulata
Convallaria majalis
Cornus canadensis
Dianella nigra
Dianella tasmanica
Diphyleia cymosa
Disporum smithii
Dracunculus vulgaris
Fragaria
Fuchsia
Iris foetidissima
Mitchella repens
Pachyphragma macrophyllum
Paeonia mascula subsp. *triternata*
Phytolacca americana
Phytolacca polyandra
Podophyllum hexandrum
Polygonatum × *hybridum*
Smilacina racemosa
Uvularia grandiflora

Low-allergen perennials

Acanthus mollis
Aegopodium podagraria
Agapanthus campanulatus
Ajuga reptans
Alcea rosea
Alchemilla mollis
Allium
Anchusa azurea
Anemone × *hybrida*
Armeria maritima
Aquilegia
Aruncus dioicus
Asphodeline lutea
Astilbe
Astrantia
Baptisia australis
Bergenia
Brunnera
Camassia
Campanula persicifolia
Cardamine
Corydalis
Crambe
Crocosmia
Delphinium
Dicentra
Dierama
Digitalis
Dryas
Epilobium
Epimedium
Eremurus
Eryngium
Filipendula
Foeniculum
Galtonia
Gentiana asclepiadea
Geranium ssp.
Geum
Gladiolus
Glycyrrhiza
Helianthemum
Hemerocallis
Heuchera
× *Heucherella*
Houttuynia
Hyssopus
Iberis
Iris sibirica
Kirengeshoma palmata
Kniphofia
Lamium
Linum
Liriope
Lysimachia
Lythrum
Macleaya
Melissa
Mentha
Mertensia pulmonarioides
Monarda
Nepeta
Omphalodes
Origanum
Paeonia
Papaver
Penstemon
Phlox paniculata
Physostegia virginiana
Platycodon grandiflorus
Polemonium caeruleum
Potentilla
Prunella
Pulmonaria
Rodgersia
Rosmarinus
Salvia
Saxifraga
Scabiosa
Schizostylis
Scrophularia aquatica
Sidalcea
Sisyrinchium striatum
Stachys
Symphytum
Thalictrum
Tellima
Tiarella
Tradescantia × *andersoniana*
Trollius × *cultorum*
Valeriana
Verbena
Veronica
Vinca
Viola

High-allergen perennials

Achillea millefolium
Aconitum spp.
Alstroemeria spp.
Anaphalis spp.
Anemone nemorosa
Angelica archangelica
Arctotis
Argyranthemum frutesens
Armoracia rusticana
Arnica montana
Artemesia spp.
Arum spp.
Aster spp.
Bellis perennis
Caltha palustris
Catananche caerulea
Centurea spp.
Chamaemelum nobile
Chelidonum majus
Coreopsis spp.
Cortaderia selloana
Dactylis spp.
Dianthus spp.
Dictamnus albus
Echinacea purpurea
Echinops spp.
Elymus spp.
Erigeron spp.
Erysimum spp.
Euphorbia spp.
Festuca spp.
Gaillardia spp.
Gazania spp.
Gerbera
Hakonechloa spp.
Helenium autumnale
Helianthus spp.
Helictotrichon sempervirens
Helleborus spp.
Heracleum mantegazzanium
Holcus spp.
Hordeum jubatum
Imperata cylindrica
Lathyrus odoratus
Lavandula angustifolia
Ligularia spp.
Lilium spp.
Lupinus spp.
Microseris ringens
Milium spp.
Osteospermum spp.
Pennisetum orientale
Persicaria spp.
Phaenosperma
Phalaris arundinacea
Pilosella
Plantago spp.
Primula (many)
Pulsatilla vulgaris
Ranunculus spp.
Ruta graveolens
Rumex spp.
Santolina chamaecyparissus
Senecio jacobea
Sesleria

Solidago spp.
× *Solidaster*
Stipa gigantea
Stokesia laevis
Uncinia
Veratrum spp.
Zantedeschia aethiopica

Perennials which attract butterflies

Ajuga
Arabis
Armeria
Aubrieta
Aster
Aurinia
Calamintha
Centranthus
Cephalaria
Chrysanthemum
Coreopsis
Dahlia
Echinacea
Echinops
Erigeron
Eryngium
Helenium
Hesperis
Hyssopus
Iberis
Knautia
Lavandula
Lunaria
Melissa
Mentha
Nepeta
Phlox paniculata
Saponaria
Scabiosa
Sedum
Solidago
Thymus

Perennials which attract bees

Allium
Alstroemeria
Althaea
Anchusa
Anemone
Asclepias
Calamintha
Camassia
Campanula
Centaurea
Clematis
Colchicum
Coreopsis
Cosmos
Crocus
Dahlia
Doronicum
Echinacea
Echinops
Epilobium
Eranthis
Eryngium
Fuchsia
Galanthus
Galega
Galtonia
Gypsophila
Helenium
Helianthemum
Helianthus
Heliopsis
Hyacinthus
Hyssopus
Iberis
Inula
Lavandula
Ligularia
Lupinus
Lythrum
Malva
Mellitis
Mirabilis
Monarda
Nepeta
Oenothera
Origanum
Polemonium
Potentilla
Rudbeckia
Salvia
Scabiosa
Sedum
Senecio
Sidalcea
Stachys
Thymus
Verbascum
Veronica

Perennials for seaside gardens

Achillea
Acanthus
Alstroemeria
Amaryllis belladonna
Anaphalis
Anchusa
Anemone
Anthemis
Anthericum
Armeria
Artemesia
Aster (dwarf)
Bergenia
Campanula (dwarf)
Catananche
Celmisia
Centaurea
Centranthus
Crambe
Crocosmia
Cynoglossum
Dianthus
Dierama
Echinacea
Echinops
Erigeron
Erodium
Eryngium
Euphorbia
Fascicularia
Filipendula
Geranium
Glaucium
Gypsophila
Heuchera
Hieracium
Iris
Kniphofia
Lathyrus
Lavatera
Libertia
Limonium
Linaria
Lupinus
Lychnis flos-jovis
Melissa
Mertensia virginica
Mimulus
Morina
Myosotidium
Nerine
Oenothera
Origanum
Osteospermum
Penstemon
Perovskia
Phormium
Phygelius
Physostegia
Potentilla
Pulsatilla
Romneya coulteri
Salvia
Scabiosa
Schizostylis
Scrophularia
Sedum
Senecio
Sisyrinchium
Stachys
Stokesia
Tritonia
Veronica
Viscaria
Yucca
Zantedeschia

Rabbit-proof perennials

Acanthus
Aconitum
Agapanthus
Alchemilla
Anaphalis
Anemone
Aquilegia
Aster
Astilbe
Bergenia
Brunnera
Campanula lactiflora
Campanula latifolia
Cardiocrinum
Clematis
Colchicum
Convallaria
Cortaderia
Corydalis
Crinum
Crocosmia
Cyclamen
Cynara
Dahlia
Delphinium
Digitalis
Doronicum
Epimedium
Eranthis
Eupatorium
Euphorbia
Fuchsia
Galanthus
Gentiana asclepiadea
Geranium
Hedychium
Helenium
Helianthus
Helleborus
Hemerocallis
Hosta
Houttuynia
Iris
Kirengeshoma
Kniphofia
Lamium
Lavatera
Leucojum
Liriope
Lupinus
Luzula
Lysimachia
Malva
Melissa
Miscanthus
Narcissus
Nepeta
Omphalodes
Orchis
Paeonia
Papaver
Phormium
Phytolacca
Polygonatum
Polygonum
Pulmonaria
Rheum
Romneya
Rosmarinus
Ruta
Saxifraga geum
Saxifraga × *umbrosa*
Sedum
Stachys olympica
Tellima
Tradescantia
Trillium
Trollius
Tulipa
Verbena
Vinca
Yucca
Zantedeschia

Deer-resistant perennials

Acanthus
Aconitum
Agapanthus
Agave
Allium
Amaryllis
Aquilegia
Artemesia
Arum
Astilbe

Campanula
Carex
Centaurea
Ceratostigma
Clematis
Cortaderia
Crinum
Crocosmia
Delphinium
Dicentra
Digitalis
Epimedium
Euphorbia
Ferns
Festuca glauca
Filipendula
Gaillardia
Geranium
Helianthus
Helichrysum
Helleborus
Hosta
Iris
Kniphofia
Lavandula
Leucanthemum × *superbum*
Leucojum
Liriope
Lupinus
Lychnis coronaria
Melianthus
Melissa
Melittis
Mentha
Mirabilis
Myosotis
Narcissus
Nepeta
Origanum
Paeonia
Papaver
Polygonatum
Potentilla
Pulmonaria
Romneya coulteri
Rudbeckia
Salvia
Satureja
Scabiosa
Sisyrinchium
Tellima
Thalictrum
Tiarella
Trillium
Veratrum
Vinca
Yucca

Poisonous perennials

All parts are poisonous, unless specified

Aconitum
Actaea
Amaryllis
Anemone blanda
Anemone nemorosa
Anemone ranunculoides
Anemone rivularis
Aquilegia
Arisaema
Arnica
Arum
Asclepias
Calla palustris (fruits)
Chaerophyllum hirsutum 'Roseum'
Colchicum
Cyclamen persicum
Convallaria majalis (seeds)
Coriaria terminalis (fruits)
Crinum × *powellii*
Delphinium
Dendranthema weyrichii
Dendranthema yezoense
Dicentra
Dictamnus
Digitalis
Echium
Eranthis
Euphorbia
Galanthus
Helenium
Helleborus
Iris
Lathyrus (seeds)
Lupinus (seeds)
Narcissus (bulb)
Nuphar lutea
Ornithogalum
Paeonia
Paris quadrifolia (fruits)
Physalis alkengi
Phytolacca
Podophyllum
Polygonatum × *hybridum*
Ranunculus ficaria
Ricinus (seeds)
Rumex
Scopolia (root)
Sedum
Senecio
Symphytum
Trollius europaeus
Tulipa
Veratrum
Vinca

Perennials which may cause skin irritation

Aconitum
Alstroemeria
Amsonia
Aquilegia
Arisaema
Arum
Borago
Caltha
Chamaemelum
Chelidonum
Cichorium
Clematis
Delphinium
Dendranthema
Dicentra
Echium
Euphorbia
Helenium
Helianthus
Helleborus
Heracleum
Hyacinthus
Iris
Lobelia
Macleaya
Myosotis
Narcissus
Onosma
Ornithogalum
Pelargonium
Pentaglottis
Persicaria
Phytolacca
Podophyllum
Primula elatior
Primula obconica
Pulmonaria
Ranunculus
Rumex
Ruta
Symphytum
Tanacetum
Tradescantia × *andersoniana*
Tulipa
Veratrum

Perennials which seed freely

Achillea millefolium
Alchemilla mollis
Allium christophii
Anthericum
Antirrhinum
Aquilegia (all)
Asphodeline
Asplenium
Aster novae-belgii
Astrantia major
Bellis
Brunnera
Bupleurum
Campanula latifolium
Campanula persicifolia
Campanula trachelium
Centaurea montana
Cephalaria
Chelidonum
Cicerbita
Cirsium
Corydalis lutea
Corydalis ochroleuca
Crepis
Cynara
Digitalis (most)
Echinops
Echium
Epilobium
Erigeron compositus
Erodium
Euphorbia characias
Galtonia
Geranium pratense
Geranium pyrenaicum 'Bill Wallis'
Glaucium
Helleborus orientalis
Hesperis matrionalis
Hieracium
Isatis tinctoria
Juncus
Lamium galeobdolon
Lamium maculatum
Linaria
Lotus
Lychnis chalcedonica
Lychnis coronaria
Lychnis flos-cuculi
Lythrum salicaria
Lythrum virgatum
Malva
Marrubium supinum
Meconopsis cambrica
Melissa officinalis
Milium effusum
Myrrhis odorata
Nectaroscordum siculum
Oenothera fruticosa
Oxalis acetosella
Papaver
Parahebe
Pentaglottis
Phytolacca
Pilosella
Plantago
Polemonium
Pulmonaria
Rumex
Senecio cineraria
Senecio uniflora
Sisyrinchium
× *Solidaster*
Telekia
Valeriana
Verbascum
Verbena

Short-lived perennials

Achillea ptarmica
Aethionema
Agastache
Alcea
Anagallis
Anchusa
Antirrhinum
Aquiegia
Arabis
Asarina procumbens
Baptisia australis
Begonia grandis
Belamcanda chinensis
Bupleurum falcatum
Calamintha nepeta
Campanula pulla
Campanula pyramidalis
Carlina acaulis
Catananche aerulea
Claytonia
Coreopsis
Crepis
Delphinium Pacific hybrids
Dianthus
Diascia
Dicentra spectabilis
Dictamnus albus
Erigeron
Erinus
Eryngium giganteum
Erysimum
Gaillardia
Gaura
Glaucium
Gypsophila
Hedysarum
Hesperis
Isatis tinctoria
Lavatera
Leontopodium
Linum
Lobelia
Lotus
Lupinus
Lychnis × *arkwrightii*
Lychnis coronaria
Malva
Matthiola
Meconopsis betonicifolia
Meconopsis grandis
Megacarpaea
Mimulus
Oenothera
Orthrosanthus
Papaver atlanticum
Papaver croceum
Papaver 'Fireball'
Papaver fourei
Papaver rupifragum
Polemonium

Primula capitata
Rehmannia
Rudbeckia
Salvia argentea
Salvia coccinea
Salvia pratensis
Sanguisorba albiflora
Scabiosa atropurpurea
Semiaquilegia ecalcarata
Senecio cineraria
Silene dioica
Silene uniflora
Sisyrinchium
Stylophorum
Symphyandra
Tanacetum
Verbascum bombiciferum
Viola

Invasive perennials

Acanthus hungaricus
Acanthus mollis
Acanthus spinosus
Achillea ptarmica
Aegopodium podagraria
Anemone × *hybrida*
Arisarum proboscideum
Arum italicum
Aruncus dioicus
Campanula persicifolia
Campanula pulla
Campanula rotundifolia
Campanula takesimana
Cardamine pentaphyllos
Cardamine pratensis
Ceratostigma plumbaginoides
Chamaemelum nobile
Cirsium rivulare
Commelina coelestis
Convallaria
Convolvulus altheoides
Cornus canadensis
Dicentra 'Pearl Drops'
Eomecon chionanthum
Epilobium angustifolium
Galium odoratum
Geranium himalayense
Gladiolus papilio
Glyceria maxima
Helianthus decapetalus
Helianthus doronicoides
Helianthus 'Lemon Queen'
Lamium galeobdolon
Houttuynia cordata
Hylomecon japonicum
Inula hookeri
Leonotis dysophyllus
Leonotis leonurus
Lilium bulbiferum
Linaria triornithophora
Lotus corniculatus
Lysimachia ciliata
Lysimachia nummularia
Lysimachia punctata
Maianthemum bifolium
Malvastrum lateritium
Mentha × *gracilis*
Mertensia implicissima
Mertensia pulmonarioides
Milium effusum
Muscari armeniacum
Myosotis scorpioides
Nectaroscordum siculum
Oenothera speciosa
Ornithogalum nutans
Ornithogalum thyrsoides
Ornithogalum tetraphylla
Oxalis acetosella
Oxalis pes-caprae
Oxalis tetraphylla
Persicaria affinis
Persicaria capitata
Petasites japonicus
Phygelius aequalis
Physalis alkengi
Physostegia virginiana
Plectranthus ciliatus
Pontederia cordata
Pratia pedunculata
Prunella grandiflora
Ranunculus acris
Ranunculus ficaria
Ranunculus repens
Sanguisorba canadensis
Sanguisorba obtusa
Sanguisorba officinalis
Sanguisorba tenuifolia
Saponaria officinalis
Saxifraga × *urbium*
Scopolia carniolica
Symphytum ibericum
Symphytum orientale
Symphytum × *uplandicum*
Telekia speciosa
Tiarella cordifolia
Tricyrtis formosana
Tricyrtis latifolia
Trifolium repens

Perennials which require to be lifted and divided regularly

Achillea
Aster amellus
Aster ericoides
Aster thomsonii
Astilbe
Bergenia
Camassia
Campanula persicifolia
Campanula pulla
Coreopsis
Crocosmia
Crocus
Doronicum
Dracunculus
Erigeron
Fritillaria imperialis
Geum
Gladiolus communis
Gladiolus papilio
Helenium
Helianthus
Heliopsis
Hemerocallis
Heuchera
Liatris
Muscari
Narcissus
Nerine
Ophiopogon
Ornithogalum
Phlox paniculata
Polygonatum x hybridum
Schizostylis
Sisyrinchium
Stachys byzantina
Tradescantia × *andersoniana*

Perennials which resent transplantation

Aciphylla
Aconitum
Agapanthus
Alstroemeria
Anemone × *hybrida*
Angelica
Anthemis
Aquilegia
Aristaea
Asclepias
Baptisia
Brunsvigia
Campanula lactiflora
Catananche
Centranthus
Cephalaria
Chaerophyllum
Claytonia
Clivia
Crambe
Crepis
Crinum
Cynara
Dictamnus
Dierama
Echinops
Echium
Eriogonum
Eryngium
Euphorbia
Fascicularia
Ferula
Foeniculum
Galega
Gentiana
Gerbera
Glaucium
Glycyrrhiza
Gypsophila
Hacquetia
Hedysarum
Hesperis
Isatis
Incarvillea
Lathyrus
Limonium
Linum
Lupinus
Megacarpaea
Mertensia
Myrrhis
Oenothera
Ostrowskia magnifica
Paeonia
Papaver orientale
Pentaglottis
Platycodon
Pulsatilla
Scabiosa
Thermopsis
Trillium
Tropaeolum polyphyllum

BIBLIOGRAPHY

General Reference:

Berry, S. and Bradley, S. *Best Plants for your Garden* Anness Publishing. London. 1996.

Bird, R. *The Complete Book of Hardy Perennials* Ward Lock. London. 1993.

Bloom, A. *Alan Bloom's Selected Garden Plants* Jarrold. Norwich. 1968.

Bremness, L. Contributing Editor *Herbs D.K. Pocket Encyclopaedia* Dorling Kindersley London. 1990.

Brickell, C. Editor-in-chief: *The Royal Horticultural Society Gardeners' Encyclopedia of Plants and Flowers* Dorling Kindersley. London, 1994.

Brickell, C. Editor-in-chief. *The Royal Horticultural Society A-Z Encyclopedia of Garden Plants* Dorling Kindersley. London, 1997.

Cooke, I. *The Plantfinder's Guide to Tender Perennials* David & Charles. Newton Abbot. 1998.

Elliott, J. *The Smaller Perennials* B.T. Batsford. London. 1997.

Godet, J-D. *Plants and Flowers of Great Britain and Europe* Arboris Press. Bern. 1991.

Griffiths, M. *Index of Garden Plants* derived from *The New Royal Horticultural Society Dictionary of Gardening* Macmillan Press. Basingstoke. 1994.

Harris, T.Y. *Alpine Plants of Australia* Watson Ferguson. Brisbane. 1970.

Hessayon, D.G. *The Bulb Expert* Expert Books. London. 1995.

Hessayon, D.G. *The Flower Expert* Expert Books. London 1997.

Hessayon, D.G. *The Rock and Water Garden Expert* Expert Books. London. 1997.

Heywood, V.H. Consultant Editor. *Flowering Plants of the World* Oxford University Press. 1978.

Jellito, L and Schacht, W. *Hardy Herbaceous Perennials* in two volumes Third Edition revised by Schacht, W. and Fessler, A., Timber Press Inc. Portland, Oregon. 1990.

Kidd, M.M. *South African Wild Flower Guide No 3* Cape Peninsula. 2nd Ed. Oxford University Press. 1996.

Kohlein, F. and Menzel, P. *The Encyclopaedia of Plants for Garden Situations* B.T. Batsford, Ltd. London. 1994.

Lancaster, R. *What Perennial Where?* Dorling Kindersley London. 1997.

Mathew, B. *The Larger Bulbs* B.T. Batsford. London. 1978.

Onderstall, J. *South African Wild Flower Guide No 4* Transvaal Lowveld and Escarpment. Botanical Society of South Africa. 1984.

Parker, H. Editor. Perennials. *A Royal Horticultural Society Plant Guide* Dorling Kindersley. London. 1996.

Philipson, W.R. and Hearn, D. *Rock Garden Plants of the Southern Alps* The Caxton Press. Christchurch. 1962.

Phillip, C. *The Plant Finder 1999/2000 Edition* The Royal Horticultural Society. Dorling Kindersley. London.

Phillips, R. and Rix, M. *Bulbs* Pan Books. London. 1989.

Phillips, R. and Rix, M. *Herbs* Pan Books. London. 1990.

Phillips, R. and Rix, M. *Perennials* In two volumes: *I Early-flowering; II Late-flowering* Pan Books. London. 1991.

Phillips, R. and Rix, M. *Shrubs* Pan Books. London. 1989.

Press, B. and Gibbons, B. *Wild Flowers of Britain and Europe* New Holland. London. 1993.

Redgrove, H. Editor. *An Illustrated Handbook of Bulbs and Perennials* Cassell. London. 1991.

Rice, G. *Hardy Perennials* Viking. London. 1995.

Rickett, H.W. *Wild Flowers of the United States Vol. 2 The Southeastern States* McGraw-Hill. New York. 1967.

Segall, B. Consultant. *Botanica; the Illustrated A-Z of over 10,000 garden plants, and how to grow them* Mynah. N.S.W., Australia. 1997.

Thomas, G.S. *Cuttings from my Garden Notebooks* John Murray. London. 1998.

Thomas, G.S. *Perennial Garden Plants,* or *The Modern Florilegium* J.M. Dent. London 1990.

Trehane, P. et. al. *International Code of Nomenclature for Cultivated Plants* Quarterjack Publishing. 1995.

Walters et. al. *The European Garden Flora,* in five volumes. Cambridge University Press. 1984-1998.

Books on Cultivation:

Anderton, E. and Park, R. *Growing Gladioli* Christopher Helm. London. 1989.

Bath, T. and Jones, J. *The Gardener's Guide to Growing Hardy Geraniums* David & Charles. Newton Abbot. 1994.

Bird, R. *The Cultivation of Hardy Perennials* B.T. Batsford, London, 1994.

Grenfell, D. *The Gardener's Guide to Growing Hostas* David & Charles. Newton Abbot. 1996.

Jefferson-Brown, M. and Howland, H. *The Gardener's Guide to Growing Lilies* David & Charles. Newton Abbot. 1995.

Mathew, B. *Growing Bulbs: the Complete Practical Guide* B.T. Batsford. London. 1997.

Pratt, K. and Jefferson-Brown, M. *The Gardener's Guide to Growing Fritillaries* David & Charles. Newton Abbot. 1997.

Rice, G. and Strangman, E. *The Gardener's Guide to Growing Hellebores* David & Charles. Newton Abbot. 1994.

Smith, F.C. *Growing Carnations and Pinks* Ward Lock. London. 1994.

Stebbings, G. *The Gardener's Guide to Growing Irises* David & Charles. Newton Abbot. 1997.

Books on General Topics:

Bird, R. *Woodland Gardening* Souvenir Press. London. 1992.

Bird, R. Editor and Compiler. *Plantsmen on Plants* The Hardy Plant Society. 1990.

Boddy, F.A. *Foliage Plants* David & Charles. Newton Abbot. 1973.

Boisset, C. and Walker, J. *The Garden Designer. Selecting Plants.* Reed International Books London. 1994.

Chatto, B. *The Dry Garden.* J.M.Dent. London. 1978.

Cooke, I. *The Plantfinder's Guide to Tender Perennials* David & Charles. Newton Abbot. 1998.

Evans, A. *The Peat Garden and its Plants* J.M.Dent. London. 1974.

Ferguson, N. *Right Plant, Right Place* Aura Books. 1996.

Genders, R. *The Scented Flora of the World* Robert Hale. London. 1994.

Grounds, R. *The Plantfinder's Guide to Ornamental Grasses* David & Charles. Newton Abbot. 1998.

Frohne, D. and Pfander, H.J. *A Colour Atlas of Poisonous Plants* Wolfe Publishing. 1983.

Howes, F.N. *Plants and Beekeeping* Faber & Faber. London and Boston. 1979.

Huntingdon, L. *Creating a Low-allergen Garden* Mitchell Beazley. London. 1998.

Jones, David L. *Encyclopaedia of Ferns* Thomas C. Lothian. Port Melbourne, 1987.

Lloyd, C. *Foliage Plants* Collins, London. 1973.

Lloyd, C. *The Well-tempered Garden* Collins, London. 1973.

Marion Merrell Dow. *Hayfever in the Garden.* 1994.

Paterson, A. *Plants for Shade* J.M. Dent. London. 1981.

Raven, J. *A Botanist's Garden* Collins. London. 1971.

Rice, G. *The Planting Planner* Macmillan. London. 1996.

Rogers, Barbara R. *The Dried Flower Encyclopaedia* Simon & Schuster. London. 1988.

Royal Horticultural Society, The *Award of Garden Merit Plants.* 1994.

Royal Horticultural Society, The *Award of Garden Merit Plants* First Supplement. 1994.

Royal Horticultural Society, The *A.G.M. Plants.* 1999.

Scott, G.H. *Bulbs: how to select, grow and enjoy* H.P. Books. Los Angeles. 1982.

Stary, F. and Berger, Z. *Poisonous Plants* Magna Books. Leicester. 1995.

Taylor, J. *Collecting Garden Plants* J.M. Dent. London.1988.

Taylor, J. *The Milder Garden* J.M. Dent. London 1990.

Thomas, G.S. *Colour in the Winter Garden* Weidenfeld and Nicolson. London. 1994.

Thomas, G.S. *Plants for Ground Cover* J.M.Dent and Sons Ltd. London. 1990.

Verey, R. *The Flower Arranger's Garden* Conran Octopus. London. 1992.

Monographs on Individual Families:

Barker, D.G. *Epimediums and other herbaceous Berberidaceae* The Hardy Plant Society. 1996.

Cribb, P. and Bailes, C. *Hardy Orchids* Christopher Helm. London. 1989.
Grey-Wilson, C. Poppies: *The Poppy Family in the Wild and in Cultivation* B.T. Batsford. London. 1993.
Ingram, T. *Umbellifers* The Hardy Plant Society. 1993.
Innes, C. *The World of Iridaceae* Holly Gate International Ltd. Ashington. 1985.
Kellaway, D. *Clematis and the Ranunculaceae* Pavilion Books. London. 1994.
Kohlein, F. *Saxifrages and related Genera* B. T. Batsford. London. 1984.
Reed, D. Editor. *Lilies and Related Plants* The Royal Horticultural Society Lily Group 1988/9.
Stocks, A. *Saxifragaceae* The Hardy Plant Society. 1995.

Monographs on Individual Genera:
Anderton, E.W. and Park, R., *Growing Gladioli* Christopher Helm, London, 1989.
Bartlett, M. *Gentians* Blandford Press. Poole. 1975.
Bath, T. and Jones, J. *The gardener's guide to growing Hardy Geraniums* David & Charles. Newton Abbot. 1994.
Bird, R. *Border Pinks* The Crowood Press. Marlborough. 1997.
Bird, R. *Lilies; an Illustrated Identifier and Guide to Cultivation* Apple Press. London. 1991.
Blanchard, J.W. *Narcissus; A Guide to Wild Daffodils* Alpine Garden Society. 1990.
Bond, S. *Hostas* Ward Lock. London. 1994.
Case, Frederick W., Jnr. and Case, Roberta B. *Trilliums* Timber Press. Portland, Oregon. 1997.
Clapham, S. *Primulas* David & Charles. Newton Abbot. 1971.
Clark, D. *The Hardy Fuchsia Guide* Oakleigh Publications. Monkswood. 1992.
Cobb, J.L.S. *Meconopsis* Christopher Helm. London. 1989.
Cohen, V.A. *A Guide to the Pacific Coast Irises* British Iris Society. 1967.
Cooper, A. *Pentstemons* Power Publications. Ferndown. 1996.
Crook, H.C. *Campanulas and Bellflowers in Cultivation* Blandford Press. London. 1959.
Davies, D. *Alliums: The Ornamental Onions* B.T. Batsford. London. 1992.
Erhardt, W. *Hemerocallis: Daylilies* B.T. Batsford. London. 1992.
Fuller, R. *Pansies, Violas and Violettas: The Complete Guide* The Crowood Press. Marlborough. 1990.
Goldblatt, P. *The Genus Watsonia* National Botanic Gardens, South Africa. 1989.
Green, R. *Asiatic Primulas: A Gardener's Guide* Alpine Garden Society. Pershore. 1976.
Grenfell, D. *The Gardener's Guide to Growing Hostas* David & Charles. Newton Abbot. 1996.
Grenfell, D. *The Gardener's Guide to Growing Daylilies* David & Charles. Newton Abbot 1998.
Grenfell, D. *Hostas* The Hardy Plant Society. 1993.
Hewitt, J. *Pulmonarias* The Hardy Plant Society. 1994.
Ingwersen, W. *The Dianthus* Collins. London. 1949.
Jacobs, D.L. and Jacobs, R.L. *Trilliums in Woodland and Garden Eco-Gardens* Decatur, Ga. USA.
Jefferson-Brown, M. and Howland, H. *The Gardener's Guide to Growing Lilies* David & Charles. Newton Abbot. 1995.
Jones, Joy, et. al. *Hardy Geraniums* The Hardy Plant Society. 1993.
Kohlein, F. *Iris* Christopher Helm. London. 1981.
Lewis, P. and Lynch, M. *Campanulas* Christopher Helm. London. 1989.
Liden, M. and Zetterlund, H. *Corydalis* Alpine Garden Society. Pershore. 1997.
Linnegar, S and Hewitt, J. *Irises A Wisley Handbook,* Royal Horticultural Society. Cassell. London. 1990.
Mann-Taylor, J. *Phlomis.* N.C.C.P.G. Wisley. 1998.
Matthew, B. *The Iris* B.T. Batsford. London. 1981.
Picton, Paul, *The Gardener's Guide to Growing Asters* David & Charles. Newton Abbot. 1999
Pradhan, U.C. *Himalayan Cobra Lilies: Their Botany and Culture* Primulaceae Books. Darjeeling. 1990.
Pratt, K. and Jefferson-Brown, M. *The Gardener's Guide to Growing Fritillaries* David & Charles. Newton Abbot. 1997.
Puttock, A.G. *Primulas* John Gifford. London. 1957.
Rice, G. and Strangman, E. *The Gardener's Guide to Growing Hellebores* David & Charles. Newton Abbot. 1994.
Robinson, M. *Primulas: The Complete Guide* The Crowood Press. Marlborough. 1996.
Snoeijer, Wim, *Agapanthus; a review* Gouda, The Netherlands. 1998.
Stebbings, G. *The Gardener's Guide to Growing Irises* David & Charles. Newton Abbot. 1997.
Sutton, J. *The Gardener's Guide to Growing Salvias* David & Charles. Newton Abbot. 1999.
Swindells, P. *A Plantsman's Guide to Primulas* Ward Lock. London. 1989.
Taylor, J.M. *Phlomis; the neglected genus* N.C.C.P.G. Wisley. 1998.
Turner, R. *Euphorbias: A Gardener's Guide* B.T. Batsford. London. 1995.
Way, D. *Pentstemons* The Hardy Plant Society. 1996.
Way, D. and James, P., *The Gardener's Guide to Growing Pentemons* David & Charles. Newton Abbot. 1998.
White, S. *Origanum* N.C.C.P.G. Wisley. 1998.
Yeo, C. *Salvias* Pleasant View Nursery, Newton Abbot. 1995.
Yeo, C. *Salvias 2* Pleasant View Nursery, Newton Abbot. 1997.
Yeo, P.F. *Hardy Geraniums* Croom Helm. London and Sydney. 1985.

INDEX

Picture Credits

All photographs by Marshall Craigmyle, except:

Heather Angel 1, 2, 6, 13, 14, 15, 16, 19, 20, 26, 32, 53, 64, 94, 99, 103, 110, 132, 135, 160, 169, 190, 220, 234, 273

Salamander Picture Library 9, 12, 22, 23, 42, 47, 57, 71, 76, 83, 89, 119, 124, 146, 153, 166, 173, 178, 185, 198, 203, 209, 215, 227, 239, 245, 250, 255, 262, 268, 277, 282, 286

HARDINESS ZONES

THE FIRST CONSIDERATION when choosing a perennial to be grown in the open all year round is whether it is hardy in your area. The United States of America Department of Agriculture has produced a table of eleven temperature zones (of which ten are shown on the map of Europe opposite). The map has been divided into broad climatic zones as a basis for assessing the degree of cold a plant can tolerate. The zones illustrated here are numbered from one to ten from the coldest at below -50°F (-44°C) to the warmest up to 40°F (5°C), based on the annual average minimum temperature for the zone in question. Every plant listed in the plant directory section of the book cites a hardiness zone. To establish whether your chosen perennial will be hardy in your garden, refer to the map of hardiness for your country and find the zonal rating for your area. Any plant with a zonal rating which is equal or lower to the zonal rating for your area will be hardy in your garden. Thus if your area is rated zone 7, all plants graded from zone 1 to zone 7 will survive and flower at the average minimum winter temperature there and plants graded zone 8 to zone 11 will not. However, every garden has a number of microclimates, i.e. some parts of the garden are warmer than others. It may be that your garden rating does not apply to all of your garden. So if your garden is rated zone 7, the warmest corner, such as at the foot of a south-facing wall, may well be zone 8. The only way to find out is to experiment by growing zone 8-rated plants in that site.

Zonal Temperature Ranges

ZONE 1: Below -50°F (Below -44°C)
ZONE 2: -50° to -40°F (-44° to -37°C)
ZONE 3: -40° to -30°F (-37° to -32°C)
ZONE 4: -30° to -20°F (-32° to -27°C)
ZONE 5: -20° to -10°F (-27° to -22°C)
ZONE 6: -10° to 0°F (-22° to -16°C)
ZONE 7: -0° to +10°F (-16° to -10°C)
ZONE 8: +10° to +20°F (-10° to -5°C)
ZONE 9: +20° to +32°F (-5° to 0°C)
ZONE 10: +32° to +40°F (0° to +5°C)